THE CRIMINAL PERSONALITY

The
Criminal Personality

Volume II: The Change Process

by

SAMUEL YOCHELSON, Ph.D., M.D.

Director, Program for the Investigation of Criminal Behavior
Saint Elizabeths Hospital

Clinical Professor of Psychiatry and Behavioral Sciences
George Washington University Medical School

and

STANTON E. SAMENOW, Ph.D.

Clinical Research Psychologist, Saint Elizabeths Hospital

Clinical Instructor in Psychiatry and Behavioral Sciences
George Washington University Medical School

New York ● JASON ARONSON ● London

The views expressed by the authors do not necessarily reflect the opinions, official policy, or position of Saint Elizabeths Hospital, the National Institute of Mental Health, the Alcohol, Drug Abuse, and Mental Health Administration, or the U.S. Department of Health, Education, and Welfare.

Samuel Yochelson, Ph.D., M.D.
Stanton E. Samenow, Ph.D.

ISBN: 0-87668-771-0

Library of Congress Catalog Number: 75-13507

Manufactured in the United States of America.

To Kathryn, whose love and
support made this work possible

Commentary

"Drs. Yochelson and Samenow's work constitutes an unprecedented scrutiny of criminal behavior, going beyond mere microscopic analysis. Vol. II makes good the promise expressed in Vol. I: that the fruition of fifteen years of research would be no less than an entirely new approach to understanding and modifying the criminal's thought patterns."

Jud Watkins
US Probation Officer and Training Coordinator

"Yochelson and Samenow have definitely profiled the characteristics of the errors of criminal thinking, together with their derivatives — feeling and behavior. They show persuasively that because of ingrained and pervasive errors of thinking, criminals live and act in a world with entirely different assumptive bases than those of noncriminals. The authors then proceed to develop a treatment program using a phenomenological approach. This exhaustive and painstaking study marks a turning point in the history of efforts to rehabilitate criminals."

W. Edward Naugler, M.D.

Preface

WHEN WE BEGAN WORKING with criminals fifteen years ago, we used the term *therapy,* and for several years we regarded ourselves as psychotherapists. We soon learned that criminals were feeding us what they thought we wanted to hear, as they had with others who had worked with them. They were also examining us. Indeed, the criminal's examination of a therapist is as intense as the therapist's examination of him. The criminal views therapy as a means of removing himself from jeopardy. He tries, above all, to avoid being confined in prison, even claiming a mental defect as a last resort in hope that such an evaluation will result in psychiatric hospitalization rather than imprisonment. Another objective of therapy, as far as the criminal is concerned, is to obtain the speediest possible release from confinement, be it prison or hospital. To the criminal, who does not regard himself as mentally ill, "therapy" means that it is incumbent upon the therapist to correct features that the therapist considers objectionable, while leaving the criminal's basic personality intact, so that he can pursue whatever objectives he chooses.

The criminal does not readily expose himself as a guinea pig for someone to study and is actively opposed to substantial alteration of his personality. If he participates in a study, he insists on receiving something in return. Despite the criminal's knowing that we could not affect his confinement one way or another and that our communication with him was strictly confidential, he believed that the administration would regard his spending so much time with us as proof of his desire to change and that this would hasten his release from confinement. Thus, he allowed us to gather careful histories, to provide psychiatric interpretations, and to try to deal with factors in his personality that had eventuated in crime.

To convey to the criminal that our program was not therapy as he used the term but rather that we were serious about achieving a massive change in him by an intensive and prolonged process, we began referring to our program as a "process of change" and to ourselves as "agents of change." Indeed, in the criminal's eyes, the mere change in title set us apart from therapists, and the differentiation became more obvious as we implemented new procedures.

Over a long period, we acquired increasing knowledge of the criminal's thought and action patterns, but to our great disappointment, we observed no substantial change. It became clear that if we were to achieve any success, we had to revise our procedures. With every revision, new material on criminal patterns was forthcoming; with more material available, further procedural changes were made. Milestones in the evolution of our approach were eliminating sociologic and psychologic explanations, discarding the idea of mental illness as a cause of criminality, and placing total emphasis on choice and will, thus making the criminal and no one else responsible for his behavior. A further revision of procedure was to make phenomenology operational. This resulted in the emergence of additional vital material.

The descriptive concepts of the first volume of this work, *The Criminal Personality: A Profile for Change,* emphasized the pervasive thinking errors and tactics that experience has taught us must be altered to achieve a basic change in the criminal. This volume presents a new format for making all necessary substantive and procedural alterations.

The approach presented here is a rational one. In this respect, we are in accord with the work of Glasser (reality therapy) and Ellis (rational-emotive therapy). We differ from them in being concerned primarily with the dynamics of the cognitive process—in this case, the correction of fifty-two errors that we found pervade all the criminal's thinking, no matter what the issue (see volume 1). We discarded the idea of altering only an individual pattern here or there, because we found it necessary to deal with *all* thinking patterns that could be exposed by an operational phenomenologic procedure. Replacing the fifty-two criminal thinking patterns by an entirely new set of patterns mandatory for responsible functioning is a prodigious task.

The criminal is a master at exercising control in all situations. He does this both blatantly and deceptively. Constantly making choices, he is usually successful in achieving criminal objectives in line with his choices. To change requires a responsible choice. This choice results in further responsible choices. If the criminal implements these choices, he must face consequences that are antithetic to his idea of living and are therefore initially disagreeable to him. The *enduring* of these consequences is our operational definition of will.

Our work with the criminal establishing a firm moral base rather than ignoring immorality or remaining neutral. In this program the criminal learns new thinking patterns to deter immoral thinking and behavior. He incorporates a graded series of deterrents climaxed by the most comprehensive deterrent, variously named by our criminals a "moral inventory" (after the Alcoholics Anonymous steps), an "examination of conscience," and an "exercise in self-disgust." We do not build the criminal's self-esteem. Instead, we hold a mirror up to him for him to see himself as he is. Having truly realized what he is, he acquires self-respect only after he implements new patterns in the responsible world.

We have followed some of the criminals in our program for the entire fifteen years of our investigation. Some, whose participation began later, have been followed regularly for five to ten years. We have had successes and failures, and we have learned from both. This volume describes the process of change in its present format, but we are confident that further work will improve and shorten the process.

We believe that it is feasible to institute this program on a scale broader than our present pilot effort. We indicate the difficulties of achieving change in the criminal in a forensic division such as that of Saint Elizabeths Hospital, where the staff is large and the variety of services offered is great. As an alternative to current programs, we describe the qualities and training that are necessary to select change agents in this field, and we present an outline for implementing our program both in the community and in correctional institutions.

It is our hope that others who are trying to achieve change in the criminal, even if they do not totally accept our format, will find the material and techniques presented here useful in their own programs. Criticism of concepts should be directed at the senior author. An indispensable contribution has been made by the junior author without whose understanding, ideas, and dedication these publications would not have been possible.

We should like to extend our appreciation to Norman Grossblatt for editing the entire manuscript, to John Lewin for his collation of materials and proofreading, and to Mrs. Charles Samenow for her helpful suggestions. We also thank Doretha Vaughan and Rhonda Atchinson, our typists.

Contents

THE CRIMINAL PERSONALITY

Chapter 1

A New Horizon for
Total Change of the Criminal

THE DIMENSIONS OF THE TASK of changing a criminal* to a responsible person are poorly understood. The procedures that have been used with criminals have not been effective. Crime is still very much with us and, indeed, according to statistics, is a more formidable problem today than ever before. Previous efforts at rehabilitation have failed for two main reasons: there has been insufficient knowledge of what the criminal is—his thinking processes and behavior patterns—and the techniques used have almost all been adaptations of techniques used with noncriminals. In volume 1, we presented a detailed picture of the criminal's thinking and action. Utilizing this knowledge, it was possible to develop new procedures necessary to achieve basic change and, with them, to succeed in changing some criminals into responsible citizens.

In setting before the reader the dimensions of the change process, it is necessary to review the profile of the criminal. To do so, we draw selectively from the material presented in much greater detail in volume 1.

At an early age, the criminal-to-be makes a series of choices that involve going counter to the responsible forces that prevail in all socioeconomic levels. Even in the high-crime areas, most of his contemporaries do not choose a criminal path. However, as a youngster, the criminal finds the restraints of

---

*Readers familiar with volume 1 of this work know that rather than limit our definition of a criminal to a person convicted of a crime, we have presented a more comprehensive profile of the criminal as a person whose *patterns of thinking* have led to arrestable behavior. These we have called "criminal thinking patterns." While some of the "criminal thinking patterns" may be found in the noncriminal, they lead not to arrestability but rather to ineffectiveness. All of the irresponsible thinking patterns in the criminal described in volume 1 must be altered in the change process presented in this volume. It is essential to underscore that the person with whom we are working is indeed a criminal, even though, regardless of the number or seriousness of the crimes he has committed, he regards himself as a good person. The reader is referred to volume 1 for a detailed description of criminal patterns of thinking and action.

responsible living unacceptable and even contemptible. He rejects the requirements and way of life of parents, siblings, teachers, employers, and others in his environment who are responsible.

Although he may manage to convince others that he is responsible and, through a facade of conformity, keep society at bay while pursuing his criminal objectives, he scorns such social institutions as the school, the church, and the law.

To be like the responsible children in his neighborhood and at school is to be a "nothing." The criminal child wants something different. He usually begins his violating patterns at home. Then if he cannot find the excitement that he wants in his own surroundings, he goes where he can find it. Crime does not come to the criminal-to-be; he goes to it.

Whatever his background, the criminal youngster views himself as different from others, as one of a kind. In whatever he undertakes, he has to be not only number one but a unique number one. To be like anyone else is to be a failure. If something appeals to him, this exceedingly energetic youngster works to be the best; when he tires of the endeavor, he quits. Throughout his life, the criminal is a sprinter, never a long-distance runner. Even when he does enough to rank first in a particular activity, it may mean little to him, because he wants to be a big shot for doing what others will not do, not for doing what is expected or acceptable. Thus success at school or work does not satisfy him. The things that an elementary school pupil learns do not interest him. Indeed, the criminal never develops an accurate concept of what family life is, what an education is, what a sense of community is, or what a vocation is.

Patterns of deception are established very early. Lying is a way of life. Lying patterns are habitual; the criminal needs only to change the details to accommodate a particular situation. Lies of omission are more frequent than lies of commission.

The criminal disregards other people's right to live safely, but demands that others show him the utmost respect and consideration. He breaks promises; in fact, he never regards a promise as a promise unless it is part of a larger operation to secure something for himself. It does not bother him to injure others; he rarely sees anything from another's point of view. Although society considers him harmful, the criminal believes that he is exercising a right to live as he chooses. In the pursuit of what is important to him, the criminal puts his family, teachers, employers, and other people concerned about him through worry and expense. As his violating patterns expand, they inflict a toll on society that is incalculable—not only monetarily but in terms of pervasive fear and broken hearts.

The hard-core criminal commits thousands of arrestable crimes and violates countless ethical and moral standards but he is rarely apprehended. If apprehended, he is likely to escape conviction. If convicted, he is likely to be given a light sentence or be returned to society immediately. If he is held accountable for a violation, he believes that he is the one who is violated, because being caught is an injustice and being interfered with makes him a victim, not a victimizer. He blames forces outside himself for his crime or for making him the way he is: others are responsible, not he. This position is usually reinforced by current concepts and practices and often by the judicial attitudes and decisions of those who deal with criminals.

We have described the criminal population as a different breed—a group of humans with the same physical needs as the rest of us but with an entirely different view of life and an entirely different set of thinking patterns. The criminal is oriented; i.e., he knows what he is doing and what others are doing. But he has his own reality, in which society's values and rules are absurd or unimportant. He chooses *his* reality, not ours.*

The criminal lives in a world where there is no loyalty or trust, even in relation to others like him. Untrustworthy himself, he demands that others trust him. If he happens to earn others' trust, he exploits it. He depends on others but does not see his own dependence. To him, this exhibits weakness and places him in jeopardy. He claims he can live without interdependence but demands that others provide him with whatever he wants. The criminal does not know how to get along with responsible people from day to day; he generally occupies the extremes of total withdrawal or inappropriate intimacy. He is intolerant of others' shortcomings but reacts angrily when anyone finds fault with him. Instead of friendships, the criminal seeks avenues of triumph. People are to be used, conquered, controlled like pawns, exploited, and then discarded when they can no longer serve a purpose useful to him. Only rarely does the criminal genuinely "like" another person. His liking is based on someone's agreeing with him, building him up, assisting him in his plans, or at least not interfering with him. He also "likes" someone he can exploit. His very characteristics preclude his genuinely loving anyone. He regards kindness as weakness. Although he expresses fragments of sentimentality, the criminal cold-bloodedly uses the very people he professes to love.

Criminals seem tough, but they are actually extremely fearful. The criminal child, who scorns responsible youngsters as "chicken," has fears that are more numerous and intense than theirs. Criminal youngsters fear darkness, water,

---

*The psychotic has his own reality, too, but his reality is one in which his orientation is very different. He deals with constructs of the mind that have no basis in fact. He may respond to voices. He may believe that people are after him. None of this has a factual basis. In contrast with the psychotic, the criminal is sharp, alert, and in touch with the facts of life. For example, if he thinks that people are after him, this is based on the fact that he is being sought, even though he may err with respect to the particular person seeking him.

heights, and many other things. Some of these fears persist into adulthood. The criminal must also deal with recurrent fears of getting caught for his violations. And he does have conscience fears; that is, there are some things he claims to hold inviolate. However, he does not tolerate continuing in a fearful state. In fact, he avoids even speaking of his fears, because it is "sissy," "lame," and "weak" to do so. The criminal has a remarkable capacity for eliminating fear, at least for long enough to do as he wants. The mental processes of corrosion and cutoff allow him to turn rapidly from trembling and uncertainty to composure and confidence.

Most of all, the criminal fears being put down by other people. A putdown occurs when someone fails to gratify his every desire or fulfill his every expectation. Any inconvenience is regarded as a personal affront. What a noncriminal habitually shrugs off reduces the power-thrusting, controlling criminal to a zero. The zero state, which is far more encompassing than the noncriminal's inferiority feelings, reflects the criminal's extremes in thinking and his misconception of himself and the outside world. He is either a colossus or a nothing. He regards himself as a zero when the world does not accord him the status that he thinks he deserves and things are not going according to plan. On such occasions, the criminal believes that everyone looks upon him as a nothing and that this state is permanent. The seeming finality and futility of such a state are intolerable to him, and he usually responds with criminal acts, as well as with anger and with determination to reassert his status as "somebody" rather than continue to be (by his definition) a "nobody." Life for the criminal is a series of anger reactions to surmount his fear of being a nothing. The antidote to the zero state is not constructive activity but a cutoff of fear, an angry reaction, and a search for excitement (crime). Anger is a basic component of the criminal's personality; it is pervasive, although not always apparent to others.

The pursuit of power and control pervades the criminal's thinking, conversation, and action. Power and control are sought in irresponsible ways purely for self-aggrandizement. The criminal approaches life pursuing personal triumphs, conquests, and build-ups. To achieve these, he promotes himself at the expense of others. He recognizes no limit to his personal power and control; the world is his to do with as he pleases. Whatever he does, whomever he deals with, he expects the world to adapt immediately to his wants, even when he is apprehended and confined.

The criminal expects to be an overnight success. A goal to him is an instant triumph achieved criminally, not a responsible objective achieved by hard work or talent. He disregards the future, does not plan long range (except when scheming a crime), and ignores the past (except for profiting from some mistakes in crime). He is a concrete thinker who lacks a time perspective.

When the criminal embarks on an enterprise (criminal or not), he either abandons it or develops a state of near certainty or "superoptimism." For the criminal, possibilities become accomplished facts. There are no imponderables; thinking something makes it so.

If necessary, the criminal endures some hardships and overcomes some obstacles in crime, but he refuses to endure the slightest adversities of responsible living. He refuses to do anything disagreeable unless he can envision its furthering his criminal objectives. Throughout his life, others have asked and pleaded with him to change, but he has put the burden on them to persuade him he should make the effort. The criminal lacks the thinking patterns needed to make prudent decisions. His decisions are determined largely by his pretensions, unrealistic expectations, prejudgments, and assumptions. He reads others according to his own premises and attributes to them qualities and motives they do not have. When he miscalculates, he blames others. He does not admit to or tolerate uncertainty. He is not a factfinder (except with respect to a crime and not always then). Even when he wants more information, he is reluctant to search for it because an admission of ignorance runs counter to his self-image and the image that he wants to convey to others. His lack of foresight and his failure to consider different options result in poor decision-making and in injury to others.

To even the most astute observer, the criminal looks like a mass of contradictions. He is fragmented in his thinking, having fluctuating attitudes that appear to oppose one another. He seems to be both fearless and cowardly, religious and blatant in his sinning, sexually a "King Kong" and sexually incompetent. In general, criminals lack a consistent and cohesive set of attitudes toward their place in the world.

One of the most striking features of the criminal is his view of himself as a good person. Despite all the injuries he has inflicted on others, he does not consider himself a criminal. His idea of "right" is subjective in the extreme: whatever he wants to do at a given moment is right. If at that time he considered an act wrong for him and regarded himself as an evil person, he would not act as he does. What society calls crime, the criminal regards as his work. When he is required to defend himself, he strives to convince others that they are wrong and that he is right. The criminal's view of himself as a good person constitutes an enormous obstacle to those who seek to rehabilitate him, and an examiner or agent of change encounters a formidable array of tactics that are designed in part to support this view but are actually further expressions of criminal thinking patterns.

A change agent or interviewer encounters in the criminal a person who does not tell the truth, does not listen, and does not take stock of himself. Telling the truth puts the criminal in jeopardy and makes him face unpleasant facts about himself. When he does talk, others think that they understand him but often do not. The criminal has such a different frame of reference that even simple words like *friend, love,* and *trust* have meanings radically different from conventional usage. The criminal hears but does not listen. His silence often conveys the impression that he is listening when actually he is inwardly disputatious or has his mind on something totally apart from the issue at hand. He is so busy proving he is in control and knows it all that he dismisses what others say, unless it pertains to a criminal scheme. As far as he is concerned, even listening to someone else is tantamount to being managed by that person. Another reason for not listening is to avoid considering points of view that oppose what he wants. Sometimes, the criminal assents to make others think that he is listening and agreeing; this is a convenient way to end a conversation and to get people to leave him alone without alienating them in the process. The third major obstacle to an open channel of communication is the criminal's lack of interest in the process of self-examination. He finds fault with the world but is unaccustomed to evaluating his own role in it. It is others who constitute the problem, not he.

As the criminal approaches a program for change, he brings to it the mental processes of a lifetime. He treats an agent of change as he has treated others, sizing him up and then trying to manage him. His tactic may entail a naked display of power or, more likely, ingratiating strategies that are subtle and difficult to detect. A problem that constantly besets an agent of change is knowing whether a criminal believes what he says or is only trying to score points; it is impossible to determine this at any given moment. Because of the criminal's fragmentation, he may be sincere one day and completely insincere the next. (For a discussion of fragmentation as a criminal thinking pattern, see volume 1, chapter 4.)

If he participates in a program for change, the criminal expects to change now—instantly and totally—and do it better than anyone else. Again, thinking makes it so. He also expects the change agent to do the work. Moreover, the criminal attempts to dictate the terms of the program and manage the personnel administering it. When told that he has to do things that he dislikes, he reverts to a variety of excuses. All in all, the criminal approaches a program for change as he does a criminal enterprise. He is there to convince others of his point of view rather than to learn a new one. Criminals usually enter change programs to extricate themselves from trouble and less often because of genuine (although transient) self-disgust.

This capsule description shows what kind of a person a change agent is dealing with when he undertakes to change a criminal. Society's ways of dealing with such a person are based on inadequate knowledge. The criminal's fragmentation and seeming contradictions have made it difficult for others to formulate coherent programs.

Society has dealt with criminals in four basic ways: retribution (punishment), confinement (to protect society), deterrence (new statutes and stricter enforcement), and rehabilitation. Retribution has been increasingly rejected because of the belief that a criminal should be helped to change, not condemned and punished. Confinement has been described as mere "warehousing" and viewed as destructive, and it outrages moral sensibilities because it is not constructive. A high rate of recidivism (which is underestimated according to our findings) indicates that efforts at deterrence have not worked well.* The current trend is toward rehabilitation. Many different approaches have been tried, but the professionals, and therefore society, have failed to grasp the magnitude and complexity of the task. Some efforts have focused on criminal behavior as the problem and used arrest and job records as criteria of successful rehabilitation. (We have found as many employed as unemployed criminals as not who are still engaged in crime.) Others have focused on isolated aspects of the criminal's functioning, using the same methods that have been used with noncriminals; it has been assumed that the application of intensive individual therapy, family counseling, group therapy, the therapeutic community, and other procedures to change specific features of the criminal would cause him to straighten out, much as noncriminal patients have straightened out. For example, in treating neurotics, the objective has been to leave the person intact psychologically but to alter features that are maladaptive. The criminal has been approached in the same way in an attempt to make selective alterations while keeping the basic personality intact. We have found that the scope of the change process must be far greater.

In the next chapter, we shall review in detail the efforts made by others to change the criminal. Organic treatments (psychosurgery, medication, etc.) have been unsuccessful. The numerous programs for altering an environment that is thought to produce crime have resulted in the expenditure of manpower, money, and energy but have left crime a domestic problem of top priority. Criminals have taken advantage of these programs and demanded more benefits and services, typically selecting what they want and contributing nothing productive to society. Criminals have been given more and more opportunities to change instead of long terms in confinement. Because of a trend toward community-based corrections, criminals have participated in community education and vocational training programs and have lived in community facilities, such as halfway houses, rather than in prisons. These opportunities have not resulted in change from criminal to responsible citizen. Job skills and education that criminals have acquired either have been utilized in the promotion of further crime or have been

---

* We discuss how the criminal thinks about and responds to deterrents in volume 1, chapter 6. In a section of the next chapter of this volume, we present a review of thinking by others about the deterrence issue.

abandoned altogether. With the return of criminals to the community, the number of crimes committed is extremely high. Criminals have exploited psychotherapeutic work, especially efforts to reconstruct their past to find out why they are the way they are. If a criminal did not have enough excuses for crime before psychotherapy, he has many more after it. As we pointed out in volume 1, the search for causes leads criminals to blame others for what they themselves have done and for their current situations. Other psychotherapeutic techniques that have been successful with noncriminals have been tried with criminals. Advocates of a more present-oriented, rational approach have used their techniques with criminals. Rewards and punishments of various types have been administered to criminals, through the legal process (confinement and deterrence) or through behavior modification therapy. These efforts have failed to change the thinking processes of criminals and have had, at best, only a short-lived effect on their behavior. The threat of punishment at the hands of the law has deterred only people less extreme on the continuum of crime and has had a temporary effect on chronic offenders weary of the revolving door of penal institutions. In general, criminals have used the programs to curry favor with others in order to get out of difficulty. In almost all correctional programs, criminals have been expected to identify with change agents who serve as models of responsibility. Except for lip service and some transient sentimental attachments, criminals have exploited the change agents and continued to scorn responsible living. Because of the necessity to do something rather than nothing, society persists with procedures that have failed.

For several years, we failed as others did. To succeed, we gradually developed a process of change that is extreme in its objectives and in its attention to detail. (The method of original investigation that provided so much substantive material was itself the product of extreme attention to detail.) We know that every one of the criminal's thinking processes described in volume 1 must be eliminated by choice and will and replaced. We know of no other task in human behavior as vast as this.

There are three broad prerequisites of the change process. First, the change agent must make an effective presentation to the criminal at a time when he is vulnerable and therefore wants to change. Second, the change agent must have a detailed knowledge of the criminal's thinking processes (the material presented in volume 1): he must know with whom he is dealing. Third, this knowledge must be made operational through the set of procedures to be described at length in this volume. In this chapter, we offer only a thumbnail sketch of our program, which has been successful in changing some criminals into responsible citizens. The details of how the program operates are presented in the chapters to follow.

The agent of change must deal with the "inner man," not with his environment. A change agent must begin by capitalizing on periods in which a criminal is vulnerable. The criminal has never had a firm conviction about wanting to change. At most, he has made some token efforts during brief periods in which there has been a sense of futility with his chosen life. It is during one of these periods in which the criminal is dissatisfied with himself that the agent of change must make his approach. The criminal may be vulnerable owing to an arrest or confinement. On occasion, conscience may be operative, so that momentarily the criminal is fed up with himself and his way of life: he may be offended by some feature of his own crime pattern, or he may be in a state of mind in which he does not want to harm his family anymore. The criminal must be reached when his opinion of himself as a good person is at an ebb and when he recognizes that he has failed even at being a criminal.

Not every criminal is suitable for this program. At the very beginning, a series of meetings are necessary in which the criminal has a chance to experience our procedures and learn of our program's requirements. We can assess his mental state with respect to change, and he can make his decision as to whether he wants to participate.

In the initial approach, we strive to have the criminal see himself as he is. Rather than ask him who he is, we present him with a profile of who he is. Our objective is to establish valid facts rather than listen to his self-serving reports. We let him know right away that we know how his mind works. We point out the apparent paradoxes in his thinking and actions (which at times have puzzled him as well as society) and show how they are not paradoxes but a natural outcome of the mental processes required to live the kind of life that he has chosen. We anticipate what tactics the criminal will use with us and enlighten him on these. We are aware of the misinterpretations resulting from the semantics of his speech. Our approach helps to elicit a great deal of information in a short time and works as a process of "de-lying," since we do not give him the occasion to direct the transaction with his self-serving accounts. With statements rather than open-ended questions, we present facts with which he is familiar but that he has cut off time and again. We face him with disagreeable but accurate statements about himself. Our accumulated knowledge of the criminal baffles him, impresses him, and occasionally shocks him, even to the extent that some say, "It takes one to know one," meaning that we must be criminals ourselves. In this initial contact, we establish that he is in fact a criminal, something that he does not want to consider, much less believe. Unpalatable as our approach is, it permits us to win his respect and usually his confidence in the fact that we know what we are talking about. In some, we elicit an initial willingness to strive for change.

In these early meetings, we make it clear that from our point of view nothing of the criminal's way of life is to be preserved. Putting on new clothes over old and stained ones is not enough; the old clothes must be regarded as contaminated and diseased and then discarded and destroyed. The criminal must eliminate his old patterns and become responsible in every way. We present him with the severity of the requirements of our program and with the austere life that will be his. We describe in detail what is necessary for the 180-degree shift from total irresponsibility to total integrity. Instead of the amoral stance, we have adopted a moral position and have made it the very cornerstone of our change program. In short, we give the criminal in these early meetings our view of him and of the kind of life that he will lead as a responsible person. The criminal is then faced with a decision as to whether to choose this program. Some select themselves out. If a criminal is willing to participate, we accept him whether or not he agrees entirely with our point of view.

We take the position that man has the capacity to choose. The criminal made choices early in life and continues to do so in the present. Now, he is in a position in which he has three options: more crime with all its risks (which may seem less appealing from behind bars), suicide, or total change as we define and practice it. We do not try to persuade him to change. It is his choice; it is his life. To succeed in our program, the criminal must reach a position of "no choice but to change." He must desire change for its own sake and regard this program as the only possible course for him. Change requires effort (restraining himself from what he wants to do and doing what he does not want to do) and the development of endurance, if he is to eliminate old thought and action patterns and replace them with responsible ones. The criminal needs a head, a heart, and a gut. He needs a head to evaluate himself self-critically, to learn, and to solve problems rationally and constructively. He needs a heart to give him sensitivity to other people and compassion. He needs a gut to endure the hardships of a way of life that he has heretofore scorned. These are hardships only from the unchanged criminal's point of view, such as being deprived of his preferred excitements and having to cope with daily problems of life with which he has had little concern and no experience.

This approach is totally new to most criminals and, as one man put it, as foreign as "the dark side of the moon." Those who have been exposed to psychiatry previously have had their behavior explained in terms of psychologic mechanisms and external events that they have used to justify their irresponsibility. *We do not attempt to derive causation.* We meet issues with facts, pointing out what patterns are operative. Going into how it all began takes us too far afield. In our early meetings, we eliminate sociologic and psychologic excuses. From our point of view, any criminal who clings to a victim stance indicates his lack of commitment to change.

In general, we avoid setting up causal connections between events.

Establishing such sequences may sound impressive, but it does not contribute to change. Instead we take a situation for what it is, point out the thinking errors, and teach correctives. We dissect the criminal's thinking patterns rather than focus on his behavior; although behavior as observed may be outwardly responsible, his thinking is invariably irresponsible. We are not interested in the crime for which a criminal is originally arrested. We do not address ourselves to a specific manifestation of criminality, such as check-forging, or to an isolated problem, such as impotence. We spend almost no time on such things but instead dissect all the criminal's thinking patterns that have resulted in difficulties for him and injury to society.

The topics of each session are not arbitrarily chosen. To reach the substantive material (the thinking processes), we developed a procedure to elicit without bias, interpretation, prejudgment, or explanation the total contents of mind for a prescribed period. This is the technique of phenomenologic reporting by the criminal. Thinking processes are probed down to the last detail to prevent later criminal acts. Otherwise, days, weeks, or months later, an incipient criminal idea will result in a crime. We have found stray thoughts to be of considerable significance, although they often seem inconsequential to the criminal. Dreams are treated like any other thinking. We do not unravel unconscious determinants or analyze symbols. Instead, we view them as indicators of the persistence of old patterns and the presence of new ones. The phenomenologic report is totally different from free association. Instead of saying whatever comes to mind, the criminal presents a well-ordered report of his thinking and actions over the preceding twenty-four hours. To capture as much of the thinking as possible, we ask that the criminal write notes between meetings. The phenomenologic report provides the material for which we offer corrections, in the form of both specific deterrent considerations and new concepts that constitute the substance of new thinking patterns.

In the phenomenologic report, we elicit both thinking and feelings. We have not regarded emotions as the primary cause of behavior and therefore of crime. Emotions, of course, are always present, but we emphasize concomitant thinking. In dealing with a criminal, to make feelings the focus results in multiplying his excuses, rationalizations, and self-deceptions. We probe thinking processes and regard the accompanying feelings as epiphenomena of thought. When criminal thinking processes are replaced by responsible ones, the emotions change correspondingly. (Despite current views, repeated and prolonged efforts at altering emotions have not changed thinking processes.) By altering thinking processes, we have totally eliminated both outward and inward anger in the criminal. Furthermore, the emotional experiences of fear and self-disgust have enhanced responsible functioning *after* the criminal makes responsible thinking patterns habitual.

We begin our work with the criminal on an individual basis. Groups are not advisable in the beginning because a group of unchanged criminals presents so many tactical problems that our concentrated approach is considerably diluted and the process prolonged. After learning what our view of him is and what our program requires, if a criminal decides to participate, he is asked to join a group of three or four other criminals. We have found the group method not only more economical in time but advantageous, in that one member learns from another. The group is a microcosm in the sense that each individual learns to absorb severe criticism—an ability necessary in the macrocosm of society.

A criminal must be educated in two respects. First, he must develop self-understanding. This is not achieved through deriving "insight" into what caused him to be as he is. Some self-understanding results from our careful dissection of his thinking processes, but the bulk of it *follows* change, rather than precedes it. A man comes to understand much more about himself and other people *after* he has changed his behavior than he does sitting around waiting for insight to propel him toward change. Second, the criminal requires a fundamental education about the outside world. He is beginning to function, much as an infant does, in a world foreign to him, and a whole new set of thinking processes has to be developed. Every old thinking pattern is replaced with a new way of thinking. The instruction is in many areas of living. All educating occurs in the context of life situations; it is not didactic. What seems self-evident to responsible people is new to the criminal. Education includes attention to the smallest details of daily living. The criminal learns what the restraints in life are and what initiatives are necessary. He practices those restraints and actually takes those initiatives. This very concrete thinker is trained to think conceptually both about himself and about the world. He learns to view the world as a responsible person does and to *implement* this view. His pretensions and expectations are scaled down. Above all, he comes to the recognition that life is a series of problems he has to meet and struggle with responsibly. With more and more education, the criminal develops genuine self-disgust and views himself as having been very stupid in the past. He sees how irresponsibly he has functioned, how he has inflicted injuries, and he gains a realization of all that he has yet to learn. Mounting self-disgust and a sense of stupidity are necessary to reaffirm continually the initial choice to change.

Learning to deter criminal activity is critically important, and deterring criminal *thinking* is basic to this. The possibility of apprehension has always had some deterrent value, but it is insufficient in building a new life. We instruct the criminal in a new sophisticated set of mental processes that constitute deterrents. In addition, all the new concepts of responsibility that

the criminal learns and practices constitute deterrence. In time, the criminal is able to anticipate the types of situations that will stimulate criminal thinking and to preempt them. The ultimate objective is the total elimination of criminal thinking and its replacement by responsible thinking.

Office meetings are for instruction and clarification, but the criminal learns through life experiences. Words spoken in the office are meaningless, if there is no implementation outside. Declarations of intent must be substantiated by deeds. Thus, there must be what we term the *calisthenics of change,* i.e., implementation of new thinking processes with attention to even the most minute details of living. Instruction begins with a thought fragment or a small incident. We point out and correct the error of thinking and thus go from the concrete incident to a concept that can be applied elsewhere. The criminal must learn from the present event, so that he will recognize a similar situation in the future and cope with it effectively. Finally, we become more abstract and show how the concept fits into an overall view of life. Actually, the end result is that we deal with what may be properly termed existential issues. What kind of person is the criminal? What kind of life does he want to lead? How does he expect to relate to his fellow man, and how does he expect his fellow man to relate to him? These existential questions can be considered only *after* substantial change has occurred. These issues call for choices that the criminal cannot make until he has experienced enough change to make choices.

The process of instruction requires a tremendous amount of repetition. The criminal's habitual practice of cutting off what is disagreeable or uninteresting is so automatic that hearing something once or twice never suffices. Criminals often react to an idea as though it is a brand-new revelation when, in fact, they have discussed it previously. The reason is that it has been office talk. Since the ideas do not have impact if they are not part of life experiences outside the office, repetition also is necessary to establish habits. Each time we go over what we think should be familiar ground, additional material and new considerations emerge.

In our instruction, we do not solve problems for the criminal, give advice, or direct his decision-making. The *process* of decision-making is far more important than an actual decision reached. We help the criminal understand the value of fact-finding and consider a wide range of options (which he had no need of previously). In no way do we direct him toward a particular conclusion. All that is of ultimate concern to us is whether the criminal has thought and acted responsibly. If he makes a mistake, it is carefully evaluated and he is expected to learn from it and apply it to the next experience.

The criminal has to learn and practice habits that are ordinary and routine for the noncriminal. Part of the calisthenics or selfdiscipline involves learning to deal constructively with adversity—paraphrasing Alcoholics Anonymous, to surmount what can be surmounted, to live with what cannot be changed, and to be able to tell the difference. We emphasize to the criminal the comprehensiveness of the effort that is necessary. The door must be closed all the way on old patterns of excitement-seeking. Specifically, this means no more violations and no more relationships with other criminals.

Far more important than crimelessness is the continuous implementation of new responsible patterns of thought. This program is extremely demanding in that the criminal must always strive to attack every difficulty responsibly. There can be no respite from this. Complacency is the greatest barrier to change, because in its wake comes inertia; soon after inertia, old patterns of thinking emerge, and crime is not far behind. Permanent crimelessness does not exist. Criminality must be replaced by responsibility. At no time does the criminal have it made. A self-critical implementing attitude must constantly be maintained, because there is always room for improvement. In fact, we have not yet learned the limits of the extent of change that a man can produce from within himself. It has been striking to watch extreme criminals change, in a matter of a few months, patterns that have been entrenched for decades.

As we embark on the process of effecting change, it is a case of a midget versus a monster—the midget being the program for change and the monster, the criminal's years of experiences and lifetime patterns of thinking. We work so that the midget will prevail. The criminal finds responsibility boring; it is antithetic to his whole life style. However, the amount of suffering that he experiences is inversely proportional to the degree of his commitment. A criminal who views the program as a "lifeline" does not suffer in it but approaches change with zest. A criminal who is reluctant to give up the excitements of the past and who disputes the requirements of the program suffers, being torn by the mandates of two opposing life styles.

We tell the criminal that no one knows the limits of choice and will. However, if he looks around, he sees or hears about people who, on their own or with help, have overcome tremendous obstacles and made remarkable achievements through choice and will. (Attributing such success to a strong ego or failure to a weak ego does not contribute to change.)

A fairly reliable indicator of change is the recognition that the criminal himself can see what he has accomplished by hard work and does not want to imperil it by reverting to old patterns. Moral values develop when a person acquires something honestly and prizes it. This occurs when the criminal has plugged away for an indefinite period (usually at least a year) and has built up something for himself in the responsible world that he is afraid to lose. It is a time in the criminal's life when he is developing some respect for his achievements as a consequence of how he is living. He is no longer living in one tiny corner of the world; as a responsible person, he has expanded his interests and activities and can deal more effectively with people than he ever did as a criminal. He is no longer looking over his shoulder to see whether a policeman is there because he is not getting into trouble. Furthermore, he does not miss the old excitements. Even the *thought* of how he used to be fills him with loathing. His gains are precious; he does not want to jeopardize them. And so he strives to preserve what he has worked hard to build.

An important aspect of our work with the criminal, indeed a precondition for work with him, is that we have contact with people who are important in his life. It may be a single meeting with a criminal and a girl friend or a series of regular sessions with the criminal and another person, such as his wife. These meetings take the same general format as our regular meetings with the criminal, in that there are specific problems to tackle. Sometimes, an agenda is prepared in advance. Because criminals often marry irresponsible women, we often have to instruct a wife in some of the same concepts that her husband is acquiring. If the other party is responsible, less time is devoted in the meetings to the fundamentals of responsibility, and there is more of a focus on the relationship. These meetings serve two purposes: they are a check on the integrity and completeness of the criminal's reporting, and they help in promoting a more harmonious, interdependent relationship.

One might think that as the criminal progresses in change, the material would dry up. However, more and more material emerges, even though crime is eliminated and deterrence of criminal thinking is developed. There are abundant new considerations as the criminal encounters new problems inherent in responsible living. The greatest increase in material occurs when a criminal moves from the restricted arena of confinement into the community, where there are both fewer restraints and more problems to solve. Criminals participate on a daily basis for a year after release from confinement. Some men have wanted to extend their daily contact beyond a year because they have found themselves still insecure in their new life. They are constantly faced with new decisions to make and are still developing new ways of relating to people. Those who want to and whose work schedules permit it continue to attend daily. Most, however, have daytime jobs and meet with us once a week and eventually less often.

A monitoring process is necessary. Long after all legal holds have expired, our changing people still meet with us. They seek assistance, much as noncriminals approach a therapist, with a self-critical attitude, trying to improve their functioning as responsible people. We emphasize continually that there is no room for complacency, there is always room for self-improvement. We take the view, Once a criminal, always a criminal, in the sense that unless a criminal continues to attack new problems thoughtfully, there is always a possibility that he may make irresponsible choices. In other words, change is always in process. With implementation over time, there is, of course less and less likelihood that old patterns will emerge. The criminal values his new way of life too highly.

Our subject has been a lifelong liar who cannot be believed or trusted, a practiced and secret violator in a variety of areas, an intolerant and insensitive pursuer of conquests who imposes his views and desires on others, a self-righteous believer that he is a unique number one, an exploiter of everyone, a blamer of others, a person guided by pretentions and prejudgments instead of facts, a person whose fragmentation is so pervasive that he cannot rely even on himself, a skillful strategist who devises tactics to achieve his criminal objectives, a scorner of responsibility and a ridiculer of those who are responsible, and a person whose entire thinking apparatus is designed to achieve his antisocial objectives. In addition, he has always been contemptuous of those who would attempt to counsel or change him. It is no wonder that others who have contended with such a person have failed, as we did at the start. The criminal has posed a challenge to all. With a new body of knowledge, with an emphasis on dissecting and rebuilding thinking processes, and with new procedures, we have met the challenge.

We do not view change solely in terms of such specific accomplishments as release from confinement, graduation from school, promotion on a job, or money saved in a bank. Instead, we view change as a total alteration of existing thinking patterns and implementation of new thinking patterns of responsibility.

Chapter 2

A History
of Criminal Rehabilitation

BEFORE THE NINETEENTH CENTURY, criminals and the mentally ill—both considered to be possessed by devils and evil spirits—were kept in dungeons, enchained and separated from society. Pinel (1745-1826) in France introduced reform on humane grounds. He freed the insane from their shackles and treated them as ill patients in hospitals. A comparable reform movement for criminals proceeded more slowly. One of the earliest prison reformers, John Howard (1726-1790), recommended that the insane inmates languishing in prisons be treated medically. The objective of more humane treatment applied both to the mentally ill and to the criminal, but with a time lag between the two.*

The distinction between the criminal and the insane was drawn either arbitrarily or not at all. In 1832, Pritchard introduced the concept of *moral insanity*, a forerunner of the later term, *psychopathic personality*. In 1843, the M'Naghten rule recognized the significance of psychiatric conditions in criminals, at least with regard to "responsibility" for the offense.** Gradually, the belief that criminal behavior was a symptom of psychologic disturbance came to be the enlightened liberal position (Silber 1974, p. 239).

This literature review enables the reader to contrast our work with what others in the field have done. The reader who wishes to proceed immediately to our format for change may skip this chapter.

*The early history of penal reform may be found in numerous books and articles. For example, Klare (1966) edited a book with a series of articles on how concepts of treatment of the criminal have changed, and an overview of social trends in combating crime is offered in an article by Glaser (1971).

**Later decisions, e.g., Durham v. United States, 214 F. 2d 862 (1953) and the American Law Institute Model Penal Code, Sec. 4.01 (1) (Official Draft, 1962) have continued to take the offender's mental condition into account.

In the reformist era (the late 1950s and the 1960s) when this belief became widespread, the number of patients in hospitals for the criminally insane increased. Procedures that had been applied to noncriminals who were mentally ill then began to be applied to mentally ill criminals. As Silber points out, criminals were characterized "as having the same traumatic developmental difficulties" as others with psychologic deficiencies.

Even criminals adjudged legally responsible for their crimes were regarded as products of adverse environments and psychologic disturbances. As a result of this view, the emphasis in penal institutions shifted from retribution to rehabilitation. Prisons began to offer not only more humane conditions but a battery of services and programs designed to change criminals so that they would get along in society. These included psychologic assessments; treatment by psychiatrists, psychologists, and social workers; and numerous programs of educational advancement and vocational training. The trend now is toward offering these services to criminals in the community rather than totally within the institution. Alternatives to confinement are increasingly advocated in line with the belief that prisons still do not rehabilitate.

Rehabilitative efforts have been guided by current notions of what causes crime. Those who believe that sociologic factors are the primary influences in shaping a criminal have recommended sociologic remedies. Because there is substantial disagreement as to causation, evaluations of programs have been biased by the various theoretical positions. Discussions of results have generally lacked follow-up, and where there has been follow-up, the main criteria of success have been statistical measures of recidivism and employment.

This chapter outlines the various main approaches to rehabilitation, presenting their conceptual bases and the results claimed by their proponents. Although many of these approaches have been used with drug-using criminals, we reserve discussion of their impact in this population for the literature of volume 3. The focus here is on the criminal who does not use drugs.

ORGANIC APPROACHES

Some investigators have believed that mental disorders have an organic basis, so procedures have been developed to treat such conditions organically. Organic treatments were applied to mentally ill noncriminals, and it was inevitable that the same treatments would be applied to criminals considered mentally ill. In addition, organic treatments were used on psychopaths (sociopaths) by those who thought that criminal patterns could be altered by such approaches.* This review covers organic treatments applied to criminals, without presenting physiologic or biochemical detail.

In a review of treatment approaches, Guttmacher (1951, p. 105), more than twenty years ago, called castration "the most time-honored form of treatment for sexual offenders." The first castrations labeled "psychiatric-therapeutic" and "prophylactic" were performed in Switzerland in 1907 (Kopp 1938, p. 698). Castration was also used in the early twentieth century in Denmark, Germany, Norway, Finland, and Sweden. In 1935, Hackfield claimed a "lasting cure" in 22 of 25 offenders through the use of castration. Kopp (1938, p. 701), citing a study in Switzerland, stated that only 2 of 32 castrates repeated sex crimes. According to Guttmacher (1951, p. 108), Hawke, a surgeon and medical director at the State School for Mental Defectives in Winfield, Kansas, was the "chief public proponent of castration" in the United States. Hawke reported greater stability and a decrease in sex drive in most of the 330 men on whom castration was performed. In the current literature, there is little advocacy of castration as a treatment for criminals.

"Sex suppressant" medication has been given to offenders. Chatz (1972) reported that thioridazine (a tranquilizer) and diethylstilbestrol (a synthetic drug with estrogenic properties) reduce sex drive and thus are effective in managing sex offenders in institutions and in the community. Field (1973) stated that benperiodol (a tranquilizer) abolished sexual desire and resulted in inability to obtain an erection when used on twenty-eight child-molestors.

Electroshock has also been used on criminals. Darling (1945) described three cases of psychopathic personality treated with "electric coma therapy": one criminal was unimproved, the second remained without "legal involvement" for a felony for three years, and the third was reported as "doing well" nine months after treatment. Thompson (1949, p. 539) reported that shock does not alter "the basic characteristics of the psychopathic personality." Kalinowsky and Hoch (1952) also pointed to "negative" findings in psychopaths treated with shock.

Thompson (1953, p. 138) mentioned the use of inhalation of carbon dioxide and nitrous oxide. There are few published reports on these procedures. Meduna (1958, p. 162) reported mixed and uncertain results with carbon dioxide therapy in five children with psychopathic characteristics, only one of whom remained in treatment long enough for his parents to consider him "cured."

Other forms of chemotherapy have been used to treat antisocial people. Tranquilizing medications have been administered in maximum security

---

*As we pointed out in volume 1, we do not maintain a distinction between psychopaths (sociopaths) and criminals.

hospitals and prisons. Kalina (1964) described a study in which Librium (diazepam) was administered to sixty-two psychotic state hospital maximum security inmates who were refractory to other psychotherapeutic approaches. He reported "complete remission of symptoms in terms of behavioral change" in sixty-three percent. Kalina pointed out that, although "basic psychopathology was unaltered," there was sufficient improvement in the inmates' behavior to make "their protracted detention more tolerable for all concerned." Gleser et al. (1965) reported decreased anxiety and hostility in forty-six male adolescent delinquents in a juvenile detention center who were given Librium.

Chemotherapy has been advocated for psychopaths suspected of having cortical lesions and cerebral dysrhythmia (Thompson 1953, p. 128). However, the administration of Dilantin (diphenylhydantoin sodium) to delinquent boys without brain damage, reported by Conners (1972), resulted in no overall change with respect to behavioral incidents or teacher evaluation. Recently there has been some interest in treating delinquents and criminals with lithium carbonate. Rifkin et al. (1972) reported that this drug was helpful in stabilizing mood swings in patients with "chronic, maladaptive behavior patterns." Ziskind et al. (1974) viewed lithium and cyproterone acetate (Schering AG), an antiandrogen, as promising "chemical prospects for control of sociopathic behavior."

Amphetamine therapy has been used in youngsters who present behavior problems. Levy (1966) had success with Benzedrine (amphetamine sulfate) in 225 hyperkinetic children who had been considered delinquent. Their school work improved, and delinquent behavior totally disappeared. Generally, evaluations are mixed. Bradley (1950, p. 30) found that administration of Benzedrine (racemic amphetamine) resulted in improvement in 21 of 25 children diagnosed as "psychopathic personality" and that 11 of 14 such youngsters showed comparable improvement on Dexedrine (dextro-rotatary amphetamine). Bradley concluded that both substances seemed equally effective "to a most gratifying degree in this resistant group." The improvement cited in such studies has to do mostly with greater cooperation in the institution; the underlying personalities remain unchanged (e.g., Korey 1944). Eisenberg et al. (1963) spoke of dextroamphetamine's usefulness in reducing disturbing behavior in the institution. When the drug was discontinued, however, behavior began to revert. At best, amphetamines helped in the control and management of some of these youngsters.

Another mode of investigation and treatment has been psychosurgery. This procedure was used in the 1950s on mental patients, but with few reports of its applicability to the criminal. Mayer (1948) and Kalinowsky and Hoch (1952, pp. 269, 270) cited unfavorable outcomes of psychosurgery on the criminal. Stengel (1950) reported that a prefrontal leucotomy on six psychopaths had produced one full remission of the disorder, improvement in three others, and no change in two. Stengel noted that among patients in other diagnostic groups, antisocial tendencies that were present to a small degree before surgery emerged more strongly thereafter. The early 1970s saw a renewal of interest in this procedure.

> Evidence is accumulating rapidly that chronic aggressive and assaultive behavior in man can be alleviated by the surgical interruption of particular brain circuits. Feelings of anger and hostility, as well as assaultive acts, are controlled frequently by selective brain lesions. Lesions in the posterior hypothalamus, the temporal lobe, dorsomedial thalamus, and the anterior cingulum have all been used successfully to reduce uncontrollable hostility in man. (Moyer 1971, p. 233)

Breggin and Greenberg (1972) called the California prison system a "pioneer dabbler in revamping the brains of selected inmates." These writers deplored the fact that after being discredited, psychosurgery was making a comeback in the 1970s. A news article reported amygdalotomies on three convicts (*Washington Post* 2/25/72). One inmate was viewed as markedly improved, another had "fair results," and the third showed little change. The inmate who showed the improvement was later arrested for robbery. Dr. Orlando Andy, chief of neurosurgery at the University of Mississippi, hailed the success of psychosurgery on aggressive and emotionally unstable children (*Evening Star-News* 1/19/73). Hitchcock and Cairns (1973) reported results of an amygdalotomy procedure on eighteen patients whose behavior was described as "hyperactive, destructive and rebellious." After surgery, these patients showed a decrease in "abnormal aggressive behavior." Turner (1973) stated that a posterior cingulectomy was appropriate for extreme cases in which "chronic resentful aggressiveness prevents the individual from living in society." He said that a paramedian frontal lobotomy was suitable for people who were not able to live in society because of their "impulsive behavior of an aggressive nature."*

Owing largely to controversy over the ethics, as well as the efficacy, of this form of behavioral control, there has been considerable pressure to call a halt to psychosurgery. Brown et al. (1973, p. 8) pointed out that psychosurgery, "because of its dramatic nature, has become a 'lightning rod' for concern and criticism about behavioral control." In 1973, a U.S. Senate subcommittee regarded the psychosurgery controversy as important enough to warrant hearings. The testimony was decidedly unfavorable.

---

*We are assuming that the destructive and aggressive behavior in these studies may, by our definition, rightly be called "criminal."

"Psychosurgery Assailed on Hill"

The government's chief psychiatrist said yesterday he opposes brain surgery for behavior problems—now being performed at a rate of about 500 a year—because the doctors don't know enough about the brain. (*Washington Post* 2/24/73)

In 1973, a bill was introduced into the House of Representatives (U.S. Congress—H.R. 5371) that would prohibit psychosurgery in federally connected health care facilities, with a maximum fine of ten thousand dollars for violators. Senate Joint Resolution 86 asked for a 2-year moratorium on federal aid for psychosurgery (*Medical World News* 7/20/73, p. 31).* In short, ethical considerations, legal pressures, and a lack of convincing results have restrained practitioners from using psychosurgery.

There are isolated references to other organic approaches. Rodale (1968) called for better diet. Kurtzberg et al. (1969, p. 46) recommended offering plastic surgery to disfigured criminals, "to effect changes in self-concept which will ultimately result in less antisocial behavior." One study (cited by Cavior and Howard 1973, p. 203) indicated that, for nonaddict criminals with facial deformities, recidivism of those who had plastic surgery was less than that of a control group that did not.

With regard to effectiveness and propriety, all the organic treatments are controversial. None of the studies that we reviewed reported long-range follow-up of the criminals who were treated. We turn next to a discussion of the many extensive programs to modify the criminal's environment, rather than his physical well-being.

SOCIOLOGIC APPROACHES

IMPROVING SOCIAL CONDITIONS IN THE COMMUNITY

Adverse environmental factors have long been seen as giving rise to crime. Almost any textbook in the field of criminology (or sociology) shows that there have been since the late nineteenth century numerous advocates of social programs to reduce and ultimately prevent crime. Taft's *Criminology*, which has been published in three editions since 1942, is a case in point. Taft pointed out that concern about the effect of unwholesome home conditions predated

---

*Under the National Research Service Award Act of 1974 (U.S. Congress—Public Law 93-348), a commission was established. One of its duties was "the investigation and study of the use of psychosurgery in the United States during the five-year period ending December 31, 1972."

modern psychology. Around 1915, the child-guidance movement provided services by professionals to parents and children. The school and church were seen as potential moral influences, in that they could provide character training and religious teaching. Occupation of leisure time in a constructive manner has been a major function of boys' clubs, YMCA groups, the scouting movement, and other groups for decades. In short, almost every type of measure currently advocated to improve social conditions for the purpose of eliminating and preventing crime is decades old. The same kinds of programs have been recommended and implemented again and again.

Barnes and Teeters (1959) referred to "a plethora of ecological studies of crime." These studies, conducted mostly in the 1920s and 1930s, pinpointed the areas with the greatest incidence of crime—typically, deteriorating neighborhoods. Many such gatherings of statistics confirmed the theories of a number of experts and were influential in determining where resources should be concentrated to fight and prevent crime. For more than fifty years, the clarion call has remained the same: improve social conditions and reduce crime.

> Any improved social arrangement that will make it easier for the common man to live will necessarily save a large number from crime. . . . As far as experience and logic can prove anything, it is certain that every improvement in environment will lessen crime. (Darrow 1922, p. 278)

> Before this Nation can hope to reduce crime significantly or lastingly, it must mount and maintain a massive attack against the conditions of life that underlie it. (The President's Commission on Law Enforcement and the Administration of Justice 1967, p. 60)

In 1970, former Attorney General Ramsey Clark called attention to social conditions that he stated were "fountainheads of crime." He pointed specifically to slums, racism, poverty, unemployment, pollution, poor housing, and prenatal neglect. A report on black families by the U.S. Department of Labor, Office of Policy Planning and Research (1965), presented some of the same views. During the 1960s and 1970s, federal and local governments and private enterprise developed a variety of programs to attack the conditions that were seen as causing crime.

Many social commentators have said that the problem is that some people are "locked out" of the mainstream of society because of a cycle of failure and its consequent low self-esteem (Friedenberg 1962; Goodman 1960; Havighurst 1963; Liddle 1963; Polk 1967). This cycle is said to begin in school.

For decades the schools have been called on to exert a constructive influence on delinquents.

There can be no doubt that educational treatment is essential for many delinquents, even though they be adults. The schoolroom, for the delinquent, should be the avenue to higher vocational possibilities, to better recreational resources, to appreciation of right methods of thinking. (Healy 1915, p. 175)

The emphasis both in prevention and in remediation has been on slum children. The President's Commission on Law Enforcement (1967) described the "vast resources" required to deal with disadvantaged students who might pose problems to the community. The Commission made nine recommendations:

1. Secure financial support for necessary personnel, buildings, and equipment
2. Improve the quality and quantity of teachers and facilities in the slum school
3. Combat racial and economic school segregation
4. Help slum children make up for inadequate preschool preparation
5. Deal better with behavior problems
6. Relate instructional material to conditions of life in the slums
7. Raise the aspirations and expectations of students capable of higher education
8. Review and revise present programs for students not going to college
9. Further develop job placement services in schools

(pp. 73, 74)

Some schools have performed extracurricular functions, so that at least children will not be excluded owing to a lack of food or clothing. Clothes collections, milk programs, government-subsidized lunch programs, and other social services have become the province of the school. Good teachers have been considered the number one antidote to crime, at least as far as measures the school can take are concerned (Van Dyke 1970, p. 69).

Curricula in many systems have been modified in an attempt to introduce greater flexibility and thereby meet individual needs more adequately (e.g., Eichorn 1965; Graubard 1969). Particular attention has been paid to reading programs, with the hiring of specially trained teachers (Liddle 1963). Incentive plans have been proposed which reward both teachers and students for the academic achievement of the students. Schools have expanded their facilities to include vocational training and avoid straight-jacketing all children in an academic curriculum. Some systems have organized work-study programs, so that children do not remain totally classroom bound but can integrate what they learn at school into real life. Trying to anticipate some of the social problems that students might face, educators have initiated school programs dealing with sex, liquor, and drugs. Many schools have increased their counseling staffs and acquired the services of psychologists or other mental health professionals. Teaching responsibility and citizenship through human relations courses and extracurricular activities has also been part of the effort to deal with the whole child. In the classroom itself, massive amounts of money have been poured into enrichment programs for both the restless slow and the restless gifted. Title I of the Elementary and Secondary Education Act of 1965 is one example of the U.S. Government's committing sizable funds to improve opportunities for deprived students. Advanced-placement courses have been offered to the academically talented.

In part, the attitude is that, if a student is kept involved and interested, he will not turn to crime. To maintain involvement, he must have success experienced in the classroom and not experience school as a never-ending series of frustrations, failures, and disappointments (Holt 1964). The psychology of what goes on in the classroom has received great attention. There is a constant emphasis on the need to build self-esteem.

> The most tragic thing that happens to lower-status youngsters in school is that they learn to accept the prevailing judgment of their worth. They accept and internalize the social verdict on themselves. (Friedenberg 1962, p. 117)

A national campaign to contact dropouts and assist them in returning to school was launched by President Kennedy in 1963 (U.S. HEW 1964). More than fifty-nine thousand young people were reached by professional workers, who succeeded in helping more than thirty thousand to return to school.

Many educators have believed that attention must be given to youngsters' educational needs outside the classroom, as part of an attempt to broaden horizons and to help prevent delinquency. Thus, "Big Brother" programs, "High Horizons" programs, and exposure to cultural events have been undertaken. Camping therapy has been used to teach dropouts and delinquents a sense of responsibility and self-pride (Kole and Busse 1969; *Baltimore Sun* 8/14/71).

Reckless and Dinitz (1972) described an inner-city program in which the school intervened in the lives of seventh-graders considered potential dropouts and delinquents. For a year, these youngsters participated in special, self-contained classrooms with carefully trained, dedicated teachers. The teachers adapted the curriculum to the needs of the youngsters and consulted with psychiatrists about classroom interpersonal relationships. There was also a control group of potential delinquents and dropouts who were not offered this program. The four-year follow-up indicated that the Youth Development Project did not fulfill its preventive function. Police and school data showed no difference between the two groups.

Preventive efforts have also been concentrated in job training. James H. Lincoln, President of the National Council of Juvenile Court Judges, recommended the use of massive federal aid to help to overcome the unemployment of school dropouts, which is considered "as big a problem as the atomic bomb, the biggest internal problem confronting the U.S." (Dygert 1971, p. 27). And the President's Commission (1967, p. 77) had already called for:

1. Job preparation
2. Providing information regarding job opportunities
3. Reduction of discriminatory barriers
4. Creation of new employment opportunities

Government has participated extensively in such job-training programs as Job Corps, United Planning Organization, Neighborhood Youth Corps, and Manpower Development and Training Act programs. Private enterprise, especially the automobile manufacturers, has launched campaigns to employ the "hard-core unemployed." The idea behind all these efforts has been that jobs keep people out of jail.

A footnote to the issue of opportunity is that racial discrimination has been seen as contributing to crime (President's Commission on Crime 1966, p. 798). Since the 1950s, great strides have been made in overcoming discrimination in hiring, and today there is a widespread emphasis on equal employment opportunity in the public and private sectors, although, to be sure, discrimination has not been eradicated totally.

As we mentioned in volume 1, poor housing has been seen as playing a role in the causation of crime.

> The crowding of millions of poor people with their cumulative disadvantage into the urban ghettos of our affluent and technologically advanced society not only offers the easy chance for criminal acts—it causes crime. (Clark 1970, p. 29)

Federal and government-supported private efforts to clear the slums and build anew have been huge. Most families have welcomed the opportunity to live under better conditions. Those who are irresponsible and criminal often demand the most but then do the least to maintain their new living quarters. In fact, there was a problem of such magnitude with a "small number of troublemakers" that the National Capital Housing Authority developed a screening program to weed out applicants who disrupt the lives of responsible tenants in public housing (*Washington Star News* 2/27/74).

Neighborhood programs have been part of the attempt to stem the rising tide of crime. The President's Commission on Crime (1966, p. 799), stressed the importance of "meaningful participation in society by all." Programs have been established to promote an interest in community affairs, such efforts being seen as helping to prevent crime. For families which are having problems, there are new resources for help such as a host of walk-in clinics and family service agencies.

Supervised child day-care centers, recreational opportunities (including playgrounds, parks, and fresh air camps), neighborhood youth centers, and community clubs have all been part of the crime prevention effort, while serving many other functions at the same time. Attempts have been made to encourage families to do things together. An optimistic view of the prophylactic effects of recreation was stated in 1946 by William Sadler, a psychiatrist:

> The more recreation a family has, the more parents and children play together, the less there is of delinquency among its juvenile members. Recreation must not be confined to a two-weeks' annual vacation. It must be had every day and every week-end. In my opinion, family play will do more to prevent youthful crime than all the other influences put together. (p. 127)

A statement by a director of recreation indicates how well recreational programs are working in actuality.

> We keep them off the streets all right. But many of these kids wouldn't be getting into trouble anyway. The ones who are out looking for trouble don't come in here. They are antisocial; they don't like our rules. Sometimes they stand in the shadows outside the building, but we never see them. (quoted in Van Dyke 1970)

Feldman et al. (1973) reported the results of a summer camp experience in which antisocial boys were mixed with "prosocial" boys. During the camping season, less antisocial behavior occurred than had been expected. However, there was no long-term positive effect on the antisocial youngsters, and the antisocial behavior did not rub off appreciably on the others.

Before the 1960s especially, caseworkers often sought out delinquents in their own hangouts. A publication by the New York City Youth Board (1960) described how caseworkers attempted to reach gang members. One function of the social worker was to provide such concrete, practical services as arranging for gym facilities, securing employment, and obtaining medical care for delinquents. But all this was a vehicle to establish interpersonal relationships. It was hoped that, in time, a gang would realize that the worker who rendered so many services was seriously interested in them; the relationships would then grow deeper through joint participation in various programs and activities, such as weekend camping trips and ball games. An important guiding concept was that the social worker would serve as a model with whom to identify and thus gradually guide antisocial youths toward constructive social activities. Social workers have also functioned as administrators and therapists in correctional institutions. The Task Force on Corrections (1967) pointed out that these caseworkers are often handicapped in decision-making, because they have too few hours to do justice to a large case load. Social workers also run neighborhood clinics and family service agencies in which they have the formidable task of treating delinquent youngsters and their families on an outpatient basis.

In an era of instant communication, the communication media have participated in the crime prevention campaign. Television and radio have warned about leaving keys in cars, keeping track of where one's children are, and so forth. Saturation campaigns against drug use and shoplifting have been launched in many parts of the country. Educational films have been prepared for showing in schools and churches, at community meetings, and on television. Special programs, documentaries, and theatrical productions have dramatized various dimensions of the crime problem.

In "Environmental Design and the Prevention of Behavioral Disorders and Criminality," Jeffery (1973) cited studies that focused on "environmental opportunities" for crime. He mentioned Jacob's observation that areas "hidden from public scrutiny and control" had high crime rates. Jeffery pointed out that an analysis of the Pruitt-Igoe housing development in St. Louis revealed that the stairwell design and the isolation of elevators, hallways, and lobbies all contributed to the severe crime problem that was a major factor in the demolition of the project. Jeffery's basic contention was that environmental control can change pathologic forms of behavior. He argued that crime prevention can be approached positively, once there is greater understanding of how environment and biologic organism interact. For example, he pointed out that the environment's impact on brain biochemistry can be affected by architectural design.

Technology has been regarded as having great potential for fighting crime. Caplan (quoted in Otten 1975), director of the National Institute of Law Enforcement and Criminal Justice, has pointed to some of the contributions that technology can make in the form of improved burglary and alarm systems, locks, streetlighting, and environmental design. Caplan emphasizes technology "not only because he believes in its possible benefits but also because he does not see any other very good answer."

In evaluating sociologic preventive approaches, there has been little concern with the characteristics of criminals. Instead, billions of man-hours and dollars have been poured into programs to improve man's environment. It is difficult to evaluate the success of these efforts since it is not possible to tell what has been prevented. All we do know is that no sociologic remedy or combination of remedies has resulted in a reduction of crime. Back in 1946, Teeters summed up the state of prevention programs:

> Millions of dollars have been poured into crime prevention activities. Many of these are admirable, some pretty shoddy so far as programs and personnel are concerned. Few agencies objectively appraise their work but hew away at old programs, using old skills, publishing glowing reports, and begging for more money from the public. (p. 61)

The situation has not changed much since 1946. Social programs have helped those who have wanted to help themselves. Caplan (quoted in Otten 1975) has said that better schools, improved housing, more jobs, and less discrimination are "all highly desirable on their own." But, he asserts, "they're much too basic to be tied to crime control." In spite of more programs and the expenditure of increasing amounts of money, crime continues to be a major national problem.

IMPROVEMENT OF SOCIAL CONDITIONS IN CONFINEMENT

Over the years, a change in emphasis in the penal system from punishment to rehabilitation has taken place. It has been said that the best way to prevent recidivism is to rehabilitate the criminal effectively (J. Rubin 1971). Dissatisfaction with the penal system has been expressed in many quarters for decades. In 1895, the noted psychiatrist, William A. White, stated that prisons were "constantly turning out into the community men who are depraved, debased and skilled in all the vices of criminal art in place of men received who were comparatively harmless citizens" (p. 15). White cited Gautier's vitriolic statement about the prison:

> The prison, indeed as it is organized, is a sewer throwing out into society a continuous flood of purulence, the germs of physiological and moral contagion. It poisons, brutalizes, depraves, and corrupts. It is a manufactory at once of the phthisical, the insane and the criminal. (Gautier quoted by White, pp. 15-16)

The Eastern State Penitentiary at Philadelphia, or "Cherry Hill," opened in 1929 with a commitment to reform. (For a history of reform, see Barnes and

Teeters 1959.) Prisoners were confined in separate cells to avoid contamina-
tion of each other. They were even led to their cells with hoods over their faces.
They worked in their cells, as part of the effort to reform them. Inmates also
had visiting rights. The system was criticized, because it was believed that
living in isolation was conducive to insanity. In 1921, the Auburn, N.Y.,
prison opened. Here, the ill effects of isolation were avoided. Prisoners were
allowed to communicate by day, but they were to be silent at night. The
contract labor system began in this prison. It was considered revolutionary in
1932, when Moreno introduced the concept of the prison as a "socialized
community," in which the individual prisoner would be assigned to a group
that would be most likely to help him to fulfill his needs. The prisons had their
various work programs, including prison industries and other activities,
which we shall describe.

Occasionally, poor conditions were exposed. In the mid-1960s, the public
became outraged over prison conditions, and a campaign for sweeping
reforms began. The nation's prisons were seen as being crime schools or, at
best, offering a few inadequate, archaic programs that contributed little to
rehabilitation. It was observed that criminals played the prison game of
cooperating with the authorities to expedite their release without really
changing their attitudes, or they caused so much difficulty that the institution
was eager to get rid of them.

"Juvenile Crime, Punishment: Criminal Training"

Training school officials say that children often have gone through the
state's juvenile system like mice through a maze, willing to do whatever
will speed their exit. They return to their communities neither reformed
nor rehabilitated. . . . Often the reason for discharging a youth was to get
rid of him, to end the problems he was creating for the institution. Thus,
sometimes the problem boy could get released before the one who was
behaving himself. The kid who was released was happy and the staff was
happy. (*Washington Post* 7/3/73)

Mass-circulation publications gave major coverage to the "shame of the
prisons" (e.g., *Time* 1/18/71). In 1970, the American Bar Association
launched a prison reform campaign. Goldfarb (1971, p. 45), in *Look*
magazine, referred to the prisons as the "one billion dollar a year failure."

In the 1960s and into the 1970s, discontent flared inside the prisons, and
America had to contend with prison violence; in the uprising at Attica State
Prison in September 1971, the most notorious incident, thirty-seven people
died. Reporters and other investigators began to visit prisons and ask inmates

what was wrong with the institutions (Goldfarb 1971; Ross 1972; *Washington Post* 2/22/73). Many accounts of dehumanizing and inhumane treatment of inmates were published. The call for reform was loud. Gambino (1969) termed the "hard labor" of many systems "pointless slavery." Mitford (1973) reported "alarming stories" of prison medical research in which doctors and drug companies profited at the expense of prisoner subjects. Reviewing the medical treatment of some prisoners in Alabama, a judge found neglect "that could justly be called 'barbarous' and 'shocking to the conscience'" (*Psychiatric News* 4/4/73). In 1973, a judge ordered the director of corrections for Virginia to pay more than twenty thousand dollars out of his own pocket to three former inmates of the state penitentiary, because they had been subjected to inhumane punishment (*Evening Star . . . News* 2/1/73). In desperation and outrage, critics of the penal system have called for a radical reorganization of the system or for total elimination of prisons in their modern forms. In a far-reaching report, the National Advisory Commission on Criminal Justice Standards and Goals (1973, p. 349) claimed that the major state adult institutions "represent the least promising component of corrections." The Commission advised that many of the current inmates be transferred to community-based programs and that construction of new major institutions be suspended. Their recommendations were the same for state institutions for juveniles. The Commission declared:

> The correctional institution has been poorly conceived, in that it is intended to hide rather than heal. It is the punitive, repressive arm whose function is to do the system's "dirty work." (p. 353)

This report, only the third major study of the American correctional system in the twentieth century, was received by some people as a bible for correctional reforms (*Washington Star-News* 10/15/73). Much current opinion is in the direction of not putting criminals in prison at all, if possible. Massachusetts and other states have closed some facilities, especially those for youths, and have elected to deal with offenders in the community. The Supreme Bench of Baltimore has referred selected criminals to an "offenders' clinic" rather than jail, ordering them to attend forty weekly sessions before serving probation terms.

The Patuxent Institution at Jessup, Maryland, began operating in 1955, under the Maryland Defective Delinquent Law (Boslow et al. 1959). The statute is unique, in that a psychiatrist rather than a penologist has responsibility for rehabilitation of "defective delinquents" (*Psychiatric News* 3/21/73). Patuxent was the first institution of its kind in the country; crime was viewed as the product of a mental factor but not insanity. Patuxent houses 386 nonpsychotic patients.

In some respects it is very much like a jail in that it is under the Department of Corrections and is maintained as a maximum security installation, with barred windows and doors, with inmates under a round-the-clock surveillance by a trained custodial force, and with a strict regard for the maintanance of discipline. (Boslow et al., p. 11)

Inmates there have been evaluated as intellectually deficient and/or emotionally unbalanced. They are committed to Patuxent on an indeterminate sentence. This is considered a "helpful outside motivating force." Boslow and Manne (1966, p. 26) observed that "because the indeterminate sentence is always present to reinforce motivation, the pressure on patients to understand their behavior is always present." The Patuxent program is expensive, costing approximately twelve thousand dollars per inmate per year. The staff has instituted a "graded tier system" (Boslow 1964), which awards inmates gradual privileges for desirable behavior. Vocational and educational programs are offered, as well as group therapy. The institution acts as its own paroling agent. Initially, Patuxent was greeted with acclaim as offering an entirely new concept in the treatment of offenders. In 1971, a group of militant prisoners sought writs of habeas corpus directing their release, on the grounds that Patuxent had failed in its purpose and that they were being treated unlawfully and inhumanely. The men were not released. However, in the wake of violence, the charges were investigated, and the staff was called on to defend its program (*Baltimore Sun* 8/4/71). A judge who visited the institution cited "a lack of direction at the very top" and stated that he found a prison, instead of a treatment center (*Psychiatric News* 4/4/73, p. 35). In January 1973, a bill was introduced in the Maryland legislature to close Patuxent, but it did not pass. In 1974, the state announced a second phase of its investigation, in which state officials would take testimony from inmates and employees (*Washington Post* 9/23/74). We toured Patuxent in 1974 and found an institution that appeared to have both a proper consideration for security and an interest in rehabilitation. The institution had a full complement of shops, a printing plant, recreational facilities, and classrooms. The inmates, referred to as "patients," were all eligible to participate in group therapy; some were eligible for individual therapy. Patuxent acknowledged that many patients are returned after they go out on parole. However, the supervising psychologist, Dr. Carney, stated that, after total release from the institution's control, the recidivism rate is only ten percent.

The nation's first large-scale "corrections research center" opened in 1976 at Butner, North Carolina. It is a federal facility constructed by the Bureau of Prisons. Norman Carlson (1974), Director of the Federal Bureau of Prisons, stated that the Butner institution has two basic missions: to diagnose and treat offenders with mental disorders and to "test and evaluate programs aimed at improving correctional effectiveness."

Barr (1967) recommended that correctional systems move toward implementation of "voluntary imprisonment" in much the same style as voluntary admission to mental hospitals. He proposed a plan that would encourage psychiatry and the legal system to cooperate and pool resources. In short, the trend is away from the traditional, large correctional institution, with its emphasis on punishment, and toward community rehabilitation that enlists the cooperation of the offender.

We turn now to a discussion of the types of institutional programs that are available to confined criminals.

Educational Programs

A variety of educational programs are offered in some prisons. Some institutions have libraries and their own newspapers to disseminate information and discuss problems. Trade and occupational information is often available. At one end of the educational spectrum, illiterates may be taught to read. At the other, opportunities for advanced education are increasingly available, ranging from correspondence courses to attendance at classes on college campuses. The Office of Economic Opportunity spent $3.6 million in 1971 to help criminals earn degrees. Such expenditures have stirred up considerable controversy. Prisoners at the Lorton Reformatory, near Washington, D.C., took college courses conducted at the prison by Federal City College instructors. Other inmates were permitted to leave the prison for specified periods to study at the college. Individual inmates were provided with hundreds of dollars in federal student grants and loans, although they already were receiving free tuition, free books, laboratory fees, and $10 a week each for pocket money. An editorial in the *Evening Star* and *The Washington Daily News* (2/15/73) pointed out that it cost $4,141 to "send a man to Lorton Reformatory for nine months." This, the *Star* stated, was slightly more than the expense of sending a boy to Harvard. The amount to support a youngster at the Lorton Youth Center was actually in excess of that, amounting to $6,839.

> If, on top of this, you add the Federal City College tuition and all those extras, you begin to wonder if we're not perhaps being unfair to ordinary, well-behaved but poor kids who can't go to college and don't have to go to jail.

The results of "study release" programs have not been evaluated through regular follow-up (*Washington Post* 5/20/73), but it must be noted that under the pretext of attending classes, criminals have left Lorton and engaged in crime (*Washington Star-News* 1/12/74). A variety of other educational programs have been instituted to help rehabilitate confirmed criminals. Vigrolio (1961) even reported that a group of prisoners with below-average schooling formed a debating team that vanquished teams from Harvard and other major universities.

Once the criminals return to the community, efforts are made to encourage them to further their education. In 1957, Roman wrote a book on reaching delinquents through reading. He found that through a combination of remedial reading and "tutorial group therapy," these youngsters could be helped in both reading and "psycho-social adjustment." Murphy and Murphy (1971) advocated allowing prisoners to attend college as part of a parole plan. The objective of the educational efforts is, of course, to equip criminals better to make a living and to develop talents that have previously been dormant. Education is one of a variety of programs offered with the rationale that an acceptable social experience will somehow influence prisoners "to live their lives in a socially acceptable manner after they leave prison" (Eaton 1962, p. 47).

Job Training

Because of a widespread belief that "idleness is the parent of mischief," prisoners often used to be given busy-work, such as moving piles of sand on trays from one side of the yard to the other. In time, a variety of programs emerged for more realistic vocational training. At first, this was restricted mainly to maintenance jobs in the prison itself or work in prison industries which made beds or license plates. The emphasis gradually shifted to training for jobs in the community. For example, the prison at Statesville, Illinois, had chairs to train forty-four barbers at a time. Expensive machinery and equipment, as well as instructional personnel, became part of prison programs, as society recognized that criminals must be prepared to do something vocationally useful after their release.

The Urban Coalition began to study the feasibility of bringing highly skilled private industries to Lorton Reformatory.

"Urban Unit Studies Industries at Lorton"

The concept involves getting a number of Washington area industries to build plants in or adjacent to the Lorton complex, 23 miles south of Washington in rural Virginia. The department of corrections would then train inmates to meet beginning job requirements.

Upon release, the inmates could opt for similar jobs with the same firms on the outside.... While in prison, they would belong to the appropriate labor unions and receive prevailing wages and fringe benefits. (*Washington Post* 1/12/71)

Either jobs were brought to the prisoners or prisoners were brought to the jobs.

"Jobs for Women Inmates"

Funded by a $266,347 grant from the U.S. Labor Department, the program [at the Women's Detention Center] will put women inmates serving terms of one year or less in jobs with the District government or in classes at Federal City College. (*Evening Star* 7/21/71)

As the Task Force on Corrections (1967, p. 68) pointed out, most releasing authorities require prisoners to have a job as a condition of release. One type of arrangement designed to facilitate reentry into society is the "work-release" or "work-furlough" program, in which an inmate is allowed to leave the institution to report for a job and then return at the close of the day's work. Although reformers have advocated this, the practice has been controversial because of security problems. A National Institute of Mental Health study, *Graduated Release* (1971b, p. 12) reported that in Washington, D.C., in 1969, 50 of 156 fellows on work-release had absconded or had their right to participate revoked. Five years later, it was reported that most escapes from Lorton Reformatory involved prisoners on furlough programs (*Washington Post* 9/8/74; *Washington Star-News* 9/26/74).

Some federally or privately funded organizations help released convicts get jobs. Palmer-Paulson Associates of Chicago, a manpower development company, is one of these. In a television interview, John Palmer (1972) pointed out that a man's feeling of well-being is associated with his work. He stated that his firm had been successful in aiding convicts vocationally and that fewer than fifteen percent of those worked with had returned to prison.

Some observers have been skeptical about how much job training contributes to changing criminals. De Berker (1966, p. 145) pointed out that habitual criminals may be well-educated and even skilled craftsmen, but "lack the ability to apply these skills to the task of living as free men in society." This has been confirmed in our study.

Cultural Activities

As we pointed out in chapter 4 of volume 1, many criminals have interests and talents in the arts. Some workers in corrections believe that cultivating these talents and interests will help the criminal to be socially more useful.

> That somebody missed the boat in the task of harnessing the creative gifts and talents . . . to social purposes and social satisfactions, we may be sure. (Winthrop 1965, p. 57)

It is argued that emphasizing the good features in criminals enhances their self-esteem and increases the chance of their being responsible. As for criminals who are untutored or culturally deprived, some people believe that exposure to art and music will open up new vistas to them and provide socially useful outlets. Prison art shows, drama groups, music groups, and crafts are among vehicles for self-expression and education that penal institutions and other correctional facilities offer (*Evening Star* 9/2/68 and 11/9/70,; *Correctional Programs News* 11/72). The first permanent gallery for prison art opened in Chicago (*Correctional Program News* 11/72), and artwork from inmates throughout the United States is being exhibited and sold there. Some institutions bring in performing artists to entertain inmates. The idea of rehabilitation through the arts seems to have received considerable acceptance throughout the country.

Recreation

Recreation in some form has been a part of institutional programs for a long time—if for nothing else, as a way of alleviating the monotony of prison life. The American Correctional Association (1966, p. 519) pointed out that recreation had been seen as a "safety valve for pent-up energies which might otherwise lead to disturbance." Later, it was viewed as "corrective and preventive for mental health," thus having a therapeutic value in its own right. Recreational opportunities are offered both in the institutions and in communities to those identified as delinquents and criminals. Counseling is sometimes offered with recreation (*St. Louis Post-Dispatch* 11/11/71). Wollard (1972) described ways in which recreational programs help to modify behavior. Criminals can learn to work cooperatively, to accept leadership of others, and to respond constructively to pressure. Another potential benefit of recreational therapy is that it can "guide a person toward a lifetime of constructive leisure time" (p. 117). Williams (1972, p. 140) studied recreational patterns of twenty parolees. He found that "the carryover value of prison recreation activities is not as strong as the carryover value of pre-prison recreation pursuits." In other words, what happened in prison programs had little impact. What a criminal liked before prison he liked later. Many advocates of recreational activities for rehabilitation believe that sports build character, but see Ogilvie and Tutko (1971) for an opposing view.

Religion

In prison, some identified religious teacher or clergyman is usually available. The American Correctional Association (1966, pp. 472-476) listed the functions of the clergy in a correctional institution as administering religious sacraments and special rites, providing religious education, "pastoral calling," interviewing and counseling, facilitating the inmate's relationship to his family, community programming, ministerial services to staff, and planning "extra-curricular" religious programs.

Interviewing and counseling are major functions. The role of the clergyman often is to befriend the inmate in order to establish a positive relationship with him. The rationale for an active religious program was stated by Eaton (1962, p. 47): "Touch a man's soul and convert him. He will be better able to control his evil impulses." Thus, the chaplain attempts to bring out the religious components that are already present in many criminals. To do this, most clergymen try to establish trust.

> Small friendly acts by the chaplain are essential for building up that trust which is basic to spiritual care. (Skambraks 1967, p. 107)

However, Klink (1970) has warned clergymen that friendship and compassion by themselves are not effective in counseling inmates.

> Easy and presumptuous compassion, undisciplined pity or guilt, even "love" are poor motivations for significant work. The process of re-adaptation for nearly all inmates involves stressful work which he alone must be encouraged to do. Those who would be of service to him must be willing to administer a tolerable dose of such strong medicine fully as much as they are moved to be "his friend." (p. 140)

Klink directed his remarks especially to chaplains who are working with criminals about to return to the community. Many in corrections have suggested that the clergyman can have his strongest impact at that point in the inmate's life.

> The impact of religion is especially great when the influence of the chaplain is supplemented by religious lay organizations in the community. Frequently, in advance of an inmate's release, they arrange membership in an organization and friendly contacts. (Task Force on Corrections 1967, pp. 52-53)

Family Visits and Family Counseling

The National Advisory Commission on Criminal Justice Standards and Goals (1973) advocated that prisoners have the right to private visits with their families. In a review of the controversy surrounding conjugal visits in prisons, Rieger (1973) proposed a pilot program for selected prisoners that would introduce such visits with family therapy as "components of an overall rehabilitative effort." Selsky (1962), a probation officer, deplored the fact that many institutions forget about families of offenders. He stressed the importance of family coι ıseling while a criminal is confined. Some institutions, especially me: tal hospitals and youth facilities offer family therapy. The "reintegrative' type of family therapy, in which the whole family is treated as a unit, has been used, as well as "corrective intervention" for one or more members (Task Force 1967, p. 31).

Teaching Social Skills

In confinement and in community rehabilitation, emphasis has often been placed on encouraging criminals to socialize with others. In 1972, Fort Worth Federal Correctional Institute became the first coeducational prison for adults in the United States. Coeducation was viewed as providing a more "wholesome, natural atmosphere" for correctional work (Stowers 1973). Civic organizations have encouraged criminals to participate in their functions by sponsoring activities at prisons and in the community. For example, more than seven hundred inmates in Virginia prisons were participating in a program of the Jaycees. The objective (Robertson 1972, p. 123) was to help prisoners to "make their prison environment a better one while, at the same time, developing themselves as leaders in positive ways." Youth training schools and reformatories have offered "social adjustment" and "reentry" programs. In addition, a plethora of groups have encouraged criminals to be with others like themselves and to engage in constructive problem-solving. These include Alcoholics Anonymous, Gamblers Anonymous, and Checks Anonymous.

A criminal who is supposed to be reforming may "play the role of rescuer, becoming a social worker or mission worker" (Berne 1967, p. 133). Some institutions sponsor programs in which criminals learn to counsel and instruct other prisoners. By so doing, it is thought, they can simultaneously help themselves (*Time* 1/18/71, p. 55). In a variety of programs, ex-convicts gain wide public exposure by speaking at schools, on television, and to community groups. The trend toward employing ex-convicts in such a counseling capacity is based on the belief that they can "comprehend the problems of the prisoner better than anyone who lacks the experience" (Buckley 1972), that they can provide a model and a "hope for the future." We might mention here W. Menninger's (1973) recommendation to extend the Big Brother programs, long active in the community, to institutions. Menninger stated that in offering a "therapy of friendship," Big Brothers could function as "father substitutes" for confined delinquent boys. Such relationships are seen as offering acceptance, affection, and understanding that have been lacking in the youngsters' lives—"the basic assignment of the Big Brother is to help the troubled boy learn how to love" (p. 46).

"REHABILITATION" IN THE COMMUNITY

Society has been increasingly displeased with its correctional system, especially with prisons. In the late 1960s and early 1970s, the trend among people in all walks of life has been against incarceration of lawbreakers. Some judges are reluctant to sentence men to prison, which they see as ineffective in rehabilitation. Many people believe that some convicts who are serving terms do not need to be confined. They argue that the longer a man stays in jail, the worse he is likely to become. A National Institute of Mental Health (1971a) monograph, *Community Based Correctional Programs,* listed four categories of currently used alternatives to jail: specialized units within probation and parole, nonresidential intensive treatment, residential programs, and out-of-home placements. It stated:

> The evidence obtained from experimental work in community programs, and supported by the results of experience with partial imprisonment and graduated release, the treatment of mental illness, and alternatives to processing by the criminal justice system, clearly indicates that a vast proportion of offenders could be managed in the community at least as effectively, and with much less cost, or diverted from the justice system entirely, thus returning to the community its responsibility for dealing with behavior it defines as antisocial or deviant. (p. 36)

Community alternatives, furthermore, are recommended as less costly and less damaging to the offenders than imprisonment.

Chaneles (1974) has proposed a sweeping alternative to prison: transitional communities that could be developed in American deserts and ghost towns. These enterprises would prove a boon to offenders and would benefit society. Chaneles suggested that such communities would provide opportunities for an offender to have "stable and meaningful employment," own a home, and play a role in community life. A criminal would learn skills that could help him to "live with competition and strain" and become a productive member of society.

The most frequently traveled route so far is that of probation and parole which some claim are underused. Dressler (1968), former Executive Director of the New York State Division of Parole, said that fifty percent of prison inmates should not be in prison at all. He said that thirty-five percent could be placed on parole after a brief period of confinement, provided they then received "meaningful treatment." The President's Commission (1967) urged that

> parole and probation services should be available in all jurisdictions for felons, juveniles, and those adult misdemeanants who need or can profit from community treatment. (p. 166)

The purpose of granting probationary sentences is to avoid confining a man at all and, at the same time, to supervise his rehabilitation in the community. Probation has been praised not only for its correctional merits but also for its cost-effectiveness. The purpose of parole is to integrate prisoners into the community after they have served part of a sentence. In many instances, supervision for probation and parole is minimal because of huge caseloads assigned to overburdened workers, especially in urban areas. The Task Force on Corrections (1967) pointed out that the process for deciding when to grant parole is not what it should be.

> Far too typically, overworked institutional caseworkers must attempt to gather information on a prisoner from brief interviews with him, meager institutional records, and letters to community officials. This information is often fitted into a highly stereotyped format. Frequently, the sameness of reporting style and jargon makes it very difficult for board members to understand the individual aspects of a given case and assess them wisely. This can lead to decisions which are arbitrary and unfair as well as undesirable from a correctional standpoint. (p. 63)

In the 1960s, community "halfway houses" for paroled offenders became widespread. They were to help in the transition from institution to community.

> Such houses are designed to meet the need of a released inmate for companionship and to supply him with adequate food and shelter while he struggles to establish an employment base in the community and a social base with his family and friends. The assumption is that the halfway house provides a sanctuary to which the inmate may retreat in the face of setbacks which might otherwise, were he on his own, have thrown him into erratic and perhaps criminal behavior. (NIMH 1971b, p. 2)

Washington, D.C., inaugurated the first program in the nation that allowed some convicted youthful felons to go immediately to a halfway house and bypass prison altogether. These young offenders, called "students," were to participate in a "living, learning experience" (*Evening Star* 12/29/70). The D.C. Department of Corrections also pioneered releasing adult criminals to community halfway houses. As this program began, it was locally heralded as an advance over traditional penal practices.

"Halfway Houses: A Project That Must Succeed"

Halfway house, work release and programs of prisoner training must be made to work for the plain reason that the community cannot afford to have them fail. There is no alternative. (*Sunday Star* 9/19/71)

Later, the halfway house came under fire in the Washington area, as criminals escaped, used drugs in the houses, and committed crimes while still residents *(Washington Post* 9/29/71, 11/13/71; *Washington Star-News* 1/12/74, 10/5/74, 10/29/74). The *Washington Post* on February 27, 1973, described the problems of the first two years, which resulted in a "get-tough" policy:

"Get-Tough Policy Saves Youth House"

Washington's 2-year-old experiment in therapeutic community rehabilitation for young offenders—the first such project in the nation—has saved itself from an embarrassing demise by getting tough with drugsters and rule-breakers. . . .

"This is rehabilitation at its best," Mayor Walter E. Washington declared at the opening ceremony.

Five months later, a quarter of the house's residents were on drugs . . . and 21 of the first 24 residents either escaped or were returned to prison for committing new crimes or major infractions of house rules. . . .

Discipline broke down in the house, and there were increased incidents of thievery, alcohol use and curfew violations. Counselors said they found themselves thinking more about their own job futures than the goals of the inmates. . . .

In 1971, only six youths successfully completed the program, while last year [under the get-tough policy] 25 were "graduated."

A policy was instituted whereby the group would be punished for an infraction by one member unless that offender came forward and confessed. Recidivism by halfway-house residents continued to be a problem. In 1974, 405 of 857 halfway-house inmates in Washington, D.C., were arrested for committing new crimes (*Washington Star-News* 1/20/75).

In other parts of the nation, halfway houses and other efforts at community-based corrections are underway. Vasoli and Fahey (1970) described a center in Gary, Indiana. This halfway house had "ample money, a pool of available jobs, intensive but not oppressive supervision, [and] acceptable physical facilities." Despite these favorable conditions, some of the youths plotted crimes on the premises. Despite intensive daily supervision nearly one-fourth of the residents committed crimes that came to the attention of the authorities. Finally, this project, initially proposed as a "striking correctional tour de force," closed.

Grygier et al. (1970) were dubious about the effectiveness of Canadian halfway houses. These investigators claimed that the more lenient of these institutions may "actually support the antisocial way of life."

> The halfway houses that make most demands on the offenders are most often criticized by them, especially by those who go back to prison; but it is possible that the houses making no such demands actually support the antisocial way of life adopted by their clients, especially if this involves alcoholism, drug addiction, or prostitution. To some offenders unconditional acceptance is a prerequisite of treatment; to others it is the license to continue their pattern of behavior. (pp. 290, 291)

Lamb and Goertzel (1974) evaluated Ellsworth House, a community rehabilitation center, whose program combined behavior modification, vocational rehabilitation, and confrontation. Contrasting residents there with a comparison group, they found in a six-month follow-up that recidivism was actually higher among the Ellsworth group. After another six months had passed, Ellsworth's recidivism was slightly less than that among the control group, owing to a tightening of supervision by the staff. Clearly, if reducing recidivism significantly was a goal, it was not being met in this community effort. Perhaps the research on programs designed to ease the transition from prison to free community is best summed up in the NIMH report *Graduated Release* (1971b). After pointing out that administering agencies believe in their own programs, the authors of the NIMH review stated:

> The more rigorous the methodology used with research and experiments undertaken in regard to pre-release, work release, and halfway houses,

the more ambivalent or negative are the findings regarding the efficacy of such programs. (p. 23)

This publication endorsed graduated-release programs, because offenders are thereby spared some of the "devastating consequences of incarceration" and can achieve something constructive.

The Juvenile Justice and Delinquency Prevention Act of 1974 (U.S. Congress—Public Law 93-415) set up a federal agency to offer grants to states which developed programs and services "designed to prevent juvenile delinquency, to divert juveniles from the juvenile justice system, and to provide community-based alternatives to juvenile detention and correctional facilities." This meant that money would be available for a variety of community programs: foster-care homes, group homes, halfway houses, youth service bureaus, and so forth.

Former District of Columbia police chief Jerry Wilson (1974) put the movement for community corrections into perspective, on the basis of his own experience. He pointed out that first-offenders rarely go to trial, much less to prison; thus, the issue of prison vs. community rehabilitation is not applicable to them. However, well-intentioned programs to help more serious and frequent offenders move from prison back into civilian life were being "subverted," according to Wilson.*

> Corrections administrators supplanted judges as the effective authorities over length of sentences actually being served in prison.

> Soon, in such widely separated places as California, Massachusetts and the District of Columbia, police and prosecutors were complaining that a lot of dangerous criminals were out on the streets committing new crimes while "serving" their sentences in community corrections modes. (Wilson 1974)

Wilson argued that, for the protection of the community, imprisonment was warranted for the "minute proportion of our population [that] is creating most of the fear among us." He said that "unlimited experimentation" with community corrections is feasible only if the more serious and frequent offenders are deterred by the "legitimate and appropriate function" of prisons, which is restriction.

---

*In Wilson's city, Washington, D.C., of four thousand prison inmates on some sort of conditional release to the community, between twelve and fourteen hundred were arrested in 1974 for committing new crimes, including close to a dozen homicides (*Washington Star-News* 1/20/75).

PSYCHIATRIC APPROACHES

PSYCHOANALYSIS

As Campbell (1971, p. 34) pointed out, Freud wrote no books or articles on the criminal.* He did not attempt to apply his concepts and procedures to criminal behavior. But Freud's followers have tried to do this, and psychoanalytic procedures have been modified to fit criminals.

In a book dealing with the criminal, Alexander and Staub (1931, p. 73) defined the task of therapy as helping a person to "gain the upper hand over the unconscious by means of the conscious part of the personality." Psychologic "sickness" was conceived of as a product of the constant pressure of unconscious motives that are not accessible to the conscious ego. The "new orientation" toward delinquency, described by Healy and Bronner (1936, p. 2), was to see it as representing "the expression of desires and urges which are otherwise unsatisfied." Attention was drawn to the effects of early experiences, particularly in the family circle. In treating delinquents in the 1930s, Healy and Bronner attempted to develop "the delinquent's insight into the real sources of his unsocial behavior." The frame of reference was basically psychoanalytic.

Eissler (1950, p. 99) cited the criminal's "incapacity of loving or of turning with positive feelings toward a partner" as an obstacle to treatment. This has been described in the analytic situation as the criminal's failure to establish a positive transference. To facilitate this transference, Eissler advocated that the analyst provide gratification to the delinquent patient in the form of various assurances and also money.

> I have never yet treated a male delinquent in the course of whose treatment it did not at some time become necessary to give him money. Not until he had received money was he able to develop the positive feelings toward the analyst, which made the further course of therapy possible. (Eissler, p. 115)

It is noteworthy that, in almost all psychologic approaches to the criminal, analytic or otherwise, authors have warned of the pitfalls of largely unconscious countertransference reactions (e.g., Ward et al. 1958). These arise when the therapist's own attitudes and emotions interfere with treatment. As part of its continuing educational program, the American Psychiatric Association at its 1972 meeting presented a morning-long

---

*Freud did write one article on motivation of criminal acts, "Criminals From a Sense of Guilt," but this was not about criminals *per se* (see *Standard Edition* 14:332-340).

videotaped session entitled "Conscious and Countertransference Reactions to Violent Patients." Shapiro and Ross (1971) reported that the staff members in an institution profited from sensitivity training, in that they became more in touch with their own attitudes toward patients and toward each other.* Some practitioners, like Eissler, have been apologetic for abandoning their positions of moral neutrality. In other words, if something was going wrong in the treatment of a criminal, many practitioners were more ready to blame themselves than their particular approach or the patient.

In practice, pure psychoanalysis has rarely been used in the treatment of criminals (e.g., Friedlander 1947). Glover (1960, p. 319) said he had seldom seen "true completed psycho-analyses in criminology."

> The uses of psycho-analysis in research and in methods of prevention far outweigh its uses in pure form as a method of treating pathological delinquency. (p. 324)

Procedural modifications have been necessary, owing to the personality of criminals. The analytic practitioner has been less of a blank screen and has been more active. Analytic theory has been seen as giving direction to work with criminals rather than serving as a blueprint for treatment. Attempts to use the procedures almost invariably met with frustration.

> All private practitioners of psychiatry see a few psychopaths in consultation. Since they generally are not amenable to treatment, they pass from view fairly quickly and it is seldom possible to study them intensively. Psychoanalysis rarely has turned its microscope upon them as they generally have neither patience, willingness nor emotional capacity to be analyzed. (Greenacre 1945, pp. 495, 496)

In describing the efforts to use analytic techniques to treat criminals, one must begin with Aichhorn's 1935 book, *Wayward Youth*. He viewed delinquency as a symptom and accordingly focused on the cause more than on the behavior itself. The emphasis in treatment was on making unconscious processes conscious and then helping youngsters to do some emotional relearning through an accepting therapist, who could serve as an identification model. The climate of the residential setting was a permissive one: "Our motto was: as far as possible, let the boys alone" (p. 172).

---

*Fenton (1973, p. 125) advocated sensitivity training to help employees of correctional institutions to "see themselves and others more realistically, to become more understanding of their own likes and dislikes, to learn about prejudices and enthusiasms in themselves and others, and to become better aware of how they themselves affect other people."

From the very beginning we felt intuitively that above all we must see that the boys and girls from fourteen to eighteen had a good time. We did not treat them as dissocial or criminal individuals from whom society needed protection; they were human beings who had found life too hard, whose antagonism to society was justified, and for whom an environment must be created in which they could feel comfortable. (p. 149)

Even the most aggressive boys were to be shown a kindness that would serve as a corrective to earlier experiences. The delinquents interpreted kindness as weakness and did as they pleased; the result was that "practically all the furniture in the building was destroyed, the window panes broken, the doors nearly kicked to pieces" (p. 173). Throughout all this, Aichhorn insisted that the boys be allowed to "work out their aggression." Aichhorn's work served as a frame of reference and an inspiration for at least three decades.

The work of Redl and Wineman (1951) was influenced by Aichhorn's endeavors. These authors have written numerous articles and books. Perhaps their best knows is *Children Who Hate*, a volume describing their residential treatment of delinquents between eight and eleven years old. Although basically analytic in outlook, the authors were not totally bound to a particular theory or procedure. They faithfully recorded their experiences and observations. They also viewed delinquent behavior as a symptom. In their dealings with these youngsters, they painted a vivid picture of "the mechanized warfare with change agents." They related how the children could get the staff "exactly where they wanted us" with their "unerring scent for strategy":

While [these] seemingly dull, or at least non-communicative, children still didn't talk much, they seemed to be aware of all the ropes and shenanigans that the most skillful attorney-at-law could hope to call his own. (p. 177)

Their perceptive observations led to their major contribution, a description of the delinquent ego and how it operates. Redl and Wineman pointed out that the delinquent's ego operates effectively but "in the service of the wrong goal."

Far from being helpless, the ego of these children is suddenly a rather shrewd appraiser of that part of reality which might be dangerous to their impulsive exploits and becomes an efficient manipulator of the world around them as well as an energetic protector of delinquent fun against the voice of their own conscience. (p. 144)

Their treatment was geared to dealing with this "hypertrophically developed ego," as they called it. This entailed attending to the "whole child in the total life situation." They concluded that education and love did not suffice and that these children were beyond the reach of education. They saw standard psychiatric interview techniques as not meeting even the "minimum condition [necessary to] begin to take hold" in work with these youngsters. Even behavior in play therapy was restless and aggressive. Redl and Wineman called for a new approach.

> Psychiatry can no longer afford to rest on its laurels of public acclaim for its potentials. The children who hate certainly can remind us of the hard fact that they are not approachable through "straight psychiatry." (p. 242)

> It seems that there is no way out of the dilemma but the invention of a new design, which offers us opportunities of Strategy in a different dimension than either good education or a thorough psychiatric treatment in themselves seem to grant. (p. 245)

Theirs is a most candid and perceptive account of an attempt that failed to effect change in delinquents.

We should emphasize in this review of analytic applications the importance attached to the process of identification to effect change. The theory behind this is that the criminal has lacked satisfactory models for behavior and that psychotherapy gives him the opportunity for new learning by offering him a suitable model. The importance of the therapist as a model has been stressed repeatedly by almost all schools of practice.

> When ... the therapist by his firmness and understanding supplies a parent figure in whom reality elements of authority and love are experienced, considerable relief is afforded. The delinquent's psychological acceptance of this now emotionally palpable father figure is brought about by the urgency of his own dependency needs. The figure of a directing authority relieves the insecurity and allows a glimpse of a parent who may serve as an ego-ideal. (Bromberg and Rodgers 1946, p. 683)

> You, counselor, are his best—and last—shot before the streets claim him again. ... I would say that the age thirteen or fourteen appears to be particularly crucial. Up to that time the counselor's chances of putting himself over as a credible identification model are far better than with boys in the fifteen to seventeen age range. (Henry 1972, pp. 27, 80)

Many, if not most, workers in mental health have at one time or another used some psychoanalytic concepts, language, and techniques in their work with criminals. Today, very few analysts, if any, treat this population. Psychiatrists, except for those in forensic settings, generally choose not to deal with them. Some practitioners have used approaches whose roots are in psychoanalysis, such as Janov in his primal therapy (1970):

> In some respects, primal therapy has returned full circle to early Freud. It was Freud who stressed the importance of early childhood experience in neurosis and he who understood the relationship of repressed feeling to mental aberration. (p. 206)

> Feeling is what this therapy is all about. We are not simply involved with today's feelings, but those old feelings which keep us from feeling the present. We are after the feeling of feeling—something which the neurotic has left behind, yet which intrudes into his life each and every day. . . . Instead of an "analysis" of feeling, the objective is to directly *experience* feelings which have long been blocked off. The cure involves no more than feeling them [the primal feelings]. (p. 386)

Janov (1972, p. 19) claimed that primal therapy is the "only cure" for mental illness, rendering "all other psychologic theories obsolete and invalid." He was certain that his work could result in tremendous strides in eliminating crime and in treating successfully those who are already criminals (pp. 280-281). Analytic concepts have formed the guidelines for a wide variety of treatments other than traditional individual psychotherapy. For example, Kagan and Zucker (1970) reported a psychiatrist's treatment of a thirteen-year-old sociopath, whose parents were treated by a rabbi. "Uncovering motivations" played a major role in both parts of the therapy.

Generally, psychiatry has taken a modest or dim view of its results with criminals, at least up to the late 1960s, when mental health professionals inaugurated a plethora of programs to treat drug users, and psychotherapeutic programs in prisons and hospitals were staffed to treat people whose antisocial conduct was a community problem. In 1947, Friedlander stated that

> psychiatrists who happen to see delinquent cases in their practice or in an out-patient department remark on the impossibility of treating them on account of their unreliability and unresponsiveness. (pp. 222-223)

This opinion has been articulated many times since.

In my experience, the schizophrenic patient has a better chance of obtaining proper therapy than a delinquent. (Eissler 1950, p. 120)

They are beyond the reach of education and they are below the grip of the psychiatric interview technique. (Redl and Wineman 1951, p. 240)

From the therapeutic side we require to admit that we have not, as yet, developed any adequate methods whereby we can deal satisfactorily with such [psychopathic] cases. (Henderson 1951, p. 86)

In 1960, Bennett (p. 224) pointed out that using analytic concepts as guides to therapeutic procedure had resulted in fewer successes with delinquent youngsters than with neurotics. Hendrickson and Holmes (1960, p. 174) observed, "The usual kind of verbal, analytic interpretations have limited applicability in the treatment of delinquents." Schmideberg (1960, p. 160) stated flatly, "Methods suitable for neurotics and psychotics are not effective with criminals."* She observed that criminals use insight to justify crime rather than to facilitate behavior change. Coodley (1961, p. 637) said that delinquents "cannot assimilate and apply insights developed in treatment" because of a lack of "adequate ego-integration." Glover (1960, p. 35) indicated that very few analyses of "anti-social types" have been conducted and that in this whole field there has been "an astonishing dearth of psycho-analytic workers."

The truth is that psycho-analysis has acquired much more prestige in criminology than is justified by the amount of actual work it has done in the field. Apart from a few pioneering studies and some fragmentary records mostly of non-criminal cases its influence is largely *indirect*, through the percolation to the field of delinquency of some metapsychological generalizations on infantile development, unconscious mechanisms and institutions, and unconsciously motivated behavior. (p. 312)

PSYCHOANALYTIC GROUPS

Group therapy for criminals has been offered in a variety of settings with therapists using an analytic conceptual framework and modified analytic

---

*Guze (1976) presented data from a fifteen-year study that affirms the correctness of observations such as those by Schmideberg. Methods that are effective with neurotics and psychotics are ineffective with criminals largely because criminals do not fall diagnostically into neurotic or psychotic categories: "Sociopathy, alcoholism, and drug dependence are the psychiatric disorders characteristically associated with serious crime. Schizophrenia, primary affective disorders, anxiety neurosis, obsessional neurosis, phobic neurosis, and brain syndromes are not" (p. 124).

techniques. Basically, however, the same format has been used for criminals as for noncriminals. Again, most therapists quickly encounter the transference dilemma.

> [Young delinquents] resent any situation which seems to resemble the parent-child struggle with which they are battling both externally and internally. (Abrahams 1956, p. 286)

The fundamental problem for these practitioners and for all others is that of motivation for treatment. Criminals often have to be forced into treatment by making their freedom contingent on their participation in therapy. Boslow and Manne (1966) at Patuxent made no bones about the fact that indeterminate sentencing puts continuous pressure on patients to understand their behavior.

Therapists have had difficulty in winning criminals' acceptance and trust, which are thought necessary for treatment. Schulman (1956, p. 201), like Eissler (1950), described how a therapist has to meet some "narcissistic needs" through "novelty and surprise." He gave his delinquents favors and refreshments from time to time. Other writers have commented on the importance of meeting the "oral needs" of delinquents.

> Most delinquent boys are tremendously and assertively oral, and they frequently demand the therapist love and feed them in a concrete sense such as asking for a party, picnic or something to eat. It is at times hard for a beginning therapist to see that these requests are attempts to escape from an intense longing to be truly loved or from intense anger at parents who did not meet the boys' nurturant needs. (Averill et al. 1973, p. 20)

According to Rachman (1969), a group leader needs to address himself to this very issue. By showing kindness and meeting some of these "nurturant needs," he is more likely to win acceptance.

The emphasis in group work is on achieving insight, which is to be accomplished in part by the open expression of feelings or, as Uehling (1962) termed it, "turning repression into expression." The expression of feelings is encouraged as an alternative to acting out. The proponents of group analytic therapy (Rachman 1969; Schulman 1956; Tec 1956) are all keenly aware of their role as models. They believe that a rudimentary value system will emerge through the process of identification. Interpretations of behavior, of course, reflect the psychoanalytic orientation of the therapists.

> During the next to the last hour, the group regressed to oral gratification. Vern brought with him a large bag of popcorn which he refused to share

with anyone until the end of the hour. . . . Their eating seemed to express
their intention to provide their own gratification since I would no longer
nurture them. (Averill et al. 1973, p. 69)

Another example is reported by Rappaport (1971, p. 494) of a man who, as a
child, had been told by other boys he had a small penis. He believed that if he
"stroked off," or masturbated, he would make it bigger. The therapist then
pointed out how, as an adult, the man "stroked" other people in the sense of
manipulating them. This was seen as a product of the early notions of organ
inferiority. All behavior is seen through analytic glasses.

While I was impressed by the manifestation of what seems to correspond
to a reanimated oedipus complex, I noted at the same time that some of
the boys regressed to occasional abandonment into anal-aggressive talk
or oral passivity and withdrawal; thus, the latter two corresponded more
to a preoedipal pattern of behavior. (Tec 1956, p. 420)

Those who use group techniques list the following advantages:

1. Recognition of similarity of problems by group members
2. Influence exerted by each member on the others to develop understanding
3. Support and encouragement of each other in times of stress
4. Fostering of a sense of identity

However, some writers indicate that group therapy by itself is not likely to
produce change in the criminal. They perceive group work as creating anxiety
in criminals, which makes them more amenable to "deeper" therapy.

It should be emphasized . . . that the depth of emotional distortion in the
character-disordered delinquent precludes the effective use of group
psychotherapy as the sole treatment method. (Schulman 1956, p. 212)

Slavson (1950, p. 230) did not consider psychopathic personalities suitable for
group treatment. However, in his 1965 book, *Reclaiming the Delinquent*, he
did argue that what he termed "para-analytic" group therapy was suitable for
nearly all adolescents, few of whom he regarded as "full-blown" or
"constitutional" psychopaths (p. 738). Slavson set forth his theory and
techniques for working with a residential population of teen-aged delinquents. He viewed delinquents as "fixated in early childhood or even infancy."
Thus, he regarded the treatment objective in terms of "advancing the
psychologic maturity of our boys." Slavson believed that a criminal youngster

was a victim of his environment, his past upbringing, and his resulting character structure.

> Individuation, so essential for psychological maturity, was denied them, and as a result, they remained helpless in dealing with their tyrannical raw, instinctive impulses in the face of external stress and internal strains. Having no resources, they acted on (infantile) impulsiveness. (p. 122)

Slavson enlisted their "natural curiosity" to explore their past in a quest to shed light on "deeper intrapsychic urges." The setting was permissive and "even the most bizarre acting out" was permitted to bring forth "unrestricted verbalization of past acts and relations." Slavson proclaimed:

> We threw the light of understanding upon their acts, and they recognized this as the source of their salvation. (p. 739)

Slavson cited some favorable outcomes of treatment. He maintained that the boys in his groups were "accepted" and therefore able to "relax," that their sense of masculinity was enhanced, and that free group participation helped in "establishing identity." Here, as in the other psychoanalytic work to which we have referred, it was mainly the light of understanding by which change was measured.

Some therapists use analytic methods, but modify them when working with criminals. Borriello (1973) stated that group psychotherapy with patients who have "acting-out character disorders" has often failed because techniques for neurotics and psychotics have been used. He reported working with such character disorders using a "basically analytic" method but adapting it to a here-and-now approach.

> The here-and now is stressed because it allows for the emergence of relationships of the immediate moment. The interactive material lays bare such psychodynamics as projection, denial, identification, rationalization, transference, and so on. Transference is not only to the therapist but to the other group members as well. . . . Initially, the focus of the transference analysis is around the group members and later the therapist. (p. 6)

Rather than "the more traditional passive-caring type of involvement," Borriello pointed out the necessity for "firm, persistent, active-caring involvement." He stated that with this approach patients explore emotional experience and learn to cope with the feeling, not to act it out. A set of "group mores" emerges from this type of group therapy. Borriello stated that twenty-

six patients who have been treated in this manner and released from the hospital are "socially effective."

Some practitioners have voiced their disenchantment with analytically oriented group work. Brandes (Brandes and Gardner 1973, p. 68) said that sociopathic and asocial youngsters who "cannot apply inner controls to their own behavior" should not be treated "in dynamic groups that depend on verbal communication of thoughts and feelings." Ernst and Keating (1964) described why they became discouraged with analytic group therapy:

> Attempts to use what is sometimes referred to as psychoanalytic type group psychotherapy were not particularly successful in the hands of this author. ... In the prison groups personally observed (by E), it early became evident that prisoners took advantage of such conceptual orientations as voluntary group cohesion and group support. For example, statements of therapists like "attendance at group meetings is voluntary," "this is your group," "talk about whatever you want," were racketeered with. Attempts to steer talk onto presumably more worthwhile subjects were frequently countered by the "rules" of the group therapy; the inmates had learned these rules from the books on group therapy which they purloined from the staff medical library. In other words, discovering that therapists were enjoined to follow certain directions and advised against other procedures, many inmate-patients figured out how to exploit the situation. ... Accordingly having been robbed, embezzled from, conned, [having] watched group members made to buy protection, witnessed rat-packing [the hot seat technique] and having had my mental "til" tapped, I decided that treating a person for an illness had less to do with
> 1. The rules of group therapy, or,
> 2. Whether treatment was compulsory or voluntary. (pp. 975, 976)

NONANALYTIC GROUPS

In the 1950s, group therapy with criminals was relatively new. The first effort at guided group interaction was the Highfields project with male adolescents in New Jersey, initiated in 1950 (J. Rubin 1971). Weeks (1958) described this as a residential setting, offering a therapeutic climate of "informality and permissiveness." The two main criteria of change were remaining out of confinement and attitude change (to be assessed by a standardized attitude scale). The highfields adolescents were contrasted with those in a reformatory. Weeks maintained that Highfields was more successful at rehabilitation than the reformatory.

Sixty-three in every 100 Highfields boys, in contrast to forty-seven in every 100 [reformatory] boys, complete their treatment and do not get into further difficulty serious enough to require that they be institutionalized. (p. 118)

However, Weeks pointed out that the attitudes of Highfields boys toward family and the law and their general outlook on life changed little. Weeks thought that perhaps the attitude scale did not pick up the changes.

McCorkle's 1953 study of 312 institutions indicated that of those replying, forty-eight percent of the training schools and reformatories and fourteen percent of the prisons had programs that they called "group therapy." The term *group therapy* was being used to embrace a wide variety of procedures, including groups using psychoanalytically-oriented methods, lecture-discussion formats, music, athletics, and so on. Some writers, although acknowledging that they lack a comprehensive understanding of the psychopath, believed that groups were at least a good place for controlled observation (Thorpe and Smith 1952, p. 33). Others have stated that group therapy is the method of choice because criminals do so poorly in individual therapy (*Psychiatric News* 4/4/73). Group treatment has been seen as economical with respect to distribution of staff resources; this has made it attractive.

> For practical reasons, we really have never had the problem of making a choice between group or individual psychotherapy, since a compelling need has been to have as many inmates in therapy at the same time as possible. (Boslow et al. 1961)

The initial and perhaps most important obstacle to effective group therapy of any kind is that, as with any other program, most criminals participate because they are forced to or because they see it as a step toward getting out. Boslow et al. (1961) described how the attitude toward group therapy at Patuxent changed from hostility to a clamoring for it. Part of this shift might have been due to a recognition by some of the men that there was something wrong with them, but Boslow cited another factor:

> Perhaps above all, there was the threat of the indeterminate sentence. After a while it became clear to all inmates that those who got out were the ones who had been in therapy and who had at least managed to convince the professional staff that in some way they had benefited from it.

Boslow went on to say that, once the inmates were in therapy, they at least had to "make a show of accepting it." Aside from the motivation problem, the obstacle cited most frequently is probably the criminals' untruthfulness. Problems stemming from this have been described repeatedly in the literature—"seduction by flattery," diversions, power struggles, conning, expecting the therapist to do it all, and the "gimme" syndrome, or constantly asking for privileges and favors (Thorpe and Smith 1952; Abrahams 1956; Boslow et al. 1961; Carney 1972). Another problem often referred to is that group meetings are consumed by endless complaints and grievances. Boslow et al. (1961) maintained that this is a problem especially where there is not sufficient staff to keep administrative and therapeutic functions separate. To remedy this, Boslow held a session each week for the sole purpose of allowing patients to air their complaints, in the expectation the the other meetings would be devoted to self-examination rather than griping.

Nonanalytic practitioners have recognized that "structure" is important for criminals (e.g., Burke and Lee 1964). Some therapists are didactic and hold discussions to educate. The "lecture-discussion" method was used in some fifty-three percent of the institutions that responded to McCorkle's 1953 survey. Snyder and Sechrest (1963) have described the structuring done by a therapist working with "defective delinquents":

> The role of the therapist was that of a guiding, manipulating leader who interacted minimally but did not hesitate to structure and organize when necessary. At times the therapist instructed in a truly didactic fashion. . . . Each of the sessions began with a predetermined topic selected on the basis of its concrete applicability to the lives of the inmates. (p. 528)

Although this was the approach to a group of people of subnormal intelligence, variants have been used with groups of criminals of average intelligence. In descriptions of the group process, terminology varies but the concepts are basically alike with respect to the stages of therapy. Thorpe and Smith (1952) described an initial stage of "testing" the therapist. This was followed by "group centered testing operations" and finally "acceptance operations" in which the therapist was recognized as an authority and a resource person as well as "a good father figure." In most of these groups, expression of feeling and insight are the principal objectives, although analytic interpretation (if used at all) is not the focus.

One of the great innovations in group therapy has been the introduction of the "therapeutic community" by Maxwell Jones (1953). The guiding concept was to utilize the whole patient "culture" to foster "healthy" personalities by changing social attitudes. Patients could be dealt with economically. In daily meetings with the staff many patients could be treated at once and they could serve as treatment resources to each other. Treatment would begin from the moment a patient set foot in the institution. Jones (1953) stated that a person with a "severe character disorder" who was antisocial was unsuitable for analytic treatment but could be resocialized in the therapeutic community. In the "process of acculturation," considerable use was made of educational methods to develop self-understanding.

> Our use of daily discussion groups with the entire patient population, documentary films, psychodramas, etc., represent an attempt to develop such [educational] methods; the main principle involved is that social problems and real life situations are either raised in discussion or acted out in psychodrama. The whole group attempts to arrive at a constructive attitude in relation to the problem raised. . . . However, in our educational procedure individual responses cannot be separated from the group climate. What appears to matter most is the degree of "group learning"—the extent to which the community accepts an idea which then becomes an integral part of the group culture. (p. 160)

Jones pointed out repeatedly the policy of "the weight of group acceptance" in this form of treatment which he described as "democratic" and "equalitarian" (1965, p. 8). At Henderson Hospital in England, Jones set up a twenty-four-hour intensive residential "living and learning" situation (described in Whiteley et al. 1973). The residents were basically antisocial or psychopathic. The entire community met regularly, and the members also met in small groups for psychotherapy. Henderson was to be a place where problems could be solved democratically, with each person being responsible for himself. A follow-up of 122 cases over two to four years revealed that 47.6 percent of the participants could not be located. However, of the 52.4 percent who were followed, 40.1 percent had not been convicted of a crime or returned to a mental hospital.

Slavson (1954) described an "orthopedagogic or therapeutic community" that he operated for delinquents at the Hawthorne-Cedar Knolls School—a participatory democracy in human relations, with communal meetings and committees of residents to run things. Slavson believed that graduated amounts of freedom, status, participation, and responsibility would build self-esteem so that a person could see himself as "constructive and creative" and thus not have the need to respond to others with hostility or to act out. Clark and Yeomans (1969) reported that fifteen patients diagnosed as sociopaths participated in a therapeutic community at Fraser House in Sydney, Australia. They observed that these patients tended to enter treatment feeling "less ill" than the others did but left feeling worse. The objective had been to make them more uncomfortable about themselves and more realistic about the outside world. Apparently this happened, but how these men functioned afterward in life outside Fraser is not reported.

Two therapeutic communities in the United States have received considerable attention, one at a state hospital and the other at a prison. At the Utah State Hospital (Kiger 1963, 1964, 1966, 1967, 1970), maximum security criminal wards were combined with general psychiatric wards, the sexes were integrated, and the therapeutic community wards were unlocked to "eliminate the stigma of the security or criminal ward." Five basic principles articulated by Maxwell Jones guided the staff's efforts: bilateral communication, confrontation, decision-making by consensus, multiple leadership, and the operation of "learning, living groups." Peer pressure was to supplant the more traditional authority relationships. In effect, patients were to "become therapists," instead of "passive recipients" of therapy. The staff relinquished some of its former role in favor of putting faith in the patients' abilities to make decisions. Privileges were to be earned by assuming responsibilities; if one patient abused a privilege, the entire group was to suffer. Inappropriate behavior was often dealt with by "instant therapy," which involved a massive confrontation and application of pressure by the other community members. Notable in this program was the power that resided in a group called the "patient posse." The psychopath was seen as having a "zealous inclination to protect his own comfort and hard-earned privileges," so it was the patients rather than the staff who performed security functions. Apparently, this zeal was known to get out of hand.

> Sometimes enthusiasm has to be curbed. The community was sympathetic when this group requested flashlights to better examine nooks and crannies on the grounds or downtown, but their reaction was sharply negative when bicycles were suggested. (Kiger 1964, p. 659)

On this unit, the staff believed that elements of the unpredictable should be introduced that called for very deliberate "manipulations."*

> Occasionally the staff should utilize manipulatory maneuvers by making changes from time to time in order to maintain an atmosphere of the unpredictable. This serves a useful measure in preventing processes from becoming too static, whereupon the psychopath not only loses his enthusiasm but is inclined to fall back into his old patterns of behavior. (Kiger 1966, p. 12)

---

*Ingram et al. (1970) also spoke of the need to introduce frequent changes to keep institutionalized delinquents from being bored. An experimental program was established at the National Training School for Boys, Washington, D.C. Excursions, building models for slot-car racing, special tournaments, weight-lifting, psychodrama, and other novel and exciting activities were introduced to maintain a "circus-like atmosphere."

Consequently, anxiety was introduced through such measures as spinning a roulette wheel or tossing dice, by which the psychopaths became the manipulated instead of the manipulators. According to Kiger (1966), psychopaths function very well in a therapeutic community, for two reasons: characteristics that seem to be detrimental "can often be turned into positive treatment trends"; and it is in the nature of the process itself that

> the kicks ordinarily gained through the psychopath's manipulatory and undermining efforts are removed through exposure. Pressures from others usually result and it is well known that the psychopath follows a path which is more comfortable to him because it is least anxiety producing. Rather than buck the program, he tends to become a part of it. (p. 12)

Nowhere in these accounts of therapeutic communities is follow-up mentioned. The Utah State Hospital does not maintain a complete follow-up, because patients pass into the care of community centers around the state, making follow-up extremely difficult or impossible (Smith 1973). Kiger (1966) indicated that among the indicators of improvement are better handling of anxiety, delaying of gratification, decreased blaming of others, and assuming more responsibility. He acknowledged that one possible treatment outcome is, "Some manifest no apparent improvement; others just become better psychopaths."

At the impetus of Maxwell Jones, a therapeutic community (described by Briggs 1973) was established at the minimum security prison in Chino, California. (Jones was retained as primary consultant to the project.)

> It was necessary to establish an atmosphere in which a group of rebellious, active, bright young men could evolve a system and a way of life which would allow them opportunities to examine the effects of their behavior on one another, on the total community, and on small segments of it. . . . In this process, they might discover for themselves the futility of their delinquency and learn alternatives. (p. 111)

The community consisted of approximately sixty residents (the prison had approximately fifteen hundred inmates in all). Early community meetings were little more than gripe sessions. The residents' work area, a laundry, was beset with various rackets. The men in the community collected "an impressive arsenal of weapons" to be used to "protect" one of their members against inmates not in the project. As Briggs indicated, although delinquent behavior manifested itself, in time those in charge began to see definite stages in a process of prisoner change. First, residents started to realize that old ways of behaving were futile. They then became more observant of what others around them were doing. Finally, they experimented with new roles and behavior patterns. Furthermore, they desired to help others to change. A follow-up was conducted of the community residents. A misdemeanor resulting in a fine, probation, or jail sentence under ninety days was not counted as an "unfavorable" outcome nor was being assigned to a short-term narcotic treatment unit. To be evaluated as "unfavorable," a former resident had to have committed a felony. On this basis, the community members functioned better than a control group that had not participated in the therapeutic community.

Elsewhere the term *therapeutic community* has been used in an altogether different manner. Tait (1968) expressed a hope that a "family therapeutic community" might become the "sort of 'workbench' for studying delinquency that the psychoanalytic couch has been for studying psychoneuroses" (p. 49). He suggested that a housing project have staff members observe, understand, and guide families "to stimulate better solutions to individual and family problems" (p. 45). The residents of the "family hospital" would be those with one or more children considered potentially delinquent.

Maxwell Jones proposed the extension of his concepts into what he called a "systems approach" to a prison. He advocated establishing a group climate within the institution where there would be shared decision-making. He recommended "the bringing together of involved individuals, which makes social interaction, the expression of feeling, and social learning possible." This, like the therapeutic community, was proposed as a "living-learning" situation (1973, p. 80).*

Psychodrama, a form of group therapy, has been defined as the "spontaneous acting out of various types of problems in a warm permissive group setting" (Kole 1968). It is seen as being useful diagnostically and therapeutically for patients or clients (Lassner 1950) and also for staff training (Kole 1968).

> It frequently reveals the core of a man's problem and starts him on a new way of thinking. While a complete reshaping of the inmate's personality cannot be expected in the course of a few sessions, it may be safely said that the most acute symptoms of personality maladjustment tend to

---

*Jones wrote earlier (1962, p. 85) about the application of social psychiatry to prisons. His emphasis was on developing an inmate-staff community that would modify "the antitherapeutic factors in the social organization of the prison." Then, in 1968, Jones wrote a volume "to attempt theoretical formulation of some of the concepts used in therapeutic community practice." This work dealt mostly with the mental hospital environment and then with the community at large.

> disappear in the course of psychodrama sessions. . . . and that a sort of palliative cure has been achieved in most cases. (Lassner 1950, p. 90)

Corsini (1958) reported that changes in behavior can come about as a result of one psychodramatic incident. This technique emphasized "emotional understanding" rather than intellectual understanding. Corsini described the type of expression desirable in psychodrama.

> You must throw yourself into the situation, say what first comes to your mind, over-act, let go, become spontaneous and free, give release to your feelings, use the worst language and the strongest expressions and develop the situation to its utmost. Don't hesitate to use physical force, strike or kick or threaten if you want to, just let yourself go completely. (1951, p. 325)

The therapist, after giving these instructions, would maintain control of the session, terminating it at an appropriate time, and then later, perhaps in another session, analyze what had happened. One of the major benefits reported is that a criminal can act out something he wants to do short of actually doing it. Thus, he can discover what the consequences of the behavior would be (Pankratz and Buchan 1965). This may set up a deterrent for the future (Yablonsky 1960). Corsini is an enthusiastic advocate of this mode of treatment.

> I am absolutely convinced that the method of action participation is far superior to any other method for group therapy, at least in prison. (1951, p. 326)

Carpenter and Sandberg (1973, p. 247) stated that psychodrama was effective with delinquents in "cutting through defenses to reach the feelings of loneliness and yearning for love," or at least it had the potential to do this. These authors reported that getting delinquents to attend meetings was a problem and that once they were there, they were often unwilling to participate.

Another direction in group treatment is the self-help group. We shall reserve discussion of the criminal's participation in Alcoholics Anonymous for volume 3. But we should at least mention here the existence of such organizations as Gamblers Anonymous and Checks Anonymous. The only reference we have found to these self-help groups are in newspapers and magazines (e.g., Trippett 1970; *Washington Post* 12/3/72; *Fairfax Journal* 6/11/73). Professional literature on techniques and outcome appears to be lacking.

We subsume in this discussion of group work family therapy, which we also mentioned as a sociologic measure. Attempts are made to deal with psychologic processes of individual members as well as the dynamics of group interaction in the family. Some professionals, especially those treating delinquents, insist that parents be involved in family therapy.

> Since the youthful delinquent is often the symptom of his family's pathology, treatment of the family as a unit holds the most promise for effective change. (Freeman and Savastano 1970, p. 271)

Family therapy may assume any of the formats discussed in this section. The choice of technique depends on the orientation of the therapist.

Finally, for the encounter methods that have been used in group work with criminals, we reserve discussion for the section on existential approaches.

RATIONAL THERAPY

A major trend in the mental health profession in the 1960s that is even stronger in the 1970s has been away from causation and the reconstruction of early experience and toward the questions of how man can cope realistically with problems here and now and prevent future difficulties. Work along these lines has been mostly with noncriminals who are responsible and have a moral base. Techniques developed with noncriminals have been applied to criminals with little, if any, modification. Therapists in the rational school do not use a medical model or a mental illness framework. Rogers (1951) and Glasser (1965) for example, regard diagnosis as a waste of time and money even in work with chronic mental patients. Glasser and others view illness as an operationally unsound concept. They believe that, if the idea of sickness is communicated, the patient may passively sit back and wait for a cure. Not only is mental illness rejected, but so are other "determining" factors. Arriving at causal formations is seen as an unproductive exercise that gives patients excuses for maintaining the status quo.

Because Glasser's reality therapy is so well known, we shall discuss it as a prototype of the rational, pragmatic approaches. Glasser believes that the therapist must "scrupulously" avoid giving the patient excuses; thus, blaming others is not permitted. Instead of being viewed as a "victim of others' misconduct," a patient is regarded as "responsible."

> Responsibility is here defined as the ability to fulfill one's needs, and to do so *in a way that does not deprive others of the ability to fulfill their needs.* (p. 13)

There is no searching for reasons "why." In fact, Glasser insists, "Knowledge of cause has nothing to do with therapy" (p. 53). The rational therapist asks, *"What? What* are you doing—not *why* are you doing it" (p. 32). Glasser believes that patients ask why as part of an effort not to change. Furthermore, he maintains that the insights derived from such a quest are unproductive.

> What good comes from discovering that you are afraid to assert yourself because you had a domineering father? (p. 50)

> In Reality Therapy we emphasize behavior; we do not depend upon insight to change attitudes because in many cases it never will. (p. 51)

Glasser is interested in the present and in conscious, rational thinking, not feelings. He considers searching for unconscious determinants to be "detrimental to therapy." A therapist using reality therapy has to be "involved" and revealing of himself. Rather than being a "blank screen," he participates in a dialogue and makes his value system explicit.

Glasser (p. 68) claimed an eighty percent success rate in his use of reality therapy at a school for delinquent girls. Reward and punishment played a role in a privilege system in which increased responsibility was met with increased freedom and vice versa. In addition, the girls knew that they had to behave appropriately if they ever wanted to get out. For example, a girl was told that she would not be paroled until she raised her cosmetology grade, so she worked harder and performed more satisfactorily. Disciples of Glasser at the Reality Therapy Institute in Los Angeles lack data on the effectiveness of reality therapy with chronic offenders.

Others have worked along similar lines. In his pastoral counseling, Drakeford (1967) evaluated the usefulness of integrity therapy, a method of treatment growing out of the work of the psychologist Mowrer. This too is a rational approach to life's problems. Drakeford was even more emphatic than Glasser about spelling out a firm moral stand and emphasizing the positive aspects of conscience. Rather than trying to expunge guilt, Drakeford emphasized the "goodness of guilt" (p. 31). He viewed guilt as the consequence of a violation of conscience. He called it an "early warning signal" that will help to "save [a person] from a course of self-defeating behaviors" (p. 43). Drakeford's work was mainly with noncriminals. However, in his chapter "The Problem of the Sociopath," he surmised that the principles of integrity therapy, if given a "rigid and prolonged application" (p. 77), could be effective with this type of patient.

Harold Greenwald (1967) has worked in a different manner in his active psychotherapy. Keeping his values to himself, he, in a sense, attempts to meet psychopaths on their own ground.

The basic treatment plan that I follow . . . is to try to indicate to each patient the fact that he and I are not so different; there are similarities between us. (p. 371)

His position has been that both therapist and patient have to deal with similar problems, drives and feelings, but that the therapist "gets away with it," whereas the psychopath does not.

I made much more money off call girls [through his writing and a movie] than you ever will, and you, you schmuck, you can get arrested any day and be sent to jail for 10 years, whereas I get respect, honor, and admiration. (p. 371)

Having heard the therapist make this type of statement, the psychopath becomes curious as to how Greenwald has managed successfully. When this occurs, Greenwald views the psychopath as amenable to learning self-control and understanding the "self-destructive" aspects of his behavior. By the latter, he meant the psychopath's propensity for continually getting into trouble.

In rational-emotive therapy, Albert Ellis (1967, p. 21) unconditionally accepts a patient, "no matter what are his crimes or his choices of avoidant behavior." The therapist tells the patient that he is acting undesirably but that "he is never a louse nor a worm, never anything but an unfortunately fallible but still essentially acceptable *human.*" Ellis (1976) has emphasized the importance of personal choice. He has sharply criticized theories of causation that blame others for an individual's problems: "You create your own disturbance." Ellis has opposed the "deification of feelings" and, in his work, engages in "cognitive restructuring." In rational-emotive therapy, the task is to dispute the irrational ideas of his clients and to assist them to accept reality gracefully. Ellis agrees with Cleckley that the psychopath is out of touch with reality and is basically psychotic. He maintains that the criminal must be convinced that he is really being self-destructive and that he could enjoy life more if he were to change his attitudes toward himself and the world. It appears that Ellis applies similar techniques to the criminal and noncriminal. This seems to be because he does not regard the thinking patterns of the criminal as distinctively different from those of the noncriminal. Actually, nearly all of Ellis' writings concern themselves with treatment of noncriminals.

Other therapists have their own set of rational techniques (e.g., attitude therapy, Folsom and Taubee 1967), but we do not find references to the use of these techniques with criminals. One school of therapy that has been applied to many groups is now being used with criminals: transactional analysis.

Berne (1967, pp. 132ff) described the "underworld games" that criminals play—"Cops and Robbers" and, in prison, "Want Out," "Bum Rap," and "Good Behavior." He analyzed "ego states" or, less technically, the "parent," "child," and "adult" parts of the personality. The objective is to have a patient become aware of the "game" that he is playing, so that he can be in a position to relinquish it and engage in different types of transactions. Ernst and Keating (1964) reported their use of transactional analysis with forensic patients at Vacaville, California. They stated that the origins of the "cops and robbers" game is seen in the normal two-to-four-year-old game of "hide-and-seek," in which the objective is to be "found and caught." In bringing out the operations of the child, parent, and adult parts of the personality in a criminal's transactions, the therapists assisted the criminal, so that he could make different choices.

> The design of the therapist is to cure the offender of his repetitively carried out conversational transactions which lead to loss of behavioral options. Recognition of alternative behavioral choices provides the inmate with a markedly improved measure of control over his day to day situations. ... Two of the major advantages the so-called antisocial person gives up on cure are, 1. Playing "cops and robbers" with its attendant gratifications, and 2. The use of "go-directly-to-jail" to solve external or internal life stresses. (p. 979)

No follow-up or detailed analysis of results was reported. Martin Groder has used transactional analysis at the U.S. Penitentiary at Marion, Illinois. Inmates voluntarily joined a "peer culture" which participated in transactional group analysis. Criminals who stuck with the program could choose to be trained as "paraprofessional clinicians." Groder reported (unpublished manuscript) the "disappearance of infraction behavior" in all. Of the first "cadre" of ten inmates who spent more than two years in the program, only two are regarded as still psychopathic.

EXISTENTIALISM

We include the existential school of psychotherapy here, because it is a relatively recent and significant development. Only in one instance have we found its concepts or techniques specifically applied by others to criminals (sociopaths). Although undoubtedly there are criminals among the patients treated by therapists, they appear not to have been recognized as such. Because of their failure to distinguish between criminal and noncriminal, practitioners may not have achieved positive results as frequently as they might have if they had screened out the criminals. This is not the place to present the complex historical background of existential therapy; a more detailed discussion of how some aspects of existentialism are related to our approach will be presented in later chapters.

Existentialism adds some important dimensions to psychotherapy, but it is often difficult to specify how the concepts are made operational. Much of the writing seems academic, and one is often left with little that is functional.

> I wonder if other people share my reaction to existential writing—I am deeply impressed, even moved, by the ideas, but when I am finished I am hard put to specify what I have learned. (Murray 1964, p. 17)

> I found myself frequently irritated by what I experienced as an overblown, vague, pseudo-poetic, and floridly self-indulgent style. . . . "I bend my being like a contortionist to engage the client in an existential crisis that will precipitate an intrapsychic metamorphosis." . . . While such sentences communicate to some readers, they do not to this reviewer, who would have wished that the author had taken seriously the words of Camus which he quotes: "Every ambiguity, every misunderstanding, leads to death; clear language and simple words are the only salvation from this death." (Greenwald 1973, p. 26, in a review of Richard Johnson's *Existential Man*)

The lack of clarity of concepts and the often turgid writing make it difficult to extract something usable. Despite the difficulty of absorbing many of the concepts, some people have been attracted to existentialism. Spiegelberg (1972, p. 359) has pointed out that it has actually become a fad to call oneself an existentialist.

> It is certainly true that phenomenology and existentialism have had a fatal appeal for a good many band-wagon climbers and free-loaders on the fringes of scientific psychology and psychiatry who try to profit from the prestige of the new movement by name-dropping or even without it.

Will and choice formerly were ill-defined concepts that were in disrepute for a long time in psychology, because they were entangled in metaphysical speculation or exploited for moralizing (Farber 1966). The existential approach "puts decision and will back into the center of the picture" (May 1966, p. 43) and emphasizes man's capacity to choose.

> The possibility of choice is ever present. At any point in time there are a variety of alternatives of action; at least more than one is always available to any individual. (McEvoy 1967, p. 1)

Personal responsibility is the cornerstone of existentialism. Writers like Frankl (1967, p. 60) have declared that man can and must take a stand toward conditions—"the conditions do not determine me, but I determine whether I yield to them or brave them." May's concept of *intentionality* also gets at man's power to make things happen, man's actively "knowing and forming reality" (1969, p. 230). This freedom to choose and to have an impact, rather than to be a victim of forces outside the self, rejects determinism and challenges much that is traditional in psychology.

> Man is neither the pawn of the environment nor the creature of instincts, needs, and drives. Instead, he has the freedom to choose, and he alone is responsible for his own existence. He can transcend both his physical environment and his physical body if he chooses. Whatever he does it is his choice. Man himself determines what he will be and do. (Hall and Lindzey 1970, p. 565)

> *Existential phenomenology* has acted as a challenge to traditional psychology. . . . It has brought home to the routine-psychologist that he knows everything except the main thing. The "main thing" to these existential phenomenologists is the way man chooses his attitudes towards life, death, the world and—as the case would have it—the transcendental. (Strasser 1965, p. 105)

Existentialists do not emphasize etiology. The three "basic existential concerns," according to Goldberg and Goldberg (1973, p. 69), are "What is life? What is man? Who am I?"

Most investigators (see chapter 2 of volume 1) have regarded criminals or psychopaths as not having free will and not being able to act differently from the way they act. Thompson (1953), stressing the importance of biologic factors in the etiology of criminal behavior, stated that

> the psychopathic criminal thinks and believes that he has complete freedom of the will, whereas in the main issues of his conduct he has none. (pp. 3-4)

The sociologic school sees behavior as determined by external forces and criminality as largely a product of the environment. Taft and England (1964, p. 222) went so far as to say that those who resist the "deterministic" position and view man as master of his choices "introduce into behavior an element of caprice scarcely tolerable to the scientific approach." Adherents to the analytic position regard unconscious forces and experiences as determinants of conduct. It is significant, however, that although so many practitioners are deterministic in orientation, they nonetheless treat their patients as though they have a choice.

> It is quite possible that most of us split our minds a little. As metapsychologist or philosopher, one may hold to the doctrine of determinism, but as practical people we act as though we can choose and we encourage our patients to act likewise. (Sutherland 1962, p. 375).

Gatch and Temerlin (1965, p. 31) pointed out that the therapist "assumes determinism because explanation is difficult or impossible without it." But the therapist then holds the patient responsible for what the latter did or what he is about to do, as though he has free choice. Gelso (1970, p. 275) observed that determinism is useful for objective analyses of behavior, but that "few people can live as if they were determined objects." He cited Kierkegaard's comment that a philosopher who creates a deterministic system is like a man who builds a great castle and then goes to live in an adjoining barn.

The broad objective of existential therapy is to embark on a joint quest for meaning (Mullan and Sangiuliano 1961), not to treat an illness (Bugental 1964, p. 201). *Meaning* is a very vague word, and each writer defines it differently. In an essay "What is Meant by Meaning?" (1966) Frankl stated that there is no universal meaning to life but that man can find meaning in three ways: "by what he gives to the world in terms of his creation," "by what he takes from the world in terms of encounters and experiences," and "by the stand he takes when faced with the a fate he cannot change" (p. 23). Controversy surrounds the issue of whether meaning has any objectivity. Sartre (1953) maintained that we are our choices, but other writers such as Feldman (1963, p. 125), spoke of a "moral imperative," and Frankl (1966, p. 24) declared that meaning is to be "found rather than given." Related to considerations of meaning is *authenticity,* another word often heard but not easily defined. Feldman (1963, p. 125) believed that one achieves an "authentic existence" by "facing up to one's inner feelings of dread, taking responsibility for self and having a sense of commitment." One also achieves authenticity by fulfilling one's potential or through what Maslow (1954) called a process of "self-actualization."*

Existential psychotherapy is concerned with the search for meaning. Its method is phenomenology. Explanation is considered to be of no import and

---

*Assagioli (1973, p. 143) warned about misunderstanding what is meant by "authenticity": "Many, in fact, behave badly and excuse themselves on the score of being authentic. But this is often the authenticity of the cave man."

even misleading. Rather, it is the report of what a person is experiencing that is the prime consideration.

> [Practitioners] are so preoccupied with attempts to fit the phenomenon into their multifarious theories that they do not take the time to make sure of the nature of the phenomenon which they have observed. (Howard 1966, p. 228)

The emphasis is on conscious attention rather than unconscious content. The patient describes phenomena as they are, so that the phenomenologist can "know the physiognomy of the things as it strikes his patient" (Van Den Berg 1955, p. 102). As Giorgi (1968) pointed out, phenomenology helps to overcome the "subject-object split" and does justice to the whole person. Man's relation to the world is considered without the reductionism of either psychoanalysis or behaviorism. The proponents of existential psychology maintain that all attempts at explanation, judgment, and causal formulation must be dropped in favor of understanding the patient. May (1966, p. 26) called for a "disciplined effort to clear one's mind of the presuppositions that so often cause us to see in the patient only our own theories or the dogmas of our own systems." The objective is to reconstruct a patient's inner world of experience without the bias of interpretation. Phenomenology as a method in psychiatry entails "the unbiased contemplation of phenomena, putting aside intellectual consideration" (Ellenberger 1958, p. 96, citing Husserl's principle). The emphasis is on a patient's psychologic reality (Van Den Berg, 1955). Phenomenology as a method has been considered "especially well suited for initial exploration of uncharted areas in psychology" (Feldman 1963, p. 123). We shall discuss phenomenology as it relates to our work with the criminal in chapter 5.

Spiegelberg (1972, p. 232) credited Binswanger with being the major "trailblazer for a new approach in phenomenological psychopathology." In phenomenologic analysis, the focus is on the here and now, but there is also a "peeling back" of "layers of experience," so that one can understand what constitutes the present experience (Howard 1966, p. 228). Experience itself is valued. Thus, a patient is not told that his feelings are really a cloak for something opposite. Rather, there is a search for "new possibilities." Binswanger believed that existential analysis required illumination of a patient's entire life history in psychoanalytic fashion. A biographic investigation using analytic methods was to be the procedure to understand "existential modes" as the patient changed in relation to the world, his self, and his own body.* In contrast with existential analysis, existential

---

*Hall and Lindzey (1970, p. 568), citing Medard and Boss, explained, "Genetic understanding can only come to the fore *after* one understands the present phenomena in their own right."

psychotherapy, although also concerned with inner experience and issues of meaning, does not entail exploration of the past. The "new elements" of existential psychotherapy, analytic or not, were enumerated by Heuscher (1964, p. 164) in an article purporting to answer the question "What is Existential Psychotherapy?": emphasis on the here and now, fullness of present experience, content rather than causal relationships, subjective awareness and appreciation of choice, freedom and the human need for meaningfulness, and qualities rather than quantities. For an example of themes important to an existential psychotherapist, we cite the work of Viktor Frankl (1962, 1965, 1966, 1967).

As we pointed out above, Frankl sees meaning as something to be discovered, not invented. As Frankl (1967, p. 12) puts it, "meaning sets the pace for being." *Logos* is "the objective correlate to the subjective phenomenon called human existence" (p. 64), and Frankl's psychotherapy is called "logotherapy." Frankl takes issue with people like Sartre, who fail to see the objective aspect of meaning.

> Unfortunately, this objectivity is frequently neglected by some of those writers who call themselves existentialists. Though they never weary of repeating ad nauseam than man is "being in the world," they seem to forget that meaning is also "in the world" and thus not merely a subjective factor (1967, p. 44)

Frankl rejects Sartre's existentialism as "nothing but a new kind of nihilism" (Spiegelberg 1972, p. 346). Frankl says (1962) that man is "questioned by life" (p. 111) and must discover meaning, with the answer lying in "right action and right conduct" (p. 77) or conscience. The therapeutic process reorients a man attitudinally. The process is not a search for happiness: "we are not here to enjoy ourselves." The therapist does not "impose value judgments" but instead guides a patient to find new meanings for existence. Through such techniques as "paradoxical intention" (1967), he helps patients to restore perspective and view their problems with detachment and sometimes "a touch of humor."

> Through the right attitude unchangeable suffering is transmuted into a heroic and victorious achievement. (1967, p. 90)

Frankl does not work with criminals and thus offers no data on them. He simply refers to them as being in an "existential vacuum" (1962, p. 109).

Encounter groups have been called "existential" for several reasons. Rogers (1971, p. 166) stated that they have a "clearly existential implication" in their tendency to focus on the present. Ellenberger (1958) maintained that "the decisive inner experience" emanating from an encounter can add meaning to a person's life.

> An encounter can bring a sudden liberation from ignorance or illusion, enlarge the spiritual horizon, and give a new meaning to life. (p. 119)

The encounter movement stresses the fact that man has a choice (Gardner and Jeans 1962). He has the freedom to take a positive stance toward life, even in the face of adversity. Schutz (1967, p. 219), for example, noted that a person's having had unfortunate childhood experiences is less important than the view that the person has taken of himself since those experiences. In other words, self-concept is important. Encounter-group therapists believe that a concrete experience at a "critical moment" can lead "the whole personality [to be] restructured" (Ellenberger 1958).

> Time and time again, I have seen individuals choose a whole new direction for their lives—philosophically, vocationally and intellectually—as a result of an encounter group experience. (Rogers 1971, p. 70)

Encounter groups work through the novelty and impact of immediate experience—the unexpected happening and release of feeling—and not through the analysis of "transference" and its insights. In fact, Schutz (1967, p. 93) has maintained that "significant change can occur without insight." Although the emphasis is on an immediate encounter or confrontation, formulations are often made in terms of past experience. The choice of a particular type of encounter is based on an assessment of problems earlier in life (Schutz, 1967). For example, screaming for "release" is acted out here and now, to give vent to "a stifled desire to shout back at a parental figure" (p. 73). There are perhaps as many encounter techniques as there are therapists, some verbal and some physical.

Dy (1974) is the only writer we have found who has distinguished between noncriminal and criminal in the application of encounter or sensitivity therapy. He called for deemphasizing "sensitivity-type approaches, particularly the ones that encourage 'If it feels good, do it' behavior."

> It has been my experience that inmates are somewhat different from the inhibited, overpolite people for whom sensitivity therapy has proven useful. Inmates do not need encouragement to be impulsive, violently expressive, and narcissistically hedonistic. (p. 1152)

Most accounts of encounter groups emphasize catharsis, rather than restructuring thinking processes. Desirable outcomes are to accept oneself as one is (Sangiuliano 1963), to "accept, respect, and love ourselves more" (Schutz 1967, p. 222), and to develop a concept of oneself as a capable human being. Whether what is learned in the encounter group is transferred to life outside, even by noncriminals, is controversial. Techniques are often crudely concrete. For example, a way of putting oneself in another's place is to change seats with him (literally) and pretend to be the other person for the moment. In the case of a criminal, already a very concrete thinker, even if he behaves differently in the group, there is little likelihood of significant carryover to life outside the group setting.

Other forms of treatment claim to have an existential orientation. Psychodrama is one. Here, the actor's full involvement in the act is called for, with an emphasis on what Moreno (1959) called "existential validation."

The more thoroughly and honestly subjective the experiences are acted out the more thoroughly accurate they become. (pp. 215-216)

Moreno wrote that "every psychodramatic session is an existential experience" that offers "fundamental information for a sound theory of existence" (p. 217).

DETERRENCE

The controversy as to whether punishing one person deters another from committing a criminal act remains unresolved. Partisans on both sides of the issue have presented their views, which have been based more on personal value judgments than on facts. Statistics are often bandied about in support of a particular value judgment. Not enough is known to evaluate the effectiveness of deterrents dispassionately, and the positions taken are not based on an understanding of the criminal mind. When investigators have tried to conduct studies, follow-up has been insufficient or totally lacking. Furthermore, no one has been able to determine how many people are actually deterred. Crime figures cannot show this, because they reveal only the number *not* deterred.

The argument favoring punishment as a deterrent has been couched in moralistic terms. Early writers—notably Becarria, Hume, and Bentham—maintained that "example is the most important end of all" (Bentham quoted by McConnell 1912, p. 61). In 1896, Tallack, in his book on penology and prevention, stated that "penal deterrence [is] essential to tame the ruffian, and to warn the dangerous elements in the community" (p. 176). The basic position has been that evil-doers must be punished, thus warning potential doers of evil. A modern version is a statement by Hotis (1972) of the FBI Office of Legal Counsel:

Even conceding that punishment may be ineffective with respect to a particular offender, it may yet serve the larger goal of general deterrence. However much we dislike the practice, criminal sentences provide a useful example to others of what they might expect should they violate society's rules. (p. 24)

Hotis went on to say that the deterrent effect might be mitigated by the "long, drawn-out war" that the criminal wages with society through interminable series of petitions, writs, and hearings.

At first, arguments against punishment as a deterrent were based on personal values. Although Tallack fundamentally believed in deterrence, he opposed long confinement on moral grounds.

Experience proves that all long imprisonments tend, from various causes, to defeat their own object, whether for deterrence or reformation. (p. 230)

In the noted Isaac Ray Lectures Award Series of 1961, David Bazelon, Chief Judge of the U.S. Court of Appeals, scored the retributive aspects of punishment and took the position that it is basically immoral.

We punish only because we do not yet know well enough what else to do. ... This unfortunate person must be sacrificed to the common good—he must be punished as an example to all, to keep all the rest of us from committing his crime. ... Now clearly the convicted prisoner was not deterred by the threat of punishment from committing the crime which placed him in prison. ... Any rational justification of punishment as deterrence must depend on its show-effect, its supposed effect on others. I need not labor the point that the individual so used is a scapegoat, a sacrificial victim. (Bazelon 1961, p. 4)

Members of the mental health profession also have argued against punishment, contending that deterrence is ineffective because of psychologic factors operating in the individual criminal. Menninger and others have seen criminality as symptomatic of mental illness; they do not believe that punishment cures illness. Menninger (1968, 1973) has said that society's practice of punishing is itself a crime, in view of the "torture" that he sees being inflicted on the offenders. Alexander and Staub (1931, p. 208) recommended "the abolition of all forms of punishment" for neurotic criminals. They advocated that such criminals be turned over to a "special agency for psychoanalytically minded reeducation, or to a psychoanalyst for treatment." Zimring (1971) stated that "the person who acts on impulse is less likely to spend time thinking of consequences, and if the association between act and consequence cannot be fully realized in the span of time consumed by an impulse decision, such action will be insulated from the accretive impact of punishment threats" (p. 38). In other words, deterrence is not effective if the life style is impulsive. Many examining experts would conclude that deterrence did not work because the offender was mentally ill.

There have been sociologic arguments against deterrence. One is that inasmuch as an offender does not have much of a stake in society, he has little to lose by committing a crime. The Illinois Commission on Sex Offenders (1963) put it this way:

> A sizable segment of our populace has no status to preserve, no employment of any consequence, little understanding of social responsibility and virtually no self-esteem. Respectable citizens seem always amazed to find that convicts, upon release, "have not learned their lesson." (p. 16)

The Zimring report (1971, p. 49) took issue with this, arguing that even those in the lower socioeconomic segment of society fear the prospect of the social stigma associated with an arrest for a crime. The report went on to say that there is no reason to believe that such people would consider their investment in the social system to be less worth protecting than that of more well-to-to citizens.

Another argument against punishment as a deterrent is that criminals are not sufficiently apprehensive about the risk of getting caught. In 1938, Von Hentig pointed out that "human nature" is often not responsive to the "menace of punishment," particularly in the criminal for whom crime "pays."

> What we do know is that the detection rate of the serious crimes is rather low. Crime pays, as far as the theory of probabilities is concerned, and no movie-propaganda can alter the picture. The criminal is much better acquainted with the inefficiency of our detection-machinery than professors of criminology or social statistics. . . . The criminal does not retreat, he improves his techniques and gets away with it. (pp. 560-561)

Salzman (1961, p. 182) described criminals' "feeling of special privilege and exemption from natural law of cause and effect"—a notion supported by the low risk of arrest.* Referring to the issue of perceived risk, Wolfenden (1960, p. 142) in a lecture on crime and sin, pointed out that it was "the certainty of

---

*We have discussed this idea in chapter 6 of volume 1, as a component of "superoptimism."

apprehension rather than the weight of the penalty which deterred." Wolfenden stated that to keep this principle in mind was to assume "the right attitude, nationally, about legislation."

For thousands of years, man has resorted to religious teaching as a guide to right or wrong. There is always the hope of reaching even the most sinful and deterring sinful conduct. Hirschi and Stark (1969) addressed themselves to this subject in an article entitled, "Hellfire and Delinquency." They quoted Teeters, a criminologist, who stated more than 20 years ago:

> If there are any studies whatsoever that show up the value of religious training as a deterrent to crime, delinquency, immorality, or unethical conduct, this writer has never seen them. (p. 203)

Hirschi and Stark's study showed that a person's adherence to moral and ethical principles was not related to church attendance. In addition, they found that a person who believed in the devil and life after death was as likely to commit delinquent acts as a nonbeliever.

To a great extent, attitudes about deterrence have changed with the times.* The decade of the 1960s was an era of greater leniency, of what some have called "permissiveness." The tide of public opinion began to turn gradually—influenced by a rising crime rate, liberal judicial decisions, prisoner demands that resulted in violence, and especially the assassinations of John and Robert Kennedy and Martin Luther King, Jr.—toward stronger enforcement, more convictions, and stiffer penalties.** In an address on fighting crime and drugs, President Richard Nixon (1973) advocated the following:

1. Restricting the use of the insanity defense
2. Restoring the death penalty for some federal crimes
3. Life imprisonment for a second drug felony
4. Minimum sentence of 5 years for any seller of heroin
5. Opposing the legalization, possession, or use of marijuana

Carlson (1974), Director of the Federal Bureau of Prisons, reported that the

---

* More than twenty years ago, Glueck (1952) noted that "every few years there seems to be a swing of the pendulum between the extremes of a repressive point of view toward crime and a curative and rehabilitative attitude" (p. 167).

** Numerous items in the press reflect the swing in public opinion: *U.S. News and World Report* 3/23/70; *National Observer* 2/8/71; *Evening Star* 9/1/71; and *Washington Post* 1/15/73. In addition, a Gallup Poll in 1973 *(Washington Post* 2/11/73 reported that sixty-seven percent of those interviewed favored life imprisonment for "hard drug sellers."

inmate population in federal prisons has continued to rise as a result of an increased rate of commitment and longer sentences imposed by federal courts. Attorney General William Saxbe (*Washington Post* 8/28/74) warned that unless urban police chiefs gain better control over crime, there could be pressure for tougher measures, perhaps even creation of a national police force. He called for a concerted effort to apprehend and convict "career criminals."

Statistics on recidivism of career criminals have led to opposite conclusions about deterrence. It is argued, on the one hand, that penalties should be increased and enforcement strengthened to remove these people from society and on the other hand, that nothing appears to deter the career criminals. People use the latter argument against imposition of the death penalty, which they already oppose on moral grounds. Unlike other crime statistics (reporting incidence of crime, arrest, and causation), which are unreliable, the recidivism statistics are reliable and are taken seriously. After a criminal has been arrested repeatedly, the judicial system decides to deal more severely with him.* When statistics show that criminals are being released only to be rearrested soon, there is public pressure to take stronger measures to keep actual recidivists off the street longer and thus try to deter potential recidivists.**

A major shortcoming of relying on statistics in this area is that it is not possible to determine how many people actually have been diverted from crime by deterrents of any kind. Tittle (1974, p. 391) has pointed out that the effectiveness of deterrents should not be evaluated only from the standpoint of recidivism; the more important question is whether potential criminals are deterred. He observed that imprisonment might fail as a "specific deterrent" of recidivists but succeed as a "general deterrent" of others.

The issue of capital punishment exemplified the changes in opinion and sentiment of the public. In 1895, psychiatrist William A. White voiced his abhorrence of this practice.

> I wish to assert myself as most emphatically opposed to its use for any reason or under any circumstances. . . . I ask you wherein lies the justice of

---

*A chronic offender was sentenced to three years in jail for stealing two packages of pork chops worth $3.71 (*Washington Post* 12/17/71). " 'I'm a firm believer in rehabilitation but only up to a point,' Judge——— said as he emphasized [that the offender] has a record of more than 50 arrests since 1957."

**A branch of the District of Columbia police department found (*Washington Post* 6/20/72) that rearrest of criminals on release status in Washington had gone up ninety-four percent in one year. After this and similar reports, the local newspapers noted that there was more scrutiny of release practices.

society which in its midst, and then in cold blood takes the lives of the
criminals which its errors have produced? (p. 13)

The implementation of the death penalty waned and came nearly to a
complete halt in the 1960s because of the controversy around it and an
impending judicial decision by the Supreme Court. Again, moral pronouncements were strong—"Our greatest need is reverence for life" (Clark 1970, p.
337). The Supreme Court tried to eliminate the arbitrariness of the imposition
of capital punishment in its 1972 decision.* As of September 1975, the Court
was still considering the issue. More than half the states have since enacted
new, mandatory death penalties, mostly for specific crimes, such as
skyjacking, kidnapping that involves the death of a victim, and murder of an
on-duty policeman. In 1977, the death penalty was carried out for the first
time in ten years.

Statistics have been presented to support both sides of the debate on
whether the death penalty deters. A Massachusetts legislative committee
(cited by Bedau 1971) concluded that the death penalty was not a deterrent to
crime. However, a dissenting minority argued that this conclusion was not
supported adequately by data, in that the death penalty had not been enforced
in Massachusetts since 1947. Sellin (1961, p. 6), a sociologist, citing statistics,
pointed out that increases and decreases in homicide rates "depend on
demographic, social, economic and political conditions" and not on the
practice of a state with respect to capital punishment. To hope that a change
could be brought about by applying the death penalty, Sellin said, "is to grasp
at a straw."

In the arguments against punishment, the welfare of criminals has been
emphasized repeatedly, but comparatively little has been said about the
welfare of society. James Wilson (1973), a professor of government at
Harvard, asked:

> If rehabilitation is the object, and if there is little or no evidence that
> available correctional systems will produce much rehabilitation, why
> should any offender be sent to any institution? But to turn them free on
> the grounds that society does not know how to make them better is to fail
> to protect society from those crimes they may commit again and to violate
> society's moral concern for criminality and thus to undermine society's
> conception of what constitutes proper conduct. [Because the correctional
> system had not reduced recidivism], we would view the correctional

*In Furman v. Georgia, the court decided that, in the three specific cases before it, the death
penalty constituted cruel and unusual punishment, violating the Eighth and Fourteenth
Amendments. However, the court's decision in these three cases did not resolve the issue for all
time (*Journal of Criminal Law, Criminology and Police Science* 1972, p. 492).

system as having a very different function—namely, to isolate and to punish. It is a measure of our confusion that such a statement will strike many enlightened readers today as cruel, even barbaric. It is not. It is merely a recognition that society at a minimum must be able to protect itself from dangerous offenders and to impose some costs (other than the stigma and inconvenience of an arrest and court appearance) on criminal acts; it is also a frank admission that society really does not know how to do much else. (p. 53)

Noting that two-thirds of all people arrested for felonies are repeaters, Guze (1976) called for a "more effective program of imprisonment and rehabilitation" for the recidivist. Having observed that criminal recidivism is markedly less after age forty, Guze proposed:

Imprisonment until middle age, at least for recidivist criminals, should result in a major reduction in recidivism after discharge from prison. This course of action, if adopted, would be justified by the pessimism surrounding current rehabilitation practices and accomplishments. Unless more effective procedures are developed for rehabilitating convicted criminals, it may offer the only hope of reducing this important component of serious crimes. (p. 137)

REWARD AND PUNISHMENT

The use of reward and punishment goes back centuries. They have been used by the tutored and untutored alike in trying to control behavior. The beginnings of the more formal scientific aspects of this work are attributed to Pavlov, who conditioned dogs in Russia during the early part of this century, and to Watson and Skinner in the United States. Since then, psychologists have studied, under controlled conditions, how learning takes place. Behavioral therapy may be defined as "the systematic application of the psychological principles of learning in the modification of human deviant behavior" (Stumphauzer 1973, p. ix). As an approach to dealing with criminals, it is both old and new. Penal institutions have long meted out rewards and punishments. However, the scientific attempt to establish new patterns of behavior is relatively recent. Behavioral techniques have been heralded as having great promise for the treatment of criminals (e.g., Schwitzgebel 1971). Burchard (1973) explained how behavior modification differs from other forms of treatment:

Although behavior modification programs differ markedly in terms of specific procedures they utilize, each one is usually based on the general assumption that there is a functional relationship between antisocial behavior and the environment in which it occurs. . . . Instead of trying to change the person through some type of periodic psychotherapeutic or verbal mediation, the focus is on changing the environment so that appropriate behaviors are strengthened or weakened. In general, the environment is arranged so that adaptive behavior is strengthened through rewarding consequences, and maladaptive or antisocial behavior is weakened through nonrewarding and/or punishing consequences. (pp. 111-112)

Critics of present correctional procedures have contended that rehabilitation efforts fail "largely because of the utter irrelevancy of the rewards and punishments employed" (Schmauk 1970, p. 334). Now, with the behavioral approach, careful formulations are made as to what must be changed and how. The desired behavior is the learning and performance of new skills, whether academic, vocational, or social. Behavior modification has been used to teach "predelinquents" such specific habits as good posture and conversational skills (Maloney et al. 1972). Reinforcement contingencies are established to "pay off" the desired behavior, and old behavior patterns are "extinguished" through nonreinforcement or, in some cases, punishment. The focus is on the behavior itself, not on thinking processes. Ayllon and Azrin (1968), Wolpe (1969), Gardner (1971), to mention only a few, have written about the application of behavioral techniques to noncriminals and have reported success in eliminating a wide variety of maladaptive behaviors. Our focus here is entirely on the application of behavior modification to criminals.

The objective is to teach a criminal a new set of responses. The behaviorists are not interested so much in *why* a criminal is the way he is. They devote a few words to it in their writing, saying essentially that he failed to make it in society because of social, racial, and other handicaps and consequently was not paid off by the usual reward system. In settings where behavioral therapy is the treatment of choice, it pervades the milieu with an emphasis on teaching "skills" so that a person can become part of society (e.g., NIMH 1973; Fixsen et al. 1973; Phillips et al. 1973; Kirigin et al. 1975).

Behavioral therapy may be part of a total-environment approach in a residential setting, or it may be a set of techniques used selectively on an individual basis. Cautela (1973) has described the technique of covert sensitization. For example, a youthful offender may be treated for car-stealing through aversive imagery:

You are walking down the street. You notice a real sharp sports car. You walk toward it with the idea of stealing it. As you're walking toward it you start to get a funny feeling in your stomach. You feel sick to your stomach and you have a slight pain in your gut. As you keep walking, you really start to feel sick, and food starts coming up in your mouth. You're just about to reach for the handle of the door and you can't hold it any longer. You vomit all over your hand, the car door, the upholstery inside, all over your clothes. The smell starts to get to you and you keep puking from it. It's all over the place. It's dripping from your mouth. You turn around and run away and then you start to feel better. (p. 310)

Here, the subject himself constructs the situation through images. In another conditioning paradigm, the subject is presented with a stimulus by another person. For example, child-molesters at the Connecticut Correctional Institution have been treated by exposure to slides of youngsters paired with electric shock (Wolfe and Marino 1974). Stoudenmire (1973) has described successful treatment of voyeurism in a forty-four-year-old man who had been peeping since the age of thirteen.

An example of a behavior modification program conducted with delinquents outside an institution is that of Schwitzgebel (1964). He and his investigators frequented areas where delinquent boys congregated. They tried to make a "positive initial contact" and then create a "nurturant atmosphere" in the laboratory. Four interviewers met with the boys—a psychologist, a graduate student in education, a priest, and a graduate student in social work. The participants were rewarded for talking about themselves into tape recorders. Throughout the project, socially acceptable behavior was rewarded with gifts. An overall objective of the project was to have the investigators and boys involved in tasks that might be effective in reducing crime. To help cut down on auto thefts a boy might be aided in getting his driver's license. Then he could legitimately borrow a car and drive. The experimental group was compared with a control group on probation which had not participated in the study. The control group had almost twice as many arrests over a three-year period after the study. There was no statistical difference in the number of experimental and control subjects incarcerated.

An example of a program within an institution to modify delinquent behavior is the study conducted at the National Training School for Boys (NTS). The design and results of the federally funded project are reported in two volumes, CASE I (Cohen et al. 1967) and *A New Learning Environment* (Cohen and Filipczak 1971). CASE stands for "contingencies applicable to special education." We shall discuss here the more recent study, in which a representative sample of forty-one boys participated. Cohen and Filipczak (1971) described their objectives in the following manner:

Positive expansion of the academic and social repertoires of forty-one incarcerated adolescents through the use of operantly formulated contingency systems and the design of a special environment. (p. xix)

The principal method was to "develop school apparatus and procedures to help the student learn how to teach himself." An incentive plan for learning was established in which points worth one cent each were contingent on performance. Points could be converted into material or such social reinforcers as private rooms, programs for leisure time, and special foods. The boys, designated as "Student Educational Researchers," were being paid to learn—"like most of us, they were willing to work for money" (p. 8). Money was chosen because it is the reward "available in a free enterprise democracy" and the investigators were trying to make the NTS experience a microcosm of the outside world. The program was voluntary and individualized. Purportedly, there was total environmental control twenty-four hours a day. Points were awarded for desirable behavior. Those who did nothing to earn points went on relief, which meant living under standard prison conditions with loss of privacy, standard meals, and so on. Only a few elected relief and did so for a very short time. Those who worked could live comparatively well. Their cafeteria resembled a restaurant: menus and flowers were on the tables and hors d'oeuvres were offered for special meals. The learning of new skills and habits covered both academic subjects (programmed materials) and social skills, including even such practical considerations as how to eat chicken. In terms of academic results, Cohen pointed out that IQ changes reflected "across-the-board increases in the demonstration of ability" (p. 132). There was a mean gain of 12.5 in IQ. With respect to changing delinquent behavior during the one-year program the investigators reported:

> The following data indicate that CASE students stayed out of trouble longer than a similar group processed by the National Training School. During the first year the recidivist rate was two-thirds less than the norm. The data indicate that by the third year the total recidivist rate for CASE students may be near the norm. The CASE program evidently delayed the delinquent's return to incarceration, but his behavior would require additional maintenance in the real world for the CASE experience to remain effective after the first year in preventing recidivism. (pp. 133-134)

Thus, the follow-up indicates that CASE participants made some academic advances, but that delinquent patterns were not altered over the long run. At a Maryland junior high school, Cohen set up a similar project called PREP (Preparation through Responsive Educational Programs). The participants—children with academic and social programs—were not called "delinquent," although many of them had fought in the hallways, run away from home, thrown things in the classroom, stolen, and so on.* We were told

*One variant of the usual paradigm in which the authority conditions the subject was described by Gray et al. (1974). Incorrigible junior high school students were trained as "behavioral engineers"

during a visit to the project that the youngsters were behaving better but that it could not yet be ascertained whether personality change was occurring. The follow-up of the first two years' effort showed seven out of thirty-four dropping out of school and others with spotty work records after graduation. The investigators believed that this was because the youngsters had not had sufficient exposure to the project, which was so new.

In short, what has happened with behavior modification is similar to what has happened with other methods used originally with noncriminals. There is a voluminous literature on the application of behavioral procedures to a variety of psychiatric disorders in noncriminals. These same techniques have been applied to criminals.

> Most procedures discussed ... are acknowledged to be drawn from the token economy. ... Clearly, then, it would take only a slight adaptation of the token economy ... for institutionalized psychotics to make it applicable to delinquents in a large institution. (Rimm and Masters 1974, p. 253)

In 1973 and 1974, the use of behavior modification techniques with criminals created a furor. An American Civil Liberties Union lawsuit (*Psychiatric News* 2/20/74, p. 16) sought abolition of START (Special Treatment and Rehabilitative Training), an experimental behavior-modification program for aggressive inmates at the U.S. Bureau of Prisons medical center in Springfield, Missouri. It was argued in court that START was punitive, not therapeutic. This program was discontinued (*APA Monitor* 4/74, p. 1). Shortly thereafter, the Law Enforcement Assistance Administration announced withdrawal of support for programs involving behavior modification. A moral-ethical issue has been that behavior modification is being used as a management device, rather than as a therapeutic tool (*APA Monitor* 4/74, p. 4). It was charged that behavior modification made prisoners more docile but did not change them. That is, inmates cooperate because such programs offer them a way to gain freedom (*Washington Post* 8/11/74).

It has been suggested that there is nothing new about behavior modification. Shah (1973, p. 34) has observed that it could be said that all therapies are "behavioral," in that "the client's behavior ... is the only reality

---

to control the behavior of parents, teachers, and other children. The objective was "to instill within the students a feeling of power, the ability to control the controllers, i.e., his teachers and the school" (p. 45). The rationale was that through the exercise of such control would come "a new feeling of self-confidence." Results of the project in terms of hard data on academic improvement and lessened disruption of the classroom were not presented.

the therapist can deal with and modify." Parents use it with children, employers with employees, teachers with students. Federal Bureau of Prisons Director Norman Carlson (1974), observed that all the programs of the Bureau of Prisons could be called "behavior modification," in that they are designed to change or modify behavior. It has been said that behavior modification does more to help the institution to control the inmate than it does to promote change (*Washington Post* 7/3/73). Wattenberg (1973, p. 392) has pointed out that although behavior modification produces results in controlled conditions, the question is what happens when the control no longer exists. In addition, it is possible that participation is governed by a criminal's desire to beat the system. Wattenberg stated that a criminal may try to con the authority by acquiring rewards on his own terms, thus turning the treatment procedure into a "battle of wits." He observed that a few delinquents in one program forged the records on the basis of which they were rewarded.

CRITERIA FOR FOLLOW-UP STUDIES

A survey of various efforts to rehabilitate criminals shows a lack of follow-up, which is critical in determining the validity of procedures. To be sure, it is not easy to continue to study this population. If one goes beyond looking at official records of arrest and wants to talk with criminals themselves, a number of obstacles are encountered. Criminals are often hard to track down, because they move around and may live under an alias or have no phone. A criminal may make an appointment but then fail to keep it. He may not return a questionnaire, even if he can do so anonymously in an addressed, prestamped envelope. There is the perennial problem of the lack of full disclosure, even if a criminal is contacted. Robins (1966), a sociologist, studied a group of five hundred people, thirty years after they were seen as problem children at a clinic. That she succeeded in locating ninety percent of this population was a testimony to the thoroughness and hard work of a large research staff. She stated that her study provided no answers about prevention and treatment.

Many accounts are only descriptive and do not offer an evaluation of results. Some of the literature contains subjective impressions as to what occurred that was beneficial. These may be as nonspecific as speaking of "prisoner enthusiasm" or of "positive" results (cited by Mintz 1971, p. 264) or as global as "remolding a self-concept" (Uehling 1962, p. 48). We have referred to reports like Slavson's (1965, p. 726) in which patients met a therapist's criterion of improvement, such as "an improved identity," but in which the criminal behavior itself continued in some cases.

Some programs rely on before-and-after self-reporting for evaluation. The problem here is twofold: it is difficult to obtain honest disclosure, and there is a lack of depth. We have encountered several studies that used this method of follow-up with criminals (Lassner 1950; Weeks 1958; review in NIMH 1971b).

The major criterion of the success of a program is the criminals' later records of arrest or return to prison (e.g., Jew et al. 1972).

> Unfortunately, follow-up studies of "treatment" and "prevention" have had very little alternative besides using the so-called hard data of records of action taken in individual cases, which largely represent the variations in the decision-making process of the caretakers—to take action or not to take action. (Reckless and Dinitz 1972, p. 160)

In 1946, Murphy et al. (p. 688) pointed out the tremendous numbers of crimes committed of which officials have no knowledge. For example, although 114 boys committed a minimum of 6,416 infractions over a five-year period, only 95 violations were a "matter of official complaint"—less than 1.5% of the total. Murphy stated that "absence of court appearance is far from an indication that [a person] is free from misconduct."

Another criterion for follow-up is institutional adjustment. How a man behaves in prison is the chief determinant of parole and probation decisions, simply because there is little else to go on. Most corrections officials recognize the shortcomings of this criterion, although they may have nothing better to offer. As Amos (1971) of the U.S. Parole Board pointed out, good behavior in prison is no guarantee of anything. Some studies are published about criminals who have not yet been released. Thus, institutional adjustment becomes the sole criterion of change, with no data on the endurance of the change (Snyder and Sechrest 1963; Persons 1966).

Still another method of evaluation is to try to assess adjustment in the community as indicated by such activities as going to school, holding a job, and saving money. Some programs are very explicit about the goals to be achieved but acknowledge that these objectives fall short of personality change.

> No attempt is made to restructure the total personality. . . . If a released or paroled patient no longer compulsively repeats earlier violations of the law, we consider that our therapeutic goal has been achieved. (Boslow and Manne 1966, pp. 26-27)

In this statement, the elimination of antisocial behavior is the objective. If a criminal does not come to the attention of the authorities, he is evaluated by the institution as changed.

SHORTCOMINGS OF MENTAL HEALTH FACILITIES

Particularly since the early 1960s, the nation's mental institutions have been inundated with "socially deviant" people. Whittet (1968, p. 131) observed that prison and hospital often "take in each other's washing." The community wants psychiatric institutions to provide answers that other segments of society have failed to provide, especially where its youth is involved. The 1973-4 report of the well-known Sheppard and Enoch Pratt Hospital in Baltimore, Maryland attests to the demands being made on mental institutions to treat this part of the population, especially the teenage group. Next to depression, the symptoms of greatest frequency in patients under seventeen are drug abuse, hostile aggression, and running away. Speaking of inpatient admissions at the University of Michigan's adolescent psychiatric service, D. Miller (1973, p. 195) reported "a radical change in the last decade in symptom presentation." Inpatients admitted to the service usually have a "characterological diagnosis," whereas adolescents with schizophrenic reactions are treated in a day-care or outpatient service. The most frequent symptoms of the inpatients are drug abuse, running away, suicide attempts, and promiscuity among girls.

The dilemma faced by mental hospitals has been described in an excellent but infrequently cited study by Miller and Kenney (1966). These investigators attributed the change in the type of patients coming to hospitals to the fact that society has been tending to "psychologize problems of living." They pointed to the great demand for adolescent hospital services that has resulted from efforts to bail youngsters out of trouble and stated that the community was knocking at the door of psychiatry to provide a magical solution. Diagnosis, treatment, and follow-up of 247 adolescents admitted to the hospital revealed the nature of the problem in treating what were mostly youths with behavior disorders. Traditional psychiatric methods failed, because the patients rejected them and hospital staff members had had to function as "disciplinarian, limit-setter, authoritative counselor, and, in some cases, jailer." Miller and Kenney concluded that "no one has ever demonstrated that problems of delinquency can be successfully treated on a large scale in a psychiatric facility. We cannot treat misbehavior" (p. 47). Silber (1974), in a more recent article, called attention to the wrong "set" of the mental hospital treating the criminal.

> Mental hospitals have the wrong "set" for treating felons: they perceive the patient as helpless and disturbed. Most criminals are not out of contact with reality, but rather are deviant in social values and behavior. (p. 241)

Groder commented generally on the severe obstacles and frustrations of psychiatric practitioners in working with criminals.

> The unsophisticated civilian entering into a relationship with someone who is busy making fools of others and themselves soon finds himself in an "Alice in Wonderland," topsy turvy world where nothing is as it seems, all apples are poisoned, all princesses are really witches, all ogres are really kind men, etc., etc. The common observations related to this are that a variety of methods of psychotherapy which had some validity and usefulness in the civilian population, when brought into institutions and used with incarcerated individuals of this type had results opposite to those expected or hoped for and that the projects proved failures, many times unpredictably so. For instance, much research has indicated that a variety of forms of group therapy when used in incarcerated circumstances contributed to the maintenance of antisocial orientations because of an incredible amount of misdirection, non-inclusion of important data, game playing and ritual performance that groups typically deteriorate into with these types of individuals as members and with unsophisticated group leaders as leaders. In similar ways, individual forms of counseling, educational methods, occupations methods, religious methods, philosophical methods, self-motivation methods, etc. are almost universally brought to naught by this capacity to make a fool out of anything; the better the thing made a fool of, the more delicious the temporary pleasure. (pp. 9-10)

A major factor in the failure of mental health professionals to treat the criminal successfully is that practitioners have viewed criminals and noncriminals as being made of the same fabric and thus have applied many of the same techniques to both.

> Mentally ill people who have committed violent and serious offenses against society are not a group apart from other mentally ill persons who have not translated their emotional conflicts into overt assault upon others. They run the same gamut of psychiatric disorders as psychiatric patients in general. Moreover, psychotic murderers respond to the same methods of care and treatment as other mental hospital patients. (Weihofen 1960, p. 530—citing a 1952 study by Cruvant and Waldrop)

This statement, contained in a publication of the legal profession, exemplifies what lawyers and mental health professionals have believed. As it has turned out, methods that have worked with noncriminals have not been effective with criminals.

In some circles, there has been disenchantment with what the mental health field has to offer the criminal. Judge Bazelon, proponent of the Durham rule, which gave many criminals the opportunity for psychologic treatment rather than imprisonment, expressed doubt that psychologists have anything of value to offer in corrections (*Washington Post* 1/22/72). Psychologist Robert Hare (1970) expressed somewhat the same opinion:

> With few exceptions, the traditional forms of psychotherapy, including psychoanalysis, group therapy, client-centered therapy, psychodrama, have proved ineffective in the treatment of psychopathy. Nor have the biological therapies, including psychosurgery, electroshock therapy, and the use of various drugs, fared much better. (p. 110)

An outsider to the mental health profession, columnist William Raspberry (1973), commented that

> until we gain more confidence in the healers of the mind, maybe we'll just have to be candid enough to say that we believe criminal insanity of the violent sort is incurable, and that lifetime confinement—or perhaps death—is the only thing that will satisfy us.

The recidivism problem attests to the failure of institutions and current treatment programs. What often baffles workers in the correctional field is that the approach taken does not frequently seem to make any ultimate difference. Roberts (1968) studied staff attitudes and practices in two California youth conservation camps—one offering "a controlled-guidance and work training type of program" and the other a "permissive-interpersonal and therapeutic community orientation." Of course, the youngsters had a more favorable attitude toward the latter. However, parole violation figures showed few differences between the two camps. Roberts concluded:

> Perhaps the main lesson of the foregoing analysis is that although "positive" treatment programs clearly seem to elicit a more cooperative and accommodating response from wards while in camp, any assumption that these in-camp attitudes or behaviors are necessarily carried back by the ward to the community environment and will affect his behavior there must remain subject to question. (pp. 81-82)

In the 1970s, the social consciousness of many people has been directed toward the reform of social institutions; prisons have been of special concern. However, the emphasis has been on agencies and institutions and not on the nature of the person who is the inmate. Carlson (1974), speaking on the state of knowledge in the corrections field, ended his statement to a U.S. House of Representatives committee by saying that relatively little is known about how to assist offenders in so altering their life style that "when released from custody, they can live a law-abiding life in society." Florida congressman Claude Pepper (Kilpatrick 1969) expressed the hope that a new, independent agency might "lead the states, counties and cities out of the medieval grip of penology in which our local jurisdictions appear to be mired." Summarizing how he sees the various programs that have purported to treat this very difficult population, Wattenberg (1973) said:

> Projects vary in size, range and sophistication. There has been recognition of the validity of multiple-ingredient programs. Two contrasting observations, by now familiar to readers, are in order: When one is close to almost any of the programs one is impressed with the sincerity of those individuals they have helped, but it is apparent from the fact that the problem continues to grow that there is as yet no solution. (p. 388)

Much has been offered criminals, but they have rejected it. Warburton (1965) said of thirty-eight "psychopathic male criminals" what has been discouragingly true of the group as a whole:

> All their attitudes, humour, odd remarks, insinuations and casual conversation carried the implication that they want this life and were determined to go on with it. (p. 135)

We end this review by citing a comprehensive study by Martinson (1974), a sociologist. Of late, this study has received considerable attention. Focusing on recidivism, he and his colleagues studied the entire spectrum of rehabilitative programs, by evaluating the results of 231 methodologically sound reports. They found that no form of rehabilitation worked to reduce recidivism—not educational and skill improvement, not individual counseling, not group counseling, not milieu therapy, not medical treatment, not intensive supervision in the community, not individual psychotherapy in the community, not shorter sentences. Martinson stated that the "theory of crime as disease" and the strategy of offering treatment to cure that disease appear to be a flawed approach.

> We know almost nothing about the "deterrent effect," largely because "treatment" theories have so dominated our research, and "deterrence" theories have been relegated to the status of a historical curiosity. . . . It is possible that there is indeed something that works . . . something that deters rather than cures. (p. 50)

CONCLUSION

Despite the application of the approaches described in this chapter, crime is still very much with us. Sociologically inspired programs have neither altered the criminal's way of life nor changed what he wants out of life. The material in chapter 3 of volume 1 demonstrates that the criminal's fundamental objectives are not determined by social conditions. He has scorned as "slaves" and "suckers" responsible people who work hard, without guarantees, to achieve modest objectives. Although a criminal may go to school and hold jobs, this merely permits him to maintain a respectable front, to keep others off his back, and to use the activity itself as an arena for crime or criminal equivalents. If a criminal utilizes community programs at all, he exploits them for his own gain. In short, the environment does not cause crime and altering the environment does not cure crime. Criminality resides within the individual. Thus our quarrel is not with social programs that improve human life but with the belief that these will reduce crime.

The human mind wants to understand and explain cause and effect. Psychoanalytic theory is appealing because its concepts enable one to explain almost any behavior. We found such explanations to be more often clever than correct. In chapter 1 of volume 1, we described our experiences in using the psychoanalytic approach to reach the inner man. We succeeded in developing a psychiatrically sophisticated criminal who used interpretations as justification for crime. "Insight" became "incite." It justified his behavior by blaming others for his plight and incited him to further crime.

As we reported, we conducted groups, learned from criminals about other groups in which they participated, and observed different kinds of groups within institutions. In chapter 11, we shall describe the shortcomings of the therapeutic community, which has become increasingly popular in treating criminals. When groups of criminals are granted decision-making powers, they promote their own self-serving, irresponsible objectives. It is not surprising that criminal groups that are entrusted with authority become overly zealous in the exercise of power, as did the patients at the Utah State Hospital unit described above. As a group leader, a criminal has an even wider arena for criminal equivalents. We believe that the therapeutic community has potential for the treatment of noncriminals; for criminals, it becomes merely one more criminal operation.

In chapter 11, we shall also discuss the deficiencies of psychodrama for use with criminals. The concreteness of the lessons learned, the reliance on insight, and the emphasis on catharsis not only fail to promote basic change, but contribute to the perpetuation of old patterns. We have worked with criminals considered by their therapists to be the most astute psychodrama participants. Unknown to the psychodrama therapists, the same criminals were actively in crime while still in the hospital.

Criminals can and should be worked with in groups. However, practitioners have used the same procedures and concepts that have been successful with noncriminals with lack of positive results. They apply the techniques they know best to a very different population, which does not respond constructively.

We believe that the movement to emphasize reason rather than emotion is a step in the right direction, certainly with criminals. Like Glasser (1965), we do not analyze feelings, and we do not ferret out unconscious determinants. We also share Glasser's view that "happiness" is an objective of therapy only if it is defined as "deep-seated satisfaction" within the context of responsibility. A major shortcoming of reality therapy as applied to criminals is that although concrete responsible objectives are spelled out, conceptualization is lacking when it comes to teaching the thinking processes that apply outside the immediate situation.* Nevertheless, Glasser and his followers have made a sound beginning by using a rational procedure and stressing responsible behavior. To produce that responsible behavior, a criminal must be equipped with a whole new set of mental processes. That is what we offer in our program.

Our most basic criticism of procedures that are termed "existential" is the one that we have made repeatedly. There appears to be no distinction between criminal and noncriminal when it comes to reporting what is actually done. The question is whether the practitioners make such a distinction even to themselves. We know of no writer who calls himself an existential therapist and claims that he is effecting basic change in criminals. Either practitioners are not working with this group, or they are treating criminals and noncriminals alike in their practices. A problem in the existential approach is the treatment of meaning. Sartre's "we are our choices" can be used to justify or legitimize almost anything a person does, including a criminal act. One need only read Sartre's book on Genet (1963) to see that he, in fact, does this (see also Goodman 1960, and Cooper 1971). Most practitioners work with

---

*For example, Barr (1974), of the Reality Therapy Institute, described the case of Eric, who had a "history of minor disciplinary problems" and was a marijuana smoker. The problem that concerned Eric was how to respond to a draft induction notice. His therapist helped him to evaluate the options. Eric chose to go into the service. However, he later "changed his commitment," went AWOL twice, and landed in a military psychiatric ward. Barr stated that if the therapist had interviewed Eric on that ward, he would have started at that point to help Eric in mapping out options for further courses of action. The problem, from our point of view, is that Eric did not learn processes of decision-making that he could apply across the board. There was no broad base of responsibility, so what his therapist did with him was situation-specific.

people who already have a moral base and some sense of values, whereas responsibility and morality are strangers to the criminal. For example, Frankl's techniques appear to assume that a person is operating from a base of responsibility. His very language of achievement and suffering would mean entirely different things to a responsible person and to a criminal, for whom achievement is conquest of another person and suffering is having to live without his excitements. One would have to go beyond the worthless fragments of a criminal's conscience to establish values. A will to meaning and the objective of giving meaning to life could not be established in a criminal without a total destruction of criminal thinking processes and the incorporation of new ones. The self-actualization ideas of some writers also would not apply to criminals. To help a noncriminal to lead a more authentic existence, in which he actualizes his potential and accepts himself, is certainly worthwhile. However, these objectives translate into something different in work with criminals. That is, one would be seeking a more authentic criminal, a man actualizing his criminal potential and accepting himself as a criminal. We shall indicate later how our approach has existential elements, not by design but as an outcome of continuing revisions of method. We did not board the bandwagon and call ourselves "existentialists"; rather, we found, after the fact, that some issues arising in our work may be termed "existential" in their concern. We shall show how we have made some of the abstractions of existentialism operational and vivid to criminals in the process of change.

With respect to behavior modification, we find it to be a simplistic way of dealing with a complex problem. Learning particular skills and changing isolated behavioral patterns do not produce basic change in criminals. Using conditioning with criminals is like trying to stave off a tidal wave with a bucket. No system of reward and punishment by itself can penetrate and change the thinking processes described in volume 1. Teaching a criminal how to interact agreeably with his teachers or employers and training him with vocational know-how do not reach the inner man. Manipulating external contingencies and giving rewards do not touch the core of the problem. The criminal is still a criminal. He learns new skills or habits easily enough but uses them to further criminal objectives. He satisfies society's requirements in a token manner, but the payoffs that society offers do not satisfy him. A criminal child may value the greater freedom that he earns when he cooperates at home and at school. But he uses that freedom to advance objectives that cause harm to others. We have yet to find one study that reports basic and lasting change in criminal subjects. Although impressive results have been achieved with behavior modification in noncriminals, this has not been the case with criminals.

The debate over the effectiveness of deterrents is likely to continue much as it has for centuries. It probably will not be resolved as long as personal value judgments determine the position taken. We hope that the material in volume 1, especially in chapter 6, has shed some light on the intermittent effectiveness of deterrents at different points on the criminal continuum. In chapter 9 of this volume, we shall explain the development of transitory and then permanent deterrents in the process of change.

Finally, we agree that our institutions need reform and that criminals deserve humane treatment. However, our proposal for reform is in a sense more radical than any other suggested. Our program departs sharply from those now in existence, which purport to rehabilitate people who have never been "habilitated." In chapter 13 of this volume, we shall present a description of the kind of institution that we consider necessary to do the job—a facility based on our concepts and techniques that has a coordinated program for "habilitation" of the criminal.*

*As this book went to press, more and more the cries of disillusionment with rehabilitation were being heard. Holden (1975) described this trend: "The American criminal justice system, and the social scholars who concern themselves with it, are now in the midst of what one of them calls a "massive retreat" from rehabilitation. Disillusionment is such that there are no programs, either within prisons or in communities, whose worth has not come into question.... The disillusionment with "rehabilitation," at least in its present forms, has been so deep that is has caused many prominent social scientists and penologists to abandon cherished philosophies in a matter of a few years" (pp. 815-816).

BIBLIOGRAPHY

Abrahams, D. Y. (1956). Observations on transference in a group of teen-age 'delinquents.' *International Journal of Group Psychotherapy* 6:286-290.

Aichhorn, A. (1935). *Wayward Youth*. New York: Viking.

Alexander, F., and Staub, H. (1931). *The Criminal, The Judge, and The Public*. New York: Macmillan.

American Correctional Association. (1966). *Manual of Correctional Standards*. Washington, D.C.: American Correctional Association.

American Psychiatric Association (1972). "Conscious and countertransference reactions to violent patients." A continuing education videotape special session presented at the 125th annual meeting of the American Psychiatric Association, Dallas, Texas.

Amos, W. E. (1971). Talk delivered at the District of Columbia Psychological Association meeting December 6, Washington, D.C.

APA Monitor (4/74). Behavior modification under fire, p. 1.

Assagioli, R. (1973). *The Act of Will*. New York: Viking.

Averill, S.; Cadman, S. C.; Craig, L. P.; and Linden, R. E. (1973). Group psychotherapy with young delinquents. *Bulletin of the Menninger Clinic* 37:1-70.

Ayllon, T., and Azrin, N. (1968). *The Token Economy*. New York: Appleton-Century-Crofts.

Baltimore Sun (8/4/71). Psychologists defend Patuxent.

Baltimore Sun (8/14/71). Seattle tries wilderness program for dropouts.

Barnes, H. E., and Teeters, N. K. (1959). *New Horizons in Criminology*. Englewood Cliffs, New Jersey: Prentice-Hall.

Barr, N. I. (1967). Voluntary imprisonment: its usefulness in the rehabilitation of criminal offenders. *American Journal of Psychiatry* 124:170-178.

Barr, N. I. (1974). The responsible world of reality therapy. *Psychology Today* 7 (February):64ff.

Bazelon, D. (1961). Equal justice for the unequal. Lecture 3 of the American Psychiatric Association Isaac Ray Lectureship Award Series.

Bedau, H. A. (1971). The death penalty in America. *Federal Probation*, 35(June):32-43.

Bennett, I. (1960). *Delinquent and Neurotic Children*. New York: Basic Books.

Berne, E. (1967). *Games People Play*. New York: Grove.

Borriello, J. F. (1973). Patients with acting-out character disorders. *American Journal of Psychiatry* 27:4-14.

Boslow, H. M. (1964). The team approach in a psychiatrically oriented correctional institution. *Prison Journal* 44:37-42.

Boslow, H. M.; Rosenthal, D.; and Gliedman, L. H. (1959). The Maryland defective delinquency law. *British Journal of Delinquency* 10:5-13.

Boslow, H. M.; Rosenthal, D.; Kandel, A.; and Manne, S. H. (1961). Methods and experiences in group treatment of defective delinquents in Maryland. *Journal of Social Therapy* 7:65-75.

Boslow, H. M., and Manne, S. H. (1966). Mental health in action: treating adult offenders at Patuxent institution. *Crime and Delinquency* 12:22-28.

Bradley, C. (1950). Benzedrine and dexedrine in the treatment of children's behavior disorders. *Pediatrics* 5:24-37.

Brandes, N. S. (1973). Outpatients. In *Group Therapy for the Adolescent*, ed. Brandes, N. S., and Gardner, M. L., pp. 63-82. New York: Jason Aronson.

Breggin, P. R., and Greenberg, D. S. (1972). Return of the lobotomy. *Washington Post*, March 12, p. C1.

Briggs, D. (1973). Chino, California. In *Dealing with Deviants*, ed. Whiteley, S., Briggs, D., and Turner, M. New York: Schocken.

Bromberg, W., and Rodgers, T. C. (1946). Authority in the treatment of delinquents. *American Journal of Orthopsychiatry* 16:672-685.

Brown, B. S.; Wienckowski, L. A.; and Bivens, L. W. (1973). *Psychosurgery: Perspective on a Current Issue*. DHEW Publication No. (ADM) 74-76.

Washington, D.C.: U.S. Government Printing Office.

Buckley, M. (1972). Enter: the ex-con. *Federal Probation* 36 (December):24-31.

Bugental, J. F. T. (1964). The nature of the therapeutic task in intensive psychotherapy. *Journal of Existentialism* 5:199-204.

Burchard, J. (1973). Behavior modification with the delinquent offender. ed. Irvine, L. M., and Brelje, T. B. In *Law, Psychiatry and the Mentally Disordered Offender*, vol. 2, pp. 111-119. Springfield, Illinois: Charles C Thomas.

Burke, J. L., and Lee, H. (1964). An acting-out patient in a psychotic group. *International Journal of Group Psychotherapy* 14:194-202.

Campbell, H. E. (1971). Freud in the American scene. *Rocky Mountain Medical Journal*, 68 (June):33-36.

Carlson, N. A. (1974). Statement before the House Committe on the Judiciary Subcommittee on Courts, Civil Liberties and the Administration of Justice concerning "Behavior Modification" and the Federal Center for Correctional Research, Butner, North Carolina, February 27.

Carney, F. L. (1972). Some recurrent therapeutic issues in group psychotherapy with criminal patients. *American Journal of Psychotherapy* 26:34-41.

Carpenter, P., and Sandberg, S. (1973). 'The things inside': psychodrama with delinquent adolescents. *Psychotherapy: Theory, Research and Practice* 10:245-247.

Cautela, J. R. (1973). Covert sensitization. In *Behavior Therapy with Delinquents*, ed. Stumphauzer, J. S., pp. 302-314. Springfield, Illinois: Charles C Thomas.

Cavior, N., and Howard, L. R. (1973). Facial attractiveness and juvenile delinquency among black and white offenders. *Journal of Abnormal Psychology* 1:202-213.

Chaneles, S. (1974). Open prisons: urban convicts can turn ghost towns into rural communities. *Psychology Today* 7 (April):30 ff.

Chatz, T. L. (1972). Recognizing and treating dangerous sex offenders. *International Journal of Offender Therapy and Comparative Criminology* 16:109-115.

Clark, A. W., and Yeomans, N. T. (1969). *Fraser House: Theory, Practice and Evaluation of a Therapeutic Community*. New York: Springer.

Clark, R. (1970). *Crime in America*. New York: Simon and Schuster.

Cohen, H., and Filipczak, J. (1971). *A New Learning Environment*. San Francisco: Jossey-Bass.

Cohen, H.; Filipczak, J.; and Bis, J. S. (1967). *CASE I: An Initial Study of Contingencies Applicable to Special Education*. Silver Spring, Maryland: Educational Facility Press.

Conners, C. K. (1972). Symposium: behavior modification by drugs II:

psychological effects of stimulant drugs in children with minimal brain dysfunction. *Pediatrics* 49:702-708.

Coodley, A. E. (1961). Current aspects of delinquency and addiction. *Archives of General Psychiatry* 4:632-640.

Cooper, D. G. (1971). Sartre on Genet. In *Reason and Violence*, Laing, R. D. and Cooper, D. G., London: Tavistock, pp. 67-90.

Correctional Programs News (1972). 1 (November).

Corsini, R. (1951). The method of psychodrama in prison. *Group Psychotherapy* 3:321-326.

—— (1958). Psychodrama with a psychopath. *Group Psychotherapy* 11:33-39.

Darling, H. F. (1945). Shock treatment in psychopathic personality. *Journal of Nervous and Mental Disease* 101:247-250.

Darrow, C. (1922). *Crime: Its Cause and Treatment*. New York: Crowell.

De Berker, P. (1966). The sociology of change in penal institutions. In *Changing Concepts of Crime and Its Treatment*, ed. Klare, H. J., pp. 139-154. Oxford: Pergamon.

Drakeford, J. W. (1967). *Integrity Therapy*. Nashville: Broadman.

Dressler, D. (1968). We have too many people in jail. *This Week Magazine*, June 9, 4-9.

Dy, A. J. (1974). Correctional psychiatry and phase psychotherapy. *American Journal of Psychiatry* 131:1150-1152.

Dygert, J. H. (1971). We must give jobs to school dropouts. *Parade*, August 29, p. 27.

Eaton, J. W. (1962). *Stone Walls Not a Prison Make*. Springfield, Illinois: Charles C Thomas.

Eichorn, J. R. (1965). Delinquency and the educational system. In *Juvenile Delinquency*, ed. Quay, H. C., pp. 298-337. Princeton: Van Nostrand.

Eisenberg, L.; Lachman, R.; Molling, P. A.; Lockner, A.; Mizelle, J. D.; and Conners, C. K. (1963). A psychopharmacologic experiment in a training school for delinquent boys: methods, problems, findings. *American Journal of Orthopsychiatry* 33:431-447.

Eissler, K. R. (1950). Ego-psychological implications of the psychoanalytic treatment of delinquents. *Psychoanalytic Study of the Child* 5:97-121.

Ellenberger, H. F. (1958). A clinical introduction to psychiatric phenomenology and existential analysis. In *Existence: A New Dimension in Psychiatry and Psychology*, ed. May, R., et al., pp. 92-124. New York: Basic Books.

Ellis, A. (1967). Psychotherapy and moral laxity. *Psychiatric Opinion* 4:18-21.

Ellis, A. (1976). Workshop presented at the United States District Court sponsored by the Office of the Probation Officer in Washington, D.C., April 8.

Ernst, F. H., and Keating, W. C. (1964). Psychiatric treatment of the California felon. *American Journal of Psychiatry* 120:974-979.

Evening Star (9/2/68). Convicts' art show brings in $24,075.

——— (11/9/70). Prison actors dramatize drug world.

——— (12/29/70). Youth facility an alternate to jail term.

——— (7/21/71). Jobs for women inmates.

——— (9/1/71). The crime problem.

Evening Star and The Washington Daily News (1/19/73). Psychosurgeon hails success on children.

——— (2/1/73). Prisoners win damages from corrections head.

——— (2/15/73). Lorton's favored fifty.

Fairfax Journal (6/11/73). Losing 50 grand and liking it.

Farber, L. H. (1966). *The Ways of the Will.* New York: Harper.

Feldman, M. J. (1963). Queries on existential psychotherapy. *International Journal of Social Psychiatry* 9:121-126.

Feldman, R. A.; Wodarski, J. S.; Goodman, M.; and Flax, N. (1973). Prosocial and antisocial boys together. *Social Work* 18:26-37.

Fenton, N. (1973). Sensitivity training in prison management. *Human Relations in Adult Corrections*, pp. 120-129. Springfield, Illinois: Charles C Thomas.

Field, L. H. (1973). Benperidol in the treatment of sexual offenders. *Medicine, Science and the Law* 13:195-196.

Fixsen, D. L.; Wolf, M. M.; and Phillips, E. L. (1973). Achievement place: a teaching-family model of community-based group homes for youth in trouble. In *Behavior Change*, ed. Hemerlynck, L. A., et al., pp. 241-268. Champaign, Illinois: Research Press.

Folsom, J. C., and Taubee, E. S. (1967). Attitude therapy. *Journal of the Fort Logan Mental Health Center* 4:47-57.

Frankl, V. (1962). *Man's Search for Meaning: An Introduction to Logotherapy.* Boston: Beacon.

——— (1965). *The Doctor and the Soul.* New York: Knopf.

——— (1966). What is meant by meaning. *Journal of Existentialism* 7:21-28.

——— (1967). *Psychotherapy and Existentialism.* New York: Simon and Schuster.

Freeman, B., and Savastano, G. (1970). The affluent youthful offender. *Crime and Delinquency* 16:264-272.

Friedenberg, E. Z. (1962). *The Vanishing Adolescent.* New York: Dell.

Friedlander, K. (1947). *The Psycho-analytical Approach to Juvenile Delinquency.* London: Kegan Paul, Trench, Trubner.

Gambino, R. (1969). Crime and punishment—toward a policy for our time. *Ethical Forum* 12:1-18.

Gardner, W. I. (1971). *Behavior Modification in Mental Retardation.* Chicago: Aldine-Atherton.

Garner, H. H., and Jeans, R. F. (1962). Confrontation technique in psychotherapy: some existential implications. *Journal of Existential Psychiatry* 2:393-408.

Gatch, V., and Temerlin, M. (1965). The belief in psychic determinism and the behavior of the psychotherapist. *Review of Existential Psychology and Psychiatry* 5:16-33.

Gelso, C. J. (1970). Two different worlds: a paradox in counseling and psychotherapy. *Journal of Counseling Psychology* 17:271-278.

Giorgi, A. (1965). Existential phenomenology and the psychology of the human person. *Review of Existential Psychology and Psychiatry* 8:102-116.

Glaser, D. (1971). From revenge to resocialization: changing perspectives in combating crime. *American Scholar* 40:654-661.

Glasser, W. (1965). *Reality Therapy.* New York: Harper.

Gleser, G. C.; Gottschalk, L. A.; Fox, R.; and Lippert, W. (1965). Immediate changes in affect with chlordiazepoxide. *Archives of General Psychiatry* 13:291-295.

Glover, E. (1960). *The Roots of Crime.* New York: International Universities Press.

Glueck, S. (1952). *Crime and Correction: Selected Papers.* Cambridge, Massachusetts: Addison-Wesley.

Goldberg, C., and Goldberg, M. (1973). *The Human Circle.* Chicago: Nelson-Hall.

Goldfarb, R. L. (1971). Voices from inside the prisons. *Potomac (Washington Post)*, November 21, pp. 40-47.

——— (1971). Why don't we tear down our prisons? *Look*, July 27, pp. 45-47.

Goodman, P. (1960). *Growing Up Absurd.* New York: Vintage.

Graubard, P. S. (1969). Teaching strategies and techniques for the education of disruptive groups and individuals. In *Children Against Schools*, pp. 329-355. Chicago: Follett.

Gray, F.; Graubard, P. S.; and Rosenberg, H. (1974). Little brother is changing you. *Psychology Today* 7 (March):42-46.

Greenacre, P. (1945). Conscience in the psychopath. *American Journal of Orthopsychiatry* 15:495-509.

Greenwald, H. (1967). Treatment of the psychopath. In *Active Psychotherapy*, pp. 363-377. New York: Atherton.

——— (1973). From client-centered to therapist-centered. *Contemporary Psychology* 18:26.

Groder, M. G. (n.d.). Asklepieion—an effective treatment method for incarcerated character disorders. n.p.

Grygier, T.; Nease, B.; and Anderson, C. S. (1970). An exploratory study of halfway houses. *Crime and Delinquency* 16:280-291.

Guttmacher, M. S. (1951). *Sex Offenders.* New York: Norton.

Guze, S. B. (1976). *Criminality and Psychiatric Disorders.* New York: Oxford University Press.

Hackfield, A. W. (1935). The ameliorative effects of therapeutic castration in habitual sex offenders. *Journal of Nervous and Mental Disease* 82: 15-29.

Hall, C. S., and Lindzey, G. (1970). *Theories of Personality.* 2nd ed. New York: Wiley.

Hare, R. D. (1970). *Psychopathy: Theory and Research.* New York: Wiley.

Havighurst, R. J. (1963). Research on the school work-study program in the prevention of juvenile delinquency. In *Role of the School in Prevention of Juvenile Delinquency,* pp. 27-45. U. S. Department of Health, Education and Welfare, Washington, D.C.

Healy, W. (1915). *The Individual Delinquent.* Boston: Little, Brown.

Healy, W., and Bronner, A. F. (1936). *New Light on Delinquency and Its Treatment.* New Haven: Yale University Press.

Henderson, D. (1951). Psychopathic states. *British Journal of Delinquency* 2:84-87.

Hendrickson, W. J., and Holmes, D. J. (1960). Institutional psychotherapy of the delinquent. In *Progress in Psychotherapy,* vol. 5, ed., Masserman, J., and Moreno, J. L., pp. 169-170. New York: Grune & Stratton.

Henry, N. (1972). *When Mother Is a Prefix: New Directions in Youth Correction.* New York: Behavioral Publications.

Heuscher, J. E. (1964). What is existential psychotherapy? *Review of Existential Psychology and Psychiatry* 4:158-167.

Hirschi, T., and Stark, R. (1969). Hellfire and delinquency. *Social Problems* 17:202-213.

Hitchcock, E.,and Cairns, V. (1973). Amgdalotomy. *Postgraduate Medical Journal* 49:894-904.

Holden, C. (1975). Prisons: faith in 'rehabilitation' is suffering a collapse. *Science,* 188 (May 23): 815-817.

Holt, J. (1964). *How Children Fail.* New York: Delta.

Hotis, J. B. (1972). A law enforcement officer looks at sentencing. *Federal Probation,* 36(March):23-26.

Howard, D. (1966). Hallucination: a phenomenological analysis. *Review of Existential Psychology and Psychiatry* 6:211-229.

Illinois Commission on Sex Offenders (1963). Report to members of the 73rd General Assembly, State of Illinois (March).

Ingram, G. L. (1970). An experimental program for the psychopathic delinquent: looking in the 'correctional wastebasket.' *Journal of Research in Crime and Delinquency* 7:24-30.

Janov, A. (1970). *The Primal Scream.* New York: Putnams.

——— (1972). *The Primal Revolution.* New York: Simon and Schuster.

Jeffery, C. R. (1973). Environmental design and the prevention of behavioral disorders and criminality. Talk presented at Centre of Criminology, University of Toronto, January 25.

Jew, C. G.; Clanon, T. L.; and Mattocks, A. L. (1972). The effectiveness of group psychotherapy in a correctional institution. *American Journal of Psychiatry* 129:602-605.

Jones, M. (1953). *The Therapeutic Community.* New York: Basic Books.

——— (1962). *Social Psychiatry in the Community, in Hospitals, and in Prisons.* Springfield, Illinois: Charles C Thomas.

——— (1965). A passing glance at the therapeutic community in 1964. *International Journal of Group Psychotherapy* 15:5-10.

——— (1968). *Beyond the Therapeutic Community.* New Haven: Yale University Press.

——— and Weeks, M. (1973). Systems approach to a correctional institution. In *Law, Psychiatry and the Mentally Disordered Offender,* vol. 2, ed. Irvine, L. M., and Brelje, T. B., pp. 73-81. Springfield, Illinois: Charles C Thomas.

Journal of Criminal Law, Criminology and Police Science (1972). Cruel and unusual punishment 63:484-492.

Kagan, H. E., and Zucker, A. H. (1970). Treatment of a 'corrupted family' by rabbi and psychiatrist. *Journal of Religion and Health* 9:22-34.

Kalina, R. K. (1964). Diazepam: its role in a prison setting. *Diseases of the Nervous System* 25:101-106.

Kalinowsky, L. B., and Hoch, P. H. (1952). *Shock Treatments, Psychosurgery and Other Somatic Treatments in Psychiatry.* New York: Grune and Stratton.

Kiger, R. S. (1963). An approach to the 'therapeutic community' in a decentralized state hospital. Presented at Colorado State Hospital, Pueblo, Colorado, May 2.

——— (1964). New programs solve old problems. *Mental Hospitals* 15:657-662.

——— (1966). Myth of the psychopath. (Unpublished manuscript).

——— (1967). Treating the psychopathic patient in a therapeutic community. *Hospital and Community Psychiatry* 18:191-196.

——— (1970). The therapeutic community in a maximum security hospital—treatment implications. Presented at the Institute on Law, Psychiatry and the Mentally Disordered Offender, Southern Illinois University, Carbondale, Illinois, November.

Kilpatrick, J. J. (1969). Claude Pepper has seasoned views on crime. *Evening Star,* September 2.

Kirigin, K.; Phillips, E. L.; Fixsen, D. L.; Atwater, J.; Taubman, M.; and Wolf, M. M. (1975). Evaluation of the overall achievement place program. Paper presented at the 83rd convention of the American Psychological Association at Chicago.

Klare, H. J., ed. (1966). *Changing Concepts of Crime and Its Treatment.* Oxford: Pergamon.

Klink, T. W. (1970). The religious community and the returning inmate. In *Community Mental Health: The Role of Church and Temple,* ed. Clinebell, H. J., pp. 136-142. Nashville: Abingdon.

Kole, D. M. (1968). Psychodrama in counselor training. *Camps and Conferences.* Fall, 1968, pp. 6ff.

———, and Busse, H. (1969). Trail camping for delinquents. *Hospital and Community Psychiatry* 20:40-43.

Kopp, M. E. (1938). Surgical treatment as sex crime prevention measure. *Journal of Law and Criminology* 28:692-706.

Korey, S. R. (1944). The effects of benzedrine sulfate on the behavior of psychopathic and neurotic juvenile delinquents. *Psychiatric Quarterly* 18:127-137.

Kurtzberg, R.; Safar, H.; and Mandell, W. (1969). Plastic surgery in corrections. *Federal Probation* 33:44-47.

Lamb, R. H., and Goertzel, V. (1974). Ellsworth house: a community alternative to jail. *American Journal of Psychiatry* 131:64-68.

Lassner, R. (1950). Psychodrama in prison. *Group Psychotherapy* 3:77-91.

Levy, S. (1966). The hyperkinetic child—a forgotten entity: its diagnosis and treatment. *International Journal of Neuropsychiatry* 2:330-336.

Liddle, G. P. (1963). Existing and projected research on reading in relationship to juvenile delinquency. In *Role of the School in Prevention of Juvenile Delinquency,* pp. 46-68. Washington, D.C.: U.S. Department of Health, Education and Welfare.

McConnell, R. M. (1912). *Criminal Responsibility and Social Constraint.* New York: Scribner's.

McCorkle, L. W. (1953). The present status of group therapy in United States correctional institutions. *International Journal of Group Psychotherapy* 3:79-87.

McEvoy, T. L. (1967). The existential dynamics of free choice. *Journal of Existentialism* 8:1-17.

Maloney, D. M.; Harper, T. M.; Braukmann, C. J.; Fixsen, D. L.; Phillips, E. L.; and Wolf, M. M. (1972). The effects of training pre-delinquent girls on conversation and posture behaviors by teaching-parent and juvenile peers. Paper presented at the 80th convention of the American Psychological Association, Honolulu.

Martinson, R. (1974). What works?—questions and answers about prison reform. *Public Interest*, Spring 1974, pp. 22-54.

Maslow, A. (1954). *Motivation and Personality*. New York: Harper.

May, R. (1966). The emergence of existential psychology. In *Existential Psychology*, pp. 11-51. New York: Random House.

————— (1969). *Love and Will*. New York: Norton.

May, R.; Angel, E.; Ellenberger, H. F. (1958). *Existence: A New Dimension in Psychiatry and Psychology*. New York: Basic Books.

Mayer, E. E. (1948). Prefrontal lobotomy and the courts. *Journal of Criminal Law and Criminology* 38:576-583.

Meduna, L. J. (1958). *Carbon Dioxide Therapy*. Springfield, Illinois: Charles C Thomas

Medical World News (7/20/73). Psychosurgery: cons, Congress and the APA get into the act, pp. 31-32.

Menninger, K. (1968). *The Crime of Punishment*. New York: Viking.

————— (1973). *Whatever Became of Sin?* New York: Hawthorn.

Menninger, W. C. (1973). The therapy of friendship in the big brother program. In *Human Relations in Adult Corrections*, ed., Fenton, N., pp. 42-53. Springfield, Illinois: Charles C Thomas.

Miller, D. (1973). The development of psychiatric treatment services for adolescents. In *Current Issues in Adolescent Psychiatry*, ed. Schooler, J. C., pp. 189-202. New York: Bruner/Mazel.

Miller, R. B., and Kenney, E. (1966). Adolescent delinquency and the myth of hospital treatment. *Crime and Delinquency* 12:38-48.

Mintz, E. E. (1971). *Marathon Groups: Reality and Symbol*, pp. 263-264. New York: Appleton-Century Crofts.

Mitford, J. (1973). Experiments behind bars: doctors, drug companies, and prisoners. *Atlantic Monthly* 231 (January):64-73.

Moreno, J. L. (1959). Existentialism, daseinsanalyse, and psychodrama. *Psychodrama* vol. 2, pp. 207-217. New York: Beacon House.

Moyer, K. E. (1971). A preliminary physiological model of aggressive behavior. In *The Physiology of Aggression and Defeat*, ed. Eleftheriou, B. E., and Scott, J. P., pp. 223-265. New York: Plenum.

Mullan, H., and Sangiuliano, I. (1961). The subjective phenomenon in existential psychotherapy. *Journal of Existential Psychiatry* 2:17-34.

Murphy, F. J.; Shirley, M. M.; and Witmer, H. L. (1946). The incidence of hidden delinquency. *American Journal of Orthopsychiatry* 16:686-696.

Murphy, M. L., and Murphy, M. (1971). College as a parole plan. *Federal Probation*, 35 (March):45-48.

Murray, E. J. (1964). Psychology's paperbacks. *Contemporary Psychology* 9:10-17.

National Advisory Commission on Criminal Justice Standards and Goals (1973). *Corrections.* Washington, D.C.: Government Printing Office.

National Institute of Mental Health (1971a) *Community Based Correctional Programs.* Public Health Service Publication No. 2130. Washington, D.C.: U.S. Government Printing Office.

——— (1971b). *Graduated Release.* Public Health Service Publication No. 2128. Washington, D.C.: U.S. Government Printing Office.

——— (1973). *Achievement Place: A Model for Delinquency Treatment.* NIMH Research Report 1, 1973. Washington, D.C.: U.S. Government Printing Office.

National Observer (2/8/71). Police say they will 'monitor' judges deemed lenient about punishment.

New York City Youth Board (1960). *Reaching the Fighting Gang.* New York: New York City Youth Board.

Nixon, R. M. (1973). Text of Nixon's address on fighting crime and drugs. *Washington Post*, March 11.

Ogilvie, B. C., and Tutko, T. A. (1971). Sport: if you want to build character, try something else. *Psychology Today* 5 (October):60-63.

Otten, A. L. (1975). Politics and people: crime fighting. *Wall Street Journal*, January 16, p. 10.

Palmer, J. (1972). Transcript of interview from "The Today Show," WMAQ TV, Chicago, Illinois, December 20.

Pankratz, L. D., and Buchan, G. (1965). Exploring psychodramatic techniques with defective delinquents. *Group Psychotherapy* 18:136-141.

Persons, R. W. (1966). Psychological and behavioral change on delinquents following psychotherapy. *Journal of Clinical Psychology* 22:337-340.

Phillips, E. L.; Fixsen, D. L.; and Wolf, M. M. (1973). Behavior shaping works for delinquents: achievement place. *Psychology Today* 7(June):75-79.

Polk, K. (1967). *Nonmetropolitan Delinquency.* Washington, D.C.: U.S. Government Printing Office.

President's Commission on Crime in the District of Columbia. (1966). *Report.* Washington, D.C.: U.S. Government Printing Office.

President's Commission on Law Enforcement and the Administration of Justice (1967). *The Challenge of Crime in a Free Society.* Washington, D.C.: U.S. Government Printing Office.

Psychiatric News (3/21/73). 'Defective delinquent' still an elusive concept in Maryland, p. 5.

——— (4/4/73). Court hits lack of medical, psychiatric care at prisons.

——— (4/4/73). Offenders' clinic established for antisocial criminals, p. 20.

——— (4/4/73). Patuxent institution—the problem of direction, p. 3.

———— (2/20/74). ACLU lawsuit seeks abolition of behavior modification unit, p. 16.

Rachman, A. W. (1969). Talking it out rather than fighting it out: prevention of a delinquent gang war by group therapy intervention. *International Journal of Group Psychotherapy* 19:167-175.

Rappaport, R. G. (1971). Group therapy in prisons. *International Journal of Group Psychotherapy* 21:489-496.

Raspberry, W. (1973). How should we treat the criminally insane? *Washington Post*, November 9.

Reckless, W. C., and Dinitz, S. (1972). *The Prevention of Juvenile Delinquency*. Columbus: Ohio State University Press.

Redl, F., and Wineman, D. (1951). *Children Who Hate*. Glencoe, Illinois: Free Press.

Rieger, W. (1973). A proposal for a trial of family therapy and conjugal visits in prison. *American Journal of Orthopsychiatry* 43:117-122.

Rifkin, A.; Quitkin, F.; Carrillo, C.; Blumberg, A. G.; and Klein, D. F. (1972). Lithium carbonate in emotionally unstable character disorder. *Archives of General Psychiatry* 27:519-523.

Rimm, D. C., and Masters, J. C. (1974). *Behavior Therapy: Techniques and Empirical Findings*. New York: Academic Press.

Roberts, C. F. (1968). Rehabilitative influences in California youth conservation camps. *California Youth Authority*, Research Report No. 54, April 19.

Robertson, W. B. (1972). The jaycees go to prison. *Therapeutic Recreation Journal* 6:123-124.

Robins, L. N. (1966). *Deviant Children Grown Up*. Baltimore: Williams & Wilkins.

Rodale, J. I. (1968). *Natural Health, Sugar and the Criminal Mind*. New York: Pyramid.

Rogers, C. R. (1951). *Client-Centered Therapy*. Boston: Houghton Mifflin.

———— (1971). *Encounter Groups*. London: Allen Lane.

Roman, M. (1957). *Reaching Delinquents Through Reading*. Springfield, Illinois: Charles C Thomas.

Ross, S. (1972). A rap with a lifer. *Parade*, February 27, pp. 7-9.

Rubin, J. (1971). Psychiatry and corrections: president's perspective. *Psychiatric Institute Foundation News*, March, pp. 1-3.

Sadler, W. S. (1946). Preinstitutional recognition and management of the potential delinquent. In *Contemporary Criminal Hygiene*, ed. Seliger, R. V., et al., pp. 107-129. Baltimore: Oakridge.

St. Louis Post Dispatch (11/11/71). Delinquency curtailed by team counseling.

Salzman, L. (1961). Guilt, responsibility and the unconscious. *Comprehensive Psychiatry* 2:179-187.

Sangiuliano, I. S. (1963). The experience of psychotherapy. *Journal of Existential Psychiatry* 3:255-262.

Sartre, J.-P. (1953). *Existential Psychoanalysis*. Chicago: Gateway.

——— (1963). *Saint Genet, Actor and Martyr*. New York: Braziller.

Schmauk, F. J. (1970). Punishment, arousal, and avoidance learning in sociopaths. *Journal of Abnormal Psychology* 76:325-335.

Schmideberg, M. (1960). Psychiatric study and psychotherapeutic study of criminals. In *Progress in Psychotherapy*, vol. 5, ed. Masserman, J., and Moreno, J. L., pp. 156-160. New York: Grune & Stratton.

Schulman, I. (1956). Delinquents. In *The Fields of Group Psychotherapy*, ed. Slavson, S. R., pp. 196-214. New York: International Universities Press.

Schutz, W. C. (1967). *Joy*. New York: Grove.

Schwitzgebel, R. K. (1964). *Streetcorner Research*. Cambridge, Massachusetts: Harvard University Press.

———ed. (1971). *Development and Legal Regulation of Coercive Behavior Modification Techniques with Offenders*. Public Health Service No. 2067. Washington, D.C.: U.S. Government Printing Office.

Sellin, T. (1961). Capital punishment. *Federal Probation* 25 (September):3-10.

Selsky, C. S. (1962). Postcommitment family counseling. *Federal Probation*, 6 (September):41-43.

Shah, S. A. (1973). Some basic principles and concepts of behavior modification. In *Behavior Therapy with Delinquents*, ed. Stumphauzer, J. S., pp. 21-36. Springfield, Illinois: Charles C Thomas.

Shapiro, J. L., and Ross, R. R. (1971). Sensitivity training for staff in an institution for adolescent offenders. *Journal of Applied Behavioral Science* 7:710-723.

Sheppard and Enoch Pratt Hospital. *Annual Report 1973-1974*. Baltimore, Maryland.

Silber, D. E. (1974). Controversy concerning the criminal justice system and its implications for the role of mental health workers. *American Psychologist* 29:239-244.

Skambraks, M. (1967). Pastoral care in a German juvenile prison. *International Journal of Offender Therapy* 11:104-107.

Slavson, S. R. (1950). *Analytic Group Psychotherapy with Children, Adolescents and Adults*. New York: Columbia University Press.

——— (1954). *Re-educating the Delinquent Through Group and Community Participation*. New York: Collier.

——— (1965). *Reclaiming the Delinquent*. New York: The Free Press.

Smith, G. (1973). Personal communication. Utah State Hospital, Provo, Utah, February 15.

Snyder, R., and Sechrest, L. (1963). An experimental study of directive group therapy with defective delinquents. In *Group Psychotherapy and Group Function*, ed. Rosenbaum, M., and Berger, M., pp. 525-534. New York: Basic Books.

Spiegelberg, H. (1972). *Phenomenology in Psychology and Psychiatry*. Evanston, Illinois: Northwestern University Press.

Stengel, E. (1950). Follow-up investigation of 330 cases treated by prefrontal leucotomy. *Journal of Mental Science* 96:633-662.

Stoudenmire, J. (1973). Behavioral treatment of voyeurism and possible symptom substitution. *Psychotherapy: Theory, Research and Practice* 10:328-330.

Stowers, C. (1973). A coed prison without bars. *Parade*, February 11, pp. 8-9.

Strasser, S. (1965). Phenomenologies and psychologies. *Review of Existential Psychology and Psychiatry* 5:80-105.

Stumphauzer, J. S., ed. (1973). *Behavior Therapy with Delinquents*. Springfield, Illinois: Charles C Thomas.

Sunday Star (9/19/71). Halfway houses: a project that must succeed.

Sutherland, R. L. (1962). Choosing—as therapeutic aim, method and philosophy. *Journal of Existential Psychiatry* 2:371-392.

Taft, D. R. (1956). *Criminology*. 3rd ed. New York: Macmillan.

——— and England, R. W. (1964). *Criminology*. 4th ed. New York: Macmillan.

Tait, C. D. (1968). A 'therapeutic community' for selected families. *Mental Hygiene* 52:45-49.

Tallack, W. (1896). *Penological and Preventive Principles*. London: Wertheimer, Lea.

Task Force on Corrections (1967). *Task Force Report: Corrections*. Washington, D.C.: U.S. Government Printing Office.

Tec, L. (1956). A psychiatrist as a participant observer in a group of 'delinquent' boys. *International Journal of Group Psychotherapy* 6:418-429.

Teeters, N. K. (1946). Fundamentals of crime prevention. In *Contemporary Criminal Hygiene*, ed. Seliger, R., et al., pp. 56-73. Baltimore: Oakridge.

Thompson, G. N. (1949). Electroshock and other therapeutic considerations in sexual psychopathy. *Journal of Nervous and Mental Disease* 109:531-539.

——— (1953). *The Psychopathic Delinquent and Criminal*. Springfield, Illinois: Charles C Thomas.

Thorpe, J. J., and Smith, B. (1952). Operational sequence in group therapy with young offenders. *International Journal of Group Psychotherapy* 2:24-33.

Time (1/18/71). The shame of the prisons, pp. 48-55.

Tittle, C. R. (1974). Prisons and rehabilitation: the inevitability of disfavor. *Social Problems* 21:385-395.

Trippett, F. (1970). The suckers. *Look*, May 19, pp. 34-41.

Turner, E. (1973). Custom psychosurgery. *Postgraduate Medical Journal* 49:834-844.

Uehling, H. F. (1962). Group therapy turns repression into expression for prison inmates. *Federal Probation* 26 (March):43-49.

U.S. Congress, 93rd. H.R. 5371. House of Representatives, March 7, 1973.

U.S. Congress, 93rd. Public Law 93-348. National Research Service Award Act of 1974, July 12, 1974.

U.S. Congress, 93rd. Public Law 93-415. Juvenile Justice and Delinquency Prevention Act of 1974, September 7, 1974.

U.S. Department of Health, Education and Welfare (Office of Education) (1964). *The 1963 Dropout Campaign*. Washington, D.C.: U.S. Government Printing Office.

U.S. Department of Labor (Office of Policy Planning and Research) (1965). *The Negro Family*. Washington, D.C.: U.S. Government Printing Office.

U.S. News and World Report (3/23/70). Citizens' war on crime: spreading across U.S., pp. 55-58.

Van Den Berg, J. H. (1955). *The Phenomenological Approach to Psychiatry*. Springfield, Illinois: Charles C Thomas.

Van Dyke, H. T. (1970). *Juvenile Delinquency*. Boston: Ginn.

Vasoli, R. H., and Fahey, F. J. (1970). Halfway house for reformatory releasees. *Crime and Delinquency* 16:292-304.

Vigrolio, T. (1961). These prison debaters will challenge anyone! *Federal Probation* 25 (March):27-31.

Von Hentig, H. (1938). The limits of deterrence. *Journal of Criminal Law and Criminology* 29:555-561.

Warburton, F. W. (1965). Observations on a sample of psychopathic American criminals. *Behaviour Research and Therapy* 3: 129-135.

Ward, J. L.; Rubenfeld, S.; and Shellow, R. (1958). Countertransference as a factor in the delinquent's resistance to psychotherapy. *Group Psychotherapy* 11: 229-243.

Washington Post (1/12/71). Urban unit studies industries at Lorton.

——— (9/29/71). Police charge convict, 31, in slaying of two.

——— (11/13/71). Coverup of escape is charged.

——— (12/17/71). Chronic offender gets 3 years for $3.71 theft.

——— (1/22/72). Worth of psychology for criminals queried.

——— (2/25/72). Brain surgery is tested on 3 California convicts.

—— (6/20/72). Rearrests in District rise 94 percent.

—— (12/3/72). Iowa convict group helps to curb bad-check writers.

—— (2/11/73). Sixty-seven percent back life terms for hard drug sellers.

—— (2/22/73). Slayer speaks up.

—— (2/24/73). Psychosurgery assailed on Hill.

—— (2/27/73). Get-tough policy saves youth house.

—— (1/15/73). Rockefeller bill would give life terms to drug pushers.

—— (5/20/73). Jail cell to campus: the uneasy life of a prisoner-student.

—— (7/3/73). Juvenile crime, punishment: criminal training.

—— (8/11/74). Virginia prison tests behavior modification.

—— (8/28/74). Saxbe sees prospect of U.S. police.

—— (9/8/74). Lorton furloughs: more liberal than U.S. policy.

—— (9/23/74). Patuxent probe phase II set.

Washington Star-News (10/15/73). Study asks prison leniency.

—— (1/12/74). Bank holdup charged to 3 Lorton inmates.

—— (1/12/74). Pair arrested in rape-slaying.

—— (2/27/74). Miseries mount in the projects.

—— (9/26/74). Furloughed Lorton killer nabbed by FBI.

—— (10/5/74). Store man in shootout blasts criminals' release.

—— (10/29/74). Two more halfway house inmates arrested here.

—— (1/20/75). Prisoners: Lorton releases rile officialdom.

Wattenberg, W. W. (1973). *The Adolescent Years.* 2nd ed. New York: Harcourt Brace Janovich.

Weeks, H. A. (1958). *Youthful Offenders at Highfields.* Ann Arbor: The University of Michigan Press.

Weihofen, H. (1960). Treatment of insane prisoners. *Law Forum* (University of Illinois), 1960 (Winter):524-532.

White, W. A. (1895). The criminal: his social and legal status and the philosophy of reformation. Reprinted from *Transactions of the New York Medical Association.* Concord: Republican Press Association.

Whiteley, S.; Briggs, D.; and Turner, M. (1973). *Dealing with Deviants.* New York: Schocken.

Whittet, M. M. (1968). Medico-legal considerations of the A9 murder. *British Journal of Medical Psychology* 41:125-138.

Wicker, T. (1972). Prisoners, not guinea pigs. *New York Times*, December 31.

Williams, L. R. (1972). An analysis of the recreational pursuits of selected parolees from a state correctional institution in Pennsylvania. *Therapeutic Recreation Journal* 6:134-140.

Wilson, J. Q. (1973). If every criminal knew he would be punished if caught. *New York Times Magazine*, January 28, pp. 52-56.

Wilson, J. V. (1974). Detention and crime prevention. *Washington Post*, November 7.

Winthrop, H. (1965). Creativity in the criminal. *Journal of Social Psychology* 65:41-58.

Wolfe, R., and Marino, D. (1974). A program of behavioral treatment for incarcerated pedophiles. n.p.

Wolfenden, J. (1960). Crime and sin. *British Medical Journal* 2 (July 9):140-142.

Wollard, G. (1972). Recreation in a prison environment. *Therapeutic Recreation Journal* 6:115-118.

Wolpe, J. (1969). *The Practice of Behavior Therapy*. Elmsford, New York: Pergamon.

Yablonsky, L. (1960). Sociopathology of the violent gang and its treatment. In *Progress in Psychotherapy*, vol. 5, ed. Masserman, J., and Moreno, J. L., pp. 161-168. New York: Grune & Stratton.

Zimring, F. E. (1971). *Perspectives on Deterrence*. Public Health Service Publication No. 2056. Washington, D.C.: U.S. Government Printing Office.

Ziskind, E.; Parker, D. A.; Syndulko, K.; Maltzman, I.; and Jens, R. (1974). Sociopaths: diagnosis and psychophysiology. Paper presented at the 127th annual meeting of the American Psychiatric Association, Detroit, May.

Chapter 3

First Contacts
with the Criminal

THE INITIAL SESSION

IN THE BEGINNING, we selected criminals from the forensic division at Saint Elizabeths (see chapter 1 of volume 1). All but one criminal accepted an invitation to participate in our interviews or program for change; they all believed that participation offered an opportunity to curry favor and achieve some self-serving objective. As time passed, we gained a reputation among the criminals housed at the hospital for being dedicated and knowledgeable. On our walks through the grounds, criminals approached us inquiring about our program. We were also contacted on the forensic wards where we were interviewing pretrial criminals confined for observation. Some criminals who had become familiar with our methods explained them to others and referred those whom they regarded as amenable to our approach. Some participants have come to us from outside the hospital, at the suggestion of criminals who have had contact with us and believed that we offered something different and potentially helpful. Some have located us through community referrals by such people as school guidance counselors or through parole and probation officers.

For the criminal to fulfill our requirements for meetings was often difficult, because of the fragmentation of his mind. Many criminals telephoned us and eagerly asked for and were given appointments, only to break them, often without even bothering to call. In some cases after we had seen a man for a couple of sessions, he dropped out with no explanation or notice. We eventually realized that this happened because criminals who were in some kind of difficulty had entered the program only to recruit us to help them out of their trouble. When they saw that we did not offer such assistance, they terminated their contact with us. Sometimes, we seemed to reach a man in confinement effectively, but then, when he knew that he was being discharged, he avoided us. The following is a description of an extreme instance of such behavior.

Confined at the hospital as an NGBRI (not guilty by reason of insanity), C* talked with us in almost fifty meetings during the course of a year. In the second session, he asked whether we would accept him in our program. Not only had C heard about us from other criminals, but he also had read that a judge had permitted a man to enter our program as an alternative to prison. We did not commit ourselves to accepting C but said that we would evaluate his suitability. (At that time, we had decided to work with criminals only after they were released from maximum security and could attend daily meetings with us.)

Over the months that we saw C in confinement, he appeared to be facing up more fully to the spectrum and frequency of his criminality. Indeed, at several meetings, he cried after viewing his life as a waste. We warned him during this time that we had seen early flushes of enthusiasm about our program wear off once a criminal was back in the community.

Up to this point, we had had only two objectives: to help C maintain an unfavorable picture of himself and to indicate to him the kind of life that he would have to live if he were in our program. After nearly a year's exposure to our approach, there seemed to be visible, intense self-disgust. The self-disgust turned out to be temporary, lasting until the time when C thought that the chances of his getting out were favorable. He then said that because of political factors, he did not want to meet with us—it would jeopardize his release. He promised, however, to see us after he left the hospital. We sent a letter to him by personal messenger, but C returned it unopened. His objective had been achieved: he was on the street. This terminated all interest in change.

Usually, our procedures are efficient enough to avoid such a waste of time. We did, however, benefit from contact with C in two ways: his case, like all the others, presented opportunities for us to learn, and through C we were introduced to some well-known criminals from whom we obtained much valuable information.

We have never refused a request to see us; however, we seriously consider as potential candidates only those criminals who are immediately available. If a

---

*Throughout this volume, criminals cited in examples will be identified simply as "C."

criminal's participation will be delayed by legal or other factors, the chances are that fragmentation and the desire either to avoid or to get out of confinement will outweigh the desire to be in the program. The objective is to select the criminal when he is vulnerable.

Specific age, background, and socioeconomic features do not preclude participation in the program. We work with blacks and whites, old and young, those from culturally deprived backgrounds and those from affluent homes, grade school dropouts and college graduates. Some have been charged with serious crimes like homicide; a few have never been arrested, although they have been arrestable for years. Some have considerable psychiatric sophistication as a result of experience with clinics and hospitals; others know very little about psychiatry.

Criminals seek us for a variety of reasons. Basically, they want to use us for a self-serving purpose. Their overriding objective usually is to avoid or to be released from confinement. Criminals who are not in confinement and who have not been arrested may be having other difficulties with which they want help. Some, who perceive their world as collapsing as a result of their behavior, come to us because wives or girl friends threaten to leave them or because others (such as parents) are seeking to apply restraints to them and are threatening them with unpleasant consequences if they do not change. They come out of a desire to placate others and make life easier for themselves.

Many criminals seek the best of both worlds. They want to get by in the responsible world, enjoying the comforts and convenience of family and home while preserving the excitements of their criminal activities. In a sense, they desire a change program to help them to become freer or safer in crime. They want to be more successful in getting away with what they do, so that others are not suspicious and antagonistic. If they at least appear responsible to others, they will enjoy some of the comforts of home and family and gain the esteem of others. In addition, if they come to see us, they not only enhance their good opinions of themselves, but in the future can tell others that they gave the program a try, thus demonstrating their good intentions. By having a fling at token treatment, they convince themselves that they cannot change and are destined for crime. This helps to erode their feeble resistance to committing criminal acts. After all, they have tried and failed; what more can they do?

Some criminals come to us because they are fed up with themselves and want to change. They may have failed as criminals (in that they have been apprehended). With the walls closing in on them, they have reviewed their lives and reassessed their good opinions of themselves. They see how they have wasted opportunities.

"When I look at what I've done with my life, I want to throw up. . . . I've thrown away most of what I could have become."

Some come to us tired after years of the strain of crime's daily grind. They are weary of discord at home, the burdens of lying and deceit, and the constant need to look over their shoulders for the police.

"I've lived in fear all my life and there must be something better. . . . I've lived in poverty in Tennessee and all the way up to the mansions of Houston, Texas, but what have I got to show for it, nothing but years of a deranged way of thinking and acting and living with nothing left but scars inside plus hate, bitterness, rebellion, a shell that I have built for myself and the walls around it. . . . I hope [Dr. Y.] can tear them all down and help me release myself from my self-made prison. I feel like a fool thinking this way after all these years of the past, but I guess I have been a bigger fool for living by crime as I have."

Some criminals have viewed their dealings with us as a challenge. They have heard about us and our methods from others. They view talking with us as exciting, their objective being to prove that they can fool and then ridicule us.

Any or all of these reasons for seeking us out may be operating. Actually, we pay little attention to their stated reasons for wanting contact with us because we know that it is impossible to discern whether a man is dedicated to change. We know that our methods will permit a more rapid and accurate evaluation of motivation than other methods. We have never denied anyone an initial contact, although we recognize that a criminal comes to us for reasons we have already described: desiring to get out of difficulty, being in a transient state of discouragement or self-disgust, or seeing us as a challenge. We know that he is not coming to change; he does not know what change is as we view it. At best, the criminal wants to continue without the hassles of arrest. He comes to us believing that he is a good person who has met with misfortune, but not a criminal. Indeed, from the beginning, we know that the odds are that he will not continue with us once he discovers what we have to offer and what our requirements are.

If the outcome is to be favorable, the most important condition at the beginning—although it is by no means a guarantee—is *the presence of a legal restraint on the criminal's total freedom*. We have succeeded only if this condition obtained initially. To be sure, when there was no external leverage, we reduced the seriousness of crimes committed by the criminal, at least for a while. But to effect total and basic change, which is the ultimate goal, there must be something hanging over a man's head that threatens his freedom.

Three charges were pending in court against eighteen-year-old C. He was accepted into our program on the grounds that he remain indefinitely on probation. C was accountable to us for twenty-four hours of his time every day. The threat of jail for noncooperation was always present. C remained in the program without any confinement whatsoever, implemented the program, and after a year of daily participation, established that he was becoming a responsible person.

*   *   *

C, sixteen years old, was referred to us by a guidance counselor who saw his falling grades, noted increasing teacher complaints, and as a confidant of C, knew about some of his criminal acts. C had never been arrested, despite many arrestable offenses. His parents were unaware of his activities and were not at all convinced that he needed our program. We saw C for almost thirty hours. With respect to his swindling, lying, and other irresponsible patterns, C commented, "I consider these things wrong and immoral, but fun." He saw no reason to change his life style other than to stay out of drug sales, which imperiled him the most. C told us that he realized he was supposed to be disgusted with himself but that he did not know how to achieve this state, despite our having spent hours reviewing his criminal patterns and the injury he had done to others. We agreed that our program was not for him at this time.

Things were going for C as he wanted them to. He was getting away with violating and enjoyed pitting himself against the school authorities. He was far from the "every avenue closed" position of the criminal in the preceding illustration.

Our first interview with the criminal lasts approximately three hours. In most cases, he has been dealt with cursorily and perfunctorily by other interviewers. Indeed, some of our subjects were confined for as much as ninety days for determination of competency and responsibility and in that entire period talked with a doctor individually only briefly. The magnitude of our task requires much time, because a large amount of material must be covered and a series of obstacles must be overcome. After a three-hour meeting a criminal cannot truthfully say that we did not give him sufficient attention. That he is being taken seriously becomes evident when he discovers that this is only the first of two or three such meetings. The time being alloted to him is in stark contrast to his previous experiences with change agents.

With privileged communication guaranteed, we have found it advantageous, in about half the cases in which one criminal has been referred to us by another, to hold the initial interview in the presence of both. We once held a productive initial meeting with a criminal and, with his consent, the guidance counselor who had referred him. She had proved in the past that she respected confidentiality. In these situations, all parties learned and contributed a great deal.

Our work is more difficult, of course, when a criminal is unwillingly brought to us, especially when he takes a stance like the following:

> "I am here because my brother is being seen. I don't have any problems. Why should I listen to a shrink? I'm coming here because I hate my stepfather. Without my parents I would be free. My problem is I don't like my parents."

This is especially likely to be what an agent of change encounters with a youthful offender whose parents or school authorities send him for an evaluation. He lacks the vulnerability described earlier. We do not permit him to determine the course of the discussion, for if we did, we would get self-serving stories, excuses, and lies of commission and omission. We would only be adding to the series of people whom he has controlled. There is, however, always the possibility that with our techniques, we can bring out the facts of his life and increase his vulnerability.

We start by doing something that is extraordinary in the experience of the criminal: we talk for approximately a half-hour to describe our format. The criminal is permitted to interrupt, but this has seldom happened.

We ignore the criminal's immediate problem, which would be presented in a self-serving way. Furthermore, we do not take histories, which we now know would be inaccurate because of the way the criminal represents events and others' attitudes. We do not diagnose and label because we firmly believe that this practice conceals more than it reveals. We do not administer tests, questionnaires, or any other self-reporting instrument. Perhaps most striking to the criminal is that we can tell him a great deal about himself, although we have never met him or read his record in advance. (In fact, we request referring sources not to send advance information about the criminal and to inform him that they have not sent it.) We tell the criminal that he fits into a profile common to *all* criminals; we present the profile and apply it to him rather than ask him open-ended questions.

We make it clear that we maintain privileged communication (which we define). We shall play no role in decision-making or administrative or legal matters. We dictate, in his presence if he wishes and for our use only, the material we obtain from him. It is then kept in a locked file that is accessible to him upon request. In the office, he is permitted to read our notes.

We state that we know that he is wary of us and is examining us as much as, if not more than, we are examining him. We know he views us as square and ignorant except when a favorable reputation has preceded us.

We discuss the spirit in which the meeting is to be conducted: we shall be truthful and courteous, and we expect the criminal to be. From our first sentence, we indicate that we are direct, that we "tell it like it is" and do not, as the criminal puts it, "come from the side." Our repeated emphasis is on establishing facts, especially because we are dealing with a person who offers only the version of events that best serves his advantage (that is, reduces his personal jeopardy and makes him look good). We state bluntly that throughout his life the criminal has dealt with the world untruthfully, habitually lying both by commission and omission. We inform him that inasmuch as we already know his tactics, game-playing only wastes time. We dip into the material (chapter 8 of volume 1) that describes tactics for preventing effective transactions. We assert that silence is not golden in our office and that agreement many be only a tactic to score points. Our procedure then is to make statements and have the criminal confirm or deny them.

"Our technique is different. I am not interested in mother, father, school, and work. I don't find that very useful. In due course, were you to be in this program, this would come out. The technique I am using is not to ask questions. It is to tell you who you are, even though I have never met you. People are different—black and white, old and young, school dropout and college graduate. Some use guns, some use conning. The things we're interested in are different from all of this. We have found many things. If you find that what I say isn't so, please tell me."

Early in the meeting, it is essential to inform the criminal that complaining about and blaming his criminality on the circumstances of life is an exercise in futility when used with us. We go on to say that the room is too small for two crybabies and that we shall not sob with him about the injustices and adversities that he has suffered. Indeed, he has injured far more than he has been injured. In other words, we want only facts and not a victim stance colored by sociologic and psychologic excuses.

As a further means of identifying our position, we indicate that we are not fascinated by crime. The criminal is surprised to find that we pay no attention to the crime with which he has been charged. This baffles him, because he is used to being asked about it or other crimes. There are two very practical reasons for not taking a crime history. An account of crimes committed does not invade the inner person. *Crimes are the outcomes of thinking processes, and it is the thinking processes that are our focus.* Secondly, every recounting of crime is exciting and stimulates more criminal thinking; crime talk is thus antithetic to our serious purpose of a clear, rational discussion of the fabric of the criminal's mind. We go even further and express our contempt for the criminal's whole way of life, saying that he represents a menace to us and our families; that we have no respect, liking, or compassion for a person who constitutes such a danger; and that he should be confined and if he remains unchanged, buried for life. Of course, at the same time, we indicate that although we dislike what he stands for, we are committed to helping a person such as he help himself to change into a responsible person.

Our approach entails a forthright, orderly presentation of facts. We are firm, but low-key, conducting ourselves with a quiet confidence based on our knowledge. This attitude prevails throughout all of our contacts with the criminal.

In the opening half hour, the criminal may respond at any point, but few do. There is little to take issue with because the agent of change is talking a great deal about himself and his own position. Most criminals are intrigued and baffled by this approach. The least that is happening is that the criminal is getting a picture of a person with an approach unlike anything he has encountered before. We are aware that he is examining us and do all we can to help facilitate this examination. We want to put our cards on the table right away and have him know as much as possible about us.

Having established who we are, we probe some specific facets of the criminal's makeup. We know that he has been a violator all his life. If we know of an offense that he has committed, we indicate that this represents only the tip of the iceberg of violation. One does not suddenly commit his first crime at the age of, say, twenty-seven; there is a long history that began very early. The details of the crime do not intrigue us at all. We do not discuss it or ask the criminal to discuss it. Instead, we inform him that we know that particular *patterns* must be present and that we want to look at them.

We are now ready to discuss specific violating patterns in the criminal's life—lying, theft, assault, and sexual patterns.

We state that the lying pattern begins as early as he can recall, and we trace it through to adulthood. This included lies of commission and omission, various illicit ways of accomplishing his objectives, and a general lack of accountability. We describe the criminal's unreliability and his attempts to avoid facing the consequences of his lies when confronted. The discussion embraces lying about a multitude of infractions—household chores left undone, school assignments neglected, not being home at the proper time, truancy and so forth.

"When you were five, six, seven, eight years old, there were certain sneaky things you did that you kept from those around you, such as parents and teachers. If these things had been known, life would have been harder for you. These sneaky things include the very early capacity to lie. This began at a very early age."

We have to confront squarely the fact that the criminal has never regarded himself as a liar.

"Even though you have been a liar all your life, you never viewed yourself as one. In fact, you have become very angry whenever someone calls you a liar."

At every turn, we drive home the point, trying to make the criminal view himself as he is. We point out that, to the criminal, lying is as natural as breathing. Crime necessitates lying. No criminal could survive as a truthful person and still maintain his way of life. Lying is a device to solve problems. It also is exciting in itself; the criminal gets a charge out of putting something over on others. We mention a few of the forms that lying takes, pointing out that it occurs mostly by omission. We talk about the fact that some lies are deliberately contrived but most occur spontaneously out of habit. In fact, the criminal is a better spontaneous liar than he is a contriving liar. We indicate that lying has grown from the childhood patterns into large conning operations in which the criminal misrepresents himself and takes advantage of innocent people. We bring the lying pattern up to date. If we are seeing a criminal confined at Saint Elizabeths, we assert that we are aware of the fraudulent way in which he gained admission to the hospital. In his coming to see us, we know that the criminal had every intention of lying. He may be seeking help; but help, as he defines it, is to have us dig him out of a hole. If a criminal claims that he is being totally truthful with us, even though he has lied all his life, we say that we are neither cynical nor gullible on this issue and that only time will tell whether he is being truthful.

A natural sequel to talking about the lying pattern is the discussion of property crimes. In the criminal's life, there has always been one kind of thievery or another. As a child, he began with petty thefts at home, stealing from mother's purse or taking change from father's pockets. The pattern was soon operative outside the home in stealing from stores and borrowing money or other things and not repaying or returning them. In pursuing this issue, we define theft as secretly and deceptively extracting things from others that do not belong to oneself. We state that if the criminal were apprehended for every instance of a property crime, he would be incarcerated for a long time. In this discussion, we move into vandalism, shoplifting, breaking and entering, and ultimately conning. We further assert that the early patterns expanded rapidly and the types of offenses are many. Again, it is patterns and not details of particular crimes that are the focus. Criminals readily acknowledge stealing, but they may say that they have never committed particular kinds of thefts, for example, armed robbery or breaking and entering. We establish that although they have not done it, they thought about it but were restrained, largely by the fear of getting caught. We also establish that there have been fantasies of thefts that were never seriously considered, because they were impractical. In short, even if the criminal were stealing all the time, his thefts would represent only a fraction of what went through his mind.

We then get into the assault pattern. From those who actually engaged in much fighting and used weapons, we get no opposition to the idea of an assault pattern. The others all admit to a few fights but resist the idea of a pattern. This latter group, however, pushed others around and intimidated them to get their way. Those who stopped short of actual assault did so only because they were afraid of getting hurt. Their thinking was loaded with violence of an extreme form. One criminal youth thought of grabbing a paddle and smashing his father over the head; the fact that his father was bigger and stronger than he deterred him.

The discussion then turns to sexual patterns. Before he was ten, the criminal was searching for opportunities to engage in sexual activity. In almost seventy-five percent of our population, this occurred before the age of ten. Whether he actually engaged in it depended on availability of partners, social restraints, and his own confidence in his sexual adequacy. Furtive early sex play was followed by increasing desire for more advanced activity. In most cases, it has been easy to bring out the early attempts at intercourse, in some cases involving coercion of the partner. We establish the voyeuristic and exhibitionistic aspects of sexual activity. The criminal has always considered himself sexually irresistible or at least wanted others to view him this way. We then establish that the criminal is actually incompetent in performance, there being a high incidence of premature ejaculation and impotence. The criminal enjoys the sensuality of the sex act less than he enjoys using sex to exploit others and achieve a buildup for himself. It is the conquest that matters. We then discuss such specific sexual patterns as rape, pimping and prostitution, and child-molestation. Included in this presentation is the exploitation of sexual partners. We probe thinking patterns related to sexuality. As is true with property and assault offenses, much has been deterred, at least temporarily.

Although we defer discussion of drug-using criminals to volume 3, we should note here that when dealing with them we spend considerable time discussing the relationship of lying and property, assault, and sex offenses to drugs (including alcohol). Our approach to drugs is different from anything that they have encountered previously.

After the property, assault, and sexual patterns have been described, we make some general statements about the scope and frequency of crime. That the criminal has eluded apprehension for most of his offenses indicates that a clever mind was operating in the direction of flagrant irresponsibility and violation. We then introduce the television camera idea.

"If a man commits a crime of the sort you have, there has been a long history of violation. You are a first-offender only in the sense that it is the first time you have been caught. If you viewed yourself as though we had a videotape camera covering every minute of your life, you would see that a lot of things have happened that were the seeds of what brought you here. You are about thirty years old, I would guess—right? [C responds with exact age.] Of course, this idea is ridiculous, in that you would have to watch the TV tape for thirty years. But if we had that TV tape, we would find a lot of things for which you could have been in trouble. Right or wrong?"

We use the television camera analogy to get rid of the "first offender" position and to underscore the concept of *patterns* of violation. This technique is useful in having the criminal face up to the extent of his arrestable criminality over a lifetime. If we had this videotape, it would show a huge number of violations. If legal authorities were to regard such a tape as firm evidence and convict and penalize the criminal accordingly, he would spend the rest of his life in confinement. Indeed, it is beyond the criminal's ability to recall each one of his offenses. He is surprised at the amount of criminality we bring out. He is surprised because he does not think in our terms. He regards the unseen taking of something from someone as natural, not as a theft. Concealing information to protect himself is a matter of survival, not a matter of lying. Once we clarify what we mean by a "theft," a "lie," and so forth, we find that the criminal acknowledges the patterns readily. In fact, after his presentation, he readily admits that he has done enough to be locked up for life, were it all known.

Generally, however, the criminal finds our procedure most disagreeable. To our discussion of his criminal patterns, one man responded:

"It is degrading to consider a 'larceny *pattern.*' The words spell doom and punishment. You have your own personal opinion of yourself."

One criminal described in writing his reaction to our initial interview.

"You and I can never have free and open communication, because I won't permit it. It flies in direct contradiction to my nature. I don't doubt *your* sincerity and candor, but if I really did have completely free and open communication with you, I couldn't . . . do the secret things I really want to do. . . . Lying is so automatic with me, it seeps out through my pores. Free and open communication on my part is just not possible, and even if it were, I wouldn't allow it."

Because criminals do not like the picture we paint of them, some are inclined to minimize, divert, qualify, and distort.

> "There were no strong urges to steal when I was very young. At ten or eleven, I and some friends stole some grapes from a neighborhood store more than once. It was a lark."

In these three sentences, there are two attempts to minimize an early stealing pattern. The criminal dismisses it as a "lark," and then, instead of owning up to the frequency of the pattern, he says only that it occurred "more than once." Vagueness is likely to permeate a great deal of what the criminal says—"I suppose," "I guess," "perhaps," "not necessarily," and so forth. All this is grist for the mill, because it enables the agent of change to make some further statements about how the criminal operates and what kind of person he is.

> "You are the kind of person who shows others what a big man you are, how you fear nothing. Yet you are the type of individual who is afraid to face up to the facts of life."

> "Forgive my bluntness for the way I characterized you. Can it be that this is the first time someone else has brought these things out? Are you willing to bring more things out and let me guide you in it? It might be refreshing for you to do this. I know that these patterns are present. They had to be there. It is a matter of whether you are willing to disclose them."

The major obstacle here is that the criminal does not think that he is a criminal. Although the TV camera could theoretically put him behind bars for many lifetimes, deep within he regards himself as a basically good person. To be sure, he may adopt our terminology and refer to himself as a "criminal," but this is assent, not his real view of himself. As far as he is concerned, others who do wrong things are the criminals, not he. For example, he may contend that crime involves violence and that because he is not violent, he is not a criminal. He may even express hatred for criminals who commit particular kinds of crimes. However, he severely objects to anyone calling him a criminal. He does not even like to use the word when talking about himself. One man put it rather delicately: "I have never believed and do not believe that I am a malefactor." Typical is another criminal who, despite his four dozen rapes and numerous other violations, declared that "never in a thousand years" would he consider himself a criminal.

We know that the criminal regards himself as a decent person. He is sentimental toward his family. He likes babies, children, animals, and old people and may go out of his way to assist them. He has artistic and musical interests and talents. He believes that he has helped many people, some through donations of the proceeds of his crimes. In addition, he may think that he is a moral person, on the grounds that he believes in God and occasionally prays. A small number of criminals may add to this the fact that they attend church. We bring all this out, and then we indicate our view that dirt cannot be masked by perfume.

"I am not interested in your good points. You do not go to jail for those. These good points as you view them do not begin to compensate for all the damage you have done and injury you have inflicted. These assets are comparable with those of a man with normal blood pressure and a good heart who is dying of cancer. The assets are worthless in the face of the liabilities."

We underscore that all his life he has been a criminal, using our definition of criminality. That is, he has always been a violator of the moral and legal standards of society. The criminal may contend that he has often thought about living differently and at times has really wanted to be responsible. Our rejoinder is that wanting to be a decent person for a few minutes or hours a week does not make him one. Here, or at some other point in the discussion of his sentimentality, we have seen a criminal fight back tears. At such times, we deal him one more blow by saying that he lacks the guts to cry.

While discussing the soft side of the criminal, we point out his fearfulness. The criminal has been a fearful person all his life with a broader spectrum of fears than the noncriminal. He has kept his fears to himself, because he is afraid to let others know that he is anything but tough. Because we cannot be sure of what he fears, we list a number of fears common to criminals and have him confirm or deny each one—heights, physical injury, darkness, deep water, etc. We point out how fearful the criminal is of fear itself and that the tougher the criminal, the more fearful. In some cases, fear restrains him temporarily from violation. However, the criminal refuses to live with fear and to allow it to be a guide to responsible living. A search for excitement overrides fear, and so fear is cut off.

In this discussion, we point out that the criminal's greatest fear is that of being put down. He views trivial inconveniences as major personal affronts. The agent of change must emphasize the criminal's vulnerability to putdowns. The criminal has a glass jaw which shatters easily when he thinks that another person has given him the slightest tap. Yet he expects others to absorb all the abuse that he hands out. His life is a continuing process of building himself up, being deflated by what he construes as a putdown, and building himself up again through crime. This discussion enables us to tell the criminal that we know that there are times when he thinks of himself as an absolute nothing. We describe the nothingness, the transparency, and the permanence of the zero state. The criminal goes back and forth from an overvalued to an undervalued concept of himself.

We then go on to make a series of statements about how differently from others the criminal has viewed the world. Early in life, he dealt with the world differently from the way in which his family and peers did. A life of responsible relationships with family, playmates, school, and community was contemptible to him. He wanted to be bigger and older and do more exciting things than his contemporaries. He searched for kicks in the world mainly through doing what was forbidden. Even as a very young child, he sought out the forbidden; he was not dragged into it by peer pressure. The criminal violated primarily for the excitement and the buildup rather than for the proceeds.

> "You could have gone to your parents for the things you needed. The things you stole you certainly could have afforded to buy or have your parents buy for you. Stealing added spice to life."

A statement of this nature is unquestionably true of the youngster from an affluent home. But it also holds in most instances for the ghetto dweller. Impoverished people find honest means to meet life's requirements. Indeed, the mothers of some of our criminals held two jobs to make ends meet and provide for their children. Their self-respect ruled out thoughts of stealing or even living off welfare. We go on to observe that the proceeds, if any, of a crime—whether dollars, objects, or sexual conquests—define its magnitude but are not the most important goal of the crime to the criminal. Most important is the excitement to be derived in an otherwise boring world. However, the criminal may find the proceeds useful in further criminality; a stolen gun may figure in later criminal acts. In addition, the proceeds allow the criminal to disport himself as a big shot with expensive clothes, big cars, and lavish living quarters. Appearing to be a man of means and accomplishment, he tries to influence and exploit others. And when he gives away the proceeds, he is the biggest shot of all.

The criminal prides himself on being a powerful figure who controls others. We point out to him that, although he has used others, he too has been used. He may be impervious to others' suggestions and persuasions that he become responsible, but he is a sucker when it comes to others' suggestions for criminal enterprises. He involves himself in mutually exploitative relationships in which each person uses the other but does not regard himself as being used. He views himself as controlling while he is being controlled by another like himself.

As we go through this procedure, we find that the criminal objects to our viewing him as "just like all the others." When we assert that common criminal patterns and thinking processes common to all criminals must be present in him, he may vociferously argue that he is different. He insists on his uniqueness. This may be expressed blatantly—"There is no other human being in the world like me"—or it may be said less directly. This gives us the opportunity to state that *every* criminal believes that he is one of a kind and thus different from all others, criminal or not. Obviously, he is not unique because every criminal considers himself unique.

If the agent of change is working in a mental health facility, sooner or later he has to confront the mental illness issue. This usually arises in the discussion of criminal patterns and should be dealt with the first time it comes up and elaborated on in later meetings. The term *mental illness* may be used in different ways. We often encounter it in a statement by a criminal that he was not in control of himself and acted on impulse. Or we may hear a sophisticated presentation of his psychotic disorder. It may take a simpler form. We have heard a criminal say that he is mentally ill because he does not get along with people. In the crudest presentation of this issue that we have encountered, a man said that he was mentally ill on the grounds that he kept committing crime after crime. In all these views, the criminal merely is seizing on what the psychiatric profession, the news media, and lay people have accepted as fact. These may all be half beliefs, rather than excuses, which can be shaken easily by presenting the leading ideas from chapter 6 of volume 1. Here, we may refer to a specific crime as the clearest way of putting our view across. The criminal had recurring thoughts about committing the crime at issue, and these desires took the form of schemes. Because of external or internal deterrents, the schemes were not implemented. But, with increasing desire, fear decreased, and the criminal chose a time and place for implementation. This was not impulse; it was premeditation. The desires were strong, the circumstances were favorable, the deterrents corroded and were then totally removed, and the act was committed. The criminal who claims that he lacked self-control has always viewed himself as on top of things and in control of others, even after an arrest. In fact, he is so much in control of himself that he has effectively malingered to convince others that he is mentally ill, thereby beating a charge and gaining hospital admission instead of a prison sentence. The many ramifications of our position on mental illness are explored in later meetings.

During the initial contact, we include a discussion of how changeable the criminal appears to others. Owing to his fragmentation, he appears to be a mass of contradictions. He fails to sustain his intentions even in crime. We apply the fragmentation concept to the present transaction by informing the criminal that his statement of sincerity about wanting to change is not convincing. We expect that he will undergo changes of mind. Only time will permit an accurate evaluation. When we describe his thinking during transient nonarrestable phases, the criminal reacts with surprise to our discussing freely that which was his secret. We describe his phases of monasticism, in which he vows to be a very pure person. We mention that he has had suicidal thoughts during the times that he has regarded himself as a failure in life. He has dealt with these brief phases by cutoff and a resurgence of criminal activity.

In the first interview, we cannot possibly cover all the material presented here. Spending three hours permits us to include most of it, but even then we may have to leave some for another meeting. At any rate, it is more effective to develop a few patterns clearly than to bombard the criminal with the entire array of concepts.

At the conclusion of the first meeting, we request feedback about our procedures. The general response is that our approach was new, interesting, stimulating, and relevant. It contained a number of surprises. First of all, the criminal is surprised that we did so much talking. As one man commented, "Usually I do all the talking." He is also surprised that we did not take the conventional history. We are often told that the criminal is astonished by our knowing things about him that he believed no one knew. During the interview, in fact, he may ask, "Where did you learn all this?" Some assert that we must have read their case records. A fifteen-year-old declared, "You must have talked to a lot of boys," and added, "You know how to ask the right questions." Actually, we had made statements, not asked questions. The basic response of the criminal is that he was totally unprepared for this. We had "peeped his hole card"; we saw right through him. The biggest surprise is that we presented a view of him as a criminal. He expresses some astonishment that he lasted through a three-hour ordeal. He tells us that he has revealed more to us than to anyone else. Actually he did not reveal much spontaneously. Our procedure established facts that he thought were unknown to others. Some men tell us that we made them face up to more than they ever had before. We know that this new self-awareness fades quickly if not followed up. Throughout his life, the criminal has been interrogated and interviewed by many people—school teachers, counselors, law enforcement officers, lawyers, judges, and in some cases mental health professionals. Rarely has anyone made a favorable impression on him. Those who did were the ones that the criminal regarded as lenient, in his corner. The criminal who has had previous experience with psychiatrists is surprised and usually pleased by our departure from traditional methods. Even with such positive feedback, we cannot be certain of our initial impact because it is always possible that the criminal is simply trying to ingratiate himself and score points.

No criminal likes what we say. No person likes to hear himself being torn down, which is what the criminal experiences. The slicker, more educated conman type of criminal seems to dislike our approach more than the street criminal, who does less conning. The reason is that we strike at the heart of this major pattern. We do this by dealing with the criminal firmly and abruptly, telling him, even before he opens his mouth, that we do not like him. He is, in a sense, defeated, because such a statement on our part makes conning useless in influencing us to like or accept him. The criminal rarely responds with anger to an agent of change whom he perceives as knowledgeable and forthright. The negative feedback usually is neither direct nor expressed on the spot; it comes out later that we are too "pushy" or "opinionated." Viewing his experience with us retrospectively, one man said that he had first viewed us as "conceited asses." After another meeting, it seemed to him almost as though we were reading his mind, we were so accurate. The third phase of his reactions came after several meetings, when he concluded that we knew more than he did about how his own mind operated. His final response, just before going to prison, was that we were in a position to offer something valuable to him. This type of evaluation is typical.

Occasionally in an initial interview, a criminal does not cooperate with us. He may remain silent, because he continues to believe that disclosure will jeopardize him. Some turn the transaction into a contest and refuse to submit to our approach. A few decide that because they cannot recruit us to help them out of a jam, there is no point in continuing the association. These people have no interest in becoming responsible. They see enough of our approach in a few hours to conclude that they do not want any more.

We invite all criminals to see us again. Nearly all say they will return, but of course not all do. If, during the initial meeting, a criminal asks about joining our program, we indicate that more meetings are necessary for him to learn about what the program will require.

FURTHER SESSIONS

After the first interview, it is assumed that the criminal knows that he is being confronted with a definite point of view on the nature of the criminal. He knows that he is regarded as a criminal. In a straightforward, unsparing, but calm manner we have informed him of our knowledge of him. All along, the criminal has been looking for "a hole in the dike" (as one man described it) or a weak spot in the presentation, so that he could take the offensive and control the transaction as he has done so successfully in the past. We invite him to comment on our views, specifically to state objections, raise whatever issues he chooses, and add any information he wishes. We respond to each of his comments with a further elaboration of our discoveries about the criminal mind.

If the criminal starts to catalogue his crimes or go into details about any particular crime (usually the one last committed or the one that resulted in his incarceration), we listen briefly. We then point out that we know that he has committed many crimes but are far more interested in life patterns and thinking patterns than in the details of the offenses. We do not want him to believe that we are fascinated by his crimes. Nor do we permit the discussion to be sidetracked by these details. We have found that his responses give us multiple openings for introducing further descriptions of his thinking errors and his tactics. Indeed, the more he talks, the more opportunities we have to demonstrate to him that we are aware of his patterns of thought and action. We describe these patterns as he has shown them at home, at school, at work, in the community, and in society in general (see chapter 3 of volume 1).

During later prolonged meetings, we inform the criminal what this program requires of him so that he can make an informed choice as to whether to participate. The description of the end results of the change process—a 180-degree change from the way he has always thought and acted—is shocking to him. We realize that several meetings with us can give him no real comprehension of what is presented either in terms of his criminal makeup or in terms of the nature of the change process. It will take months of daily work for this to be understood. But we do lay out a perspective and provide some information. Whatever understanding the criminal obtains is not operational at this point but sets the stage for later corrections of thinking errors in daily living.

We continue to invite feedback as we go along. We know that the criminal has been finding the picture we are painting of him disagreeable. In fact, after each session, he goes through a process of wondering why he continues to participate in a procedure that he finds so unpleasant. One man reported saying to himself after each meeting, "Why is this fool getting me to present what I do? He is full of b.s.; I'm not going to do that." Then, once again, he would find himself revealing more, some of which he had never told anyone. We have asked some of the criminals who have a flair for writing to record their thinking after our sessions. This spurs them to think about what has been said rather than cut it off without further thought. It also provides us with useful information for later sessions. The following statement, which the criminal called "Baptism by Fire," is a lucid account of one man's reaction to our initial approach.

> "The compact and forceful introduction has the advantage of shock in opening up the person you're talking to. That doesn't mean he's going to bare his soul or be candid with you. But his reaction will tell you something about the person he is. . . . I want to come back to one other

point. The clear, flat statement by you that 'I'm here for my own purposes. I'm not going to do a thing to help you get out of here'—stated in the flat, unemotional and self-interested way you stated it—does a great deal to clear the air and to eliminate a lot of con because, up to that point the criminal mind—mine included—has got to be asking itself 'How can I use this big wheel egghead to level my way out of here?' ... After you've made the statement undercutting that, my immediate reaction was—well, what the hell is he doing here, why should I help him, what am I getting out of it, why should I talk to this guy?"

We are always aware that the feedback itself may be part of the criminal's effort to con. Time will tell whether he was sincere. This individual realized that his tendency to con was so automatic that anything he said might be a part of this pattern.

"Some of my writing is an attempt to seriously discuss the issues we've developed in our talks, but as I'm sure you're aware, part of my writing (as with everything else I do) is con. In other words, if you want me to write, boy will I write. I'll fill up as many pages as I can. I'll really give you something to read. It's the old story of finding out what the teacher wants and giving it to him. ... I'm finding that much of what I say, write and do with you is both half con and half truth."

This statement provided us with a context in which to discuss the automaticity of lying and how even a part of the truth can be a con.

We continue to control the sessions by bringing up patterns of thought and action and thereby keep the discussion from wandering. We come to each meeting prepared to discuss a particular theme, but we would rather that the criminal bring up things he wants to discuss than impose a topic of our own. We are fully prepared to deal with any issue he raises. Every statement or question by him allows us to demonstrate more of our attitude and bring out more facts about criminal thinking processes. Thus, we are continuing in the style of earlier sessions but presenting most of our material now in the context of his contributions.

Usually, the criminal welcomes our directness. However, he may show some reluctance to talk after the initial contact because he does not want to suffer any more blows to his self-image. He may claim that, "I have told you everything." We respond that we certainly know enough about him to realize that this is not the case. It is his practice to tell us a bit of the "truth" and then to regard himself as totally truthful. We know that the channel is not wide open so we launch into a full discussion of what the wide-open channel is. We take up the criminal's lifelong secrecy, recognizing that secrecy has been necessary to reduce personal jeopardy. It has other functions, such as helping him to preserve his sense of uniqueness and superiority over others. We say that we know that he wants to maintain this secrecy with us, because he regards exposure as threatening. We go on to say that if he acts like a patient who has an ailment but forbids an examination, we can accomplish nothing. We again emphasize the criminal's cowardice in facing up to the facts of his life. Here, the criminal is increasingly vulnerable and frightened as we "peep his hole card." One man posed his dilemma: "How can I be blunt without exposing myself too much?" The criminal does not want to reveal more and more, only to be "torn apart," as he puts it. So he continues to fence and uses the many tactics that block communication.

The agent of change must have reasonable expectations with respect to the channel of communication. We do not anticipate a wide-open channel during the first several meetings, but we do attempt to open it further than it is when we begin. Occasionally, the channel is surprisingly wide open. Some men are so impressed by our approach that they take us into their confidence right away and reveal something very intimate. In one such instance, a criminal informed us in an early meeting of his plans for escape, which he later implemented successfully. But by and large, this does not happen. Our position is that we have the time and patience to wait and see whether the criminal is being truthful. We know that lying is automatic, that the criminal is fragmented, and that he is still evaluating us before revealing himself more fully. While not convinced by the stated intentions of a brazen liar, we do not dismiss him. We have nothing to lose by continuing our transactions. In time, the criminal realizes that he must meet our standards; in other words, a wide-open channel is mandatory. If the channel is closed, we are not the losers; we do not bear the consequences of his attempting to deceive us. If the channel opens, this shows some acceptance of our approach by the criminal. Emphasis on the channel issue is a part of the preview of what will be required in our program.

Right at the beginning we often choose to address ourselves to the control feature of the closed channel. The criminal initially approaches us expecting to "put us in his pocket," as one man put it, just as he has tried to manage everyone else and to convince others of his point of view. The criminal is so intent on proving that he is correct that he fails to listen to what is said. This reflects his lack of receptivity, another barrier to a wide-open channel. We request that the criminal listen carefully, consider the issue thoroughly, and reach his own conclusion. Our urging him to listen may go unheeded. He may deliberately attempt to provoke us and engage in battle. Some have suggested that we must ourselves be criminals since we know so much about criminals. They have claimed that we judge them unfairly and that because of our approach, we put them in jeopardy. Our response to the criminal's tactics, irrespective of their crudeness, is to listen and then continue stating the facts as we see them, using each tactic to illustrate further the fabric of the criminal. This is done firmly, but calmly, and sometimes with humor, which can be disarming. We have found it best to tell the criminal frankly that he will have to abdicate control. Rather than allow the criminal to run the meetings, we will take the initiative, at least for the time being. Although he will not understand at first the reasons for this, they should be presented.

As new obstacles appear, we are prepared to handle them. A combination of knowledgeability and flexibility is important. With experience, we learn to recognize a tactic when it is used and to shift gears to deal with it. Otherwise, we could be diverted from the central issue or locked into a debate that ends in a power struggle. Each of us would be seeking a victory, when there should be no contest at all.

When the criminal tries to dominate, it is because he is unwilling to accept our view of him. He believes that we are cutting him down, that we are being unfair in calling him "criminal." As more than one has put it: "It's hard to believe you are talking about me." He insists that if he really believed that he was a criminal, he could not live with himself. When pressed on the issue of his criminality, he retorts that no one is perfect, that everyone has criminality in him, and that every man is basically out for himself. We point out the fallacies in this "larceny in every soul" argument. We present the concept of the continuum of criminality (see chapter 4 of volume 1), pointing out that, of course, one can find others who are as criminal as he but that there are *degrees* of irresponsibility. Most people are basically responsible. Some do entertain larcenous ideas but usually deter them promptly rather than implement them. The criminal may introduce the idea that everyone is "out for himself," meaning that everyone who tries to advance his own self-interest is a criminal. We make clear that the criminal's self-interest involves a quest for excitement and conquest at the expense of others—those are not the self-interests of responsible people.

A criminal who has been in jail may acknowledge that he is a criminal to the extent that he may admit that the facts of his life include an arrest. But he still believes that he was right in doing what he did and objects to our view of him. A violent man told us he was basically nonviolent at heart:

> "My natural inclinations are not to be violent. I am deathly afraid of people. I am bitter and hateful but I don't mean these things. I love and care about people though my actions deny this. Most of the things I have done *I haven't wanted to do.*"

Another man, who had committed hundreds of rapes and thefts and was heavily involved in drug traffic, stated, "All my life I have been out to help and not hurt anybody." As an example of how he had shown consideration for others, he cited the occasion when a girl whom he had raped was on the witness stand and he told his lawyers not to interrogate her because he wanted to spare her discomfort. The criminal continues to extol his good deeds to show that he is not all bad, thereby maintaining his image of himself as a good person.

A criminal may present his holding a job or going to school as an indication of his responsibility, but we put the emphasis on his irresponsibility on the job, at school, and elsewhere. The religious factor looms large in many a criminal's self-appraisal. We take issue with the criminal's contention that he is a religious person. He is a phony: he observes some rituals, but he has no concept of religion as a way of life. Religious people do not steal, assault, exploit, or ask God to aid them in their crimes.

To prop up his view of his decency, the criminal may tell us that he experiences guilt feelings. If he does, we are unsparingly blunt in our response. We tell him that if he is trying to demonstrate his sensitivity and humanity, his actions override this consideration. We point out that whatever guilt exists in him is transient and gets cut off. Guilt or no guilt, he continues to violate and injure. As far as we are concerned, he does not experience enough guilt. If he did and sustained it, there would be less criminality. Rather than build up the criminal's self-image as many others have attempted to do, we view that image itself as totally criminal. From the criminal's past experience with therapists, he may have the idea that a change agent tries to make people comfortable by removing guilt, fear, and tension. We inform him that we do the opposite. We make fear operative as a guide to responsible living, increase his tensions, and view guilt as favorable to achieve change. We realize that he does not understand the full import of this statement, but he knows where we stand.

In talking about his view of himself as a good person, we again bring up the diversity and pervasiveness of the individual's criminality. We go into a discussion of criminal patterns, often spending as much as three hours on any one of them. We thoroughly probe both his thinking and action, demonstrating the continuity and expanding nature of his criminality throughout life. We can trace one of his acts, such as burglary, and show the scores of additional criminal transactions that ensue from it—reckless driving during the getaway, the purchase of drugs for the celebration, the exploitation of a woman, the misrepresentation of the source of the funds, fights, and so forth. If we are estimating the number of offenses of all kinds, we are talking in terms of thousands of violations per criminal. He is obviously astonished at this, because he has never regarded his behavior as criminal.

The criminal's reaction to our attempt to delineate his criminality exhaustively is often shock. One very articulate criminal wrote this analysis of the television camera idea:

"By the constant application of the TV camera concept I think we achieve three things.
1. The full awareness of our criminality.
2. It is a self-motivated police watch over our actions. . . . It is a forced exercise of will. How can I cheat on TV? It is better than God's watchful eye. For a machine is merciless and unforgiving.
3. . . . It registers my deeds and plays it back to my conscious reasoning. . . . It is a continuous exercise in self-restraint."

That is one man's appraisal of the potential that this concept could have if he lived as though the camera were watching him. In practice, the criminal does not live that way, so the agent of change has to keep reminding him of what the camera sees.

After the discussion of the diversity and pervasiveness of the subject's criminality, we bring up the suffering that he has caused others. We discuss his lack of concept of injury (chapter 5 of volume 1), pointing out that any one criminal act has repercussions, just as though one dropped a stone into a pond and watched concentric ripples spread out. We might take stealing from a department store as an example, citing the expense to the store of replacing stolen items, the money spent for surveillance, the higher insurance costs, and the passing on of all the costs of the thefts, so that even his mother, when she shops, must now pay more for the very same items that he stole.

As we expand upon the criminal's injuring of other people, he blames forces outside himself. We know that these forces are not causal but that he uses them for his accountability explanations. Many people whom he has talked with before have believed his excuses. (As we pointed out in volume 1, the victim stance appears in many guises.) The criminal often traces his current situation back to one event that he represents as causing all his difficulties. Thus, when a man claims that his problems began with the death of his father, we are quick to bring out that the criminal patterns existed before his father's death, that his siblings did not take a criminal path, and that most children who lose a parent do not become criminals. Whatever aspect of the victim stance he presents, we point out that he chose to act in a particular way and that his difficulty is the consequence of his choice. For every situation we hold the criminal accountable.

A sophisticated criminal may offer the psychologic excuse that something in him made him want to get caught. We point out how he schemed and weighed risks so as *not* to get caught. He even postponed crimes when circumstances were not favorable. It is true that superoptimism sometimes led him to miscalculate and resulted in apprehension. But, we observe, once apprehended he did everything possible to avoid conviction, and once confined he battled for his release.

The criminal may claim to be "paranoid," offering this as an explanation of his criminal behavior. All this means is that he is suspicious, as indeed he must be, because of the ever-present danger of detection for his crimes. We discount any material that he raises about an irresistible impulse, compulsion, loss of control, and so forth (see material from chapter 6 of volume 1).

Criminals often revert to talking about being victims of their feelings. Those who have had previous therapy may have talked mainly in these terms. This gives us an opportunity to emphasize that our program requires a subordination of feeling to reason. At this time, such a statement means little because they have collected excuses based on other therapist formulations in terms of feelings and unconscious forces acting on them.

> C learned in a therapy group that he committed crimes because he wanted to punish his mother. He hated her at the same time he loved her. On an unconscious level, he was getting even with her because he blamed her for the death of his father.

> "Through my ten years of therapy, I accounted for my criminal behavior in a multitude of ways. I was showing anger to one parent first, then the other. It was a way to compensate for my homosexual fears. It was an instance of what Reich called "moral masochism." It was Fromm's flight from freedom. It was dependency. Finally, in despair, I arrived at the only conclusion possible, that I was a hopeless case of sociopathic personality."

This man used his being a "hopeless case" as a justification for what he did. After all, if nothing could be done for him, he was a victim of his condition. Both these men had picked up new excuses that they had never thought of on their own.

After hearing us eliminate his sociologic and psychologic excuses, a criminal may say that he must be as he is because of a genetic factor—he was born this way. This excuse must also be dismantled. We counter by stating that, even if the need for excitement were of a genetic origin, thinking patterns are learned, and choices are made. In addition, some genetic patterns are correctable. Virtually any victim story, no matter how entrenched, can be shaken.

The techniques that we describe in this chapter are so powerful that in only a few interviews we eliminated a genuine half belief that a man had held for thirteen years.

> C was convicted of first degree murder. After the outcomes of several trials were reversed by technical errors, he was sent to Saint Elizabeths by

civil commitment, the criminal charge having being dismissed. For years he had been claiming that he had had a blackout before the crime and amnesia after. Now, thirteen years later, immune from prosecution, C expressed interest in talking with us. We demonstrated that we knew the kind of person that C must have been before the homicide. After three meetings, C, sufficiently impressed by our procedures, rendered a clear, precise account of the homicide. He chose to commit the crime, there were no blackouts, hallucinations, or subsequent amnesia. This did not emerge in a single confession; rather, as we successfully dealt with a number of his tactics, his confidence in us grew, and he came forth with the material in stages. From C's point of view, to have done this earlier would have been foolhardy. When he was on death row awaiting electrocution, it worked in his favor for him to push the facts of the event out of mind and stick to his blackout-amnesia story. Ten years later, when he was out of danger, in a kind of backlash of conscience, he began to have hallucinations, some of which were voices condemning the crime. Voices began to tell him what he had known was true, but had refused to look at.

In true amnesia, a person struggles to recall what occurred. This, however, was an effort *not* to recall. A mental illness story became a well-entrenched half belief, because adhering to it and convincing others of it saved this man's life. Most victim excuses offered by the criminal are much easier to eliminate because the criminal never even half believed them. Nevertheless, ideas that become genuine half beliefs also fall by the wayside when we use our techniques.

Throughout our meetings, the more we present things from his point of view, the less the criminal dissents. That is, he appreciates that although we do not agree with his premises of life, we at least know what they are. During our presentation, we inform the criminal that he may have a high IQ, but he has an equally high SQ, or stupidity quotient. The SQ idea applies in several ways. He lives a life in which he is constantly in jeopardy and winds up like a monkey in a cage. More importantly, he continually wastes physical and mental energy in excitement-seeking but never achieves contentment or peace of mind. His high SQ also shows up in his unrealistic expectations and his pretensions. In his criminal view of the world, if he is not number one he is nothing, and the slightest disappointment can reduce him to a zero. Although the stupidity quotient idea is contrived, it is often effective; it indicates that we know how the criminal views himself, although we, by no means, share his view. Actually, he *is* bright and has potential, but his talents and abilities are directed toward objectives that are detrimental to others and ultimately to himself. Of course, he does not see it this way and contends that we do not understand him. Whenever a criminal is faced with an opposing point of view and is trying to preserve his stance, he says, "You don't understand." This really refers to the fact that we do not agree with him.

The overall purpose of the presentation thus far in these interviews is to show the criminal how destructive he is to himself and others. We strive to establish in him a view that his behavior is contemptible and his way of life futile. He has already held this view occasionally but only shallowly and without impact. That occasional view is very different from the self-disgust that must be developed in the process of change. If a criminal continues to believe that he is a good person (or "not that bad" a person), no headway in change is feasible because there is little to change. The criminal must be totally fed up with himself.

> "If I'm ever going to make it, if I'm ever going to be able to live with myself, if I'm, ever going to be able to stand myself, I'm going to have to keep swimming in my own vomit; the moment I get my nose out of it, I begin to think I'm a swan instead of the filthy, slimy leech I really am."

This point of view contrasts with that of a teen-ager who was not much influenced by our presentation:

> "I know I'm terrible and all that stuff, but it doesn't bother me. I know I'm supposed to become disgusted with myself, but I don't know how I'm supposed to do it."

This boy did not see any need for basic change, because he was enjoying what he was doing. He had not had to face the consequences of his lying, stealing, exploiting, and drug-trafficking, as does a criminal who is arrested.

Even when a man realizes that he must "swim in his own vomit," he cuts off the thought when he is away from us and gives it little further consideration.

> "When I sat down to read what I had written, it all seemed unreal—as if it had all happened to someone else and wasn't important anyway, and why read this crap and why go on writing—it's meaningless, it all happened to someone else and far away. The moment we finish talking, something sets in, divorcing me more and more from what I am, building up a thicker and thicker protective wall between me and the vision of my rottenness, calming me, making me satisfied with myself. Writing breaks through it, but the second I stop writing, stop examining my sores, it begins building up again—cutting me off from my own rottenness."

We expect this cutoff and must counter it in each meeting by relentlessly pursuing the personal inventory. Time and again, the criminal has experienced futility and despair. There have been islands in his life when he has wanted to be responsible and has envied honest men. We seek to tap and sustain something that has occasionally been present briefly, but has been cut off each time.

PRESENTING THE PROGRAM OVERVIEW

When a criminal has sought help from others in the past, he has wanted assistance in getting out of a jam. By this time in his contact with us, he usually realizes that there is no hope of such assistance. However, he still has misconceptions of what a program for change entails. Many criminals want only to be more successful as criminals. They think of change in terms of taking fewer risks and staying out of the heavier action—being so-called misdemeanor criminals rather than felons. They think about going to school or working to achieve an appearance of respectability. They plan to abstain from the more dangerous enterprises—which might involve guns, trafficking in drugs, and so on—and thereby to minimize their chances of arrest. They are typified by a man who conveyed his intention to live "high on the hog" by gambling, writing numbers, and bootlegging. If he were apprehended, he thought, the penalty for these offenses would be relatively light—a two-year sentence at most and early release for good behavior. He intended to avoid any activity in which there might be violence. We responded that his appetite for excitement would grow in time and that patterns would expand. With his fragmentation and suggestibility, we knew that his intentions would go by the boards if something exciting came up and he would eventually go beyond misdemeanors. He did, later, commit armed robbery. We informed this man, and others like him, that with this outlook, they would not follow through in our program, which demands *total* change. Getting away with things on the side while maintaining a front of respectability is not what we mean by change.

Some criminals want to change to get rid of specific characteristics that they themselves find offensive. In chapter 1 of volume 1, we described our use of conventional psychiatric techniques to treat a child-molester. The result was that he left children alone but continued in almost every other kind of crime. Some criminals seek relief of psychosomatic symptoms, so that they can be more comfortable in their functioning. And some isolate a particular problem—impotence, drug use, temper, and so on—and ask for assistance with it.

Many criminals have the notion that change will occur through a miracle. They expect the change agent to do all the work, and they expect change to occur overnight. Not only does the criminal want a miracle, he also wants a guarantee that he will like the change brought about. The only guarantee we offer is that our techniques can do the job if he makes the choice to do the necessary learning and implementing. From our point of view, the program's requirements are clear, the concepts accurate and detailed, and the procedures effective. There can be no failure if the criminal commits himself. To show the criminal that this total basic change is possible and has in fact occurred, we have him talk with men who have successfully participated in our program.

A related obstacle is the criminal's superoptimism about change. Once he has stated that he wants to change, it is as though nothing more is needed—thinking it makes it so. A decision to be noncriminal automatically washes out the past and ensures success.

> "When I get out of [confinement], it is a new chapter. I am an entirely different person. I have much more confidence."

The criminal gives no consideration to the effort that is mandatory, because he has no concept of it. He thinks that mastering the program consists of grasping two or three points. We have seen criminals try to build themselves up as brilliant people who rapidly comprehend everything. We then inform them of the comprehensiveness of the change that is required. The problem is the person himself—the way he thinks—and not any one aspect of his life, such as drugs or sex. At the beginning, the criminal does not realize, as one man later puts it, that "it's thinking, not drinking. It's thugs, not drugs." The criminal must be so different at the end of the program from the kind of person he was at the beginning as to be unrecognizable. Current thinking patterns must be destroyed and replaced with new ones. Every nook and cranny of the criminal's thinking must be invaded. Nothing of his present mode of thinking is to be preserved. We purport to change the "death style" of a criminal to the "life style" of a responsible person. It is a strong, sweeping indictment to say that there is nothing worth saving in the criminal's thinking patterns. It means that the criminal has to realize that he is rotten to the core. One of our people who grasped the idea expressed it this way:

> "Somehow you do have to excavate the foundation, because, until you do, anything you try to build on the same site will stand on a rotten and insecure footing. . . . Once the demolition is accomplished—and it would seem a long and arduous process—after all, I've been building on this rotten foundation for thirty-two years—then the basis for a decent life can be established and the framework erected."

We are not recruiters for this program. We clarify what our program requires and present a rational view of the criminal's options. The choice lies entirely with him; it is his life. We say that it does not matter to us if he assents or scores points, because it is *he* who will return to old patterns and wind up in confinement. Time will tell whether he has the dedication to achieve responsibility. If he chooses to go in our direction and commits himself to doing what we require, we shall show him the way by teaching and correcting. This is a far cry from trying to sell him on a program or persuade him of anything.

Our discussion is in terms of free choice and the application of will. The criminal has made choices all his life. In crime, he had to choose between his desire to do what he wanted to do and his fear of the consequences. Now, he can choose to establish a new way of life. There is a pitfall in putting it this way. If the criminal is told that crime is a matter of choice and that he must make a different choice, he is likely to say that *choosing* to be responsible is all that is necessary. He leaves out the will to endure the consequences of that choice. But even choice and will are insufficient for change. The criminal needs new knowledge and the further learning that comes with the implementation of that knowledge. Admittedly, up to now, all this is just words to the criminal. But he does comprehend that we are ruling out excuses and are insisting that he is personally responsible for whatever course he takes and that we consider him responsible for his thoughts as well as his actions. We point out that he desires, promotes, and even contrives various kinds of thoughts that he finds exciting. He can change that; he is not a victim of the thoughts that pass through his mind. The burden of decision rests solely with him.

We try to make the criminal comprehend the monumental importance of his choice. He has three options: continued crime, suicide, and change. He can continue his old way and die early or spend his life in and out of confinement—a sort of living death. He can kill himself, which in a sense is the greatest crime, because he will injure others if he succeeds and compound his problems if he fails. Or he can choose a life that he has envied at times but generally scorned. The last option amounts to giving up what he has known all his life for a way of life that he knows nothing about, and doing it with no guarantees of happiness. Usually, at this point, none of the three options is very attractive. Some criminals are ready to reject the criminal path that has brought them where they are. But they do not want to commit suicide, and they have no desire to suffer to attain something that does not appeal to them.

The issue is which way of life is the lesser of two evils. The criminal may contend that he does not have a choice, inasmuch as he is so entrenched in his way of life. Although many patterns are habitual, all are products of choice. For example, in driving a car, a series of choices are made; however, we make them so automatically that they require no deliberate thought, and we usually do not think in terms of choice. Commitment, even slavery, to a program requiring responsibility is necessary to achieve real freedom. To the criminal, freedom is what we consider anarchy—doing what one wants, without regard for rules or other people, and trampling anyone who gets in the way. The criminal is far from certain that he desires to live in a "penitentiary" of restraints called laws, rules, and social customs. He does not understand that people put on their own handcuffs and willingly live within legal and social restraints, so as to have a maximum of freedom to develop and achieve. Some criminals have given us a clear, unequivocal no to the option of change. They have told us that they would rather go to prison than change. In fact, they were prepared to do so with the outlook that at least their way of life allowed them to do what they wanted, even if they had to spend some time in confinement. They decided that they would rather "rule in hell than serve in heaven."

The criminal cannot change to something amorphous, so we must give him an overview of what a 180-degree shift to responsible living entails. He is told that his affirmation of a new way of life will deprive him of the excitement that has been the oxygen of his life. There must be an immediate cessation of criminal activity—no gambling, drinking, lying, or associating with other criminals, and no involvement with women for the time being (unless, of course, it is with his wife). The door must be totally shut to violation, because even a slight opening will eventually result in a serious crime. That certain habits are longstanding is meaningless; the criminal can desist from them. No excuses are accepted for manifestations of criminality.

The criminal will be required to attend this program daily for a year, participating in a group and giving valid reports. In these meetings, the wide-open channel must be scrupulously adhered to. The criminal will learn phenomenologic reporting, so that all the contents of his mind are revealed.

Our program has its roots in a core of moral values that has endured for centuries. The criminal will be expected to function impeccably in line with that morality. The program has to permeate every thought and every act during every waking moment, with attention to every detail. Being in this program is like being pregnant—it is all or nothing. The criminal can no more be a little bit moral than a woman can be a little bit pregnant. He must go from one extreme to another: from total irresponsibility to total integrity.

The criminal does not change through talk in our office but through life's experiences. There is no suffering in the mere exchange of words, but he may consider himself to be suffering as he lives without criminal excitement while surmounting the problems of responsibility. We inform the criminal very early about the difficulties of living as a responsible person. In a sense, being responsible is more of a struggle than being a criminal, because life consists of distressing situations, problem-solving, and decision-making, most of which the criminal ignores or defers. If the criminal thinks that he has been bored in the past, he will experience periods of intense boredom as he learns to live a kind of life that he previously scorned. The criminal will have to learn that effort, as we use the term, means not doing what he wants to do and doing what he does not want to do. This is totally foreign to him; he has usually done what he wanted to do and ignored what others expected of him. He must start now to learn the responsible patterns of thinking and action that he should have begun to master as a child. In the process of education and implementation, he will make many mistakes. We can guarantee that his course will not be smooth and that he will wonder many times whether the whole enterprise is worth it. However, this program calls for surmounting discouragement and dealing constructively with adversity. In fact, even the concept of adversity requires redefinition. The criminal has regarded things' not going his way as adversity; he will now have to recognize his own limitations and those of the outside world. He will have to do the best he can and be the unsung hero rather than the big shot. We offer no guarantees about the future, except that with diligent implementation and increasing commitment, the effort and endurance will become less and less difficult, just as the effort in driving a car becomes less as habits become automatic.

We will not dictate the decisions that the criminal makes, but we will teach him how to make choices responsibly. We do not try to determine the specific outcome of decision-making. What is important is the process by which a decision is made. We do not know what the criminal's ultimate station in life will be, nor do we care, so long as it is responsible. Personally, we value a responsible waiter above an irresponsible executive. We assure the criminal that he will not be an overnight success. Through hard work, he will progress as far as his talents and intelligence permit. It will be up to him to generate responsible initiatives from within and to make his own way in the world. We will not do this for him. Again, we remind him that we will not help to dig him out of holes. The outcome of all this hard work is something that he is totally unfamiliar with—the self-respect and peace of mind to be derived from cleanliness.

We do not expect the criminal to understand what we have said until he lives it. Talk is easy, and at this point we know that we are presenting ideas that he does not fully comprehend. Knowing that he has changes of mind, we do not equate sincerity with conviction. He will be able to demonstrate conviction by his implementation of this program. A halfhearted desire to "give the program a try" is unacceptable. Such an attitude implies that the criminal will stick with it only as long as it is agreeable to him. However, his comfort or happiness is of no importance in the process of change. He does not set the conditions of the program.

The criminal must realize at the very outset that we provide him with massive resources and that he must pay a price to depart from the program. Therefore, an important condition is specified early. If a criminal is on probation or parole, he is assured that privileged communication will be maintained throughout. However, he is also informed that if after a reasonable period of time (usually a few months) we find that he is using us (which would be manifested by a closed channel and arrestable behavior of which the authorities have no knowledge), a report will be submitted to the proper authority—judge, probation officer, or parole officer. The report will state that further continuation in the program by him is pointless because he is persisting in a criminal pattern of action thus using the program as a shield for his activities. It is clearly understood in advance by the criminal that specific reasons for this decision will not be provided to the authorities. Thus, if he has been committing crimes, he can be positive that we shall not inform about them. We are, after all, change agents, not law enforcers. If he shows continued lack of cooperation, rendering our efforts useless, we shall terminate his participation in the program and report this. Our judgment as to the conditions for termination is based solely on our ability to assess the degree of change. The criminal must clearly understand these conditions in advance.

We invite the criminal to voice his doubts, and he usually does if the channel is open. We realize that his transient despair about his present life style is not the same as a desire for cleanliness. A criminal may see his present life as futile, but still be unsure as to whether he wants to go to the extremes that our program requires.

> "I don't know whether I want to adjust to a life when the best I can hope for is the satisfaction of achievement."

> "Do you honestly think there is anything out there that can give me what I want?"

> "The road to impeccability is the path from the bottom of the deepest valley to the peak of the highest mountain. I am not sure I want to travel it."

These attitudes are to be expected when one is telling a man that he must change from what he has known all his life to something entirely foreign. Criminals who decide to participate in our program eventually view themselves as having no other choice. It is a choice of no choice. Most have participated in other programs that have been ineffective. This program, with its very different approach, is the criminal's lifeline.

By discovering who we are, learning what we know about him, and being informed early of what is involved, the criminal is in a better position to choose whether he wants to participate. Some, after hearing what we are offering, find our whole concept of basic change repugnant.

> As C was in confinement, his mind pored over ideas of rape, robbery, shooting, and stabbing. He stated that he had no use for suckers and slaves who do the "crap" of school, work, and so on. He stated that he had the right to do as he wished and that nobody had the right to stop him. Even though he often wondered why he is the way he is and said that he was "fucked up," he did not want to live differently.

For such a man, happiness is living the kind of life that he has always lived. Our program could offer him nothing that he wanted. Our techniques allowed us to detect this relatively early rather than waste countless hours working with him.

There are criminals who desire a change out of convenience rather than conviction. They want to change only if it is easy. Some decide that they will not participate because they believe that it might prolong their stay in confinement. Some demand guarantees that cannot be offered. They want us to guarantee results and how long they will take, overlooking the fact that the outcome depends more on their efforts than on ours. Many decide to go their own way because they do not want the result that is the objective of our program or else do not want to go through the strenuous process to achieve that result.

The criminal, fragmented as he is, shifts positions. A man may be totally sincere at the moment about wanting our program, but there may be at the same time a reservation about the totality of the commitment. In fact, sincerity about change or about anything else in the criminal is always limited because of his fragmentation. We may find in the selection process that a criminal who respects us, admires our knowledge, and believes that the program makes sense soon decides that none of it applies to him, accurate as it is. Some reject us but later return and ask to participate.

One of the reasons that we have not excluded criminals from our program once they were in it is that we know how changeable their minds are. We have had long experience with the criminal's shifting states of mind and poor decision-making. We know that he may change his mind and resolve to reenter. Even when a criminal states that he is quitting the program, he is aware of his own changeability and knows that our door remains open.

As we look at the criminal population, we realize that only a small percentage is going to make the change that we are talking about. We estimate that ten to twenty percent of the criminals who are interviewed when vulnerable will accept the program and implement it. Another ten to twenty percent will accept it and later drop out.

Criminals who want to enter our program still are not fully convinced that the program will work for them; they choose this course because it is their last resort. We accept them, knowing full well that there will be violations in the early stages. We realize that the channel has not been fully open during the selection process, but this does not disqualify those who express a desire to be in the program.

Really then, we do not disqualify criminals from our program. What we have described as a selection process involves selection only inasmuch as the criminal decides whether or not to select our program. He gets a foretaste of what is in store for him and decides whether this is what he wants.

Chapter 4

Choice and Will

FREEDOM VERSUS DETERMINISM

THE FREEDOM-VERSUS-DETERMINISM CONTROVERSY has engaged the attention of theologians, scientists, philosophers, lawyers, psychologists, and many others, all from somewhat different perspectives. Before Freud, the common view of human nature was that man has the capacity to make choices and to implement them. Bromberg (1948, p. 11) pointed out that the "ecclesiastical concept of moral responsibility" asserted that man was responsible before God. Royce (1961, p. 209) cited Sorokin's observation that, through the centuries, "human thinking has dipped into determinism periodically but has always returned to the conviction that man has free choice."

Various terms have been used in discussing self-determination—*will, free will, choice, volition, voluntary action*, and others. The semantic quagmire can be difficult to escape. Will is often defined in terms of choice, there being no clear distinction between the two. In some instances, definitions are so broad as to obscure what the writer wants to convey.

In this chapter, we do not concern ourselves with the centuries of thought on the freedom-determinism controversy. This is not a survey of philosophical ideas on choice and will. Instead, we provide background information pertinent to our development of choice and will in a program for basic change in the criminal.

There have been a variety of deterministic views of human behavior. Determinism did not start with Freud. In the Middle Ages, wrongdoing was considered to be due to possession by Satanic forces out of the realm of human control. The idea that man is a product of his experience and education is also old. Spinoza, in the seventeenth century, maintained that, because man's actions are products of memory and education, will is not free.

He implied that behavior is guided by forces of which man is ignorant.

> Men think themselves free because they are conscious of their volitions
> and desires, but are ignorant of the causes by which they are led to wish
> and desire. (Spinoza, cited in Durant 1953, p. 136)

Interest in the unconscious has been traced back to Plato. In the early
nineteenth century, Herbart spoke of ideas that are forced out of
consciousness and designated them "inhibited ideas" (Schultz 1969). In the
wake of Freud's study of unconscious mental processes, determinism became
operational and therapy gained an ascendant position.

> The deeply rooted belief in psychic freedom and choice ... is quite
> unscientific and must give ground before the claims of a determinism
> which governs mental life. (Cited in May 1969, p. 183)

There was no place for choice and will in a system stressing the dynamics of
unconscious motivation. Erickson (1973) observed that "free will has been
viewed as an outworn or at least fruitless notion." Ricoeur (1967) stated, that
"it's not by chance that the word 'volition' is absent from the Freudian
glossary." The behavioral psychologists are also determinists. They assert that
"no behavior is free" (Skinner 1953, p. 111).

> If we are to use the methods of science in the field of human affairs, we
> must assume that behavior is lawful and determined. We must expect to
> discover that what a man does is the result of specifiable conditions and
> that once these conditions have been discovered, we can anticipate and to
> some extent determine his actions. (Skinner 1953, p. 6)

As a reaction to the deterministic position, there has been a renewed
emphasis on free choice. Allport (1955) was critical of the fact that one could
look through one hundred psychology books and find neither will nor choice
mentioned.

> It is customary for the psychologist, as for other scientists, to proceed
> within the framework of strict determinism, and to build barriers between
> himself and common sense lest common sense infect psychology with its
> belief in freedom. (pp. 82, 83)

Allport pointed out that psychology was increasingly concerned with choice,
which "revived the problem of freedom." May (1953, p. 162) asserted that the
freedom-determinism dichotomy is false and that freedom is shown in "how
we relate to the deterministic realities of life":

> The pattern and the style in which you build your house are products of

how you, with an element of freedom, use the reality of the given materials. (p. 163)

A number of writers have pointed out that even the therapists who are determinists in their theoretic orientation function as though their parents are free agents in making choices (Wheelis 1958; Coleman 1965; Sutherland 1962; Gatch and Temerlin 1965; May 1966; Ricoeur 1967; Erickson 1973).

The individual in psychotherapy probably cannot grow without the exercise of his choice-making capacity; the ego cannot be strengthened without decision and choice. As a matter of fact, unless the patient has made the basic choice that he wants psychotherapy and has decided to devote all his resources to the therapeutic effort, personal change is limited. (Temerlin 1965)

In other words, total adherence to a strict determinism would mean that their patients were all helpless victims.

CHOICE

Some writers and practitioners have viewed the capacity to choose as a defining quality of man. Royce (1961, p. 208) pointed out that existentialists emphasize free choice and do so to an extreme. Sartre (1953) took the position that man *is* his choices, with the "choice of being" as the fundamental choice. This view of choice as basic to defining man is also expressed by Edwards (1965):

There is no self lying "outside" choice which causes choices to occur; but since I am my choices when they do occur, I am thus the cause of and responsible for the actions which issue from my choices. It is thus inappropriate to think of my choices as things which happen *to me*, because there is "me" lying outside them from which they can be completely distinguished, and to which they happen. On the other hand, it is most appropriate to think of the *actions* which follow upon my choices as happening *because of me*, since I *am* the choices from which these actions issue. (p. 286)

In his writing on logotherapy, Frankl (1965) spoke of man's "intrinsically human capacity to take a stand" in the face of conditions not of his own making. Feldman (1963) stated that "man becomes what he is through his decisions." Peters (1956) has pointed out how undermining the deterministic position can be, as people begin to doubt the value of their efforts once they "become wise to the causes suggested for them." Carrying this further, a person may suppose mistakenly that, if one can find out the cause of an action, it will absolve him of any responsibility for his choice. (In chapter 1 of volume 1, we pointed out how such absolution occurred regularly during psychoanalytic treatment of criminals.)

A number of psychotherapists who set themselves apart from the determinism of Freud often fall back on the unconscious and early experiences for explanation. Hobbs (1955, p. 12) observed that client-centered therapy, although it does not *emphasize* psychodynamics, does share with psychoanalysis the view that unconscious motivation and childhood experiences are important considerations in therapy. One part of rational-emotive therapy (Ellis 1970, p. 57) is to show the patient "how to understand the antecedents of his behavior." The encounter movement makes extensive use of past determinants of behavior. Schutz (1967, p. 88), for example, described "working through" unresolved feelings from childhood. Other nonpsychoanalytic therapists also sift through past events for determinants of present conduct, for example, Stampfl and Lewis in their implosive therapy (1973).

The idea of choice is not particularly abstruse to the layman. The term has operational significance in that we make innumerable small choices every day. We make more important choices at critical times in our lives—sometimes a series of choices that determine a basic course. One finds, for example, an account of a youth raised in a deprived environment, who could easily have joined the delinquent youngsters in his area, but instead "chose to take the other path, leading, hopefully, to when he can be of service to others" (Raspberry 1973). As we shall point out, this ability to determine, to choose, our actions is often considered to be the same as will.

WILL

Will, as described by philosophers, has characteristically been discussed in terms of mental functions or faculties. There were few, if any, truly operational aspects of will in such a description that could be used in psychology. In 1900, Pfander (cited by Spiegelberg 1960) published a psychologic analysis of will. It was an early attempt to describe a process from the inside of a person in terms of subjective and conscious components rather than such objective concomitants of thought as physiologic factors. Schoen (1931) stated that the "realm of will" is composed of reflexes, instincts, habits, and voluntary action. William James (1950, p. 562) said that the "effort of attention is the essential phenomenon of will." The determination aspect of will has been described by Vesey (1961), who speaks of the exercise of will when a person is trying to hang on to the edge of a cliff despite unbearable pain in his fingers. Will is evidenced in the person's "encouraging himself not to give in, not to release his grasp."

In many writings, *will* appears to be synonymous with *choice*. Locke in the seventeenth century and Low two hundred years later have said approximately the same thing:

> And is that faculty [will] anything more in effect than a power; the power of the mind to determine its thought, to the producing, continuing, or stopping any action, as far as it depends on us? (Locke 1952, p. 181)

> The Will has one function only: it rejects or accepts ideas and stops or releases impulses. In either case, it says either "yes" or "no" to the idea or the impulse. (Low 1963, p. 132)

Jonathan Edwards, the eighteenth-century New England clergyman, defined will as the "faculty or power or principle of the mind by which it is capable of choosing." Numerous other modern writers have the same view:

> Volition is the power of choice between means by which an end is obtained. (Moore 1948, p. 343)

> In my opinion, will, as the capacity to make and implement choices, is the culmination of all psychological functions. (Arieti 1972, p. 2)

In a book devoted entirely to the subject of will, Assagioli (1973) described the "directive and regulatory function" of the will:

> The function of the will is similar to that performed by the helmsman of a ship. He knows what the ship's course should be, and keeps her steadily on it, despite the drifts caused by the wind and current. (p. 10)

Assagioli's development of his psychology of will is so comprehensive that it is hard to see how it can have operational value. He described almost two dozen "qualities" of will that embrace many different aspects of mental functioning.

Both Assagioli and May (1969) have said that the Victorian conception of will power is not in line with what they mean by will. Assagioli called it a "caricature" of the concept of will. May (p. 183) stated that Victorian will power had turned out to be "a web of rationalization and self-deceit" that resulted in the suppression of wishes, drives, and instincts. *Will power*, as commonly used now, refers to a person's doing something "against the grain." It is reflected in a person's tenacity in doing what is disagreeable but necessary or not doing something that one wants to do.

Will power may then be defined as effort directed and controlled toward an end, the accomplishment of which requires the overcoming of present desires and impulses. ... For will power to be present, the end to be achieved must be of a nature that counteracts already present tendencies or habits. (Schoen 1931, p. 165)

Will power is the name we give to fiats that run counter to our appetites or inclinations. (Farber 1966, p. 2)

Rothschild (1934, p. 170) said that will power is exerted when there is conflict between "a particular act and the individual as a whole." Will power helps a person to make a moral choice; when he comes to terms with the conflict, he no longer needs will power. Rothschild's emphasis is on the elimination of the requirement of will power, rather than on its effective use.

Rank (1950), in developing a therapy of will, used the term to refer to self-determination and spoke of the creative aspect of will as it won out over the "biological, sexual instinct." He called for the "rehabilitation of will" in psychology.

Why must we always deny the will, call it now God, now fate, or attribute it to an "id." In other words, the essential problem of psychology is our abolition of the fact of will. (p. 10)

Farber (1966) defined will as a "responsible mover ... which pushes actively toward its goal" (p. 35). He pointed out why, in many circles, will had fallen into disrepute:

Even a cursory inspection of this scholarship will reveal that on the one hand the topic of will has been endlessly exploited for all manner of self-serving moralizing and on the other hand came increasingly to be the speculative plaything of the academicians who tinkered with it so whimsically it would be difficult for the reader to know will had any relevance to human considerations. Thus, either as an ingredient of moral coercion or as a fruitless academic venture in philosophical or theological academicism, the subject of will gradually lost its connection with existence. (p. 29)

Like Rank many years later, Farber believed that will should be restored to a place of respectability, and he discussed psychopathology in terms of "disorders of will." Wheelis (1958) also lamented the "partial eclipse" of will.

In psychology [will] has lost its position as a primary mental function and has become an epiphenomenon. ... Knowledgeable moderns put their backs to the couch, and in so doing they fail occasionally to put their shoulders to the wheel. As will has been devalued, so has courage. . . . In our understanding of human nature we have gained determinism and lost determination—though these two things are neither coordinate nor incompatible. (p. 44)

In short, the terms *choice* and *will* are generally fuzzy and not operational. One problem is semantic; it is often difficult to comprehend each definition and hence difficult to know what each writer is saying. Another problem is that a discrepancy exists between theory and practice. Practitioners who emphasize choice or will often resort to determinism for explanations. And practitioners who are determinists must have recourse to choice and will; otherwise, their patients would not deal with immediate problems. Thus, the antideterminists fall back on determinism, and the determinists use choice and will. In an effective program for change a clear, precise concept of the nature of choice and will is necessary. In our program for change, we attempt to define *choice* and *will* unambiguously and without reliance on determinism, so that they can be effectively operational—so that they can be implemented by the criminal.

CHOICE AND WILL IN
THE PROGRAM FOR CHANGE

CHOICE

In this section, we shall describe the change process in terms of choice. In volume 1, we discussed the elimination of sociologic and psychologic factors as excuses for crime and showed that accountability-reasoning which emphasizes factors outside the criminal's control is invalid. The criminal *chooses* the criminal path in his search for power and control and for the excitement to be derived from doing the forbidden, be it by stealth or force. Living a criminal life requires many other choices. The criminal chooses to cut off his past, not to consider the future, to ignore injury to others, to rely on prejudgment, to refuse to factfind, and to perpetuate all the other thinking errors. Each error leads to the choice of another error. This concept of choice negates what others have termed impulsive action.

Although irresponsible thinking and action patterns (which are the products of choices) are firmly entrenched, the criminal has the capacity to choose to eliminate these patterns and develop new ones. Change requires a commitment—a choice in and of itself—and then further choices to implement the commitment.

The criminal is, at the very least, reluctant to choose to destroy his way of living. As his thinking processes are evaluated in our program for change, he is faced with more and more totally alien choices on the road to responsibility. It is difficult for him to affirm a commitment to change, because he does not know what new choices will be called for and he is opposed to, or at best uncertain about, the kind of life that these choices will lead to.

When the criminal enters the program, it is most likely to be the result of a forced choice. He may be offered by the court the alternative of confinement or our program for change. If this is not the case, he may be pressured by others to seek help for an isolated problem or he may believe that he will get into further difficulty if he does not change some specific aspect of his behavior—stop using drugs or control his temper. If he is not in jeopardy of confinement, he has the free choice of rejecting the program, once he hears what it requires. Whether the choice to change is forced or free, it will not be sustained unless a number of other appropriate choices are made as time goes by.

Just stating that he chooses to change is of course of no greater significance than a decision to diet. Either must be affirmed by doing what is necessary to implement the choice. The most important choice at the outset occurs when a criminal decides whether to subject himself to our procedures. If he elects to, this ensures that there will be many other choices on different levels that will be open to him. Our procedure of phenomenologic reporting elicits material leading to numerous choices, major and minor, as we deal with each twenty-four-hour period of the criminal's thinking and action. Examples of major choices are whether to rejoin his family or whether to continue his education. Associated with each of these choices are subsidiary choices. Whether to get a job is another major choice, and its subsidiary choices are where to look for a job, the type of work, the salary, and fringe benefits. There is another set of choices to be made while at work: shall he be prompt, subordinate himself to the requirements of the job, pay attention to detail, plan for the long term, show concern for others, work as part of a team, exert effort, or work overtime? In speaking of echelons of choice, we point out that there are physical and mental limitations. It is necessary to explore with the criminal what the realistic limitations of his choices are. Some choices that he makes are eliminated; these are unrealistic choices, often prompted by the criminal's desire for power and his desire to be an immediate success, a unique number one.

When others have discussed choice with the criminal, the focus has usually been establishing particular objectives. That is, they have tried to induce the criminal to choose to stay out of crime, to work, to go to school. What they failed to understand is that such objectives cannot be achieved in the criminal through choice alone. Given the criminal's thinking patterns, those choices do not work out, because the criminal knows neither what they imply nor how to implement them responsibly. To expect a criminal to choose to work and then actually to function responsibly is absurd. The criminal is not equipped with the thinking processes for functioning at work interdependently, with integrity, with loyalty, with a sense of obligation. Such major choices are at best sincere intentions. Owing both to the criminal's lack of knowledge about how to implement them and to his fragmentation, these sincere intentions cannot possibly last. Choosing a particular objective, such as working, is only the first feeble step in the process of change. Without the thinking processes that are necessary to achieve a responsible objective, the choice of that objective by itself is futile. It is commonly assumed, for example, that once a man chooses to work, if given the proper skills, he will work effectively. Again and again, this has proved not to be the case. If he is to work effectively, the criminal must also choose to learn new ways to think and act and then implement that choice.

Our program requires that the criminal learn to think in a totally new way in order to implement the choice responsibly. We know that there is nothing to prevent the criminal from choosing to learn new thinking processes. When he learns a new thinking pattern, the program requires that he choose to make it a habitual part of his daily life. Without these steps, there can be no constructive results. The choices that the criminal makes in our program are based on reason, not on feelings. The thinking processes that he must learn are rational correctives of lifelong thinking errors; these can be changed explicitly and directly by a rational process of learning and implementing correctives.

The material in chapter 5 of volume 1 exemplifies the considerations that are subject to choice. The criminal can choose to learn correctives for his automatic thinking errors, and such a choice is necessary if he is to implement the major choices in life—choices concerning work, school, etc. The criminal can choose to participate with us in a wide-open channel of communication. He can choose to disclose fully, to listen with an open mind, and to criticize himself along the lines of responsible functioning. It is a matter of choice for him to eliminate "I can't" thinking; when he says that he can't, this is an assertion of choice—he chooses to be unwilling. The objective of change is reachable; he can become responsible, even though to do so has many disagreeable aspects. Elimination of victim excuses is a matter of choice; the criminal has the capacity to examine his own role in various situations and not to blame others. The criminal can choose to attain a new perspective on time. In crime, he has chosen to learn from mistakes; in planning crimes, he has to some extent anticipated problems in the future. He has the capacity to do the same with respect to responsible considerations. The criminal has thought about other people's reactions when planning a crime; now he can choose to put himself in the place of others within a totally new context, and he can choose to think responsibly before he acts, so that he does not injure others. Fulfilling obligations and taking responsible initiatives are matters of choice.

He has acted as though he owns others and as though he has no obligations to them. Now he can choose to learn what an obligation is and how obligations constitute an important part of life. He has been intolerant of fear and has cut it off; now he can choose to live with fear and let it be a guide to responsible living. To trust and have faith in a change agent is a matter of choice. In fact, it is an essential choice as he begins to learn about a way of life totally foreign to him; if there is not some degree of choosing to take things on faith in the early stages of this program, progress is not possible. Closely related is a choice to be interdependent (beginning in the relationship with the change agent) and to abdicate power and control over others; he can choose to function interdependently at home, at work, in the program, wherever he goes.

Another choice is to do what is responsible, regardless of whether he is interested, likes it, or is given a guarantee of success. To be responsible, he must choose to see himself as he is. This means that he must adopt a different view of himself; he must choose to alter the victim and "I can't" stance, to discard his pretensions, and to see himself and the outside world realistically. Part of this choice involves accepting the picture we present of him as a criminal. If he does not hold the mirror to himself and see himself for what he is, then he is choosing to continue his old way of life. One of his most significant choices is to exert effort in our program. Effort means doing what is necessary for responsible functioning, whether or not it makes him happy or comfortable. It also means abstaining from whatever he wants to do that is opposed to responsibility. Effort calls for deterring criminal thinking—clearly a matter of choice. Finally, in dealing with daily situations, the criminal can choose to fact-find, consider different responsible options, and thereby make informed, responsible decisions.

We have taken the themes of chapter 5, volume 1 and described them in terms of choice, but the concepts of chapters 4, 6, 7, and 8 could be presented in a similar manner. For example, the pattern of anger described in chapter 4 is subject to choice, as is the pattern of deterrence in chapter 6 and the tactic of diversion in chapter 8. Each correction for a thinking error can be presented in terms of choice. Thus, there are an enormous number of choices to be made.

As the criminal is being taught new thinking processes, the ultimate choices recurrently come into focus: what kind of life does he want, or does he want to live at all? Again, we can take work as an example. Once the criminal has spent some time on the job, he may decide that he does not like working in a subordinate position, earning little money, having to take orders. As we obtain his thinking about whether to work, we introduce more far-reaching considerations—namely, his alternatives in life. When he resists responsible choices, we bring up the ultimate choice among the three options: crime, suicide, or change. We repeatedly make an issue of this ultimate choice.

At the beginning, the criminal is most likely to say that he chooses change, especially because he is being forced into it by the threat of confinement.

However, to present him with the three options at the beginning of our contact with him and expect him to choose would be unreasonable. The criminal has to have experiences in life before he can make an informed choice of this magnitude. He cannot know whether he really wants a responsible life until he has had some experience in implementing responsible patterns of thought and action. He can be more informed in making his choice once he learns more about what functioning responsibly entails.

Of course, the choice to learn new thinking processes is only one step in change. This choice gains effectiveness only through implementation. Implementation is itself an option to be chosen.

WILL

We have had doubts as to whether to use the term *will* at all in our work. Because of its widespread usage, it is appropriate to discuss its applicability to our program. We present here an operational concept of will; however, we do not use the word *will* itself in our daily work with the criminal.

The idea of will power comes closest to our meaning. The noncriminal exerts will power in many instances to accomplish an objective. Occasionally, human interest stories in the press describe a person's tremendous determination and endurance in achieving an objective. The emphasis is usually on determination, whereas in our work we emphasize what has to be endured—the price to be paid for achieving a responsible objective.

"Garbage Man to Ph.D."

Raised in a home in which Italian was the dominant language, flunking out of high school at 16, deprived of a laborer's career by his back injury, ——— somehow found ... the determination to make a better life for himself. (*Evening Star* 6/9/71)

This news item told how a young adult earned a Ph.D., despite appearing "doomed to a bleak world of obscurity" in a city ghetto. The emphasis was on will power in the sense of determination to get ahead. However, there was also will power in his being able to endure beginning at the bottom, relatively late in life with physical and scholastic disabilities, and struggling to subsist while attending school.

The endurance aspect of will power is more readily seen in situations in which people overcome physical pain or a crippling disability and achieve something worthwhile, as did John Gunther's son, who, debilitated by a fatal cancer, graduated from Harvard. This kind of will power directed toward a responsible objective is totally foreign to the criminal.

In his criminal activities, the criminal has made choices and implemented them, often overcoming substantial obstacles. However, responsible objectives have been scorned. As we have said, when he makes a choice to be responsible, it is at best a statement of intention. Responsible choices are so new to him that he does not truly understand them until he begins to implement them. His choice to change is opposed by a formidable barrier—a lifelong pattern of criminal thought and action. If he means to become a responsible person, a high price has to be paid. He will have to participate in a program that is not concerned with his happiness or comfort. It requires him to endure a life that he will find (at least for a while) banal and excruciatingly boring. He must live without his criminal excitements, which are the oxygen of his life. He must exist without crime, without criminal associates, without drugs or alcohol, without irresponsible sex, and, for a while, without control over his own money. He cannot be persuaded or exhorted to do this. He cannot accomplish the many necessary changes solely by a show of great determination. Rather, he has to *develop* endurance as he experiences the problems of his new life. Endurance cannot be taught by someone else.

Endurance means giving up being the big shot, the unique number one, the overnight success. It means abidicating power and control and living as an ordinary person. Endurance means having to take orders from others. Endurance calls for learning and implementing the most elementary habits, something most schoolchildren do automatically.*

Endurance means living with more fear and guilt, not less. It means having to absorb and learn from what have always been considered putdowns. Endurance means living with and learning from criticism, not automatically rejecting it. Endurance means deterring criminal thinking.

Endurance means that the criminal does what has to be done to achieve a responsible objective, whether he feels like it or not. In fact, in his new way of life, feelings are subordinated to reason. Endurance initially means swallowing anger, then eliminating it by disciplining one's thinking. The criminal often has to do what he dislikes and refrain from doing what he likes if it is incompatible with responsibility. He will have to see a project through and function as a team member, rather than as the captain.

In living with others, the criminal will have to endure revealing himself— telling the truth, subjecting his work to scrutiny and evaluation by others. Endurance means often living without recognition, even for a job well done. It means receiving no medals for doing what is expected. To endure means to run up against an array of new problems as one deals with family, friends, co-workers, and society at large. It means working tirelessly to achieve an objective—surmounting obstacles rather than quitting. Endurance means

---

*Numerous examples of this are offered in chapters 7 and 8 as we discuss correctives for particular thinking errors.

that the criminal fulfills obligations, even if they seem unnecessary and burdensome. It means not deferring the responsible, but being on top of things and taking responsible initiatives, whether or not there is interest in them. Endurance requires tremendous self-discipline along all these lines, as well as in the correction of all the other characteristic thinking errors described in volume 1.

To become responsible, the criminal must repudiate his life and his image of himself in thought and action. In doing so, he suffers. *It is the endurance of such suffering that we call will.* Some criminals fail to implement the choice to become responsible, even though the choice itself is sincere. They fail because they do not want to endure the consequences of the many choices required. In fact, the phenomenon of fragmentation can be viewed as the failure to endure the consequences of their choices.

In the change process, as we shall show, endurance plays a dominant role in the early and middle stages. As the criminal continues in the program he learns the skill of endurance, or perhaps it could be better said that he achieves new degrees of endurance. As he builds a life for himself and achieves objectives responsibly, the criminal ceases to regard himself as suffering and has less and less desire for criminal excitement. Choice and will are truly complementary. A choice cannot be implemented without endurance or will. In turn, the more successful the implementation, the stronger the affirmation of the basic choice to be responsible.

In summary, our approach requires rationally formulated choices to achieve total responsibility. The choices are free (within an externally imposed framework of responsibility), but the criminal has to learn what they are. Each choice leads to other choices. Rational, responsible choices require giving up the excitements of irresponsible living. Thus, for a while, the criminal lives in a kind of no-man's-land. He must deny himself all familiar pleasures. Deprived of his previous excitements, he must function in what he has heretofore viewed as a dull, meaningless void. What has been known as will power is less the determination to see a choice through than it is the endurance of the consequences of that rational, responsible, free choice. If the criminal does not develop endurance, others may conclude that he did not have the determination to begin with. That is not necessarily true. Often, the determination is strong; but without the necessary endurance, it wanes.

BIBLIOGRAPHY

Allport, G. W. (1955). *Becoming.* New Haven: Yale University Press.

Arieti, S. (1972). *The Will to Be Human.* New York: Quadrangle.

Assagioli, R. (1973). *The Act of Will.* New York: Viking.

Bromberg, W. (1948). *Crime and the Mind.* Philadelphia: Lippincott.

Coleman, J. C. (1965). Conflicting views of man's basic nature. In *Humanistic Viewpoints in Psychology,* ed. Severin, F. T., pp. 54-60. New York: McGraw-Hill.

Durant, W. (1953). *The Story of Philosophy.* New York: Simon and Schuster.

Edwards, R. B. (1965). Agency without a substantive self. *Monist* 49:273-289.

Ellis, A. (1970). Rational-emotive therapy. In *Four Psychotherapies,* ed. Herscher, L., pp. 47-83. New York: Appleton-Century-Crofts.

Erickson, R. C. (1973). 'Free will' and clinical research. *Psychotherapy: Theory, Research and Practice* 10: 10-13.

Evening Star (6/9/71). Garbage man to Ph.D.

Farber, L. H. (1966). *The Ways of the Will.* New York: Harper.

Feldman, M. J. (1963). Queries on existential psychotherapy. *International Journal of Social Psychiatry* 9:121-126.

Frankl, V. (1965). The concept of man in logotherapy. *Journal of Existentialism* 6:53-69.

Gatch, V., and Temerlin, M. (1965). The belief in psychic determinism and the behavior of the psychotherapist. *Review of Existential Psychology and Psychiatry* 5: 16-33.

Hobbs, N. (1955). Client-centered therapy. In *Six Approaches to Psychotherapy,* ed. McCary, J. L., and Sheer, D. E., pp. 9-60. New York: Dryden.

James, W. (1950). *The Principles of Psychology,* vol. 2. New York: Dover.

Locke, J. (1952). Concerning human understanding. In *Great Books,* vol. 35, p. 181. Chicago: Britannica.

Low, A. A. (1963). *Mental Health Through Will-Training.* Boston: Christopher.

May, R. (1953). *Man's Search for Himself.* New York: Norton.

——— (1966). The emergence of existential psychology. In *Existential Psychology.* New York: Random.

———(1969). *Love and Will.* New York: Norton.

Moore, T. V. (1948). *The Driving Forces of Human Nature and Their Adjustment.* New York: Grune and Stratton.

Muelder, W.G., and Sears, L., eds. (1940). *The Development of American Philosophy.* Boston: Houghton Mifflin.

Peters, R. S. (1956). Motives and motivation. *Philosophy* 31:117-130.

Rank, O. (1950). *Will Therapy and Truth and Reality.* New York: Knopf.

Raspberry, W. (1973). Write when you get some news . . . *Washington Post,* May 9.

Ricoeur, P. (1967). Philosophy of will and action. In *Phenomenology of Will and Action,* ed. Straus, E. W., and Griffith, R. pp. 7-60. The Second Lexington Conference on Pure and Applied Phenomenology. Pittsburg: Duquesne University Press.

Rothschild, R. (1934). *Reality and Illusion.* New York: Harcourt Brace.

Royce, J. E. (1961). *Man and His Nature*. New York: McGraw-Hill.

Sartre, J. P. (1953). *Existential Psychoanalysis*. Chicago: Gateway.

Schoen, M. (1931). *Human Nature*. New York: Harper.

Schultz, D. P. (1969). *A History of Modern Psychology*. New York: Academic Press.

Schutz, W. C. (1967). *Joy*. New York: Grove.

Skinner, B. F. (1953). *Science and Human Behavior*. New York: Macmillan.

Spiegelberg, H. (1960). *The Phenomenological Movement*, vol. 1. The Hague: Martinus Nijhoff.

Stampfl, T. G., and Lewis, D. J. (1973). Implosive therapy. In *Direct Psychotherapy*, vol. 1, ed. Jurjevich, R. R., pp. 83-105. Coral Gables, Florida: University of Miami Press.

Sutherland, R. L. (1962). Choosing—as therapeutic aim, method and philosophy. *Journal of Existential Psychiatry* 2:371-393.

Temerlin, M. (1965). On choice and responsibility in humanistic psychotherapy. In *Humanistic Viewpoints in Psychology*, ed. Severin, F. T., pp. 68-69. New York: McGraw-Hill.

Vesey, G. N. A. (1961). Volition. *Philosophy* 36:352-365.

Wheelis, A. (1958). *The Quest for Identity*. New York: Norton.

Chapter 5

The Phenomenologic Approach in a Program for Basic Change of the Criminal

THIS CHAPTER DESCRIBES procedures that have provided us with the contents of the criminal's thinking. It is this material that is necessary in order to correct the errors of thinking described in chapters 4, 5, and 6 of volume 1. The errors are not correctable by using sociologic discussion or by probing the unconscious to bring out suppressed feelings or other psychologic factos thought to be causative. The thinking errors emerge as they are reported by the criminal in his account of life's experiences as soon after the experience as possible. Our examination of thinking processes has extended to the most detailed reporting in which we elicit the conscious incipient thinking and later apply correctives. We are particularly interested in the incipient thinking even if it has been eliminated temporarily by corrosion and cutoff, because it recurs and is likely to find expression later in criminal action.

Having abandoned psychologic techniques, we found it necessary to develop procedures that would provide the raw data of thinking. We discovered that by excluding interpretations and explanations, we were obtaining material that phenomenologists had insisted was the *only* material valid for consideration. Phenomenology in its broadest terms eliminates psychologic theorizing and deals directly with life's experiences that are registered in conscious awareness and are therefore reportable. We had developed our particular implementation of the phenomenologic method before we labeled our process phenomenologic. Thus we included ourselves in that group of workers who have limited their data to what has been known as phenomenology.

Modern phenomenologic psychology in clinical practice emphasizes understanding an event in terms of its multiple meanings as the individual experiences it. The major portion of the writing on technique is directed toward how the clinician reaches an understanding of his patient. In volume 1, we emphasized how crucial it is that we understand the criminal's experience by using the data of experience rather than interpretations imposed by him or us. In this volume, the emphasis is on how the criminal is trained to report his thinking so that the contents of his mind are available to the change agent in a manner that promotes understanding, although not necessarily agreement. We do not structure the criminal's experience or impose our interpretations. Rather, we provide a format whereby he can most effectively communicate that experience. Keen (1975, p. 69) has said that phenomenology as a therapeutic style "encourages the patient, quite explicitly, to focus on that same crucial nexus of how he is every day rather than directing his attention toward the provocative, but esoteric, 'realities' of traditional therapies." We believe that our phenomenologic procedure achieves this result. Before describing that procedure, we present a capsule history of the phenomenologic method.

AN HISTORICAL NOTE
ON PHENOMENOLOGY

Before describing the phenomenologic approach used in our program, we think it may be helpful to the reader to present some background on phenomenology itself, although this very limited treatment of the subject cannot do full justice to either philosophers or therapists. In 1960, Herbert Spiegelberg, a contemporary expert on phenomenology, published a two-volume work, *The Phenomenological Movement*. In 1972, he published *Phenomenology in Psychology and Psychiatry*, which provided a guide to the main phenomenologic current in those fields. Spiegelberg stated that phenomenology in the twentieth century "has influenced psychology and psychiatry more than any other movement in philosophy." Some of the practitioners included in this book did not consider themselves as phenomenologists when they did the bulk of their work, but their methodologies were in part phenomenologic. For example, Carl Rogers "took an intense interest" in his clients' descriptions of the phenomenologic world, which was "not only the main causal factor for man's behavior but was also the main point of attack for the therapeutic process" (p. 152). As Spiegelberg pointed out, although Rogers never deliberately tried to practice phenomenology, it did serve as a "methodological ally."

We have found ourselves in the same position as Rogers. We did not set out to be phenomenologic, but after failing with other procedures, we slowly developed a method that turned out to be deeply rooted in phenomenology. Thus, like Rogers and others, we found, after the fact, that we were using a method that can properly be termed "phenomenologic." For a truly authoritative history and perspective of the entire phenomenologic movement, we refer the reader to Spiegelberg's work.

To the philosopher, phenomenology refers to a process of gathering valid data by looking at mental phenomena as they appear in awareness without making judgments. Collins (1952, p. 28) acclaimed Husserl's 1913 definitive work on phenomenology as "the outstanding philosophical event of the years just preceding World War I." Husserl suggested that a phenomenologic psychology was needed to "fill the gap between philosophy and the best psychology of the day" (Spiegelberg 1960). The emphasis was limited to the mental data as they are experienced. Consciously experienced thoughts were of prime importance. Husserl (1931, p. 111) called for experience to be "set in brackets, untested but also uncontested." In other words, what was to be valued was naive observation, as opposed to "unclarified notions, unexamined assumptions, and loose argumentation" (Collins, p. 28). Spiegelberg (1972, p. 13) observed that although Husserl, with his "science of intentional consciousness," had provided direction for the future, there was still little *specific* application of phenomenoogy to psychology.

In the late nineteenth century and the first quarter of the twentieth century, Brentano emphasized "descriptive," rather than "genetic," psychology. He maintained that any causal study of psychologic phenomena was useless until the psychologist "clarified and described what it was he wanted to explain" (Spiegelberg 1960, p. 38). With this emphasis, psychology became an "autonomous enterprise," no longer "taking its cue from the other natural sciences." Brentano expressed his emphasis on description before explanation when he said that there is

> no hearing without something heard, no believing without something believed, no hoping without something hoped, no striving without something striven for, no joy without something we feel joyous about. (Spiegelberg 1960, p. 41)

As Lonergan (1956) put it, phenomenology per se is a "highly purified empiricism" that one cannot do much with because it only provides data. Spiegelberg (1972) pointed out that the philosophers had little direct influence on psychology and psychiatry. They had not instructed psychologists "to carry out specific research or suggest fruitful areas for study."

Phenomenology became useful as it was employed to obtain the broadest possible perspective in the study of man. It was seen as humanizing psychology, in that it generated an investigation of the whole person (Giorgi 1965). Writing in the first half of the twentieth century, Jaspers described the phenomenologic method as a device to obtain the most complete and careful description of what is experienced in the minds of both the healthy and the sick. Thus, Jaspers has been called the "Brentano of phenomenological psychopathology" (Spiegelberg 1972, p. 191). Phenomenology became an aid in the psychiatrist's effort to gain a more intimate understanding of the experience of his patient—to enter more fully into the patient's existence. The method was effective, because it relied on the "unbiased contemplation of phenomena" (Ellenberger 1958). Value judgments, causation, background, and other intellectual considerations were to be set aside.

Existential psychotherapy and existential analysis (Daseinsanalysis) emphasized first the acquisition of suitable data of experience. The therapist then derives issues of "meaning" to assist the patient to get his bearings in the world. As we pointed out in the historical overview of existentialism in chapter 2, some existential concepts are applied to psychotherapy without recourse to phenomenology or psychoanalysis. According to Spiegelberg (1972, p. 158), Rollo May is perhaps "the most influential native American spokesman for an existential phenomenology." For May, phenomenology (which preceded existentialism) has the task of "bridging the gap between theory and psychotherapy while also providing a new basis for the best insights in Freudian psychoanalysis through a better understanding of the fundamental nature of man, transference, and the unconscious" (Spiegelberg, p. 158). Thus, for May, phenomenology is not the central procedure or primary tool. It offers one way of getting data to be used in a basically analytic enterprise.

In his logotherapy, Frankl (1967) has claimed to be making a phenomenologic investigation.

> Our task is to resort to a phenomenological investigation of the immediate data of actual life experience. In a phenomenological way, the logotherapist might widen and broaden the visual field of his patients in terms of meanings and values, making them loom large, as it were. (p. 14).

Frankl circumscribes areas in which his patients need help. He seeks the "immediate data" with respect to these. In selecting particular issues on which to work, he tries to help a patient find or rediscover meaning in life. Like Rogers, May, and others, Frankl has not been interested in phenomenology for its own sake. Rather, as Spiegelberg (1972, pp. 352, 353) pointed out, Frankl "consulted it in reaching his conclusions" and has used it in his work as a "minor auxiliary."

The Daseinsanalysts (Boss 1963) maintain that their work is based on phenomenology and that they work with phenomenologic methods.* However, their method of data collection is the same as that of the psychoanalyst; the basic rule of free association is followed. The existential analyst points out that although he uses psychoanalytic methods, he is not

---

*The literal translation of "daseins" is "to be (sein) there (da)," but its popular translation, according to Boss (1963, p. 2) is "existence."

bound by psychoanalytic theory. It does appear that although he uses data somewhat different from Frankl's, to a great extent he shares Frankl's objectives. The existential analysts use biographic investigation. They retrieve material from the past and treat it as data presently at hand. They pool material from early experience with present material and then regard all of it as material to be worked out in the here and now. These practitioners do not stick to the natural phenomenologic data of the here and now.

In summary, we can say that the contribution of phenomenology to psychiatry and psychology is that it has helped in getting away from preconceptions, interpretations, and assumptions. By looking at the "untested but also uncontested" data of experience, the clinician understands his patient better. Spiegelberg (1972) put it this way:

Phenomenology is not afraid of variety. As such it has not only encouraged and supported the exploration of neglected and overlooked phenomena but has actively participated in spotting them. (p. 362)

Spiegelberg (1972) has described the quickness, in the historical stream, of professionals to embrace phenomenology and existentialism. In our study, only after we developed a procedure did we realize that it was phenomenologic. Out of necessity, we had arrived at a method that fits the requirements of phenomenology—an emphasis on the data of personal experience and on description rather than explanation. We have adhered faithfully to the facts of experience here and now, and have distinguished this from experiences in the past. Nowhere else have we found others adhering to the raw data that Husserl emphasized as the authentic data for further study.

AN OPERATIONAL PHENOMENOLOGIC
APPROACH WITH THE CRIMINAL

We have gone to unusual lengths to elicit all the criminal's thinking in detail, because we have found that the irresponsible thought of today often turns out to be the irresponsible act, or crime, of tomorrow. It has turned out that criminal thinking *not* immediately followed by crime is as important as criminal thinking that is immediately implemented. In other words, incipient criminal ideas more frequently than not result in crime. An extreme case of this is a criminal who recurrently thought about counterfeiting. As a child, he started using tracing paper to copy money; fifteen years later, he made plates and launched a counterfeiting operation. All crimes have had their origins in thinking that has recurred and been initially deterred (see chapter 6 of volume 1). By eliciting the details of thinking, we teach the criminal an elaborate set of deterrents, so that criminal thinking patterns are eventually totally eliminated. We have found that the only opportunity to effect change is through the procedure for reporting that we have developed.

In chapter 1 of volume 1, we described how we began with traditional methods of reporting and failed. Having a criminal talk about how things are going or give his free associations during a session did not permit us to probe the thinking processes that had adverse consequences for the criminal and society. One criminal made the following statement about his thinking:

> "There hasn't been a day in my life that I haven't had to deter homicide and suicide for the last fifteen years. I've had thoughts of homicide and suicide at the same time."

He then described his thoughts of wiring himself with dynamite and entering the U.S. Senate chambers, grabbing a gun, and shooting. He also described his thoughts about shooting everyone at the hotel where he worked. Such information is not volunteered readily. An agent of change who lacks the techniques to tap this thinking misses a crucial datum of experience.

Most of our early work was done with men who were in confinement for the greater part of the day. They would come in and say, "Nothing happened." However, we knew that their minds were extremely busy during the entire period. The objective was to find out what the stream of thinking was. In 1966, we reached a point at which we thought that it might be helpful to have the criminal report every thought that had passed through his mind. We sought to elicit the complete contents of mind without limiting the data. Increasingly, we stuck to the here and now, rather than probed past experiences or searched for causes. We worked eclectically, focusing on the criminal's ongoing thinking to discover errors. At the time, we did not label this "phenomenologic reporting."

As a result of our gradual shift in procedure, new vistas opened in terms of available material. In fact, the phenomenologic approach permitted us to derive much of the material in volume 1. By having the criminal observe his own thinking and report the full range of that thinking, we saw the colliding desires and choices, the contradictions, the thinking errors, and the way of making decisions. Later in our work, we realized that a truly phenomenologic approach had evolved. The information of value was the raw data of his thinking. During the selection process, the criminal was informed that this very detailed reporting was essential for participation and progress in our program. We had a surfeit of experience in which the criminal failed to report what later was to result in criminal activity. If he had something in mind from which he did not want to be deterred, he closed the channel. In addition, anything that he thought would betray weakness, lower our opinion of him, or deflate his own self-image was unlikely to be revealed. We knew that, if change were to take place, the criminal should not be the one to decide what information was important or relevant. Thus, we required that he report the total contents of his mind, so that we could learn how he thinks and apply corrective measures.

The criminal has to be *trained* in reporting. It is, at the beginning, automatic for him to engage in circumvention, circumlocution ("rounding" or "gaming" in his language), withholding, and in other ways presenting only what furthers his own objectives. Now, he has to habituate the self-discipline of conscientiously supplying the raw data of thought and action. What we require is analogous to a computer printout of his thinking. Such a printout reveals, to a knowledgeable authority, the criminal's characteristic thinking errors and tactics. It gives data to the agent of change and thus provides a field in which to alter thinking patterns. When the raw data of mental experience are brought out, the criminal's excuses for being the way he is fall by the wayside. With the printout, the criminal can see the cutoff of fear, scheming, lack of endurance, and failure to plan for the long term.

The criminal learns that we expect reporting without reservation, addition, subtraction, or interpretive slant. We teach him to present the raw data of thinking, without forcing it into his own prejudgments and conclusions about what we want (even though we want to know what those prejudgments, opinions, and conclusions are *as they occur* in his thinking). Instruction in phenomenologic reporting occurs each day, from the time the criminal enters the program. We do not lecture the criminal on phenomenology, nor do we even use the term *phenomenologic reporting* with him. In conversation with him, we speak simply of his "report." We use the criminal's daily experience to teach this kind of reporting. When he gives his reports early in the program, we evaluate them for completeness and attention to detail. We ask questions to elicit more material. Virtually anything that he reports reveals characteristic thinking errors. At first, the criminal is astonished at material that is brought out and how we use it. Later, when complete reporting is habitual, we continue to provide the commentary, but we do not have to struggle with him to bring out all the data. His brevity of reporting does not necessarily indicate an attempt at deliberate concealment, but instead a lack of knowledge and skill as to what this kind of reporting entails. When the criminal implements what he learns, the concept of the wide-open channel becomes clear—total disclosure, receptivity, and self-criticism. The criminal learns to be self-critical by being receptive to, and then applying to himself, our criticisms of him.

In looking at the criminal's report of twenty-four hours of thinking, we are selective in the data we attend to and develop. The thinking that is relevant to change bears on the themes developed in volume 1—fear, anger, building oneself up, failure to trust, and deferment. The kind of thinking that is not relevant includes the minor details of a day, such as whether he buys a

Rachmaninoff or Rolling Stones album (although we might question whether, on his budget, he should buy records at all) and whether he chooses lemon pie or apple pie.

The criminal makes daily notes of the previous twenty-four hours' thought and acting. These notes, which are brought to the sessions, provide the substance of the report. Writing such notes accomplishes more than a reminder, however. Notes are a tool in the change process. The mere process of writing them requires self-monitoring and self-criticism. They help to keep the criminal alert to criminal thinking, which makes deterrence easier. Without notes, the reporting is largely in terms of actions and the specific thoughts that bear on them; we do not get the stray thoughts, recurrent ideas, inner debates, and incipient criminal ideas. Without the raw data of thinking in fine detail, we miss opportunities for teaching. One criminal who had participated in our program at a time when notes were not required was surprised later to find out how much they helped him in deterring criminal thinking. The practice of writing them made him scrutinize his current thinking and long-range objectives much more carefully. He commented, "The more I write, the more progress I make." All have found the notes valuable. The absence of notes indicates a lack of self-monitoring and consequently a lack of implementation of the program.

Early in the program, a report brings forth a tremendous amount of criminal thinking.

> On Monday, C reported thinking and action from Friday afternoon to Monday morning. C reported thinking about eloping and living with the former girlfriend of another criminal. In his mind, he saw her, introduced himself, misrepresented who he was, charmed her, and moved in. After thinking about this, a stream of criminal thinking was unleashed, which included kidnapping, bank robbery, and rape. Later, in watching a basketball game, he thought about how he would have dealt with a highly contested situation—namely, by firing the coach. He described watching the legs of the cheerleaders. During the weekend, there was thinking about eloping from the institution. This did not occur at the time, but he had escaped before. The thinking this time was soon followed by unauthorized leave from the grounds and later by a stream of irresponsible behavior.

This was only a small part of C's very complete report for one day. To give an example of a more detailed written report, we present a criminal's writeup of his thinking and action in one situation.

> "Went out and had dinner at a restaurant—had steak and potatoes, etc. $1.95. Very good. Saw very attractive, young girl of foreign descent, approximately 19 or 20 years of age—immediately decided to pursue and

capture—made no opening gambit—merely ascertained her age from the waiter—will find out her name directly on next visit—it is legal so far and will try not to be irresponsible in this regards but I am definitely seeking a sexual partner and she would do quite nicely—judging from outward appearance—we shall see—will have to be very discreet and use finesse as the people of her culture on the average are very moral and protective in regards to young female offspring and I doubt if they would approve of anything even resembling irresponsibility with an uncouth American bum [by his standards]. A major factor here that is unknown at this point, is the girl, and she may have an emotional commitment elsewhere already and also simply may not be attracted to me—I have plan B—which is Linda, young white female American, who is a waitress in same restaurant appears to be accessible—we shall see—It is hard to cultivate two females at the same time in the same locale, without showing your hand—guard against it with any female—also interesting to note that I went to the restaurant for the purpose of seducing Linda, but changed my choice after viewing this flower, whom I had not seen on my first visit . . . when I first spotted Linda and made a mental note of the fact—I am truly a predator and an animal with a considerable degree of cunning and guile—I am not happy with this fact and I shall have to be honest as I possibly can with everybody—realizing that honesty and 'confession' is another technique of mine to gain ingress to a person's psyche and there I start manipulating to gain control."

C did not pursue either of the women at the time. His thinking about "cultivating" females and "manipulating to gain control," however, was soon enacted elsewhere, a felony being committed in the process. With our earlier procedures, the details of this thinking would have been missed. The criminal would simply have noted that he had dinner at the restaurant and left it at that. Here, we had the incipient thinking to work with. We obviously were not successful, because the criminal wanted to go his own way more than he wanted to be in this program. However, in most cases, we can take a single episode and spend many sessions on relevant deterrent considerations, such as injury to others, power and control, and many of the other topics treated in volume 1. Although C did not remain in the program long enough to learn and implement new thinking patterns sufficiently (which would have had a significant, lasting deterrent effect), in the brief course of his participation, a number of crimes were deterred. An excerpt from notes made by the same criminal shows the course of criminal thinking and the response to temptation at a time when he was implementing a part of the program.

"Work went well. I decided to be not tempted on viewing objects, property or people. Waiter offered me shot of booze with my o.j. [orange juice]. Refused on grounds it was not vodka—which shows how ethically particular I am about what I drink—not that I also considered it as a violation—I did—but I may? have accepted if the situation were safe. I embellished my reporting which is a nice euphemistic way of saying I am a lousy 2-bit liar at the click of a pen or any opportunity—went to [tavern] 2 beers ($2.66) went home—arrived 1:40—changed clothes took mace and razor [for self-protection] and went to get food. . . . half drunk—got home and bed at 4:40. . . . Work went well—had anger at ——— about housekeeping report—wanted to 'knock the back caps off his teeth' thought it through and reasoned it out and anger disappeared plus I realized I wouldn't be doing housekeeping report much longer—and there would always be something disagreeable about any job. Took it easy at work but was vigilant not to goof off. . . . Went to ——— and had one vodka and juice and salt and one beer. Watched topless girls do their thing—observed incident. Talked with guy, lied about my job. . . . [It was] a real temptation at work to cop wallet with I.D. account. . . . found Playboy, confiscated and took it home, read Playboy till 3 a.m."

These were among notes quickly jotted down on a three-by-five pad. They provided the basis for a full morning's meeting that had mainly to do with specific methods of deterring violation and irresponsibility and a wide range of other considerations.

We do not deliberately bring up the past to explain what is happening now. Long ago, we discovered that asking why yields only self-serving rationalizations and other forms of accountability thinking. It is not productive of clarification and new learning. If, however, in the course of a day's thinking the criminal thinks about past events, these are immediate valid data. In the excerpted interview above, the criminal recalled previous attempts on his part to conquer and exploit women. Thus, rather than going on a fishing expedition for causative factors, we get the criminal's report of his stream of consecutive thoughts, which contain considerations of past and future as they relate to present experience. As the criminal changes, there is a greater tendency for him to reflect on the past and to apply what he learns to the present and future.

It could be argued that ours is not a *pure* phenomenologic approach, in that we emphasize patterns inherent in individual thoughts, thought sequences, and experiences. We may view a thought sequence as a manifestation of a power-thrusting pattern. Phenomenologically, the criminal does not report the experience of being a big shot or something comparable. However, it is apparent to us that power is a component of what he has reported. Habituation eliminates some components from the report. This does not mean that they are relegated to the unconscious. Driving a car is analogous. This is done by rote, but it involves a series of maneuvers that the driver does not think about; they are automatic. A report might include thoughts about surmounting traffic jams en route to a destination, but not thoughts about the habitual features of accelerating, braking, signaling, and steering. In the criminal's report, a single thought invariably turns out to be a manifestation of a pattern, not an isolated instance. The pattern (usually formulated in our terms) resides within the thought, thought sequence, or act, even if it is not experienced by the criminal. Thus, we do depart from pure phenomenology. It is not the thought itself that is important, but the broader criminal thinking pattern.

Phenomenologic reporting permits us to elicit intention, purpose, and objective as they occur in thinking. We do not take an outcome or consequence of behavior and then impute intention. That is, we do not try to explain an effect by attributing a cause after the fact.

C was angry at his wife for asking him to repair something in the house. He was also angry that she did not fix him what he wanted for dinner. Enraged, he threw a bottle of syrup through a window. In a session with us, another criminal, listening to C's report, observed that C's intention had been to intimidate his wife. C replied that there had been no such intention in his thinking. In fact, in his state of mind, he would have thrown something even if she had not been there.

C's behavior did intimidate his wife, but he had behaved in similar fashion many times before with others. Had the focus of the meeting been intimidation, we would have neglected the central issue, which was the power thrust and its components. The problem was C, and not the relationship between C and his wife. The phenomenologic approach led us to the putdown-anger-violence pattern rather than to a discussion of C's relationship with his wife, toward whom he was actually very tender in a fragmented way. Viewing the consequences of C's behavior as the central problem would have led to consideration of a totally different set of factors and diverted us from the basic criminal pattern. Looking at consequences and imputing causation limits the areas for change. Probing ongoing thinking opens up many important considerations. For example, phenomenologic reporting has brought out premeditation in crimes that appeared to have been committed on impulse.

At this point, the difference between free association and our procedure of phenomenologic reporting should be clear. In earlier work with this population, we found that, by encouraging the criminal to say whatever came to mind, we were being diverted from relevant material to self-serving material, which is the criminal's stock in trade. What was required was organized and straightforward reporting of the previous twenty-four hours' mental experiences, so that we could dissect ongoing mental processes and have them as a basis for new teaching and implementation.

Of course, in any one report, there is too much material to be handled in a single session (even one that lasts for three hours). To deal most effectively with twenty-four hours of thoughts, actions, and afterthoughts, we must select what we think is important, rather than leave it to the unchanged criminal to make that determination. We choose a focus from all the data of the phenomenologic report. We bring out and highlight features that the criminal often finds unpalatable or regards as insignificant. Criminals are astonished when we select a passing thought and develop it into a theme for the entire meeting.

> C reported fleeting anger toward his father, who disapproved of C's allowing his friend Eric to drive an old broken down car belonging to C's family.

> We spent considerable time on this anger fragment. Upon inquiry, we determined that the car had been bought from an estate sale and had no title. Second, the car was uninsured and had not been inspected. Third, Eric's license was not valid, and finally, C wanted to allow Eric, a frequent drug user, to have free access to the car. The consequences were obvious if there were an accident involving a car with no title or insurance and driven by a person with an invalid license. None of these considerations entered C's mind as he thought about his father's attitude toward Eric's driving the automobile. Neither C nor other members of the group were used to thinking in such terms.

We belabored a passing thought with the objective of making a general point about how the criminal assesses situations and makes decisions in life. There was no psychologizing about C's anger and whether it was justified by the facts of the situation.

We use the phenomenologic report to point out specific thinking processes that must be altered. To begin, we get all the details of both thinking and action. No detail or drifting of the mind during a day is too trivial. We then focus on a specific incident or thought and identify the error. We say "the error" as if there were only one; in fact, it is one of many. For teaching purposes, we select one error at a time, although we may cover several errors in a session. We show that the selected error is a manifestation of a broad *pattern* in the criminal's life that constantly occurs in his thinking and action. We introduce and generalize corrective concepts which the criminal can apply not only in comparable situations but in all situations. It is easy to anticipate events that will call for application of the new concepts in the future. Each new concept then is discussed in a more general context—a philosophic overview of a changed life that the criminal must evolve.

If we did not use the phenomenologic approach but had to depend on what the criminal thought was worth discussing, the endeavor at change would be altogether futile. Starting from the details of the twenty-four-hour report, we move on to a generalization and conceptualization of his character in relation to the noncriminal, the social world as it is, and finally the crucial issue of the nature of existence and responsible reality. It is in this overview that we become involved in issues of meaning that concern the existential psychotherapists. Of course, one cannot present this new *Weltanschauung*, unless one begins with the criminal's concrete data of experience. Without the phenomenologic report as a base, talking about a new philosophy of life is as effective as preaching a sermon to the criminal.

In the beginning phase of our work with the criminal, we do not get much meat, in the sense of a detailed report of thinking. It is not only because the criminal is not trained in this, but also because he is busy digging himself out of holes that he has created in the past. It is when such problems are eliminated that we begin to get at the substance of the ongoing processes. Another phase in which there is a dearth of material with respect to thinking occurs when a criminal is well along in the program but still resides in confinement. When he encounters the same circumstances day after day and is contending with them responsibly, his reporting becomes sparse. With greater freedom, more of the criminal's unchanged thinking is exposed. Because the criminal has many new life situations to face, the reports become longer and more detailed. More errors are revealed that provide us with numerous opportunities for correction. In chapter 10, we shall discuss how a reduction in confinement usually results in more violation.

In the later stages of change, the reporting is often so complete that there are far too many details about responsible considerations to cover. Nevertheless, our practice is to encourage as complete a report as is possible within the time constraints of the session. It is better to tell all than to determine in advance what has merit, because it is precisely some of the things that the criminal may discard that the agent of change finds highly significant.

Criminals have developed three formats of reporting. They may report events and thinking chronologically. They may decide to report thematically, grouping material under such headings as *family, work,* and *criminal thinking*. Or they may present events, actions, and conversations as they occurred, and then express the thinking that attended each. We accept any of these methods of reporting, as long as the important thinking is brought out. Whichever format is used, we explore in detail the thinking relative to the program's new set of requirements for living.

A condensation in procedure is necessary when the agent meets with the criminal on a weekly basis. Only a limited amount of what has happened can be covered, so the contents of mind are subjected to a process of filtration to bring out what is most significant. Notes are still required. At this stage, the criminal has a self-critical attitude. He is unlikely to close the channel, because he now very much wants to improve his own functioning. The report is still indispensable for bringing out concrete details of thinking, but now in a more circumscribed manner.

There are times at which the report is devoid of criminal thinking or uncertainty about decisions to be made. We then review some aspect of the report and show its ramifications now and in the future. In other words, our major input is to develop additional material for discussion. If the criminal has handled a situation responsibly in thinking and action, we may review the factors that contributed to a responsible solution. We bring in the past to review old patterns and consider what still needs to be done to correct thinking errors. We also discuss what could go awry in a comparable situation and how the criminal might respond. There is a constant emphasis on preparing the criminal to deal with obstructions and adversities that may arise. The following edited excerpts from dictations of two of our meetings with a criminal show this process. C had been in the program for about two months. We recognize that, at this point, the reader may not fully understand the outcome toward which the approach is directed.

C decided to watch television. It was a film about two fellows, one black and one white, who set sail around the world with no cares—the ocean and faraway places, an escape from the "mundane" (a term C uses frequently). He did not talk about the substance of the film which was the personal relationship between these two fellows that ended in the possibility of homicide. There were problems, to be sure, but C wasn't thinking about that aspect. He was thinking about the escape from the mundane. In this state of mind, his thinking turned to homosexuality with a partner. The thinking rapidly changed and he thought of the excitement of past associations, but also about their dangers. Then his thinking turned to viewing himself as a homosexual, which at this time was offensive to him.

C remembered a cross-country trip to California with two fellows with whom there was no homosexuality. Again, he had no responsibility, no concerns, no thoughts for the fact that they were spending his parents' money, and that they were drifting. In fact, he recalled that they had a setup of a pipe with a brew of hashish, which could be passed from one to another. Again, there was nostalgic excitement. C caught himself at this point and asked, "Where is this leading me?" There was a reversal of thinking for a brief period, but that passed. And then there was excitement as he thought of his first injection of Methedrine, which had given him one of the most striking drug experiences he has had.

Then came another kind of thinking. It was the vascillation of debate. C summarized all this and said that on the one hand, he had pleasurable thoughts of being out of the responsible world, but on the other hand, he considered the pleasure of being a part of society. In this state of alternating thoughts, he fell asleep. When he awoke this morning, his first thinking was, "Here we go again—problems." Then he thought about how to avoid, rather than face, difficulties. At this time, the temptation of escape through drugs entered his mind.

At this time, I as the A.C. had a choice to make. We had covered the point about the fragmentation of thinking: that doesn't help C, but it helps us. But how could we be of value after this presentation? I elected, because of the limitation of time, to go from the specific to the general and to talk of the larger dimensions of the meaning of life itself—the quality of existence, the choice of responsibility or crime. It unfolded that a responsible way of life has its rewards, which are certainly not those of being a big shot, getting medals, or being a hero. It is simply acting responsibly, hoping to advance as far as possible in domestic, social, economic, and communal aspects of life. There is no limit to where one can go, provided that he is responsible. The comparison of what has happened to C as a criminal and to others was brought out sharply. . . .

I continued this subject the next day. I went into the details of his escape thinking. It is obvious that, when C thought of his past drug experiences, past travels—when he thought of the criminal solution to the boredom— he talked about escape as a sense of relief from mundane problems. . . .

How do we in the responsible world view him and view ourselves? We don't even see that there are problems in the mundane. We take them for granted. We are confronted with a swarm of problems everyday— insulating a house, having an auto repaired, getting rid of a painter. . . . We see the criminal like C gambling, stealing, failing in school. We see the problems that he is producing for himself and others. We see the injuries.

But everything that the criminal does in his escape from the mundane is producing a host of problems within himself . . . when he fails, is exposed, or is arrested. These problems are ever-present, and he has got to see them. Let us take, for example, the TV show that he saw of a black and a white traveling around the world. . . . It did involve an interrelationship between two fellows that almost ended in murder. It was a struggle all the way. They were struggling with each other, not with the "mundane." C could view it only as escaping from the mundane, and actually he did not emphasize that one almost killed the other. What I'm trying to bring out is that there's no such thing as problemlessness. The problems are there. For the criminal, there is an enormous amount of getting himself into and out of jams. For the responsible person, there are different kinds of problems. But C talks only about escape to a life without problems.

What we have to do is to get into the details of his escape thinking: how escaping compounds rather than solves problems.

We took C's viewing a film on TV and elicited all his thinking. Then, we explored with C the multiple problems that had emerged in his life when he attempted to escape from responsibility. That produced an opportunity to discuss with him the fact that escape only causes the very difficulties that he was in the program to eliminate. That ultimately took us into a discussion of effort, endurance, and the totality of life's struggles. The major theme could have been approached in many ways; in fact, it was, inasmuch as it continued to arise in later sessions. Many situations occurred in which C had to choose between acting responsibly and escaping, which meant seeking criminal excitement. In later chapters, we shall develop further how in our day-to-day work we go from the concrete to the general to the abstract.

In summary, we work with the raw data of thinking. We extract thinking errors, establishing the fact that each error is a part of a broader criminal pattern. We teach the criminal new correctives, responsible thinking patterns here and now, and prepare him for future situations. He learns not only to deter current criminal thinking, but to anticipate what is to come and to preempt that thinking from even occurring. With phenomenologic reporting, it is possible today to correct thinking errors that otherwise will result in crimes tomorrow. As the criminal implements the program, we watch his reports change from thoughts of criminal solutions for problems to thoughts of responsible ones.

This chapter describes only the procedure for obtaining the raw data of thinking. It does not describe the difficulties inherent in the change process. The specific corrective procedures and how the criminal implements them will be presented later.

BIBLIOGRAPHY

Boss, M. (1963). *Psychoanalysis and Daseinsanalysis.* New York: Basic Books.
Collins, J. (1952). *The Existentialists.* Chicago: Henry Regnery.

Ellenberger, H. F. (1958). A clinical introduction to psychiatric phenomenology and existential analysis. In *Existence: A New Dimension in Psychiatry and Psychology,* ed. May, R., et al., pp. 92-127. New York: Basic Books.

Fankl, V. E. (1967). *Psychotherapy and Existentialism.* New York: Washington Square.

Giorgi, A. (1965). Phenomenology and experimental psychology. *Review of Existential Psychology and Psychiatry* 5: 228-238.

Husserl, E. (1931). *Ideas: General Introduction to Pure Phenomenology.* New York: Macmillan.

Keen, E. (1975). *A Primer for Phenomenological Psychology.* New York: Holt, Rinehart and Winston.

Lonergan, B. J. F. (1956). *Insight: A Study of Human Understanding.* New York: Philosophical Library.

Spiegelberg, H. (1960). *The Phenomenological Movement,* vol. 1. The Hague: Martinus Nijhoff.

———(1972). *Phenomenology in Psychology and Psychiatry.* Evanston, Illinois: Northwestern University Press.

Chapter 6

The Group Format

MANY FORMS OF GROUP THERAPY such as the therapeutic community, psychodrama, encounter and sensitivity groups have been used successfully with noncriminals. They have also been used with criminals (see chapter 2). We shall describe later (chapter 11) how criminals have exploited these various treatment formats, not to become responsible citizens but to their own advantage. What has been effective with the noncriminal has failed to achieve significant, lasting change with the criminal.

To avert the chaos and anarchy that many people who work with criminals regularly experience, it is necessary to have a well-organized, disciplined format. Gradually, over the years, we have developed such a format, creating a curriculum and an agenda for group instruction. Group work offers a greater number of criminals the opportunity to participate in the program and gives the participants not only the opportunity to learn from one another's experience but also to see that each commits the same errors as the others. Group work also provides an arena in which change can be directly observed by the A.C. (agent of change).

Before he participates in a group, the criminal has had substantial exposure to the A.C. In one-to-one individual meetings, he has been faced directly with the A.C.'s view of his criminal personality and with the presentation of a set of exacting requirements for participation in the program. By the time he is ready to enter a group, the criminal knows that the change agent is thoroughly aware of the fabric of the criminal mind and has specific procedures to effect change. The criminal learned in the initial contact that the approach was very different, and he is aware that the group experience also promises to be very different from anything that he has encountered before. He realizes that he is not being allowed to set conditions or revise the format of the program to suit his own purposes.

The criminal enters a group with three to five other participants. Attendance in this group every weekday is part of a disciplined life in which time is programmed. A criminal is rarely excused from a meeting, and then only for an extraordinary reason, such as a family emergency. The group meets for three hours a day, five days a week, for at least a year. The composition of this group will change as criminals progress and leave the intensive program for a less intensive contact with the A.C. Criminals occasionally return to a group meeting to assess their further progress in the presence of others, including some of their fellow group members. The same format may be used in such a follow-up group, meeting once or twice a week.

Each session begins with the phenomenologic report, organized chronologically, thematically, or in a sequence with acts followed by attendant thinking (as explained in chapter 5). The order of presentation is rotated among group members. This sequence is altered when there is a crisis in that a criminal with a crisis will report first. The more criminals in the group, the less time is available for each member to report. Under these circumstances, each criminal presents only a part of his report or some members defer their presentation and are the first to report the next day.

Two different patterns have been followed in developing the material from the reports. In some cases, the A.C. and the group members listen to an entire report from start to finish. More commonly, the A.C. asks for comments and raises issues about each part in turn. Often, a report is not completed, and the A.C. checks to see whether all the major issues were discussed. If not, material is held over to the next meeting. A note is dictated on each report, and it is always available to the criminal. If the material is especially important, it is dictated in front of the group.

During a meeting, the criminal not only thinks about what he has reported earlier but also listens intently to the reports of others in the group. He considers how in the past he has dealt with situations similar to theirs and learns how a responsible person functions. After the meeting, he takes an inventory of his criminal patterns and contrasts them with the new responsible patterns that have been presented to him and discussed in the group. He is amazed at the discrepancy between his and others' thinking and action. At the next day's meeting, he begins his report with a review of his thinking about what he learned the day before. This is a relatively recent addition to our format. It indicates whether homework has been done between meetings. Indeed, thinking about and reporting the relevance of the previous day's meeting to his own life show that change is occurring.

Each criminal is required to state what he has learned from the daily reports of the others. He may raise further questions and seek clarification, point out thinking errors, suggest corrections, or comment on the adequacy and completeness of the reporting. If a decision is being made, others in the group contribute by raising questions about the effectiveness of the decision-making process or by suggesting additional options for consideration. The A.C. does not seek a criminal's advice and criticism of others as much as he expects each criminal to indicate how the issues raised in the report apply to himself. The question asked of each criminal is What did you learn? In time, it becomes routine for the criminal to apply to himself what others reveal about their lives, past and present. The experience of one corresponds to the experiences of other group members, even though the details of a specific situation are peculiar to the one reporting. Because criminals all have the same patterns of thinking (described in volume 1), the report of one is a mirror for all. A new group member often sees the reports of others as reflecting only their problems, and not at all relevant to his. This initial attitude is vigorously dealt with by demonstrating that concrete experiences are exemplary of general patterns common to all criminals.

It is important to emphasize that our group format does not utilize the techniques of encounter or confrontation. Instead of verbal attack, ventilation of feelings, or heated confrontation, our program stresses a thoughtful, rational approach to identifying thinking errors and replacing them with responsible reasoning. The agent of change conducts himself with firmness and, occasionally, intensity, but never with anger. The criminal is taught this same conduct to deal with situations in which confrontation is imposed on him by others outside the group.

As we have indicated, the direction of the discussion in this program is not up for grabs. The time is too precious and the task too important not to make every moment count. The A.C.'s job is to identify and correct the criminal's thinking errors. In every experience described in the phenomenologic report, many errors are often evident to the A.C. Time does not allow the extraction of every error from every experience of every criminal, so the A.C. focuses on those he thinks most important. A specific error is identified, and its repercussions in other situations are discussed. This means moving from the details of a concrete experience to formulation of some general principles. We go beyond this to more abstract considerations—such as what the implications of the thinking errors are in dealing with one's fellow man.

C was describing business at a store that he was charged with closing each evening. Business was not good on a particular Thursday, so he closed a little early. C was in the rear of the store, working on some accounts. No one else was around. A woman knocked at the front door. C did not answer, but the rapping continued. He went out and told her that the store was closed. She had wanted to purchase cigarettes. He shut the door and then heard rocks being thrown at a screen on the side of the store. C went outside and found that the woman was drunk. Her young boy was throwing the stones. C asked her to tell the youngster to stop. She insisted on the cigarettes. C was angry, because stones were being thrown and because she was wasting his time. He returned to the back of the store and heard a loud crash. The boy had hurled a stone through a $125 window. C physically detained the woman, but she was so drunk that she began to make a pass at him. C told her that she must pay. Soon, two men who knew the woman came running over, wanting to know what was going on. They saw him trying to ward off her advances and saw the broken window. C explained to them what had happened, and they promised to take care of it.

As C reported this situation, he brought out the fact that he had been angry. He realized that the best thing to have done would have been to sell the woman cigarettes and get rid of her. But, in an angry state, he had yielded to no one. The consequences were a broken window and much inconvenience. Another option would have been to call the police before things went as far as they did. In his anger, he took no constructive steps whatsoever.* In the group meeting, the A.C. and other group members generalized from this situation to the broader issue of how to deal with people who are irresponsible and threatening. The discussion was then turned to a view of life—what one expects from other people, what responsible self-interest requires in this world, what is worth protecting and standing up for. This is the kind of discussion that evolves out of the criminal's reporting a single incident. There is no imputing of motives or other form of purely speculative psychologizing. These are viewed as diversionary. We are openly critical of attempts at psychologizing.

The other group members are asked to contribute to the discussion in terms of comparable incidents and problems that they have faced. Implementation of the program requires factfinding, increasing the range of options considered, and precludes prejudgments. Thus, the A.C. invites the criminal to raise issues along these lines.

We do not comment on nor forbid the use of street language and profanity. Because we do not use either, criminals in the group tend not to. A new member quickly realizes this and conforms. It is not that the criminal identifies with the A.C., but rather that he is accommodating himself in so many ways to fulfill the program's requirements that when he sees that the meetings are being conducted in a particular style, refraining from street language or profanity poses no difficulty. At first, he restrains himself, and

*The reader may not see much reason to fault C for the way he reacted. However, the anger shown in this situation was a manifestation of a behavior pattern that later wound up in his shooting a suspicious looking person who entered his store.

then profanity and street language drop out, not only from usage in the group, but elsewhere.* This is reflection of the fact that the format of these meetings is more like that of a disciplined school than that of a free-expression group.

The main function of the group is not advice-giving. Some unchanged criminals are all too ready to do this and present themselves as experts in the process. This is indicative of their pattern outside. On the other hand, some new members who may be verbal outside are silent in the group. The requirements of the group format, however, elicit participation by the latter, and their verbalizations are evaluated for relevance to the issues. Both types of group members are expected to contribute to discussions as others in the group present their reports.

Criminals see each other outside the hours of the group meetings. In the early days of our work, they lived in the same facilities in the hospital. Now, when we work with criminals not in confinement, they still eat together, ride together to and from meetings, and in some cases work at the same place. The issue quickly arises in a group as to whether one ought to snitch, or inform, on another member. Our position is that to withhold any of one's thinking, regardless of whom it concerns, violates the wide-open channel. We require each group member, in his report, to disclose his every observation and thought about other group members. Failure to do this indicates insufficient participation in the group and is taken seriously. We regard this kind of reporting as essential to self-help, not as snitching.

In the group, self-criticism is emphasized more than criticism of others because self-criticism is basic to the wide-open channel. As we have said, constructive criticism of other group members is encouraged, but its substance and intent are closely examined. More often than not, it is the critic who is criticized.

> C1 had a severe problem with his sinuses. When he sneezed, it made a loud noise. C2 found this offensive and criticized C1. In return, C1 criticized C2, saying that small matters of "form" and politeness were always important to C2 than more major issues. That is, C2 used this exaggerated show of politeness and concern for the way things were done as a device of his conning.

From such seemingly minor issues as a sneeze emerge criminal patterns of thinking.

Newcomers fit in well if they join a group with a well-indoctrinated nucleus. Of course, lifelong thinking errors and tactics present the usual barriers to

---

*The decrease in profanity has been observed and commented on by others, especially members of the criminal's family.

effective functioning in a group. The new member is receptive, but only selectively. Hearing another man report his criminal thoughts may excite rather than disgust him. Determined to be number one in the group, he may look for opportunities to put others down, which also diverts others from examining him. He may offer advice to build himself up. The A.C. can be sure, if these patterns are visible in the group, that they are also present outside. As these patterns are reviewed according to the format for identifying and correcting thinking errors, they are in evidence less and less both within the group and outside. Bringing an unchanged criminal into a group of people immersed in the change process helps to open the channel, because he sees that everyone is operating this way, and there are pressures for him to function similarly. In time, disclosure, receptivity, and self-criticism (which constitute the wide-open channel) are practiced everywhere, not just in the office. With us, and eventually outside, the criminal's excuses, his emphasis on feelings, his blaming others, drop out as he gets down to the business of reporting in minute detail all that is actually happening in his daily life and as his report is subjected to microscopic dissection and correction. Distrust and competition wane as explicit correctives are taught and interdependence develops among group members. This does not mean that the objective is to have a harmonious, smoothly running group; indeed, if a criminal puts on a show of cooperation to score points, the A.C. will find it out in time. The interdependence that the A.C. seeks to foster comes about through the correction of thinking errors, not through pretense.

We have stated the advantages of the open group mainly in terms of the newer members' learning from the old. However, there is also a notable advantage to the older members in such an arrangement. When an unchanged criminal enters the group, the other members have an opportunity to assess themselves again and again. The new member is a stark reminder to every other member of his own past.

Often, genuine concern emerges in which one criminal becomes fearful for another who appears to be heading in the wrong direction.

> C was insisting that a beer a day was perfectly alright for him. He said that as long as he was not thinking about committing crimes, he did not have to worry about such small things. There was some intransigence in this position, a dogmatism about doing things his way, which genuinely worried other members of C's group. They knew all too well the dire consequences that such an attitude had had in their own lives. They also were aware that in the past C had gone on drunken binges and committed many violations. They had developed respect and fondness for C, because of the changes that he had made in his life. Yet they feared that owing to his continuing criminal pride, he was going to throw away his gains. In

fact, one group member was so fearful for C that he composed in his mind an imaginary letter to C, telling him that he was drifting off course and would wind up in disaster.

Concern by group members about one another poses no problem, unless it beclouds reason.

When a criminal elects to leave the program, it produces a crisis for those who remain. The criminal who is substantially advanced in change is frightened by a group member's choice to lead an irresponsible life. He knows that what happens to other group members could easily happen to him.

When C1 quit the program, C2 regarded this as a warning of what could happen to him. He thought about, how throughout his life, he had made similar choices, opting for the irresponsible. He realized that he could easily follow C2's path. He became extremely frightened as he considered the consequences of such a decision. C2 was truly sorry that C1 was throwing his life away. But he resolved that he was going to benefit from this situation. C1's disaster was C2's opportunity to put himself in the place of another person and thereby learn. Even though C1's life was not valuable to C1, C2 thought very differently about his own life.

This experience brought C2 again to the realization that he was not self-sufficient and that this program was indeed his lifeline.

The A.C. should not be guided by theories of group dynamics. Clever interpretations based on such theories only divert from teaching the basics of responsibility, and intragroup struggles are analyzed at the expense of substantive issues of the program. There are, of course, distinct dynamics that are immediately obvious. However, anything that happens within the group is treated in the same manner as an experience elsewhere. For example, a verbal attack on another group member is viewed in the same light as a power thrust outside the group. The same corrections are applied to thinking errors inside as outside the group. If a criminal is showing old patterns within the group, it is certain that he is functioning similarly outside. One must not, however, make the reverse assumption. That is, although errors are not evident in his interactions with group members, the criminal may still be making those errors outside. If the latter is the case, this eventually emerges in the criminal's daily reports or else it is observed and reported by others (group members, family, or, if he is arrested, the police).

This well-planned and disciplined format prevents most of the chaos that we experienced in our early groups. In chapter 1 of volume 1, we recounted our early experiences in which criminals functioned together more as gangs than as constructive therapeutic groups. We described how we had to contend with point-scoring, criminal talk, power and control maneuvers, and the many other tactics that impeded change. One of the most formidable barriers to change was that each criminal insisted that his problems were different from those of all the others. Each found ways to set himself apart from the others, freely offered advice, but never applied it to himself. When we observe this behavior in the group, we routinely treat it in the context of thinking errors. With our direct and focused format, a great deal of such tactics as verbal sparring, diversion, and digression is minimized.

We have been through the storms attending the open-ended therapy groups in which we asked criminals to express themselves, where there was no agenda, and where we applied traditional psychiatric techniques. Now, we have a format that other change agents can apply and that they will find functional for implementing a specific, pragmatic, and relevant curriculum in which the criminal's thinking errors are identified and corrected.

Chapter 7

Correctives for Automatic Errors of Thinking

THE TERM *RESPONSIBILITY* has been used in so many ways that it has become almost meaningless. In daily living, it may refer to something specific, such as an obligation, a duty, or a chore. It may pertain to accountability in the legal sense of being responsible for a crime. In our program for change, responsibility is defined as the result of the implementation of the new thinking patterns that are necessary for the criminal to be an effective, constructive person of total integrity.

To begin with, the criminal is responsible for deciding whether he wants to become an effective, constructive person. That is, he himself must choose the kind of life he wants. But this simply means that he is accountable for making a choice. We go further and describe responsibility as a new homeostasis. To achieve this state, the criminal has to learn the mental processes through which he can become responsible and then implement what he learns. Clearly, responsibility goes beyond crimelessness, a state that cannot exist alone because it would amount to a vacuum in the criminal's thinking. His busy mind is either operating with the old criminal thinking patterns or occupied with a new set of mental processes—those necessary for responsible thinking and actions.

The criminal's thinking processes preclude responsible thinking and actions because they have been developed to fulfill criminal objectives and indeed are essential for achieving what he wants in life. He lacks the thinking patterns necessary to live responsibly. The criminal has heard the word "responsibility" throughout his life; he has even used it himself, but usually only to satisfy others.

> "I do not like the word 'responsible': that is your word; it is not mine. It conveys something to you—to me it conveys only a very general idea. It's too easy a word to hide behind, to parrot."

The criminal's view of responsibility is based on misconceptions. If asked, he describes responsibility in terms of isolated, concrete acts, such as attending church, helping someone in trouble, being on time for work, or paying a bill. The criminal believes, furthermore, that if he is responsible in one area, this makes him responsible in all. When confronted with a more extensive definition of responsibility, such as ours, the criminal regards it as a state of saintliness. One man said of his sister, who functioned responsibly, "She could have been in a monastery." He regarded her daily patterns of living as impossible for him to emulate. No matter how much a criminal might admire a responsible person, he has never sustained a desire for that person's way of life for himself.

We present here the specific correctives for the criminal's thinking patterns. The reader will note that the major headings in this chapter parallel the automatic errors of thinking in chapter 5 of volume 1. All the correctives are interrelated and inevitably overlap. Because errors of thinking compound one another, an agent of change should not expect to correct a pattern merely by introducing a single corrective. The A.C. must in time bring out the interrelatedness of all the concepts presented here. However, for clarity in presentation and for teaching purposes in working with criminals, especially in the early phases of change, each corrective is discussed separately. As change progresses, the criminal is taught that each corrective contains the seeds of all the others.

The correctives have two basic functions. First, they serve as deterrents to crime and irresponsibility. Second, by replacing old patterns, they provide a base for an entirely new way of functioning. Initially, the correctives are like fire extinguishers. When criminal thoughts occur, the criminal goes through a reasoning process in which he applies these principles by thinking about injury to others, achieving a time perspective, and, when appropriate, implementing any of the other fourteen correctives. In time, these correctives become fireproofing as the criminal incorporates them into his thinking and implements them. When new mental processes are implemented and become habitual, they do not have to be deliberately called on to extinguish thoughts of violation. In fact, the fire-extinguishing function, useful as it is, will not achieve the objective of total change: if the criminal wants to violate, he will cut off the correctives just as he has eliminated other deterrents in the past. The thinking processes described in this chapter eventually are the foundation of a new way of life and a new philosophy of life.

The correctives stress the primacy of reason over feeling. The word *feeling* is often used when one is referring to thinking. If one man asks another, "How do you feel about the economy?" he is really asking him what he *thinks* about the economy. If economic conditions are poor, some agitation may accompany his response and a heated debate may ensue. But it is his *thoughts* that are being elicited and expressed. Whatever emotions accompany an issue, there is concurrent ideation, and it is usually ideation that provides the substance of the discussion and triggers an emotional response.

Many mental health professionals use feelings as the currency of their transactions. They value the expression of feeling and strive to alter feeling through insight. In phenomenologic reports, we obtain both thinking and feeling, but we do not regard emotions as primary causes and as something to correct in themselves. Everyone has feelings. Expression of them (catharsis) offers some relief. For the criminal, catharsis is of only transient value because his emotional state of thinking changes so quickly (fragmentation). Furthermore, emotional expression does not produce any change in his criminal patterns. We have found that the criminal uses insights about feelings to excuse whatever he thinks and does. He uses fear, anger, depression, or any other emotion to justify heinous acts. We provide the criminal with even more excuses when we probe the origin of his feelings. A criminal who had undergone more than ten years of psychoanalytic psychotherapy with a prestigious therapist evaluated that approach in the light of his experience with us:

> "I had believed in reason and logic. Plato and Aristotle were my teachers, but my psychiatrist taught me to distrust all that. 'You are rationalizing,' he would say. 'Stop thinking. Start feeling.' So I spent about three or four years 'getting in touch with my feelings.' I am very much in touch with my feelings now after ten years of psychotherapy; but I am now in a security ward of a mental hospital on a Federal Court order because I am a suspected criminal, insane or both. 'Getting in touch with my feelings' obviously did not prevent the devastating injury I had inflicted upon others and myself. . . . I know I must 'think' now; but I have forgotten how. 'I feel; therefore I am' was my claim to existence for so many years now. How to go back suddenly to 'Cogito, ergo sum'? I cannot. Or, is it that I don't want to?"

Emotional experience is a vital part of life for both criminals and noncriminals. But we have learned that feelings are altered once thinking patterns change. In that sense, feelings are epiphenomena of thinking.

We do not focus on feelings in working with the criminal. Instead, we concentrate on thinking for two main reasons: first, in accountability situations, the criminal resorts to feelings to justify whatever he does; and second, feelings are intangible and difficult to work with.* It is more

---

*Low (1973, pp. 834-835) pointed out how illusory feelings are even in the noncriminal: "I want you to know that your feelings are not facts. They merely pretend to reveal facts. Your feelings deceive you. . . . Thoughts alone possess the quality of truth and falseness."

productive to work with the thinking components of fear or anger, for example, than with their emotional expression. In every instance, we have eliminated feelings from consideration in the change process and have focused on the thinking that accompanies them. We do not await a change in the criminal's feelings before he implements the program. We have found that feelings often do not change with insight, but that they do with new experiences. In short, feelings are altered in our program by a rational process—the correction of thinking errors and the implementation of the correctives.

We attempted to teach the correctives for thinking errors didactically, introducing each one in a classroom format. Because criminals seemed to understand the material, we expected them to implement what they had learned. The didactic approach failed. First, it was not sufficiently tied in with their daily experience. Second, these men dismissed what they had heard and proceeded to do as they pleased, using their thinking errors as excuses just as earlier they had used sociologic and psychologic excuses. Erroneously we interpreted the criminal's verbal grasp of the material as an indicator of progress. We derived a sense of accomplishment from his comprehending the correctives that we were teaching. Our assessment was incorrect: despite his understanding of the material, the criminal persisted with the same thinking errors. Finally, we recognized that this material had to be applied to life situations, so as to serve as more than an academic exercise. Therefore, we addressed ourselves to the criminal's immediate life experiences, which were far more vital to him than didactic presentations of concepts. By examining the data of twenty-four hours of thinking, we could easily and rapidly identify the errors of thinking. Opportunities exist right from the beginning to correct these, because when the criminal speaks about anything, he makes habitual errors.

As the reader becomes familiar with the contents of this chapter, he is likely to find himself thinking that the correctives are self-evident. However, concepts that are obvious to the noncriminal are foreign to the criminal. We were confounded by the presence of these thinking errors in criminals who were college graduates. Naively, we had believed that no one could graduate from college, thinking as they did. The correctives are actually patterns of thinking that any responsible teen-ager uses automatically; but to the criminal, they are new. Our criminals have had to learn through explicit instruction what a responsible child gradually acquires simply through life's experiences.

Although the correctives appear here in a form that may seem didactic, in our program for change they are applied to life situations as those situations are reported phenomenologically. Chapter 10 demonstrates how the correctives, once offered, are implemented and change actually occurs.

The reader will find that we refer repeatedly to *elimination* of thinking errors. He may question whether elimination refers to suppression of old patterns or to their complete disappearance. The question of whether a particular criminal pattern still resides within an individual is purely speculative. We have found that consequent to persistent and prolonged implementation of the corrections for thinking errors and other deterrents (see chapter 9), old thinking patterns occur less frequently and finally disappear, at least as far as reliable phenomenologic reporting reveals. We have worked with people whose criminal thinking occurred dozens, and sometimes hundreds, of times a day, but who now report, after years of follow-up, that such thinking no longer occurs. Even transient thoughts of theft, assault, visiting with criminal associates, or engaging in a myriad of other violations do not enter awareness. As we shall develop in chapter 10, the criminal must not become complacent about his change. We emphasize that as long as he lives there is always the potential for a resurgence of old patterns. Although from our experience we believe that they have been eliminated, we are not complacent and realize that a recurrence is possible. However, from an operational standpoint, one does not find these old patterns in the changed criminal's thinking or action.

OPENING THE CHANNEL WIDE

The first and foremost mental requisite of responsible thinking and action is having a wide-open channel. Change cannot occur without total disclosure, receptivity to others' points of view, and the maintenance of a self-critical attitude. All this is antithetical to the criminal's life style, unless utilized in the interest of a self-serving objective. The criminal has lived a life of secrecy, preserving his sense of uniqueness, and enhancing his power by keeping others in the dark about his thinking and activities. He has rarely listened to others, because he has not wanted to invite opinions that would deter him from his chosen course of action. Rather than be self-critical, he has criticized others and done what he regarded as necessary to achieve his criminal objectives and, as a byproduct, to maintain a misconceived image of himself. Total destruction of these patterns is mandatory for change.

The agent of change is severely limited in what he can accomplish if the criminal controls the transaction by opening and closing the channel to suit his own purposes. In fact, one could accurately view the establishment of the wide-open channel as the product of the criminal's first exercise in the new pattern of abdication of control. All three components of the channel— disclosure, receptivity, and self-criticism—must be in "good working order," because deficient functioning in one affects the others. For example, if a person is not self-critical, he will not receive what others say to him, unless it is agreeable. The wide-open channel is the phenomenologic approach in operation, supplying the agent of change with the details of the criminal's struggle with himself and the outside world.

DISCLOSURE

The criminal discloses whatever part of the truth will best serve his purposes and conceals the rest. In this program for change there is no part of his thinking or action that he may reserve as "my business." Reporting even the seemingly most insignificant thoughts is necessary, regardless of the light in which it puts him. In chapter 5, we described our specifications for phenomenologic reporting. Such a report is a *sine qua non* of our program for change, in that it defines "total disclosure." It is the most important corrective for the closed channel.

The criminal is required to report his thinking about disclosure. He informs the A.C. and the group how he arrives at a decision to disclose. Of course, there is always the possibility that a clever criminal will do this to score points and divert the A.C. from other thinking that he is concealing. This is a form of "con" that uses telling a part of the truth as its best tactic.

It takes time to learn how to report in the prescribed manner. Obviously, the criminal has to learn to select relevant material; otherwise, twenty-four hours of thinking and actions would take twenty-four hours or more to present. The criminal has to learn what is worth putting under the microscope during the limited time available to him in each day's meeting.

> C went into great detail about going fishing. He described everything he did, right down to the colors and stripes of the fish he caught. Then he made passing references to his father-in-law's being taken to the hospital and his own remaining at the hospital for many hours. However, there was not a word about C's thoughts during all those hours.

C emphasized details about a situation that did not bring out thinking errors. He failed to disclose his thinking in a much more important situation. With persistent probing, we elicited from him his homicidal thinking about his father-in-law.

It is to be expected that the initial reporting will be unsatisfactory and sometimes wearisome. The criminal cannot very well focus on material that reveals thinking errors before he has learned what those thinking errors are. At first, the A.C. is more likely to hear about the jams that the criminal is in and little more. The time that it takes to master the proper method of reporting is determined by the criminal's attitude. A criminal who is strongly committed to the program picks it up very rapidly, whereas a criminal who is fighting the requirements progresses much more slowly, if he progresses at all.

RECEPTIVITY

Receptivity is the second component of the wide-open channel. All his life, the criminal has been the omniscient one. He has viewed people through a tubular scope, focusing only on what was commensurate with his criminal objectives and ignoring anything contrary to those objectives. In relationships with others, he has looked upon himself as the person with wisdom and experience and, therefore, as the teacher rather than the student. He has regarded even listening to another's viewpoint as tantamount to being controlled, unless he has had some immediate gain in mind. Although the criminal is receptive to a new criminal M.O., it is, indeed, a formidable task to indoctrinate him into being equally receptive to a brand-new way of thinking. Receptivity is not a matter of tolerating and assenting to what others say. Rather, the criminal has to think seriously about totally new material pertinent to a foreign way of living. In addition to receiving the substance of the program's material, the criminal must be open to others' criticisms of his functioning, and not regard them as putdowns.

There are several indicators of how well the criminal is receiving the comments of the A.C. and other criminals in his group. Some make notes, indicating that they are paying attention. When the channel is wide open, the criminal is actively thinking about the material, raising questions, and, where appropriate, discussing his ideas with others. After a meeting, he takes a theme, ponders it, and spontaneously raises issues at the next meeting. The most important criterion of receptivity is whether the material is retained and implemented over time. The process of ingestion and regurgitation to please the A.C. is counterproductive. We do not expect the criminal to be a believing, uncritical listener. Rather, we require that, as a receptive person, he considers what he is hearing and tries it out—implements it. The corrective will not be incorporated into his thinking until he has some experiential evidence of its merit.

SELF-CRITICISM

The third component of the wide-open channel is self-critical thinking, which takes the place of the production of self-serving reports and statements. This calls for the criminal to abandon the victor-victim perspective. We stress the view that a criminal, in responding to a situation, has to assume that he was fully responsible for what happened, whether he actually was or not.

There was the beginning of an antagonism in the group. C1 claimed that C2 was ignoring him and not even saying "hello" in the morning. C2 maintained that C1 was unfriendly and unresponsive. Actually there was evidence of both. Operationally to achieve a result, each had to consider himself totally to blame. By assuming full responsibility, each criminal had to focus on his changing, not on excuses.

Each criminal was being asked to assume the burden of responsibility for rectifying the situation. The assumption of total responsibility increases the likelihood that self-criticism will result in correction. Self-criticism without ensuing correction is merely confession, and confession by itself ensures nothing in the way of lasting change.

We teach the criminal to develop a distrust of his own thinking and action. After being exposed to a critical evaluation day after day in the group, the criminal acquires the habit of self-criticism. The following incidents show how the criminal eventually subjects all that he does to self-criticism.

> C was working very hard at a restaurant.* Within a year, he had risen from busboy to bartender to waiter, and he was now being considered for manager. C asked himself over and over whether his striving for excellence was an expression of his old tendency to prove that he could take over and do the best job. Was he trying to show that he could do something else that no one else could?
>
> *   *   *
>
> C pulled off the road after he saw a woman hit a dog with her car. The woman was upset, and C talked with her. He then wondered whether this was a friendly act or another of his old efforts to build up his opinion of himself as a good person, without any compassion for the woman.
>
> *   *   *
>
> C was told by an acquaintance that he had a sarcastic sense of humor. He believed that he had no intention to offend others. In fact, his comments usually drew a laugh. He began to wonder whether he was reverting to his pattern of getting laughs by tearing others down.

On the face of it, each of these points may seem to be small, especially when juxtaposed with the seriousness of the criminal's major errors of thought and action. However, it is just such an alertness to old patterns that is a deterrent to crime itself and a promoter of change. Eventually, self-critical thinking that is repeatedly practiced becomes a way of life for the criminal. He views himself critically at all times, even in watching a movie.

> C was viewing a film about the Rothschild family. He observed a family that had its roots in the ghetto. Through hard work, it built a financial

---

*This chapter contains many examples of situations at restaurants. The reader may think that we are referring to one criminal repeatedly. Actually, the restaurant business has been the one in which most of our criminals have found jobs. Although the setting in many examples is the same, different criminals are involved.

empire. As the story was presented, he saw that this was accomplished through effort, persistence, integrity, and sound decision-making. He then questioned himself about his own values, asking himself, "Where am I going?"

C saw the sharp contrast between how the hero in the movie dealt with life and how he, C, had functioned. The self-critical attitude eventually becomes so entrenched that a criminal may criticize the A.C. for not being sufficiently critical of him.

OPEN CHANNEL ELSEWHERE

It is insufficient for the wide-open channel to be in effect only in the office. It must be implemented outside. Since the total disclosure of the phenomenologic report is not suitable or desirable elsewhere, the criminal has to be taught what is appropriate disclosure in different situations: his boss will not be privy to the same information as his wife, and so forth. But in all that he chooses to disclose to others, he must demonstrate integrity and avoid deceptions of any kind. The criminal cannot permit himself the minor lies that might be relatively insignificant for the noncriminal, because a departure from the program's standards of integrity invariably opens the door to further irresponsibility and, in time, violation.

Just as he is receptive to us and to others in the group, so must he be receptive to people outside. The criminal learns to be open-minded, even when listening to those whose advice he has shunned for years. He has much to learn about responsible living, and he must adopt the attitude that he can learn from every situation. Instead of being put down and reacting with anger when others say something contrary to his point of view, the criminal monitors himself to ensure that he is giving careful consideration to their words.

The criminal learns to take criticism from others, instead of reacting only by justifying what he thinks. Naturally, he is more receptive to others' criticism when he himself is being self-critical. In the process of change, criminals sometimes carry their self-criticism to such excess that they are paralyzed in taking initiatives. When a criminal is wary of offering a woman in his office a light for her cigarette because she might misconstrue the offer, he is taking it to an extreme. We have to teach flexibility when self-criticism becomes a barrier to effective functioning.

We have set forth the correctives for the closed channel, stating the necessary changes in thinking and action. In the early meetings, the A.C. lacks a wide-open channel, because the criminal has had no experience with it. Because of the criminal's fragmented states, there continues to be considerable opening and closing of the channel. Only time will tell whether the channel has been open during a given period. When total disclosure, receptivity, and self-criticism become habitual, the A.C. can rely on the criminal's judgment in selecting material to present. As he progresses, the criminal becomes aware of features that he knows need correction, and he emphasizes these in thematic reports. It is no putdown for him to bring out unfavorable aspects of his functioning, because his evaluation of himself is now based on responsible performance.

ELIMINATION OF THE VICTIM STANCE

Both the criminal and the noncriminal may be victims of misfortune. Either could be afflicted by a serious illness, a crime, or a natural disaster. A person who is truly a victim is not at fault; he has not knowingly contributed to the event. A man who has locked his car and taken the keys is a victim if that car is stolen; he has done what he could to prevent a theft. However, if he leaves the keys, he has not taken every preventive measure and has contributed to the possibility of a theft; in this instance, we do not view him as a victim because he did not take every necessary precaution. Some responsible people blame others for their misfortunes just as the criminal does, but it is not part of a criminal pattern. A careful dissection is required of the numerous patterns by which the criminal blames others and presents himself as a victim. In the relatively rare cases in which a criminal truly is a victim and played no part in what happened to him, the issue is how to deal with adversity (a topic to be discussed later).

In crime, the criminal does not think of anyone's being a victim at all—either himself or the person whom he is about to victimize. The victim stance is a prepared accountability tactic. The criminal has available a variety of excuses, some of which he has used so often that they are half beliefs. The victim stance takes its grossest form when the criminal is apprehended in a crime. He then says that he is a victim: someone informed, another person slipped up, or a police car happened to pull up. However, the criminal does not depend on such a crude expression of being a victim for long. He has a plethora of other excuses according to which he is a victim of individuals, events, institutions, and even natural forces, past and present. He readily shifts from one form of the victim position to another.

When the criminal envisions himself a victim of a mishap in the course of a crime, our position is that what happened was a consequence of his own choices. He chose to commit the crime; but his superoptimistic thinking led him to misjudge the situation and resulted in his arrest.

Criminals quickly revert to sociologic excuses, claiming that their acts and personalities are consequences of unfavorable environmental circumstances. Our position is that the criminal has victimized the environment more than it has victimized him. Beginning as a child, he dismissed numerous opportunities that society offered. Other children chose to study in school, to associate with responsible youngsters, to acquire job skills. The criminal took a different course. Performing minimally in school, he learned little; but he later faults society for not giving him the chance for an education. He chose to associate with criminal children in the neighborhood and sometimes left his neighborhood to do so; however, he later claims that he responded to peer pressure that led him into crime. He spurned opportunities for vocational training, but asserts that society deprived him of a chance to earn a decent living. In all these claims, he maintains that somehow the world was out of step with *him*. He has made his own choices all along, but when held accountable he claims that he had no choice. Furthermore, many of those who experienced stresses similar to his or worse made different choices, including the choice to live responsibly.

The racial excuse is a special case of the sociologic victim stance. Obviously, racial discrimination persists in society. But the criminal has used the racial factor, usually after all other excuses have failed, to excuse his violating behavior. Race is his last-ditch effort to oppose us. When a criminal progresses in change, he no longer resorts to this. He thinks about others of his race, including members of his own family, who have made choices different from his. Instead of seeing himself as oppressed, he is struck by the fact that he has oppressed and victimized others of his race and has done nothing constructive to remedy injustices to his people.

C, who was black, used to invoke racism almost any time he was held accountable by a white man for anything. He had exploited others, black and white, and had been violent. Before he came to our program, he considered "whitey" responsible for all his misfortunes. As he implemented the program, we had a different problem with C: he became extremely critical of the tactics used by racial militants and tended to exaggerate their number and lump people into that category who did not belong there.

We worked with C, and he developed a more realistic perspective. In a few cases, a criminal is so wedded to the racial excuse that we are prevented from probing further. That is, it is more rigid than the half belief, which can be and is easily shattered in most criminals.* If a criminal steadfastly opposes us on racial grounds, work with him will be unsuccessful.

*A half belief is the outcome of a criminal's adhering to a self-justification that he originally knew had little truth, but because he has used it so often, he almost comes to believe it (see chapter 4 of volume 1).

The criminal glides easily from sociologic to psychologic excuses, faulting his parents for what they did. As stated previously, our view is that mothers and fathers are victims of their children, as well as vice versa. Much of his parents' behavior was determined by what the criminal did as a child. Parents were often more punitive than they wanted to be, because of the behavior of their youngsters. The criminal faults his parents for not communicating although he did not want them to know what he was doing. When his perplexed parents tried to supervise him more closely, he complained that they were too restrictive. In families where parents were absent, overly harsh, indifferent, or whatever else they might have been, most of the children still chose to lead responsible lives. In other words, we nullify formulations of cause and effect and concentrate on the criminal's choices, the risks that he took, and the contributions that he made to situations, even when they were adverse.

> "I used to think that if [my parents] had given me more love, I wouldn't be where I am today, but now I wonder if having been the kind of son I am didn't also lead them to where they are."

That statement was made by a criminal who was beginning to agree with our position as he reviewed his early upbringing. Even when parents have obvious faults, we focus on the criminal's contributions to adverse situations.

> C's father was a fairly heavy drinker. When he drank, he became irritable, unpleasant, and generally hard to get along with. C used to get angry, walk out, and slam the door. Repeatedly, he became embroiled in verbal tiffs with his father, and the relationship, which was already not good, deteriorated further. As we worked with C, he developed a more balanced view of his father and recognized that his own attitude was making the relationship worse. Accepting his father's shortcomings, C decided to ignore them or else respond with good-natured humor. Once C began doing this, his father recognized the change in C's attitude and became less contentious and easier to live with.

We paid no attention to C's complaints about his father, emphasizing instead how C compounded the difficulties. A change in C's attitude did not cure his father's drinking, but it did diminish the friction in the household that was mounting with each confrontation.

Another form of the psychologic excuse is the criminal's justification of what he does in terms of his feelings. He describes them as though they were beyond his control, almost as though they were alien intruders, undermining his good self.

"I always regarded my feelings as being absolute. I had nothing to do with their being there."

The criminal takes responsibility for his good feelings when he wants recognition for his good qualities. But when he is held accountable, he says that his feelings are beyond his control. He may then be diagnosed as mentally ill, thus becoming a victim of an illness for which someone else is to offer a cure. Earlier in this chapter, we discussed feelings in the format of this program. Feelings invariably accompany thinking. In crime, the criminal routinely subordinates emotion to thought. A basic tenet of our program is that thought and feeling (as an epiphenomenon of thought) are both subject to the criminal's control.

When he realizes that talking about feelings gains him no sympathy, the criminal may contend that he is the victim of his own thinking processes. A sophisticated criminal couches this in psychologic language and talks about "character structure," "incurable psychopathy," and so forth. In other words, he asserts that his thinking *leads* him into crime and thus into difficulty. Our response is that he has shown control over his thoughts in crime, just as he has over his feelings. Furthermore, he has chosen not to develop thinking patterns necessary for responsible functioning.

Another category of victim excuse (in addition to the sociologic and psychologic) is the claim that he is at a disadvantage because of his criminal record. He says that others are suspicious of him, that no one will give him a break, and that it is impossible for him to get a job. He may assert that the frustration from such rejection has driven him to commit more crimes out of desperation. Fifteen years experience in this field has shown us that such claims are not true. The attitude toward giving ex-convicts opportunities has been improving. All the criminals with whom we have dealt have been able to find jobs—not just any jobs, but jobs that permitted them to attend our program for a half day, every day. Many employers are eager to assist a criminal who reveals something of his past and states his intention to change.* The complaint of being denied opportunities is heard mainly from criminals who fail to pursue opportunities, quit after one or two inquiries, or refuse to take jobs that they regard as beneath them. When a criminal complains that others are suspicious of him, he is correct; this is a consequence of his criminality, and he will have to tolerate people's suspicions of him even long after he is well on the path toward change.

Another type of victim excuse sometimes heard is a genetic excuse. The criminal may say that he was "born to lose" and blame fate, as did the criminal

---

*The problem arises for the prospective employer when he is impressed by a criminal who presents himself as wanting to change but has no such intention.

who said he was born in the wrong year on the wrong day at the wrong time. The more educated criminal may argue that his chromosomes made him a criminal. We insist, however, that his thinking errors are not genetic in origin, but rather were learned. Genetics does not preclude learning a new set of thinking processes. The criminal may claim that he has an unusually strong sex drive, the result of a biologic condition that he cannot help. We have demonstrated that the sex drive of which he speaks is the reflection of a pervasive pattern of seeking conquests. When his criminal patterns of thought and action are eliminated, his urgent desire for sexual activity decreases. This has been true in all cases with which we have dealt. Meanwhile, we teach the criminal to divert his thinking from sex and direct it elsewhere, this being a temporary remedy.

Whether the victim stance takes a sociologic, psychologic, genetic, or other form, we have four main ways of countering it. First, we trace the pattern of the criminal's choices to show that he played a determining role in arriving at his present station in life. Second, we demonstrate that others subjected to similar or worse stresses did not turn out as he did because they made different choices. Third, we prove that he is a victimizer far more than a victim. Finally, when he says that he is a victim, we observe that he is opposing responsibility. To give up the victim stance, he has to want a different way of life. A person cannot be committed to responsibility while maintaining that he is a victim, and offering excuses for a lifetime of irresponsibility.

It is a sign of change when a criminal is accountable for his shortcomings and does not blame others for them. Blaming others is absent in the changed criminal to the extent that even when things over which he has no control do happen, he self-critically examines his own thinking and action, rather than fault another person.

C, a very light-skinned Negro working as a busboy, was assigned a group of customers with crewcuts, whom he sized up as being from a rural area. As it turned out, they were from Iowa. In the course of conversation, they asked him what his nationality was. He quietly said, "Negro." The pleasant tone of the conversation quickly vanished, and there was a perceptible chill in their manner. But C decided that they would get not only good service, but "superservice." He did this, and they thawed out a bit. Their bill would have warranted a $4 tip, but C discovered that they left only $1.35. He was not angry, but he did a lot of thinking as to why this was. He thought that perhaps they did not know what percentage of the bill was customary as a tip. Or perhaps, as tourists, they were short of money. He also gave considerable thought to how he might have served them even better, wondering whether he had slipped up somewhere.

C did not think about being a victim of racial discrimination. His old pattern would have been to get angry at being asked his "nationality." At the first suggestion of racial prejudice, in his mind he would have gotten even and then perhaps gone so far as to put something in the customers' food to make them sick. In C's assessment of his own contribution to the situation, all victim thinking was eliminated.

ELIMINATION OF THE "I CAN'T" ATTITUDE

In common parlance among responsible people, the phrase *I can't* connotes either an incapacity or prohibition stemming from within the speaker. In the criminal's usage, it connotes neither. In his daily life, the criminal rarely says "I can't" as a statement of incapacity. To do so is at odds with his self-image as a powerful person totally in control. To him, saying that he cannot do something is self-derogatory. If someone else challenges him by telling him that he "can't," this is a putdown, which he fears and which therefore might draw an angry response.

The criminal may turn down a proposition that seems too risky. Saying "I can't" in such a situation means that he does not want to jeopardize himself by an act in which he thinks that apprehension is likely. He may also say "I can't" when asked to do something along responsible lines that he dislikes doing or does not want to be bothered with. If asked to trim a hedge, he may say "I can't." In situations like this, "I can't" is so habitual that he says it without even thinking about it. This may be due to his perfectionism: he "can't" trim the hedge because it would not meet his unreasonably high standard. Most likely, he would say "I can't" to hedge-trimming because it is boring and there are other things he prefers to do.

"I can't" may indicate a prejudgment about something that the criminal has never previously done. A criminal child's school counselor may suggest that he begin study of a language. The youngster responds that he "can't" learn the language, when in fact he has never tried and knows nothing of what it entails.

The "I can't" theme is common in accountability situations, where it serves as a variation of the victim theme. It is sometimes couched in psychologic terms. When the criminal refers to feelings, needs, impulses, and compulsions, the A.C. is confronted with a statement of helplessness. This is either out-and-out malingering, or it is feeding people what the criminal thinks they want to hear. As the criminal presents it, "I can't" fits in well with the current psychologic thinking of many people. Many observers have described the criminal in terms of his inability to do various things (Freyhan 1955, p. 19; Cameron 1963, p. 652; White and Watt 1973, p. 326). A criminal may use "I can't" so frequently to refer to his incapacity to be responsible that this becomes a half belief. The views of experts, when widely accepted, reinforce the "I can't" notion.

Ultimately, the criminal may assert to an A.C. that he "can't" change because of his thinking patterns. It is true that, given the criminal's thinking processes, criminal behavior is the only possible product. The error is the contention that these mental processes are immutable. If the thinking processes are destroyed and new ones learned, a different product will result—responsible behavior. The idea that the criminal "can't" change is not a matter of conviction; when he is questioned closely about this, he admits that ability is not the issue.

"I can't" expresses unwillingness—"I won't." Predicated on a series of prior decisions to live a criminal life, it is a refusal to utilize his potential in behalf of living responsibly. In the process of change, the "I can't" theme may arise with respect to the elimination of virtually any thinking pattern or habit. The criminal asserts that he cannot change because, despite fleeting desires to do so, he wants a supply of something that the responsible world does not provide, namely, criminal excitement. What the criminal misses is stated in terms of "needs": "I need sex"; "I need a drink." He says that his needs are not being met and uses this to justify not changing. "I need" is another form of "I can't."

"I can't" represents failure to make a choice to live responsibly. It reveals the criminal's unwillingness to learn and implement new thinking patterns. An A.C. has to make it clear early in the program that there are no "can'ts." The only accurate use of the word "can't" is that the criminal cannot live responsibly and also enjoy criminal excitements.

The criminal may acknowledge that success in the program is within the realm of possibility. But then he wonders what, if he has to give up so much, the use of living is. The "I can't" is really a response to a program that from his viewpoint takes away everything his life is based on, leaving him with nothing. He has regarded responsible people as "suckers," "slaves," and "squares." To live as they do would reduce him to a zero. As one man put it: "Take my crime away and you take my world away." The criminal does not know what the rewards of responsible living are because he has never lived responsibly. Faced with an unappealing way of life, he says that he "can't" change.

An A.C. must meet the criminal's "I can't" early, because such a position is incompatible with the implementation of the free choice to participate in this program. If a man has eliminated crime or suicide as possible options, total change is his only remaining option; it is his lifeline. The criminal has chosen from the beginning the path that he wants to follow, and all else is a consequence of that decision. "I can't" in this program opens the door to crime. It is a statement of "I won't" and an acknowledgment that criminal thinking is competing and gaining the upper hand.

A problem that arises in many cases is that the changing criminal believes that his mind should be devoid of criminal thoughts. Because this does not happen rapidly, he regards the continuing occurrence of criminal thinking as evidence that he truly is unable to change. This view reflects the criminal's requirements for instant success. The A.C. deals with this by instructing the criminal in the mental processes of deterrence (chapter 9). The criminal is taught to expect that criminal thoughts will recur for a while, but that if he acquires and implements new thinking patterns, they eventually will preempt the occurrence of such thoughts.

If the criminal elects the program, then all excuses must be eliminated in favor of a mental set of "I can" and then a mental set of "I must." Having adopted this position, he must put forth initiatives and effort to implement new knowledge and destroy old patterns. In this undertaking, what he likes, is interested in, or feels is irrelevant. It has no role in the decision to be responsible, because it is used only to support the "I can't." The corrective for this thinking error is the *attitude* of doing the difficult now and the impossible later. Many of the things that the criminal insists that he cannot do, he does quite easily once he makes the effort. The "I can't" corrective, then, is more than the elimination of excuses; it is *doing*.

ACHIEVING A TIME PERSPECTIVE

The responsible person has an awareness of time perspective early in childhood; it becomes highly developed by adolescence. However, this is totally antithetic to the criminal's pursuit of his objectives. To think of the past or to view responsibly the long-range consequences of his actions deters criminal thinking and action. Consequently, this is a pattern that the criminal does not develop. Incarceration is not conducive to this kind of learning. The criminal has no more interest in changing his life style after prison than he did before. From his experience of arrest and confinement he learns only to be more careful in future crimes. He may learn from the past to be a "better" criminal, but more often he does not, because in his superoptimistic way, the criminal cuts off past experience, taking chances to achieve his immediate objective.

The criminal does not learn from experience what society wants him to learn in order to become a responsible person. Nor does the criminal conceive of the present as a time to build a responsible future. In fact, given his mental processes, he does not have the equipment to plan a responsible future. The future is not important to him, except for a big score in crime. A vague intention to become a responsible person one day is always deferred, because the more he gets away with, the bigger is his appetite for crime; thus the day of straightening out never arrives.

We formerly believed that schemers could be turned into planners. The criminal thinks ahead in planning crime, so we thought that perhaps he could utilize this facility in planning responsibly for the future. Such a view turned out to be simplistic and valueless. Criminal scheming is directed toward an irresponsible objective and is totally incompatible with responsible planning. For the latter, new thinking processes are necessary.

In meeting with the A.C., the criminal does not understand why he should be branded with the hot iron of the past. His attitude is, let bygones be bygones. As we have indicated, the A.C. must dwell intensively on past patterns so that the criminal will learn from his errors of the past and develop and sustain self-disgust. Keeping the past in mind is necessary for the correction of the criminal's tubular vision. Such review facilitates reflection and moral inventory (processes to be described in chapter 9). The criminal is trained to look into the mirror and relive the harm he did. Still, he complains that the A.C. is hanging him repeatedly when a single hanging is sufficient. The reason for the repeated hangings is that facing up to his past again and again is necessary if the criminal is to discard old patterns. He cannot realistically evaluate his progress in the program without contrasting present thinking and action with what has been characteristic of him earlier. As the criminal presents reports of his thinking and actions, he reveals how characteristically he eliminates consideration of even the recent past.

> To justify corrosion in his responsible performance, C began quarreling about the strictness of the program's requirements. Over several weeks, his expenditures had been excessive, and he had lied about money, done some drinking, deceived a girl, and begun wishing for sex with an irresponsible girl friend whom he had long ago given up. He was also experiencing anger and a decrease in efficiency at work. He was aware that he was on the brink of arrest. In reflecting on his situation, C commented, "In a split second, how much you can undo!"

This statement indicated a total failure to take the past into account. With the criminal, nothing happens in a split second (see our discussion of impulse in chapter 6 of volume 1). There is a corrosion of responsible behavior. The split second is merely an event in a chain of events. Introducing this perspective was a sobering corrective for C's faulty time perspective.

The criminal's tubular vision has led him to view the future only when preparing for a crime. In the meetings, we teach the criminal how to broaden the scope of his thinking. Consideration of the future is intimately related to all the other correctives. If a person is accustomed to taking the future into account, he anticipates possible consequences of his behavior. When he puts himself in the place of others, he is likely to evaluate what might harm them and thus avoid actually injuring them. Thinking about the future is necessary for sound decision-making and enables a person to establish responsible goals. The criminal has never set goals toward which he worked responsibly. To him, a goal is a big score. The criminal has been mired in the muddy waters of nonachievement, because he has had unrealistic notions of how success is achieved. In his zeal for pie in the sky, he has often sacrificed bread on the table. His failure to think realistically and to consider the future is illustrated by the following situation:

C was planning to organize his own company and develop an apartment project. However, having no capital, he had to obtain a construction loan for nearly eighty percent of the funds at a high rate of interest. To raise the other twenty percent he had to take out a short-term loan, also at high interest. C then talked about mortgaging the land that he already partly owned. While talking about this ambitious project, C was about to become unemployed, having already resigned his current job. C figured that with his own company he would receive contracts to manage property and, with the income from this, would have a cash flow for his company.

At twenty-eight, this criminal was determined to be an overnight success in real estate. About to quit his job, with his wife and two children to support, and with two thousand dollars in debts, he was contemplating a venture costing hundreds of thousands of dollars, all of which he would have to borrow. Even if he could have done this, he would have had no way to feed his family. C expressed admiration of others who had sacrificed and struggled for years to make significant achievements, but he was uncertain that what they did had no application to him. He regarded himself as unique and as sure to succeed immediately. Finally, as a concession to us, he agreed to find a job and defer the formation of his company. Such token talk proved to be worthless. In fact, C eventually dropped out of the program, was unemployed indefinitely thereafter, and had no legitimate source of income.

When the criminal embarks on the change process, he is apt to view crimelessness as the goal. This is not a viable objective because it is a negative purpose. It points toward what he will not do, rather than what he will do. As we have said, there is no such state as crimelessness. A vacuum cannot exist in the criminal's life or in anyone else's. The elimination of old thinking patterns has to be followed by the learning and implementation of the new thinking patterns of responsibility. The A.C. has to teach the criminal what a responsible goal is. The criminal learns that excessive pretensions disappear, once they pass through the filter of logic and reason. One has concurrent goals in life. There is no point at which one has arrived and can sit back complacently without any problems. New problems are always emerging, and with them, goals are constantly being revised. The responsible person works toward many objectives simultaneously. He has a continuous series of problems to be solved on many fronts, frequently all at the same time— vocational, domestic, financial, and social. Some responsible people do live from day to day, with little regard for the future, but their failure to plan ahead is not at the expense of being responsible. They may remain content without setting long-range goals, but such a mode of living does not satisfy the energetic, ambitious criminal, even after he has advanced in the process of change.

When the criminal was young, he wanted to be older than he was. In line with this desire, he tried to be the big man who would achieve status by doing what others would not do. As he grew older, the criminal believed that he was not to be in this world for long. He saw his end as being not far off and expected to die early. Old age was not a concern. This was not unrealistic in that many criminals have had associates who were killed in crime. Now as he becomes responsible, for the first time in his life, the criminal thinks about the process of aging and begins to prepare for the contingencies in life. He develops a concept of aging in a longer life.

As the criminal adopts a time perspective, he learns the necessity of patience. In crime, he was patient and deferred gratification in that he schemed and then postponed a crime to await the best opportunity. As the criminal views society, he wants to accomplish immediately what others take years to do. Failing this, he regards himself as a nothing. We have to correct this instancy feature of zero-state thinking, in which he has the idea that without immediate impact he is nothing and will accomplish nothing for the rest of his life. He must learn that patience has its rewards, that the tortoise can beat the hare. We have to lessen his sense of urgency and teach him that life's problems are not resolved responsibly by precipitous action and snap decisions. One man reflected that he was becoming aware that life does not consist of emergencies. In the past, he was the one who turned everything into an emergency.

Taking this approach does not mean that we condone or contribute to the criminal's pattern of deferring what needs to be done. Instead, we teach him to distinguish between when it is advantageous to put off something and when there is nothing to be gained by delay. For example, before making a decision, it is often useful to suspend judgment in order to acquire more information. However, in other situations, it is obligatory to attend to matters promptly. In particular, there is to be no deferring when it comes to implementing our program. A criminal in this program cannot succeed if he is like the overweight man who says that he will feast tonight and begin his diet tomorrow. Sometimes, a criminal is quick to grasp our material but slow to do anything with it. Because he cannot be a finished product immediately, he may put off trying at all. In the program, there must be a "do it" attitude. We insist that the criminal take responsible initiatives and fulfill obligations. We demonstrate to him that delay only compounds problems. This is something that he knows through long experience but, like so much else, has cut off. All his life, the criminal has had the vague idea that he will straighten out one day. Now that day is here.

EFFORT

In common parlance, *effort* and *energy* are often used interchangeably. For example, it makes little difference in meaning whether someone speaks of the efforts or the energy needed to paint a house. For the purpose of changing criminals, we have found it helpful to make a conceptual distinction when using the words *effort* and *energy*.

A person who works in his garden for several hours on a hot day is expending a great deal of energy. If he enjoys what he is doing, then, by our definition, it is not *effort*. If he sweats over the lawn and shrubs, but prefers to be swimming and really dislikes what he is doing, we regard this as *effort*. We define *effort* as either doing what one does not want to do or refraining from doing what one wants to do in behalf of a responsible objective. Responsible people must do things that run counter to their desires. No matter what one's station in life, living from day to day in a responsible manner requires some drudgery—doing what one does not want to do. The responsible person does what is contrary to his desires so habitually that it is not necessary for him to think in terms of effort. The effort required in not doing what one wants to do involves more than backing away from some situations. It entails not seeking them out initially. Deterrence is an integral part of effort.

The criminal has never exerted effort toward anything responsible. In crime, he has done things that he preferred not to do, but these have been necessary for the successful execution of a crime. When effort has been applied, the overriding consideration has been the score at the end of the crime. However, in such cases, doing things that go against the grain has not been a struggle and therefore, from our point of view, has not involved effort. The criminal may appear to be applying effort, when actually he is playing both sides of the street, using ostensibly responsible behavior as a cover for criminality. Such effort is made with the expectation of recognition by others; it enhances his opinion of himself as a good person.

Throughout his life, the criminal has refused to face the disagreeable, which requires effort. Anything not contributing to his quest for excitement, either immediately or in the long run, was boring and therefore disagreeable. The criminal has viewed answering a letter as disagreeable and, therefore, an effort, unless it somehow furthered a criminal scheme. Of course, the noncriminal and criminal may find the same obligations disagreeable. The noncriminal may put them off or otherwise manage to avoid them, but he does not resort to a criminal solution. The criminal has been intolerant of the disagreeable, has defaulted, and has sought excitement by doing the forbidden. In this program, there is much that is disagreeable because the oxygen of his life, criminal excitement, has been taken away.

On the basis of the criminal's phenomenologic report, we teach correctives for the lack of effort. A criminal may say, "I don't feel like going to work." This calls for a discussion of how one surmounts boredom that is a consequence of a lack of criminal excitement. Many other themes are brought in, but the emphasis is on how the criminal, to implement this program, must push himself through boredom, disinterest, and fatigue. It is characteristic of the criminal to be exhausted in the face of responsible tasks. Yet, if something exciting appeals to him, energy is suddenly available, no matter how tired he has said he is.

> As he began our program, C was insistent on going to bed before 10 p.m. He was afraid that he would get too tired and physically rundown from coming to our meetings daily and then commuting a long distance to work unless he got at least eight hours of sleep. He found that even with this he had to push himself to function satisfactorily at work. Yet, some nights he would stay up until 3 a.m. engaging in criminal talk, then get three hours of sleep and manage a considerable output of energy for the rest of the twenty-four-hour period. Later, as he became committed to the program, C eliminated the criminal talk but still had a very busy schedule, which allowed him a maximum of five or six hours of sleep per night. Tremendous energy was available both for work and for the rest of living.

Once the criminal understands that his fatigue is produced by a mental state of anger and self-pity and decides to do what is essential, energy is available. When he pushes himself, fatigue lifts. When a criminal is committed to this program, the energy becomes available for its implementation. The theme of exerting oneself applies everywhere, including the meetings with the A.C. Here the criminal is required to push himself to be present for three hours every day, to report in microscopic detail his thinking and action, to accept criticism, and to implement the correctives offered.

An attitude is developed in this program that one must push oneself to meet the inevitable impediments and adversities. A responsible attitude toward adversity is reflected eloquently in a statement by William James.

The world thus finds in the heroic man its worthy match and mate; and the effort which he is able to put forth to hold himself erect and keep his heart unshaken is the direct measure of his worth and function in the game of human life. He can *stand* the Universe. He can meet it and keep up his faith in it in the presence of those same features which lay his weaker brethren low. He can still find a zest in it, not by 'ostrich-like forgetfulness,' but by pure inward willingness to face the world with those deterrent objects there. And hereby he becomes one of the masters and lords of life. (1950, pp. 578-579)

Instances are legion of people who, despite great handicaps, attain noteworthy goals. Their efforts require endurance of tremendous physical or mental pain. It is endurance, or will, that maintains effort.

Some years ago, we saw a patient at Saint Elizabeths, who was in his fifties, taking halting steps, trying to find his way around the grounds, bumping into things. The man was blind. A year later, we saw the same man moving briskly around. He was able to cross the street, because he was attuned to noise and vibration and so could get his bearings. One day, the man was struck by an automobile. He suffered two broken arms, two broken legs, and fractured ribs. He recovered and eventually returned to his brisk pace.

The criminal learns that effort means pushing himself as hard as he can toward objectives that are attainable. He also learns to accept his limitations gracefully. The motto of Alcoholics Anonymous, taken from Reinhold Niebuhr, is a sound corrective for the criminal.

O God, give us serenity to accept what cannot be changed, courage to change what should be changed, and wisdom to distinguish the one from the other.

The substance of this message is vital to change. It is in stark contrast to the criminal's thinking.

I have no frustrations,
And the reason is to wit,
If at first I don't succeed,
I quit.

Pushing oneself is necessary for the habituation of new thinking processes and actions. The ultimate objective is making a habit of pushing oneself. In time, this becomes so natural to the criminal that not to drive himself seems strange. For the criminal, relaxation means complacency, and in this program, with these people, there is no room for a letup in effort. The criminal has always been energetic and ambitious. As a responsible person, he still has drive, and thus the need for continuous effort to direct it in a responsible fashion.

The criminal may state that he will make an "honest effort". As soon as an agent of change hears this phrase, he knows that either the commitment to the program is shaky or the criminal does not understand the concept of effort. By our definition, effort is honest. If the criminal is committed to change, he will be making responsible efforts along many lines. "Honest effort" has the ring of a half-try; there is a latent "I can't" in such a phrase that portends that if things do not work out, the criminal can always say that he tried but failed. With a dedication to change and an understanding of effort, as we define it, there is no issue of honest effort.

The criminal may decide that the way to demonstrate effort is to elect to do specific tasks purely as a matter of self-discipline. One man bought two bottles of soda and, instead of drinking them both, saved one for the next day. He also decided to refrain from masturbation. We take the position that such contrived tests are not significant beyond the act themselves. We have been through them with criminals, and they have not been effective, because there has been no carryover. Such self-discipline does not transfer to life in general.

Early in the process of change, the program's requirements are met with anger and self-pity, so that the criminal sees nothing useful resulting from making the effort to live in a manner that he has scorned all his life. The anger often is directed toward his job, because it is a condition of this program that the criminal start in a low position. One man spoke of "looking forward with dread" to his part-time work each day at a bank. He insisted that it was "stupid to stand in a little box all day" as a teller. After the bank closed, he worked part-time at a department store: "I go there with the attitude that I hate it." We do not take the position that the criminal must like his job. Liking is totally irrelevant for these people, who have used not liking something as an excuse to avoid the responsible. Rather, the criminal is taught to consider the long-range objective and maintain a perspective that extends beyond the mundane details of the job itself. A low-level job, no matter how menial, offers an arena for change. The criminal can exercise a self-discipline that has heretofore been lacking. He has the opportunity to develop sound work habits, to function with people harmoniously, to handle money responsibly, and to support himself and his family honestly.

During the early contact, the A.C. informs the criminal as to what he may expect. To the criminal, at this time the description of the disciplined life he will be leading is just words. As he implements the program, he learns what effort entails. One man commented, "I never thought it would be so hard to be decent."

The A.C. must not only meet the criminal's objections to putting forth effort but also his self-pity with its complaints of boredom and fatigue. Previously, the criminal has wanted others to give him reasons for living in our world and making efforts to do things our way. As long as the criminal regards everything as a burden or something to put up with, or does things to please the A.C., this is tokenism, not change. If the criminal is truly fed up with himself, then he is thankful to start life anew; there is satisfaction in redemption. Rather than being begged, cajoled, or persuaded by the A.C., the criminal has to persuade himself. The criminal can talk himself into things and out of things. Once he makes a responsible choice, he can talk himself into making the effort to implement it. There must be a *self-generated enthusiasm* to assume the initiatives to come to grips with problems and solve them responsibly.

> C began work as a second chainman in a surveying crew. Subject to many allergies, he worked in mosquito-laden fields grossing seventy dollars a week. Even with a strep throat and a 102-degree fever, he showed up for work. Within a year or so, he was a partner in a crack surveying team, earning $115 a week. He then became the first instrument man, earning in excess of $150 a week, and in line for a job as a crew chief. In addition to working six days a week on his regular job, he often spent Sundays on outside projects with his former crew chief. C saved $3,000 in less than two years.

C approached his work with zest, even when the conditions were extremely unpleasant. Stamina was not something that he already had. In fact, he had never in his life stuck to anything that required effort. Rather, he developed stamina, along with a great deal of expertise in his field, and both paid off in a relatively short time.

Effort is the decision to get down to business and to implement change thoroughly twenty-four hours a day. Every one of our criminals admits that it is not hard to live up to the principles of the program if he implements them. He is perfectly capable of effort, but there has been no reason to exert it in behalf of a way of life that he has scorned. If the criminal applies effort from the very beginning and approaches change by viewing it as an opportunity, he rapidly reaches a point where he says, "It is not hard." That is, he does not experience what he is doing as making an effort: "The harder I try, the easier it gets." There is less struggle and suffering as he habituates new thinking patterns and deters the old ones. Effort is not experienced as effort when one truly wants something badly enough and works for it.

As he embarks on our program, the criminal may believe that the responsible person has it made, in the sense that he has no more worries. It is his idea that one day he too will arrive and have no further problems. But, as we have pointed out, the criminal has not even known what constitutes a problem for the responsible person. To the criminal, a problem is being thwarted in achieving a criminal objective. Now, he has to progress to a new echelon of suffering, as he learns that responsibility entails meeting a *series* of problems and struggling with them. Deferred gratification, when it is finally achieved, is only the beginning of more troubles. A person struggles through law school and a clerkship and becomes a practicing attorney. This is just the beginning of other problems as he has to respond to a variety of professional and personal pressures. The tensionless state that the criminal envisions is possible only in death. The criminal learns in this program that his idea of Nirvana is a misconception and that he must put forth effort as long as he lives. As the criminal comes to realize this, we hear, "If this is life, it's a hell of a life." He wonders whether it is worth living a life in which one problem gives way to another. Although the noncriminal is used to this and accepts it, the criminal rejects it. Furthermore, the criminal discovers that there are no rewards for coping with problems; rather, it is expected.

> "When I do these things, there are no medals. There is no fun when I do the things I am expected to do; there are no kicks. . . . One gets snowed under with one problem after another."

The criminal has viewed himself as effortlessly reaching a summit from which he could look down, much like a king sitting on a throne and giving commands. His perspective shifts as he learns that even a king has problems and must make efforts to surmount adversities. As a person's assigned authority increases, the number of problems that he has also increases.

The following examples indicate the types of situations our people have met that have required considerable effort.

Vocational Difficulties

A half-dozen fellows in C's company were appointed management trainees and received a pay raise. However, C was told that he could not at that time advance beyond being a salesman. C had worked very hard and was disappointed about the failure to earn more money and the lack of promotion. However, he showed no anger and did not argue. Instead, he decided to do some fact-finding. He inquired as to why the store's wage commission had decided as it had. His behavior was totally appropriate and without self-pity. C found out that because he was still on probation by the court, he could not be promoted, even though the store had trusted him to the point of asking him to bank several thousand dollars each day. When it became evident that there would be no reversal of the decision, C looked for another job on his days off. Later, he gave notice and moved to another firm, where he advanced rapidly.

C's previous pattern would have been to raise a commotion about being unjustly treated, insult the store's personnel, and then quit. For the duration of the episode, he would also have stolen intermittently from the store. Instead, he endured the uncertainty about his status within the company, made the effort to ascertain the facts, and acted responsibly throughout.

Marital Problems

Before his change in this program, C had married Cynthia, who stole, lied, was unfaithful, and showed the entire range of criminal characteristics. As C became more responsible, Cynthia became more and more difficult to live with, and C saw through her more and more. She neglected and abused their infant son, was unaccountable for her time and money, and generally was a poor mother and wife. For a while, she lived with another man, leaving C to take care of the baby. She openly flaunted her infidelity. Her abuse of C reached the point where she struck him in the face with a belt and told him that he had better not go to sleep, or he would be in danger. This was one of many efforts on Cynthia's part to provoke him so that he would leave and she could claim that he deserted her. Throughout the innumerable incidents of verbal and physical abuse, C remained calm. His only physical action was to restrain her when she had a weapon in her hand. At no time did he become angry.

C's earlier pattern would have been to abuse his wife verbally or physically, leave the house, and go to a bus station to pick up a woman for sex. In the present situation, he endured the abuse and lived with the hope that by so doing he could be in a better position to effect changes in his wife's attitude so that they could live in harmony. Regardless of the fact that she eventually left him, C's self-discipline in the situation was important to his changing.

Financial Problems

Working as a salesman at a furniture store, C had some lean months financially during which his expenses exceeded his earnings. In addition to supporting himself, he had to pay support for his two children. As a result, he had to supplement his income by scrubbing floors and doing other menial labor during spare time. Despite this long period in which he was discouraged, he did not resign. His persistence paid off: he progressed to the point of being number 2 of 185 salesmen in the district. There was another period of lean times, but he endured this and emerged from it to earn $20,000 annually, with a zest for further progress.

Earlier in life, C had never persisted at anything, especially if he had to endure any adversity. It had been beneath him to scrub floors or to work at any job where he could not be in charge. Consideration about supporting his family was minimal. He had been so uncaring about his wife and children that he brought other women into the house at night and had sex with them. In short, the effort and endurance shown as a furniture salesman had been totally alien to him.

Death and Child Care

C remarried after a separation from his wife. He conscientiously paid child support to his ex-wife for their daughters. In fact, he contributed more than the court required. C maintained a cordial relationship with his former wife and, for the first time, showed tremendous interest in being with his children. His ex-wife was diagnosed as having cancer. For the duration of her illness, C devoted time every week to her, buoying her spirits and doing whatever was possible to make her comfortable. Gradually, C assumed more and more responsibility for the children. He helped in providing a housekeeper for them and spent nearly all his leisure time with them. He was at his former wife's bedside as she entered the final phase of her illness. He promised to care for the children and gave her unwavering emotional support in final hours. During this time, C missed more than two weeks of work. When she passed away, C took the children into his home and functioned as a devoted father.

This may not sound very remarkable for a noncriminal, but it was in utter contrast to the way C had lived before this program. He was a person who, as he described it, "whooped and hollered" whenever something did not go his way. Worse than that, he was violent and in one instance had committed a homicide when a particular situation had not worked out according to his wishes.

Less dramatic incidents in day-to-day living also show how important the application of effort is. One criminal had purchased a new automobile with serious defects. The continuing problems with the vehicle caused him and his wife much inconvenience. They had to drive the car some distance to the dealership, rent a car, and spend considerable money. The criminal made an effort to be patient in the way he conducted himself and in his response to his exasperated wife. He learned how necessary it was to make the effort to keep accurate financial records and to retain and file receipts of work done. All this was new to him. Although suffering a loss with respect to the car, he gained in the long run in what he had learned.

As we explained earlier, it is artificial to abstract a corrective for separate treatment. This is probably nowhere more obvious than in the case of effort. Throughout this program, the corrective described here is closely related to fulfilling obligations, to relating interdependently with others, and to all the other correctives for thinking errors.

PUTTING ONESELF IN ANOTHER'S POSITION: THE COGNITIVE CORRELATE OF EMPATHY

A goal of therapeutic efforts with many patients is empathy, in which one considers what other people are feeling. Empathy is defined mainly in terms of feelings.

The ability to know how others feel. (Hutt et al. 1966, p. 292)

What happens in empathy may be phrased in this way: "How would I feel under the same circumstances?" (Alexander and Ross 1952, p. 315)

Changes in feelings, as we have mentioned earlier, are invariably the result of changes in cognitive processes. In working with the criminal, we help him to learn to be empathic expeditiously by rational methods. If a criminal takes another's thinking into account, he also is being considerate of that person's feelings.

The correction of the thinking error of failing to put oneself in another's place is mandatory for the criminal, although not for the noncriminal. To be sure, the noncriminal is at a disadvantage in relationships and in decisionmaking if he fails to consider the position of others. However, for him such an error does not result in serious social consequences. In the criminal, this thinking error must be corrected because it contributes to crime, and hence, to injury to others.

The criminal does put himself in another's place in his criminal operations; the successful execution of a crime depends on it. He capitalizes on his capacity to pick up cues in order to anticipate how his victim will react. This is the essence of a proficient con operation, and it plays a role in all other types of crimes. However, he rarely takes others' thoughts and feelings into account in any responsible way. To do so would interfere with his criminal actions.

One dimension of this thinking error is that the criminal lacks accurate, cumulative knowledge of a person. Even if he lives with a particular person, each encounter with that person is treated *de novo*, as if there were no history to the relationship. It is as though the criminal does not know the person and is unaware of how he thinks. This makes it even more unlikely for him to put himself in that person's place. The criminal does not develop an accurate concept even of his parents. That is, he does not view them in the way that responsible people do. As a child, he approaches each transaction with them anew, considering only what it is that he wants at the particular time.

Learning consideration for others is a fundamental process that begins for most people in early childhood. The youngster is taught to think in terms of how other people will respond to what he does. Putting oneself in another's position is a habit for most people and does not require a deliberate effort. It is a pattern built into the social order. The parent thinks about how his child will react, and the child often anticipates how his parent will behave. Enlightened employers, when working out matters of company policy, find it necessary to understand the thinking of their employees, so they include worker representatives on policy committees. Currently, students are appointed to school and university management boards and participate in the formulation of educational policies. A speaker's selection of a topic is based in part on how he gauges the interests and attitudes of his audience. The criminal rarely thinks of, and almost never does, even the little things that responsible people do to please others.

> C was not aware that Mother's Day was approaching until he heard it over the radio. Then, he thought about sending his mother some flowers. Because she lived in a rural area of a distant state, he found this prohibitive in cost. So he did nothing to remember her on Mother's Day.

Most criminals fail even to think of such kindnesses, unless it is for a self-serving objective. Out of sentimentality, they occasionally perform a favor for someone whom they neglect or exploit the other 364 days of the year. They have no idea that good will is built on small acts of consideration. As C reported the Mother's Day episode, the group raised questions, and he recalled other, comparable events. His parents had once sent him ten dollars for his birthday, and he thanked them by calling them collect over a distance of more than one thousand five hundred miles. Identifying C's thinking error of failing to consider others was the first step; rectifying it was the next.

The following incident shows the type of learning that takes place as we dissect patterns of thinking and action.

C was due to appear in court. He phoned to advise us that he would not be able to be there because he had hurt his arm and it was very painful, needing medical attention. His attorney told him to call the court and inform them. The lawyer then called us to find out whether C had really broken his arm, as reported. We told him that all we knew was that he had said that he had hurt his arm. The attorney then asked C to get a note from the physician. Inwardly, C blazed with anger at his lawyer. The attitude that he revealed to us was, "What right did he have to question me?" He was so angry that he failed to find out later in the day whether he was free or to be sent to jail.

There were many thinking errors in this episode, including anger, a lack of receptivity, and a failure to be self-critical. The most prominent thinking error was C's failure to put himself in the lawyer's place. He failed to recognize that it was not only the lawyer's prerogative, but also his duty, to question why C had been absent from court. The attorney was simply doing his job by trying to ascertain the facts. Had C considered the situation from a standpoint other than that of his own immediate objective, he might have antagonized fewer people and perhaps restored some lost credibility.

Every day, the criminal makes errors in which he fails to put himself in another's place. The following are examples in which we chose to focus on this error among the many that were brought out in phenomenologic reports.

C's wife, who did not drive often, asked C to accompany her while she went shopping. She particularly liked to go to bazaars in hopes of picking up bargains. C refused to go and insisted that his wife find her own way. He was angry at her requests and considered her presumptuous even to ask him to go. He did not want to put up with her wasting time, buying what he considered frivolous items, and spending endless time deliberating over even the smallest purchase. C had other things he wanted to do.

C's indignation was evident, even as he reported to us what had taken place. This is only one of many situations in which he had failed to consider his wife's wishes. We focused on this thinking error many times, with the result that C eventually changed his thinking and action.

C decided to accompany his wife without his usual protests and objections. In fact, on this trip, he started to pay attention to the merchandise. He thought about what might make attractive gifts for other people. He purchased a piece of jewelry for a relative, a gift for his wife's grandson, and an item that he thought his boss might like to have.

C not only put himself in his wife's place, but also began to think of what might please other people. Another criminal showed the same error when he went to meet with his probation officer.

> When C appeared to meet the probation officer, he found that the man was not there. Before leaving, C asked the secretary her name. She wanted to know why he was asking. He found himself getting angry, thinking about what right she had to question him. C replied that he wanted it on record that he had appeared on the right date at the right time. He expected to be able to refer by name to the secretary, with whom he was leaving that message. The secretary replied by giving only her first name. This made C even angrier.

We pointed out that C failed to think about why this girl was being so cautious. A probable reason was that in her position she encountered many criminals with whom she did not want any involvement. Consequently, she may have decided to be discreet about revealing her full name. Considering the situation in this light was foreign to C; he was put down and angry about her refusal to accede to his request.

The details of daily living furnish innumerable opportunities to apply this corrective. The many transactions within a household provide a laboratory for implementation. The criminal who is married has been accustomed to pushing his wife around and rarely considering her opinion, whether it be on a decision as to what kind of vacuum cleaner to purchase, or about how to allocate a paycheck. He now has the chance to improve his relationship with his wife. The smallest transaction offers an opportunity to put himself in another's position.

> "Again, as you said, even sitting in a chair and thinking may deprive my wife of the company she wants. But when I'm sitting and thinking, that's what I want to be doing, and where my wants are involved, I simply never think of others. And I don't think things through that far. It surprised me that just sitting and thinking could affect someone else."

In the process of change, a criminal may criticize his wife for making some of the same errors that he is now correcting in himself. One criminal faulted his wife for her inflexibility and dogmatism, an observation that was accurate. However, what he failed to consider was that she was not that way when they married. Because he had been irresponsible in so many ways and had made such poor decisions, his wife had had to take over, and she did so with increasing firmness. If the criminal had had this perspective, he would have understood what she had to do out of necessity, rather than criticized her for trying to do her best.

Another aspect of the corrective for this thinking error is for the criminal to understand how people function in particular roles. This applies particularly at work.

> When C began working at a restaurant, he was contemptuous of the entire staff. He regarded the owner as shortsighted, the management as stupid, the waiters as incompetent, and the bartender as inefficient. He was most critical of the busboys, whom he regarded almost as infrahuman. Even though he himself was a busboy, C regarded himself superior to everyone who worked there, regardless of station. He believed that he was brighter, more knowledgeable, and more efficient.

We picked apart error after error as C reported his thinking after each evening's work at the restaurant. The uniqueness, sense of ownership, criminal pride, lack of trust, failure to be interdependent, and many other errors were all evident to us. After several months of participating in this program, C began to put himself more and more in the place of others, especially as he gained experience as busboy, bartender, and waiter. One day, he reflected during a phenomenologic report, "Busboys are human beings." He had gradually arrived at this conclusion. His thinking had evolved to a point where he concluded that he was not so superior, and the others were not so stupid. In fact, he stopped criticizing the busboys and did his utmost to assist them.

Here is another example in which a criminal thought only of his own wishes, and not of how another person was expected to function:

> Sandra and C had been "romantically" involved for some time before Sandra became a hospital employee. Once she began work at the hospital, Sandra was wary of being seen on the hospital grounds with C, a forensic service patient. She knew that there was a policy that staff did not fraternize socially with patients during working hours in any way outside the job requirements. C had wanted Sandra to eat with him in the general hospital cafeteria, but Sandra proposed instead that they eat on C's ward as they had in the past during visiting hours. C angrily expressed his displeasure to Sandra.

There was total failure by C to consider how hospital employees function. He wanted Sandra to make compromises for him without any thought as to how this might affect others' perceptions of Sandra. This is part of a general pattern in which the criminal not only fails to see people as other responsible people view them but lacks any understanding of how others function in today's world.

C was infatuated with a particular woman. He became irate when he saw her kissing other people on greeting them. What C viewed as sexual was nothing more than a reflection of the bright, breezy, outgoing personality of a young woman who was functioning no differently from her peers.

Had C not made this thinking error, he might have realized that what the woman was doing was not in the least bit sexual, and not jumped to a conclusion based on his criminal reality.

In the process of change, the criminal constantly has extreme and unrealistic views of people. For example, his boss is either an irresponsible fool or the wisest and most responsible person. Yet he does not have any realistic concept of what a boss's role is. People are perceived as gods or devils, whereas they are neither—just fallible people with assets and liabilities. The criminal has never viewed people in a balanced way. This important lesson is learned partially through putting himself in the place of others. What the criminal must incorporate into his thinking is succinctly expressed in an often quoted old Indian saying:

> Grant that I may not criticize my neighbor until I have walked a mile in his moccasins.

As he puts himself in the other's place, the criminal comes to understand how responsible people view him—something that he has ignored before, unless the opinion were favorable. While he was violating, it was habitual for him to cut off others' adverse reactions, so that he could proceed undeterred. Now, rather than cut off unfavorable opinions, he utilizes them as stimuli for improvement. When he finds that he is still being eyed with suspicion, rather than responding with outrage, he puts himself in the position of the distrustful observer. He keeps in mind that because he is a criminal, it is reasonable that he be viewed with suspicion.

Putting himself in another's place is a corrective that the criminal can practice by himself.

> One night, C spent four hours setting for himself the tasks of putting himself in the place of other people in his life. He began with his childhood, and he thought of his past behavior and all his victims. He went from family to wife to strangers whom he had pushed around and intimidated. He did this with each major area of life. So absorbed in this was he that he took scarcely a break, except for a drink of water, until midnight when he finally stopped. He then went to bed and dreamed about being victimized himself by a bunch of criminals.

We have found that an exercise in which the criminal puts himself in the place of victims of crimes in which he has not participated also enhances his self-disgust and can be repeated productively many times.

C was watching a television program in which there was considerable violence. He detached himself from this, concentrating instead on the victim. In this particular episode, a young man who had everything going for him went into crime. He took up with a divorced girl who was well-respected in the community, and he was finally caught for bond theft. C could think only about the lonely girl whose life was shattered. He related this to episodes in his life.

*   *   *

C read about a teen-aged girl who was the victim of a savage crime and died because of it. He thought about this girl as an individual—her love of life, her vocational aspirations, and her scholastic ambitions, all of which the newspapers described. He also put himself in the place of her parents, siblings, and schoolmates. As C did this, his own rape-homicide thinking filled him with disgust for himself, as well as for the girl's assailant.

The corrective of putting oneself in another's place has been used by every one of our changed criminals. It is such a new idea to the criminal that it even made a considerable impact in the days when we were teaching the correctives didactically rather than applying them specifically to daily thoughts and actions. When we have inquired of criminals several years after their participation in the intensive part of the program as to which corrective made the greatest impact, we have received interesting answers. Some criminals do not remember any of the correctives by name (even though they are implementing them every day) but, if there is one that stands out strongly in their minds, it is this one. As the criminal increasingly puts himself in the place of other people, he realizes ever more sharply how he has affected people throughout his life, and there is greater impetus for further change. Because of this correction in his thinking, he truly develops empathy.

SENSITIZATION TO INJURING OTHERS

Before the 1970s, society viewed injury stemming from crimes mostly in terms of the physical damage inflicted by assaults, rapes, and homicides. Then the concept of injury expanded to include monetary loss and property damage. During the early 1970s, more attention has been given to the extent of injury; it has expanded to take into account other consequences, such as emotional damage. Laws have reflected society's views. That is, there are gradations of the seriousness of crimes, the most serious being homicide and the least being the so-called victimless crimes, such as gambling.

Early in our work, we expanded the concept of injury far beyond its current usage. For effecting change in the criminal, every type of injury, tangible and intangible, must be considered as a possible consequence of *every* crime. Our view is that there is no such thing as a victimless crime. For example, as a consequence of gambling, referred to as a victimless crime by Rogers (1971), a family may have to do without something it needs. In fact, families may become destitute as a consequence of gambling. Gambling is often supported by theft, which has a toll of injuries of its own.

Our concept of the victim of a crime also extends beyond the common view. The victims of crimes are not limited to the direct targets of the criminal but include the family of the immediate victim, the criminal's own family if he is apprehended, the community, and society at large.

If society's view of injury is limited, then the criminal by comparison has virtually no concept at all of the many injuries that he inflicts or of how serious those injuries are. For him it is illogical to view himself as injuring others, because he does not regard himself as a criminal, but instead as a very decent person. In fact, rather than regard himself as harming another person, he often places the blame on the victim. If a store is robbed, then the store is at fault for not having better security. If a man is mugged, he should not have been where he was in the first place. If a girl is raped, she should not have been so friendly. There are only two types of situations in which the criminal views himself as injuring others: in the zero state and when he is held accountable. When he is in a zero state, there is a global degradation of himself. One element of his disgust with himself in such a state is that he has harmed others. But the zero state is transient, and his regret about injury is brief. The time at which the criminal is most likely to talk about how he has injured others is when he is held accountable. It is obvious to the criminal that he has harmed his immediate victim when a physical injury occurs. But he divests himself of responsibility and blames the victim or some aspect of the circumstances surrounding the crime. His acknowledgement that he has harmed another person is mainly self-serving. He regrets what he did mainly because he got caught. Even in an accountability situation, a criminal sometimes makes statements that appear callous, showing what others regard as an astonishing lack of sensitivity and awareness. When an interviewer was talking to a criminal about how, over the years, he had hurt his mother by what he did, the criminal replied, "I'm in prison. My mother isn't." He did not view his mother, who had made significant sacrifices for him, as being injured by anything he had done.

If someone does something to injure the criminal, he is put down and angry. The same is true if anyone harms a person toward whom the criminal has a sentimental attachment. But he does not view himself as a victimizer of others.

From the criminal's phenomenologic report, we dissect patterns of thought and action that result in injury to others, and we introduce correctives. We focus the TV camera on patterns of action operative in the past and in the present. As the process of change progresses, we address ourselves mainly to the criminal's current thinking. His irresponsible ideas, if implemented, would result in extensive injury to others. The objective is his application of the corrective before a violation occurs rather than a post mortem after injuries have been inflicted.

Correction entails showing the criminal the full impact of a criminal act. Discussions with him extend beyond legally defined crimes to include such patterns as lying. If a criminal promises to meet someone at nine o'clock to repay him some money and fails to do so, injury has occurred. The person not only is still out of money but has been inconvenienced by having to go to the meeting place, wait, and have his day disrupted. Attendant to this is the victim's worrying about whether he will be repaid, having to spend more time contacting the debtor, taking more time to meet again, and so on. Thus, the consequences of a single lie, which on its face seems relatively innocuous, are sizable.

A chain of injuries stems from every crime beginning with the immediate victim, and extending to the victim's family, the criminal's own family, the people in the neighborhood, the community at large, and society in general. In a breaking and entering, objects are destroyed and property is taken. The financial loss from this is only the beginning. There is often a loss of objects of sentimental value, which cannot be replaced. Further expenses are incurred when the victim's insurance premium is raised and when he decides to increase his security system. The victim has to spend his time talking with the police and insurance agents and shopping for replacements. An even larger time commitment is required if he has to lose hours from work to appear in court. Still, this is only time and money. The emotional consequences are often more serious. To have the sanctity of one's home invaded is especially shattering. The victim never again leaves his home unattended without fear.

> Although I have taken new security measures, I am left with a sense of insecurity and a new reality: that lights and locks do not a fortress make, and the only things really separating Them [the burglars] from me are double-paned windows. That reality greets me each time I return home and ask myself: Has anyone been here? And at night now, as I lie in bed, listening to the walls creak and settle, the thought, What was that? no longer occurs. Instead, I now wonder, Who is that? (Curry 1974)

This touches only on the injuries to the immediate victim. It takes only a single incident to produce a climate of fear in a neighborhood. The residue of living in fear is perhaps the most enduring and costly aspect of such a crime.

The scope of injury is broadened still further if one considers the total cost of similar crimes that occur tens of thousands of times across the country every year. It was estimated (*Washington Post* 4/6/75) that in the Washington, D.C., area alone a home or office was burglarized every twelve seconds in 1973. A tremendous expense is borne by taxpayers for additional police, more judges, the maintenance of correctional facilities, and their adjunctive programs. The criminal's own family shares in the cost.

All this holds true for thefts from businesses. The establishments victimized spend more and more for security—cameras for surveillance, guards, plainclothesmen, and iron grilles. Stores that suffer greatly from theft find insurance premiums skyrocketing, especially in high-crime areas. Some of the stores cannot withstand the high losses and fail to survive. The consequences to customers are considerable, because the losses from thefts are passed on to them. The criminal's own mother spends perhaps ten percent more for an item in a store because he, and people like him, have been stealing. When large stores go out of business in high-crime areas, consumers have to go farther to shop or pay much higher prices at smaller neighborhood stores.

When viewing the consequences of an assault, the criminal faults the immediate victim for interfering with him or in some way posing a challenge or threat. Once again, he does not think in terms of the injury that he inflicts, or he does so in only a very limited manner—the blood spilled. The consequences of an assault are physical and emotional. Our criminal groups, in the process of change, have pointed out the far-reaching effects on the victim's family and friends. In addition, they have cited the impact on the neighborhood and society at large. A climate of fear blankets the area of the crime. Not only do residents spend their money on elaborate security devices, but they do not go out at night. When they travel, they often go by car, even though their destination is within walking distance. Some citizens become frightened enough to arm themselves. The chain of consequences is without end, as a person's or community's entire way of life adapts to what is perceived as an ever-present danger.

Sex crimes have similar consequences. There has been considerable attention paid lately to the dilemma of rape victims, who suffer not only the physical attack and its emotional consequences but also the degradation and humiliation of the aftermath—physical examination, investigation by police, and questioning on the witness stand in court. There is sometimes lasting disruption of the victim's sexual life and emotional relationship with men. The damage may be more traumatic when the victim is a minor.

The so-called white collar crimes also cause tremendous anguish. One can take the case of a couple whose invested savings are embezzled. Money that has been earned through hard work over the years disappears, and with it their security. To attempt to recover the money, the victims have to pay further sums to lawyers. The physical and emotional stress is great in such proceedings, which may wear on for months or even years. Such a crime can virtually destroy the patterns of people's lives. They live with a pervasive distrust of the individuals and institutions that have always seemed reliable.

In teaching the criminal this greatly expanded concept of injury to others, we discuss his reactions if a member of his family were injured by a crime. Of course, his response is, "If I could get that s.o.b., I'd kill him." How he has victimized his own family is also cogently developed in group meetings. In chapter 3 of volume 1, we pointed out how the criminal exploits his family from early in his youth. He did not start out with the intention of exploiting his parents, but he has done so time and again. He has made all kinds of demands on them, and usually they have accommodated him. Many have spared themselves no expense in trying to do what they thought was best for their children. Mothers have taken two jobs to provide their criminal youngsters with whatever they wanted, thinking that this might prevent their stealing. Parents have given their criminal offspring money, have covered for them, and have repeatedly bailed them out of trouble. They have clung to the hope that they could be instrumental in helping their children to straighten out. But by their way of life, the criminals have destroyed their parents' faith, shattered their hopes, and broken their hearts. In reviewing the past, we focus the TV camera on the many injuries that the criminal's own family has suffered as a consequence of his acts. When faced with this, the criminal sees himself as he is, and experiences remorse. One of our men recalled his intimidation of his younger brother.

"When we were kids, Matt got fifty cents for his birthday. I knew the day before that he was getting it. I was saving football trading cards at the same time and I remember how excited I was the night before thinking of how I could con Matt out of his money and all the penny football cards I could buy with it. Why, I might even get whole teams. The next day, half bullying, half con, I got the money and bought the cards. What bothers me most about this memory is the sick, twisted excitement I had the night before. Matt really felt the loss of that fifty cents. I know he did. It was a bright, shiny present and he had lots of use he would have liked to put it to. . . . If he gave his consent it was unwillingly, and he felt the loss keenly. It was a theft. I didn't even think of the stealing, of the way my brother would feel. I just saw his money as being mine."

Self-disgust is a consequence of this type of review. It is a prod to implementing correctives and serves as a deterrent to further injury.

In the daily meetings, the criminal's phenomenologic report contains instances in which he caused injury to others, but did not recognize it as such. One criminal and his friend walked out of a bar without paying a bill. We discussed this as a theft with consequent injury to the owner and ultimately to customers who might have to pay higher prices. We extended the discussion of injury to the criminal's stealing patterns throughout life. Often, the injury is not inflicted through an arrestable crime, but rather through a lie, an anger reaction, or failure to consider the other person.

> C told a small lie with respect to an error that he had made in food preparation while working as a cook. He put mashed potatoes on a dish instead of French fries. He said to the waitress that he thought the fries were an extra order in addition to the mashed potatoes.

The criminal failed to consider the injury to the waitress (putting her on the spot with the customer) or the inconvenience to the customer. Furthermore, his pattern of lying was deleterious to the necessary teamwork required at the restaurant. In another situation, a confined criminal left the grounds without authorization in order to have sex. Afterwards, on the basis of many experiences with people who have been caught for such a violation, we traced through the potential multiple injuries had he been caught this time. First would have been the people whom he would have let down—in this case, the doctors vouching for him in legal matters, others in the program, and his family. Second would have been future victims, because this incident would have been only the crack in the door to a resumption of patterns in which there would be more victims. Third, there ultimately would be injury to himself, because he would be returning to a life of crime with all its hazards.

As change occurs, the criminal makes reparations when possible, deters violations, and considers in advance the consequences of criminal thinking. Now there is the thinking: What will happen if I have sex with her? What will happen if I don't tell the truth?

> C was visiting his wife at the hospital. He was on his way to the cafeteria to get a snack when a janitor yelled at him abruptly and rudely not to walk on a freshly waxed floor. C's thinking was, "I'm going to shove my fist down his throat." Then he thought about the consequences, mainly in terms of what such assaultive behavior had resulted in throughout his life. He simply moved to the edge of the floor and said nothing.
>
> *   *   *
>
> C went to a university library, where he read and listened to some music. He looked around and saw many appealing girls. He thought about how

he would like to pick one up and take her to bed. Then he stopped himself and thought of the consequences this kind of thinking had had in the past. He had kept a "stable" of young girls (he was in his forties), had exploited them sexually and economically, and had psychologically hurt them. He decided to stop looking around at girls and concentrate on reading and music.

When the criminal applies this corrective, conscience becomes operative. (We pointed out in chapter 6 of volume 1 that the criminal has a conscience, but that internal deterrents, or conscience fears, are not sustained.) Now, the criminal learns the value of guilt. He cannot undo all the harm that he has caused, but, by developing a broad concept of injury, he can avoid doing more harm in the future. Applying the correctives that we have discussed, he develops a genuine compassion for others who are injured by people operating as he did.

An acquaintance of C's was killed in a holdup while transporting money from his employer to a deposit box. C attended the funeral and thought about how this young man was cut down by criminals. He reflected on how he had planned an arrangement to holdup an establishment. C thought about many other things he had done to injure others. He was so upset that he could not tolerate sitting in the funeral parlor for long. His wife wanted to stay there for a while, but he wanted to leave. He was disturbed by the death of this man, the effect on the victim's family, and, most of all, the things he recalled about his own life, in which he had harmed others.

This criminal's compassion was without value because he did not demonstrate it responsibly in other ways.

As the criminal functions responsibly, he increasingly expresses concern for members of his family whom he has injured. Demonstrating a complete change of attitude, he is considerate of them and helpful. One criminal was so worried about his father's drinking that he prodded his father into seeking professional counseling. Another was extremely solicitous of his wife and children, whom he had deserted years earlier, despite the fact that his wife was asking nothing from him. A third began visiting an uncle, aunt, and half-brother, who had done so much for him in his youth but whom he had exploited and discarded. Still another man looked up his nine-year-old son, whom he had not seen since the boy was an infant. Such actions are typical of all changing criminals in our group. In the past, their concern was transient; now it is sustained.

In summary, our concept of injury is brand new to the criminal and is broader even than society's view of injury. We are not saying that our view need necessarily be adopted by society, but it is necessary to regard injury this comprehensively when one is operating a program to change criminals. The scope of the corrective is analogous to the casting of a pebble into a calm lake. Just as there are ever-widening ripples once the pebble strikes the water, so there are ever-widening repercussions of a criminal act. These extend far beyond physical injury and monetary loss. The victims of a single crime are invariably numerous. The criminal, by learning and implementing this corrective, understands the full impact of his crime patterns, and this understanding leads to application of deterrents.

OBLIGATION

It is obvious to the responsible person that he should try to avoid injuring others. The obligation not to injure is a negative one, but obligation has positive requirements as well, and they are essential to the criminal's effective adaptation to society.

Instead of viewing himself as obligated to others, the criminal functions as though the entire world is obligated to him. He perceives being obligated as being controlled and used. Obligations interfere with what he wants. As far as the criminal is concerned, those who honor obligations are suckers and slaves. When the criminal *appears* to fulfill an obligation, it is usually in the service of a criminal objective (such as a con job in which he does many things preparatory to later exploitation) or to build up his opinion of himself as a good person. The criminal affirms obligations when fulfilling them helps him receive the benefits of both worlds. That is, he does what he must to coexist with responsible people. Holding a job and bringing home a paycheck satisfy requirements of the family and signify to others that he is functioning responsibly. In a sense, he buys off others by doing something for them, rather than acting out of any moral imperative. By holding the responsible world at bay in this manner, he has greater leeway for criminal operations.

For teaching purposes, we speak of two types of obligation. One is the musts of daily life in which there is little or no choice; this relates mainly to what others expect. The second is an inner or moral sense of obligation. With respect to the first, many things expected of us are monotonous and onerous. Fulfilling these is a part of life. Onerous tasks are so habitual that the responsible person does not regard them as obligations. A person who has a job is obligated to report to work on time, to carry out particular duties, and to conduct himself properly. In the course of his work, he has to do some things that he is not eager to do and, in some cases, that are disagreeable. By having taken the job, he has entered into a kind of contract, even if it is not a formal written one. The idea of a contract pervades many undertakings, even though the parties do not think in terms of a contract. A man who purchases a home for his family imposes on himself obligations of ownership that extend beyond paying the mortgage and taxes. He has to keep it in repair both inside and outside. Most homeowners alter their life style upon purchasing a home because they consider themselves obligated to maintain it, almost as though they have contracted to do so. They mow lawns, wash windows, change furnace filters, paint. Home maintenance is a self-imposed obligation, not a binding contract, but the person acts as though there is a contract to do the things that are required. The concept of contract is so all-encompassing that it applies in virtually every area of life. Even in deriving pleasure, obligation is involved. If a person has a boat, he is obliged to register, insure, and maintain it. In a sexual relationship, there is obligation for mutual physical and emotional satisfaction. The criminal has never thought in these terms. As far as he is concerned, people and possessions exist solely for his use.

The criminal may question us about our fulfilling obligations that we do not think we should have to fulfill. Thus, there is a discussion of obeying laws that we think are unjust or abiding by decisions with which we disagree. The responsible view that we teach is to obey laws even when we are not totally in accord with them. This does not mean that one should totally capitulate to the existing system. Rather, one has the option of working responsibly to change it.

For each individual there is a wide latitude of choice as to what he obligates himself to do. He may choose to undertake specific tasks that he thinks will be personally fulfilling to him. Some people believe that they should be active in their churches or involved in community politics. Such people perceive these obligations as part of a moral imperative. For them, it is a matter of the "shoulds" of life, rather than the "musts." One's inner sense of obligation is based on an evaluation of what his relationship is to another person. Sometimes we do things that are of no immediate advantage to us, solely because they engender good will. We also have ideals that we consider ourselves obligated to fulfill. People dedicate themselves to causes out of an inner moral urging, and they act without fanfare or demand for recognition. It is obligation as they experience it. Some people contribute a portion of their income to charity, because they are committed to helping those less fortunate. They do not view this as obligation; rather, helping others is part of their lives. Others might see them as making great sacrifices, but they believe that being charitable enriches their own lives.

Each time one fulfills an obligation, he himself is ultimately one of the beneficiaries.

C's wife had repeatedly reminded C to fix a lamp that had not been working for a long time. C had put off repairing it again and again and each time had objected to his wife's "nagging" him about it.

As a result of defaulting on such obligations, C's house was in disarray and his wife was out of sorts. Once C began fulfilling domestic obligations, the atmosphere changed from one of friction to one of harmony. With the obligatory chores taken care of, C and his wife spent less time arguing and had more time for less onerous jobs. Thus, C and his wife both benefited. Incidents like this occur daily in the criminal's life.

Obligation is the antithesis of control. It is a new concept to the criminal, especially because he has considered living in obligation as being vulnerable to control by others. For example, he has regarded the dutiful husband as one controlled by his wife. That the criminal should take this view is understandable, because he has controlled and exploited those who, out of a sense of obligation, have helped him.

In the course of change, the criminal must be cognizant of his old patterns when he does something for another person. It has been his custom to obligate others by helping them out, while at the same time building up his opinion of himself. Now the question is, If he helps a responsible person and is sincere now, will he not become fragmented later and eventually exploit the recipient of his favor?

It is mandatory that the criminal do nothing to help another criminal. This invariably leads to trouble—if not now, then later. Doing a favor for a criminal establishes anticipated exploitation, if not in the giver, then in the recipient. (See the discussion of obligation in chapter 5 of volume 1.)

We do not preach to the criminal about obligation, but through his reports we examine his relationships and transactions with others and apply the concept. The following situation exemplifies a criminal's not considering obligation at all, but instead permitting his own wishes of the moment to be the important factor in decision-making.

C had been holding a particular job for eleven months. He had asked his employer for permission to attend a two week conference related to his field. The boss turned him down because things on the job were in turmoil at the time. C thought about quitting immediately, so that he could attend the conference and then move on to some other position. He was dissatisfied with his present job because of the salary, hours, and working conditions. The most important drawback to the work, as he viewed it, was that there was hardly any opportunity to advance. He was growing restless and dissatisfied about not having the chance to learn new skills and assume greater responsibility. Consequently, he was ready to quit, figuring that he had little to lose.

There were many thinking errors with respect to making this one decision. We emphasized that C was considering neither his obligation to his employer nor his own long-range future. He was very much needed in the firm and had committed himself to this employer to complete specified assignments. Furthermore, he was preparing to resign with no definite job in prospect. C acknowledged that it would be inconsiderate to leave at this time. However, he failed to recognize that staying on the job was to his advantage. Because of his spotty employment record, it was doubtful that someone else would be eager to hire him. In recent years, he had not remained at any job for more than ten months. In addition, it was unlikely that his present employer would recommend him favorably for a position elsewhere if he left abruptly at such a critical time. After much discussion of his thinking errors and after being exposed to a new way of thinking, C decided not only that he was obligated to his employer to stay, but that he, too, would benefit by remaining on the job, at least until he helped to put the office in order.

Again we note that, as in implementing any of the other correctives, the criminal may go to extremes. A sense of obligation can be too burdensome. A person can be so occupied in fulfilling what he considers to be obligations that he overlooks other matters. A man can be so caught up in obligations at work that he neglects his wife and children. Obligation becomes a burden when a person is so consumed by it that he is crippled in his functioning elsewhere. The ideal is a balanced, rationally determined evaluation of what is obligatory.

The criminal can learn only by doing. In the final analysis, it is his choice. We explain his choices to him. The ultimate objective is for the criminal to be cognizant of obligations as they run through his life, so that he automatically fulfills them. In fact, if implemented, the thinking processes become so habitual that the criminal does not view obligation as obligation. Obligation has then become an ingrained pattern, a natural part of responsible living.

ELIMINATION OF THE
OWNERSHIP ATTITUDE

The criminal believes that it is proper for him to take possession by stealth or force of anything he chooses. Ownership thinking is expressed in both crime and nonarrestable activities. When the criminal enters a room, he views all the contents as belonging to him. When he sees an attractive woman, he regards her as his bed partner. This sense of ownership is the extreme expression of the control function. With respect to people, it is a relatively sustained attitude. Whether he appears domineering or subservient, the criminal's ownership thinking is still very much present, although his outward demeanor does not always reflect it. The sense of ownership may strike others as so removed from reality as to be psychotic. It is far from that. The criminal's thinking and action reflect a calculated world view in which his rights, desires, and objectives preempt those of others. Ever since childhood, he has dealt with parents, playmates, teachers, and employers in ownership terms. With time, this thinking pattern has strengthened. It reflects itself in his attitude toward debts and toward the law. If he repays a debt, he views the lender as required to make further loans to him—that is, to be further exploited by him. The criminal has abused society, all the while insisting on what he regards as his rights. "His rights" to him has meant the license to do as he pleases without accountability. He has failed to learn that one person's liberty (his rights) ends where the next person's nose begins. Regarding the law, his attitude is, Break it if it suits your purpose, and use it to your own advantage whenever possible.

The criminal actually owns very little legitimately. What he has stolen from others far outweighs that which he has earned. From our perspective as change agents, the criminal owes the world far more than it owes him. Although it is an overstatement, our uncompromising stance during the process of change remains that the world owes the criminal absolutely nothing. This view is essential to fostering an attitude in the criminal that he must earn his place in the scheme of things.

In the early phase of the program, each day's phenomenologic report invariably contains many instances of the ownership error. That it is remarkably persistent is not surprising inasmuch as it is so integral a part of the pervasive power and control patterns. The criminal is used to taking people for granted and prejudging how they will and ought to function. Everywhere he goes, he expects others to satisfy his wishes.

> C was not feeling well. While getting ready for bed, he asked his wife to bring him a glass of orange juice. She set it down on his crowded night table. C was angry at the way she did this, because he thought it was likely to spill. In a fury, he threw the object closest at hand, his glasses. The orange juice spilled, and his wife cried. Even though his eyeglasses did not break, he had done his damage.

This situation contained within it a manifestation of ownership. We probe such incidents because, despite their seemingly innocuous nature, there are important errors requiring attention. This criminal had virtually enslaved his wife. The orange-juice incident highlighted one aspect of a massive ownership pattern that C was in the process of correcting.

In eliminating ownership thinking, prejudgments and assumptions are replaced by fact-finding and consideration of others. The corrective entails the criminal's recognition that not everyone will like him or do what he wants. This is a difficult lesson for the criminal, who has expected everyone to accede to his wishes and has forced or conned others into doing so whenever they have opposed him. The corrective for the ownership error is accepting people as individuals and recognizing that they have their own tastes, preferences, and ways of doing things. As the criminal has learned to be receptive to others who differ from him, he has found that he has become better informed in the process and gotten along with others more harmoniously.

It is not hard to correct the ownership error with respect to crime. That is, the criminal readily understands the flawed thinking in his thefts, assaults, and sexual crimes. This is in part because the A.C. repeatedly confronts him with the injuries resulting from his ownership thinking. It is more difficult to correct ownership as it plays a role in the ordinary course of day-to-day relations with other people, especially when arrestability is not at issue. The criminal accepts that he does not own the property in a store, but it takes him longer to accept the fact that he does not own the proprietor.

Correcting the ownership error entails learning about social boundaries. Basic to this is the concept that people are accountable to each other for what they say and do; they do not step on other people to achieve their own objectives. Another aspect of such boundaries is that people are entitled to privacy. Previously, the criminal has equated privacy with secrecy. For him, secrecy has been a source of power and necessary for his survival. Yet he has not granted others privacy; he has considered it his right to know whatever he wants about others. In the correction of the ownership attitude, the criminal learns the difference between privacy and his own style of secrecy.

Once the criminal understands that he does not own other people, he comes to realize that he may even owe them something. His view of a debt is then altered. He learns that he does not own people to the extent that they *have* to lend him anything. A lender is doing him a favor, rather than fulfilling a mandate. In short, the criminal progresses from a view of owning people to one in which he realizes that he has no claim on others and that in fact they may have some claims on him.

Some criminals have gone from one extreme to another, failing to take initiatives because they equated assertiveness with ownership and shrinking from acting in situations in which it is in their legitimate self-interest to do so.

Through constructive initiatives, supported and maintained by effort, the criminal accomplishes things and legitimately owns some items in the material world. Ownership of material goods is earned, but ownership never applies to people. Rather than owning others, he is obligated to them. As one criminal said, "I used to think the world had to qualify for me. Now I have to qualify for the world."

SELF-GENERATION OF
RESPONSIBLE INITIATIVES

Initiative is not foreign to the criminal. He is extremely active and independent in pursuing what he wants. He shows resourcefulness and initiative in crime, learning from others and picking out the place, the time, and the victim while taking what he thinks are the necessary precautions. In clinical descriptions, however, the criminal is sometimes characterized as passive-aggressive, partly because others see him failing to initiate responsible actions. Rather than doing things for himself, he appears to be passive-dependent, that is, to rely on others to do things for him. The description of the passive-dependent personality sounds very much like a characterization of a criminal.

> There is little or no awareness that some benefits might have to be earned rather than just received. . . . [They] present themselves as angry, injured parties who have not been treated fairly or been appreciated. . . . Conflicts with authority are a predictable feature. (Solomon and Patch 1971, pp. 232-233)

The designation "passive-dependent" reflects the viewpoint of the person doing the labeling. The label is sometimes applied because of the criminal's outward demeanor. He is considered passive if he is bland, shoulder-shrugging, and generally nonresponsive. From the noncriminal's point of view, the criminal is passive when it comes to doing what society expects. However, the criminal regards himself as anything but passive or dependent.

With respect to responsible initiatives, the criminal is passive, if one wants to use this word. He has no desire even to begin to do things that do not offer excitement. The criminal may show a responsible initiative solely to impress others or to enhance his opinion of himself as a good person. What appears to be a responsible initiative by a criminal is usually an act intended to facilitate criminal activity. His actions may seem responsible, but they are not.

We speak of initiative in a broad sense to mean embarking on a new way of life and in a narrower sense as making a start at implementing specific new thinking processes in everyday living. We distinguish between initiatives as thrusts for power and control and initiatives directed toward responsible objectives. To become a responsible person, the criminal is required to make some beginnings that are nonexploitative and that do not result in immediate payoffs. A responsible initiative entails starting something and continuing it. If a criminal visits two businesses looking for a job and then stops, that is not an initiative, but typical of his pattern of starting and quickly abandoning his objective. Initiatives are worthless if not continued. In the past, the criminal did not sustain initiatives because they did not offer the excitement he sought. Anything that did not lead to quick personal aggrandizement was not considered worth pursuing. Now, it is necessary to become a long-distance runner, instead of a sprinter.

The reader may wonder what motivation there is for a criminal to take initiatives that he has previously disdained. Certainly there is no inner need, in the sense of a sustained drive or motive, acting as a catalyst. The motivation develops only after the initiative is taken.

> C, a professional man, had his license to practice temporarily revoked, owing to his criminal activities. Having joined our program, he was required to take the initiative of finding a job. Viewing himself solely as a white-collar man, it was a putdown even to have to consider what he regarded as unskilled and menial work. However, he had little choice. C found a job as a cook in a restaurant. He had no interest in this work; indeed, he had contempt for it and dreaded it when he began. However, our program required that whether he liked it, was interested in it, or "felt" anything else about it, he was expected to function responsibly. As C worked there, he became increasingly interested in the business and in his job. He tried to improve his efficiency and even began to think about a career in the restaurant business.

Here were two stages of initiatives. The first was his looking for a job on his own—an initiative mandated by the program's requirements, and not at all related to personal preference, feelings, or interest. The second was actually a set of initiatives generated by C's growing interest in the work. The motivation developed as a consequence of initiatives and in turn led to further initiatives.

There are numerous barriers to be overcome in the criminal's taking responsible initiatives. One is that he often enlists other people to do things for him. Thus, he is called "dependent," but this is viewing his behavior from the outside, not from the criminal's position. Getting others to take initiatives in his behalf is part of his exploitative pattern. By acting this way, he controls them. Characteristically, when a criminal enters this program, he asks someone else, such as a probation officer, to locate a job for him. He is accustomed to having others do for him what he does not want to bother doing himself. In this program, the criminal is required to find employment on his own and to do other things without enlisting people to act in his behalf.

A major obstacle to initiative is that the criminal lacks basic knowledge. He does not know how to do many things that are second nature to the responsible teen-ager. When he starts on his own to look for a job, he is grossly uninformed and inefficient. Even very intelligent criminals do not think of looking in the newspaper, calling employment bureaus, or consulting government agencies or other people who might be of assistance. It is essential that the criminal approach prospective employers with integrity both in interviews and in filling out job applications. In this program, the criminal takes the initiative in fact-finding. It may well be the first time in his life that he determines in advance the specifics of salary, social security and tax deductions, and fringe benefits. Few criminals have ever looked into these before.

> C was injured in a job-related accident. Only after he was disabled did he realize that his employer, in violation of the law, had not offered his employees workmen's compensation. This meant that C, his wife, and their children went weeks without income as C sought legal advice for eventual reimbursement. In the same job, C had no medical insurance. Furthermore, the wage schedule was such that C had been paid a flat weekly rate regardless of the number of hours he worked. He had received the same paycheck for 65 hours as for 40.

C's daily reports brought out all these facts. As he sought a new job, C learned the necessity of determining in advance all the specifics of wages, deductions, and benefits. The lack of knowledge for taking initiatives is pervasive. As one man said, "With a million dollars, I wouldn't know how to get twenty dollars worth of groceries and get twenty dollars worth of value." This was not a comment on inflation, but a reflection on his lack of knowledge.

Another barrier to initiative is that the criminal wants a *guarantee* that his initiatives will result in success. His fear that he will not achieve perfection results in his stalling and defaulting on what he ought to be doing. The criminal is likely to go through a phase in which he is not engaging in crime but not being constructive, either. In this state, he is like a person who has purchased tennis equipment but will not venture out on the court to play because he is not of tournament caliber. When the criminal has something new to do, even if it is to switch from a manual to an electric typewriter, he may be fearful. In this program, as in life, there are no guarantees. All that an A.C. can possibly promise a criminal is that if he makes sustained initiatives, he will progress toward becoming a responsible person. There is, however, no guarantee of the outcome of any specific initiative.

The criminal's feelings are another impediment to initiative. He shrinks from social initiatives because he is afraid. Part of his fear arises because he is still prejudging situations according to criminal expectations. He shies away from a responsible group because he fears that he will not be a stunning conversationalist and that he will therefore be rejected. He says that he avoids initiatives because he is depressed or anxious. The attitude engendered by this program is one of *doing*, regardless of feelings.

An important factor that continues to hamper the criminal even after he is well on the way to change is his assessment of the risks in interacting with responsible people. He has chosen to function in a totally different kind of world and does not share many interests with responsible people. Consequently, he is ill at ease and fails to broaden his social base, even when doors are open to him. In responsible company, the formerly fast-talking criminal experiences an awkwardness that can be almost paralyzing. He is afraid that his lack of knowledge of the responsible world will result in his making a fool of himself. An additional but less prominent inhibition is the fear that responsible people will shun him on learning about his past. To be sure, this sometimes happens. Far more often, however, if the criminal relates his background to others, he is credited and sometimes admired for his candor and for striving to overcome his past.

The criminal defers on some initiatives because he does not want to burn bridges to the past. The following example shows how this thwarted one man's attempt to build up his business responsibly.

> C was having many problems with Fred, a long-time friend, to whom he had given an important position in his store. Fred was coming to work late and going home early, leaving tasks undone. He was driving with a fraudulent license, spending time with married women, and using marijuana. Of greatest concern to C was clear evidence that Fred was stealing money from the store's cash register.

> We had talked with C many times about the need to overhaul his labor force, which included Fred and two other irresponsible, drug-using employees. Although C saw the wisdom of doing this, he deferred initiatives in this direction. He kept overlooking the things that Fred did, until much money was missing from Fred's register. C had considered this man a friend for many years. The two had been in crime together, and C was still reluctant to sever one of the last ties to his former life.

C was seriously trying to revive a failing business, working seven days a week to make it respectable and profitable. His lack of initiative in this area was undermining his objective.

Another striking aspect of the lack of initiative that requires correction is the criminal's failure to take the necessary steps toward achieving a responsible objective. In crime, there was no hesitation; but, as he ventures into new areas, the criminal does not do that which is in his responsible self-interest. It is common, for example, for the criminal to call someone to get information, find that the person is temporarily unavailable, leave a message, and then wait indefinitely for the person to call back. He figures that once he has made the effort, it is up to the other party to contact him. We have seen a criminal wait for days to be called on a matter as important as financing his mortgage. He does not take into account that the person he is trying to call might not have received the message, might have been otherwise occupied, or might have forgotten to return the call. In responsible endeavors, the criminal is not the same go-getter that he was in crime.

Not taking initiatives in responsible activities is perhaps the thinking error that persists the longest. In the phenomenologic report, attention is centered on all the thinking and acting patterns that preempt or hamper responsible initiatives—relying on others, lack of fact-finding, perfectionism, desire for guarantees, fear of putdowns, contrary feelings, association with other criminals, and lack of responsible self-interest. Change does not occur by osmosis. The criminal learns by doing. When a criminal is advanced in change, he not only makes a beginning where essential, but he also searches for new areas in which to generate initiatives. He generates as much voltage in responsible initiatives as he did in criminality.

This program requires that, when a criminal does take a responsible initiative in his own self-interest, he do so in a totally responsible manner. Our requirements of the criminal along these lines are more demanding than the requirements that many in the responsible world make of themselves and others. What is responsible self-interest for others is not necessarily responsible for our changing criminals. The criminal is not to advance himself by exploiting or injuring someone else. He is not to lie (either by omission or commission), con others, or otherwise exploit people and situations. Some activities that might be standard operating procedures in the course of an ordinary business transaction for some businessmen are to be rejected by the changing criminal, even if it means loss of a job. It has been our experience that the changing criminal has never lost a job because he has adhered to standards of total integrity and refused to participate in questionable business practices. In fact, he has been valued even more by his employer for adhering to principle.

FEAR AS A GUIDE
TO RESPONSIBLE LIVING

That of which I stand most in fear is fear. Montaigne

Nothing is so much to be feared as fear. Thoreau

The only thing we have to fear is fear itself. F. D. Roosevelt

These quotations emphasize the negative aspects of fear. In the mental health profession, fear is commonly viewed as disabling. Most clinicians take the position that fear, often termed "anxiety," is undesirable and must be eliminated. Popular writings describe people's battles against fear, the enemy (Freeman 1951; Piersall and Hirshberg 1955). In clinical treatment, many practitioners probe for sources of fear with the objective of providing the patient with insight to reduce fear.

Some writers point out that fear has beneficial aspects. Henderson (1939) referred to the "Jekyll or Hyde," characteristic of fear, but most authors continue to emphasize "Hyde," the harmful aspects.

Some of the ancient philosophers took a different view of fear, regarding it as a positive force in life.

> For to fear some things is even right and noble, and it is base not to fear them. . . . The man, then, who faces and who fears the right things and from the right motive, in the right way and at the right time, and who feels confidence under the corresponding conditions, is brave. (Aristotle 1952, p. 361)

Despite the modern emphasis on viewing fear as an enemy, a few writers have presented a more balanced view and have pointed out the usefulness of fear.

> All of the inventions and discoveries of human civilization are in a sense by-products of our fears and worries. Men were afraid of the dark. They learned the art of fire and discovered the secrets of electricity. . . . If we were to take away man's capacity to fear, we would take away, also, his capacity to grow, since fear is often the stimulus to growth, the goad to invention. (Liebman 1946, pp. 81-82)

Still, since it is the person who is impaired by fear in his daily functioning who comes to the mental health clinic seeking relief, the emphasis in the clinical literature and in the mass media continues to be fear's disabling qualities.*

We view the way people cope with fear as ranging along a continuum. At one extreme is the person severely disabled by fear, who may be truly mentally ill. At the other extreme is the criminal, who refuses to tolerate fear. He cuts off fear that impedes him. In the middle is the person who is not paralyzed by fear and does not cut it off, but rather is stable and responsible and lets fear serve as a guide or even an incentive. To such a person, fear is an asset. Fear as a guide to responsible living is a fundamental consideration of this program. The mental health practitioner views fear as disabling people from behaving

---

*A nationally televised education program (White 1975), "Anxiety: The Endless Crisis," part of the Public Broadcasting System's series, *The Thin Edge*, pointed out that stress and its attendant anxiety were necessary for survival and for surmounting problems, although the emphasis was more on how fear disrupts normal functioning.

responsibly, and the criminal similarly regards fear as disabling him from pursuing his objectives. Fear aborts his quest for excitement, and so it is cut off.

The mental health practitioner, in treating a patient, probes the patient's guilts and fears. These are uncovered and used to explain troubling symptoms. The objective is to eliminate these guilts and fears, which are viewed as causing the distress. Sometimes, patients are left with the idea that all fear or guilt is bad. Our objective with the criminal is not to eliminate fear and guilt but rather to put them in perspective with regard to the right thing at the right time.

Although the fears that are part of the criminal's new learning are cognitive, they may also elicit a visceral response. In the change process, he may experience concomitant psychosomatic symptoms. Our view is that it is better for him to live in such distress than to cut off fear. Fears are introduced into thinking processes through the establishment of deterrents (see chapter 9). Fear of punishment now and in the future is important, especially at first. But it is insufficient: as long as the criminal has gained nothing, he has nothing of material or interpersonal substance to lose by going to prison. In time, fear of punishment is not merely fear of the loss of freedom, but fear of the loss of all that he is building in life—friendships, material acquisitions, and, most important, self-respect. In the change process, the fear of returning to his former criminal life may be even greater than the fear of suicide. The criminal is frightened about what is going to happen to him in the future. In this program, the role of fear in life is set forth rationally. The criminal learns what he should fear and then learns to deal with fear in a rational manner. Fear stimulates *responsible* problem-solving. When fear is cut off, the criminal is irresponsible.

An important category of deterrent fears consists of those related to conscience. Guilt over wrongdoing is a manifestation of fear. Most therapists want to rid their patients of guilt, as well as of other fears. A few writers have distinguished between guilt that is neurotic and should be removed and guilt that is constructive.

> It is important for young analysts, particularly, to avoid the error made by so many laymen to the effect that psychoanalysis "removes" anxiety and guilt. ... Psychoanalysis can indeed alleviate certain guilt feelings that are attached to the idea of an aggression that the individual never committed; it cannot remove guilt feelings properly attached to the aggressions that a person does commit or has committed. Many of the unconscious guilt feelings that people experience are attached to the wrong thing, and one of our objectives might be said to be to get the

patient's guilt feeling attached to the "right" things. (Menninger and Holzman 1973, p. 174)

In the noncriminal, neurotic guilt is relieved. But the criminal has not been guilty about what Menninger and Holzman termed the "right things."* In him, this guilt must be established. We share Drakeford's (1967, p. 31) view that there is a "goodness of guilt." The criminal's statements that he has "guilt feelings" are often attempts to feed the A.C. what he thinks the A.C. wants to hear. Genuine experiences of guilt do occur, but they are transient, isolated fragments about a few specific acts. The capacity to experience guilt is not an enduring deterrent to the criminal. Indeed, the fact that the criminal experiences transient guilt promotes his regard for himself as a humane person. In this program, guilt must be functional. The criminal comes to experience guilt about the people whom he has injured. More importantly he becomes so used to considering other people that he avoids injuring others and so has less to be guilty about. Fear preempts injurious action.**

The criminal learns to regard fear in a totally new way. Fear formerly was essential for survival in crime, and, to the extent that it made him aware of danger, it was a guide. In this program, he discovers that fear is a positive force behind a variety of necessary responsible activities. We schedule annual medical and dental checkups out of fear of disease. Fear leads to preventive care. Out of fear for our families, we subscribe to life insurance. Fear is a factor in social programs. Special funds are made available to educate disadvantaged children for fear that they will not have the educational opportunities necessary to become responsible, productive citizens. The fear of pollution spurs advances in technology. Fear of an energy shortage accelerates conservation measures, as well as efforts to develop substitutes for oil and natural gas. The noncriminal does not think about medical examinations, life insurance, and social and technologic advances in terms of the fears that are operative. In daily living, such fears have been expressed as "concerns" or "worries" and then have been met with constructive efforts. They are so much a part of life that no one considers them fears. The essential point for the criminal to internalize is that fear is an ally, not an enemy, in the lives of responsible people.

---

*Salzman (1961, p. 186) also differentiated "guilt as a neurotic defensive maneuver" from "guilt as an awareness of personal responsibility." It is the latter that the criminal lacks.

**What is mandatory for the criminal, Jeanne Binstock (1973, p. 73) describes as a practice to be avoided in child-rearing: "Internal guilt has replaced external guilt; instead of feeling guilty when they have done something defined as evil, they feel guilty when they have only thought of doing something evil or have failed to do something good." The "overinjection of guilt" that Binstock describes is exactly what we consider imperative for change in the criminal.

One kind of fear to eliminate is the criminal's fear of a putdown. His daily reports provide numerous opportunities to make corrections.

> Over the years, C grew progressively more distant from his brother, who became a responsible person and was making a career in the police department. A gradual rift between the two had become a chasm and there was infrequent contact. C's brother did not know of any of C's recent activities and arrests. All he knew was that C had had a "nervous breakdown" and had been hospitalized. Now, well along in the program for change, C was reflecting on how he had been responsible for the alienation of his brother, and he wanted to make amends. But he was so frightened about dealing with his brother that he postponed contacting him for months. C thought that his brother might want nothing more to do with him if the truth came out.

Because C feared rejection, he was deferring making contact with his brother. The fear was so strong that it stood in the way of C's arriving at a realistic plan as to how to approach his brother. He thought that he should either tell him nothing or tell him every detail of his life. Finally, after much discussion, C decided that as a first step, he would write to his brother and propose to get together. He realized that it was possible that the brother might want no part of a relationship with him, but if that were so, C would have to accept it as a consequence of how he had acted. It was not long until the relationship was restored.

If a criminal achieves responsibility, does his best work, and tries to meet the demands of life calmly and rationally, he does not regard a criticism as a putdown. His daily reports offer many opportunities to examine the criminal's responses to criticism. Indeed, in this program, he is constantly being criticized. He could regard this process as putdown after putdown. However, the criminal learns to evaluate the merits of criticisms. If they are valid, there is a chance for self-improvement. The criminal also learns to consider the source of criticisms to determine their merits. A person with a realistic view of himself and realistic expectations of the world is difficult to put down.

The position of this program on living with fear is uncompromising.

> C was slicing onions in a slicer. It was set at the recommended cutting edge. Yet onions were breaking off, resulting in an insufficient number of rings and a waste of onion, which could not otherwise be used. C was working at an establishment in which the manager was extremely cost-conscious. C thought about how the manager would regard his performance with this slicer and was frightened.

C began to wonder whether all of his life was to be this way. Must he always live as a crawling, timorous person? We pointed out that C had two choices. He could either remain afraid and be responsible or cut off fear and commit a crime.

We have deliberately fostered excessive fearfulness as the lesser of two evils. We know the consequences of a criminal's not being sufficiently fearful. The criminal has been a creature of extremes. In the change process, this is also true. We have found that the criminal passes through a phase in which he is excessively afraid, much as the neurotic is. One criminal was so fearful that he was not being economical enough that he was reluctant to spend money on medicine that he needed. Another was so fearful of making a fool of himself at a church function that he refused to attend. We mentioned earlier how responsible initiatives can be paralyzed by fear. When fear is excessive to a point of disability, we provide the criminal with a perspective so that he can achieve a more balanced assessment of his own situation. It is a matter mainly of reevaluating his expectations of himself and other people, rather than of encouraging him to be less fearful.

In short, the criminal learns to be guided by fear so that it becomes an asset in living responsibly. A major teaching is that fear is an incentive for self-improvement. Fear prods one to analyze a task, decide how best to carry it out, and marshal the resources to do so. Ultimately, fear is incorporated into a philosophy of life in which it is used to make sound decisions to achieve responsible objectives. With respect to criminal patterns, there is no middle ground. The criminal must live in fear of returning to these patterns, as others have had to live in fear of him when he was in active crime.

EXPERIENCE BREEDS INTEREST
IN RESPONSIBLE LIVING

The criminal's primary interests lie in doing the forbidden, which offers excitement and the possibility of conquest and triumph. Some criminals have almost no other interests. Many, however, are interested in such pursuits as sports, music, art, and nature. Some of these interests are discovered accidentally in confinement, where the criminal is bored and looks for time-fillers. Although when not in crime or confinement, he may look to such interests to relieve boredom, they are usually casual and transient. Many criminals are gifted in the arts but never have utilized their talents constructively in a sustained manner. One criminal was well on his way to a career in major league baseball, but that interest gave way to crime.

Interest in sports or the arts is of little consequence in whether a criminal learns to live responsibly. The problem to society is the criminal's lack of interest in functioning responsibly at home, in the community, or at a job.

A. S. Neill stated in *Summerhill:* "I cannot compel an interest in the children, when the interest does not originate in them" (p. 163). He maintained that a child must spontaneously desire to engage in a particular activity—that the interest must arise from within. We agree with Neill that interest cannot be compelled. But our view is that interest in responsible functioning can be developed, provided that correctives are substituted for criminal thinking processes. Interest in anything usually originates and develops as a consequence of experience. We may watch someone playing tennis and think that it looks like fun. But we do not know whether we are truly interested in participating without taking a racquet in hand, going to the court, and playing. Similarly, we do not know whether we are interested in Shakespeare unless we are exposed to his writings. Valentine (1956, p. 248), in his book on the "normal child," quoted a student as saying about chemistry that "it is exciting; you never know what is going to happen next!" The student could not have been excited about chemistry if he had not first had experience with it. Interest emerges from the knowledge that arises from doing.

It is of little importance whether a criminal is interested in Shakespeare, tennis, or chemistry. However, to achieve responsible thinking and action, a start must be made, no matter whether he is interested initially. When the criminal comes to us, he knows only one way of life—his way. Although acquainted with responsible people, he is ignorant as to how they think and live. An analogy is the person who has eaten only vegetables and fruit. He knows about meat but has not tried it. Whether he is interested in eating meat is not ascertainable until he has gained knowledge of its taste through eating it. The criminal does not have experience in responsible living. For the criminal who has selected our program, the issue of whether he is interested in being responsible is not relevant. Having ruled out suicide and a return to crime, he has one remaining option—to implement the program, become responsible, and then see whether interest grows.

We distinguish between two types of interest: the obligatory and the optional. To be responsible, the criminal is obligated to participate in family functions and chores. He must also budget carefully, perform conscientiously at work, and be accountable to others. Most criminals, once they make a start, develop interest in the obligatory and sometimes go beyond what is required.

C had never taken care of his possessions; he was always acquiring new ones and giving away old ones. Now, in our program, he and his wife had saved money and purchased a house. C spent many hours outside manicuring his lawn. In addition, C voluntarily mowed two other lawns as a favor to some elderly neighbors. Formerly, he had regarded lawn care as boring and a total waste of time.

This is not to say that a person who tries something in which he is uninterested is guaranteed to develop an interest. But our experience has been dramatic in seeing criminals become interested after making a beginning. Even if interest fails to develop or remains minimal, there are things that the criminal must do. He may have no particular interest in housecleaning, but he has no other option. For a balanced life, it is obligatory that he develop other interests. Here, there are many options, and he will choose his leisure activities on the basis of personal taste. Many begin with something with which they have some familiarity—photography, reading, music, or tennis. At no time do we suggest, request, or require development of a specific interest. Our emphasis is on *doing*, with interest as the consequence of the doing. A criminal may try out new things, but it is not incumbent on him to continue. We have found that, once our people take the initiative and give something a fair trial, they usually persist. In fact, they sometimes overdo, becoming so involved in a new activity that more pressing matters are deferred. This deferment must then be attended to, to achieve a balance.

Occasionally the criminal says that he is not interested in something, because he believes that he will fail to be an immediate success at it. The fear of a putdown restrains him from developing interests. Another common obstacle to developing interest in the responsible is the criminal's recourse to feelings. If reason yields to feelings, he may never begin an activity. As he implements the program, the criminal finds again and again that feelings often change *after* one has embarked on an activity and acquired knowledge. A person likes or dislikes something only if he knows something about it through experience. With respect to the obligatory interests, liking is irrelevant. But with regard to the optional interests, he may not experience enthusiasm until after he develops some skill and regards himself as proficient.

The attitude that the criminal must adopt is that he has to immerse himself in something, stick with it, and allow interests to develop. This applies to all parts of his life. For example, with his spouse, the criminal does not know what tenderness is. Without experience, he does not know how tenderness can contribute to a marriage. Although he may lack the feelings or interest that he thinks he should have, the criminal can nevertheless show tenderness to his wife. Despite initial awkwardness, one of our men made a sustained deliberate effort to do this. He was surprised to find that, with practice, tenderness became second nature and far outweighed sexual intercourse in frequency and importance in his marriage. The result was a more gratifying, richer marital relationship. Vocationally, the criminal characteristically says that he does not know where his interests lie. This is not necessarily an excuse to avoid work. It is an accurate statement, inasmuch as he has never stuck to anything long enough to get involved, and thus interest has never developed. One criminal, after working as a clerk-typist for several months, found that he looked forward to his job each day and enjoyed being part of a team. He stated, "I like what I am doing because I know the work." The liking part of it came only after the development of knowledge and skill. Knowledge not only generates interest, but also enhances self-confidence and makes advancement more likely.

That the criminal is changing is indicated when he immerses himself with zest in new, responsible activities, sticks with them, develops some expertise, and derives confidence from what he is doing. Only then can he validly gauge his degree of interest.

INTERDEPENDENCE

Dependence is regarded as normal in both children and adults. Although positive aspects of dependence have been recognized, it is the negative aspects that have been stressed. Dependent people are often regarded as immature. In psychiatry, they are termed "passive-dependent" if their dependence is such that they are fixated at an early developmental stage and are not self-sufficient. Great emphasis has been placed on pathologic excesses of dependence, including parasitism, which breeds resentment and retaliation by others and maladaptation in most spheres of life. The dependence built into feminine roles in our society has come under attack by the women's liberation movement. Independence is generally regarded as desirable and useful, but its excesses have been viewed as overcompensations for dependence.

Control, ownership, and all the other characteristics that we have described are opposed to dependence with respect to the criminal. Lacking experience in cooperative relationships, he has no concept of teamwork. He considers dependence contemptible; it is not at all congruent with his self-image. The criminal fails to recognize that he is in fact dependent on others. Yet he is angered when someone proves to undependable.

If one has a realistic view of the world, he acknowledges both the dependence and independent features of interdependent relationships. Not only do we depend on other people, but others depend on us. To be dependable is to fulfill the dependence requirements of others. This view of life is new to the criminal.

Interdependence is a component of almost all relationships; it is taught everywhere, although the term is not used. Family units have a network of interdependent relationships. The primary-school child studies interdependence in school when he learns how a farm works or how the early American colonists struggled to survive. He experiences interdependence in cooperative projects. He depends on his classmates, and they on him, in team sports.

Interdependence characterizes relationships throughout the animal world. Even insects depend on one another.*

In our program, the criminal learns that interdependence fosters an independence and freedom that are different from those that he has experienced. From society's point of view, the criminal hems himself in, always having to look over his shoulder for the policeman. The criminal's idea of independence and freedom results in anarchy and massive injury to others. As he implements the program, he gradually learns new definitions of independence and freedom. He learns that, by living interdependently within the constraints of responsibility, he can achieve a greater and more fulfilling freedom.

It is essential, in learning about interdependence, for the criminal to understand that dependence is part of life and therefore is not a putdown. However, it is a matter of being dependent on others for the right things at the right time. In responsible living, parasitism is not interdependence. The criminal is not to exploit others or get them to do things for him that he is capable of doing himself. He learns to depend on people for some things and realizes that they in turn depend on him.

Through the dissection of criminal patterns, the criminal is taught the nature of interdependence. For example, he initially describes his employer in terms of the authority that the employer wields. In this program, he learns to consider the massive network of interdependent relationships between the employer and the workers and their ties to society at large. The criminal's tubular vision is expanded beyond the power aspect to an understanding of how people depend on each other to get a job done.

> We discussed with C, a cook, the massive interdependence in running a restaurant between the franchise owner, the regional manager, the resident manager, the cook, the waiters, the cashier, and the customer. We could have gone beyond this to include the sources, processing, packaging and delivery of food—a long chain of interdependent relationships.

In discussions with this man, we carefully scrutinized his relationships with

---

*Winchester (1964), a biologist, pointed out: "The social insects have a highly developed organization with a distribution of tasks among members of the group and a sharing of the benefits of their labors. ... Through social unity the insects have power. ... The social group of honeybees is called the colony. ... Each worker seems to assume some specific task at which it works exclusively, although the task may change as the need becomes greater in other fields. ... When the new workers emerge from their cells they take over the duties within the hive and free the older workers for field duty." (pp. 303-305)

waiters and all other personnel, so that he would develop the necessary attitudes to function as a team member.

The criminal has not known what sharing is. One man mused, "I don't even know what it means." His orientation to any transaction had been, What's in it for me? He learns to share not only materially, but also in the exchange of ideas and emotional attitudes. He has not known how to have a discussion in which ideas are shared with a responsible person. It has been his practice to be secretive and to tune out what others said, unless it agreed with his own point of view. Learning to exchange ideas is a brand-new skill. In the past, when the criminal scorned an idea, he scorned the person who held it. Interdependence demands listening to and considering others' ideas, as well as tolerating disagreements.

With other people, the criminal has either been overly familiar or completely aloof. We have seen both extremes in criminals who have been in the program only a short time. At work, some criminals put themselves on a first-name basis with others too quickly, flirt with women, and start telling others how to function. In contrast, some keep to themselves to the point where they are not considered part of the team. Learning how to gauge the appropriate degree of closeness and intimacy requires a great deal of experience.

Interdependence involves learning what friendship is. A good definition of friendship is offered by Douvan and Adelson.

> The friendship we have in mind is characterized by mutual trust; it permits a fairly free expression of emotion; it allows the shedding of privacies (although not inappropriately); it can absorb, within limits, conflict between the pair; it involves the discussion of personally crucial themes; it provides occasions to enrich and enlarge the self through the encounter of differences. (1966, p. 176)

By that definition, the criminal has no friends at all. Even in crime, he lacks friends, having instead collaborators in criminal schemes who often do not remain loyal. Faith, loyalty, and trust between longstanding, responsible friends has no counterpart in the criminal world. Companionship for its own sake and liking of one another based on sustained sharing of interests do not exist.

For criminals who have families, one of the best laboratories for the implementation of interdependence is the home. As the changing criminal moves toward interdependence for the first time in his marriage, adjustments have to be made. The criminal learns to abdicate control for a more equitable give-and-take relationship. At the same time, he gradually assumes some of the duties on which he has previously defaulted and becomes a partner in decision-making. The road to domestic interdependence is bumpy. Even in the criminal who is well along in change, a residue of control patterns persists at home more than it does elsewhere. Some criminals still come home expecting the family to accommodate to their moods and wishes. Such criminals think that because they have worked hard and are functioning well outside the home, they are entitled to this. We have sought outside information on the criminal's interdependence and dependability. To obtain this and to foster interdependence at home, we have met with criminals and their spouses.

As with the other correctives, some criminals go from one extreme to another in implementation. Once the criminal realizes that in the past he has assisted other people mostly to benefit himself, he may distrust himself to the extent of refraining from helping anyone; this is his attempt to eliminate the old patterns of obligating others and building himself up. To prevent unwarranted intimacy, the criminal may back away from people to an almost absurd extent. We have seen a criminal afraid to take his date's arm as they crossed the street for fear that that she would think that he was taking unwarranted liberties. Because of his fear that he is still trying to control others, he may not assert himself where it is in his legitimate self-interest to do so.

> C had been assigned to coordinate his work with Larry. However, the team was split up to work in different areas, and this resulted in a loss of efficiency. C had qualms about talking to Larry and then to the supervisor, because he was fearful that this might be part of his old pattern of trying to run things. Finally, he talked with the proper people, and the two were able to resume their former effective, interdependent teamwork.

Sometimes, the criminal's distrust of himself poses an obstacle to interdependence with the A.C. Being alert to the power-thrusting component within himself, the criminal concludes that expression of disagreement with the A.C. is to be avoided, because this once again might be his former one-upmanship pattern. The criminal may concentrate on the power dynamic at the expense of a substantive issue. As he subjects his thinking and action to our criticism and correction, the criminal learns to differentiate between old-pattern behavior and assertion in his own responsible self-interest, which is a legitimate part of interdependent functioning.

Arenas for implementing interdependent living are everywhere. Home and work may be more personally demanding, but the same skills are required everywhere. The criminal learns to get along with the car dealer who inconveniences him, the restaurant waiter who delays him, the cleaner who fails to remove a spot. Part of interdependence is making allowances for the faults of others—indeed, anticipating them. The noncriminal may be able to afford anger in situations where he is inconvenienced. The criminal in the process of change cannot risk it. Even in the most adverse circumstances, he must function calmly and rationally, so as to get along with others. Most important is that he learn that interdependability is a major part of interdependence. That is, he has to show others that they can count on him. The implementation of all the other correctives fosters interdependence. Trust, fulfilling obligations, taking initiatives, and putting oneself in another's position are especially important.

TRUST

The criminal's way of life mandates that he trust no one. His active distrust of others has been regarded as suspicion and labeled "paranoid." The criminal often applies this term to himself, especially when talking to mental health practitioners. However, his suspicion is a consequence of things he is doing now and that he has done before; therefore it is not paranoia. Indeed, this suspicion serves him well in avoiding apprehension.

The criminal insists that he does trust people. What he means is that he trusts those who will collaborate with him in a criminal enterprise and who will not snitch. He might say that he trusts God, but his trust in God is to get him out of a jam, and that is about the extent of it.

For most of his life, the criminal has distrusted responsible people, whether parents, teachers, employers, or anyone else. Why should he trust them, when they oppose what he seeks in life and he is equally opposed to their pallid existence? To trust someone is to become his victim. To trust is to risk being betrayed or, if not betrayed, used. Despite this view, the criminal demands that others trust him, even in the light of his criminality. When others do not trust him, he is put down and angered, often to the point of retaliating. If he says that he will be at a designated place at an agreed-on time, he thinks that he should be believed and trusted, despite the fact that he seldom honors such commitments. One criminal expressed it well when he said, "I am honest, because when I say I will meet somebody, I always add, 'if I have time.' " Then, if he does not show up, he still is trustworthy, because he at least warned the other person.

Trust or faith is quite different from suggestibility. Criminals trust other criminals to the point of gullibility when a criminal enterprise is proposed. By trust and faith, we do not mean this at all. Our frame of reference is the trust shown in responsible living. In the criminal, such trust is impossible, given his thinking patterns.

Our view is that it is not possible to live responsibly without trusting other people to fulfill particular functions. If one were untrusting, he would not go to doctors, put his money in the bank, allow his spouse discretion in household spending, take advice from others, nor share confidences. (And most criminals do none of these.) Trust is subscribing on faith to what selected people say or do, particularly when we do not have their knowledge and experience. This is apparent in the selection of a physician, whose advice we follow because we believe he has the knowledge and experience that we lack. We take prescribed medicine, even though we know nothing about pharmacology. Whenever we elect a person to a public office, we entrust him with representing our interests. In hiring a carpenter for home repairs, we trust that he is competent and knows his business. We do indeed change doctors, elect new officials, or engage different carpenters, when our trust turns out to have been unjustified by their performances. What we are describing is an obligatory trust that is built into daily living. In the criminal, we do not find this kind of trust. The contacts that he has had with people whom he says he trusts are based more on the prospects of exploitation than on faith in their judgment, integrity, or experience.

Trust is optional to the extent that we make choices as to whom to trust with what. We do this on the basis of our estimation of who has our interests at heart or who will fulfill his part of an agreement. We are discriminating. We might discuss a marital problem with one person, but not another. We confide the details of our financial position to some people, but not others.

The criminal's first experience in an authentic, trusting relationship begins with the agent of change. We do not try to persuade the criminal to believe uncritically all that we have to say. Giving the criminal a rationale for implementing this program does not work. Lacking previous experience with what we are describing, he is in no position to assess accurately the validity of the program's requirements. For this program to work, he must have sufficient faith in us to decide to implement new patterns of thought and action. It is only by doing so that he can determine whether his trust in us is warranted. In other words, the criminal is asked, not to become a believer, but to become a doer, so that he can find out for himself and decide how trustworthy the A.C. is.

It is incumbent on the A.C. never to violate the criminal's trust. By our daily conduct, we have demonstrated to the criminal that he has not misplaced his trust. We show our trustworthiness by not violating privileged communication, by the way in which we handle the money that he entrusts to us, by the forthright manner in which we deal with him in a wide-open channel, and in the many other transactions that we have with him every day.

Early in the program, the major indicator of the criminal's trust in the A.C. is the extent to which the channel is open. The criminal's faith in the A.C. is bolstered as he implements the program. When the A.C.'s predictions about the outcomes of specific patterns of thought and action turn out to be accurate, the criminal's faith increases. In time, the A.C.'s statements about the consequences and rewards of responsible living no longer need to be taken on faith, because the criminal begins to experience the effects himself.

The process of extending trust from the A.C. to the outside world is accomplished by correcting errors that are brought out in the phenomenologic report. Formerly, the criminal did not trust people unless he was sure that he could control them. Now, we carefully evaluate a variety of situations to assist the criminal in arriving at a decision as to who can be trusted for specific purposes.

Learning who to trust is not a matter for a snap judgment, but instead requires fact-finding. The question of whom to trust seems complex to the criminal as he realizes that a person whom he trusts with one secret is not trustworthy in all respects. That is, he might share work-related confidences with a co-worker and find that the confidence is kept. But the same co-worker may turn out to be a gossip about domestic affairs. The criminal, of all people, should realize that no one shows his hand all at once. However, he has to learn that personalities unfold over time and that deciding whom to trust is a slow process.

There is not only the issue of whom to trust; the criminal must demonstrate to others that he himself is worthy of being trusted. Trust is a two-way street, in that as he learns to trust others, the criminal is trusted by them in return. This is a slowly evolving process at home, at work, and everywhere else the criminal goes. For the criminal as well as the noncriminal, progress in responsible living requires trusting others and being considered trustworthy by them.

REPLACEMENT OF PRETENSIONS
WITH REASONABLE EXPECTATIONS

The criminal's view of himself as a conqueror, his sense of ownership toward people and objects, and his belief in his uniqueness are all parts of his pretentiousness. As far as he is concerned, he is entitled to top status in anything he chooses. In crime, it is a big score as measured by the proceeds or outcome. In confinement, it is a big score in the form of being the big shot of the penitentiary, violating, and getting out. In daily life, the big score is having a high position, even though he is not qualified.

The obvious, visible accoutrements of such an existence are luxurious living quarters, expensive clothes, big cars, and rolls of money flashed and given away. There are criminals who regard such material items as unnecessary. Some look disparagingly at those who con their way to such affluence. For them, conquest by force is valued more, regardless of the proceeds. Whether a criminal uses slickness or muscle, he considers himself above the responsible people who plod along, striving to achieve modest objectives. To be like them is to be nothing at all.

Some of the criminal's *tensions* are the result of *pretensions*. When he meets an obstacle to achieving what he wants, he considers it an injustice and a putdown. The tension is anger, which is expressed verbally or physically in criminal activity. If deterrence is operating, the tension may be expressed in the form of psychosomatic symptoms. By violating, the criminal can relieve his headaches, palpitations, dizziness, stomach distress, and fatigue.

It is a Herculean task to help a criminal to begin from the bottom and progress to a point where he has responsibly earned the things that he wants and have him acquire a sense of perspective of his place in the scheme of things. For the criminal's pretensions to be lowered, he must view himself and the world more realistically. We do not require the criminal to surrender all his ultimate objectives; rather, we assess each in terms of whether it is based on excessive pretensions. Ambitions are pretensions either if they are clearly beyond reach or if the criminal superoptimistically thinks that they are as good as accomplished merely because he has ordained it.

There are qualitative and quantitative aspects to the alteration of pretensions and expectations. There has to be a change in *what* he expects and in *how much* he expects. At issue is what constitutes a success or a setback. The criminal's idea of success is a continuing flow of triumphs. In our program, he learns of the little successes that result from meeting day-to-day problems at home, at work, and with friends. Even if he reaches the top, problems do not cease there; they only multiply. Just as in his former life the criminal derived greater excitement from executing a crime than he did from its proceeds, he is to find in living responsibly that the *process of achieving* offers as much, if not more, satisfaction than the achievement itself. That is, when one is successful in one objective, he does not stop there, but moves on to the next. It is the doing that has significance, more than the ultimate result, which serves only as a catalyst for the solving of more problems and the achievement of other goals.

Having realistic expectations is a *sine qua non* for the criminal's achieving responsibility. However, the A.C. needs to be careful that the criminal does not latch on to the notion that all that is required is a revision of expectations. This by itself does not guarantee success in anything. A revision of expectations is only a prelude to the necessary initiative and hard work.

Characteristically, the criminal has construed success and failure in terms of personal triumphs and defeats. We use the words *setback* and *failure* in a totally different sense from the criminal. To him, a setback is not being on top; it is the putdown that results when his expectations are not fulfilled. In the context of the daily phenomenologic reports, an entirely new perspective is developed. The criminal learns that setbacks are inevitable in the human condition; they are not a disgrace. In fact, the person who has never failed cannot have tried very hard initially. A person must fall short of success to become aware of his limitations. He may be restrained by his own shortcomings or by circumstances and therefore have to settle for less than what he wants. The perspective that the criminal gradually develops is that setbacks are not putdowns but important events in life from which one grows. He recognizes that people learn far more from setbacks than from successes. Failure can be a guide and an inspiration—a critical factor in achieving future successes. Through falling short of success, one learns how to improve. In our work with the criminal, we go from a specific incident in his life to the nature of life itself. The history of mankind abounds with trial and error, success and failure. In all human enterprises—medicine, agriculture, electronics, and everything else—setbacks have bred successes.

We encourage the criminal to strive for excellence, but in a way that differs from his previous conception. An ordinary person can do an excellent job. The criminal thinks that he must be better than anyone else could possibly be—a unique number one. We emphasize the effort component rather than the immediate outcome of the effort. The certainty that one has striven for excellence and has done his best in so doing is the basis for satisfaction and self-respect. The criminal has never before regarded this as a success. He has never known the satisfaction that results from doing a job well. Excellence in the ordinary is at first repugnant to him. It becomes more valuable as he implements the program and begins to record small achievements as a result of responsible thinking and action. A promotion at a job, a commendation from a customer, and praise from his wife are all ordinary events, but each spells success in its own way.

Of considerable utility in reducing expectations is Murphy's Law: If anything can go wrong, it will. This is not introduced to foster undue pessimism but to establish a state of preparedness. With Murphy's Law in mind, expectations are scaled down to a more realistic magnitude. Operating under Murphy's Law reduces reactions of indignation when things do not go one's way in life. One criminal, after half a year in the program, introduced a corollary to Murphy's Law: "If it isn't one damn thing, it's another." This is in line with the idea that life entails continually facing problems that require solution. If the criminal incorporates Murphy's Law and its corollary into his view of life, he is not put down or angered when his expectations are not fulfilled. Instead, he takes disappointments and occasionally a tragedy in stride. One caution to the criminal is that he needs to distinguish between Murphy's Law and his own carelessness. That is, he can keep many things from going wrong. We offer the following example of how a criminal trained himself to apply Murphy's Law and its corollary to a trying work situation.

C was the manager of a low-income housing project. His days were filled with people quarreling and complaining and with property being vandalized and requiring repair. The project was operated on a shoestring budget. This meant that maintenance was a patchwork job, with no preventive measures. There was a never-ending series of crises with equipment—the breakdown of elevators, air conditioners, trash compacters, and security devices. In addition, the custodian, who was competent when sober, was drunk much of the time and neglected his duties. The property deteriorated. C had to cope with both outsiders and residents who vandalized the property, broke lights, marred walls, abused appliances, and discarded trash in the halls. He also had to deal with tenants who did not pay rent and those who complained that things did not work. No sooner was one problem settled, than others emerged. C responded to nearly all difficulties with anger. When the anger was not expressed directly, it was displaced into psychosomatic symptoms.

C finally recognized that he was working at a place where Murphy's Law was in effect all the time. His phenomenologic reports provided many opportunities to identify and correct pretensions and unrealistic expectations. He learned that he could not shame the custodian into sobriety or mobilize the tenants into responsibility. Furthermore, he acquired a mental set of expecting problems to occur and then handling them as well as he could with the limited funds and personnel available to him. Some of his pretensions about making the housing project a showpiece for the city underwent revision.

On the basis of his daily reports, the criminal's expectations are identified and evaluated. Perhaps his wife is not a gourmet cook. Perhaps his boss does not give him the commendation that he thinks he is due. Perhaps a friend is not as trustworthy as he had thought. The criminal learns to see things more objectively; when he does so, disappointments are not putdowns.

The criminal's expectations are corrected on two levels. Those that are scrutinized first are the clearly outlandish ones. These are the expectations that are related especially to crimes and are the most easily corrected. It is not difficult to show how flawed his thinking is when he expects to take possession of everything that he wants through crime. On the second level, however, once a criminal has stopped violating and is doing all that he thinks he should, he expects everything to operate like a well-oiled machine. What he considers reasonable expectations are still unreasonable.

C came home from work, tired after a long day. He sat in his chair and read the paper. However, his tranquility did not last long, as his children chased through the house and his wife, who was preparing dinner, asked him to get something for her that she could not reach. C did not outwardly show anger, but he was upset. His thinking was that, after he had spent the whole day doing what he was supposed to do, he was entitled to come home and have a peaceful evening.

Clearly, this was an unreasonable expectation, given the facts that his wife, who also worked, was trying to get dinner on the table and that their two young children were home. His thinking was that everything should fall into place to accommodate him, simply because he worked. Although many noncriminals might have reacted the same way, it was important to go into the details of this event with C, because in the past when C had become frustrated in comparable situations, his anger had resulted in drinking, violence, and drugs.

An overriding problem of major importance early in the change process is the criminal's discontent that results from expecting the same high voltage out of responsible living that he experienced in crime. Expectations of this sort will not and cannot be met. In the past, a high pitch of excitement with women has been sought through conquest. Now the criminal seeks his satisfaction in a responsible relationship with a girl friend or wife. Sex no longer has the impact that it had before, when it was achieved by conning or force. Instead, it is pleasurable and gratifying with a responsible, consenting partner. The criminal learns that responsible people have their enthusiasms and excitements. But enthusiasm over a football team, a trip, a new piece of furniture, or a garden is in an utterly different category from the excitement of breaking and entering, obscene phone calls, or pimping. To the extent that the criminal expects to find in responsible living a counterpart to criminal excitement, he is disappointed, self-pitying, and angry.

As the criminal implements the correctives for responsible thinking and action, he becomes more realistic about how others see him, what they expect of him, and what he can expect in return. His view of himself as a collossus gives way to a more modest self-image of a person who is doing his best to function responsibly in his pursuit of progress. The idea of a big success overnight is replaced by more modest and realistic ideas as to what success is and how one achieves it. Furthermore, the little problems of daily living begin to overshadow his former criminal grand plans for the future.

C was walking around in a two dollar Salvation Army sport coat, rather than in a three-hundred-dollar suit, to which he had been accustomed as a criminal. He was debating whether to spend thirty cents for an ice cream bar instead of thirty dollars for lunch.

At this point, which was early in the program, C regarded his station in life as more successful than any that he had previously enjoyed. To be sure, he was a parolee, working as a busboy in a restaurant, renting a small room, depending on walking or buses, and owning only two complete changes of clothing. However, in contrast with years of living high and fraudulently while injuring others, he viewed himself as living with integrity for the first time. To him this constituted success.

In short, progress requires that the criminal abandon his pretensions, scale down his expectations, and think and act like an ordinary human being. Functioning effectively as an ordinary person always has the possibility of leading to extraordinary accomplishments.

SOUND DECISION-MAKING

In the pursuit of criminal objectives, the criminal makes decisions, many of which are sound. Most of his decisions result in success for him, in that he commits an extraordinary number of crimes without being apprehended. Many of his crimes are specifically planned, with decisions made as to time and place. Others may not be schemed in detail, but they are programmed in the sense that the criminal has made basic decisions as to what to do if a particular situation arises. For example, in an armed holdup, he has determined beforehand that he will not shoot unless he is endangered physically. The basic decision in crime is to achieve his objective by obtaining as much as he can at the least possible risk to himself. If he is apprehended or becomes a suspect, his decisions were inept. (We have described in volume 1 the cutoff of deterrents, superoptimism, and other factors that contribute to his faulty decisions in crime.)

In the program of change, the decision-making processes that the criminal has developed in crime cannot be utilized. He must begin from scratch to learn to make decisions in areas in which he never made decisions before. We are confronted with the task of teaching the rudiments of sound decision-making. We know that the criminal defers, defaults, prejudges, superoptimistically believes that events will happen as he ordains, jumps to rapid conclusions, and is reluctant to ask questions of responsible people because he does not want to appear ignorant. With such thinking processes, he is not equipped to function responsibly.

The criminal is untutored in the way society is organized and does not even know what resources are available to him for living responsibly. He is unfamiliar with community services, religious and educational opportunities, consumer information, and vocational services. It is indeed striking, when one has worked with a very shrewd criminal who has been successful in crime, to learn how helpless and uninformed he is with respect to making some of the simplest decisions. The noncriminal decides what time to leave home to get to work promptly. He decides to notify someone at his place of work if he is delayed. When he gets to work, he decides on an agenda for the day. He decides how economical he should be at lunch, with respect to both time and money. He decides to call his wife if he is going to get home late. He makes numerous decisions with respect to his work and in interpersonal transactions. By the time he leaves his job, he has made dozens of decisions, whether he is a white-collar worker or an unskilled laborer. Most of these decisions are so routine that he does not have to stop and consider them. For example, it is habitual for him to notify the office if he is unexpectedly delayed. There is no decision to be made, as he views it. Similarly, he does not have to decide that he is going to arrange his work schedule; he simply does it. Although it involves a decision, he does not regard it as one. This kind of functioning is foreign to the criminal. The criminal also makes decisions at work, but these are self-serving. He arrives at work whenever it is convenient for him. He regards the work itself as insignificant, unless he can use it as a vehicle to enhance his sense of power and control. A con man may make decisions to act responsibly with respect to particular situations. He does this, however, to achieve a criminal objective, not as a way of life.

Early in the change process, the criminal's decisions are seriously flawed, because all that he has to work with are the decision-making patterns that he used in crime. He relies on shrewdness rather than prudence, and consequently makes mistake after mistake. This case illustrates the point:

C was given funds by his parents to open a small store. He ran it heavily into debt because of his irresponsibility and criminality. C left the area, and the store continued to be managed incompetently by others. Three years later, C returned to the area, joined our program, stayed out of crime, and was functioning responsibly. He was still beset by a series of problems, because he did not know how to make sound decisions. In this store, C knew nothing about purchasing; there was no system for ordering and no device for inventory determination. Thus, he was constantly at a loss as to whether there was an oversupply, a shortage, or a reduced inventory due to thefts. His work force consisted of colleagues in crime who maintained that they were honest, but were not. C knew nothing about recruiting responsible help. When an employment agency (whose existence he learned of through someone else) sent him applicants, he selected the first one who appealed to him without checking references or knowing anything about the person, except what was on the application. When shopping for a security system, C purchased equipment from the first solicitor who walked in. He made decisions about vending machines and food stamps with little knowledge. He was altogether in the dark about accounting procedures and tax decisions.

As C's daily reports to the group revealed his thinking and action, considerations about the store were very prominent. Although the other criminals, who were further along in the change process, knew nothing about operating a store, they were able to suggest that he seek facts, weigh options, and take long-range considerations into account. As a result of C's participation in the group during this period of crimelessness, he tripled the store's gross income and then had sufficient funds to reduce accumulated debts. However, when C was finally able to draw a reasonable salary, the A.C. and the group had to begin from scratch with him about financial decisions. It was as though all that he had learned about operating the business had no application to his personal finances. The store was a moderately complex operation. But the fundamentals of decision-making taught here applied to the most minute decisions in the lives of all the criminals in the group.

Without the correctives for the other thinking errors described in this chapter, responsible decision-making is not possible. But, even if all the other errors are corrected, decision-making must still be dealt with separately. The criminal must learn to ask questions. He must become a student in the kindergarten of decision-making rather than the know-it-all whose every desire is magically translated into a successful result. He must be prepared to accommodate himself to results that are not always what he had hoped for and to deal responsibly with unexpected problems that require new decisions. While maintaining strict integrity, he must acquire the flexibility and open-mindedness necessary to profit from errors. He must learn to reveal what is relevant to obtain the best information. Every decision will have its short-term and long-term aspects. Tubular vision and concrete thinking will not yield the most effective decisions. The criminal must learn not to defer for the sake of putting things off, but to defer when it is necessary to acquire more facts for decision-making.

Teaching a criminal to make sound decisions has many dimensions. Learning how to get information is one of the most basic. All his life, the criminal has regarded asking a question as something to be avoided, because it showed him up as ignorant. In the past, assumptions were made, instead of facts being gathered. Thinking something made it so. It was the proclivity of the criminal to think something, exclude other considerations, establish it as a firm opinion, and believe it to be a fact. Having decided that something was in the bag, the criminal had no need to find facts or consider others' views. Thus, all discussion of a decision-making process would have been irrelevant. When things did not go as the criminal was certain they would, he viewed it as an injustice and blamed others. Now, he learns that it is necessary to admit ignorance, at least to himself, and then to take responsible measures to become informed.

As he opens the channel with other people, the criminal discovers how ignorant he has been in matters of responsible living. Instead of operating on the basis of prejudgments, he listens to people for the first time. His appraisal of people becomes increasingly conceptual and decreasingly based on instantaneous subjective reactions. From the daily reports, the A.C. identifies errors that the criminal makes.

> C was permitted to interview applicants for a job at his place of employment. One was a woman whom he found physically attractive. C thought that perhaps he should eliminate her from the competition, because she might constitute a problem for him.

The range of C's thinking was narrow. He was evaluating the applicant solely in terms of how she might affect him. In trying to correct the error of using women, he was making an erroneous decision with respect to the business, which at that time should have been uppermost in his mind. To be sure, he might earlier have done the opposite—that is, hire her only because she had a desirable body. This would have been in line with previous criminal patterns. Although he was now thinking more responsibly, the scope of his thinking still was not broad enough.

In making decisions, the criminal has never been much concerned with details. Instead, his grand schemes for what he wants to accomplish have guided him. What he scorns as trivial details usually have turned out to be basic considerations.

> C expected to work for his Ph.D. and make a unique contribution to knowledge. He was a middle-aged college dropout, had no reliable source of income, and was in debt. Yet, he aspired to earn his degree while working full-time, maintaining an active social life, attending our program, and going to a variety of cultural events. The details of whether he could survive financially, even be admitted to graduate school, and find enough time to do what he wanted to (as well as what he had to) were unimportant to him. After several months, he learned that his grand plan was not working out. He had not had even the time to complete an undergraduate course necessary for his bachelor's degree. Faced with his errors of thinking, C acknowledged, "I can talk quite a bit about Plato, but I can't make a decision about anything in my life."

In the everyday tasks of life, the criminal also lacks basic information. When one criminal went shopping for a pair of blue jeans, he had no idea what size he wore, what kind he wanted, how much they would cost, or even what store to go to. He had never actually shopped for something. He had procured his clothes through buying stolen goods, trading clothes, being given clothes by his parents and other criminals, or uncritically buying whatever was most expensive. Criminals have no knowledge of how to keep track of money. Few have saved or bothered to keep a checkbook. Some have simply ignored bills and other financial obligations. The criminal has to start at the beginning to learn how to make financial decisions. Even the criminal who has been employed regularly lacks a knowledge of his financial position, and responsible decisions are therefore impossible.

> We were talking with C about his future at his job. He stated that he earned between $5500 and $6500 a year. We knew that his pay was $118 a week and that he was getting time and a half for the sixth day, so his gross income must be about $154 a week. We asked C to multiply $154 by 52. This came to over $8000, and he anticipated a raise of $520. His entire perspective changed. C had never viewed himself a earning that much money. He had no idea of what he was earning and so was not able to make realistic plans.

C was thinking about the financial future of his family, but was not even utilizing the information available. Finally he sought additional facts and talked with his employer about opportunities for advancement in the business.

The criminal has not been aware that information often requires verification. Filing a tax return is an example. Many criminals do not bother to file at all, whether they have worked or not. Some submit tax returns, but invariably do so inaccurately. Now, as they make out their income tax returns, some for the first time, questions arise. The criminal is likely to consult the first person available and take his advice as that of an authority. It does not occur to him to call the Internal Revenue Service or double check in some other way the accuracy of his information. The criminal shows the same pattern in making inquiries regarding how to obtain what is legitimately due him, such as pensions or social security payments. He uncritically accepts the first answer he receives. In crime, he was suggestible and acted on tips, often without checking them out. He now learns to go to a reliable and knowledgeable source for information.

A major task for the A.C. is to develop in the criminal the habit of considering options. The criminal has made few actual decisions, if by decision one means choosing among alternative course of action; he has approached each situation with concrete thinking, tubular vision, and prejudgments. When he has to make responsible decisions about matters new to him, he is at a loss. Often, he considers only one course of action. One criminal was purchasing a fence for his home. He called one company and decided that the price was too high. He gave up without even considering calling other firms. The following is another example:

> C wanted to get his wife a gift for Valentine's Day. The family already had one large console color television set. C decided to purchase a portable set, so that his wife could have one handy in the kitchen. He decided on a portable set of a particular brand from a particular store. He chose the dealer on the basis of the fact that the set would be delivered. There was no consideration of price or of the dealer's reputation (which was very unsavory). C was planning to buy the television set at a time when he was not working and was depleting the family's savings.

C failed to consider options all along the way: the timing of the purchase of the set (including whether to buy it at all), the brand, the dealer, and the screen size. He was truly amazed when he found that he could buy a better brand at a lower price from another dealer. The responsible person would be equally amazed at the criminal's failure to consider alternative courses in making even the most routine and seemingly insignificant decisions.

> C went to a bookstore, searching for a particular textbook that he had not found elsewhere. He located only one copy in the whole store. He decided to hide it within the store while he looked elsewhere for a paperback edition.

C was not aware of other options. He might have asked a clerk to hold the book for him. If this had not been feasible, he might have offered to put down a refundable deposit. Again and again, it is striking how elementary the teaching of the criminal must be.

> C had worked, saved money, and rented an apartment and was functioning responsibly. But working at the job he had was frustrating, owing to the owner's irascibility and occasionally unethical conduct. C finally had to make it clear that he could not make the kinds of compromises that the owner wanted. The consequence was that C was transferred to an office of the same firm in another area. C wanted to leave the company altogether, but his employer prevailed on him to remain. However, C announced his intention to look elsewhere. As C talked about this situation, he related how the manager of another branch of the company did a good business without having to follow the owner's unethical practices. The option of C's doing the same thing did not occur to him. It never entered his mind that the same end could be achieved by

different means. That is, by operating like the other regional manager, he could achieve the same results.

C's tubular vision blinded him to a possibility that was obvious to us. Actually, it works both ways: the criminal needs to consider options to know in which areas to seek facts, but he must find facts in order to establish more options. Both skills are foreign to him.

Related to the consideration of options is the establishment of priorities. The criminal has no concept of this whatsoever, especially in his management of time and money. In this program, he learns to set priorities, and this in time becomes a habit.

In decision-making, a responsible time perspective is essential. In describing the error of instancy, we pointed out that the criminal is unwilling to apply effort toward a long-range objective. Developing a long-range view reduces fragmentation, in that the criminal does not make important decisions solely on the basis of here and now. In crime, the criminal considered the future sufficiently to defer decisions to gather more information if he needed it; in other matters, he failed to consider long-range consequences. In the interests of a more prudent decision, it is sometimes wise to delay action. If the criminal is required to make a decision, it is often reasonable for him to suspend judgment in the interest of a wiser decision later. He has to endure the tension of ambiguity and the lack of closure until he has sufficient information on which to base a decision. In effective decision-making, there has to be what William James (1950), called a "rational balancing of the books." To achieve this, one has to have time to determine the options and to consider consequences. Whereas a prompt decision is desirable, in the long run it is often advantageous to delay until the best decision can be made. We do not encourage the criminal to be a perfectionist or to defer unnecessarily. Rather, we help him to acquire a sense of timing in decision-making. He learns that there are decisions for which one could acquire more data *ad infinitum*, but that at some reasonable point a decision must be made. One is rarely one hundred percent certain in a decision of any complexity. In fact, it sometimes takes great effort and courage to come to a decision when there are imponderables and risks involved. This is totally new to the criminal, who has been operating throughout his life on the basis of superoptimism with respect to anything he undertakes. In this matter of timing, there are considerations besides whether one has the needed information. The proper climate and circumstances are also important. When to ask the boss for a raise, for example, involves determining when the boss is in a receptive mood.

The state of mind in which decisions are reached is important. The criminal learns to defer decision-making not only until he has the facts, but also until he is composed and calm enough to evaluate them. Anger precludes logical thinking and thus results in poor decisions. In working with any criminal, it is possible to discuss innumerable examples of unfortunate consequences of decisions made in anger and haste. The costs are often high when decisions are based on feelings, whether anger or sentiment.

Not every decision has to pass through the process of fact-finding and sorting out options. Some decisions are less complex than others. The criminal learns which decisions do not require excessive fact-finding. In the process of change, he makes for the first time many of the decisions that responsible people have long grown accustomed to making. For the criminal, the process is not at all automatic. He still must deliberately and carefully evaluate his course of action—fact-finding, weighing options, thinking about the long range, and verifying information. All the other correctives for thinking errors must be applied to decision-making.

The agent of change does not make the criminal's decisions *for* him. Criminals do not function as automatons or extensions of the A.C. We help them to evaluate the process by which they make decisions. What matters is that the process by which a decision is reached is responsible. If we think that the criminal is about to make an unwise decision, we raise many questions and present other options. However, we do not instruct him to follow a particular course, because, in the end, it is he who must make the choice and bear the consequences.

BIBLIOGRAPHY

Alexander, F., and Ross, H., eds. (1952). *Dynamic Psychiatry*. Chicago: University of Chicago Press.

Aristotle (1952). *Nichomachean Ethics. Great Books of the Western World*, vol. 9. Chicago: Britannica.

Binstock, J. (1973). Requiem for momism. *Intellectual Digest* 3: 72-73.

Cameron, N. (1963). *Personality Development and Psychopathology*. Boston: Houghton-Mifflin.

Curry, W. N. (1974). Aftermath of a burglary. *Washington Post*, November 28.

Douvan, E., and Adelson, J. (1966). *The Adolescent Experience*. New York: Wiley.

Drakeford, J. W. (1967). *Integrity Therapy*. Nashville: Broadman.

Freeman, L. (1951). *Fight Against Fears*. New York: Crown.

Freyhan, F. A. (1955). Psychopathic personalities. In *Oxford Loose Leaf Medicine*, pp. 239-256. Fair Lawn, New Jersey: Oxford University Press.

Henderson, D. K. (1939). *Psychopathic States*. New York: Norton.

Hutt, M. L.; Isaacson, R. L.; and Blum, M. L. (1966). *Psychology: The Science of Interpersonal Behavior*. New York: Harper and Row.

James, W. (1950). *The Principles of Psychology*, vol. 2. New York: Dover.

Liebman, J. L. (1946). *Peace of Mind.* New York: Simon and Schuster.

Low, A. A. (1973). Recovery, incorporated: mental health through will training. In *Direct Psychotherapy*, vol. 2, ed. R. R. Jurjevich, pp. 818-843. Coral Gables, Florida: University of Miami Press.

Menninger, K., and Holzman, P. S. (1973). *Theory of Psychoanalytic Technique.* New York: Basic Books.

Neill, A. S. (1960). *Summerhill: A Radical Approach to Child Rearing.* New York: Hart.

Piersall, J., and Hirshberg, A. (1955). *Fear Strikes Out.* Boston: Little, Brown.

Rogers, J. G. (1971). Victimless crimes: how one city has changed the rules. *Parade*, November 21, pp. 12-16.

Salzman, L. (1961). Guilt, responsibility and the unconscious. *Comprehensive Psychiatry* 2:179-187.

Solomon, P., and Patch, V. (1971). *Handbook of Psychiatry.* Los Altos: Lange.

Valentine, C. W. (1956). *The Normal Child.* Baltimore: Penguin.

Washington Post (4/6/75). Victims of burglary: intangible losses.

White, J. M. (1975). Worry worry worry worry. *Washington Post*, May 12.

White, R. W., and Watt, N. F. (1973). *The Abnormal Personality*, 4th ed. New York: Ronald.

Winchester, A. M. (1964). *Biology: And Its Relation to Mankind*, 3rd ed. New York: Van Nostrand.

Chapter 8

Correction of
Other Thinking Errors

IN THIS CHAPTER, we shall demonstrate how we correct twelve thinking errors described in "Criminal Thinking Patterns" (chapter 4 of volume 1) and two of several thinking patterns presented in "From Idea Through Execution" (chapter 6 of volume 1). The thinking patterns covered in this chapter all contain automatic errors, but correction of those errors alone does not produce the desired change. Additional correctives are needed. For example, power and control persist even after the automatic error of ownership is eliminated. Similarly, fragmentation is not totally eliminated by a criminal's adopting a responsible time perspective. This chapter describes correctives applied to thinking errors more complex than those described in the last chapter.

After describing the rationale for the correctives in each case, we include illustrations of old and new thinking patterns in a given criminal. By presenting the details of specific examples, we hope that the reader will understand more clearly the corrective concepts—how they are used and how their implementation results in change. We have chosen illustrations that do not include arrestable acts or even thinking about arrestable acts. The situations we cite may appear to be common and not dangerous, but in the criminal this ordinary thinking inevitably results in arrestability. For effective change to take place, errors must be recognized in change *when they are incipient* because the incipient thoughts of today result in the arrestable acts of tomorrow.

When we propose a corrective, it should not be interpreted as meaning that this corrective alone produces change. It is usually combined with other correctives. A criminal thinking error is part of a pattern expressed often in different contexts and requires many corrections frequently repeated until a more responsible thinking pattern replaces it.

REDISTRIBUTION OF ENERGY

In volume 1, we described the extent of the criminal's physical and mental activity. In the process of change, when responsibility is required, the A.C. constantly hears the criminal complaining about how tired he is although previously, in his criminal life, he has displayed tremendous energy, often sleeping only a few hours out of every twenty-four. Clearly, to a great extent, available energy depends on what he chooses to concentrate on doing. He is tired when he is required to do things that he does not want to do. In chapter 7, we emphasized the importance of eliminating "I can't" from the criminal's life and the importance of doing what is necessary in a responsible manner even if contrary to his feelings or interest. Criminals who view this program as a lifeline implement these new patterns of thought and action and invariably are surprised that they do accomplish what they had previously considered impossible. In our program, all participants work eight hours per day (some six or seven days per week), spend four hours with us, and still fulfill their home responsibilities. In the process of change, they are tired at times but never exhausted. They have little time to sleep but do not complain of disabling fatigue. Interest in living responsibly grows as they gain more experience doing it. Our people agree that they function better when overscheduled than when underscheduled. The more they have to do, the harder they work, the more they earn, and, interestingly, the more energy they find they have available. We have found that, when our people have gone into saleswork, invariably they have been busy with more than selling. When business is slow they straighten and arrange merchandise, memorize the stock, and do some cleanup work. They also think about how to improve their performance, and they reflect on the change process. When the criminal has his day heavily programmed, there is much less criminal thinking than when he is idle, because "I am too busy doing and thinking of the things I have to do."

One problem that sometimes occurs is that the criminal becomes too focused on one part of life and defaults in others. He puts great effort into his work, often devoting evenings and weekends to it. As a consequence, he neglects obligations to other people and has to postpone things that he has planned. The criminal has always been a very intense person who pours his energy into one objective to the exclusion of other considerations. This is an expression of the tubular vision to which we have referred; the same pattern now characterizes him as he functions responsibly.

Old Pattern

C became involved with his latest girlfriend to the exclusion of many other commitments for which he stated that he had no time or energy. He did not visit his mother and even neglected to talk to her on Mother's Day. He did not return to his minimum security ward at the proper time. He defaulted on looking for lodging in the community. C dropped his interests in sports and music. He resumed using drugs in small amounts. Because of this focus on the girl, there was a series of self-made emergencies, culminating in his being excluded from hospital residence and having to find living quarters immediately. C accounted for these events to us by saying, "I get carried away." This was a statement of the fact that he had been so preoccupied with the girl that little else had even entered his mind.

C's energy was consumed in his relationship with his girl friend and in concurrent irresponsible thought and action that resulted in his having to dig himself out of holes. This pattern was a consideration in daily meetings, and slowly change occurred. C began to direct his energy toward home and work. Later, he expanded his sphere of concern, but did so slowly.

The Corrective Applied

C applied himself diligently to a full-time job. He had had a reconciliation with his former wife and two children. With both husband and wife employed, the couple bought a house, and now there were many demands on C's time and energy. There were chores around the house, activities with the children, and overtime work at the office. C was learning to handle many different situations at once and no longer was carried away. Energy was abundant as he attended to more tasks than he had earlier.

In responsible living, the criminal learns to "bounce many balls at once." Spending time with his family, paying bills, visiting relatives, helping neighbors, playing with children, running errands, keeping a checkbook, and a myriad of other routine responsibilities are fulfilled, in addition to those at work. This balance in life is foreign to the unchanged criminal. Thus if his energy appears to be disproportionately expended on one situation or in one part of life, this is carefully considered in the group, and usually time-budgeting is the result.

The criminal sometimes goes to the other extreme. Instead of focusing on one task or set of problems, he tries to do everything at once. Consequently, he is not systematic or effective at any undertaking. The corrective for this is establishing priorities with respect to the expenditure of energy and time so as to do a competent job at whatever he undertakes. Otherwise, he will skip from one thing to another and become disaffected with everything. If this occurs in the case of a responsible person, he becomes ineffective; in the case of a criminal, the immediate outcome is irresponsibility and the ultimate outcome crime.

In the past, the criminal's energy has been expended first in irresponsible activity and then in trying to extricate himself from the problems that he has created. Now, in change, the criminal's tremendous energy is an asset. He requires challenge and diversity and is always searching for something to do. In our program, we help him to harness that energy and direct it to constructive, purposeful activity. With such abundant energy available, the criminal is required to do more than comply with or conform to the requirements of this program. He must attack this program as though it were a life-and-death matter. This is analogous to professional sports, in which an athlete must practice constantly and concentrate totally; if he lets up, his performance suffers and he is no longer successful. Of course, the rechanneling of energy by itself does not produce a responsible outcome. For energy to be responsibly redirected, many other changes must occur first, including the correction of the thinking errors now to be presented.

ELIMINATION OF ANGER

Anger is pervasive in the criminal. It is abundantly expressed, although often it is not at all visible to the observer, extreme as it might be. Anger is a consequence of fear, especially of the fear of a putdown. We have described in chapter 7 how the criminal's perception of what constitutes a putdown is altered in the change process. More is required, however, than insight into what constitutes a putdown. Anger requires separate and continuing attention as the criminal reports his daily experiences. Every reference to anger is really a reference to the thinking processes preceding and during the anger state. Anger as *emotion* cannot be dealt with rationally, but anger as *thinking* can be.

We review with the criminal the many costs of his anger as it has operated throughout his life. Injury to others is the most serious consequence. However, there have been other costs—illogical thinking, impaired problem-solving, a decrement in the quality of performance, diminution of energy for the task at hand, and alienation of other people.

Traditional psychotherapy calls for expression of anger.

In the permissive atmosphere of the therapeutic situation, the patient brings up his problems and expresses the hostility, fear, guilt and other emotions that center around them. Often, as he "talks out" his problems, hostility or fear or other feelings of which he was totally unaware will come to the surface. This "release"—verbal expression—of true emotional feeling is considered essential to effective psychotherapy; it paves the way for the development of insight and positive action toward the solution of his problems. For until the patient "gets these feelings off his chest" the tension and conflict connected with them operate as blocks to any learning of new, more adjustive attitudes. (Coleman 1964, p. 565)

As we have said repeatedly, we do not depend on insight to lead to positive action, for such insight *follows* change. Repressed hostility in the criminal's unconscious is not a problem. Rather, he has a low threshold and is all too ready to flare up in anger. When he ventilates his anger, the anger does not diminish, but increases.* Consequently, we have found that we must take the opposite approach. Just as we eliminate not only crime but criminal thinking, so do we eliminate not only the outward expression of anger but also its internal manifestations. This is because we regard every anger reaction as an indicator of vulnerability to violation. Anger reflects an underlying state in which violation is likely.

We have found only one other author who has stressed the importance of *eliminating* anger. In a book that has received too little notice, Hauck (1967) asserted that anger is "not legitimate" in human beings. He stressed the importance of reason in dealing with daily life.

By reasoning soundly we prevent our frustrations from getting to the point where anger is created and then drained off. (p. 111)

Hauck maintained that man can control anger and prevent it.

Properly instructed, it is perfectly possible to raise children who will not get angry over most normally provoking situations. . . . The idea that one can be as solid as the Rock of Gibraltar and as peaceful as a sunny day, both at the same time is absolutely foreign to the angry child. Yet such is the lesson he will have to learn if he is to have a peaceful life and if this ever is to be a peaceful world. (pp. 100-101)

For the criminal, anger is the crack in the door to irresponsibility and eventually leads to crime. Therefore, it must be eliminated. At first, the criminal must deter its expression. But suppression is only a step along the way; anger may be displaced and find its expression in some other form, such

---

*Moyer (1972, p. 37) also pointed out the danger of catharsis or ventilation of aggression: "Space does not permit a review of the vast research on the general problem of catharsis as a means of reducing tendencies to hostility. However, it is clear that it is by no means generally effective and there is much additional evidence that aggression either vicarious or otherwise may increase the tendency to further aggression."

as psychosomatic symptoms. Displacement of anger is not a satisfactory resolution, because the anger is still present. With anger eliminated, displacement is unnecessary.

The criminal learns new processes of deterrence to apply to anger. (These processes, the same ones that he applies to criminal thinking, are described in the next chapter.) When he describes an anger reaction in his daily report, we examine the attendant thinking processes, point out the costs of anger, and bring in his contribution to the situation that angered him.

Old Pattern

C was working in a store when the cash register jammed. In a rage, he called up the repair company and demanded that the agent come to the store immediately and fix the register. The agent did not show up that day or the next. C phoned the company again, became loud and profane, and threatened action if the machine were not fixed.

The group pointed out to C, as he related the incident, that his reaction had been a lifelong pattern that alienated others and resulted in injury. In this instance, C had undercut his own objective of getting the register fixed. His automatic thinking errors were identified—ownership, not seeing things from another's point of view, unrealistic expectations, failure to find facts, and prejudgment. In line with our emphasis on mental preparation for the future, C began to anticipate what might happen and to think rationally before he was in the situation (preemptive deterrence).

The Corrective Applied

C realized that he had been angry enough to assault the company's agent had he shown up. Having reviewed the consequences of anger in the past, C planned a different response. He phoned the company again. In a quiet, courteous manner, he reminded the agent that the register had been repaired not long before and that the same problem had recurred. In response to this call, the agent arrived in four hours. C received prompt service, this time at no charge.

If a criminal shares the common view that anger is an inherent, irreversible aspect of the mind and a natural part of life, this vitiates efforts to lessen anger, because he is excusing it. A changed attitude is mandatory: he will forevermore have problems to solve, but no matter what they are, they can be solved rationally. Anger is *never necessary* to solve a problem.

The criminal often justifies anger on the grounds that only through anger can he get people to do his bidding. Our position is that action can be generated without anger and that the costs of displaying anger far outweigh the advantages. Furthermore, firmness and insistence on one's position are usually as effective as anger, and often more so.

Repeatedly, we demonstrate how anger impedes the criminal's performance.

> C was angry about failing to obtain proper information from his boss relative to a problem at work. He did not show this outwardly, and yet it had its effect as he was interviewing people for a job with the firm. One girl was applying for a job as a barmaid. C saw that, despite her claims of proficiency, the girl was not experienced. He regarded her as conning him and thought that she should not even be considered for the position. Abruptly, but without an outward expression of anger, he returned her application to her, and she broke down in tears and went to the manager. The manager smoothed things over and then pointed out to C that he had handled the situation in such a way that the management was left open to a charge of discriminating against women. The group suggested that C could have accepted the girl's application and told her that she would be notified later of the action taken. But, because he was already angry about something else, C's thinking was not clear and there was a decrement in his performance.

Although the cause-effect relationship might seem indirect here, this situation is typical of how the criminal functions. Anger is often present, though not expressed. It affects much of what the criminal does in areas totally unrelated to the issue about which he is angry.

In an angry state of mind, the criminal magnifies the significance of everything that goes wrong.

> C had had little success in obtaining the kind of job that he wanted and continued to work as a salesman in a department store. He admitted being angry inside, although he tried not to let it interfere with his work. Nevertheless, his performance had not been as good, and he was making errors in sales transactions. Finally, C began to resent being there. In the group, he emphatically said, "I don't want to do it any more. I don't want to be a robot on a machine treadmill. The human being is not meant to be a machine." In an examination of his state of anger, it became apparent that C was increasingly angry at everything that was not going his way, and therefore anyone or anything could be a target for the expression of

that anger. C stated, "There is anger because I am not getting where I want to go. There is no relief from all I have to do." At this point, even putting on a shirt with a slightly worn collar was an occasion for anger.

C was angry because his unrealistic expectations were not being met, and thus he was put down. The costs of the anger were a decrement in his efficiency and accuracy at work, alienation of others, psychosomatic symptoms, and illogical thinking about his future. This was a dangerous state of mind because of C's proclivity for violence and other types of crimes. The channel had been partially closed, and C had not brought out his anger until it had mounted to a point of great intensity. Ideally, correctives are applied at the first indication of an angry state. Here, it was a sizable job to correct errors that had compounded one another. As it turned out, in this case, it was too late. C had already decided that he would not put up with the machine treadmill any longer. He dropped out of the program and returned to his earlier mode of existence. Because he had been a voluntary participant in the program, there was no leverage to hold him.

Interestingly, the criminal in change sometimes has a short fuse with others who are irresponsible.

It took C an hour to complete a typing job that should have taken ten minutes. He realized that he had made too many errors, and so, without anger, he retyped the copy. Then he found out that one of the people in the office who was notoriously unreliable and incompetent had once again provided erroneous information. C had the wrong signature on the page and had to retype it again. He was angry but did not express it. He was fed up with the irresponsibility of the other person. With this anger, there was the "to hell with it" attitude, followed by criminal thinking. These manifestations were then dealt with in the group.

C had to learn to handle irresponsible people in a responsible manner. Understanding that anger often elicits anger, C learned to take a position and maintain it firmly. The danger in the persistence of an anger reaction (as might have happened in the above situation) was an increasing probability that C would see himself as a victim of his co-worker's irresponsibility. In the past, this would have resulted in indignation and retaliation.

When the criminal is deprived of excitement, he is very likely to react with self-pity. He builds up a list of grievances that have little merit and is angry at the way life is treating him. We examine this angry self-pity, clarifying how the criminal has contributed to the state of mind and reviewing its consequences in the past.

Old Pattern

C complained about having to travel by bus to and from school and then spending more time riding the bus to the other side of the city to see us. He objected to having too little time for lunch, about the dullness of his courses, about the separation from his girlfriend, who was going to school elsewhere, and about a variety of other aspects of his life. Although he did not express anger in a visible manner, the angry state of mind was brought out in the group meeting. Attending the anger was the thought of quitting the program, and this was followed by a surge of criminal thinking—getting drunk, finding a prostitute, and returning to his former criminal haunts.

C's state of mind was, If this is life, it's a hell of a life. However, C acknowledged that no other option was acceptable. Consequently, he became more reflective and one day came to the group meeting observing about himself, "I was in the self-pity bag."

The Corrective Applied

C was describing his thinking about the inconveniences of his daily routine. He admitted having experienced flashes of anger from time to time, but then he gave himself a talking to. C thought about how, after years of confinement, he had an opportunity to make something of his life. Rather than emphasizing the hardships of attending this program and school, he stressed the opportunities. Instead of being angry at his girl friend's geographic remoteness, he thought about how important her education was to her. By thinking things through, he eliminated anger reactions.

In time, C no longer experienced even momentary flashes of anger toward the inconveniences of life. To him, anger signified a return to prison. Eliminating anger (and self-pity) became a life-or-death matter.

Sometimes, the criminal who has shown a prominent assault pattern reports that he has experienced anger at *himself*, as though this represented a massive change. However, our experience is replete with examples that demonstrate that such anger does not add to one's effectiveness, but reduces it.

C got angry at himself for mixing up orders as he worked behind the counter. He became sullen and silent. In the group meeting, C readily acknowledged that this reaction antagonized others and resulted in a decrease in his performance.

The corrective here is the view that one does make errors, but that one's energy should be directed to remedying the situation and not spent in anger at oneself which detracts from problem-solving and leads to discouragement, a "to hell with it" attitude, and finally criminal thinking. (For discussion of anger and its attendant criminal thinking and action patterns, see chapter 4 of volume 1.)

Early in the process of change, the criminal at times avoids meeting a situation responsibly because of fear that he will become angry. This is a victim position: he fears that he will be a victim of his feelings. One man did not want to visit his wife's relatives, because he was afraid that he would become angry. This fear of an anger reaction was not undesirable, but a more desirable response would have been to think the situation through in advance and deter the anger, rather than avoid an obligation to his wife.

The criminal learns to monitor anger in himself and apply deterrence. Eventually, as he implements the correctives for thinking errors, he preempts much anger by approaching situations mentally prepared and rationally, allowing fear to guide him, rather than responding to each disappointment in life as a personal affront. Anger can be eliminated by choice: "If I decide that I will not be angry and I am prepared for things, I find that I am not angry."

> C pointed out that at work he was not too efficient, because he was thinking about matters not pertinent to his job. Consequently, others were reminding him of his inefficiency, although this was done in a warm, friendly manner. What struck C was, "I wanted to be angry." He was used to striking out at people who made demands of him. C stated that he did not become angry because he reasoned. He had thought that if he was not being effective, it was because he was not concentrating, and that he was responsible for each error he made. Not being angry was strange and unnatural.

In the past, C would have asserted himself with anger and indignation. He would have lashed out at others and tried to control the situation. Here, through the application of reason, he had robbed himself of his anger.

Our criminals succeed in eliminating anger. This includes the elimination of *any* internal state that has anger at its core—resentment, hostility, irritability, and annoyance (all of which *in the criminal* are potentially dangerous). The result is not bland, colorless, unemotional people; they never become that. Nor does the elimination of anger mean that they become doormats for others' use. Rather, because they fully implement the new mental processes of responsibility, the changing criminals are on the way to being "as solid as the Rock of Gibraltar and as peaceful as a sunny day, both at the same time."

ELIMINATION OF CRIMINAL PRIDE

Criminal pride refers to the criminal's image of himself as powerful and unique. He uses the word *pride* without the adjective *criminal*. More commonly, he speaks of "respect," which he believes that criminals should accord him in all endeavors, criminal or not, and others should accord him because he is a powerful figure.

The criminal insists on doing things his own way and acts in a manner that he professes is "standing on principle." When he has an objective, achieving it becomes an all-or-nothing matter—the sole determinant of his worth as a person. The cost of criminal pride is great. The criminal has adhered to an attitude of "if I bend, I break" to avoid being a nothing. Accordingly, if there has been any perceived threat to him, he has stood his ground. When put down, he has retaliated and injured others. People have paid with their lives because a criminal's pride has been affronted.

In our meetings, criminal pride is expressed in the way the criminal interacts with the A.C. and the other group members. If something is said that he does not quite understand or a word is used that he does not know, the criminal does not ask for clarification. He acts in a smug, self-satisfied way, indicating that what others in the group have to say is of little interest to him. He avers that he knows all there is to know about any issue that is brought up. When challenged, instead of being receptive and self-critical, he tries to tear others down. He sloughs off irresponsibility, claiming that confessing to wrong-doing is all that is necessary. When others are concerned about him, he may condescendingly thank them but implies or says outright that they need not worry about him.

The criminal's notion of manhood is a cornerstone of his pride. In our program, this notion is taken out of the realm of sexuality and physical toughness and is redefined. Manhood has much more to do with a man's facing life's problems responsibly and doing his best to solve them.

Old Pattern

C received a message from his landlord asking him when he intended to move. C met with his landlord that evening, and what was to have been a discussion quickly developed into a confrontation. There was an argument over back rent. The landlord approached C menacingly with a weapon, and C punched him in the face. C turned away and stalked down the street toward his home. A policeman apprehended him and charged him with assault. In the discussion of the incident with us, C remained firm in the position that he would not tolerate anyone's talking to him the way the landlord had. Furthermore, he was going to stand up to anyone who threatened him in any way. C delivered a tirade on what manhood was and insisted that he was not to be faulted for acting as he had with the landlord. Being a man meant fighting back.

In this discussion, the group tried repeatedly to point out that C's idea of manhood had often resulted in his committing serious crimes, including homicide, and that it would inevitably do so again. However, C was not receptive; he was standing on principle. In later discussions, he slowly began to accept the program's view that it takes more of a man to avoid a fight than to uphold one's sense of pride by retaliation.

The Corrective Applied (first stage)

C's two-year-old complained about being kicked by the boy downstairs, who was older. This happened several times. C stayed away from the boy's father, who had a bad reputation, but did talk with the boy's mother. She screamed profanities at him. Her husband, who was drunk, came out of the house with a knife in one hand and a stick in the other. C quietly told him not to touch him and walked away. However, C reported, "I was smoking." Anger was blazing within.

At this stage of the change process, C avoided serious consequences by leaving the scene. Criminal pride, however, was still present, manifested by anger at himself for walking away. The presence of anger even in this form still constituted a potential danger.

The Corrective Applied (second stage)

C was shopping in the neighborhood with his wife. They came face to face with the son of the landlord with whom C had the fight. The son was abusive to C and made some insulting comments to his wife. C had been thinking repeatedly about this type of situation, because of the discussion in our daily sessions. He reported no anger then or later. Very quietly, he had taken his wife by the hand and calmly walked away.

There was no defending his manhood in C's thinking. In this situation, and thereafter, his thinking was that fighting and seeking other women were not badges of manhood. Rather, these patterns would surely lead to his return to jail. C came to the belief that a man remains loyal to his wife and avoids a fight, no matter how much he has been provoked.

The criminal, with his pretensions and unrealistic expectations, is ever insisting on his rights. This is another major element of criminal pride. If anyone tries to stop him from exercising his rights, that person is sooner or later assaulted either verbally or physically. By putting himself in the place of others, considering the injuries that he has inflicted, and reviewing his violation of trust, he sees that in pursuit of what he has considered his right to do as he pleased, he has violated the rights of others.

Criminal pride is so deeply embedded that virtually any challenge to the criminal poses a threat to his entire self-image. In this program, the criminal's self-concept is gradually altered, so that he regards someone's challenging him in a totally different light.

> C was waiting for one of the other criminals to give him a ride. He wanted to read for a while, so he asked our secretary for a key to one of the offices. She asked him why he wanted the key. C did not regard this as the "great" C's being challenged. Instead, he explained to her that he wanted a place to read where he would not bother anyone and where he would not be distracted. C realized that it was her responsibility to ask him why he wanted access to an office. This small detail denoted a major change.

Formerly, if C had wanted to do something, he had regarded it as his right. If others tried to impede him, it had led to verbal and then physical altercations. C no longer was trying to prop up his image of himself as a powerful figure by regarding each such incident as a personal challenge. At this stage of the change process, his pride was based on the small accomplishments that he was making in earning a living honestly, putting some money aside, and functioning without injuring others.

As criminal patterns are eliminated and replaced by responsible ones, a self-respect develops that is quite different from the criminal pride of the past, in that it is based on the substance of responsible achievement. Clearly, this self-respect cannot be taught. It is a *consequence* of change.

ALTERATION OF ZERO-STATE THINKING

When the world does not comply with the criminal's decision as to how he should achieve his excitement, he regards himself as a nothing. "Take my excitement away and you take my world away." Being anything less than the unique number one reduces his image of himself to that of a zero. In the extreme form of this state, he believes that the entire world sees him as a nothing and that his existence is permanently futile. He regards himself not as a criminal but as a good person who, nevertheless, is a nothing. When he believes that he has no good in him at all, then he is a suicidal risk.

In the change process, the criminal has bursts of enthusiasm followed by periods of what he calls "depression," which include elements of discouragement, boredom, and anger. We have seen some zero states with pronounced suicidal thinking, but more often we find that the zero state is not this extreme. Thus, we might call it a "near-zero state." When the criminal presents himself to us, it is in terms of a mood, a state of despair with anger. We do not talk about a mood, but rather discuss the thinking preceding and during it.

In the process of change, near-zero states are dangerous, because the criminal will not endure them indefinitely. In this state, no matter how much he has gained in responsibility, he takes a negative view of life. He asserts that living in this social order makes his life meaningless: "If I am to be responsible, as you define it, I will live permanently in this state and I will be nothing the rest of my life. This I will not do." His solution to such thinking is irresponsibility, which immediately lifts his mood, alters his thinking, and makes him more energetic. He is more satisfied with life as he resumes an irresponsible course that sooner or later will result in his being arrestable.

Faced with this situation again and again, we see as our chief and immediate objective helping the criminal alter this thought pattern so that he exercises responsible judgment. Ignoring the mood and talking reason, we evaluate his past life, his present dilemma, and his future course.

The difficulty that most observers have is that they see the same apparent state in both criminal and noncriminal, but do not fully comprehend how differently the same state is dealt with by each. The responsible person manages such distress without major violations. But the criminal reacts to this state as though his whole life were imperiled and turns to his old source of excitement, crime. The responsible person summons up the courage to continue, in the hope that somehow things will straighten out. Asking the criminal to do that is like asking him to inoculate himself voluntarily with leprosy.

Our task is to present the criminal with a dissection of the cognitive components of the zero state. He views his past, in which near-zero states have resulted in criminality. He considers the outcome if he persists in the same patterns in the future. In the present, we reason with him as to how to deal with the irreversibly gloomy state in which he perceives himself. The criminal's choice as to whether to accept or reject this approach depends on his relationship to the group and to the A.C.

To counter his view that he is a transparent nothing, the criminal is asked to consider how responsible people regard him. He can draw on experiences that he has had with his own family. He is commended by others when not in crime and is admired as a person striving to go straight. Others exhort him to persevere in responsible endeavors when the going gets tough. Society's view of him changes, however, when he is high on crime* and thereby finding what

---

*In fact, a street term for this state of mind is a "natural high." Without drugs, the criminal attains the natural high by a stream of criminal thinking in which power and control are central.

he considers his meaning in life. The family regards his return to crime with sadness. For them, it is a tragedy. Some people view the criminal as a menace and advocate limiting his freedom. Others perceive him as a victim, persist in excusing him, and try to offer him help, for example, find a job. Because he persists in his criminality, eventually almost everyone gives up on him and regards him as a zero—that is, as worthless. Thus, what began as a misconception of himself becomes a self-fulfilling prophecy.

In the zero state, the criminal's thinking is antagonistic to the program. There are many ideas of criminal activity which he is temporarily deterring. If he were not deterring them, he would not be in a zero state. Confronted with this state of mind, the A.C. straightforwardly presents the choices to him. The criminal life is what he was in the process of altering. This is where his choice is critical and where *will* becomes an operational concept. The criminal can choose to endure the suffering of change, he can elect to return to his criminal way of life, or he can decide to kill himself.

The near-zero state occurs in the process of change. Many criminals in the group have attested to these states and to the consequences when they responded with criminal behavior or suicidal thinking.

We introduce a variety of appropriate correctives: acquiring a responsible time perspective, being guided by fear, lowering excessive expectations, making rational decisions on the basis of facts, and, especially, avoiding injury to others. To apply these, effort is mandatory, and the criminal must implement the program with Murphy's Law in mind. When all seems dark and futile, faith (not necessarily religious) is necessary.

We emphasize the criminal's misconception of himself. Without building up his opinion of himself as a good person, we reappraise his assets that he underrates. His view that his failure is obvious to everyone is erroneous. The outside world is not paying nearly as much attention to him as he thinks it is. Others in the group dispute the criminal's idea that this depression is a permanent state of being. They have lived through it many times.

When this state appears, the A.C. deals with it as with other issues, treating it calmly and rationally, and without cajoling or pleading. If, at this point, the A.C. shows concern, makes concessions, grants exceptions, accepts the criminal's excuses, or gives credence to his complaints, then he will become ineffective. At such a time, the criminal resorts to self-pity, anger, and a recitation of injustices. The A.C. responds to none of this empathically or sympathetically. What the criminal in such a state must realize is that it is his problem, no one else's. The A.C. or the group will not solve it for him but will help him solve it for himself. If the criminal sees that he can get sympathy in a zero state, he will later exploit it by claiming to be in a zero state, when in reality he is only trying to justify his failure to implement the program. This state will become a new psychologic excuse.

The criminal will meet adversities again and again. The issue is whether he will permit his morale to drop to a point where he will no longer tolerate the near-zero state or will take constructive steps to implement the program despite his feelings.

The following illustrates what may happen when a criminal experiences a near-zero state. Bored, angry, and tense, a criminal was thinking about the insufficiencies of responsible living that deprived him of the excitements that he very much desired. A series of events occurred in the store that he managed.

> When C returned to work, he found that the instructions he had given an employee to clean the refrigerator had not been executed. Instead, another employee was doing it. C was angry about this and then became irritable with customers. The first employee requested twenty minutes off to run an errand. C's anger was boiling. He told her that she could have the time off but need not bother to return, except to collect her final paycheck. C was then informed that a man who had made a purchase was standing near the doorway filing his nails. Viewing him as a potential shoplifter, C was angry again. He approached the man and told him to leave. The man refused, at which point C's anger was raging. He threatened to call the police. The man then replied that he was considering making another purchase and began to curse C, castigate the store, and raise a commotion that the other customers could hear. C stated that during the weekend he was also angry outside of work. He was angry at his parents, regarded his own friends as "ridiculous," and was angry at not having an available sex partner. Furthermore, he was angry at his own liver. C had had several attacks of hepatitis during the preceding couple of years, and, as a consequence, his doctor told him not to drink any alcoholic beverages.

Basically, C did not like the way the world was. He stated, "I go around goddamning everything." As he viewed life, he was being handed defeat after defeat and therefore was angry at everyone. His failure to gain control by anger resulted in a zero state. Life held no hope of improvement. Faced with this situation, C then had to consider the options: self-destruction, a return to crime, or perseverance in change. The dangers of the zero state were clear. At the time, C was deterring many irresponsible actions, some of which would have resulted in his being arrestable. (For a discussion of the steady stream of criminal ideas, see chapter 6 of volume 1.) Indeed, without such deterrence, a zero state would not have occurred, because the criminal would have been high on crime. In the past, violations had often been preceded by similar states of mind. His pattern had been to say to hell with it, to cut off his fears of what might happen, and to pursue his criminal excitements. Thus, C's options were clarified. In addition, he was required to assess his contribution to the present series of events that had gone awry. It had been his lack of care in employee selection that had led him to hire an incompetent and irresponsible employee. *He* had approached the customer, looking for a fight. *He* had contributed to many of the family difficulties that were now angering him. And *he* had chosen his own friends, whom he now regarded as ridiculous. Most absurd had been C's anger about not being able to drink. Owing to his use of drugs and alcohol, *he* had impaired his *own* health. Perspective was restored; the world was not being unfair to C, but rather C was experiencing a series of consequences of his own criminal patterns.

The correctives for the zero state are offered in the manner indicated by the above illustration. The criminal's options in life are reviewed. There is an attempt to assess his contribution to his present situation and to restore perspective. Other correctives are brought in as appropriate—time perspective, decision-making, and so forth. As the criminal changes, he continues to have periods of despair, but they become more like the depression of the noncriminal, rather than the global hopelessness that is a prelude to violation.

ELIMINATION OF CRIMINAL POWER AND CONTROL

The criminal's antidote to putdowns and to the intolerable zero state is the exertion of power and control over others. What he subjectively perceives as conquest and triumph provides him with self-esteem. The resulting excitement is a "high," a state qualitatively no different from a drug-induced high. From a nothing, he is transformed into a victor—a powerful figure who has demonstrated his superiority by overcoming and managing others. Illegitimate and illegal extractions of property, intimidation, physical and verbal abuse, and deception are among the means that he uses. The fact that others are used and exploited is of no consequence to the criminal, nor are the injuries inflicted even on those whom he claims to love.

Power and control are parts of the social order. However, responsible power and control are acquired within a framework of integrity by proper training, effort, and accomplishment. The criminal seeks power and control in antisocial ways for self-esteem, rather than for a socially useful purpose.

Early in the change process, the daily phenomenologic reports reveal the criminal's power and control patterns that pervade relationships with everyone—family, neighbors, work associates, and others. Because the power and control patterns are so habitual, the criminal does not think about their exploitative and injurious effects. He knows that he is using people, but he views this as his right.

Our first task is to make him aware of the extent of his search for power and control, the ways in which he conducts that quest, the purposes it serves, and its effect on others. Within a twenty-four-hour period, there may well be a half dozen expressions of power and control in his behavior and far more in his thinking. The casual observer might regard as innocuous some of the criminal's behavior that has an unrevealed power component.

In this section, our illustrations exclude obvious arrestable power-thrusting. Instead, we have selected nonarrestable and sometimes subtle manifestations of power and control, because these best convey the flavor of the corrective process. If we limited ourselves to eradicating power and control only as expressed in arrestable actions, we would be neglecting the incipient expressions that, although not arrestable at the time, lead to crime.

To ask the criminal to surrender his insatiable quest for power and control is to ask him to deprive himself of oxygen.

"My immediate reaction to giving up control for the sake of control is that I'd be turning myself into little people. And here enters the ego. I oppose myself to all the little people of the world—to all the puppets manipulated by the master puppeteer—me. I need the thought of controlling others so that I won't have to face how very ordinary I am."

In countless episodes reported in the daily meetings, the criminal shows how crucial is the maintenance of control.

Old Pattern

C and his wife had eight houseplants, because his wife wanted something alive that she could care for and they did not want to have a child or a pet. C's wife wanted to buy some more plants. C believed that this would crowd the appartment. His wife insisted that she wanted them. C was angry as he thought about how she was getting her own way. From there, he went on to thinking about other instances in which her desires prevailed.

Clearly, the issue was not houseplants, but that C must have his way. The danger in this situation became apparent, in that C asserted emphatically at one point that he had "had it" with his wife.

"Lately I've been taking a lot of crap from my wife, and my initial reaction is that if I take it for a while, appear contrite, get a job, and work for a while, she'll drop her guard and I'll be in control again. But, if things get too hot, if she dishes out more crap than I'm willing to take, I'm just going to take off."

This was characteristic of the criminal's attitude when he failed to maintain control. He had to learn to view the many transactions between him and his wife in terms other than who was controlling whom. For example, in the houseplant incident, he was put down because he thought that his wife was controlling him. She had no such intention in mind, but was expressing her desire for something that she wanted. She had to do this firmly because in the past if she were at all tentative in asking for something, C would ride roughshod over her and she would retract her request. C had to understand that if his mild mannered wife was now expressing her wishes more strongly, it was largely because of him. He had to consider how he defaulted on obligations to her and how theirs was anything but an interdependent relationship. Putting himself in her place, he realized that he had so controlled her that over the years she had rarely expressed an opinion counter to his, much less fought him openly on an issue. Gradually, C learned to evaluate differences between him and his wife on the merits of an issue, not on the basis of control.

The Corrective Applied

C's mother-in-law was coming to visit for a few days. His wife wanted the apartment scrubbed—all dust removed, everything in place, and the floors gleaming. C at first resented his wife's imposing burdensome cleaning chores on him. However, he stopped to think about how his mother-in-law had done everything to make him comfortable when he had visited her. He also put himself in his mother-in-law's place to consider how pleased she would be to see that her daughter was such a fine housekeeper.

The desire to be a big shot persists. It is one thing for the criminal to deter thoughts of crime, lies, and other f rms of irresponsibility, but when some of his cherished ambitions are regarded as manifestations of criminal thinking, he is initially resistant.

C stated, "I want my own operation. I am not very comfortable working for someone else." He pointed out that even though he was only in his twenties, he resented working for others in such institutions as banks or government agencies and did not want to work in commercial establishments. In fact, he remarked that he wanted to "disappear" whenever an acquaintance saw him working as a sales clerk at a store. He believed that he had talents to run things better than anyone else and resented his lack of authority over others. Instead, everyone else was telling him what to do.

On first thought, one would not fault a young man for being ambitious enough to want to be an entrepreneur. However, C had quit any number of jobs precisely because he lacked power and control over others, as does anyone who starts at the bottom. Because he did not have the authority he wanted, his attitude was, To hell with it, and he found what he desired in irresponsibility and, eventually, crime. There was nothing wrong with his ambition to have his own business. Rather, it was his view of the way in which this would happen that showed an error in thinking. To C, it was his right to be the power figure in any enterprise of which he was a part. A review of the costs to others and himself of this drive to be the top man was the beginning of his reducing his unrealistic pretensions, adopting a responsible time perspective, and applying effort so that he might make some constructive accomplishments and legitimately acquire power that he could use to benefit others.

Many aspects of the criminal's functioning are reviewed in the light of his wanting to be a big shot.

Old Pattern

C came to the meeting in a three-piece, fashionable suit. He claimed that he really had "nothing to wear," because his clothes were two years old. He stated that he needed to buy more clothing for work. C considered it "economical" to reduce his expenditure for a suit from four hundred dollars to two hundred dollars and for a tie from twenty-five dollars to twelve dollars. The group severely criticized his extravagance. C replied, "I would rather die than wear a four-dollar tie."

C was required to consider the consequences of this attitude. Because he had believed that he was entitled to whatever he wanted and had tried to control others through misrepresenting himself as a man of means, C had landed in prison. It was necessary for C to consider himself as a parolee who had accomplished nothing honestly in his life, not as C, the big shot for whom only the best was good enough. The program required that C carry only a small amount of money on his person and that he budget so as to live strictly within his means.

The Corrective Applied

C was spending a few idle moments by the river before going to work. He spotted an ice cream vendor and started toward him. Then he paused and thought about spending twenty-five cents on the ice cream. He was overweight and he knew that he should avoid it. Furthermore, he thought, perhaps the discipline of not spending the money would be the best course.

Because of his changing view of himself, this man, who had readily spent four hundred dollars and more on a suit, was now in conflict over spending twenty-five cents on ice cream.

Power and control are so pervasive and automatic in the criminal's functioning that he is often unaware of their prominence in almost every thought and act. In fact, what appears to be virtuous to some observers often turns out to be a power thrust.

C's expression of power was to charm people with his suave, polite, and articulate manner. This was not contrived by him, but was a part of his personality. He could make a friend on the first contact.

On its face, C's affinity for people was an asset. Yet his was a long history of impressing people and being singled out by them, only to exploit them later. In the group, C was not faulted for being polite. Rather, he was required to consider how he had gained the admiration of others, only to injure them later. It was essential for him to remain alert to the use to which he put personality assets.

Through daily phenomenologic reporting, the criminal monitors himself and is monitored by the group so closely that he becomes wary of any thinking or action that reflects former patterns of power and control. In fact, he may be reluctant to assert himself legitimately, for fear of trying to control others.

C's employer had found C to be performing very diligently. The employer also recognized that C had a good mind and therefore began asking him for his observations and advice about running the business. The employer asked C to evaluate the inside stealing that was going on and to appraise various employees. Because of his position, C had well-informed judgments, as well as accurate information. However, he kept putting his employer off, because he was fearful that by answering the questions, he would really be trying to take over from the boss.

C had to learn to discriminate between the power that came to him legitimately through achievement and the power derived from irresponsible self-aggrandizement at the expense of others. This criminal commented, "Power is like a knife." He elaborated by saying that just as a knife may be used to injure someone or to cut bread, so power could be used for evil or good. In every instance, criminals well advanced in change have been apprehensive about the acquisition of power, continually questioning whether they have earned it legitimately, have acquired it in a criminal manner, or are using it responsibly by adhering to the principles of our program.

As he makes progress, the criminal acquires a concept of responsible leadership. Before, to lead meant simply to dominate others. Now, the criminal comes to understand that leadership has its opportunities and responsibilities. Power carries with it new problems and burdens. Most importantly, situations that the criminal used to view mainly in terms of power and control are regarded as opportunities to be of service. As he puts himself in the place of others, learns what obligation is, and recognizes the nature of interdependent living, power is no longer pursued for its own sake.

UNIQUENESS IN PERSPECTIVE

The criminal's sense of personal power derives in part from his belief that he is unique. Everyone has some clearly distinguishing characteristics. The responsible person may be outstanding in one way or another, but in most respects he evaluates himself as average, or normal. The criminal views his personality as one of a kind, not duplicable, and unique, like a fingerprint. He therefore believes that he is never fully understood, deserves special consideration, and should not be inhibited in any way from whatever he wants to do. This thinking elevates him above all other people, regardless of his own station in life, even when confined. When he performs quite well or even acceptably, the criminal views himself as the unique number one, who knows more than others and does things better than they. Even if he chooses to avoid a task, he believes that he could outperform anyone else with very little effort, if he only cared to. Part of the sense of uniqueness is a belief that what applies to others does not apply to him. In his way of life, he has believed that laws that apply to others do not to him. He is above the law. Also contributing to the criminal's sense of uniqueness is his secrecy. The criminal believes that although others are open books to him, he is a mystery to them. He does not reveal himself to people, and yet he thinks he has their numbers or knows a great deal about them. Furthermore, he believes that he is singular because others have no idea of how much he knows.

Responsible people refer to those who are pedestrian or run-of-the-mill as ordinary. To the criminal, anyone who is not a criminal is ordinary. In his opinion, to be ordinary is to be a zero. One criminal expressed this idea when he exclaimed, "I'd rather be dead than just a mail-sorter." The criminal is certain that what ordinary people have accomplished is within his capability. He can do anything they can and do it better. The ordinary person is square (stupid), because he is missing out. The criminal has something that the ordinary person does not have—his criminal excitements. Furthermore, ordinary people have many problems as they plod on from day to day, but he has only one problem—will he get caught? The criminal's sense of uniqueness is rarely articulated in precisely this manner. However, when he is probed, he expresses his contempt for the ordinary, and his sense of uniqueness is evident.

To a criminal who is certain of his uniqueness, placing him in a group of other criminals does not offer him much. In his estimation, whatever applies to other group members has no applicability to him. As other criminals present their reports, the new group member is bored. His thoughts are far off, because he believes that listening to someone else's thoughts has little bearing on his life.

It does not take much teaching or lecturing to deal effectively with the criminal's sense of uniqueness. As daily reports of each group member are discussed, he is drawn into the dialogue and in instance after instance provides material similar to what others are offering. Although the groups are heterogeneous with respect to age, race, education, and social background, striking similarities of thinking and experience emerge among all the members. It is illuminating for a white, middle-class criminal to be confronted with the fact that from the standpoint of thinking patterns, he is no different from a black ghetto criminal, and vice versa. The errors of thinking are common to all criminals, regardless of early experiences and milieu. Just as striking is that the criminal who uses force and resorts to violence discovers that he has the same thinking patterns as the conman whom he disdains for being chicken and weak. Conversely, the conman who considers himself above the brutality of the violent criminal finds that he is not so different after all. Similarly, the drug-user and the criminal nonuser share the same thinking patterns.

Even after the basic similarities are established, the criminal persists in searching for differences that will demonstrate that he is unique.

> C1 considered himself different from C2, despite the fact that he acknowledged some common characteristics. C1 stated that C2 had never really thought about living responsibly, but he had. Furthermore, C1 asserted that C2 had "enjoyed" crime more than he. C1 claimed that he was totally different from C2 because of this "philosophic difference." C1 failed to consider that he and C2 were both criminals cut of the same cloth and that their similarities far outweighed their differences.

Several weeks of daily discussion of one another's experiences makes the point persuasively that the criminal is not unique. There remains, however, the belief that he is not an ordinary person. The criminal still has many pretensions. He states, "Anything I want to do, I will do." He means this; it is not idle boasting. He scoffs at hard work and step-by-step progress. Because of his extraordinary talents and abilities, he plans to attain overnight what others work a lifetime for.

Old Pattern

C believed that the people who took a long time to accomplish things were either lazy or fools. He thought that he knew more than doctors, lawyers, teachers, or anyone else. Furthermore, he believed that others did not understand how special he was in his abilities and talents. He often said to himself, "How many supermen can there be? I am it!" C was certain that he could perform brilliantly and be an instant success in whatever he undertook.

The Corrective Applied

In the process of change, this elementary school dropout who had spent many years confined finally got out in the world and began to make his way. Participating in this program, C began to face his limitations, which he had never considered present. In attending vocational training classes, he discovered that he was not so gifted. In fact, he had to struggle to spell some of the most elementary words correctly. He had no unique talents. Rather, because of poor study habits and tremendous educational deficiencies, he had to work hard to pass what others considered easy courses. In finding a job, C was not as irresistible to employers as he had imagined. On his own, he found that some of the routines of life that he had scorned were necessary. He had to go to the grocery store, clean his room, do his laundry, mend his clothes, and cook. He was supporting himself not in an impressive and influential position, but as a truck-driver. Slowly, there came a realization that he was far from a unique number one. In fact, he was learning things about how to get along in the world that many people half his age already knew.

C was having to function as an ordinary person. This was quite at odds with the superman image that he had held earlier.

What is noteworthy is that from time to time the criminal expresses his admiration for those who work hard to achieve their objectives, but he still thinks that he is so capable that what applies to others does not apply to him.

C was contrasting himself with a fellow at work. The latter was working on two master's degrees simultaneously and was planning to go to law school full-time. C's colleague was twenty-eight years old, a low-key person, and one who C believed would go far because of his aptitude and initiative. In contrast, C, in thinking about his own career, stated that he did not think about going to school and later receiving a salary. Rather, he was thinking in terms of immediate, large returns on investments for which he planned to borrow the capital. He daydreamed about a large estate with a swimming pool at the end of a spacious terrace.

Unknowingly, the world sometimes supports the criminal's idea of uniqueness.

C, an unemployed college dropout, finally went to look for a job, seeking a modest desk clerk position. The employer at the first place he tried said that there were no jobs available but added, "A man like you should be up on Capitol Hill." The fact was that C was articulate and regularly impressed people on first meeting. Here was one more reaction that fed an already inflated self-concept.

In the group, this incident was viewed as another instance of C's getting his foot in the door, sometimes in high places, and later betraying the trust initially placed in him. As C was required to think about his thinking and his actual performance in life, he realized, "I must adjust my thinking." He admitted that he used to curse the fact that he was not born wealthy. He had always wanted what a lot of money would buy but did not consider it necessary to work for it, as his peers did. Here he was, the same age as his friend but with no skills, with little job experience, unemployed, and with a family on welfare. This was a sobering perspective for this unique number one, who reflected that he wished that he had taken seriously a high-school locker-room motto: "The potential is interesting. The performance is everything."

Part of the criminal's experience in change is observing ordinary people and profiting from how they handle life situations. By watching others, a criminal who is self-critical rapidly comes to recognize his own deficiencies.

C was on a long bus ride. Two men on the bus began to fight. One had a gun, and it was a truly alarming situation for the passengers. The driver remained calm. He stopped the bus, walked up to the men and separated them. He stated that they had two options: he would drop them off at the police station or let them leave the bus then and there to settle their dispute. He then told each man where to sit, and the bus continued on its way. The driver was not visibly upset. There was no cursing or other manifestation of anger. He appeared to be completely unruffled.

C began to think about how he had responded to the unexpected. He recalled his past attempts to assert his authority and control over others through anger and violence. He wondered how he would have reacted had he been that bus driver. The noncriminal routinely learns from what other people do. The criminal has to be taught to do that. In this program, he becomes aware of how much he has to learn from the ordinary people whom he has scorned.

At times, especially early in change, the criminal balks at doing what ordinary people do. It does not offer him the excitement he wants.

> C and his wife spent the afternoon with a friend and the friend's children. The youngsters had fun playing on the swings and slides, while the adults sat around and talked. Everyone had a good time, C reported, except him. He hated it.

The unique number one experiences a combination of despair and anger at such outings. He then has to evaluate (probably for the hundredth time) what he wants out of life. Does he think that he is superior to these ordinary people? Is his life to be a continuing series of excitements or conquests? Will he learn to see people for what they are? Does he realize the consequences of his having placed himself apart from everyone and having regarded himself as superior? Will he settle for a life of hard work, modest achievements, and self-respect? One criminal, as he thought about all this, reflected:

> "I think of myself as superior to those around me. I say that I'm willing to live *like* ordinary people. Yet I don't realize that I *am* just ordinary people and am not doing as well with my life as those around me are doing with theirs."

A kind of humility, totally foreign to the criminal, develops as a consequence of such realization.

At no point is the criminal discouraged from pursuing excellence. Ordinariness and excellence are not mutually exclusive. An ordinary person should do an excellent job. What is eliminated is the criminal's idea that he can do such a marvelous job that no one can be his equal—that he is a unique number one.

REDUCTION OF CRIMINAL PERFECTIONISM

Perfectionism is an expression of the criminal's sense of uniqueness and of his search for power and control. At one time or another, many criminals contemplate the perfect crime. No single crime is truly perfect, in the sense that it is the ultimate big score. But the tendency toward perfectionism in crime pays off, as indicated by the criminal's infrequent arrests in the face of his having committed hundreds of crimes. Perfectionism also pays off in his conning schemes as he wins others' approval and trust.

Perfectionism in a responsible activity is far less common than it is in crime. When the criminal applies himself to a task, the product is often remarkably good. But the criminal is usually sloppy when given a responsible assignment, because he disdains that task. Perfectionism is *visible* mostly in the nonarrestable measures that he takes to impress others and to assure himself that he is indeed a unique number one. His clothes may be fashionable and immaculately clean and well pressed. His car may gleam, and his apartment may be neat and spotless. Criminals who do not care especially about cars, clothes, or living quarters show comparable perfectionism in other ways.

Not infrequently, the criminal begins a task, intending to do a perfect job. He usually does not finish it. This may be because something more exciting attracts his interest or because he does not think that he will achieve the standard of perfection that he has set for himself. The criminal makes a production out of a simple requirement. To do a reasonably competent job gives him no satisfaction. He wants to do the best job, better than anyone else could conceivably do. To him, not achieving perfect results is equivalent to failure. He quits, both because he falls short of his own standard and because he wants to avoid the possibility of criticism by others. Although he shuns others' criticisms, he is quick to fault what others do and will detect and exaggerate even a tiny flaw.

In this program, perfectionism is required with respect to functioning responsibly, but this does not mean that perfection is required for each individual task. The criminal has to learn to determine what is worth being perfectionistic about. One criminal was so indiscriminate that he dropped a piece of paper on the street and, having littered, had the idea, "I will never change." More often, the problem is that, for the first time in his life, the criminal has to solve problems responsibly on many fronts at once. He becomes extremely tense because he cannot achieve the desired perfect results in every endeavor.

> At work, C's baskets were filled with papers requiring processing. C would work as hard as he could to clear them. One or two people told him that he was pushing himself too hard. Still C was dissatisfied whenever there was work remaining at the end of the day. The work continued to pile up, no matter how hard he worked to reduce the stack. Then he began working overtime on evenings and weekends. He liked the idea of earning extra money for overtime, but still was very tense over the fact that he could not complete all the work.

This was not C's former type of perfectionism, in which he wanted to show that he was better than anyone else. Rather, he was really doubting that he was doing his best. A risk in reducing the criminal's tenseness in instances like C's above is that there will be too little concern about the quality of performance. Optimally, the criminal needs to establish a middle point—working hard and doing his best without being excessively tense over factors beyond his control.

Sometimes, the criminal is so tense about making mistakes that there is a loss of efficiency in performance. This may apply to work or to family life. Perfectionism of this sort has a neurotic quality, because the criminal is experiencing more tension than is warranted by the demands of the job.

> C, as he typed, payed attention to the rhythm of the typing. Everyone in the office knew that he was intent on producing a perfect copy. Repeatedly, he was told that this was not necessary for the kind of assignment he was doing. But C remained tense about making errors. For example, one day he typed a clean copy of an invoice except that a comma was crowded between two letters. C was berating himself because he had not left quite enough space.

C had to learn to moderate his perfectionism. The objective was to maintain a standard of performance but to avoid doing unnecessary retyping that then would reduce his overall productivity for the day.

The criminal has always expected things to go according to his plan. Now he learns that if things do not go perfectly, he is to take them in stride. Indeed, he is to be faulted if he expects perfection in others.

> C went shopping. He readily found all the items that he needed. It was a generally pleasant afternoon, until he picked up a pair of pants from the tailor and discovered that one of the alterations required redoing. Although this was the only thing that went wrong on the shopping trip, C reported that it had been "totally ruined."

C's perspective was all wrong. He was reacting to one small incident as though a major catastrophe had occurred. Had he kept Murphy's Law—If anything can go wrong, it will—in mind, he would not have expected perfection.

> C had worked hard during the week and had spent all of Saturday shopping and cleaning. He looked forward to a day of rest on Sunday. However, in the apartment above him were twelve Cub Scouts who were wrestling and running around, shattering the peacefulness of his Sunday. C became more and more agitated. Then his thinking was, "What do I work so hard for? What is it all worth?"

These panics occur in criminals when things do not go just right. C was responsible, but angry. He did not find other constructive activities to divert him, but spent the day in an irritable, disconsolate state. The potential danger was that C might say, To hell with it, if things did not go perfectly. Irresponsibility would then ensue. In him, such irresponsibility inevitably would result in crime. The correction offered was that, upon realizing the situation, C could have taken his wife and children somewhere and still have a pleasant day. He did not have to make the day a total waste for all concerned, simply because things did not go perfectly.

In the process of change, the criminal tends to apply to others the standards that are applied to him in the program. People must be perfect—impeccable in their integrity—or the criminal perceives them as seriously flawed. He begins to see criminality everywhere. If his child tells a lie, it is criminal. If his wife types a personal letter at her job, it is criminal. If a fellow worker takes a day of sick leave when he is not sick, it is criminal. The criminal learns balance and proportion in his evaluation of others, realizing that an instance of irresponsibility in an otherwise responsible person does not make him a criminal.

The criminal's former perfectionism was in the interest of being the unique number one in whatever he did. Excellence continues to be a goal in many situations, but the criminal now believes that there is merit in a merely competent job. He does not need to prove in every situation that he is better than anyone else.

SENTIMENTALITY IN PERSPECTIVE

Sentimentality is present in varying degrees in the thought and action of all people, responsible and irresponsible. In the criminal, it is a major component of his self-concept: he is a good person and not a criminal despite his long history of major crimes.

The criminal's sentimentality reveals itself, for example, as a professed love for a relative and in compassion for babies, the disabled, the elderly, and pets. Much more of this is present in his thinking than in his actions. Many regard themselves as religious and pray sporadically; some irregularly attend church. Many criminals have artistic aptitudes and interests that from time to time are expressed in music, art, and poetry.

The criminal's sentimentality is fragmented. It is quickly eliminated in a search for excitement, although it may reemerge during the course of a crime. Early in the change process, the criminal gives great weight to the good deeds that he has done and to his noble ideals. At first, we thought that criminals were stressing these features solely to impress us. But, in time, we learned that in their daily criminal life, they utilized sentimentality to build up their opinions of themselves as good people.

> "I not only think of myself as a good person, but I *am* a nice guy. When I'm doing things for others my personality is that of a nice guy doing good things, and the concern I feel for others is *real*."

One of the essential things for the criminal to recognize is that his sentimentality is not an enduring personality feature. It is readily cut off in favor of competing criminal excitements. Kindness toward others does not last.

> C said that he was sorry for a customer who received a small portion of spaghetti and paid a lot for it. Although he was capable of this genuine concern for a person, there was no concern whatsoever for the terrified recipients of his obscene phone calls. When offered a chance to obtain a free Christmas tree if he would cut his own, C stated emphatically that he would not consider destroying a living thing. Yet he had hundreds of thoughts of destroying people by killing them.

The criminal must face up to the fact that, although he considers himself merciful (for example, to the poor), he is merciless in the treatment of others who hinder him in his objectives. Furthermore, although he espouses altruistic ideals, he readily sacrifices others in his pursuit of criminal objectives. The criminal who is distressed by the cry of a child is not distressed by evidence of neglect of his own children. He, who charitably gives away proceeds from crime, does not sustain a charitable attitude toward his own family.

Responsible self-interest calls for the abandonment of the pattern of giving things away. In the past, the criminal has done this out of sentimentality. He has also given things away as part of a con when planning a score, to build up his opinion of himself as a good person, and to enhance his personal power (a criminal equivalent). The changing criminal in this program works hard and does not earn an especially high salary. In fact, he is learning to stretch a limited income to meet his basic needs and then to have some left over to begin the discipline of saving. It is necessary that he be far more discriminating than he used to be about the situations and the people to whom he gives money or gifts. We do not fault the quality of generosity, but clearly such donations must be compatible with the criminal's long-range responsible self-interest.

It is not only the transitoriness of such sentimental attitudes that the criminal must face, but also the fact that the goodness of his sentimentality is totally eclipsed by the harm that he has done. His reluctance to kill an insect pales in significance when contrasted with his shooting a human. His donation to a beggar is far outweighed by the financial hardships that he inflicts on his family. The value of his artistic talents, which can beautify the environment, is diminished by his damage to the property of others.

The criminal is required to consider how sentimentality has actually made crime easier for him. It has been a redeeming feature, part of his good opinion of himself. As one criminal said about his ideals and kind deeds, "You have to have these to live." The criminal's sentimentality makes it easier for him to live with himself. We shall say more about this in the next section as we describe the correctives for the criminal's building a good opinion of himself.

The sentimentality of many criminals is expressed in religious observance. In this program, they are confronted with how they invoked God at their convenience to help them get away with crimes, to help them remain undetected, and to help them out of the many jams into which they get themselves. Religious sentimentality has had no impact on their way of life. In this program, they learn that they cannot depend primarily on religious sentimentality to become moral. First, they must acquire the thinking processes necessary to lead a moral life. This program supports the criminal's religious beliefs and observance. However, religion is not an effective substitute for learning and implementing the principles of this program, all of which are compatible with religion.

C met a responsible girl who was very much wrapped up in her religious faith. C had long discussions with her about religion and began reading the Bible. He told us that he had accepted Christ and that to "live in Christ" was the way to prevent sin. C devised his own prayers and asked God for the strength to combat sin. We had no objection to his religious study and observance. We questioned, however, whether C was depending on faith alone, rather than faith and reason, to *achieve* responsibility. Did he expect to draw his strength from Christ or from himself? Would he rely on God to answer his prayers and default on making his own initiatives? In short, did he expect to become responsible through religion alone?

Our position was that religion could be an asset or liability in change. C's girlfriend believed that if she made a slip, through repentance she would gain forgiveness and return to Christ. For C, who did not have the responsible foundation that his girlfriend had, confession and contrition could well serve as a way to permit himself deviations from the program, because he could always expect forgiveness by God. In fact, when C did violate, he told us that he needed to "be stronger in Christ"; that was the solution. Our response was to ask him how one does this—does he wait for a force outside himself to produce change? Gradually, C began to understand that he could use acceptance of Christ and "God's will" as "copouts." (After all, if something were God's will, what could C do about it?) C recognized that religion had a great deal to offer, but that the program stood on its own merits. Failure to implement it would make a mockery out of religion.

Sentimentality, however expressed, must be an enduring personality feature. Otherwise, it is of no value.

Old Pattern

While shopping with his wife, C was frightened when she reported a sudden loss of vision in her left eye. He thought about the possibility of a brain tumor and was fearful of what the future might bring. This triggered a flood of sentiment toward her and thinking about how empty life would be for him if something happened to her.

In their marriage, C's sentimentality had been transient and of little value in promoting a mutually satisfying relationship. In fact, within the same week as his wife's loss of vision, C had denounced her as ignorant, dogmatic, and uncompromising. This wife, whom he would miss so badly if something happened to her, was the same wife whom he had earlier thought of assaulting and deserting.

The Corrective Applied

In ensuing months, C went out of his way to be thoughtful of his wife, who, it turned out, did not have a serious medical problem. Increasingly, C thought about how much she had suffered at his hands. Whenever there was a difference of opinion between them, C went to the extreme of yielding to her, rather than trying to control her. Whatever the issue— money, sex, a household chore, their schedule for the day—C tried to see it from her point of view. A genuine and lasting sentimental bond was developing between them as C showed his wife every consideration. In time, C neither yielded nor dominated completely. Decisions were arrived at by discussion and compromise.

Sentimentality no longer was being expressed in isolated instances and then cut off. There was a more enduring mutual concern.

In the changing criminal, sentimentality results in constructive, responsible living patterns. Sentimentality toward a mother acquires substance because it is shown in a sustained, concerned, helpful attitude toward her. Sentimentality toward a child extends beyond an affectionate pat or buying a present; it is expressed by developing a family life and shouldering the burdens of being a parent, as well as by partaking of the pleasures of family living. A notable phenomenon is that the unchanged criminal does not care about his illegitimate children; but, as he becomes responsible, he does as much for them as he can. Sentimentality is now a constructive, enduring part of the criminal's personality and plays a lasting role in his life. It is no longer a factor in promoting criminal action.

CHANGING THE CRIMINAL'S VIEW OF HIMSELF AS A GOOD PERSON

We have not seen a criminal who has truly regarded himself as evil or, for that matter, as a criminal. Rather, the criminal views himself not only as a good person, but as more moral and righteous than others. He is kind to babies, loves animals, and is helpful to elderly people and the disabled. He believes in God, prays sporadically, and occasionally attends religious services. He not only appreciates the aesthetic productions of others, but is artistically creative himself. He believes in the brotherhood of man and in the Golden Rule and espouses many noble ideals. As long as he retains his good opinion of himself, he assumes that he has a kind of license to commit arrestable acts, none of which he thinks he has to justify. If he is held accountable by others, he regards himself as being wronged, not as having done wrong. Supporting him in this view are myriad sociologic and psychologic excuses articulated by influential and intellectual people. These excuses allow him to appear as a decent person who, owing to circumstances beyond his control, ran afoul of the law. In fact, the criminal takes this position so regularly that it becomes a half belief. (For a discussion of the half belief, see chapter 4 of volume 1.) The fact that his belief in his innate goodness is reinforced by society becomes a formidable obstacle in change. Occasionally, the criminal experiences transient guilt, and he uses this to demonstrate that he is human after all.

It is precisely the criminal's sentimentality, kind acts, creativity, and aesthetic sensitivity that have encouraged others to regard him as having potential for good. We do not fault his specific deeds, but we do fault his appraisal of himself as a total person. When the criminal's inner good is emphasized, supervision is lax, confinement is brief (or avoided), and deterrence is weakened. This gives him added room for criminal maneuvering.

Instead of good qualities eventually blotting out the evil, we have found that the good qualities are necessary if the criminal is to continue to do evil. It is essential for the criminal to consider himself part of the human race. Strip him of his good qualities, and crime is impossible to sustain. As one criminal observed, "Doing good makes me feel better about robbing." It in no way diminished the amount of robbing that he did. The criminal must maintain a good opinion of himself. Otherwise, he considers suicide.

Early in the change process, the criminal's phenomenologic reports reveal a substantial attempt to build up the good in himself and to deemphasize his criminal thinking. He is trying to hold on to his view of himself as a decent person. Consequently, it is essential to clarify how building up the good has been indispensable in facilitating crime. The fact is that good deeds have been so important to the criminal that he has gone out of his way to do them, sometimes delaying and imperiling the successful execution of a crime. The sentimentality is then cut off and the crime committed. If the sentimentality returns, with a good opinion of himself prevailing, the criminal then gives away the proceeds or sells them at a price far below their retail cost. Throughout his life, among his sources of triumph in crime have been the crime itself, the conquest, and his demonstration of generosity afterwards.

The criminal's associations with responsible people have also been partially for the purpose of promoting a favorable self-image. Even as a youngster, he maintained regular contact with at least one responsible peer. In part, this reflected his admiration of the noncriminal, even though he did not want to live the boring life of a responsible person. Because he had responsible associates, others, especially his parents and teachers, thought better of him and this promoted his thinking well of himself. Out of sentimentality, some of these relationships continued into adult life. Yet, given a promising opportunity, the criminal exploited these very people.

Religion is another part of life from which the criminal has derived a sense of innate goodness. While considering himself a believer in God, he still persevered in his criminal way of life, calling on God's assistance to be bailed out of difficulty. It did not make any difference to the criminal what he was praying for or whether he lived by the religious precepts that he mouthed to others. What mattered in his viewing himself as good was that he believed in God.

In trying to achieve change, we contrast criminal acts and their effects with good acts and their effects. This amounts to composing a balance sheet of good and evil. In every case, the balance is overwhelmingly negative. The good intentions are worthless, because they are so easily cut off in the interest of crime. In the course of change, the criminal is required daily to make a moral inventory of conscience, so that he dwells heavily on the harm that he has inflicted. (This procedure is described in the next chapter.)

As the criminal surveys his life, he expresses much remorse that is genuine. By doing so, he demonstrates to others (as well as to himself) that he is not so bad, in that he does experience guilt. We show how transient that guilt is.

In gambling, C cheated and used a variety of deceptive devices to win money, sometimes from people who could ill afford to be gambling. On more than one occasion, he won money from a father with several children at home to feed. To assuage his own guilt, C loaned the father the money he had just won.

It was not clear whether C really experienced guilt or just said that he did. If the guilt was genuine, its existence supported his view of himself as a humane person. It did not deter gambling or further criminality. If guilt is to be of any value, it must do more than support the criminal's favorable image of himself. It must be functional in promoting a discontinuation of the pattern that he admits to being guilty of.

Many of the criminal's generous acts and noble sentiments have been known only to him and to the immediate recipients of his kindness. In most instances, the criminal has not desired public recognition, because he has not wanted to be considered soft or weak. In fact, he has actually been ashamed of some of the very qualities that contributed to his favorable view of himself.

The danger of the good deed is that it reinforces the criminal's belief that he is not a criminal. The position of this program is that the criminal's evil is not removed by good works. Rather it is the evil itself that must be attacked at its roots. Doing extra chores at home, helping the teacher at school, and staying overtime at work may all be genuine expressions of thoughtfulness and concern. At the same time, such acts meticulously and diligently carried out help place the criminal above suspicion and thereby facilitate his remaining undetected in his criminality. It is difficult to disentangle sentimentality for its own sake from that which is either part of a conning operation or an attempt to play both sides of the street, that is, to appear respectable while being in crime.

As he begins to implement the program, the criminal thinks well of himself for doing the expected. That is, he is a good person in that he shows up for an appointment on time, pays a bill, or helps his wife. In the past, he has expected medals when he has done what another person asked him to do. Now he learns not to expect any credit for performing the routine duties that responsible people carry out automatically without self-commendation or reward by others.

Building up a good opinion of himself is so automatic that the criminal has to be alert to the possibility that, unless he takes preemptive measures, he may turn a kindness into a self-serving act.

C was owed money by a fellow worker. The latter came to C to pay the debt. However, C said that he did not have to pay him right then. In his daily report, C stated that, in his thinking, he was regarding himself as extremely generous.

There were two issues here. One was whether C acted wisely. Postponing payment of the debt was against C's responsible self-interest, because he was on a limited budget. The other issue was whether this transaction would turn into an instance of C's ingratiating himself with another person and obligating that person in the process. The criminal becomes increasingly aware that the features of his personality that impress some people are the very ones that are instrumental in exploiting others.

We do not take the view that the criminal should *forever* discontinue kind and charitable acts. But he should *temporarily*—until his criminal patterns have been altered. As change occurs, the criminal is increasingly self-critical and often wonders about the genuineness of the nice things that he does for people: did he really mean what he said or was it just another occasion for him to praise himself and set another person up for later use?

By now, it is clear to the reader that ours is not a program for raising the self-esteem of the unchanged criminal. We do just the opposite, as we show the criminal how much harm he has done to others and how wasteful his life has been. As the criminal implements this program, he does see tangible results. The rewards of responsible living are both material and spiritual. Valued most is the sense of cleanliness. It is on the basis of this that the criminal begins to have a legitimate opinion of himself as a good person.

LEARNING TO THINK
CONCEPTUALLY

It did not surprise us to find that criminals who were elementary school dropouts thought mainly in concrete terms. But it did surprise us to learn that criminals who are college graduates and professional people are as concrete in important areas of life as are elementary school dropouts. We are not referring to the concreteness found in young children or in some psychotics. Criminals can conceptualize classes of objects (furniture, clothes, categories of food) and can conceptualize in some academic fields of interest to them. What they lack are fundamental concepts of family, education, time, job, money, and religion. These matters are discussed only in concrete terms, regardless of the criminal's education. Conceptualization either has never developed or, in a few cases, developed early and atrophied through disuse. Crime itself involves very little conceptualization, because each criminal act is a concrete event and requires separate consideration. Conceptualization of the nature of a family, a career, and social institutions, when developed, help achieve responsibility. One might think that, if a criminal prayed sporadically or went to church, he would have some concept of what religion is all about. Instead, we found that the criminal might remember details from his catechism, a few proverbs, or Bible stories, but that was all. Conceptualization of religion in terms of personal ethics is nonexistent, because it is antithetical to crime.

In his early reporting, the criminal's focus is limited to a series of concrete events. Obviously, the criminal will not learn from experience if he perceives only individual events and does not generalize or conceptualize from them. As each concrete event is presented, it is the task of the agent of change to relate it to identical or similar experiences and apply it to situations that are far removed from the one presented. Each concrete event can be generalized and conceptualized to apply to a variety of people, events, institutions, and, indeed, to the nature of existence itself. For illustrative purposes, we shall present not an arrestable crime or a complex act, but only a simple pattern, to show how much can be done by considering just a small detail.

The Concrete Incident

After serving a prison term, C, a highly educated man, was reporting daily in the program. Working as a waiter, C had decided that, instead of paying busboys the customary twenty percent of his tips, he would give them twenty-five percent of his tips; not infrequently, he added a dollar extra. Consequently, the busboys who worked with C sometimes earned more than the other waiters.

This situation was utilized to bring out C's thinking with respect to money.

Old Pattern

C had embezzled and had forged and issued fraudulent checks for thousands of dollars in a variety of places before he was apprehended, convicted, and sentenced. In his life, money came and went readily, criminally obtained and just as criminally given away. One of C's great excitements was to give money away, usually in an ostentatious manner. This built up his sense of power and made him out to be a very kind and generous person. It also enhanced his control, in that the recipient was set up for C's later exploitation.

We focused attention on how C must gain experience in managing money responsibly. If he did not acquire a concept of money, other aspects of the change process would be retarded.

The Corrective Applied

It was necessary to have C turn in his earnings to the A.C. who would hold them. C was taught how to shop, pay bills, and budget. It was necessary for him to deny himself some purchases because of his tight budget and to work extra hours to earn more to make ends meet.

It took C a long time to develop a concept of money. Soon after the issue of busboy payment arose, C gave away several hundred dollars in one night. Repeated attention to financial transactions is necessary before the criminal becomes thrifty and begins to value money. In similar fashion, the lack of a concept of a family may be examined when a criminal fails to write a particular letter, the lack of a concept of work when a criminal is repeatedly tardy, and the lack of a concept of interdependence when there is an absence of consideration for a neighbor.

Most criminals are so concrete that they can see all the trees (the concrete details), but not the forest (the major themes and concepts). On the other hand, some see only a forest (in the form of a few vague themes, but still no concepts), but do not know the trees that are in it (the relevant details). At the beginning, the problem is most often the former: the criminal completely misses the big picture, because he is attending to only a few details. Later, he does not realize it when he encounters events comparable to an earlier situation, but in a different context. He persists in focusing rigidly on the concrete details, ignoring the context, and makes a faulty decision.

Working three days a week at one establishment did not provide C with sufficient income. Therefore, he took an additional part-time job. After several months, C was called by both employers. On one particular day each anticipated being so busy that C was asked to work a total of fourteen hours that day. C had planned to have the day off to practice typing in preparation for a new job. He worked the fourteen hours, but was disgruntled. He did not object to the lack of sleep or the fatigue from fourteen hours of work, but he was disappointed about not having the necessary time to prepare for the new job. C had stated months previously that, because the income was needed, he gave working top priority. What he did not take into account now was that the circumstances had changed. When he made the decision, he had no plans for a job change. He lost rest, relaxation, and his wife's company if he worked fourteen hours. Now he was losing the time that he must have if he were to improve his skills that were vital for a new job. The solution was for C to talk with both employers and establish a maximum number of hours that he would work.

C remarked that his wife could adapt to changing circumstances, but that he seemed stuck on the details. The question was whether he would carry over the lesson to new situations. Would he consider the context of events, as well as their details?

Conceptual thinking is developed as the criminal acquires experience in living responsibly. He did not have a concept of family life, because he chose not to have a family life. He did not have a concept of money, because he never valued it. He did not have a concept of morality, because his way of life was opposed to it. After the criminal has spent a year with us, subjecting his thinking to daily criticism and implementing the corrective concepts, this concrete thinker learns to think conceptually. This is as true of the criminal eighth-grade dropout as of the criminal college graduate.

ELIMINATION OF FRAGMENTATION

We have listened to tapes of criminals who have been declared schizophrenic, primarily on the basis of observations of their disconnected thinking. We have reviewed reports and attended clinical conferences in which the criminal's shifts in thinking have been deemed as pathognomonic of mental illness. We have heard it said that the criminal's shifts of mind indicate a deficit of ego strength, referring to his lack of persistence in many areas of life. What is not commonly considered is that the criminal has great persistence in criminal enterprises and, from that point of view, could be considered to have great ego strength.* The criminal's shifts in thinking can be better understood if his behavior toward an examiner were evaluated as tactical maneuvers designed to achieve an objective (see chapter 8 of volume 1). In accountability-thinking, contradictions and shifts in thought are inevitably present. These shifts may occur very suddenly, even from moment to moment, as pressures on the criminal mount. The diagnosis of mental illness is often influenced by the criminal's abrupt silences, lying, calculated vagueness, and general unresponsiveness. This is called "blocking" and is considered pathologic. In addition, when the criminal talks matter-of-factly about something that the examiner thinks should be emotionally laden, the criminal is considered to be suffering blunting, or flatness of affect, another indicator of mental illness.

With accountability not at issue and the criminal not attempting to avoid jeopardy, we have studied his thinking (retrospectively) over a twenty-four-hour period. It has become clear that his fragmentation is not a discontinuity in thought. The criminal is thoroughly aware of each thought, and his

---

*Redl and Wineman (1951, p. 141) spoke of the delinquent's "hypertrophically" developed ego functions that are "applied in the service of the wrong goal." This at least qualifies, if it does not oppose, the "weak ego" concept.

thoughts follow what is to him a logical progression. He has accepted this kind of thinking as normal for him and others. Shifts from sentimentality to violence and vice versa are common.

> C spent an hour in the group meeting, weeping in contrition over the many injuries that he had inflicted on others. Still tearful, he asked for a few moments to himself to regain his composure. As he left the room, another criminal coming in for a meeting asked him what was wrong. There followed, in response, a stream of profanity from C and a threat to assault the other man. This was followed by more tearfulness and then, within twenty-four hours, an actual assault.

*   *   *

> C wrote the following testimonial to Dr. Yochelson, who was convalescing from an illness:
> "How can I say what I really believe and feel quite deeply. You are a man, a great man, and one that isn't put on mother earth very often. . . . Seeing you is an honor; it is like going to a good college at the same time. . . . I so badly want to sign this 'your prize case,' but I can't, and I am aware of how far I am from it at this time."
> The desire to be a "prize case" did not last: C soon returned to crime.

This fragmentation appears from meeting to meeting and within meetings. Early in the change process, we never know what response we shall receive on any given day. This is, of course, also true of the people with whom the criminal lives. Situations of the following type are common:

Old Pattern

> C controlled his wife, ignoring her but using her when it was convenient. At times, there was genuine and sentimental devotion in which C considered himself in love with her. In such a state of mind, he was extremely considerate. With criminal thinking along sexual lines, C complained that he found her dogmatic, abrasive, and snappish. It was not a change in her behavior that determined this attitude; his wife was not a particularly changeable woman. Rather, she became unsatisfactory to him as soon as he preferred criminal excitement. It was then that C decided to ignore his wife, rather than subject himself to what he considered at that time unfavorable aspects of her personality. In such a frame of mind, C thought that it was better to find someone new than to endure her. Within a week, C had gone from being extremely "in love" with his wife to considering a separation.

Such rapid changes serve the criminal's purpose very well. He exaggerates the disagreeable and shifts to something that provides him with greater excitement. The choice of criminal excitement prevails at the particular moment, and other considerations are disposed of instantly, through cutoff. Obviously, C's thinking and action were fragmented, his desire for criminal action at the time being more exciting than day-to-day life with his wife.

The Corrective Applied

One or two incidents in which C was put down had distorted his view of his wife. It was typical for him to dismiss people if they did not act in accord with his wishes. C obviously had not gained a perspective of the relationship. His wife had for years elected to endure his neglect and abuse. What role had he played in her becoming abrasive and snappish? Furthermore, was he saying that these qualities obliterated the many assets that she had as a companion, friend, and wife? Was it not incumbent on him to change, to be more critical of himself and not so thin-skinned with respect to each little thing his wife said? As the meeting ended, C stated that he really did not want to leave his wife. In fact, he praised her charm, liveliness, helpfulness, and warmth and said that he was sure that the two of them would be together forever.

Within the same hour, the criminal had totally shifted his view of his wife, first dismissing her and then admiring her many fine qualities. With his concrete thinking and tubular vision, he had no perspective. It is essential for the criminal to think beyond his momentary thoughts and feelings. C began to develop a concept of what a wife should be: someone more than a servant ministering to his changing wants. Such perspective is an antidote to fragmentation.

Perspective frequently is restored by reminding the criminal of his basic options: crime, suicide, or change. It is evident that in the past the criminal has strayed from his avowed intentions of becoming responsible in that he has reacted to life more out of emotion than out of reason. Fragmentation results in part from responding to feeling and in part from the lack of an enduring core of moral values on which to base decisions. It is as though there were no course by which to steer a ship and as though the ship were rudderless and buffeted by unpredictable elements, and indeed this is what the criminal would have one think. However, he is the one who has elected to veer from the course. He has control over his feelings, but exercises it only when it benefits his criminal objectives. As we said in the preceding chapter, feelings are subjected to rational appraisal in this program. They are not unpredictable forces that set the criminal adrift from the moorings of responsibility.

The following illustration shows that the criminal is not a victim of his feelings:

> On waking up from an afternoon nap, C reported, there was spontaneous and immediate thinking about suicide. He mused that he had nothing in life and that everything was futile. He thought about coming to group meetings every morning, returning home briefly, going to work in the evening, and then starting all over again. He was approaching a zero state—nothingness now and no hope in the future. He began to cry. C then got hold of himself and stiffened his resolve. He decided that he would overcome this state of mind. He left home and, as he neared work, he made a dramatic shift in attitude. He viewed himself as having been loaded with self-pity and as responding solely on the basis of feelings. He changed from deep pessimism to a positive, zestful attitude. He did a full evening's work and stayed late at the job. He returned home, watched television, slept soundly, and came to the group meeting in a positive frame of mind.

C divested himself of a state of mind that was a clear and immediate danger. In the past, he would have sought relief in irresponsibility. In this case, he disposed of suicide and self-pity and generated a constructive attitude. The discussion in the group extended beyond this one situation. C was asked what he wanted and expected from life for the next twenty-five years or more. What did having nothing mean? What did he consider truly worth while? In part, C was complaining about a lack of self-regard. Yet he had not accomplished enough responsibly to achieve the self-respect that most responsible people have. Indeed, his choice to change from self-pity to constructive endeavor was a brick in the structure of self-respect that he could build over time as he implemented the program. In this discussion, perspective was an antidote to fragmentation.

Another aspect of the criminal's fragmentation is his basing important decisions on immediate reactions to people and events, rather than taking a long-range view.

Old Pattern

> With his small business going well at the moment, C was enthusiastic about a career in business. After a series of problems, C wanted to get rid of the business right away. He then thought that he would have nothing further to do with business, but become a lawyer instead. However, it was

the middle of the school year, and he could do nothing immediately about entering law school. After a few weeks, sales picked up. C once again became enthusiastic and talked about becoming an owner of a chain of stores.

C changed his mind repeatedly on the basis of his short-term observations.

The Corrective Applied

Throughout his life, C had acted on the basis not of responsible self-interest, but of expediency in his criminal objectives. Before, he thought of the future mainly with respect to committing a crime. However, he was now seeing that responsibility required long-range planning and information gathering. In particular, a career decision entailed evaluation of options and sound reasoning, C realized that it was imprudent to jump to a conclusion about a lifetime career solely on the basis of rapid fluctuations in sales at the store. There were discussions with C about more substantial considerations in planning for a career. Furthermore, larger issues were brought up. C was required to examine the role of a career in his life as balanced against family life, social obligation and outside interests.

Learning from reviews of the past and looking to the future provide perspective. Perspective helps to reduce fragmentation because the criminal begins to see and appreciate the fruits of his labor—a closer family life, the esteem of his colleagues at work, the trust of responsible people. Finally, responsibility becomes more than just a word; there have been benefits personally experienced. The criminal does not consider a fleeting excitement to be worth the price of impairing the sense of cleanliness that is emerging. He is increasingly inclined to deter criminal thinking that threatens, if savored, to destroy all that he is working for. As we shall point out in the next chapter, there comes a time when deterrence becomes automatic, when criminal thoughts are extremely few and the commitment to responsibility is unshakable.

ALTERING THE DIRECTION
OF SUGGESTIBILITY

Society has regarded the criminal as hard-nosed, negativistic, and closed to suggestion. This coincides with each criminal's view of himself as nobody's sucker. But other criminals know that a criminal is in fact very suggestible.

Our criminals have admitted that in crime they were excessively suggestible, sometimes to the point of gullibility. However, they were easily influenced only if it was along lines to which they were already predisposed.

Every criminal has been resistant to suggestions that he function responsibly. These have been scorned, because they did not offer him opportunities for the excitement that he wanted. Clearly, these patterns of suggestibility and contrasuggestibility must be reversed. Our objective, therefore, is two-fold: to achieve contrasuggestibility to crime to the point of effective deterrence, and to achieve receptivity to suggestion in responsible living.

Our process of change is both an exercise in deterrence of criminal thinking and action and an education in responsible thinking and action. It has been our experience that, immediately upon the criminal's admission to the program, there is at least a temporary cessation of criminal action, but still, of course, much criminal thinking—the only kind of thinking in which he is practiced. The first step is for the criminal to avoid situations that automatically prompt criminal thinking. These include exposure to movies, television programs, periodicals, and books that contain accounts of crimes. As one criminal commented, "When I read about trouble, I think trouble." Thus, exposure to crime stories, even in the newspapers, is discouraged. Where suggestive material cannot be avoided, the criminal is directed not to savor such material or expand on it in his thinking. Of course, the criminal does not immediately begin to avoid everything having to do with crime. But, in time, he sees the wisdom of such avoidance as a temporary measure to preempt criminal thinking. Later in the change process, as responsible patterns of thinking and action are being habituated, it is not necessary for the criminal to avoid everything that could be suggestive of criminality. Indeed, in watching movies and television programs, the changing criminal is interested primarily in character profiles, the techniques of plot development, and technical aspects. Toward criminal action itself, he assumes an anticrime position. He does this spontaneously; we do not require it.

From experience, the criminal knows that he is suggestible to other criminals who offer him propositions and want him to join them. If he is confined, it is not possible to stay away from other criminals because he is surrounded by them. But he is required to remain distant and not to engage in criminal talk. He quietly assumes an anticrime position without being a missionary about it. His general demeanor involves being pleasant to other criminals but uninvolved with them. Both in and out of confinement, merely talking about crime is exciting. To refuse to join other criminals in conversation or action is to burn a bridge to the only life the criminal has known. This program requires that all these old ties be severed.

There is considerable resistance in the criminal to giving up ties with other criminals, especially those whom he has known for a long time. As one criminal put it, "I loathe crime, but I loathe to close the door on it. When I close it, I regret it." In reporting to the group, the criminal builds up other criminals as having good qualities and being a help to him. Because he fails to consider them criminals, he invariably creates more difficulties for himself.

Old Pattern

A great deal of C's money had been stolen by his employees, some of whom were old friends of his. C had known one of them for more than a decade. Despite repeated evidence of their irresponsibility, C defended keeping them on his staff, maintaining that help was hard to find, that he could do worse, that they were not bad people, and so on. C had chosen to live with another old friend who was a criminal. C was left with large long-distance phone bills and substantial debts incurred by his roommate.

The Corrective Applied

The facts were finally convincing even to C. His defense of his old friends was weakened by the substantial losses and inconveniences that he had suffered. C was required to examine carefully the relationships that he had had with criminals in which each exploited the other. There followed a discussion of the implications of C's resistance to viewing them as criminals. It was suggested that C did not regard himself as a criminal, inasmuch as he refused to recognize as criminal the features that were common to him and his friends. C's continuing association with criminals indicated that he was still suggestible to excitement along irresponsible lines.

The requirement for severing ties with other criminals is so absolute that the criminal eventually realizes that even saying casually to an unchanged criminal, "See ya' later," an innocuous enough expression, constitutes invitation for a resumption of the contact and indicates to the other party that he is still open to suggestion along criminal lines.

Resistance is equally great when it comes to giving up contact with irresponsible women. The criminal has elaborate justifications and, in some cases, half beliefs with respect to their decency. A review of his past is rarely sufficient to discourage him from maintaining old ties or establishing new ones with irresponsible women. Repeated incidents, in the course of change, are necessary to convince him that the costs of such affiliations are too high and that they are incompatible with becoming responsible. Among the things that have occurred upon the criminal's rejoining old associates, are talking about crime, drinking, prowling for women, and even participating in crime in a minor role—being the driver of a car for example.

We are referring primarily to a pattern of avoidance that keeps the criminal from being exposed to situations in which he might be suggestible. Staying out of neighborhoods where criminals are known to congregate, not contacting criminal associates, and staying away from anything that is likely to stir up criminal excitement are insufficient measures in themselves for dealing with suggestibility. Important as this pattern is, avoidance only reduces some types of external stimulation to which the criminal is suggestible. It does not eliminate the inner state of mind which makes a criminal suggestible. Even criminals who have gone to extreme measures to avoid experiences that could stimulate criminal thinking still encounter situations that trigger it. This has to be the case, because the criminal can view virtually any situation as an opportunity for crime. In chapter 9, we shall describe five processes of deterrence that criminals learn to use both preemptively and when confronted immediately by events that could stir up criminal thinking. Ultimately, of course, the criminal reaches a point at which there is nothing but disdain for himself as a criminal and indifference toward others who are criminal. Then he is not dependent on avoidance or on an elaborate set of deterrents.

In his days of active crime, whenever it suited his purpose, the criminal did some things that ostensibly were responsible, but he had little interest in them. He was extremely suggestible to what others had to say. He accepted suggestions and acted on them, because he did not care enough to evaluate them or to seek facts on his own. By perfunctorily doing what someone suggested, he avoided default. For example, if an officemate advised him to use one procedure rather than another, he did it. There would be no checking to determine whether it was authorized or more efficient; there would be only uncritical acceptance of the other person's word.

The criminal's suggestibility is repeatedly demonstrated in selecting a job, searching for a companion, resuming an old friendship, or making a new friend. In the group meetings, each of these processes is subjected to careful reasoning in which prejudgments are questioned and fact-finding is stressed. Judgment in financial matters is often at issue.

Old Pattern

C had always had the idea of making a fortune in the stock market. He had never studied the market and knew very little about securities. One day, C read in the newspapers about the development of a natural resource in a particular region. He immediately concluded that a small airline going to that area would be a sure money-maker. He was so suggestible that he was prepared to call a broker and place an order for stock in the airline.

This type of situation is treated in the following manner: The criminal's experiences in similar situations in the past are reviewed, with emphasis on how *suggestibility has overwhelmed judgment*. The present situation is evaluated with respect to errors of thinking in the decision-making process. Finally, there is consideration of what might happen if the criminal went ahead and acted as he had planned, including thinking about the worst possible consequences.

The Corrective Applied

There was a review of many decisions that C had made because he wanted a big score. Pretensions and superoptimism had been his guides, rather than reasoning based on facts. In the stock situation, C had available only five hundred dollars, most of which he would need once he was released from the hospital. He did not have sufficient resources to risk anything in the market. If C had had the requisite funds, the corrective would have been further fact-finding. C had no facts about the airline's financial position or about whether it was expected to play a significant role in the development of the region. Finally, he knew nothing about the attractiveness of this stock, compared with others. C thought about his financial needs on leaving the hospital: a deposit on an apartment and the first month's rent, basic supplies and furnishings for the apartment, living expenses while he was going to school, and money for busfare both to attend this program and to go to school. C concluded that, although he would have sufficient money for these items (through social security and some savings), his reserves would be exhausted if he bought stock. Furthermore, if he had no savings at all and if his social security check came late, he would have to borrow money. Therefore, he decided that any stock venture at this time was unwise. Although he did not act, the ideas about big deals occurred for many months thereafter.

Through evaluations of this type, suggestibility gives way to a balanced, rational consideration of options.

If the criminal resists suggestions of a responsible nature or quickly assents to them before he has given them thought, this indicates a closed channel. As the channel is closing, the A.C. receives no feedback about suggestions offered by him or others in the group. Eventually, there is irresponsible activity, which comes to light sooner or later. The factors contributing to irresponsibility are many, but they inevitably go back to the competition between excitement and the dullness of responsible living. With the channel closed, the criminal is not receptive to suggestion about responsible living, and change does not progress. When this occurs, the basic options (crime, suicide, change) are repeated, and the stipulation that he be returned to the probation or parole officer for noncooperation is again a subject for discussion.

As the criminal changes, he increasingly asks the group for suggestions as to how to handle particular situations. He so distrusts his own thinking that he actively seeks out the opinions and advice of others. He also does more and more of this outside the group. This is the new form that suggestibility takes. In an open channel with other people, he not only hears but actively solicits others' points of view, knowing that he is not bound by them. At the same time, he knows what his responsible objectives are and thoughtfully examines the merits of others' suggestions, rather than accepts them uncritically. He is not suggestible to irresponsibility, because he knows where it has led him in the past, and he is beginning to value what he has achieved too much to return to that path.

CHANGING SEXUAL PATTERNS

The criminal is more interested in conquering people for sexual use than he is in the sensuality of the sexual experience itself. Since childhood, he has regarded sexual experiences as conquests and has often achieved these through conning and coercion. His interest has truly been in sex objects for his use, not in people as sexual partners. The exception to this has been when the criminal has selected a particular female who was attractive to him, but not available. He has treated such a person with consideration, but only until he has achieved control of her, if that was feasible. The criminal has viewed himself as irresistible and to confirm this view, has used sex as a vehicle for building himself up as a sexual giant. He has indiscriminately sought young and old, married and unmarried, blacks and whites, and in most cases, males and females. His greatest excitement has been in the *pursuit* of sex, not in the sexual act itself. In fact, he has perceived his own sexual performance as insufficient. The thinking patterns behind his sexual conquests have been the same as those behind a bank robbery or any other criminal act. The sexual arena has been only one of many that he has used for the proof of power and the assertion of control.

We have not found one criminal whose sexual criminality has been based on sexual deprivation. Having a normal sexual outlet has been no answer to eliminating criminal sexual patterns. In our work with rapists, we have found that they rape even after sex with a consenting partner. Sexual irresponsibility is part of a larger pattern of irresponsibility everywhere and is never eliminated through a legitimate sexual outlet.*

Sexuality is always dealt with in the context of the criminal patterns of deception, intimidation, exploitation, and imposing demands on the sexual partner. It is these factors that are carefully evaluated, and it is the emphasis on these that produces changes in sexual patterns. Rape is one example.

C had been arrested for rape, but he insisted to us that he had not really tried to rape anyone. He defined rape as an activity in which more than one man forces a woman to have sex. Once he accepted the idea that rape was also an individual act, he said that he had raped 4 times. But again his definition was restricted to situations in which a woman put up a fight. When demanding sex, he preferred that she struggle, because this provided him with the opportunity for acquisition by force. The final stage of the act was for him to believe that he was irresistible and that she enjoyed it. We broadened the term to include any situation in which a woman was intimidated by gesture, motion, attitude, or display of a weapon so that she feared for her life and therefore complied with his demand for sex. When we applied this definition of rape, C acknowledged, "This happens all the time." On this basis, he estimated that he had committed at least 250 rapes.

Rape is not singled out for special attention. Rather, it is one of many exploitative or injurious sexual patterns that the criminal has shown throughout life. By emphasizing the show of power and the injuries (both mental and physical) inflicted on the victim, and by presenting the other correctives, we have been able to achieve in the criminal the requisite self-disgust and the implementation of new sexual patterns.

We must emphasize that the particular sexual preference, homosexual or heterosexual, is not important, so long as sexuality occurs responsibly, without exploitation, and without taking away the dignity and respect that a sexual partner should be accorded. In all criminals, unmarried or married, an important idea that is dealt with early is that proof of power is not established

---

*Freyhan (1955, p. 255) observed that sexual irresponsibility is not an isolated phenomenon in the personality. "If an individual behaves in a generally irresponsible manner, showing no regard for the feelings of others, this will be apparent in all of his activities including sexual conduct, which should not be evaluated as an isolated field of activity. The sexual behavior must be judged against the background of characterological trends instead of being classified on the basis of activity."

by having a variety of sexual partners. In no case have we found a criminal who has been loyal to one partner in thought and action. To the criminal, not having a sexual partner available is a putdown. But it goes further than that. To the "irresistible me," being without several available partners is also a putdown. The criminal believes that all women want him sexually and that it is his prerogative to give them their chance. One married criminal remarked that "hitting on a woman is expected of a man"—a reference not to assault, but to sex. What he meant was that he was not a man unless he made a pitch to every woman. Furthermore, he was not a man unless he had more than one woman.

Criminal sexual patterns are so injurious to others that we require unmarried criminals to be celibate in the early phase of their participation in the program. This is part of their shutting the door to crime. It is necessary, because, as we have said repeatedly, sexuality in the criminal is an expression of broad criminal patterns.

The twenty-four-hour report contains a complete account of all sexual thinking and action, and this account is subject to the same procedure of evaluation and correction as any other material. Dozens, sometimes hundreds, of times a day, the criminal eyes the bodies of females, centering his attention on buttocks, thighs, or breasts. He savors what he sees, encourages fantasy, and builds himself up by thinking about acquiring them. An examination of his thoughts reveals voyeurism, exhibitionism, conning, the reduction of females to slaves, violence, and, in many cases, child molestation (especially of twelve- and thirteen-year-olds). Indeed, in our early work, it was truly alarming to see that all this material was present in thinking. It became clear that, as with other crimes, a sexual crime was not a product of impulse, but an outcome of long-standing thinking patterns. Although it is true that one could not in every case have predicted the time, place, and victim of a particular sexual crime, it was always possible to have predicted that such a crime would occur, given the criminal's stream of thoughts.

The material in the twenty-four-hour reports is evaluated in terms of all the features of the criminal personality that bear on sexual patterns. We consider the role of such thinking errors as power, control, ownership, and superoptimism to demonstrate the relative unimportance of sensuality and the greater impact of conquest. It is this material that leads directly to a perspective of a lifetime of injury to others and of jeopardy to oneself. It is this evaluation that brings out the excitement of thinking and talking about sex, which, in some criminals, is equivalent to action.

The thinking during sex itself is a subject of examination. The excitement during a sexual act often has no reference to the partner. The criminal may be thinking of someone else. Of course, this is also true of some noncriminals, who during intercourse fantasize partners other than their own. Fantasying sex with the woman next door may be irresponsible, but it is not arrestable, and it does not result in injury to anyone. The criminal, however, while having intercourse fantasizes rape, child molestation, or some other act that is injurious and arrestable. It is the fantasy of a criminal activity that gives him the voltage he otherwise lacks in a sexual act.

In the process of change, sexuality is often the last outpost of criminal patterns. When the criminal is deprived of excitement in crime, he still wants to prove that he is someone. Acquiring a woman is one way to do it. He justifies new sexual adventures by insisting that he is a man and that he needs an outlet. From years of experience, we know that irresponsibility does not stay confined to sex. The choice for the criminal is whether he will risk his future for a pair of breasts or buttocks.

> C and his wife took a harbor cruise. C saw a couple of teen-age girls wearing jeans and skimpy halter tops. For an hour, he gazed at them and encouraged fantasies about them. Then he stopped and began to consider what he was doing. He realized that no other person on the boat was staring at these girls (at least not in an obvious manner). C thought about how indulgence in sexual fantasy would mean trouble now, as it had in the past. Before, such thinking had been the precursor to boredom, anger, deceptions, drugs, injury to his wife, and eventually other crimes. C considered all that was at stake and the price that he would have to pay if he continued savoring bodies in this manner. This application of logic resulted in a conclusion: the staring and indulging in fantasy were not worth it.

C was strongly criticized in the group meeting for permitting the thinking to continue for an hour. He could have preempted the thinking by realizing that there would be scantily clad women on the boat and deciding in advance to direct his attention elsewhere.

The review of past patterns is critical in the criminal's developing self-disgust. He has to be as convinced of the injury emanating from his sexual patterns as he has been of the injury resulting from his assaults. He is required to deter sexual thought, talk, and action just as he deters other criminal thought, talk, and action (see chapter 9 for a discussion of deterrents).

> In a restaurant, C was waiting on two girls. One had large breasts and looked "luscious." His heart thumped, and he experienced an erection. As he put it, "I was totally taken by the girl." However, C also experienced concurrent fear and realized that he had to meet this situation responsibly. Consequently, he took three steps:

1. He directed his attention to his work and became caught up in serving customers—going to the bar for a drink, to the machine to stamp the bill, to the kitchen for salads, and so on. It did not work. The erection was still there.
2. He tried to think about material that he was studying in school. This did not help his immediate situation at the restaurant.
3. He faced himself with the fact that he had a choice. He thought of the injuries that he had caused other women in the past and how he had put himself in jeopardy and ultimately ended up in the penitentiary. There was a rapid, kaleidoscopic review of his past. The erection subsided and did not return. From then on, he gave efficient service to the girls, and there was no more sexual thinking.

The next step was for C to program himself ahead of time, so that such struggles would not occur. Clearly, there would be other attractive female customers. The issue was how C would direct his thinking.

We are confronted with the criminal's emphasis on the necessity of relieving his erections. Characteristically, the unchanged criminal spots a desirable female. Instantly, he regards her as his. This generates exciting thinking, which is accompanied by an erection. He wants an erection. If he does not have one, he is disappointed; it reflects on his manhood as he views it. To gain an erection, he gazes at sexual areas and savors sexual thinking. When held accountable for an irresponsible sexual act, the criminal views himself as a victim of his lust and of the attendant erection. He insists that a sexual act is required to obtain relief. In the process of change, the criminal can preempt erections. He redirects his thinking along lines of responsibility, and the erection does not occur. In time, redirection and deterrence become automatic.

C was standing in line to deposit money in his bank account. He saw a girl whom he regarded as "made to order" for him. When he did not experience an erection, he missed it. Yet he was pleased that he did not have it. The absence of an erection demonstrated to him that it was possible to eliminate that which he had regarded as "natural," "manly," and automatic.

It is remarkable that within a couple of days a criminal can rid himself of troublesome erections if he sets his mind to it.

In the change process, the criminal in time finds a female companion. This program requires that he bar sexual activity from the relationship at the beginning; otherwise, early sex will overshadow everything else.

C started seeing a woman whom he had known earlier. He had always admired her and been fond of her. She was totally responsible, attractive, and bright. Discussing her in advance in the group meeting, C decided to see her once a week for companionship. There was a decision on his part not to think about sex with her, but simply to enjoy her company. This would relieve his loneliness. The relationship grew closer over a period of months. C had decided to refrain from sexuality. It was the first experience of friendship with a woman without conquest as the objective.

Because sex was not part of the early relationship, C learned and implemented many interpersonal skills that had been foreign to him. He shared his thoughts, considered another's point of view, developed concern for another person, and, for the first time, showed tenderness toward someone.

Tenderness is a new skill to be acquired. It is not learned if the criminal plunges quickly into sex before getting to know his partner. In fact, immediate sex stands in the way of the criminal's evaluating whether his partner is responsible or personally compatible with him. At first, the criminal finds the attempt to be tender contrived.

C said, "You want me to be hypocritical and be tender toward my wife when I don't feel that way." We replied, "Can't you learn to do for a human being what you already do for your cat?" C was making himself the victim of his feelings. He had said that he wanted a closer relationship with his wife, but that she was "standoffish." He agreed to put his arm around his wife, compliment her occasionally, and show affection in other ways. In time, she responded with greater warmth, and C remarked to us that his relationship with his wife was now only "twenty percent sex."

In every case, we have found that, when the conquest element drops out of a relationship, the criminal is less interested in sex. There are two reasons for this: his mind is programmed with many other things, and—by implementing such correctives as trust, interdependence, and the open channel—he is learning that there are many gratifying aspects of the relationship that overshadow sex. In fact, one criminal commented to us that "this whole sex business is overrated." He was thinking about how, of 168 hours in a week, at most 3 were given over to sex, whereas many times that number of hours were spent in sharing other types of experience with his wife. The sexual experiences that the criminal now has lack the voltage of earlier conquests. Sex is integrated into the rest of the relationship, so that the partner is treated as a person. One criminal observed, "For the first time, I'm concerned with a woman's mind. I want her to have something on the ball." If the criminal finds that in his subculture extramarital affairs appear to be a norm, he has to make a choice. He can view this from the standpoint of the excitement to be gained or from the standpoint of the injuries and often tragic impact that infidelity produces in family life.

The changing criminal who is single restrains himself in pressing for sex as he dates.

> C raised a question in the group meeting about his relationships with women. He was fearful that he might be engaging in old patterns of searching for sex and then dropping a woman after he had sex. C decided that he was not ready to marry (he was in his early twenties), but he wanted both female companionship and, eventually, sex. His question was how he could have these without becoming involved. As he described his dating patterns, it became clear that C was giving women "the rush" (as he put it). This was not the old pattern of trying to conquer them for sex. But, finding a woman attractive and interesting, he would shower her with a great deal of attention and date her several times in one week. Questions about what he "really wanted" arose quickly in the relationship. C was amenable to the idea of dating more than one woman at a time, or at least restricting the early period of dating one woman to once a week, thus not giving her the rush. Then, if he found a woman to be attractive and responsible, he might well allow himself to become involved. This might be a good experience for him, provided that he did not lead the woman into thinking that he was interested in marriage.

At this time in C's life, there was no urgency about sex. In fact, he wanted to be certain that he was avoiding his old patterns of discarding women after sexual triumphs.

In responsible sexuality, it is the responsibility that is critical, not the kind of sex. No objections are presented to homosexual relationships, as long as they are by mutual consent and are devoid of criminal patterns. With respect to masturbation, the critical issue is the nature of the attendant thinking. Does the criminal fantasize responsible sexual activity or is the fantasy of irresponsible sexuality? In his past, the criminal's masturbation fantasies have been the precursors of criminal action.

> C went to an "adult bookstore" to look at the sexually explicit books, magazines, and films. He purchased some magazines. At home, he masturbated, focusing on sexual material that contained coercion and sadism. C reported that he experienced the desire for marijuana, to enhance and sustain his sexual excitement.

C stated that he had gone to the bookstore not only for the excitement at the time, but to restock his supply of fantasies with new ones for future excitement. The objection offered was neither to the masturbation nor to the purchase of pornography. It was rather to C's having chosen to focus on what for him were criminal sexual patterns.

C lived a responsible life, diligently implementing the program. His preference was to have a consenting homosexual relationship with a responsible partner. This was done discreetly, with no exploitative or coercive aspects to the relationship. His sexual fantasies were of homosexual acts, but they did not contain elements of criminal conduct.

The important aspect of our approach to sexual patterns is that we do not make them a separate subject of consideration. The criminal's sexual life becomes responsible as he becomes responsible in other ways. That is because there is a wide carryover of the correctives for thinking errors. All such considerations as trust, injury to others, and interdependence are applied to sexual relationships as they are applied elsewhere.

ELIMINATION OF SUPEROPTIMISM

After a criminal cuts off his fears, he achieves a state of maximum certainty in which he is in control of all events and in which possibilities become accomplishments—a state of superoptimism. Superoptimism is an intrinsic aspect of the ownership pattern for which correctives are described in chapter 7. Superoptimistic thinking is itself exciting, because the criminal regards himself as already triumphant in the enterprise at hand. His failure to appraise events realistically sometimes results in a recklessness that leads to his being apprehended for a crime.

Superoptimism is well-entrenched and pervades all the criminal's thinking and action. It results in very dogmatic conclusions, because it is based on the criminal's belief that he has all the necessary information, is in control of everything, and can proceed with assurance of success. Thus, superoptimism is counterproductive to responsible decision-making, which requires fact-finding and weighing alternatives.

Early in the change process, superoptimism manifests itself in innumerable situations. When the criminal sees a woman who is attractive to him, he concludes that she is his. If he wants someone to assist him with a project, he is certain that the person is in the bag. If he is appealing a legal decision, there is no question in his mind but that the appeal will be acted on favorably. If he applies for a job, he is positive that he will be hired. In his mind, failure to achieve any of his objectives constitutes an injustice; clearly, his error lies in his presumption that he will have whatever he wants.

As the criminal begins to participate in this program—despite the information given him that the program is severe, that its duration is indeterminate, and that his thinking processes must be eliminated and new ones learned and implemented—he is certain that there is nothing to it. In his view, he has made a decision to live responsibly, and little else is required. Despite our emphasis that he lacks all the tools for change, he views this as no obstacle at all. Not only will he become responsible quickly, he believes, but he can do the job faster and more convincingly than any other criminal in this program. Furthermore, he finds absurd the requirement that he report all his thinking. Having decided that he will be responsible, why put up with the grueling day-by-day examination of thinking and the scrutiny of all its details?

In the course of time, as error after error is exposed, the criminal learns that his smugness is unjustified. It is one thing for a criminal to understand the concepts provided and another to implement them. His superoptimism is such that once he verbally grasps a new concept that is a corrective for a thinking error, he is sure that he can handle with aplomb any situation that calls for its application. This is comparable to a man's claiming to be a professional tennis player after reading a book and practicing for two days. It is jolting to the criminal to face the fact that, despite his understanding, the same thinking errors recur. It takes him a long time to learn that talking about change in an office is not synonymous with changing. Actually, he does *not* understand a new concept until it has been applied in daily experience *outside* the office.

Superoptimism asserts itself in still another way. When the criminal has corrected one error in daily living, he thinks that he has corrected all of them. He overestimates the degree of his change. Once he has deterred arrestable criminality, he thinks that a small lie, a drink, or some other infraction of the program is of little consequence. After all, he asserts, he is not raping, robbing, or otherwise breaking the law. By careful reporting and subjecting himself to a thorough evaluation of the details of his thinking, the criminal slowly learns that his superoptimism is unwarranted, in that today's incipient criminal pattern, although not cause for arrest, is the precursor of tomorrow's arrestable criminality.

The complacency that accompanies superoptimism about change is a real danger. One possibility is that, once the criminal thinks that he has changed and there is an event that shows otherwise, he is put down and angry and dismisses the entire program. If he is a voluntary participant (not sent by the court), he may drop out of the program once he figures that he has it made. Whenever the criminal believes that he has done it all, as far as changing is concerned, his performance in the group slackens. Notes are sparse, reports are incomplete, and he assumes prerogatives that result in violation.

C, on probation for manslaughter, had been sent to our program by the court. His attendance at daily meetings was sporadic because of a physical disability and, when he worked, an erratic schedule. After several months, C regarded himself as having been very conscientious about treading "a straight and narrow path." He became certain that his change was complete. He had committed no criminal acts, was not drinking, and finally had a regular job. In his superoptimistic state, there was a gradual dropping off of participation in the program. Soon, he was arrested for an assault.

We shall say more in chapter 10 about the dangers of complacency when the criminal decides too early that he is fully equipped to make decisions on his own and that he no longer needs to subject his thinking to our evaluation.

The criminal's superoptimism regarding his state of change emerges again and again. It is dealt with virtually every day in the examination of his reports. As the criminal discusses women, money, work, family, and other facets of his life, superoptimistic thinking recurs, despite the fact that he has ruled out crime.

C was excited about receiving a letter from a former girlfriend. The fact that she wrote her return address on the envelope indicated to him that she wanted him to visit. In the body of the letter, she told him in an ambiguous manner, "Try hard." C interpreted this to mean, "Try hard to visit." In his mind were thoughts of the perfect Christmas with this woman, whom he had dropped three years previously. He welcomed a reunion with her. C gave little consideration to the fact that the letter was actually reserved and noncommittal.

C prejudged the course of events. He regarded as fact what was only possibility. As it turned out, C's former girlfriend was not interested in renewing the relationship.

The criminal's superoptimism about managing money emerges repeatedly. Once he has money saved, he becomes smug and invariably returns to old patterns.

C had saved more than one thousand dollars. He decided that he had met the challenge; that is, he had demonstrated that he *could* save. Furthermore, he reasoned, he could always save in the future and be assured of available funds. In this state of certainty about his financial position, C started a spending spree, in effect repeating the very patterns that had landed him in jail. He decided that he wanted an ascot. So he purchased one for fifteen dollars at an expensive, fashionable shop. To get there, he took a cab, rather than save money by taking a bus. That night, C went out on the town and treated others to ninety dollars worth of food and drink.

In his superoptimism, C never once thought about the necessity of maintaining adequate reserves to cover fees for impending legal proceedings. His superoptimism about money was part of a broader pattern of superoptimism about change. He had reached a point at which he believed that he did not have to adhere to the strict requirements of the program. He thought, Why should I have to account to them for every cent? C began to modify the requirements of the program to suit himself. Instead of fear for his future, there was superoptimism. In a review of C's life, it was easy to demonstrate how he had used money irresponsibly, injured many people, including his parents, in the process, and wound up in the penitentiary. Saving had been perceived as a challenge by C. Now, as he saw it, there was no purpose to it. He was showing an old criminal pattern of acquiring money, though now legitimately, and giving it away to build himself up and play the big shot. The review of his past, bringing up the corrective of letting fear be a guide, and reiterating the time-perspective corrective were all important in C's once again invoking reason and deterrence and adhering to the letter of the program's requirements.

We have said that the criminal expects things to turn out as he plans, regardless of his assumptions, prejudgments, and insufficient fact-finding. A useful corrective for his superoptimism is to have the criminal anticipate that the worst will happen and plan for it. For example, what will one do if everything goes wrong at work or at home? The "worst possible case" is not simply an academic exercise. So often in life, things do not turn out as one plans; in the criminal's life, this happens with great frequency. What we are referring to here is preemptive deterrence, which we shall discuss fully in the next chapter.

When the criminal is thinking superoptimistically, the channel is partially closed. If he believes that he has all the information and all the answers, he is not receptive to others. An open channel is an important corrective for superoptimism. It requires that the criminal seek others' opinions. Another important corrective is the set of ideas that are covered in teaching the criminal responsible decision-making. It is essential that the criminal eliminate his prejudgments and assumptions and learn to seek facts and weigh alternatives. We have already described the processes by which this happens in the group.

The criminal in change confuses superoptimism and confidence. Superoptimism takes possibilities as accomplished facts and is based on misconceptions about oneself and the outside world.

C was discussing his vocational plans. In doing so, he foresaw making a quick fortune in a series of business ventures. The group challenged him on his cockiness, his view that instant wealth was a sure thing. C replied, "What you people see as arrogance, is seen by others as confidence. There is a confidence based on the fact that I can do it, whatever it is." This statement was not substantiated by anything that C had done in his life. His claim, in fact, was arrogant and, in our terminology, superoptimistic. His confidence was not based on the self-assuredness that arises from knowledge, skill, and responsible accomplishments.

In this program, confidence is based on acquiring new thinking patterns and putting them to work in life. One can approach a task or another person confidently when he has the facts at hand, knows what is required to do the job, and has some evidence from experience that he has a fair chance of success. Confidence is not the superoptimistic "thinking makes it so" of the unchanged criminal.

*   *   *

The concepts presented in this chapter and in chapter 7 cover the correctives for thinking errors that are most germane to change. When these correctives are implemented regularly, they become automatic. It becomes a part of life not to injure others, to seek facts, to think conceptually, to fulfill obligations, and to do the many other things that the correctives call for. Habituation of all the correctives constitutes the ultimate deterrent to criminality. In the next chapter, we shall amplify our discussion of choice and will by describing five processes of deterrence that the criminal uses in the process of becoming a responsible citizen.

BIBLIOGRAPHY

Coleman, J. C. (1964). *Abnormal Psychology and Modern Life.* 3rd ed. Chicago: Scott, Foresman.

Freyhan, F. A. (1955). Psychopathic personalities. In *Oxford Loose Leaf Medicine*, pp. 239-256. Fair Lawn, New Jersey: Oxford University Press.

Hauck, P. A. (1967). *The Rational Management of Children.* Roslyn Heights, N. Y. Libra.

Moyer, K. E. (1972). *A Physiological Model of Aggression: Does It Have Different Implications?* Report presented at the Houston Neurological Symposium on Neural Bases of Violence and Aggression, March 9-11. Carnegie-Mellon University Report No. 72-3.

Redl, F., and Wineman, D. (1951). *Children Who Hate.* Glencoe, Ill.: Free Press.

Chapter 9

The Process of Deterrence

WHEN A CRIMINAL COMMITS A CRIME, it is the result of his choosing to behave irresponsibly. He desires to avoid apprehension, and we have used the phrase *external deterrent* to label his fear of getting caught. At times, conscience enters his stream of thinking and inhibits crime; we have labeled this the *internal deterrent*. No criminal objective is seriously pursued without his removing the external deterrent, internal deterrent, or both. Some crimes are preempted by the operation of these deterrents, but the processes of corrosion and cutoff eventually become more pronounced, so deterrents are eliminated and crime is committed. (This is described in chapter 6 of volume 1.) We have demonstrated that whether to utilize or eliminate deterrents is the criminal's choice. Such choices are made repeatedly and very rapidly. Whereas in crime he chooses to eliminate deterrents to achieve a criminal objective more effectively, in the process of change to responsibility he must choose to utilize both external and internal deterrents to eliminate criminal thinking and criminal excitement. In change, external and internal deterrents must be used to *sustain* restraint, rather than to produce only transient restraint. In achieving total responsibility, he eliminates the corrosion and cutoff of deterrents.

In our program, the agent of change has no recourse to sociologic causes or psychologic mechanisms to alter thinking or behavior. Instead, criminal thinking patterns must be eliminated through choice and will—the endurance that stems from choice. We cannot rely on the deterrents that the criminal sometimes utilized in crime. These are easily cut off, and there are so many criminal ideas in his stream of thought that the application of the external or internal deterrent as he has practiced it is totally insufficient.* If the criminal

---

*Criminals who experienced nonpsychotic hallucinatory deterrents while active in major crime (chapter 6 of volume 1) report that these were at times potent in dissuading them from crime. In the change process, they are not active in crime; therefore, the nonpsychotic hallucinatory deterrents play no role in their thinking. We have not treated chronically hallucinatory criminals whose hallucinations, for the most part, are effectively deterring crime.

depended solely on the transient deterrents that he already had available, more than half his thinking would be consumed by invoking them many times within any given hour. Because of his concreteness, the criminal would be required to deter and deter and deter, almost constantly. Obviously, this could not continue for long. Living a life of repetitive deterrence leaves energy and opportunity for little else. Ultimately, the A.C. must achieve a state in the criminal in which the application of deterrence is automatic, leaving abundant mental energy for constructive purposes. To help the criminal to sustain responsibility, it has been necessary for us to develop more complex procedures of deterrence. These consist of detailed reasoning, preemption of the criminal idea, and finally, a comprehensive deterrent, the application of which contributes to a globally responsible view of life.

We teach these processes of deterrence within the context of the mental content derived from phenomenologic reports of thinking and actions. Before our use of such reports, we attempted to establish deterrence in a way that turned out to be nonproductive. We believed that to understand the full stream of criminal thinking, we needed to drain it out of the criminal and have him express it directly to us. We encouraged him to let this thinking run its course rather than to make any attempt to stop it. This excerpt from one of our notes shows our earlier conception:

> "Criminal thinking is automatic. Our people must permit the full flow of it until it stops. The skill is for them to let it flow, knowing that they will not do anything about it. Then that kind of thinking can be replaced with the new thinking—mainly deterrents that we have imposed."

Instead of lessening criminal thinking, this procedure increased it. Thus, there was no drainage at all. After letting his thinking run and reporting all of it, the criminal was so stimulated that attempts to apply deterrents and teach correctives for thinking errors were futile. Consequently, we ceased amplifying criminal thinking and instructed the criminal to apply deterrents as early as possible. Exercises in deterrence were conducted in our groups, but lessons in the group were of little value. Deterrents have to be applied promptly in daily experience outside the group, for this is where basic change truly takes place.

Early in our work, we invoked deterrents as devices only to deal with crises and to prevent immediate criminal action. It became increasingly clear that it is too late to deter a criminal action once a chain of criminal thinking is in progress. The criminal's mind is already crowded with irresponsible ideas, each of which is generating more ideas. At this point, deterrents rapidly corrode and then are cut off and criminal thinking is implemented. Despite the criminal's having no intention of committing a crime after engaging in a criminal fantasy, there is danger that such a fantasy will eventually result in some form of criminal behavior. This has happened repeatedly. Therefore, a criminal fantasy is not taken lightly by us; it is necessary to apply deterrents to the very first thought in a fantasy. We are convinced that failure to deter promptly makes the application of deterrents later more difficult. We have found that the smallest irresponsible idea contains the seed of major crimes. Our goal has been to destroy this seed. It is well within the capacity of the criminal, if he so chooses, to destroy the thought before it germinates. His failure to do so merely reflects his preference for criminal excitement.

Deterrents must be applied to all irresponsible thought and action patterns, even if particular thought will not result immediately in further criminal thinking and then later in criminal action. A given thought or action has totally different repercussions in the criminal and in the responsible person. If a noncriminal decides to spend seventy-five dollars on dinner for two and that constitutes overspending, he then pinches pennies elsewhere or incurs a debt that he eventually pays off. If a criminal spends seventy-five dollars on dinner for two, that act may well result in a progression from irresponsible thinking to crime. Spending seventy-five dollars for dinner for two is, of course, not an arrestable act, but for the criminal it is part of being the big shot and searching for excitement, conquest, and triumph. A continuing search for excitement results in arrestability. Deterrence of such an unwise expenditure might be prudent for the noncriminal; for the criminal in the process of change, it is vital. The thought of such an expenditure must be deterred at its very inception.

Another illustration involves the telling of a small lie. In the noncriminal it may not be noticed, but if it is, the outcome is embarrassment. A small lie by a criminal may also go undetected. However, if it is noticed, he is not embarrassed, but angered. Detected or not, such a lie leads to more lies, including lies for exploitative purposes. Therefore, all lies must be promptly deterred.

We have developed the importance of cognitive fear in responsible living (chapter 7). Fear, the keystone of deterrence, is necessary, but it does not constitute the total change process. The external deterrent (fear of apprehension) is a valid fear, but to emphasize this and not the internal deterrent can lead the criminal to conclude that we are helping him to avoid being caught. Several criminals have commented to us that our emphasis on the external deterrent in the early part of the change process helps them to become more successful in criminal enterprises. Despite this, we emphasize the external deterrent so that it is not corroded, cut off, and replaced by superoptimism. However, relying only on the external deterrent or stressing it excessively detracts from the essential objective, which is to *establish a moral base for change*. Ultimately, the criminal must think in terms of injury to others, interdependence, and the many other correctives that are essential to responsible living.

In the course of our work, we were surprised to find that the agent of change is himself an embodiment of the external deterrent. Because we are not enforcement agents, we become a conscience. To be accurate, conscience lies within a person, not outside. But we have learned that in our daily program, the criminal anticipates censure and embarrassment by the group and the A.C. if he does not fulfill requirements. There is a danger in this process in that since at first all the group members want to create a favorable image with the A.C., deterrence is occasionally practiced solely to score points and mislead the A.C. The criminal's reporting that he deterred violation may be directed toward making a good impression while covering up other thinking or actions that he is not revealing. Such efforts to score points are easily discovered—if not immediately, then later.

The usefulness of the A.C. and the group as an external deterrent may pave the way for the development of conscience. When the criminal deters through such thoughts as "I can't let that man down" or "I can't let the group down," he is beginning to show an awareness of the injury that he might inflict on others and some cognizance of the desirability of interdependence. We recognize the fragmentation inherent in such deterrence and are aware that its occurrence once or twice does not demonstrate sustained change. However, it is welcomed, in that it is a step for the criminal in thinking about how he affects other people.

We use any deterrent that will lead to responsible action. The external deterrent of avoiding apprehension or disappointing the A.C. does not achieve total change. But it is a *starting point* for acquiring thinking processes that lead to responsible self-interest, making long-range considerations, the establishment of self-respect, and, finally, the valuing of integrity and change for their own sake.

A primitive form of deterrence such as "I might get caught" inhibits criminal thinking. In a more sophisticated form (to be described), deterrence requires the criminal to *think about his thinking*. It entails applying reason to the thoughts that lead to criminal action, to fantasies ultimately expressed in some form of criminality, and to visual images (eidetic images) that accompany thoughts. Images are more stimulating than nonpictorial thoughts. Thinking about going to a bar, if it is expressed in images may include female bodies and drinking. These images are not stills, but rapid sequences that produce further thought and action. As is the case with all criminals, the criminal who thinks in images is confronted with a choice. He can obliterate images or prolong and savor them to reach a higher pitch of excitement. The application of deterrence is expressed as follows:

C recalled a vivid image of a party. A girl (whom he described in detail) appeared, and he wanted to touch her. That was the start. The thought came that this "slide" sequence was "not good" for him. So he decided to "push the button" and "see another series of slides."

C chose to direct his thinking so as not to be a victim of a "living color" fantasy. For him the thought (image) of touching the girl had in the past led to rape-homicide fantasies, and his history had included several unsuccessful attempts. The application of deterrence to images requires more determination than its application to thoughts unaccompanied by images, because of the images' vividness and immediacy.

The processes of deterrence in and of themselves are not startlingly new. What is innovative is the way these processes are taught in combination with the correction of thinking errors as the criminal becomes a responsible citizen. The criminal is required to deter criminal thought and action and report what his thinking was before, during, and after deterrency. The five processes of deterrence to be discussed in detail are

—aborting a crisis (D1)
—disposing of a persistent criminal thought by means of
a reasoning process (D2)
—preempting criminal thinking (D3)
—taking a moral inventory when no criminal thought
has come to mind (D4)
—automatic deterrence (D5)

ABORTING A CRISIS (D1)

As he begins our program, the criminal is totally unchanged. His thinking contains such a heavy flow of criminal ideas that only a small number can possibly be implemented (see chapter 6 of volume 1). From the very beginning, we have a crisis situation, and thus from the outset, we intensify the criminal's alertness to the dangers of criminal thinking. Such thinking has in the past, and will in the future, result in crime unless it is deterred. The first step in deterrence is for the criminal to regard every thought as dangerous, so dangerous that he cannot allow himself to dwell on it or debate its merits. Thinking "it's dangerous" must be prompt.

C walked into a store. A janitor waxing the floor yelled at him to watch where he was going. The instant thought was "jamming my fist down his throat." C had taken such action many times in the past. Here, he was alert that an assault spells trouble. Deterrence was prompt. He simply moved to the edge of the floor and said nothing.

In this instance, realization of danger was immediate. Deterrence (D1) is focused on the immediate consequences of the act in question—that is, injury to another person and trouble for himself. Such prompt deterrence is designed so that the thought is rejected without an elaborate review of past experiences and likely consequences. It is similar to touching a hot surface; when the person is about to make contact, he withdraws his hand because of the inevitable burn he is about to receive. One criminal called D1 the "poison" deterrent.

We have refined the "it's dangerous" formula so that the criminal links an incipient criminal thought with immediate confinement. Just to meet old associates means jail. To go to a high crime neighborhood means jail. To visit an area in which prostitution flourishes means jail.

As the criminal implements this program, he considers himself in an inner jail—a jail he erects around himself and in which he is deprived of his former excitements. One man called this "the jail within myself." The criminal has a choice between jails, our jail or society's jail. It is the dread of the latter that is a significant deterrent dozens of times a day as the criminal begins the program.

> As he entered this program, C had dozens of criminal ideas per day. He would pass an attractive female on the street, see one in a laundromat, or sit next to one on a bus and think of rape. (This man had committed hundreds of rapes.) Any time he had a minor difficulty at work, he would think of assaulting someone and quitting. Entering a store, he would think of theft. With each criminal thought, he trained himself to think of "jail." In fact, this became such a vivid fear that an image of iron bars flashed through his mind each time.

D1, the fear of jail, although unsophisticated, is effective early in the program, but insufficient in the long run.

D1 is actually commonplace with noncriminals who think of a violation but deter it immediately and give it no further thought. However, in the criminal, the same thoughts recur daily, again and again. Depending on D1 in working with the criminal is like relying on aspirin; it may relieve the symptom without remedying the underlying condition. D1 can be repeated many times a day, but it leaves little energy for constructive change. Earlier in our investigation, we depended heavily on D1. Here and there, a criminal *act* was deterred, but D1 did not eliminate *criminal thinking*.

The applicability of D1 is extended from precise thoughts that result in specific crimes to particular thinking errors, such as those accompanying anger. When the criminal is about to respond angrily, he thinks, "Don't. It's prison for me." Anger is suppressed. As we have explained, however, although D1 is a useful first step, the criminal eventually applies more powerful deterrents to anger so as to eliminate anger reactions totally.

D1 is effective for immediate deterrence. However, because the criminal has strong, recurrent desires to violate, deterrent thinking is again necessary. Within a half hour, criminal thinking may reappear three or four times, denoting a battle between the criminal desire and effort at deterrence.

Clearly, D1 does not have a lasting effect. Although it is the easiest deterrent to cut off, it temporarily serves as a vital and indispensable emergency measure to deal with crises. It gives us the time to invoke the rest of the program—that is, to change fifty-two thinking errors and teach more sophisticated deterrents. In time, the criminal must progress beyond the rather simple deterrent of the fear of jail to acquire and utilize deterrents of conscience that are based on a broad concept of what is responsible and moral. Once this has occurred, it is rarely necessary to invoke D1.

DISPOSING OF A CRIMINAL
THOUGHT BY REASONING (D2)

To impose more effective deterrence, we have introduced D2, which requires the application of reason in two stages—drawing on experiences to establish or strengthen self-disgust and then applying the lessons of the past to the future. The first stage involves a post mortem assessment and teaching after a violation or series of criminal thoughts. The second stage requires the criminal to utilize what he has learned and thus engage in reasoning before the fact. That is, just as he is about to violate, he goes through a reasoning process and deters action. We have used D2 hundreds of times with many criminals and have found it effective in eliminating criminal thinking. It is often necessary that the criminal continue to use D2 in long sessions by himself, sometimes for as long as twenty minutes. In such sessions, a flood of frightening consequences come to mind. A criminal had recurrent thoughts about taking liquor off his shelf and "getting bombed." Prompt deterrence using D1 (it's dangerous) resulted in an immediate elimination of the thinking, but it recurred a few times within a half-hour. This was the time to apply a longer spell of deterrence.

C had a bottle at hand and had taken the cap off. He thought about how his drinking had contributed to a separation between him and his wife in the past. Now they were reunited, but she was in the hospital. He thought about how disappointed she would be if he resumed drinking. Then he considered the effects of his drinking on his children, who had endured a lot of abuse from him. He began to think about how adversely they would be affected if he took to the bottle again. C remembered all the money he had wasted on alcohol and how his family had had to do without things it needed. Most vivid of all were his recollections of injuring others, both emotionally and physically, when he got into ugly moods after drinking.

After sitting there staring at the bottle and engaging in this thinking, he replaced the cap and put the liquor on the shelf.

Here is an illustration of how D2 reasoning did not emphasize the past, but instead offered a clearer picture of the present and anticipated the future:

C had permission to go to the library. However, with the change of shift, the evening nursing assistant (N.A.) would not allow him to go. There was a momentary flash of anger, which C did not express. He then began a process of reasoning, considering some of the brutal things that he had done in the past when angry. He thought about the concept of putdown and realized that the N.A.'s refusal to let him go to the library was not a putdown and that perhaps the N.A. had a good reason. He was also aware that he would have to live with this N.A. long after this incident. A broader consideration entered C's thinking: he was not an invited guest in maximum security. No matter how unfair others were, he would have to endure it. It was a price he had to pay.

When a criminal is actively pursuing a criminal objective, D2 is not likely to be applied, because he does not want to talk himself out of what he wants. When he reports that he has sought recourse to a second path of deterrence (D2) after the first (D1) has failed, this is an indication that implementation of the program is taking place. With conscientious application of D2, the criminal develops a more stable view of himself in which disgust with his past not only is readily experienced, but is actually sought, so that it will remain vivid and be a reliable guide to future thinking and action.

D2 may have a drawback. Early in the program, some criminals report that, while employing D2, they enjoy reviewing experiences because they savor the excitements and get a charge out of these memories. This, of course, is counterproductive to intensifying self-disgust.

C was thinking about how to strike up a conversation with a young girl. The next thought was how to get her into bed. To oppose this thinking, he followed our instructions and drew on his experiences with women. This produced a flood of memories of sexual adventures (mostly irresponsible). He found himself enjoying thoughts of sexy, young girls whom he had misused and who had been his slaves, giving him bubble baths and catering to his every desire.

In this instance, drawing on experiences enhanced excitement rather than promoted self-disgust. We have been able to achieve a more effective result by having the criminal direct his thinking toward the inevitable consequences of irresponsible acts. He is instructed to review not the details of his criminal performance, but the physical and emotional harm that he has inflicted on society and his family and how he has jeopardized himself. The following summarizes the thinking of the same criminal as he applied the reasoning procedures of D2 constructively:

> C began to think about how he had charmed and flattered young women so that he had them at his feet and in his bed. He thought about how he had conned, lied to, and exploited these women, leading them to believe that he was something he was not. He thought about his two marriages and the children who never knew their father. He regarded himself as a phony who never knew what love was and who had never had a responsible relationship with a woman.

As a consequence of this type of reasoning, he had less desire to approach a young woman at work. As he repeated D2, there was no desire at all. Indeed, he was confronted with mild self-disgust for having had the thought in the first place.

As the criminal implements D2 thinking, consideration of past consequences leads to thoughts about his future. D2 becomes totally effective when actual experiences are applied to thoughts of the future, both immediate and long-range: forewarned is forearmed. Mental preparation for future events is a major subject of our discussion of the criminal's phenomenologic reports. After reviewing some of the experiences of the past, he concentrates on the future.

> C still was associating with other criminals, drinking and occasionally using drugs. This was occurring just after he had rejoined his wife and two children and wanted a family life. C began to think about the costs to his family of his past criminal patterns. His wife had left him, and he had been a stranger to his children. Now he wanted to be a better father and provider. C was hoping to move his family to better surroundings and save enough money to help his children attend college. The more thought that C gave to his new objectives, the more apparent it became that he could not afford further contact with other criminals and that he had to close the door on alcohol and drugs.

PREEMPTING CRIMINAL THINKING (D3)

We developed preemptive deterrence, D3, because we found that the criminal could hardly go about his daily routine without encountering some situation that evoked memories of past exploits. There was a danger that he would find these memories exciting and want more criminal action. Preemptive deterrence entails consideration of a future probability *before* a criminal thought has occurred.

D1 is necessary during a crisis. D2 requires reasoning just before a violation. D3 requires deterrence even earlier—before a situation is at hand. It is an anticipatory deterrent. From his experience and from that of others in the group, the criminal can reasonably anticipate that particular events will happen and that particular types of people or specific individuals will be encountered. He knows that, if he chooses to frequent a criminal area, the mere sight of some people will arouse criminal thinking in him. He can predict that the people he knows will talk to him in criminal terms because their relationship to him has been based on criminality. Being aware of what is likely to occur under such circumstances, he is in a position to attack incipient criminal thinking by avoiding the situation. In this case, it is a matter of staying away from areas in which criminals are known to congregate. Of course, the criminal cannot possibly avoid every situation that might stimulate criminal thinking.

> Whenever he had a dental appointment, C used to think about using dental floss to strangle the technician. Knowing that this idea might occur to him on a forthcoming visit to the dentist, he was prepared for it. When he got there and the dental floss was used, the thought of strangling the technician did not occur to C. He had already knocked the idea out before he sat in the dentist's chair.

> Among C's serious criminal patterns was making numerous obscene phone calls. Now, he had a research job that required making phone calls. Before dialing, C thought about how he used to respond to the voices of women whom he did not know. He was prepared to stick to business in his use of the telephone. The desire for the obscene phone calls did not even appear.

These situations demonstrate the central role of fear in deterrence. C had reached a point where he feared that he might want to make an obscene phone call. The fear that occurred in advance was the preemptive deterrent.

Redirection of thinking and preemptive deterrence are two sides of the same coin. In fact, redirection of thinking inevitably occurs with *all* deterrence. This is because if criminal thinking is deterred, something must replace it. There can be no vacuum of thought. The redirection of thinking may be contrived. That is, temporarily the criminal may have to choose what to think about. Or his thoughts may naturally turn to something else—either something purely diversionary like the local football team or something constructive such as how to improve customer service at work. When the criminal uses preemption, he is simultaneously and automatically redirecting his thinking. The criminal knows that during idle time, criminal thoughts are likely to emerge. To prevent this, he can decide in advance to direct his thinking along different lines. There have been hundreds of instances in which a changing criminal remembers a crime as he passes a store or bank that he has previously robbed. He now has no desire to commit a crime. Rather, he wants to avoid even the memory of criminal excitement. Therefore, knowing where he will go, he chooses not to allow his mind to dwell on the past crime and directs his attention elsewhere.

As a way of implementing preemptive deterrence and redirection of thought, the criminal may think about the worst possible outcome of an impending situation and how he might handle it.

> Working as a waiter, C prepared himself for his day at work. He thought about patrons complaining about the food, flat drinks, the chef's carving, food being unavailable, and long waits. Knowing full well that any or all of these complaints might be registered, C thought in advance about how he could provide the best service and earn the maximum tip. Past patterns when things had gone wrong included anger, insults, ignoring the customer, and quitting. Now, he had a modus operandi so that, if Murphy's Law were operating (If anything can go wrong, it will), he was prepared to turn that adversity into a challenge to provide superservice and increase his income from tips.

Our people have found that, when they have handled such situations without conning, but with superservice (rather than just efficient service), their patrons have rewarded them more. Preemptive thinking in this situation was not limited to the mechanics of restaurant service. C knew that he would see many females, both staff and patrons. He had committed thousands of crimes, including sexual ones, that began with thoughts of breasts and buttocks, extended to voyeurism, and culminated in exhibitionism and a wide range of felonies. He successfully preempted sexual thinking by deciding not to engage in it but to direct his thinking instead toward his work. Another criminal in our program had committed serious crimes of violence. He realized that, when he was not occupied, he had recurrent desires to escape from the institution (which he had done once already) and commit crimes. He established a mental set to direct his thinking and energies toward earning money responsibly by providing a particular service to the staff.

The criminal must regard preempting minor irresponsibility and, more important, incipient criminal thinking as a matter of the utmost gravity. D3 has its fullest impact when the criminal regards preemption as of life or death importance. It is like the ex-smoker who regards having just one cigarette as causing lung cancer, the diabetic who considers eating one piece of pie as fatal, or the man who thinks of having sex with a prostitute as resulting in tertiary syphilis. For the criminal, thinking about picking up a prostitute, thinking about a three-hundred-dollar suit, or thinking about telling a lie will result in arrestable crimes with consequent injury to others and jeopardy to himself. For the responsible person, each of these events is unlikely to lead to the chain of irresponsibilities and crimes that it does for the criminal. In the process of change, the criminal must habitually think, "Sex with——means jail," "Buying a three-hundred-dollar suit means the penitentiary," "Telling a lie means the loss of everything I am working for." For him, preemption is now truly a life or death matter.

We realize that D3 does not constitute a solution, but is an intermediate stage. When preemption occurs, the criminal shifts his thinking and energy from irresponsibility to obligations at hand, or he creates new tasks for himself. Several criminals, working in restaurants, have become genuinely interested in and contributed to many aspects of restaurant operations. By directing their thoughts and energies to improving their functioning, they have proved to be of great value to their employers. What started as preemption to eliminate criminal thinking resulted in increased earnings and promotion. Initially, we did not anticipate such an outcome, but it occurred repeatedly, and we now expect this type of progress.

Without implementation of D3, the criminal becomes complacent. With constant implementation, preemption becomes habitual, and there is less need to use D3.

> When C came home from work, he regularly produced crises, angrily responding to his wife's requests or suggestions, which he viewed as control. Dinner was marked by silence or quarreling. According to our instruction, C began to practice the following thinking before he arrived home: "Watch your temper; think before you say anything. Be receptive to everything your wife says and does. Do not react immediately, but think."

This became a routine in which C trained himself to listen carefully to what his wife had to say before forming his own conclusion. In most instances, he realized that she was being helpful, not controlling. The evening meal became pleasant. After repeated preemption, the pattern of listening and controlling his temper became so habitual that it no longer required time and effort to establish a mental set.

Preempting anger is an absolute necessity in learning to implement D3. If the criminal remains realistic in his expectations, he learns not to react with anger when things go against him. Properly forearmed, he keeps in mind that Murphy's Law is unexpectedly operative. Even when something happens that an objective observer regards as unreasonable, unwarranted, and unjust, the criminal must learn to respond without anger. Then he is prepared to cope with problems constructively.

> C was the supervisor of a group of employees, several of whom were lazy and inefficient. C realized that the work would not be done as efficiently and thoroughly as he desired. Furthermore, he was well aware that those men whom he had to pressure would resent him. His view was that he would do the best he could. He knew in advance that he would be criticized for demanding that others do precisely what they had been hired to do. Bearing this in mind, C did not expect to win a popularity contest among the employees. Furthermore, no matter what happened he would not feel put down and react with anger.

Repeated deterrence is less necessary if the criminal gears his thinking to anticipate what lies ahead. When he does this, irresponsible thinking occurs much less frequently. Life is then more an effort to implement responsible thinking than an effort to deter criminal thinking. The criminal has greater freedom to devote himself to concentration on responsible problem-solving.

With repeated implementation, the correctives for thinking errors (chapters 7 and 8) are incorporated into the criminal's way of life. He refrains from criminal thought and action, because they are antithetical to the kind of life he wants to lead and the type of person he wants to become. In essence, the correctives of thinking errors constitute the substantive side of deterrence. In our series of interviews, we have found that unchanged criminals sporadically invoke some of the same deterrents that we teach. They do not sustain them. They label them in a variety of ways, some in terms of religious precepts. The difference between these unchanged criminals and those who change by means of our program is that the former find that life is a neverending struggle to apply deterrents, whereas the latter do not experience such a struggle. Within a year or two, as they implement new thinking patterns, deterrence becomes automatic. It is a built-in component of responsible living.

MORAL INVENTORY (D4)

The moral aspect of this program is present at all stages. However, in the moral inventory, or examination of conscience (D4), morality is addressed as an issue in itself. D4 was not developed by us, but rather by some members of the group. Each morning, the criminals came to the meeting with the notes from the previous day on which they based their reports. The very writing of the notes resulted in their reflecting about themselves. Having been instructed in the group meetings to review the injury that they had inflicted on others, they began on their own to engage in fifteen-minute sessions outside the group, evaluating the many ways in which they had wasted their lives. One called this process his "exercise in self-disgust." This struck us as very much like the "searching moral inventory" of Alcoholics Anonymous. It was indeed a searching moral inventory, extending far beyond the immediate events of the day.* One criminal appropriated the term "examination of conscience" from his early religious training. However, none of the D4 thinking ever took the form of religious considerations.

It is noteworthy that D4 must be implemented as an exercise in its own right, not as an immediate antidote to a criminal thought. D2 is used for that. Other members of the group, who had not made moral inventories spontaneously, heard these reports of examination of conscience. They tried it on their own but reported little impact. We therefore conducted training sessions in the D4 deterrent during the group meetings. But change occurred only if the criminals promptly implemented D4 outside the group and then reported their experiences with it the next day.

After criminals meet with us all morning, work into the evening, and arrive home late and eager to rest, they are reluctant to conduct an examination of conscience. It is not an agreeable way to end a day. We require that they engage in this examination whenever possible—on a long bus ride, during a break at work, perhaps lying in bed before sleeping. It is feasible to make a moral inventory during any period between activities.

> C had not written to his parents in many months. He stopped at a post office to buy stamps and found long lines of customers waiting at all windows. His first thought was, "Why should I wait?" Then he thought about the fact that his parents had not heard from him, and he decided that it was more important for him to purchase the stamps than to do anything else. While waiting in line, he engaged in an examination of conscience about his relationship with his parents. He thought about how disappointed in him they must be. He traced through episode after

*The process is somewhat analogous to Assagioli's (1973) exercises for strengthening the will: "Picture to yourself as vividly as possible the loss of opportunity, the damage, the pain to yourself and others which has actually occurred, and which might again occur, as a result of the present lack of strength of your will. Examine these occasions, one by one, formulating them clearly; then make a list of them in writing. Allow the feelings which these recollections and forecasts arouse to affect you intensely. Then let them evoke in you a strong urge to change this condition" (p. 36). Unfortunately Assagioli refers vaguely to "feelings" and has a very broad definition of "will."

episode in which he had misrepresented himself to them, misappropriated their money, and lied. Even after his father bailed him out of jail, C continued his criminal patterns. C thought about how his father had done everything to help him, and yet he had caused his father to suffer over the years. C realized that he was the primary source of his father's unhappiness at a time when his father was so successful in his professional life. C viewed himself as the dark shadow on his father's otherwise productive, gratifying life. He pictured himself as a little boy on a tricycle approaching a dangerous ditch near the house. A housekeeper warned him to move away, but C paid no attention. The housekeeper summoned C's father, who also warned him of the danger. C responded by throwing a rock at his father. He pictured his father's anguished look.

The following examples illustrate other circumstances under which the moral inventory has been taken:

As he worked at his office one night, C saw the housekeeper come in and collect the trash. C had no desire to approach this woman sexually, but he began to recall experiences in which any housekeeper, young or old, thin or fat, would be a figure in rape-homicide thinking. For twenty minutes, C sat in his office and focused his attention on both sexual and nonsexual aspects of his past thinking and action. He thought about the women he had followed, the women he had wanted to mutilate, his unfaithfulness to his wife, and his deceptions of people. This review continued until C was so disgusted with himself that he began to feel physically ill. He then terminated the exercise.

* * *

On a trip, C and his wife stopped at a store, where C saw a buxom woman whom he found appealing. When he returned to his car, instead of thinking further about her, C reviewed his past experiences with women. There had been disaster after disaster because of his lying, cheating, drug use, and drinking. He thought about his out-of-wedlock children whom he had neglected. As he reviewed his years of exploiting women, his disgust with himself mounted.

Although both these examinations of conscience focus on criminal patterns with women, the same type of self-inventory is taken by criminals whose criminality has included thefts, assaults, and conning.

C was saddened at the fatal shooting of a policewoman for whom he had great respect. This lady lived near him, and they had gone to school together. Even though she was on police force, C had regarded her as a fine, decent person. C began to think about his own patterns of violence in which he had used his fists, a gun, a board, or anything else at hand to overcome others in fights. He thought about how he had hurt not only the immediate victims, but their friends and families. Also going through C's mind was the memory of the Christmas he had spent confined because he had been convicted of manslaughter. He remembered how his children had to come to the jail that holiday season to see their father.

D4 is not designed to produce the state of despair characteristic of the zero state. The latter is a sense of nothingness, transparency, and permanent futility. D4 is constructive. It is a self-inventory by which the criminal can observe how far he has come and how far he must go. It is our most effective device for making the criminal face himself as a criminal.

Criminals who have used the moral inventory spontaneously have experienced rapid impact. Criminals who have been required by us to use D4 and have not applied it on their own initiative have reported impact only after it became a habitual exercise.

D4 has value only if it evokes disgust and shame based on a criminal's being truly fed up with the kind of person he has been. The moral inventory underscores how extensively the criminal has injured others. It furthers the process of change in still another way. If a moral inventory is to be of value, it has a preemptive function. Contempt for oneself as a criminal is intensified, and there is a looking to the future to ensure that one does not repeat errors of the past and cause injury to still others.

In taking moral inventories, the criminal at times reaches a state of mind in which he has a sense of futility about life in the light of the burden that he is carrying. The revulsion that he experiences toward himself for the injury that he has inflicted on others can overwhelm him to the point of suicidal thinking. At such a time, the criminal's thinking becomes so narrow that it excludes other options. Suicidal thinking is no novelty, but it has always occurred in the past when he was active in crime. Now he evaluates his thinking with an emphasis on injury to others. If he were to commit suicide, he would indeed be injuring people, especially his family, whom he has already harmed repeatedly. In other words, what he regards as a step to prevent further injury could result only in inflicting more injury. The criminal's guilt and shame about his past are directed toward constructive alternatives, rather than toward injuring others by self-destruction.

Occasionally, the criminal complains that the disagreeableness of the moral inventory discourages the exercise. We do not accept this because it bespeaks less than total implementation. The moral inventory strengthens the anticrime attitude, a prime desideratum. Continuing use of the moral inventory is an index of the implementation of correctives for errors of thinking everywhere.* D4 is a component of the criminal's lifeline.

When the criminal is not in a program for change and deters criminality, thus depriving himself of the oxygen of his life, he experiences psychosomatic symptoms—headache, fatigue, gastrointestinal distress, and multiple aches and pains. These symptoms disappear when he opts for criminal excitement— "oxygen" relieves the "anoxia." Symptoms are most prominent when the criminal is in our program but is at war with it. His itch for excitement then clashes with our absolute insistence on one hundred percent responsibility. As he starts directing his attention to implementing correctives for thinking errors, conflicts diminish and psychosomatic symptoms are fewer.

As the criminal regularly practices his moral inventory, he not only orients that inventory to his specific errors but increasingly expands it to more philosophic issues. While still engaging in an examination of conscience with accompanying self-disgust, the criminal now includes in his inventory a global assessment of the way in which he has lived his entire life. The very premises of his life are now challenged. These premises are the thinking patterns described in volume 1. More and more, the inventory concludes with how he must live in the future.

> C began to think of the many things that he had neglected throughout his life. He thought of the people whom he took for granted and how he made others do things for him. His had been a life of exploiting people, violating their trust, and in other ways injuring them. He realized that he had lived this way because of the overriding importance of his search for excitement. C realized that now was the time to develop the skills of responsibility, in order to bring about a broad-based change in every aspect of his life. He began thinking about what life would be like in the future if he failed to do this.

We have found that, as substantial change takes place, the criminal begins for the first time in his life to acquire some wisdom and to reexamine what he has always taken for granted.

> After working very hard in this program, C1 still faced the possibility of deportation from the United States because of crimes committed earlier. C2, a U.S. citizen by birth, reflected that throughout his life he had committed thousands of felonies, but was never in danger of deportation.

---

*We emphasize the deliberate nature of this examination of conscience. It is different from the criminal's day-to-day reflections in the course of events. One does not necessarily sit down to reflect; it is a more casual process. But examining one's conscience is an exercise that one chooses to engage in at a specific time.

He realized that he had always taken the rights of citizenship for granted. He thought about how he had abused the freedom and opportunities of living in the United States. These were precious assets that he had failed to utilize responsibly. This particular line of thought was a stimulus for yet another moral inventory to consider the specific crimes that he had committed and the many people whom he had injured.

Some criminals expect criminal thinking to disappear totally if they apply the deterrents. Because this does not happen, they become discouraged. In our program, no change is possible without deterrence, but deterrence alone is not enough. If he deters criminal thinking, the criminal can devote himself more single-mindedly to learning and implementing new thinking processes. Deterrence and correction of thinking errors constitute a circular process: each reinforces the other. Deterrence is an important first step. Unless a host of criminal ideas are eliminated, the criminal is not open to new concepts.

The exercise in self-disgust (the moral inventory) can become quite wearisome for the criminal well advanced in change. Some criminals have utilized a variant of this deterrent procedure. Instead of reflecting on the crimes that they have perpetrated, they imagine that they are the victims of such crimes. They are being exploited, lied to, stolen from, and assaulted. The criminal thinks of himself as being the disappointed father, the beaten-up brother, or the startled victim of a housebreaking. With such a focus, the criminal experiences more disgust and thus more impact than he does from a moral inventory in which he engages just to satisfy a routine.

A moral inventory can, of course, be utilized by the criminal for purposes other than change. He may try to feed the change agent what he thinks the agent wants to hear. He may utilize it to make a confession, and then view himself as absolved and go on to repeat the confessed offenses and commit new ones. Such an inventory has the effect of building up his opinion of himself as a good person. The danger is that a change agent will be satisfied with an impressive moral inventory and neglect to emphasize that it is *worthless* unless it is a factor in change.

In a program like this, if a criminal is not implementing change but is only attempting to extricate himself from one jam or avoid another, he may make token efforts at deterrence and change. But he eventually experiences boredom and, with it, psychosomatic symptoms. If he is seriously implementing the program, he still may complain about the grind of deterring criminal thinking and assert that life is nothing more than round after round of deterrence. Repeated deterrence is, however, part of a transitional stage. Less attention has to be paid to deterrents as the criminal corrects thinking errors and becomes responsible. With experience in responsibility, interest grows. With interest, there is enthusiasm and less need for deterrence. In criminals who are conscientious—implementing the program at every turn—we have noticed within a year a dramatic reduction from scores of criminal ideas each day to a few each week.

As the criminal makes strides in the change process, he makes many, many moral inventories, all laden with self-criticism and self-disgust for his criminality. Eventually, a point is reached at which repeatedly blasting himself yields diminishing returns; it becomes a routine with little impact. At such a time, the features of the moral inventory related to his criminality are accepted as facts of life. He has been a criminal; he has injured numerous individuals and society at large. The emphasis shifts from dwelling on past contemptible behavior to planning what must be done now and in the future to ensure responsible functioning. Of course, he must reinstitute the moral inventory if a criminal idea occurs. The practice of taking stock of himself, however, does not cease. The issue is less that of a moral inventory and more that of a self-appraisal of his functioning in the responsible world. When the criminal stops questioning himself along these lines, he becomes complacent about change, thus revealing that change has been insufficient.

A criminal occasionally protests that he wants to get rid of a specific kind of thinking, while he is doing many things to retain it. That is, the same ideas are coming to mind, and he is having to deter them again and again.

C was deterring thinking about sex with other women long after he had established a responsible and sexually satisfying relationship with his wife. C knew that he would not allow himself to make contact with another woman, because to do so would destroy himself and his family. Still, the thinking occurred. We discovered that C's idea of his manhood was being kept alive. In his thinking, he was a man if he still entertained ideas of a harem. If he were truly monogamous, he was less of a man.

C believed that there was not a ghost of a chance that he would implement his thinking about adultery. Such thinking occurred two or three times a week and lasted at the most thirty seconds each time. The A.C.'s task in such a situation is to examine carefully the criminal's desire to retain such thinking. In the case of adulterous thinking, it requires continuing effort to alter the criminal's idea of manhood and to teach him to implement more sophisticated deterrent thinking processes. He must take a moral inventory, reflect about what his idea of manhood has resulted in in the past, and take active steps to preempt such thinking in the future.

Because we emphasize the moral inventory so heavily, the criminal sometimes thinks that change will occur instantly if he takes such an inventory. One criminal reported that he had spent four hours thinking about his life of injuring others. Having done this, he expected an almost magical change. It was as though he believed that, once he had conducted the inventory, his thinking errors were already automatically replaced by the correctives. When we called this to his attention, he stated, "I have got to do something to change my mental set." This was a statement of further deferment of change. The mental set must be in process. Implementation must be immediate. The moral inventory and a mental set for the future, by themselves, do not do the job. In change, there must be instant implementation of all parts of the program.

AUTOMATIC DETERRENCE (D5)

In the thinking of criminal and noncriminal alike, ideas enter and leave awareness without conscious efforts at deterrence. Eventually, the criminal functions much like the noncriminal who deters an occasional irresponsible idea. In the noncriminal, an irresponsible thought may be consciously deterred, or it may disappear from awareness in a flash without any effort at all at deterrence. We have observed that, when the criminal is well advanced in change, criminal thoughts that were savored, elaborated on, and translated into action now enter and leave awareness without deliberate deterrence, just as they do in the noncriminal. We have labeled this phenomenon *automatic deterrence*. D5 no longer requires effort and deliberate implementation.

In this program, the criminal wants to rid himself of all criminal thinking. He often complains that such thinking comes and goes so fast that he cannot recall it. Those who have tried diligently to capture and report all criminal thinking retrieve only a small percentage of it, because the ideas appear and disappear with such speed. The significance of automatic deterrence demonstrates that a foundation for responsibility is being built.

We have discussed deterrence of thinking, but feelings are also deterred. The criminal may talk in a self-pitying manner as he lives without his old excitements. This is a state of frank boredom. He is angry at having placed the handcuffs of responsibility on himself. We turn to his *thoughts* of self-pity rather than dwell on his feelings. As his thinking is rationally evaluated and new patterns are implemented, the criminal reports a change in feelings. Deterrence of self-pity is of course no answer by itself, because it leaves a vacuum. Rather, deterrence must be combined with a redirection of thinking and action and an assiduous correction of thinking errors.

It is critical that the changing criminal not become complacent, even though criminal thinking is minimal. Even the slightest appearance of old-pattern thinking requires his attention and evaluation.

> C decided to make a project of catching and remembering the fleeting old-pattern thoughts that occurred during the course of a week. During a 7-day period, he detected 15 stray sexual thoughts (not related to sex with

his wife). This was in contrast with hundreds per day formerly. C found that not one of these old-pattern thoughts came spontaneously; they were triggered by passing through an area directly on his way to work where there were prostitutes. C decided that he should preempt these thoughts. This he successfully did by focusing his thinking on work or current events whenever he was in that location. Whenever a criminal thought was not preempted and came to mind, he experienced a flash of contempt for himself for having the thought.

It is remarkable to see a man whose mind has been filled with criminal thinking for years alter that thinking so as to be preoccupied with working out responsible solutions to problems of daily living.

C had time for a lot of thinking on a slow night at work. He was examining part of the restaurant that needed repairs and was considering how to do them. His thoughts turned to the situation in Southeast Asia. He wondered what alternatives there might be to military force as a solution to problems in that part of the world.

Instead of watching women, thinking about drugs, and being bored and angry at his routine job, C directed his thinking toward contemplating a problem at work and then toward a more impersonal issue. This is characteristic of what our changing criminals report. Criminal thinking rarely occurs, and, if it does, it is quickly dismissed. Training in deterrence is complete, but its exercise must continue indefinitely.

BIBLIOGRAPHY

Assagioli, R. (1973). *The Act of Will*. New York: Viking.

Chapter 10

Experiences During
the Change Process

OBSTACLES

THE GREATEST OBSTACLE TO EFFECTING CHANGE is that criminals oppose
change. One group of criminals who show interest in our program do so
because they are confronted with an unpalatable alternative—the prospect of
long confinement. They think that the courts will place them on probation,
especially if a rehabilitative program is available. They may be ordered to
enter our program as a condition of probation. If they have the option of
entering a less demanding program than ours, they elect that; they would
rather participate in a program that requires a meeting only once a week than
in our program, which requires meetings three hours a day, five days a week.

Another group of criminals who seek admission to our program do so to get
out of confinement. They want to be paroled from prison or discharged from a
psychiatric institution where the period of confinement is long or
indeterminate. In the early phase of our program, we worked mainly with
criminals in a psychiatric hospital; but in recent years, we have been dealing
mainly with criminals on parole or probation. Criminals who avoid a prison
sentence by being adjudged "not guilty by reason of insanity" are admitted to
a hospital. Most such criminals do not believe that they were or are mentally
ill, and they begin scheming to get out as soon as they are admitted. Some
criminals evince great interest in our program, because they expect that
participating in it will hasten their discharge. However, once they learn that
they are soon to be released into the community, their interest in our program
fades rapidly. When the law requires that they either enter our program or be
confined, they invariably choose the former.

A third group of criminals who are not confined and are not under any
court order apply for admission voluntarily, because they are discouraged by
their failures as criminals.

Obviously, the odds against us at the beginning of our work with a criminal are staggering. Whether the criminal enters the program as a forced alternative to confinement or comes to us voluntarily, he enters not knowing from experience the full extent of change required. He faces the prospect of changing to a way of life that he has scorned. One man put it this way:

> "Crime is the only real life I know. Giving up crime is a form of death to me, but it is something I want to accomplish."

It is clear that the criminal's statement that he desires to change represents his view that our program is the least of the evils of prolonged confinement, suicide, or change.

In the initial contact (chapter 3), the criminal has been told unequivocally of our evaluation of him. Psychiatric diagnosis has been set aside in favor of a blunt assessment of him as a criminal. He has been presented with a kaleidoscopic view of the requirements of the program and a description of the finished product. Still, he views ultimate change as a state of crimelessness rather than total responsibility. There is a problem even with the criminal's idea of what constitutes crimelessness. To the criminal, a crime is an act for which he has been arrested and convicted. Despite his having committed hundreds of crimes for which he was never arrested, he regards himself as a good person, not a criminal. At best, he goes along with our appraisal of him as a criminal mainly because he thinks that it is to his benefit not to antagonize the agent of change. For a while, he may truly believe that our prospectus for change has merit. But nothing in his experience permits him to understand the scope of the change that we require and what it ultimately entails.

The criminal believes that he will achieve the objectives we outline, but that he will do so in his own way. Faced with the necessity of surrendering control to us, he persists in his tactics to maintain it, even though it is in his best interest to give it up. To him, to control is to be reduced to a slave or a pawn, and this is unthinkable. To maintain control, the criminal examines us far more than we examine him. Although he is behind the eight ball, he tries to convince us that he knows what is best for himself and for others and thus constantly presses to do things his way.

The channel is at least partially closed at the beginning, and the criminal opens and closes it in his transactions with us to suit his purposes. We train him in phenomenologic reporting (chapter 5), but his diligence in implementing it varies with his changing attitude toward the program. One criminal described the reporting process as "exquisitely painful."

> "What we're discussing here is an extremely thorough scouring of the mentality, an exquisitely painful and effective washing out of the mind together with an ongoing instillation of new patterns of thought."

The process of reporting is disagreeable because the criminal regards it as submission. To disclose is to surrender. To listen to someone else's view is to surrender.

We are constantly faced with the question of whether at any given time the criminal is truthful. He lies both by omission and by commission. He tells a part of the truth and omits the rest. He tries to impress us with confessions. Once he learns the knack of reporting, he uses that criminally. He thinks that, because we value total reporting as a *sine qua non*, he will give us what he believes will satisfy our requirements, but do nothing more. For example, he violates today and decides that it was permissible, because he plans to report it tomorrow. He regards the report as all that matters, not understanding that to us this is just another form of scoring points.

> C gave long, detailed reports and criticized others for insufficiency in reporting. C's reports revealed his thinking errors and the many habits that required change. As the group began to discuss the irresponsibility that was evident from his reports, C indignantly exclaimed, "I'm reporting, aren't I?" It was as though reporting absolved him from criticism and correction.

It was obvious that C's meticulous reports would be worthless if the change process ended with reporting. Later failure to implement correctives showed that C had not learned from the errors that the report revealed.

It is especially difficult to obtain thoughtful reports from those criminals who have never been particularly reflective. Of course, like everyone else, they have a stream of thought. But it takes some special training in thinking about thinking for them to observe their thinking, retain it for the next day's meeting, and promptly implement the correctives.

Another obstacle to establishing a wide-open channel is assent. The criminal sometimes agrees with what is said merely to terminate discussion or avoid an argument. The criminal is unused to open and polite disagreement. The opposite of assent is argument for its own sake, in which criminal pride prevents him from agreeing with us on the spot. Argument is preferred to assent, because through argument we are more likely to learn where a criminal stands. Part of the training in opening the channel is having the criminal state his own position candidly and then actively listen to and consider the opinions of others.

Despite our early disposal of sociologic and psychologic excuses, the criminal still attempts to use them. When they finally are eliminated, the criminal tries to feed us what he thinks we want to hear by seeming to adopt our way of looking at things. Feeding others is automatic; he has successfully done it all his life.

"[There is] the trend to adopt your terminology whole hog both to avoid thinking for myself and to ingratiate. For example, it's easier to talk about developing a 'responsible life' than to discuss exactly what kind of a life it is you're trying to construct. This was a technique I used with great success in college—find out what the teacher wants and then give it to him—in his terms if possible. It's one of the signs of my con."

A major problem is that the criminal questions why he should be subjected to this prolonged, rigorous, and very dull method of change that we have promulgated. He acknowledges that there is merit to much of what we say about him, but he still believes that he is inherently a good person and asks why a decent fellow like him should have to go through all this.

"You shouldn't paint a completely dark picture of me. There are a few good spots here and there. I still have some decency in me. You need a true picture of me."

All along he may be thinking that he needs to change only a particular pattern, usually the one that resulted in his arrest. He does not realize that the problem is the whole person, not a particular criminal pattern. The child molester, for example, requires attention to more than his sexual patterns. In molesting children, he has schemed, conned, lied, stolen, threatened, and assaulted. In both thought and action, he has committed crimes other than child molestation. Even when the criminal understands this, he believes that crimelessness constitutes change. When he finally does see that a process of "rebirth" is required, it is a terrible blow. One criminal who came to this recognition at the age of forty-five recalled his resistance:

"I saw how much of me had to be changed. You have to give up your entire being. It was like dying and coming back to life. If I gave up everything, I wouldn't know anything. At least [in crime], I had something."

The criminal truly has to begin life all over again. The patterns of thinking that he has to learn are so foreign and the tasks so new that the change process is like "a visit to another planet," as one criminal expressed it.

All the criminal's thinking errors are obstacles to change. He makes himself the victim of his past and of his feelings. He is untrusting and untrustworthy. He does not view himself as obligated to anyone, not even us and the courts. He acts as though others are obligated to him, including us and the members of the group. He fails to consider the point of view of anyone other than those who agree with him. He regards himself as unique; therefore what applies to others is not applicable to him. His failure to think in long-range terms is a tremendous impediment to change. He automatically uses all the tactics described in chapter 8 of volume 1, such as calculated vagueness, silence, minimization, diversion, selective attention, and so on. All the features described in volume 1 must be corrected—a truly massive undertaking.

Once he hears his criminal patterns delineated and grasps a few of our concepts, the criminal believes that he has achieved total insight. Superoptimism rides high. He is certain that change will be easy and that he can accomplish it faster and better than anyone else. Periodically, he thinks that he has the key to change.

Our program encompasses all the features of a complex personality. No single factor or concept is the key to change. Each aspect of the program is like a component of a machine. Every part of the machine must function, or the machine will not operate. The criminal does not understand the magnitude of the change enterprise or of its specific requirements until he has had experience in implementing new patterns. Useful knowledge is a product of *doing*, not of talk in an office.

To have any chance of success, the criminal must begin by participating for three hours a day for at least a year. For years, we tried to do the job in less time, but were minimally successful.

C stated that, because of his family situation and job requirements, he could not attend meetings every day. He said that he would be at our office a minimum of 3 days a week and more often when it was feasible. C was under court order to participate. At first, he attended regularly, but never for more than one-and-a-half hours at a time. Problems then arose at work that made it impossible to adhere to any regular schedule. C phoned conscientiously whenever he was going to be late or could not attend. Gradually, he reduced the total number of hours he was present. We were pleasantly surprised, however, at how well C seemed to be doing. He seemed to be showing an extraordinary degree of determination to change and appeared to grasp well whatever we were able to teach him in the limited time available. Unfortunately, we were unable to obtain outside corroboration of his progress. C said that his wife did not want to meet with us and that his mother was too ill to do so. Nevertheless, C continued to impress us by attending meetings whenever possible, despite serious illnesses in the family. Eventually, C's attendance had dropped to once a week for about an hour. He apologetically said that circumstances were such that attendance was becoming more and more difficult. Although we wondered how C could be doing so well when he had not had the same intensive exposure that all the other criminals had had, we began to think that C was truly exceptional in his determination. We knew that there was much material we had not even touched on, but C seemed not only to have shut the door on violation, but to have amazingly little criminal thinking.

There was a period in which C had a number of illnesses, including pneumonia. For several weeks, he was incapacitated. Shortly after his return, C related a series of encounters between him and his landlord that strongly suggested that trouble was brewing. However, C appeared resolved to handle the situation responsibly. There was another interval—this time several days—in which we did not hear from C. We received a call from his probation officer informing us that C had been charged with the assault of his landlord.

C was ordered by the court to return to our program and attend daily. Only then did we begin to see that, because we had not had the proper opportunity to monitor C's thinking, a great deal of it had not come to light. In later sessions, we found that we were dealing with an unchanged criminal.

This was not wholly a con job by C. He did learn some of the correctives for thinking errors, and, for several months, these had provided deterrents to violation. However, we had not had the time to go through the extensive process of hearing detailed reports and introducing the bulk of the corrective concepts necessary to eliminate criminal thinking. C was no exception; like all the others, he needed the total program.

It may be difficult for others to understand how the criminal can make a *commitment* to a change process of which he is totally ignorant or a commitment to a way of life that he has rejected. The answer is that at the outset he does not truly make a commitment to change. Before a person can know whether he wants to change from one kind of life to another, he must experience something of both. A decision to become responsible is not the same as a commitment. At best, it is a tentative choice prompted either by a temporary sense of futility about life as it has been or by despair about the future. We do not call this motivation, because genuine motivation for change develops only after one has had experiences in change. There is little zest or enthusiasm (except whatever is temporarily generated in the honeymoon phase). Contrary to his desires, the criminal is required to make efforts to become an ordinary, responsible person, instead of the powerful, unique number one that he thinks he has been. Until he experiences what that new life has to offer, there can be no commitment. Education and implementation come first; then the commitment and motivation for change follow.

We dispel most of the criminal's ideas about change. Having had no experience in living responsibly, the criminal has little choice but to place his life in others' hands. In the absence of his own experience, he must rely on the judgment of the A.C., who, if nothing else, is experienced in responsible living. The criminal does not want to put his life in anyone else's hands, but at this point in his life when there is little alternative, he has to have a degree of faith. Whether that faith is well placed, each criminal eventually decides for himself.

The obstacles are many. The task is onerous. Everything is new to the criminal who enters a program that will make him the kind of person he has not wanted to be. From the outset, we are aware of the ever-present possibility that the criminal wants to score points. Although he does not understand much of what change will entail, he does understand that there is a set of conditions attached to his acceptance in this program. There must be an understanding between us, the criminal, and the law. The criminal knows that we will not shield him from the law if he chooses to continue his former style of life. We do maintain privileged communication; but the criminal knows that if he does not cooperate, we shall report this lack of cooperation to whoever has custody of him—for example, his parole or probation officer. When criminals enter the program voluntarily, we warn them that those who have not come to us through the courts have found the program not to be what they wanted and have dropped out. We do not exclude voluntary participants, but we have little expectation that they will persevere. Of course, one can make this a self-fulfilling prophecy by announcing that he expects these criminals to fail. Our acceptance of voluntary participants in the program is combined with a statement that we know that every criminal is *capable* of change, that we shall provide them with the means of changing, and that it is entirely up to them whether they do in fact change.

Probation and parole officers have been eager for a criminal to participate in a serious program that so closely monitors his thinking and action. Their follow-up, in most cases, is perfunctory, because of a large caseload. With our assumption of the task, their supervision becomes even more perfunctory. In some cases, we have not been contacted for years by these officers. In fact, probation terms have expired without our being notified and with the criminal not being seen at termination by his probation officer. When we have initiated contact, however, these officials have been most cooperative.

Our attitude, stated at the beginning and reiterated throughout the program, is that it is the criminal's life that is at stake, not ours.

THE HONEYMOON

At the outset, the criminal is attentive, enters into discussion, shows a desire to learn, and makes an effort. There is initial excitement in this new change process. The criminal believes that change will be easy, and he is certain that he will outperform the other members of the group. He will be the best reporter, the most insightful participant, and the most successful at implementation.

He has entered a group in which the other criminals are already trained in reporting and have had various degrees of exposure to our corrective concepts. Every time he opens his mouth, others point out errors that he is making. This is not a putdown to him, however. When he sees others accepting criticism, he realizes that he must do the same, as well as be critical of himself. The criminal's curiosity is whetted, and he is stimulated by the idea that there is so much to learn. In the group meetings, he is attentive and diligent. He writes down his thoughts and is alive with ideas.

> "I see more deeply when I write than when we talk, and the writing stimulates my thinking and primes my imagination. And it contributes to our discussions by giving me new ideas or variations on old ones so that sometimes, like today, I'm just bursting with things I want to talk over with you."

The criminal grows superoptimistic as he comes to believe that he knows what change is all about. He talks enthusiastically of the program to others and even tries to recruit some of his criminal associates. He thinks that he can teach others to become responsible. Acting with a fervor sometimes approaching missionary zeal, he tries to inform others in the group and outside of his discoveries. This is a nonarrestable power thrust—a criminal equivalent. Once the criminal grasps one small point, he thinks that he has mastered everything. Superoptimism grows as long as the criminal refrains from arrestable acts. The honeymoon usually is characterized by an absence of violations and a reduction in criminal thinking. We counter the superoptimism by identifying thinking errors and pointing out past instances in which these have contributed to injuring others. The criminal is repeatedly reminded that his current superoptimism about success in changing is the same superoptimism that contributed to his arrests.

Like all other honeymoons, this one ends eventually. The first flush of excitement wears off, and then the criminal finds the pace grueling and tedious. He realizes that he is starting at the bottom, not just vocationally, but in every other way. There is nothing exciting about subjecting one's thinking to microscopic examination and criticism by others day after day. There is nothing exciting about working as a busboy or being without a girlfriend. One man stated that he knew a rope would be put around his neck when he came to us. However, that rope was drawn tighter than he had expected.

> "I am dissatisfied with everything. I am dissatisfied with myself because I am in this situation. This is the lesser of two evils. It is better than what I had. I don't want to live the way I was living. It really is a prison either way, depending on how you look at it. [This program] is my prison."

Another criminal commented that everything is suicide: criminality, responsible living, and suicide itself—all are forms of suicide.

As the criminal becomes disenchanted with the program, the channel closes. He participates less. He comes late or asks to leave early. His notes for his reports are increasingly sketchy. If he remains conscientious about reporting, he is smug, expects the group to be satisfied with a complete accounting of his twenty-four hours, and then considers that his obligation is fulfilled and that no further change is needed.

Instead of being self-critical, the criminal starts to complain and criticize us as well as others: we are rigid, unrealistic, not at all understanding. We hear such statements as, "I'm at the bottom," "I am stuck," "Now I'm in the worst jail I've ever been in." There is a strong desire for action, and the criminal is bucking the restraints of the program. The initial impact of the program does not begin to equal the impact of crime. It is at this point that the voluntary participant is likely to drop out. The criminal legally bound to the program sloughs off as far as enthusiasm and participation are concerned.

Early in the development of this program, we observed the rapid ups and downs of the fragmented criminal and asked him, "Who are you today?" Now we expect these ups and downs. We know who he is—a person with a rapidly changing mind who shifts frequently in his stance about how he wants to live.

Within a few days, C, who was chafing at the program's restraints, expressed a number of different preferences as to how he wanted to live. First, he spoke ardently of living as a recluse high in the mountains; the appeal to him of a monastic existence was strong. He then talked about committing a series of major crimes, such a hijacking a 747 airliner. C then said that he did not want a life of crime, only enough excitement to keep life interesting—a "wine, women, and drugs" ideal, without any program for change to dictate to him what he could and could not do. C finally opted for the second alternative. He commited serious felonies and was apprehended and confined.

The idea of extreme and permanent self-denial now appears absurd to the criminal. He often says to himself about a particular infraction, "I'll have to stop this for a while, and then everything will be all right." The major issue for the criminal is whether or not to surrender fully to another person and to adopt a way of life totally foreign to him. This question is expressed in many forms. Often, it is a claim that we are turning him into a robot or into a replica of ourselves. Sometimes it is simply stated, "I don't want to be a goody-goody." Obviously, the basic issue is not perceived accurately. To surrender to the program is only to implement its precepts and thereby to become responsible. All his life, the criminal has refused to submit to others' guidance, wisdom, or authority. To submit to anyone reduces him to a slave; it emasculates him and makes him a nothing. Now, however, the criminal's life is on the line.

As the honeymoon is ending, the criminal begins to think that he can take liberties with the program. Because he is not arrestable, he is superoptimistic about the degree of change that has occurred. So he decides that he can skip one meeting, tell a small lie, take a drink, pick up a prostitute. Warnings from us about the absolute necessity of deterring even the thought of the smallest violation go largely unheeded. The criminal learns from experience, not from exhortations and warnings. By this time, the criminal has been exposed to enough of our ideas to have deterred major violations. Having come this far, he sees no need to be straitjacketed by the program.

> C attended a conference out of town. He decided that a drink would not harm him, so he invited a young woman to join him. One drink led to another, and the two wound up in bed. Following this incident, there was a desire for drugs and more sex with the same person. C knew that drugs were "poison" (D1) and did not seek them. Returning from the conference, C thought about how betrayed his wife and children would feel if they found out. With some astonishment, he realized how rapidly he had wiped the program out of his mind.

We have seen countless similar instances in which the criminal decided to take exception to the program's requirements. The understanding that he gains from life's experience is more convincing than any argument we can muster about the necessity of *total* implementation.

It is important that the A.C. not be misled by the harmony of the honeymoon. At times we believed that a criminal was doing so well that we expressed our approval of him and even showed him off to others. Soon thereafter, we found that basic change had not occurred. We had been thrown off by the honeymoon. The change process had, in fact, only begun.

Although at the start the criminal is doing what he is supposed to, the honeymoon itself is no prognostic indicator of ultimate change. There still is absolutely no belief by the criminal that change must be pursued for its own sake. By satisfying others, he can achieve his objectives. He believes that change is easy and, as in everything else, he wants to be number one. As the honeymoon comes to an end, it is apparent that basic criminal patterns are still operative. There is an increase in criminal thinking, and the criminal lacks the tools to deal with it. Furthermore, he still believes that a state of crimelessness constitutes basic change.

What the criminal lacks early in the program is a view that change is a life-and-death matter. So long as he does not regard this program as his life line, he is not *serious* about making the effort to change. There is no commitment, and so he is unwilling to endure the tedium and self-denial that are necessary. The self-pity, the boredom, the despair, and the sense of suffering are minimized when a criminal truly believes that this program is his only means of saving himself.

The criminal does not use the phrase *life line*; this is our term. He refers, instead, to the alternative to change as "death" or "prison." The "life line" view is not adopted on the basis of what we say. It certainly is not established in the initial contact, but is arrived at gradually with implementation.

Some criminals end the honeymoon with a divorce. They quit and do not return, although some do keep in contact with us. More often, criminals who have left the program return after they find themselves in difficulty and are again fed up with their way of life. These criminals generally continue in the program indefinitely. Divorce or separation can be prevei.ted only by the continuing exercise of authority by the court.

Not all criminals go through a honeymoon. Some contest us from the beginning. In only one case has there been sustained cooperation throughout. This was by a criminal who took the program very seriously from the outset. He had his doubts about the program's requirements and, like others, feared changing. However, he had made a choice not to return to the living death of crime. He implemented that choice right from the start, and although he made mistakes while learning to be responsible, he never sought criminal excitement. The fact that one person tenaciously adhered to this program's requirements from the start and never violated showed at least that it could be done and that the honeymoon phenomenon is not inevitable.

Incarcerated in Saint Elizabeths maximum security for an indefinite period, and with his career in shambles, and his wife about to leave him, C had reached the depths of despair. It was in this state that we found him. As we described what would be to him a long, unrelenting struggle, C was staggered by "the sheer volume of what's involved." But he realized that, without basic changes in himself, he could envision his life stretching before him as a series of jails and hospitals. He regarded himself as a passenger on a sinking ship, rapidly going down. He thought Why argue with the captain who has a plan for rescue?

C had his doubts and dissatisfactions with the program. Sometimes, he thought that there was little reason to work so hard without any guarantee that he would like what he would become more than he liked himself as a criminal. But C had ruled out being a criminal and had also ruled out suicide. There was no alternative, other than change.

C found the new life to be alien and strenuous. It required effort and endurance that he was not accustomed to. As his determination grew, there was less of a sense of struggle or suffering. The ship was going down; there was only one way out. The program was a life line, and it remained so in his thinking ever after.

ESTABLISHING THE LIFELINE

INTENSIFYING AND SUSTAINING SELF-DISGUST

The degree to which a criminal regards the program as a life line is in part a function of the intensity of his self-disgust. There cannot be either a choice or a commitment to change without self-disgust. Usually the form of the self-disgust is cognitive at first. In this program, we are not influenced by feelings but rely on the reasoning process from which is derived a sustained view of oneself as an injuring person and a failure in life—a criminal. There needs to be a continuing appraisal by the criminal of himself as no good. Self-disgust is not based on the self-deception of zero state thinking; rather it is a self-evaluation based on the facts of one's past.

"You pointed out so vividly things I wouldn't look at. These were exactly the things I have wanted to forget."

To achieve self-disgust, the criminal's fear must be elicited by the A.C. and other group members. This is done unremittingly. A vivid picture of his sordid past makes the criminal fear what he might do to others and to himself, now and in the future. Although he is not sweating and shuddering, fear is present. In some criminals, the self-disgust remains cognitive throughout change. But, in most, there eventually are visceral concomitants. When emotional concomitants of self-disgust are present, we do not discourage them. Criminals have reported wanting to vomit when the dregs of old patterns have been brought up for review. One criminal was sickened by the thought of the smell of the burning sulfur from matches used for cooking drugs. Another criminal felt ill as he thought of the stench of musty "adult bookstores" where he had spent a great deal of time recharging his rape-homicide fantasies. As we pointed out in the preceding chapter, some criminals think in images. These can be extremely powerful in reinforcing self-disgust.

After several sessions of reviewing past patterns, C had imagined the image of a spider and a web. He pictured himself caught in the web with the spider attacking. This produced an experience of such helplessness and panic that he was almost physically sick. He knew that this symbolized his being picked apart in the early meetings with the A.C. However, he was well aware that, throughout his life, the roles had been reversed. He had been the spider trapping innocent victims in his web.

The terror of being in either role—victim or victimizer—was extremely disturbing. C thought it strange that he could jump from one extreme to another—from spider to victim. We pointed out that it was characteristic of every criminal to think in simplistic extremes. For him not to be the spider meant only that he could be a victim; in this program's self-evaluation process, he was no victim. It was suggested that C could develop the concept of himself as the spider without the accompanying terror. It was essential that he adopt a view of himself as a victimizer. If he were fed up with this role, then he could set his sights on becoming a constructive, responsible person.

The perspective that we establish is that even dozens of good deeds do not cancel out one crime. No matter how many good features the criminal has, they are eclipsed by his criminality. In fact, the criminal's assets eventually serve as factors in self-disgust, because they have been used criminally. A bright mind or a particular skill or aptitude has been utilized in the service of criminal objectives. Although society acknowledges the criminal's intelligence, his behavior is usually adjudged stupid. A review of his life demonstrates that he has nothing to show except years of disappointing and injuring others and jeopardizing himself. One criminal who used his considerable intelligence successfully in crime but who wound up in jail, observed:

"My life has proven that I'm not too intelligent. I'm one of life's failures any way you rack it up."

It is difficult to determine the extent of self-disgust accurately when a reward-punishment factor is operating. At issue is how one can assess the genuineness of self-disgust when the criminal is trying to avoid confinement by being in a program that views self-disgust as vital to change. The criminal might feign self-disgust while having every intention of continuing his criminality. The problem is in the same category as How do you know whether the criminal is telling the truth? As we have stated previously, an A.C. does not know definitely. However, this is an intensive program and requires participation for a long time. If the criminal's self-disgust is temporary or fraudulent, this will be revealed *in time* by his tactics, by his reporting, and ultimately by his failure to implement.

Self-disgust becomes more intense as the criminal has more responsible experiences enabling him to contrast life now and in the past. Current experiences present occasions for moral inventories of the past. Self-disgust is sustained by repeated moral inventories that reach far back into the criminal's life. In turn, the mounting self-disgust prompts more implementation and learning. The process snowballs. For example, the more thoughtfully the criminal treats his wife, the more harmonious and gratifying is the relationship. As the criminal reports the details of the transactions between him and his wife, there is an increasingly sharp contrast between his present affection and consideration and his former control and abuse. He is struck for the first time by the pervasive criminality of his earlier relationship.

When old patterns persist, we provide a perspective that will increase self-disgust and preempts their repetition.

> C flared up at his wife for buying the wrong thing at the store. He complained about her stupidity and said that she never did things right. At this point in his report, we asked C to compose a mental balance sheet comparing her integrity and fidelity in life with his. We then asked him to put himself in the place of the judge hearing a divorce case involving him and his wife. C quickly realized that there would be little to say in his favor. He said that it was absurd even to begin to compare his wife's devotion and loyalty with the way he had acted during the course of their marriage.

Whether such discussions are of ultimate value can be evaluated only by how the criminal acts in the future. Will he again get angry if his wife makes some minor mistake? *Self-disgust is worthless unless it preempts repetition of criminal patterns of thought and action.*

With rising self-disgust, there is a reaffirmation of the basic choice to change and a strengthening of will (endurance). The criminal is prompted to do even more to improve his relationship with other people. Furthermore, a strong sense of self-disgust is vital to the self-respect that he will eventually experience as a responsible person.

SELF-DENIAL

Self-denial is required by this program. In exercising effort in the course of change, the criminal must refrain from doing many things that he wants to do and must do even more things that he dislikes doing. He must sever ties with criminal associates. He must not engage in sex during the early phase of the program (except with his wife, if he is married). Spending money in his customary manner is interdicted. He is not to engage in talk about crime. He is denied the secrecy that has been so important to him, but instead is held strictly accountable for his every thought and action. He must deter anger. He must monitor his thinking and must not lie. He is not to ignore criticism, but instead he must seriously evaluate it. He is even denied the pleasures of criminal fantasy. By far the major self-denial is the elimination of criminal excitement. The criminal has made a choice. Now he has to endure the consequences of that choice—the exercise of will.

One criminal said that the self-denial required in this program is worse than the agony that he suffered undergoing withdrawal from drugs. After the criminal's initial superoptimism and the harmony of the honeymoon, he finds the change process excruciatingly slow; every step seems a monumental undertaking. With the absence of excitement, the criminal thinks that he is on a treadmill to oblivion or that he is engaged in a task similar to rolling a boulder endlessly up a mountain. He is angry, bored, and depressed and has psychosomatic symptoms. Nothing in life gives him satisfaction—not his family, not his job, not this program.

When self-denial is protested, the honeymoon may draw to an end. Early in the change process, a crisis occurs whenever the criminal insists on something that he wants that is imprudent, short-sighted, or irrelevant. Later in the change process, this does not occur.

For the first time in the first two months of this program, C failed to disclose an important event. He informed us later that he had inquired about a used car that was for sale. Eleven years old, it had a blue book value of $250. The owner had improved it, replacing the motor, and was asking $350. C learned that insurance would cost $300.

Realizing that we would object to such an expenditure, C was angry before ever mentioning it to us. At work, he was careless and inefficient, spilling a load of dishes. At the meeting with us, he was argumentative and sullen. C insisted that he could afford the car. He contended that he was employed and was expecting social security payments for the next nine months.

Could he afford the car? He had entrusted us with all his money—$920. To spend $650 for the car and insurance would leave him with $270. He had applied for an apartment that required a security deposit, the first month's rent, and furnishings. He would then be in debt.

This program requires economy, budgeting, and long-range planning. C had not done any comparison shopping. Others in this program with better paying jobs were managing without a car. They had financial reserves and could meet emergencies. It was pointless to hold C's money were he to demand it for imprudent expenditures. The desire for a car was an old pattern—I want what I want when I want it—preferring luxuries to necessities. He had been accustomed to new cars. In the past, for example, he had criminally acquired a new automobile by conning a woman. We did not endorse him to his probation officer as totally implementing this program.

C was initially silent, self-pitying, and angry. The following day, he agreed with our assessment. There was no evidence of a continuing desire for the car.*

When the criminal longs for past criminal excitements but restrains himself from criminal action, he experiences such psychosomatic symptoms as dizziness, headaches, gastrointestinal distress, palpitations, and sweating. As change agents, we offer no sympathy, because we believe that it is preferable for the criminal to live with his symptoms than to violate. We know that he can find instant relief by seeking excitement.

> C complained of headaches, dizziness, and general tension. One Friday, he left our office and went to visit a woman whom he had started to flirt with at work. He planned to spend only a short time at her place, but instead stayed the whole night without notifying his wife that he would not be home. C and the woman spent the evening talking and drinking and then had sex. When he returned home Saturday morning, he snidely replied to his wife's queries, "I was screwing fifty thousand women." Meeting with us early the next week, C observed, "I had surprisingly little tension over the weekend."

C's relief from physical distress was no surprise to us. In contrast, another criminal decided that despite severe psychosomatic symptoms, he would stay home and practice restraint over the weekend. This man stated on Monday morning that he had had only a few hours of sleep and spent much time crying but was refreshed and had experienced something new—a "sense of cleanliness."

We do not prescribe or suggest medication for relief of psychosomatic distress** since they attack only the symptom and not the basis. We have seen criminals who have taken various medications. The thinking responsible for the distress has not changed, no matter what drug was prescribed. The most potent antidote consists of telling the truth, correcting thinking errors, and adopting a different perspective. A criminal can reduce the incidence and intensity of psychosomatic reactions by scaling down his expectations and pretensions. When he meets life's realities responsibly, such reactions are alleviated.

> C came to the meeting in great distress. He had a severe headache, was worried about his blood pressure, and was experiencing dizziness. We spent several hours with C in discussing his unrealistic expectations about his work, family, and friends. In this context, we hammered away at how

---

*If crises of this nature persist, they indicate that the criminal is not implementing the program.
**Only when a criminal is well along in change do we recommend a mild tranquilizer for relief from tension.

one must learn to endure situations that cannot be changed and how Murphy's Law must always be reckoned with. We pointed out that a calm, rational approach is an absolute necessity for problem-solving and progress. C stated that recognizing reality and dealing with it were not palatable to him. After this long meeting in which we tried to provide some perspective, C reported an almost immediate disappearance of symptoms.

The more the criminal implements the program in his thinking and actions, the less his psychosomatic reactions recur.

The state of self-pity, always accompanied by anger, arises because the criminal perceives his life to be going badly. He blames us for requiring him to make the decision to change. He begins to doubt that he chose wisely. Yet, he is trapped, because he has ruled out a return to crime. Feeling sorry for himself, he takes few initiatives; and his performance in most of his undertakings is of poor quality. It is as if he were awaiting proof from others that he has made the right choice. The world does not give him what he wants and does not accord him the recognition that he believes he deserves. The criminal's frustration and anger become generalized. Conditions of life that may once have been acceptable are no longer so.

One day of anger and self-pity had to do initially with school. C had had an examination in laboratory science that required identification and description of slides. The one minute allotted per slide for the lab exam was not enough for him. He was angry at having insufficient time. He was especially frustrated, because he knew that he would score low and no longer rank at the top of the class. Then he wondered why he should bother at all with school. He returned to his ward at the hospital (he had "released time" for school) and just missed lunch. There was more anger. C started to boil inwardly at having to put up with living at the hospital. His resentment mounted, as he thought about the severe restraints that our program was placing on him. That morning, as C left for school, he was questioning the merits of the whole change enterprise and feeling sorry for himself, because he was living what he called an "antiseptic life." In this state of self-pity, anything was a potential target for anger. The exam had been such a target, and then, like an uncontained fire, that anger had spread. In a different frame of mind, C had been pleased to be permitted to attend school and was not especially critical of the ward living conditions. Furthermore, he had regarded this program as enabling him to achieve a new kind of personal freedom, not as imprisoning him.

A long-range perspective is repeatedly invoked when the criminal is chafing under the restraints of responsibility and its self-denial. His thinking that he might not be suited to this kind of life often leads to philosophic discussions. The following typifies the position that we take:

> "You made a choice to change, because you rejected the alternatives of crime and suicide. You are now afraid of failure. You will make mistakes in the course of change; these are not putdowns. Just as pencils have erasers so that mistakes can be corrected, you can correct your mistakes. It is a question of whether you learn from your mistakes. You will find limitations in yourself and others. Do you expect a world where things go perfectly? Will you spend your life trying to control others and becoming angry and vindicative when you cannot? Or will you endure what you cannot change and do the best you can? You complain about meaninglessness, but life is not automatically imbued with meaning. It takes effort to accomplish something worthwhile and thereby make life satisfying and meaningful. The first goal is change; with change, other goals will emerge. Long-range thinking is a necessary part of change."

Many variations on these themes are covered, as are other points designed to teach the criminal the importance of maintaining a long-range perspective. This may strike the reader as preaching. However, when these considerations are introduced in the context of daily events, they are immediate and real, not abstract pronouncements. Time and again, we return to the basics of choice and will and confront the criminal with the question of what kind of life he wants to live. This long-range view helps him to keep his eye on basic issues and not be diverted by the momentary trials of self-denial and self-pity. It is a perspective that is mandatory if he is truly to regard this program as his life line.

THE PRIMACY OF IMPLEMENTATION

> It is well said, then, that it is by *doing* just acts that the just man is produced, and by *doing* temperate acts the temperate man; without doing these no one would even have a prospect of becoming good. But most people do not *do* these, but take refuge in theory and think they are being philosophers and will become good in this way, behaving somewhat like patients who listen attentively to their doctors, but *do* none of the things they are ordered to do. As the latter will not be made well in body by such a course of treatment, the former will not be made well in soul by such a course in philosophy. (Aristotle, p. 351, italics added)

The "life line" concept is not adopted as a consequence of the A.C.'s preaching. It is adopted only as a criminal implements the program and has the opportunity to contrast responsible living with his former life. In the early phase of our work, we were encouraged by our belief that the criminal understood the ideas we were presenting. However, we soon learned that his understanding was concrete, not conceptual. He understood postmortem evaluations of specific situations, and we thought that the insight derived was indicative of change. This conclusion was short-lived: we saw criminals with insight violating as much as criminals without such insight. Clearly, there was an enormous gap between understanding (insight) and change.* We found that superoptimism contributed greatly to this. Once the criminal thought that he understood what needed to be done in order to change, he regarded it as already accomplished. Therefore, he did not generate initiatives to change and exerted no effort in behalf of change. The insight gained in the office was worthless because it was not translated into constructive action. Change could occur only through implementation, not through words spoken in our office. That is, a criminal could not truly comprehend responsible living without trying it.

In this program, three types of implementation are required. The first is in *reporting*—total disclosure, receptivity, and self-criticism. The second is in *alteration of thinking*. A criminal may fulfill all the requirements of phenomenologic reporting (the wide-open channel), but not practice the new thinking required in all forms of deterrence, particularly the moral inventory. The report is of no value if it has not led to more and more corrective thinking. Finally, there is the *activation of all the correctives* in changed thought and responsible action. Without this implementation, the most excellent report and the most reflective thinking are valueless, and the change process becomes merely token, rather than effective.

In this program, decisions are based on reason. Reason does not require great intellectual ability or a knowledge of the arts, philosophy, or literature. Many responsible people, even of less than average intelligence, think rationally and exercise sound judgment in their daily behavior. The use of reason differs from rationalization, which merely justifies what one thinks, feels, or does.

In this program, feeling is subordinate to reason. Without reason, the criminal resorts to feelings to justify any departure from the program's

---

*Despite the fact that the criminal knows from the outset that we rule out searching for insight into the causes of his criminality, he occasionally reverts to causal explanations in an attempt to provide excuses for his behavior. Because this is so automatic, it happens even when he is advanced in the change process. He returns to explaining *why* something came about, once in a while reverting in sophisticated fashion to unconscious processes for explanation. Any attempt to derive causation in this way diverts the criminal from the self-discipline required in implementing this program, because he expects that insight will lead to a miracle—that is, understanding by itself will produce a change. Then he relies excessively on the A.C. to produce change in him, rather than shouldering the burden of change himself.

requirements. Recourse to such feelings obscures issues, divests him of responsibility, and is used by him to avoid facing current problems. Feelings, of course, are present, and sometimes intense, but there is great danger in allowing them to determine decisions. The fragmented criminal vacillates in his feeling about change. The danger in the criminal's responding primarily to feelings is that, to escape the lows of responsibility's drudgery, he will cut off the program and return to the highs of criminal excitement.

Our experience in all cases has been that the criminal reports that after he changes his thinking and puts the new thinking to work, there is indeed a change in feelings. For example, if he decides to act tenderly toward his wife and actually does so, he eventually experiences stronger feelings of affection and tenderness. The tenderness that may have seemed contrived to him at first in time becomes a genuine feeling. When he decides to work on a project that he thinks is dull but permits himself to become immersed in it, he often feels differently about it. As a consequence of *doing*, the criminal learns both about himself and about the outside world. The insight and new feelings *follow* change.

A critical aspect of implementation is deterrence of criminal thinking and action. We introduce D1 (it's dangerous) and D2 (reasoning) as early as possible and, soon after, bring in D3 (preemptive deterrence) and D4 (the moral inventory). The introduction of deterrent considerations is, of course, geared to the material presented in the phenomenologic report.

In understanding deterrence, it is necessary to differentiate between a violation and a mistake. A *violation* is the outcome of criminal thinking. The criminal might be arrested, but there are also nonarrestable violations for which he might be held accountable, such as telling a lie. Deterrence is to be applied to all thinking or action that results in violation. In contrast, a *mistake* results from the criminal's lack of experience in the responsible world, as an unknowing child burns his finger when he touches a hot stove for the first time. The criminal makes hundreds of mistakes as he awkwardly tries to act in a manner new to him. It is not possible to deter mistakes any more than it is possible to prevent an infant from taking a few falls as he learns to walk.

As the criminal progresses in change, the major issue in deciding whether to deter an act is less a matter of personal jeopardy than of, Is it right? The objective is to be a person of integrity, rather than merely one who is not in danger of arrest.

C was feeling sorry for himself because he was still in confinement, without a girlfriend, and with no excitement in life. Having grounds privileges, he was out for a walk one day and encountered a man he knew who offered him drugs. Through C's mind flashed the memory of his last drug-taking and how disgused he was with himself afterward. He turned away and returned to his ward, saying to himself, "No violation." On the ward, he began reading his notes taken during the last few weeks of group meetings. He thought about how much he had progressed and realized that it would be a personal defeat for him to deviate from the program now or in the future. He also thought about what drugs had led to in the past—his injury to other people, his wife's leaving him, and his poor health. Finally, he wrote an account of the afternoon's thinking for presentation the next day in the group.

The emphasis here was not "I might get caught" (D1). In fact, this did not even cross C's mind. Instead, there was a quick experience of self-disgust, followed by an examination of conscience (D4).

Even when the criminal has shut the door on crime, the *thought* of a crime still may produce excitement. As one criminal put it, "You're always finding things to make up for what you just gave up."

C walked by a junkyard. He thought of old times when he totally rebuilt a car from parts he stole from junkyards. As he walked past this place from which he had stolen, there was no thought of stealing anything. However, he reported that thinking about past thefts gave him a "charge."

The act of stealing was not at issue, but a residue of the old criminal excitement emerged in C's thinking. There was a discussion in the group of the necessity of preempting criminal thinking, as well as a review of the injury that C had inflicted on others by his stealing.

In a later incident, C passed a store from which he had stolen. This time, there was a fleeting "charge" from the idea of stealing. As he continued on his way, C experienced disgust for having had such a thought and even greater disgust for having found the thought exciting.

There was an improvement, in that C did not dwell on memories of past crimes and savor them. However, the fleeting criminal excitement had not yet totally disappeared. Making more and more examinations of conscience intensified self-disgust and strengthened a mental set, so that criminal thinking did not appear at all in such situations in the future. The mental set formed was one in which C was determined that when he encountered situations comparable to that at the junkyard, he would redirect his thoughts elsewhere. In time, such contrived redirection was unnecessary, because C had established a firm moral base; to memories of past crimes, C responded with the same disgust as a responsible person.

The important feature of deterrence is that it is an *active process*. It requires training, implementation, and discipline. We cannot assume that a criminal will change merely because he has made moral inventories. The lessons of such inventories must be put into action; they must become part of a mental set against criminal thinking and action. In time, with the correctives for thinking errors, these deterrents operate automatically. One criminal described succinctly the eventual automaticity of deterrence when he stated, "I can deter a thought before I can truly say I've had it." That is, the mental set is so firmly entrenched that deterrence no longer requires effort—it just happens.

Optimal implementation of this program must occur against the background of a total rejection of all criminal thinking and action. If a criminal is implementing our program but at the same time has recurrent, irresponsible thinking, the speed of implementation invariably suffers. If a criminal has unequivocally rejected criminal thinking and action, he then surmounts adversities that arise both on the job and everywhere else. However, if he is actively deterring criminal thinking, he reacts to adversities irresponsibly rather than constructively.

THE DISCIPLINE REQUIRED IN CHANGE

C chose to learn tennis, a game in which he was totally inexperienced. He applied himself diligently to it, reading about it, watching others play on the hospital courts, and viewing matches on television. C practiced daily, sometimes pushing himself to do so when he did not feel like it. He was his own severest critic and tried to catch mistakes. C found that he had to restrain and finally eliminate the anger that occasionally interfered with his performance. He disciplined himself so that women on the courts did not distract him. When he had a bad day, he was persistent enough in his objective not to say to hell with it, but to continue to strive for excellence. Winning became less of a focus, and there was more emphasis on playing to improve.

What C was doing with tennis paralleled what he was doing with the rest of his life. His commitment to a goal grew the more he played. He did not complain or give in to discouragement as he pursued excellence. The self-discipline exerted on the tennis court is typical of what is necessary everywhere. Although *effort* was not necessary here, because C was working at something he wanted, a great deal of *endurance* was demonstrated. Throughout this program, there is continuous stress on both effort and endurance, so that the criminal learns and implements a type of thinking that has been foreign to him.

Above all, this program calls for disciplined responsible thinking and action. The nature of a specific task is usually less important than the discipline it entails. In our daily meetings, we appear at times to be nit-picking as we go into minute detail about what may seem to be relatively trivial issues. It is the discipline involved in attending to the details of daily living that is emphasized over and over, no matter what the context.

Early in the program, the criminal learns that we maintain a firm insistence on self-discipline. To him, this is not only foreign, but unreasonable.

> C made a case for a day off from work. First, he was very tired. He was on the go from 5:30 a.m. until after midnight. Second, he had had no time to do his laundry or stop at the cleaner's. Third, he needed time to look for an apartment. It sounded reasonable that C could productively utilize a day off. However, we asserted to C that in his thinking were ideas of utilizing the time off for break and entry and rape. Readily, C acknowledged that this was indeed the case.

In the early phase of change, we closely scrutinize even the seemingly valid reasons for the criminal's request to depart from his newly established routine. We know that the overriding plausible and obvious choice for the new man in the program is to continue habitual past criminal patterns. In the situation above, we maintained a tough position that gave top priority to a schedule that required both the discipline of long hours of work and attendance at morning meetings with us. At this point, C was required to adhere to the routine and establish self-discipline which he needed more than the day off.

While implementing new patterns of thought and action, the changing criminal establishes intermediate targets along the way. That is, he shoots for particular subgoals. He resolves to save a specified amount of money. He is determined to sell a particular quantity of merchandise at work. He decides to paint his house within a fixed time. The purpose of establishing such subgoals is to lead the criminal to practice self-discipline and to have something concrete by which to gauge accomplishment. To him, specific objectives are milestones on the road to change. However, such achievements in themselves do not constitute change. To look good may be the overriding objective. The criminal has done this all his life, deceiving parents, teachers, employers, and probation officers. Even if a criminal is sincere and not merely scoring points, he may fulfill some subgoals and still be making numerous thinking errors that show up in his decisions and interpersonal relationships.

Some criminals have regarded the work of change as finished when they have achieved tangible accomplishments such as saving a sum of money, selling a quota of merchandise, or completing a household project, or even maintaining a period of nonarrestability. Having become complacent, these men have subsequently spent their savings, sloughed off in job performance, and neglected domestic responsibilities and, ultimately, committed crimes. The fact is that there is no crucial moment in the change process or as one man put it, "no road to Damascus." The process of change requires a steady, plodding elimination of criminal thinking and action patterns and a steady, plodding construction of a responsible way of life. No single accomplishment or feature of the personality is the key to change. All features must be changed concurrently over an extended period.

The changing criminal believes that a responsible life is problemless. He thinks that one need only accomplish a particular objective or set of objectives to have it made. He is surprised and often discouraged when he discovers that as he becomes responsible, he has more worries than he had in crime. Early in change, the criminal begins to realize that a responsible life entails assuming one burden after another.

> C was working long hours because he had to stay to close the restaurant at night. His wife was ill, so he had to drive rather than have her drive him places. Having always feared driving, C dreaded this. He had a limited income, a demanding job, a sick wife, fatigue from too little sleep—and now another problem. In addition, C was deterring the many criminal ideas that came to mind and that he knew, if enacted, would make life once again exciting. In the past, life was simple; there was only one worry—getting caught. Now, he had more problems than ever before.

It does not occur to the criminal that, as long as he lives, there will be problems to solve. The criminal has avoided the disagreeable, expected things to be easy, and insisted on having his way. In this program, he wonders what there is to a life in which one plugs and plugs only to be confronted with more demands. In our initial contacts with the criminal, we warned him that life would not be easy, but he then had no understanding of what we said. Only when he is actually implementing the program does he begin to comprehend what we meant. The necessity of dealing with current problems as effectively as one can and anticipating what lies ahead is, as one man said, "a new concept of life." In the past, he was affronted if it rained when he was going on a picnic. He was insulted if his wife got sick at an inopportune time. Now he learns to accept such events as parts of life. When a criminal has progressed in change, he expects problems and responds to them, not in anger, but with resolve, hard work, and endurance to surmount what he now considers challenges.

> C had done well in working for a particular company and was asked to work at a different branch. He was pleased by the firm's confidence in him and expected to ease into the new job. Arriving there, he found a mountain of problems. The paperwork was chaos, the files unsystematized. The salesmen were new, and most knew nothing about estimating cost for company jobs. C had to work from early in the morning until late at night training office help, accompanying salesmen to job sites,

checking installation of materials, meeting builders, and updating equipment orders. At first, C was overwhelmed because his expectations had been so inaccurate. However, he decided to take each problem as a challenge and handle it responsibly. He established a series of subgoals and strove diligently to reach them, and he did not become demoralized by the magnitude of the overall task.

A plateau in the habituation process denotes complacency, insufficient implementation, and a failure to recognize that in life a constant flow of new problems require solution. In this program, as in life, the emphasis is on the *process* of achieving, not the achievement itself. Once a person accomplishes something, he is ready to move on. The responsible person always has a backlog of goals that he wants to achieve. He is never totally satisfied with his performance, but sees ways to improve. This view of life is new to the changing criminal.

It is mandatory that the criminal program his time, because for him idleness is truly the devil's playground. The following example shows what happens when time is not programmed.

C was progressing in change. He was performing conscientiously at work and was functioning well at home with his wife and children. Occasionally when he had nothing to do, C went up the block to the corner to join some fellows in an informal music group. Most of these people were irresponsible, and some were active in crime. C found that little music was played. Rather, the men hung around talking and drinking. On one of these occasions, C wandered up the block, met the group, began drinking, and then decided to call a woman who he knew from past experience was available for sex. With the prospect of sex, C bought drugs to enhance his performance and then met the girl.

With his time not programmed, C departed substantially from the path of implementing the program that he had been conscientiously following. In change, programming means less likelihood of criminal thinking and action. Of course, the programming of time is itself insufficient. The criminal has to follow through and adhere to the program. Busying oneself, even with the most routine chores, is essential.

On weekdays, C spent ten hours or more at work. Then he came home and cooked and cleaned. Several times a week, he had a date. On the weekends, he had plenty to keep him occupied. He sometimes spent a day at his parents' home, visiting and doing chores—painting, mowing the lawn, working on the car. C reported to us that there was no criminal thinking, because "I am too busy thinking of the things I have to do."

Some criminals expect boredom to disappear when they program their days fully with responsible activity. However, they find that, even though they may be busy all day, they still experience some boredom. Boredom is not relieved simply by programming responsible effort and action. Boredom arises in the first place because of the absence of criminal excitement. A criminal is bored if he does not lie, scheme, steal, search out women, and control others. The key to the elimination of boredom for the criminal is the elimination of criminal thinking and thereby the desire for criminal excitement.

In some cases, it is necessary for the criminal to formulate a time budget, just as he draws up a financial budget. He may be unrealistic in planning, but he will find this out through experience later. We have consistently found that it is far better for the criminal to overprogram than to underprogram his time. An example of a time budget follows:

Monday - Friday

6:45 a.m.	Rise
8:30 a.m.	Due at office
6:00 p.m.	Leave office
6:30-9:00 p.m.	Dinner, reading paper, etc.
9:00 p.m.	Television or reading

Saturday

8:00 a.m.	Rise.
10:00 a.m.	At office
2:00 p.m.	Leave office
3.00 p.m.	Television or other diversions, unless there is a specific activity for children

Sunday

8:00 a.m.	Rise
8:00 a.m.-Noon	Breakfast, reading paper
Noon-6:00 p.m.	With children
6:00 p.m.	Preparing for week (wash, iron), reading, television

This was an unsatisfactory time budget for any criminal, although it might have been suitable for a responsible person. Too many large blocks of time were allotted to television, reading, or unspecified diversions. C did not have enough planned activity to occupy him. Too much unbudgeted time was spent with women other than his wife and in political activities in which he was trying to be a big shot. In addition, there was no regular allocation of time to attend our program. In contrast with C's time budget was that of another criminal:

Monday-Friday

5:30 a.m.	Rise
6:45 a.m.	Leave home
8:30 a.m.	Meet with us
12:30 p.m.	Take bus to work*
3:30 p.m.	Report to work
12:00 Midnight	Leave work

Saturday and Sunday

8:00 a.m.	Rise
9:00 a.m.	Into town with wife for house-hunting, shopping; home for lunch and house chores
3:00 p.m.	Leave for work
1:30 a.m.	Arrive home.

Both criminals had family obligations, although in the second case there were no children. The second criminal had time-consuming chores on country property that he was renting. In his time budget, there were large blocks for travel, because, before his entry into this program, he had decided to rent a house that was far from the city. Even the travel time was programmed, in that C planned what he would think about. He did not permit his thoughts to wander idly. In this programming of mental activity, C was preempting criminal thinking. For five months, he chose to work seven days a week. He often found himself tired as a result of overprogramming. The first man dropped out of the program and reverted to crime. The second progressed rapidly and achieved considerable vocational and marital satisfaction. Whereas the time budget was only one of many contributions to the different outcomes, it was an essential discipline.

In discussing programming of time, the criminal says that he fears getting into a rut. The unchanged criminal believes that submitting to any routine is a putdown, because it means having to do something on others' terms. Furthermore, he views schedules as for slaves. He regards routine as, at best,

*C's job was a two-and-a-half hour bus ride from our office.

monotony. In this program, he learns that routine and monotony are not identical. A routine is a pattern of activity that is necessary for organized, effective performance. A person can follow a routine and still be productively occupied with obligations that in time become interesting.

Monotony occurs when a person is not stimulated by what he is doing. If the criminal wants to achieve success responsibly, a routine is a necessity.

For the criminal, as well as the noncriminal, there is value in setting up time targets, especially at a job where there is some monotony. Doing so helps to improve concentration. For example, one criminal was mowing his large lawn. He aimed for completion of the side yard in a half-hour and then estimated times for the remaining portions. This is similar to the responsible person's setting out on a eight hundred-mile trip and targeting arrival at specific destinations along the way for particular hours. It makes the task more palatable. For the criminal, the consequence of such discipline is that more energy, both physical and mental, is directed to the task at hand and less to criminal thinking.

COMPLACENCY

The criminal who has successfully deterred arrestable acts and who has made other changes is likely to reach a point before basic change is entrenched at which he congratulates himself on a job well done. He thinks that he has come so far that it is inconceivable that he could ever again commit a crime. He views himself as a totally changed person.

In such a complacent state of mind, the criminal does not generate new initiatives and does not vigorously attack the daily problems that arise. When this is called to his attention, he asserts that as long as he is not in crime, he has done all he needs to—change is complete. Slowly, the channel closes. Because he thinks that he knows what is necessary to be responsible, he is not receptive to others. Disclosure lessens because he does not want to be criticized. In addition, there is little spontaneous self-criticism.

Usually, the criminal's complacency is not obvious. We become aware of it only when there is a noticeable erosion of responsibility. The complacent attitude is demonstrated by this postmortem of a major deviation from the program's requirements.

C had been functioning impeccably for many weeks, paying the closest attention to expenditures of money, programming time, scrutinizing his work situation to see where he could improve, engaging in self-criticism in his interpersonal relationships, and reflecting on the themes of every meeting with us. We began to notice after a while a corrosion in C's functioning in the program. His notes began to be less complete and his reports on his thinking processes less detailed. He made several requests to leave the meetings early, because of "emergencies" at work. He became very critical of others in the group and less reflective about his own functioning.

One week after we recorded these observations, we were presented with the following situation:

> After work, C went to a nearby tavern. He bought a young woman a drink and then ordered eight brandies for the two of them. It was very late, but he thought he would phone his former girlfriend and fly to see her or wire her the money to visit him. He cashed his paycheck but vetoed both of these ideas. Instead, he called his current girlfriend, who refused to see him at that hour. Undeterred, at two a.m., C took a cab to her place. Just as he arrived at her building, he thought better of barging in and asked the cab driver to take him home. On entering his apartment, he discovered that somewhere in the night's travels he had lost all his cash—more than $150.

C's irresponsibility at the tavern did not happen suddenly. He had been conscientious in implementing the program. He prided himself on how quickly he had adapted and on the fact that he was progressing more rapidly than the other group members. But this was not enough for him; he wanted something more, something exciting and different. As he became smug about his progress, a corrosion in attitude and behavior occurred. The ultimate result of his self-satisfaction was violation, the loss of a substantial sum of money, and loss of faith in him by his girl friend and others.

An aspect of complacency is that, once the criminal overcomes a particular adversity, he views this as evidence that he has changed completely.

> C, who had knowledge of a nursing assistant's irresponsibility, was threatened by that nursing assistant. The latter took C aside and, holding a knife to his throat, said that if C ever talked, he would regret it. C avoided reacting to this in his characteristic manner—an assault or plan for revenge. Having deterred his old patterns, he had evidence that the work of change was accomplished. Shortly thereafter, C told others on the ward how they too could become responsible. C began to edit his reports to us, and slowly the channel closed. He engaged in a couple of small thefts, eloped from the hospital, and returned to crime.

The criminal has to learn that changing one pattern is only a beginning. The entire spectrum of thinking and behavior patterns must be altered.

We anticipate that complacency will appear at any time, even late in the change process. However, warning the criminal about its deleterious effect after irresponsibility has ensued has little value. It is essential to preempt complacency. One way to do this is to present the criminal with potentially disagreeable situations.

> We asked C what would happen if he were prevented by the judge or by action on a detainer in another city from being released by the hospital unconditionally. At issue was whether C would stick it out and adhere to his decision to become a responsible person, even if it meant that he was under the court's authority for several more years.

This kind of discussion is essential for a man who has always expected things to go his way. Routinely, we present possible contingencies and, for the moment, view them as inevitable. We then prepare the criminal for making decisions, in case these contingencies become realities. This is designed to challenge complacency. With Murphy's Law operating, this has evolved into more than an academic exercise. As it turned out, more than two years elapsed before C was granted an unconditional release. C was well-prepared for this and had adopted the perspective that the unconditional release was secondary and that his changing was primary. Of course, he still wanted the unconditional release, but he had the opportunity to live outside the hospital grounds (on conditional release) with few restrictions imposed by the courts.

Attempts at preemption often work as they did here. However, it appears that at some point every criminal has to suffer the consequences of complacency for himself. Only then does he realize that he does not have it made.

Complacency is best combated through the criminal's daily reporting, subjecting himself to criticism, and preparing for adversities to come. This is the major reason for meeting—to determine what has to be changed so that he can then change it.

Because the criminal must always be looking for ways in which to improve his functioning, we rarely express confidence in him or approval of his actions. If we approve of one action, he thinks that we approve of everything he does. Just as an ex-alcoholic continues (in line with Alcoholics Anonymous) to view himself as an alcoholic, no matter how many years he has abstained from liquor, so the criminal must always view himself as a criminal. There are never grounds for resting smugly on one's laurels. There is always more to be learned. Complacency, whenever it appears, indicates that change is insufficient.

INCIPIENT CRIMINALITY

The criminal makes a distinction between thought and act. He argues that he cannot be arrested for his thinking. He fails to realize that thought and act form a sequence, that they are parts of the same flow of events. At one time, we also ignored this fact. As a result of our not attending to incipient irresponsible thinking, we were faced with numerous violations. We began to believe that some violations were inevitable in the course of change, but they were not inevitable. The number of violations and the incidence of irresponsibility could be reduced by focusing on incipient irresponsible thinking. This discovery was a milestone in the evolution of our program. Once we realized that the long path to responsibility could be shortened by eliminating incipient irresponsible thinking, fewer violations occurred. We now know that violations are not inevitable. If the criminal chooses to implement this program aggressively and to *attack* each incipient irresponsible thought, violations can be deterred totally throughout the change process.

We make a major issue out of what strikes the criminal as an innocuous thought, because we know that what appears harmless on the surface will in time expand, be pervasive, and ultimately be harmful. If not deterred, the incipient irresponsible thinking inevitably results in irresponsible acts and crime.

For four months, C functioned responsibly and was diligent in deterring irresponsible thinking. Then he began to relax in this deterrence, but continued to do well in the eyes of others. He began to think about having sex with adolescent girls. The occasional thought became more frequent. There was no attempt at preemptive deterrence and no utilization of moral inventories, because C was enjoying the thoughts. With this decrease in his self-monitoring, C was open to other ideas. Thoughts of getting drunk and buying drugs ensued. During this period, C had an experience at an auto shop in which he failed to deter anger and became furious over poor service. Waiting for his car, he fumed inwardly and decided to take a walk. He passed a store where his former employer was working. He thought of how he had swindled this man and, inwardly, he gloated over this theft. Two days after C reported this thinking, we learned from his wife that he had cashed his paycheck, stolen from the family account, and purchased drugs. During the following week, there was drinking and more drugs. In addition, C lied to his wife about the money and his whereabouts and verbally abused her. We then learned that C was purchasing prescriptions from illicit sources and selling them to other criminals.

Thus, one event led to another. Failure to deter the first thoughts about adolescent girls opened the door and led to anger, drinking, lying, drug use, theft, and abuse of his wife. In less than two weeks, four months of responsible functioning were shoved aside by a competing desire for excitement. C had brought out the sexual thinking in his report and had been instructed as to the potential consequences if that thinking were not deterred. However, this instruction was ignored, because he wanted to savor that thinking, not give it up. He believed that he would not violate if he limited himself to savoring. This was incorrect and resulted in irresponsibility. Such a situation, and countless others like it demonstrate that operationally one must take the position that, *in the criminal, the thought is as criminal as the act.* This is not true of the noncriminal.

Usually, we can explore with the criminal the ramifications of his incipient irresponsibility before it develops into something more serious. Our phenomenologic approach is conducive to nipping it in the bud. A report that lacks an account of incipient thinking is not complete. Like anything else, such reporting requires training and practice before it becomes automatic. The following is an excerpt from our dictated summary of a criminal's report in which there are several examples of incipient thinking that merited attention.

> With his girlfriend (who lived in another state) uppermost in his mind, C masturbated. The girlfriend figured prominently in his fantasies, but he also included two girls in New York with whom he had had high-impact sex. This was one break in the dam. The second was that on Saturday afternoon as he walked along looking for shoes, he surveyed the girls parading around in revealing clothes. He did not make an approach toward any, nor did he include any of them in a fantasy, but this kind of girl-watching was one practice that he had been deterring, because in the past he had gone the entire route, including rape. The third event was his having an alcholic beverage at dinner without even thinking of deterring it. Whereas for months he would not even have a beer, now he had a hard drink. Trivial? Perhaps. But it gives us the opportunity to present forcefully the concept of incipient thinking and its dangers. In each of the three events, C was lowering his guard.

The criminal's reports eventually are so thorough that significant issues are ferreted out from events that seem even less important than those in C's report.

> Working as a busboy, C was offered cheesecake by a waiter. C accepted it, even though employees were not to have cheesecake without paying for it. At issue was his taking something that he knew he was not entitled to.
>
> *   *   *
>
> C dialed "0" to place a long-distance call. The operator told him that he could dial directly. C was angry, because he thought that she should make the call. At issue was C's pattern of making others do things for him and becoming angry when they did not.

*   *   *

Every day, C parked at a bank that charged a fee for daily parking. However, C parked free, because he was able to squeeze his car into a small space. He often had trouble getting the car out, but managed to do so. The issue was whether C was finding it exciting to get away with something improper, thereby beating the system.

*   *   *

C was considering taking a Sunday morning class in photography. He reported an elevation in mood as he thought about becoming a famous photographer. He reported that his fantasy gave him a high as he thought about what he considered his unique talent and the stunning productions he would turn out. The issue was whether he would put himself to the test and submit to the course requirements in order to become a competent photographer.

*   *   *

The situations in question, not very important in themselves, could have been the forerunners of criminal acts. Each involved the issue of criminal power versus integrity. The discipline involved in attending to incipient thoughts is as important as the thoughts themselves. If the criminal neglects incipient thoughts in one area, he is neglecting them in others.

A point of contention by most criminals is our requirement of abstention from alcohol. Criminals insist that there is no harm in a beer after work or a glass of sherry. In the infrequent case of a truly alcoholic criminal, we hear less disagreement. After tolerating the criminal's drinking occasionally, we saw a potential danger in one drink for the criminal that is not there for the nonalcoholic noncriminal. (Our discussion here parallels the emphasis of Alcoholics Anonymous on physical, mental, and spiritual sobriety.) The one drink, time and again, has proved to be the door opener to irresponsibility and, often, violation. Yet we constantly encounter the criminal's superoptimism that he can handle drinking. Our instructing him in the dangers is usually futile. He has to experience the consequences himself.

C had one beer at a tavern. One led to another, and then to two shots of cognac. There was then a stream of sexual thinking. The program dissolved in the alcohol, as it were, and C went to find a woman who he knew was available for sex. After staying out all night, he had to face his wife the next morning, and that produced anger and further complications.

Deterrents can be cut off without alcohol, but the process is more rapid with it. As a result of the one drink, C endangered all that he had been working for. In trying to defend his actions, the criminal submits that the problem is not the alcohol, but rather his thinking. That is correct. However, as we shall develop in volume 3, alcohol not only helps to eliminate restraints but also acts as a facilitator of the forbidden things that the criminal wants to do. Sometimes, the criminal stands on principle—that a drink will not hurt him—simply to avoid total submission to the program. Experience has shown over and over that the criminal must deter the *idea* of the first sip. Our approach now is to warn less, but instead to require the criminal to consider his past carefully and to decide whether a drink is worth the risk of destroying what he is working for.

Attention to incipient irresponsibility requires going over the same conceptual ground many times. Frequent repetition is necessary, not because the criminal fails to grasp initially what is said, but because he fails to implement it aggressively. At first, our material is viewed as words. The criminal has a lifetime of old habits to unlearn. The new concepts acquire meaning only when the criminal starts to put them to use.

> "This repetition was necessary because I know myself well enough that, because my criminal thinking is so habitual, it would assert itself. Responsibility would be overruled."

After several months of participation in the program, the criminal himself regards incipient irresponsible thinking with alarm, quickly spots it, and deters it.

> Alighting from a cab, a woman dropped some money. C called to her, but she did not hear him. He tried to catch her attention a second time and failed. Finally, she turned around, and C pointed to the money on the ground. The woman was most grateful and offered C a reward for the recovered eighty dollars. This he turned down. However, he had the thought that, if the woman had failed to turn around, the money would be his. He caught himself thinking this and was ashamed. The ensuing disgust with himself put an immediate end to any further thinking along this line.
>
> *   *   *
>
> C was never an alcoholic or even a heavy drinker. The question often arose as to whether one drink was permissible in a social situation. C refused to allow himself to drink, because he feared that, like other criminals in the group, he might then act irresponsibly. He abstained from liquor as though he were an alcoholic. Deterring a drink, although he was not a heavy drinker, was part of the *discipline* of deterrence.

Both criminals knew full well the problems that could unfold from the slightest irresponsibility. When they first participated in the program, the concept of incipient irresponsibility, or incipient criminality, was absurd to them. They could not see that the little things mattered. As one said rather skeptically, "I can't get over a gang leader's worrying about breaking the speed limit." Now he himself was not only fearful of exceeding speed limits or of any other violation of the law, but fearful that *any thought* of irresponsibility might imperil his progress and set him back on the road to a life of crime.

LESS EXTERNAL RESTRICTION OPENS THE DOOR TO IRRESPONSIBILITY

We have found that when external restraints are reduced, every criminal, no matter how much he seems to be progressing, undergoes an increase in criminal thinking and is more likely to violate. We went through a phase of disappointment in which we thought that our changing criminals were suffering setbacks or relapses. We were surprised to find that just as they were receiving privileges in confinement or were being released from confinement altogether, they threw caution aside instead of being more watchful of themselves. Criminal thinking increased, as did drinking, running around with women, gambling, and, in some cases, minor property crimes.

Some other workers in the field who have observed this phenomenon regard it as indicative of regression. They interpret the criminal's recklessness as being a manifestation of a persistent unconscious desire to be caught and punished. By studying the criminal's thinking processes, we have learned that this has never been the case. We have neither found a criminal who desired to get caught nor a criminal who was relieved by being punished. Rather than indicating a regression, the criminal's behavior indicates that he has not advanced enough; change has been insufficient.

The criminal has developed some internal restraints while he has been restrained externally. For example, he has learned to bridle his superoptimism and is aware of the dangers of corrosion and cutoff. When external restraints are reduced, his acquired internal restraints prove to be insufficient. In some cases, they become nonfunctional in the light of what he perceives as a new opportunity for excitement with less risk. Once the criminal knows that he will have more room in which to operate, we observe that old patterns, dormant for a while, are again operative. The bulk of the change process cannot occur in confinement or in any other artificial environment. It takes place when the criminal is functioning in the community.

As external restraints are reduced, the criminal thinks, Now I have it made. Deterrents corrode, the obligatory is deferred, and a celebration ensues. The mere anticipation of a change in his status results in complacency and superoptimism.

As soon as C knew he would be leaving the hospital sometime within the next two months, he was ready for action. He had the privilege of being on the hospital grounds and took liberties with this. He left the grounds without permission, went drinking, obtained drugs, and had sex. Over a period of two weeks, there were several such series of events. C reported to us what he had done in each escapade. There had been no effort on his part at deterrence. When we faced him with the immediate and long-range consequences of his actions, C became more sober and restrained himself for a while longer. In two months, C obtained his discharge from the hospital with no difficulty. The night after the court hearing, he thought that now was the time to celebrate. Again, there was liquor, drugs, and sex with an irresponsible woman whom he had previously resolved not to see again.

C had totally cut off the fears mandatory in the program. It was necessary then for C to reconsider his basic choice. Knowing what this program required, he could choose to implement it more intensively or to go his own way. In this case, he elected to continue.

Whenever a criminal is granted a reduction in restraints, there is the possibility that we have not sufficiently prepared him for it. This also applies when he is given greater authority over others or achieves greater independence.

C had become a management trainee at a department store. He was pleased with the authority given to him and was anticipating advancement within a short time. C's father reported to us that, at this time, C was becoming cocky around the house, his demeanor resembling what it was when he was in crime. He was not considerate, did not listen to others' opinions, and generally seemed headstrong, irritable, and resentful.

* * *

C moved from a small town to a city to be closer to his wife's job. With less travel time to his own work, he had more time in his department. His wife was often out, and he spent more hours alone than before the move. With time on his hands, C thought more about visiting adult bookstores. He also had a thicker phone book in the city and thought that, alone in his apartment, he had greater opportunity to make obscene phone calls.

* * *

C received a promotion at work. He was pleased at the increase in income, because of the greater freedom that he would have in not being restricted to a tight budget. Regarding the money as already in his pocket, C spent large sums on a girlfriend, in playing the big shot around town, and in treating others to drinks at bars. Exhausting his funds did not bring him back to earth. Instead, he borrowed more money at usurious rates, figuring that he could easily pay it back when he received his paycheck.

In the first situation, with increased confidence, C was showing some of his old power-thrusting. In the second, a criminal operating in a less limiting environment experienced an acceleration in criminal thinking. In the third, a criminal's promotion and raise in pay gave him greater independence to violate. Each of these situations showed that the criminal had not dealt sufficiently with the broad spectrum of criminal thinking, especially incipient thinking.

Before restraints are reduced, we anticipate what the criminal can expect later. Much time is spent warning him, to help him preempt increased criminal thinking and action. One criminal who thought carefully about what his course might be on release from the hospital expressed his anticipation of the problems ahead.

"I don't think I'll physically evade or avoid you. The probability is that I will see you but lie to you to cover up what I did, and our 'crisis' will come when I'm next arrested. As you say, there would be no regression because I wouldn't have changed in the first place. Anticipating this pattern, I am determined to change it—to stick with the program and not to go back to committing crimes. But having all the determination in the world while I'm in here means nothing. What is important is what I do out there."

This man did not violate. However, with additional freedom, he did report increased temptation and an acceleration in criminal thinking. The indoctrination of the criminal before restrictions are reduced prepares him to deal with what we have learned he should expect. In every case, preemption is emphasized. However, the criminal usually learns from the mistakes that he experiences. Because he gives up his own ideas reluctantly, he decides at some point to try his own wings. In every case, he has faltered and suffered the consequences.

There is always risk in reducing restraints. By the time our people are released, they have been trained sufficiently so that no major crime has been committed. They are monitored regularly with respect to the implementation of thinking errors and deterrents. In chapter 13, we recommend that, if our format is used elsewhere, the A.C. (who spends fifteen hours a week with the criminal) should be granted the major role in deciding at what point a criminal's restraints should be reduced.

Until we began training the criminal to spot and deter incipient criminal thinking and to preempt further criminal thinking, we believed that it was inevitable for him to violate when restraints had been lessened. We now know that the criminal can be sufficiently trained to prevent this. He can apply the same principles, whether he is in maximum security, in minimum security, or in the community. It is true that most of the learning about living responsibly will occur in the community. He will make many mistakes there. However, if he truly regards the program as his life line, he views the lifting of restraints, not as an opportunity for more criminal excitement, but as a challenge to come to terms responsibly with a world that he has never known.

WHEN THE CRIMINAL DECIDES TO GO HIS OWN WAY

We have said that the criminal is at times complacent and strays from the program's requirements, but returns to vigorous implementation. The progress is not simple and smooth for either the criminal or the agent of change. We have been through many periods in which the criminal has closed the channel, opposed us, and taken every opportunity to discredit our efforts. It is to some of these crises that we now turn.

We never play detective. We can be conned, although our techniques and format reduce the frequency of conning. At some point we discover that the criminal has been closing the channel. This becomes clear when he is absent from meetings without reasonable excuse, when the quality of his notes and reports deteriorates, and particularly when we learn of an irresponsible act. The criminal does not suddenly announce that he is quitting. A decision to leave the program is expressed in different ways. Most often, it takes the form of a declaration that he is ready to stand on his own feet.

> "I have to do things for myself. If I make mistakes, I make them. I have to make them."

*   *   *

> "Let me go and knock my head against the wall if I need to. I can't sit back. The only way to do it is to go out and fail. That's not the kind of thing I've been doing. Books can't tell you how hard it is."

There is truth in both these statements. Of course, the criminal will make mistakes, and he must learn from experience. However, the purpose of such statements is to justify both his pursuing the excitement that he wants as well as his not implementing specific program requirements. In saying that he has to have room to make mistakes on his own, the criminal is actually making allowances for himself—an attitude totally contrary to emphasis on incipient irresponsible thinking and preemptive deterrence.

The criminal's disagreement is not with the substance of the program. His argument is that we require more implementation than he considers necessary. He regards us as too rigid and demanding. He may make any requirement a bone of contention. Money is often the issue, with the criminal maintaining that he is a grown man and can manage his own money. Some assert that the program takes too much time and draws energy away from other, more pressing matters, such as job or family. The debate may be about the significance of a deviation from the program's requirements. What is really happening is that, in different ways, the criminal is demonstrating that he does not want to surrender totally to the program's requirements for change.

A criminal who has cooperated but then wants a way out is experiencing suffocation. He has, in his opinion, toed the line and, in doing everything that was required, deprived himself of excitement. Now he is bored, complacent, self-pitying, angry, superoptimistic, or any combination of these. He wants to know, What else is there in life? In this state of mind, he shows few responsible initiatives, little effort, minimal endurance, and a failure to deter criminal thinking. Some criminals resign from the program permanently, some temporarily, and others not at all, despite their differences with us. Because we have been involved in a research investigation, we have not terminated anyone's participation. In every case, when criminals have elected to drop out, we have taken them back when they requested it, no matter what the circumstances. Had we not been in research, we might not have had the time to offer some criminals numerous opportunities to participate over a period of years. Following are accounts of what happened to one criminal when he dropped out permanently and to another who left only temporarily.

The Permanent Dropout

After several months of faithful attendance at group meetings and sustained implementation of our program at his job, C, 23 years old, said that he was certain that he wanted to be responsible but was not sure that he wanted to pay the price. He said that he knew that halfway measures would not achieve responsibility; he had tried these. Although he knew that we were correct about the totality of the effort needed, he objected to the degree of suffering that he would have to endure. He insisted that we were too rigid and demanded too much. C declared that the sacrifice involved was "like dying on the cross." He said that he would just as soon be dead, but he knew that he did not have the courage to die. With this outlook, C looked for surcease from the grind of the program.

C reported receiving calls from a criminal friend. In what he termed an "aberration from responsibility," he went to the friend's house, had four beers and marijuana, got high, and began talking about prostitutes, drugs, and owning corporations. The exciting thinking and talk provided a respite from the dullness of responsible living.

The channel remained open for some time (in part because we had no legal hold on C and he knew that he could not be penalized for violation), so C reported his "aberrations from responsibility." He was familiar with the correctives and deterrents. It was his choice as to whether to implement them. The issue was what kind of life he wanted. Superficially knowledgeable about philosophy, C said quite seriously that living as a Buddhist monk would provide an answer. His discussion of his quest for what he called a "spiritual solution" was mainly tactical to shift the focus from this program. C complained that our program did not fill the emptiness that he was experiencing. We replied that Buddhism or any other kind of religion or philosophy would be of little value in relieving that emptiness if he were going to live a criminal life. C replied, "I am not giving up this program by any means." Yet, he was not implementing it as required. Instead, he was making exceptions to suit his purposes. One of the reasons for this was that he still was not completely convinced that he was a criminal. If he were not a criminal, then he could embrace some parts of the program and reject others. It need not apply totally to him.

C stated, "When I was 12 years old, I vowed never to swear allegiance to a program. Whenever I am in anything, I will not follow what they say on principle. It would somehow interfere with my independence." C made it clear that he regarded himself as the sole arbiter of his fate. He asserted that any program, by the nature of its construction, had its rigidities. C said that he did not want to argue with us, because he did not want to upset us. Thus, for a while, he had closed the channel to the extent that he did not voice his mounting reservations about the program and its application to him.

C still regarded his past as contemptible and simultaneously refused to adopt any system of moral behavior in order to break with his criminal past. C said that he wanted "spiritual peace"; he meant that he wanted a problemless existence. He did not want to struggle for anything. He desired the trappings of responsibility but refused to do what was required to achieve it. He considered himself above the mainstream of life and found it difficult even to imagine himself being straight. C reiterated that he believed in the program. He said it was hard to object to anything in it. But he was not sure that it was for him. To do all that was required would be to live a drab, colorless existence. There was recurrent thinking that little purpose was served in living at all. Both crime and responsibility were unacceptable.

One week C did not attend any of the group meetings. Finally, he came in to launch an offensive against the program. He declared, "You don't know who I am" (despite our having spent more than one thousand hours with him and his having said many times that we were the only ones who understood him). C said, furthermore, that we were not interested in him as a human being. He claimed that the program took him away from work for too long. Yet we learned that on two of the days when he was not with us he had not been at work either. C said that it was inconvenient to attend our meetings and that he derived little benefit from them. In addition, he objected to our categorizing him as a criminal. C said that he would listen to our response to what he had said. However, as we began speaking, he quickly grew angry, said he was wasting his time, and, as we were predicting that he would again wind up in serious trouble, stormed out. Six months later, C committed suicide.

The Dropout Who Returns

After a phase of intensive application of this program to his life, C gradually became less enthusiastic. He reached a state of limbo in which he was not active in crime but had many criminal thoughts. His attitude toward responsible living was, What are you supposed to do to get out of this kind of life? What does it do for you? Do you wind up in the old folks home? Or, if you wind up in jail, does it make any difference?"

C was not antagonistic to us, but was pitying himself. He said that he valued nothing and that nothing in life was worthwhile. We warned him that, in his state of dissatisfaction with himself and the world, his present abstention from crime would not continue indefinitely. C's reports became increasingly sparse. Efforts at this time to promote his long-range thinking or his taking responsible initiatives were met with indifference. C finally said, "I'd like to kill myself, but I don't have the energy to do it." He stated that we were exerting more energy in any one morning on him than "I put on myself in a week and a half." This state of mind continued: "I don't care much about living. Nothing is important. I feel trapped in a hopeless situation. I don't find any reason to live—no get up and go."

C reported that he had drunk a fifth of liquor but this only resulted in his being more depressed. He then obtained heroin, which did not lift his mood either: "Even drugs don't do any good. I never had a problem like this before." C's wife had left him, and he was living as a vagrant in a park. Finally, C turned himself in to a hospital as a drug addict and entered a methadone program. Shortly thereafter, he was permitted in the community during the day to look for a job. This he did not do, but instead was seen in major crime areas of the city. C used the hospital as a hotel while he was active in the drug world and in crime.

We had not seen C for two-and-a-half months. One day, he called and requested an appointment, saying, "I have come to my senses." He admitted that he had been in crime every day. Wi.h the seriousness of his crimes steadily increasing, C became frightened. He said that at the age of forty-three he was on a one-way street that would end at the penitentiary. Realizing this and seeing the shambles that he was making of his life were sufficient inducements to return to the program.

In the first case, the criminal arrived at the conclusion that the program, although it had merit, was not useful to him. At the age of twenty-three, he believed that he could find his own way in life. Because he was a voluntary participant, there was no legal way to hold him in the program. He was pessimistic about what life held in store for him, but he did not want to surrender totally to the severe requirements of our program or any other. He was adhering to his pledge made to himself at the age of twelve that he would be master of his own destiny. In the second case, the forty-three-year-old man had had twenty more years of experience in the daily grind of crime than the first criminal. He had been in and out of our program several times; each time, after dropping out, he had experienced legal, financial, and marital difficulties. Truly alarmed by the enormity of the crimes that he was contemplating, C returned. Apparently, his earlier exposure to the program had had some deterrent effect.

Whenever the criminal wants to go his own way, he makes that choice. We do not cajole, persuade, or entreat him to continue. If he is a voluntary participant, he does not, of course, have complete freedom of choice. If he is under the jurisdiction of the courts, he is less likely to drop out entirely, but instead will show only token cooperation.

IMPORTANCE OF FIRMNESS
IN THE AGENT OF CHANGE*

The criminal tries to use any program as a shield from the law. If he is in a program, he expects enforcement officials to be more lax in supervising him, leaving that responsibility to the A.C. He also anticipates that if he is arrested, he will not be penalized if he is already in someone else's care. Both expectations have been substantiated by experience.

At Saint Elizabeths Hospital, if a criminal, whether in minimum security or on conditional release, is again apprehended for a crime, he is confined in maximum security. A number of criminals have stated that remaining on the hospital rolls is their best protection, in that it gives them a license for crime. By this they mean that they believe (correctly in most cases) that they can

---

*Firmness in attitude as one of a number of essential qualities of the change agent will be discussed in detail in chapter 12.

commit crimes with less worry about being caught, because if apprehended, they will be returned to the hospital, which will then resume custody of them. In this way, they can avoid long prison terms.*

Many criminals who are on probation but in community rehabilitation programs also consider themselves immune from the law. Their experience has often confirmed this view. Parole or probation officers sometimes know that criminals are violating but do nothing about it. Usually the officers are occupied with heavy caseloads and leave supervision and decision-making to personnel in the programs in which the criminals are participating. Again, the criminal is shielded simply because he is enrolled in a program. It may require a serious complaint or arrest to force the probation or parole officer to take notice. Even an arrest is often insufficient grounds for confinement; the criminal must actually be brought to trial and convicted.

It is essential that the criminal who enters our program understand that it will have no option but to enter and then continue in this program.** Some criminals have been eager to leave this program, but did not, because they knew that their departure would be reported. In the preceding section, we described a forty-three-year-old criminal who left our program and returned. This happened several times. The final time, he had been apprehended for two thefts and asked to reenter this program as an alternative to jail. We accepted this man, with two conditions: that the court make his participation a condition of a long probation term and that his probation officer be notified if he were not cooperative. C called this "therapy by threat." His use of the word "threat" showed that he was superoptimistic that we were only threatening and never would actually report him. C later discovered that he had misjudged us: we reported him for noncooperation and drug use.

This happened several times. The final time, he had been apprehended for two thefts and asked to reenter this program as an alternative to jail. We accepted this man, with two conditions: that the court make his participation a condition of a long probation term and that his probation officer be notified if he were not cooperative. C called this "therapy by threat." His use of the word "threat" showed that he was superoptimistic that we were only threatening and never would actually report him. C later discovered that he had misjudged us: we reported him for noncooperation and drug use.

---

*In the last few years, some criminals have been brought to trial, convicted, and sentenced to terms intended to begin after release from the hospital. However, it has often happened that the prison term was combined with hospital confinement and that the hospital, in effect, acted as a parole officer. When the criminal was discharged from the hospital, his time in the hospital was credited against his prison sentence by the court.

**On occasion, the court has sent a criminal to us to evaluate his suitability for our program and we have rejected him, because right from the start he gave no indication that he would cooperated. Such a criminal is willing to take his chances on being placed elsewhere.

We have found that the probation or parole arrangement with the courts is not very effective unless the officers and court implement the conditions for the criminal's participation in the program.

> C had entered this program as a condition of probation. With enthusiasm, he began implementing new patterns of thought and action. Having been in the program before and having dropped out, he now believed that he had a new lease on life. He could come here, rather than go to prison. However, once again, after a honeymoon period, his performance became lackluster and he wanted criminal excitement. He was inattentive, and the quality of his reports eroded. He ceased making moral inventories. C began to drink, became argumentative with his wife, and began thinking about other women. We then learned that he had been chipping drugs. There was, in short, ample proof that he was persistently violating probation requirements. We reported C's lack of cooperation and drug violations to the probation officer. The officer had warned C earlier that if this occurred, probation would be revoked. However, the officer simply admonished C and required him to provide weekly urine samples. C then was fired from his job for poor performance. Again, the probation officer warned him that he had better mend his ways. It became clear that, short of an arrest, the officer would not take C into custody.

The officer's lax attitude weakened our leverage considerably. In contrast with this case was the following series of events:

> After C had been convicted of a felony, he was sent to our program by the courts for evaluation. C was selected for the program and was warned by his probation officer that a failure to cooperate would result in the revoking of his probation. During a period in which C decided that he did not need to be here daily and wanted to do things his way, his attendance slackened off. A word by us to the probation officer was sufficient to elicit a sharp warning to C. In no uncertain terms, C was told by the officer that there would be no second chance. C returned promptly to the program on a daily basis and adopted a different attitude toward it, resulting in effective implementation of corrective measures. Indeed, he became a model participant.

Our experience thus far has been that the lax attitude of the probation officer in the first example has been the more prevalent.

As the criminal progresses in change, legal leverage becomes less of an issue because there are rewards for change other than keeping the probation officer off his back. It is necessary that the A.C. be uncompromising in requiring the criminal to meet the program's standards. Clearly, the criminal needs us; we do not need him. One standard on which there can be no compromise is the wide-open channel. No excuse for closing it is tolerated.

> C's girlfriend was a very responsible woman. However, she was unrealistic in her management of money and made decisions that she later regretted. Early in the program, C had helped her out by giving her some money. Embarrassed at having taken the money from C, the girlfriend requested that C say nothing about their financial transaction in our meetings. Out of regard for her, C complied.

Our position was that, although on the face of it C had not broken the law, he had violated the rigid requirements of this program. A pattern of failure to disclose everything substantial for any reason is itself a violation.

Our firmness is established by our refusal to accept excuses for the criminal's irresponsibility. Our position is unapologetically moralistic.* The criminal sometimes espouses noble ideals, but expects to use criminal means to attain them. Rather than make some modest gains responsibly and ultimately achieve peace of mind, he wants to be a success by dishonest means and is willing to live with the tension of possible arrest. He blames factors outside himself for his failure to implement the program, because in the early stages he still does not want what this program offers. We repeatedly place the burden on him to function responsibly, no matter how he thinks he has been wronged by others and no matter what obstacles lie before him. We constantly confront the criminal with, "What kind of life do you want?" We inquire as to whether his solution to his complaints about boredom and suffering is, as one criminal quipped, "a felony a day." Is he willing to see himself as he is—a threat to society and a failure in life, even as a criminal? Does he have the courage to change? It is up to him. If he does, we are there to assist him. If he does not, it is *his* life, and we can let society decide how to deal with him.

Thus, the firm position has two aspects: an unyielding insistence that change requires a *total* implementation of this program, and a readiness to request legal sanctions if the criminal decides not to cooperate.

---

*This is in direct opposition to what Shakow (1975) said is desirable in a clinical psychologist. "What we want finally is a person with a distinct ethical code of his own, but who makes no judgments about the ethical codes of his clients or patients" (p. 6). Shakow did not make it clear whether this applies to working with amoral and immoral clients.

CRIMINALS' ATTITUDES TOWARD ONE ANOTHER

UNCHANGED CRIMINAL TOWARD CHANGING CRIMINAL

The greater part of our work during the first six years was with criminals who were still in confinement, most of whom had grounds privileges. A significant aspect of a criminal's experience at the hospital while he participated in our program was the attitudes expressed toward him by criminals not in our program. At first, the latter reacted with considerable skepticism. They thought that the criminal in our program was not sincere about change, that he was simply conning and up to his old tricks.

Some unchanged criminals thought that our people might be sincere about wanting to go straight, but they doubted both that this desire would last and that implementation would be sustained. The unchanged criminals had had their own sincere intentions to change, especially when they believed that apprehension for a crime was imminent, but had never sustained these intentions. Knowing of their own changeability (fragmentation), they regarded the criminal in our program as being just as changeable. Some unchanged criminals played up to the changing criminal as they saw that he was getting into the good graces of the institution's staff, thinking it would benefit them to be seen associating with him. They thought, too, that they could persuade him to put in a good word to the staff on their behalf. The unchanged criminals often asked the advice of the criminal in our program, not because they valued it, but because they desired to flatter him or sought to enlist his support in a particular power thrust or scheme for control.

Whatever the attitude or degree of association, most unchanged criminals eventually made certain that talk about crime and the commission of actual crimes was kept from the changing criminal. Because of the fear that he might inform, they regarded him as police, much in the same way that they regarded a conscientious staff person.

What happens in confinement is useful in preparing the criminal for experiences in the outside world. The attitudes of unchanged criminals in confinement are also characteristic of unchanged criminals on the street who have contact with the changing criminal early in the program. They do not play up to him, but there is the same skepticism, the same fear that he will "snitch," and the same desire for his good will. When unchanged criminals are exposed to the criminal in our program over a long period and observe that he is showing evidence of change, they adopt various attitudes. Some unchanged criminals assert that the changing criminal is being brainwashed. They may then attack the criminal's sense of manhood by asking him, "Are you letting that man run you? Are you being a spineless jellyfish?" Once the unchanged criminal realizes that the changing criminal is not merely going through a phase, they express envy mixed with doubt and then wish him well. The following excerpts from a letter by an unchanged criminal to a criminal in our program demonstrate this attitude.

> Dear——
> Was thrilled to hear of your new job. Hope you like it and make a success of it, if that's what you want. . . . All I truly want *for you* is to be straight and at peace. Your Mom is so proud of you now, and myself—keep it up! . . . I'm lucky to have your friendship.

C knew that if he continued in this program, there would be no further friendship with this or any other unchanged criminal. If he showed evidence of change but still mantained contact with other criminals, we would regard him as being likely to engage in criminal activity.

CHANGING CRIMINAL TOWARD UNCHANGED CRIMINAL

In the beginning, the changing criminal continues to associate with unchanged criminals, because he is fearful of burning the bridge to them in case he wants to rejoin them. His major job, as he sees it, especially in confinement, is to avoid arousing antagonism. He remains polite but becomes progressively less involved. Eventually, he refrains from criminal conversation, except, when asked, to take an anticrime position. One problem has been that the criminal functions as a reformer, even as a missionary who recruits others for our program. In ward meetings and activities, he very rapidly assumes center stage as a spokesman for responsibility. When a criminal acts as a teacher of others in this way, it is a criminal equivalent. In a nonarrestable power thrust, he controls others and builds up his opinion of himself. Although the advice he gives others may be sound, the very pattern of giving advice is not conducive to change. The desire to take over, albeit responsibly, is similar to his irresponsible control patterns. Therefore, the criminal is neither to accept nor to seek positions of power and is to do a minimum of socializing with other criminals.

The confined criminal in our program maintains a delicate balance. He tries on the one hand to be responsive to the staff's requirements by participating in the ward's therapeutic community and other activities, and on the other not to teach, offer advice, exert influence, or feed others what they want to hear. To be sure, nonparticipation also arouses antagonism from staff and other criminals, but this passes in time. At the least, his withdrawal results in considerable isolation, because all that he is left with on the ward is talking with responsible staff members, reading, and television. Our people have been criticized by ward staff for too little participation and, at the same time, by us for too much. The best that can be hoped for is that the criminal will use the confinement setting to observe carefully and to reflect on his own thinking and action.*

Even though the ward is not a true microcosm of the outside world, the criminal still begins to implement the program. The following incidents are indicative of how the confined criminal in our program eventually behaves toward other criminals in his immediate surroundings.

> On seeing a female visitor who was attractive, one of the criminals surmised what she would be like with "her legs spread wide open." C handled this by leaving promptly and not permitting this talk to stimulate criminal sexual thinking.
>
> *   *   *
>
> Money was being passed from one ward to another, to be used by criminals to purchase a hacksaw. Because one fellow to whom money was given appeared to be taking the money for himself and was not passing it along, C was asked by some other criminals to trace the money. C refused on the grounds that "I don't do things like that."
>
> *   *   *
>
> C reported that while he was playing cards with a criminal and a nursing assistant, a record of dirty jokes was being played. He said that he was able to tune out the record with minimal effort and concentrate on the game.
>
> *   *   *
>
> When a criminal came to C and told him about a plan for elopement, C only listened. He then decided that even listening was offering too much encouragement, and, not being interested in the conversation anyway, he terminated it.

Every day, there are incidents like these. Living among other criminals, the criminal in our program cannot be totally silent. But he can and does minimize his personal involvement.

Once the criminal is in the community, this program requires a total severance of ties with criminal associates. The criminal is made aware of this prime necessity. However, he usually learns not through our indoctrination, but through experience. If a changing criminal assists an unchanged criminal in any way or even speaks with him, it is perceived by the latter as a desire for continuing the relationship. The criminal in change eventually realizes that there is nothing in common to sustain former relationships. Our men hold new jobs, live in different noncrime locations, do not frequent crime areas, and always move in an entirely different milieu. More importantly, they

---

*We are speaking of a confinement setting where our format is not used.

develop a new set of attitudes. The criminal's old buddies eventually become more aware of these facts; even so, some still try to maintain contact. Ultimately, the changing criminal must be direct and outspoken to make it clear that he wants nothing more to do with his former criminal associates. This applies especially to irresponsible women he has known who persist in contacting him.

A young female criminal kept calling C. To entice him to her home, she used the ploy of stating that he had left some of his belongings there. C finally told her to burn or discard whatever items he had left.

Eventually, the criminals in our program share the same attitude toward unchanged criminals that most responsible people have. They want no contact with them whatsoever.

CHANGING CRIMINAL TOWARD CHANGING CRIMINAL

In the early stages of our work, we assumed that changing criminals in groups would serve as models to those just entering our program. In 1964, we observed:

"Criminals tend to look up to some leaders. A talk with another [criminal] patient who is improving is of tremendous value."

We found that we had overestimated the value of such a talk, partly because at that time the program had not been developed to its present extent. The criminal new to the program actually comprehended little that the changing criminal said. After all, the process of change and the way of life being described were totally foreign to the unchanged criminal. What could an unchanged criminal really know about effort, a time perspective, and the many other elements of the program? Furthermore, we discovered that the criminal does not use other people as models (see chapter 12). Still, we require participants well along in change to describe their experience in the program to entering criminals. After they have been in the program for a while, their reports are given with humility and thoughtfulness, not with missionary zeal or to build themselves up. The major usefulness to the newcomer is that he observes that total change is truly possible, that some have faithfully adhered to the rigorous requirements of the program and are living safer, more productive, and responsible lives. The unchanged criminal expresses admiration for this achievement, although it is not clear to him how it came about.

In the group, each criminal is skeptical about the others' sincerity, truthfulness, persistence, and diligence. A competitive element is present that is neither introduced nor fostered by us. Each criminal wants to show that he can change the fastest and the most completely. In the beginning, one berates another for mistakes not brought forth in his report or not self-critically attacked. In this way, he shows his superiority. This attitude provides substance for discussion, especially of the power and uniqueness characteristics. In our format, each criminal is asked what he has learned from the reports of others. He is required to bring out in his comments similar mistakes that he has made in the past and is still making.

The group members are not all at the same point in change. Indeed the group is deliberately constituted so that the members are all at different points in the change process (see chapter 6). The new participant soon realizes that he is competing only with himself. He becomes aware that the others in the group are not interested in downgrading him for his mistakes but in trying to learn from them. When an unchanged criminal gets into trouble, the attitude of the others is, He asked for it. This is not said in a self-righteous way, nor is there pleasure in the distress of others. Instead, there is disappointment and additional fear about themselves. In later reports, we discuss and observe whether what happened to others is a lesson for them. Do they benefit from the mistakes of others and implement correctives?

No social relationships between group members are maintained outside the group setting. At the beginning, this was surprising to us. Occasionally, some criminals work in the same establishment during the same hours. Their leisure time is limited, however, and is programmed with their families or in some other way; they choose not to spend such time with one another. As they change, they are polite to other changing criminals but prefer to develop different relationships. Generally, they want nothing to do with other criminals—changed or unchanged.

> "I simply hate criminals. I don't even like those criminals who are supposedly changed."

As we stress new initiatives in the social world (a later development), changing criminals establish relationships with responsible people. A responsible wife may take the lead in such relationships, but some of our changing criminals assume such initiatives themselves. From time to time, if group members can be of service to one another, they do so without protest, but also without great zeal.

NONCRIMINALS' ATTITUDES TOWARD CHANGING CRIMINALS

Responsible people take either of two sharply divergent attitudes toward the changing criminal. Those who know him and have been hurt by him remain skeptical, often to the point of cynicism. They may have been encouraged in the past by his brief efforts to go straight but later have been disappointed. Most have been let down too many times to believe that anything lasting will evolve from the present change effort. So they not only believe that they are being conned but state that we too are being conned. Others go overboard to help him. These people are so eager to believe that they are benefiting the criminal and society by their support that they are gullible. Consequently, in time, they too are exploited and become skeptical.

The changing criminal reacts to the skepticism of others with a sense of injustice.

> "It angers me that people infer that I will still be dishonest. Sometimes I don't feel like putting up with it."

The criminal has to learn that there is no statute of limitations with respect to the consequences of his past criminality. People will remain fearful and suspicious for a long time. Furthermore, he must expect that the least departure from total responsibility will be perceived by others as confirming their suspicions. He may also be blamed erroneously for things that happen, simply because he is in a given area. Unjust suspicions are to be expected, because the criminal's history cannot easily be erased. Even when he is unquestionably doing well, others wonder, Who is he trying to con now? The criminal must anticipate such reactions. Expecting them and realizing that he had deserved them will help them to preempt anger. Remaining unruffled, although disappointed, in the face of skepticism and even accusation is a sign of change.

Another reaction by the responsible person may be one of puzzlement and astonishment.

> C went to a family dinner and was offered hard liquor. When he refused it, he was handed a beer. When he asked for a soft drink instead, the reaction of others was, What's the matter with him? There was similar amazement when this same criminal turned down an invitation to go out on New Year's Eve in preference to spending a quiet evening at home. C said that he wanted to stay home, because the chances of getting into trouble outside were too great.

Some people meet the criminal for the first time when he applies for a job or is introduced to them socially. When he reveals his past and his current efforts to change, he is more often regarded with respect for candor and effort than with shock.

ARENAS FOR CHANGE

Whatever the criminal is engaged in offers an arena for change. In this section, we discuss four such arenas—work, money management, social relationships, and women. Self-discipline and close attention to the implementation of new patterns of thought and action are necessary everywhere. The same concepts apply to money management as apply to relationships with women, in the sense of honoring obligations, fact-finding, scaling down pretensions, and so forth. Any corrective that applies to one arena must be applied to all others to achieve total basic change.

WORK

When we are asked for reports on how criminals are doing, we do not limit our remarks to their work performance. A job in itself is no indicator of responsibility. With intelligence, drive, assertiveness, and perfectionism, many unchanged criminals rise rapidly in the world of work and engage in the same criminality as when they were not employed. In fact, as a cover, some criminals prefer to be employed at all times, while actively engaged in criminal enterprises.

To discuss career choices with the unchanged criminal is a waste of time. His ideas are based on his pretensions, and so we defer serious consideration of a career decision until he has been working responsibly for at least a year at a low-level job. Any job, no matter how menial, provides an opportunity for change to take place. In this program, all criminals must have a full-time job, in addition to the fifteen hours a week they spend with us during the first year. We do not expect the job to promote responsibility. Rather, work is a laboratory for implementing what is taught daily in the office. It is immaterial to us what skills the criminal has or acquires at work, because we regard any kind of employment as a vehicle for change. Besides requiring the learning of particular skills, jobs require cooperation with other workers, working under supervision, recognizing and accepting others' limitations, and coping with a variety of inevitable pressures, demands, adversities, and dissatisfactions.

The criminal must obtain his own job. He is not to have anyone else, even an agency, find one for him. We do not in any way sponsor a criminal in this pursuit. The most that we do is confirm that he has entered our program and corroborate any other factual information that is requested by a potential employer.

It is preferable for the criminal to begin at a low-level job, which has little power and control built into it. Unless he is dishonest in applying for a job or exploits family or other connections, the criminal is unlikely to qualify for anything better. The criminal is to answer truthfully all questions asked by a prospective employer. Rarely have employers pressed for details. Some have been astounded when the criminal volunteers them, as we require him to do. In our experience, it has not been difficult for the criminal to find a job, even during a recession, if he is not limiting his search to a position that offers power and prestige.

Even when a criminal has a highly developed skill, which many do, it is best for him to start at the bottom of the ladder in the occupation in which that skill is utilized. In some cases, it is desirable that a criminal not utilize that skill at all in his work. For example, we reject our criminals' accepting a first position in sales, even if they have had experience in that field. Although some have high potential for success because they are so verbal and persuasive, we have evidence that this facility is used initially as a criminal equivalent, that is, conning the customer.

The job assumed must be compatible with the hours of our program. A number of criminals have found low-level positions that allowed them to meet with us three hours and still work at least eight hours. Among these jobs are mail-room clerk, busboy, janitor, and short-order cook. It makes no difference what the criminal's prior training is. An attorney, suspended from practice, worked for two years as a short-order cook. It is also necessary that the criminal work at an establishment with a reputation for its integrity. We discourage criminals in our program from seeking positions where other criminals work or congregate or from applying to employees who have questionable reputations.

The job must keep the criminal totally occupied. Work that permits long periods of idleness or that is purely seasonal is discouraged. The criminal's time must be programmed; this usually means being employed by a well-structured organization. Here is an example of what occurs when there is not enough to do:

> Business had been poor for months. With periods of nothing to do on the job, C would bring a book to work and read. At this job, C could not learn about other aspects of the business, mainly because no one was there to teach him. There was a corrosion of C's morale. He did not want to quit, however, until he found another job in the same field in which there was opportunity to learn about additional aspects of the operation. Consequently, there was an expansion of thinking along criminal lines, predominantly sexual. Finally, C revealed that he had been drinking each night when he came home. C was so far along in the change process that he finally opened the channel and then requested and received more frequent meetings to monitor his thinking. C got a new job that offered new opportunities. The liquor consumption stopped immediately.

We have found that, with the tremendous energy the criminal has available to him, the heavier the workload, the less he complains of boredom and fatigue and the less the criminal thinking.

When the changing criminal knows in advance that he will have free time at work, he decides how to utilize it. In the past, the unchanged criminal welcomed slack periods of work; he daydreamed, talked with women, napped, or left the premises. Now he regards free time as an opportunity to attend to details that he has been too busy to handle, or if there is nothing else to do, he has already programmed reading to broaden his knowledge. In the past, even reading was regarded as work. An indicator of change is the criminal's filling spare time with obligatory tasks or with self-created tasks that further his development.

Formerly, the criminal used the slightest physical discomfort as an excuse for loafing on the job or for staying away from work altogether. Work now is an arena for discipline, so he puts in effort and shows endurance, despite a headache, a cold, or a sprain. He meets his obligations, despite illness or minor injury. This is the kind of discipline that this program requires in all areas at all times.

It is preferable that the job have diversity or the potential for it. Even a busboy position offers this, inasmuch as, in waiting on customers and in working with waiters and management, a daily variety of problems have to be solved. Working at a car wash, however, entails repeating exactly the same task again and again, with many slack periods in which there is nothing to do.

The job should offer an opportunity to advance within the establishment. A car wash is a dead end in this respect, but it is possible to earn a promotion from busboy to waiter, from clerk to assistant manager, or from unskilled laborer to supervisor.

Most criminals have considered themselves ready to advance at their jobs before we thought it advisable. Sometimes, after being at a job for only a few weeks, the criminal demonstrates his old pattern of thinking by indicating that he knows everything about the work and that he is better than everyone else there. At other times, the criminal may well be ready for a promotion by the company's standards, in terms of his skills and knowledge but not equipped in terms of learning and utilizing the new thinking patterns necessary to function responsibly in a more demanding position. For that reason, we caution against the criminal's seeking job advances too early. The power thrust, when enhanced by too rapid promotion with insufficient change, has been a precipitating factor in the resumption of crime—in some instances, on the job.

Some criminals satisfy the work ethic, but do not work ethically. These criminals want to work, and they actually do work, fulfill the requirements, and remain in the same position for a long time. They are then perceived to be functioning satisfactorily. These are the criminals who succeed in conveying an erroneous impression to probation officers and others. Some use their jobs as arenas for crime. They remain at their jobs for a long time, and their crimes usually remain undiscovered. In a program for change, these criminals take the trouble to report that they did not steal a piece of candy or a pen, but they do not reveal the more serious crimes that they have committed. Others actually do function without violation at work, but commit crimes elsewhere; work is a cover for crime, in that holding a job confers respectability. Our program requires that the criminal function with integrity elsewhere, that he work ethically while living ethically in all other parts of his life.

On the job, many problems arise both in the nature of the work and in interpersonal relations. Some difficulties are caused by other people, but most are consequences of the criminal's habitual thinking errors (especially not seeing things from the other person's point of view) and of his lack of knowledge of how to function responsibly. In developing the material of chapters 7, 8, and 9, we gave many examples of how thinking errors are corrected in the work setting as well as elsewhere. Instead of repeating that material here, we provide a few illustrations of the kinds of problems that arise every day.

Handling a reprimand

C was verbally blasted by one of the supervisors, who claimed that C had left early several times without permission, when in fact this was not the case. The supervisor was screaming so loudly that other salesmen and customers could hear. In the past, this would have evoked a furious reaction from C. However, he asked quietly whether he were fired. He was told that the manager would see him. C was angry but said nothing. He was not afraid of losing his job, but was unsure of how to handle the manager. He discussed this with us. The solution he arrived at was not to be called on the carpet but to request an appointment with the manager and present the history of difficulties with the supervisor. The important thing was not to react precipitately but to remain calm and set the record straight.

Coexisting with irresponsible workers

C was working as a painter on a crew where most of the men were drinking on the job and wasting a lot of time. Without success, C urged the men to work more efficiently and get the job done. Out of frustration, he reported them to the supervisor. This did not endear him to the supervisor, who did not want his subordinates to become angry at him. Our position was that C operated as a policeman, a function poorly suited to one who in the past had exerted far too much control and power over people. C had to learn that he was not going to alter the behavior of the others, but would instead only earn their ill will. He decided to stop complaining to the supervisor, because he realized that he was putting the man on the spot. Instead, C completed his fair share of the work and did not worry about what others were doing or not doing. As a result, he got along much better and still fulfilled the job requirements.

Relating to a supervisor who seems inconsistent

C's supervisor constantly told him what a fine job he was doing. In fact, C was told that he would soon receive a promotion. Weeks went by in which compliments were generously given, but there was no evidence that a promotion was in the offing. C was angry. He thought that, because he was the best employee at a particular level, the manager wanted to keep him there and thus not advance him. C thought that he was being exploited and wanted to tell the manager off. It did not occur to him to ask the manager for an appointment to discuss his future with the company. C finally did this and was given a date when he would be promoted. The promotion occurred as promised.

Coping with racial prejudice

C was eligible for a promotion, but feared that, because of his supervisor's reputed racial bigotry, he would be bypassed. C did a lot of thinking about how he should act. He resolved not to be difficult at work in any way and not even to consider walking out. Instead, he decided to redouble his efforts and show the supervisor how conscientious he was. C would give him no legitimate grounds for complaining about C's job performance. Consequently, C worked overtime and assumed extra work with eagerness, complaining about nothing. In several months, C's composure and tenacity paid off; he received the promotion.

Probably none of these four situations strikes the reader as particularly dramatic, inasmuch as they are all typical of what the responsible employee may also encounter. However, in time, even small problems become crises for he criminal, because he has not yet corrected thinking errors and mplemented new patterns of thought and action.

The criminal who has never worked or who is strongly against work presents special difficulties. He decides whether he will work on the basis of his feelings, his interest, or how hard he thinks the job is. He shows no initiative and little effort. As a result, he is careless, inefficient, and unproductive. The teaching in this program is that such a person must alter his attitude of doing the minimum and getting away with whatever he can. He must push himself, abide by the regulations, and when the work load is light, take initiatives to find things to do and then do them.

C had an extremely disagreeable job to do. He was required daily to buff the floors in two rooms, using strong chemicals in a poorly ventilated area and using defective equipment. C had reacted to the task negatively. He was angry, feeling sorry for himself, and ready to quit. In response to group discussions, C realized that he had held such an attitude at all jobs and had a dismal employment record. He knew that a continuation of the attitude would result in a deterioration not only at work, but elsewhere, and, inevitably, in crime. C decided that he had better alter his attitude and place change ahead of his feelings. Thus, he began to ask himself questions and to find fault with himself, rather than with the job. Was he running the buffer too long? Was he using the proper concentration of the solution? Was he doing everything possible to gain the cooperation of his co-workers? Pushing himself to do the best he could with the resources he had, C completed both rooms and had time left over to begin a third. And so he discovered that it was feasible to complete three rooms in one night, rather than two rooms in three nights. When the work was completed, C was still energetic and in a pleasant frame of mind.

C's self-critical attitude and initiatives resulted in improved performance. This in turn provided him with a more positive attitude toward the work, a sense of satisfaction, and commendation from others. C showed no reluctance to work at such a menial job daily and had plenty of energy left after such an enervating task.

In the process of change, the criminal each day prepares himself for the day's events. The unchanged criminal has not done this and, in fact, has had no schedule unless it was to further a criminal objective. Now, the changing criminal anticipates events and thinks about how he must perform each task with integrity and efficiency. Because all participants in our program work, this is true no matter how menial or executive their jobs. Psyching himself up for work is a new discipline that contributes to the criminal's more effective performance. This psyching up is done in every other aspect of life.

Unless the criminal anticipates what he will face each day, the old habitual patterns of thinking and action will automatically assert themselves.

C was working as a busboy at a restaurant. A girl who was not very attractive and rather sloppy sat at a table. C gave her blue cheese, which she consumed rapidly. When she asked for more, he used the term "Mademoiselle." She asked whether he was French, and he replied that he was Spanish (which was true). Then she used the word "seniorita." At this point, C was aware that he was getting into something and that he should refrain from further conversation. While waiting on other tables, he noticed that she seemed sad. He thought that he should cheer her up. Aware of what he was doing, he gave her some water and remarked that she was too pretty to be worried. At this, she smiled. Actually, she was not at all pretty, and C recognized that he was on the way to making a conquest. When he asked whether she was celebrating anything in particular, he knew for sure that he was on the make. She stated that she was down in the dumps and that she thought that it was a good idea to treat herself to a first-rate meal. C agreed. She left a two-dollar tip.

There would be nothing particularly untoward in this incident if C had been a responsible person. Here, however, C's behavior was typical of his old style in which he flattered women, ingratiated himself, and then exploited them. C knew that at his job he would be among women every day, both customers and fellow employees. It was necessary that he use deterrents and simultaneously choose to direct his thinking toward the job requirements, instead of toward the conquest of women.

A problem for the criminal is the tension that results from his perfectionism as, for the first time, he learns about many of the thinking patterns and interpersonal skills that responsible people begin acquiring when they are children. He reacts with panic to minor obstacles to his performance and must learn to take them in stride. The danger is that instead of enduring this tension as he learns a new life style, he may decide to forgo the whole change process. He may be dissatisfied because he unfavorably compares his performance with that of a co-worker who has years of experience both at that particular job and in functioning as a responsible person. The criminal has to learn to make realistic comparisons. Not being accustomed to the everyday worries of responsible living, he switches from one extreme to another—from giving no thought at all to some problems, to worrying about them incessantly.

> C described nights of tossing and turning as he was filled with nagging doubts about the adequacy of his performance at work. Was he doing well enough? Was he getting the training that he needed? Did his supervisor think well of him? What would he do after completing his training?

To be sure, such concerns are encouraged not only at work, but everywhere— provided that the standards by which he evaluates himself are realistic

> C said that he constantly had to make extraordinary efforts to do a job that satisfied him. To him, forty hours was not a workweek. He thought less of himself if he did not spend at least fifty-five hours at his desk. At one point, such a time commitment was necessary, but the job no longer required that. Yet, C retained an inflexible and unrealistic idea of what a good worker does.

It is essential that the criminal derive a positive impact from his work. Something must be gratifying in the job itself, or he will go elsewhere. As we work with a criminal, he begins employment at a low-level job; then, after a year, he shifts to a job offering more opportunity for personal development and growth. The criminal remains there if the work is challenging or eventually moves to something else in which he has talent and interest. Sometimes, he does so well at his first job that he becomes interested in it, rises within the organization, and establishes a career there.

We closely scrutinize the details of the criminal's performance at his job. As change agents, we have learned a great deal about fields unfamiliar to us. We have spent many hours discussing the problems of efficiency at a job—the problems of serving dinner to a large group of people or the options in establishing inventory procedures. These are not excursions in irrelevance. To dissect thinking errors and teach the criminal to apply correctives on the job, we have found that it is important to become knowledgeable about the job itself.

In working for someone else, the criminal is expected to develop company-mindedness and loyalty. This is not to say that he is to be an organizational automaton. Rather, the issue is his learning to subordinate his personal ambitions and dissatisfactions to the task at hand—to getting the job done. He has never done this for any sustained period or without expecting an immediate commendation. Loyalty is to be complemented by his learning to act in his own responsible self-interest whenever necessary. The major manifestation of the criminal's company-mindedness is the degree of effort that he shows in doing things that he does not want to do, such as working overtime or doing a job that he considers beneath him.

When applying for a job, all criminals in our program must inform employers of their criminal backgrounds with as much detail as requested. From time to time, they are called upon to help spot thievery within the organization. Every criminal must report criminality he observes, but we firmly object to his voluntarily taking on the assignment of detective or policeman. We have found that in such a role, the criminal derives an excitement similar to that he obtained in crime. We have termed this excitement a *criminal equivalent*. (We presented the concept of the nonarrestable criminal equivalent in chapter 7 of volume 1.)

At no time must a criminal compromise his integrity. He is expected to function with honesty, even if others around him are not doing so. There are to be no white lies, no taking sick leave unless he is genuinely incapacitated, no phony excuses for anything. In a few situations, the criminal's supervisor has asked him to act unethically. In each case, the criminal has successfully explained why he would not do this. Some have stated directly that the consequences of a lie or unethical practice are too costly for them in the light of their own history. That has been sufficient, because the supervisor had known from the beginning the background of the criminal.

Most of the criminals in our program have done well in the world of work. Having begun at the bottom, many have risen rapidly to supervisory or management positions. In other words, we have talented people, and when they are functioning responsibly, their talents are quickly recognized, and they are placed in positions of authority.

Not every product of our program has been a stunning success at his work. The positions of criminals at their jobs have ranged from a company officer who eventually earned in excess of $50,000 a year to a house painter earning less than $10,000 a year. However, no matter what his station, each criminal is totally responsible at his job. Like any other man, a criminal will rise in the vocational world as far as his talent, energy, and initiative will take him. The amount of money he makes and how rapidly he advances at work are not our essential concerns. Rather, how he does the job and relates to others will show his progress in change. We prefer that a criminal remain a store clerk who plods away responsibly rather than become a company director who operates by short cuts and unethical practices.

In short, passable or acceptable work is not satisfactory in this program. Passable work is totally consistent with criminality. The criminal has held jobs in the past just to satisfy others while remaining active in crime. The objective in this program is to do more than get by. The objective is to strive for excellence in every aspect of a responsible life. There must be integrity, loyalty, and efficiency. But, if these qualities are in evidence only at work, they are worth little in the criminal's change. Unless the new patterns of thinking and action are implemented with excellence everywhere, they do not become ingrained.

MONEY

Far more money passes through the hands of most full-time criminals in a month than a middle-class family earns in a year. Yet the criminal justifies much of his criminality on the basis of his needing money. Money has been mainly an index of the success of his crime and a tool for exploiting others. Thousands of dollars may be disposed of in a few weeks. The more the criminal acquires, the more he spends or gives away. No matter how much money he obtains in crime or earns, very soon he is broke. Clearly, the criminal has never valued money and knows nothing about its proper use. He is unfamiliar with the simple details of saving and budgeting. In this program, the criminal learns both to value and to manage money. Because of our lack of assistants, we have done all the instructing in this area. However, this aspect could well be handled by an assistant to the program.

The criminal has to account for all his money—income and expenditures.

At the beginning, a responsible person, usually his wife, supervises his handling of money. We contact whoever performs this function to check the accuracy of the criminal's report to us. This checking is necessary early in the program, because the criminal sometimes lies to and intimidates the person who is monitoring him. If there is no responsible person to oversee the criminal's financial practices, we agree to do it. He turns his pay over to us and we dispense money to him as necessary.

Each day's report includes an accounting of all money spent during the preceding twenty-four hours. The criminal's having to account for every expenditure acts as a deterrent to his financial irresponsibility. Of course, if the criminal is intent on spending money, he can do so without our knowledge by obtaining a credit, borrowing, or swindling someone.

> C began spending beyond his means as soon as he got out of prison. A week after he entered our program, with $20 on his person, he met a girl-friend at the train station. When he said that he had only $20 for the weekend, she was understanding because she knew that he had just come out of prison. The woman had $60 with her. She could have gone to the YWCA and he home. Instead, they went to a hotel for $14 a night. Deciding that this was too shabby, they wound up at a more expensive place, for $28 a night. With a bill for two nights plus meals, C very quickly was broke. He borrowed from her and wired a friend to send $75 of money that C had deposited with him for safekeeping. At work, he received another $12. By the end of the weekend, C had only enough in his pocket to take his girlfriend to the train station. His view of the weekend, as he described it in the group, was that, compared with similar episodes in the past, he had changed: he had been "economical." He pointed out to us that, even in prison, he had spent more money on women, having persuaded his family to send him $2,000 that he used to buy presents for girlfriends.

The same criminal, during a four-month honeymoon in our program, saved $2,300 and then squandered it. In time, he resumed a program of saving, amassed more than $1,000, and began to value money and to manage it prudently.

When there is active criminal thinking and the criminal has money with him, it burns a hole in his pocket.

> As C entered the program, he had 55¢ available for the first day's expenses. (He was being given two free meals at work.) First thing in the morning, C spent the 55¢ on beer. This 55¢ for beer was qualitatively no different from the $20,000 that he had spent on cars, women, and the rental of seaside cottages. In neither case was the money being spent

responsibly. Whether 55¢ or $20,000, the *pattern* of expenditure was the same.

C never developed the discipline necessary to manage money or to implement and sustain the correctives for thinking errors. He returned to crime.

Money is a burden to the criminal in this program, because it is potentially always an open sesame to further criminality. There is no way other than through experience for the criminal to learn this. We require him to draw up a budget. It is one thing to make a budget and another to follow it. Some criminals are initially enthusiastic about saving money. We do not personally hold large sums of money for them, but encourage them to open savings accounts and earn interest. Thus, they can accumulate a substantial reserve. What appeals to them is the challenge of saving—proving that they can do it. The act of saving is valued more than the money itself. Because the criminal has demonstrated that he could achieve it, the challenge has been met. He then gives the money to women, makes extravagant purchases, and in other ways returns to old patterns.

We cannot teach the criminal to value money. Valuing money is an *outgrowth* of implementing the correctives for thinking errors. The criminal's attitude toward money changes as he begins to think in long-range terms, as he alters his pretensions, as he learns to make decisions, and as he eliminates control and ownership patterns. Valuing money in a responsible way is a *consequence* of implementing the program. A criminal who was starting to value money, thought in the following manner:

> C decided to stop seeing his girlfriend, for a variety of well-thought-out reasons. He believed, however, that he would need something more than work to occupy him. He was not planning to pursue other women because he had little time or money for a social life. Moreover, he realized that he was not ready for a responsible relationship with a woman. Being a lover of music, C thought about buying a stereo phonograph. This led to a careful consideration of his financial position. He realized that in the past he had not hesitated to buy anything he wanted, whether or not he had the money. Consequently, he had landed in prison. C reasoned that an expensive purchase of any sort now would be inadvisable. He concluded, "To be solvent is to have a keystone for my freedom." Moreover, he thought, if he wanted to listen to music, he could go to the library and attend free concerts. He also decided that he would be kidding himself if he thought that a stereo set would fulfill his desire for female companionship.

In this program, the criminal develops a concept of what money can accomplish both immediately and over the long haul. The first step is to take care of basic needs, such as food and shelter. After these requirements are met, the criminal learns to plan. He considers setting the money aside to provide for the education of his children, for insurance in case of disaster and disability, and, eventually, for investment for a capital return. We do not tell criminals how to spend their money; rather, we present options that are new to them and expand the scope of their thinking. As criminals begin to value money and formulate responsible monetary objectives, they are eager to earn more. All our people have either worked for overtime pay or done some moonlighting on a second job.

Eventually, the changing criminal becomes close-fisted. As with so many other things, he goes from one extreme to another.

> C and his wife had accumulated $6,000 worth of debts. This was their financial position as C entered our program. Within two years, they had saved almost $9,000 from both their incomes. Their target was $10,000. Both had adhered to a very strict budget. When they needed something, they bought it only on sale. They watched pennies so carefully that differences between them cropped up over spending a dollar here or there. For example, one night C's wife wanted to go dancing. This was not in accord with C's rigid idea of economy. He wanted to drive without deviation toward the $10,000 goal. C was fearful that even a very small incidental expenditure would develop into a pattern of profligacy.

C's wife had been responsible in money management all along. As C put it, "She holds a nickel until the buffalo jumps off it." However, his wife had not been able to save, because, with C not working but spending their funds excessively, all her income had been used to provide the bare necessities of life and cover debts. With C functioning responsibly, they were working together as a financial management team.

In other instances, we have instructed both the criminal and his wife in money management, because neither was knowledgeable. Some couples meet with us, bringing in their bank statements, checkbooks, bills, and lists of expenditures and debts.

> C realized that he did not know how to handle money. However, his wife also spent beyond the couple's means, and more than $2,000 in debts had accumulated. Meeting with the two of them, we suggested the following:
> 1. That we obtain a complete account of indebtedness.
> 2. That the financial management temporarily be taken out of C's wife's hands, so that we could instruct C and give him experience.
> 3. That a checking account be opened at a bank near their home and all checks be deposited there before being cashed. All expenses would be paid by check, except for a weekly cash withdrawal given to C's wife for

food, cleaning, and other incidental expenses. Through paying by check, clear records of expenditures could be kept. We would teach C how to handle a checkbook properly.

4. That the two of them live off C's paycheck and use his wife's earnings to pay debts.

5. That there be no more buying on credit.

6. That a list of priorities be established for paying debts, largely according to which ones had the highest finance charges.

7. That C communicate to his wife everything that he learned, so that, within a few months, complete management could be undertaken by the two of them.

Here we were establishing accountability for all money. C's wife agreed to this arrangement, and it worked out well. In three years, their debts were paid, many important household purchases were made, and the couple had put aside $1,700. The greater the attention to the mechanics of money management, the more the couple valued money. In turn, the more they valued money, the more carefully they scrutinized their expenditures.

We do not even suggest that the criminal repay old debts that have been written off, especially if he was confined. This was unrealistic and impractical; he could never manage to do it. If called to account for an old debt, he must settle; but this has very seldom happened.

A question sometimes arises as to whether the criminal should help others in need. This is not an issue of giving to organized charity, but helping people to whom he is close, especially relatives and women.

C's brother was unemployed and had two children and a wife to support. C knew that his brother was refusing to work unless he could obtain a prestigious position. In light of the brother's lack of education and poor work record, this was a pipe dream. The brother had repeatedly refused to help himself or let others help him to get a job for which he was qualified. C's first inclination was to give his brother some money and provide him with the use of a car. C listened to counterarguments in the group: by giving his brother the money, C would only perpetuate the status quo and deprive himself of needed funds. C decided, nevertheless, to help his brother. The brother did nothing to help himself and continued indefinitely to drain C's resources.

This criminal not only ignored the advice of the group in this situation, but also decided to do things in his own way in many other situations and eventually left the program. In contrast with this is the following incident that involved a criminal who was progressing in change:

C wanted to bail his girlfriend out of temporary financial difficulty. She was between jobs and short of money. There was nothing criminal about C's loaning her the money. He had it to loan and had legitimately earned it. The question was whether it was prudent in the light of his own upcoming financial obligations. After thinking about this, C decided that he could not afford to make the loan. But he rejected loaning the money on other grounds as well; he thought that, by trying to help this woman, he might again be trying to build himself up as her rescuer and to gain control of her, as he had done with so many women in the past.

If this situation had occurred before C's participation in this program, C would not have hesitated to give the money to his girl friend, not simply to loan it. Money had never meant anything to him, so giving it away would have resulted in a buildup for him and indebtedness for the other party. The criminal who is progressing in change in this program adheres to the adage, "Neither a borrower nor a lender be." He has learned for the first time in his life how to manage money, and he values his money because he has worked hard and honestly to acquire it.

SOCIAL RELATIONSHIPS

Once he has severed his ties to the criminal world, the criminal complains of loneliness. To him, loneliness is not a lack of companionship but rather a void resulting from the lack of criminal excitement. A partial remedy is for him to take initiatives and meet new people. However, in the early stages of this program, the criminal has little opportunity for this because his time is programmed. Early in change, every one of our criminals has limited himself to a routine that he follows regularly, occupying himself mostly with work, family, and daily group meetings. Therefore, we have not attempted to encourage social initiatives early in the change process. Some criminals do not try to develop a broader social life until well after they have completed the demanding first year of our program.

When we help criminals to grapple with taking social initiatives, we find two opposite patterns. Some sit back and wait for others to come to them. Their reticence is attributable to their lack of experience in functioning with responsible people. They are, therefore, ill at ease and awkward in their approach. Other criminals have always had great facility in socializing. These are the criminals who have good manners, charm, and savoir-faire and have capitalized on them. Each group now faces the same challenge: building responsible relationships for the first time and basing those relationships on common interests, trust, truthfulness, and concern for others. Criminals in both groups must learn the same social skills. It is more difficult, however, to instruct the charmers, who regard each person who comes along as another sucker for them to exploit. These criminals not only have to learn new patterns, but also must unlearn habits that are praised by others who do not know of their criminal makeup.

Even if the criminal is reticent and tries to insulate himself socially, he nevertheless has casual social transactions that he must learn to handle.*

> While getting a haircut, C found that the barber was upset about the death of his mother and was talking about her funeral. C was uncomfortable. He was now sensitive enough to know that he should respond, but he did not know how. He managed to blurt out a statement of sympathy and then switched the topic of conversation.

The criminal who is facile in social relationships also has to learn to respond to people in a way that is different from his old habits.

> At C's job, the manager's wife dropped by. She did not have a place to sit as she chatted with the staff. C jokingly pointed to his lap. The rest of that evening, C pondered his behavior. He concluded that it must have been a desire for action that produced his response. He became frightened that he might be on the road to crime.

The criminal has to learn to fit his responses to the situation. He has to discriminate between being friendly and intimate, between being interested and intrusive, between being complimentary and obsequious.

In observing responsible people functioning from day to day, the criminal is struck that those who have never heard of our program appear to function according to its principles. Moreover, they do so without suffering the sense of deprivation of excitement that he experiences.

> A woman at work was saying that people have to start at the bottom and gradually work their way up in life. As she was talking about this, C thought "Gee, she might have been talking to Dr. Yochelson," although he knew that she had not.
>
> *   *   *
>
> C asked the cashier at the store where he worked if she ever thought of stealing some of the money and altering the records. She replied dryly, "I look at the money as my work." She did not even regard the money as money. It was as though she were counting paper clips.

*Although it is not necessary to change a pattern of social reticence in the noncriminal, it is vital to do so in the criminal. Mastering skills of responsible social relationship is an essential part of his establishing a new life style.

As we pointed out earlier, the criminal does not establish friendships with other group members. Most begin to extend their social world within their own families. They have relatives, usually in the area, whom they have not seen for years or have met only at the funerals of other family members. Many of these are people who were good to the criminal when he was a youngster, but then he took advantage of them and then ignored and avoided them altogether. Social initiatives gradually expand to include neighbors and co-workers. Sometimes, the criminal strikes up a relationship with responsible people whom he once knew but long ago abandoned. Early in the course of the criminal's new social forays, these embryonic relationships often intensify very quickly, at least on the criminal's part. The criminal sometimes channels so much time and energy into his social life that he ignores other obligations. Here, as elsewhere, he learns moderation—that friendships develop gradually. It takes time for people to know and trust one another. This is especially true when the criminal renews contact with people whom he let down earlier. For the first time, the criminal learns that friendship entails fulfilling obligations, truthfulness, a surrender of control, and putting himself in the position of others.

Social relations are totally different from anything the criminal has ever experienced. Previously, the criminal has had as his primary objectives self-aggrandizement and the exploitation of others. Now, there are new objectives, including recreation, seeking information, utilizing leisure time constructively, and, most important, the life-enriching dimensions of harmonious interpersonal relationships that develop from sharing, giving, and learning to receive. Eventually, by putting himself in the place of others, the criminal acquires sensitivity to other people's needs. The more the criminal implements this program, the more he attends to the finer points of relationships, the small courtesies and pleasantries. This is done out of respect or fondness for a person, rather than for personal gain.

The criminal learns to be discriminating in his social contacts. Some responsible people who are good company for others may not be suitable for him. He may have neighbors who get drunk while watching sports on television each weekend. These people may be generally responsible, but the criminal will get little from their company without drinking, which he cannot afford to do. Furthermore, if responsible people occasionally do something irresponsible, the criminal has to refrain from that activity. This is not a matter of setting himself above others morally. What would be an isolated instance of irresponsibility for one person is likely to open the door to continuing irresponsibility and arrestability for the criminal. The criminal has to make continual appraisals if he is to develop relationships that offer him the greatest potential for growth.

An aspect that emerges repeatedly in the criminal's social learning is his bigotry toward responsible people. Throughout his life, he has mostly scorned responsible relatives, responsible peers, responsible co-workers, and any other responsible people with whom he has had contact. With his bigoted attitude, the criminal has invalidly built himself up as being better than others. This attitude must be changed. With experience in living responsibly, this bigotry disappears and is replaced by admiration for responsible people. The criminal also seizes on a specific feature by which he builds himself up at others' expense, such as color, religion, or national origin. In the group, the criminal learns to evaluate people on the basis of their personal qualities. As he associates with responsible people of different ethnic backgrounds (among them some in our group), this prejudice gradually fades.

WOMEN

In chapter 8, we described the alteration of sexual patterns in the changing criminal. Here we shall emphasize the *process* by which the criminal's relationships with women serve as an arena for change, rather than discuss specific sexual patterns that are altered.

The unchanged criminal, as we begin working with him, is continuing to pursue women for exploitative purposes. This is true of criminals who are single, married (either to irresponsible or responsible women), living in common-law relationships, and separated from their families. Whether married or not, they are rarely satisfied with having one woman; they consider it an intrinsic part of their manhood to have a stable of women available for sex. Those who have liaisons with irresponsible women are using these women for sex and money and regard themselves as being in total control of the relationships. However, they do not realize that they are themselves being used in much the same manner.

In listening to the unchanged criminal's daily reports, we find that sex occupies more of his thinking than any other topic on any given day. He thinks of having sex with any woman whom he encounters and considers himself irresistible to her. This includes total strangers whom he passes on the street. In his thinking, there is no limit to the license he has in securing women.

Nothing can be done to alter these patterns immediately. A substantial period is required for change. Clearly, as he begins our program, the criminal is not equipped for a relationship with a responsible person. Therefore, we impose restraints on him. Criminals who are unattached are, for the first few months, to refrain from sex and from any other kind of involvement with women. This they have done for as long as a full year. A criminal who is married or is living with a woman is required to restrict his relationships with females to that one woman. Because there is voluminous sexual thinking, it is essential that the criminal apply deterrents very early in the change process (chapter 9).

Just as the criminal has had to start from the bottom at his job, so he has had to start from scratch to find and relate to a responsible woman. This has entailed probing, waiting, and taking things slowly to find one who not only is attractive to him and personally compatible, but is responsible. Fact-finding with respect to a person's responsibility has been more than a one-date proposition; usually it has taken months. When the criminal finds a responsible woman who appeals to him, she becomes a vehicle for his change, in that, for the first time, he must abdicate control, function interdependently, fulfill obligations, and implement the many other important correctives that are essential to a responsible adult relationship.

In the daily reports, many different issues arise as the criminal shifts from seeking sexual conquests to establishing an interdependent, constructive relationship. Power, ownership, and anger reactions are among the subjects of frequent discussion and correction. In our daily work, it is easiest to correct patterns in criminals who are married to responsible women. The married criminal who changes in this program develops a loyalty toward his wife that he never had before toward her or anyone else. The process of change has the roughest course when the criminal is married to an irresponsible woman who opposes his changing because he will no longer be the exciting person that he once was. Unchanged, the criminal abandoned one woman after another. Now, the opposite occurs and he stays with his mate even in relationships with little chance of success. Even in the face of infidelity and physical abuse by his spouse, the criminal has clung to the hope that if he changed, he could have a family life. In every case in which the criminal's wife has been irresponsible, a separation has occurred, always at the wife's initiative.

The criminal's entire approach to women changes as his thinking patterns are altered. Sex, which was of overriding importance, is now integrated into the total relationship. Over a period of many weeks, the unmarried criminal develops a responsible relationship with a woman that may include sex. Married and unmarried criminals both report far less urgency and frequency of sexual activity than at any other time in their lives. This is both because they have so much else to occupy them and because sex is less exciting now that the conquest element has been eliminated. Extramarital sex is deterred, because the criminal does not want to sacrifice gains for which he has worked long and hard. Tenderness overshadows sex in the relationship. As one criminal commented, "A flower can be more expressive than a caress."

The unchanged criminal avoids the word *love* except when he refers to sex or when he is sentimental in a fragmented way toward someone important in his life, such as a mother who has stood by him or done things for him. In the process of change, the criminal learns an altogether new form of interpersonal relationship that emphasizes concern, obligation, trust, interdependence, and openness. The changing criminal now fulfills the basic requirements of a love relationship, but, interestingly enough, he still avoids the word *love*.

Of course, the criminal still has much to learn, even when he has eliminated old patterns and is habituating new ones. Many problems with the women in his life continue to arise and are discussed in the meetings. The themes that emerge include concerns typical of those arising in responsible relationships—disagreements about raising children, differences over money, problems with relatives, particular difficulties that wives or girlfriends are having, and problems in social relationships. Throughout the change process, there remains a strong emphasis on deterrence. That is because insufficient change manifesting itself in irresponsibility is reflected most immediately in thinking and action patterns with women. As we pointed out in chapter 8, the last bastion of criminality usually appears in relationships with women. As the criminal implements our program and uses the correctives and the more sophisticated deterrents, he eventually reaches a point at which his thinking processes are similar to those of responsible men who have sexual thinking about women other than their wives. These thoughts quickly come to mind and are just as quickly deterred.

Our description of what occurs with the heterosexual criminal also applies to the criminal who is homosexual. A person's sexual preference makes no difference in this program. Rather, it is the responsible quality of the relationship that is important. The homosexual has to alter the same patterns as the heterosexual criminal who has pursued, conquered, and then abandoned partners. The homosexual is sexually continent at the outset of the change process until he learns to evaluate people as people, not simply as sex objects for his use. The criminal who is a homosexual must apply the correctives for thinking errors, so that he develops an interdependent, constructive relationship before sex occurs. He is then ready to engage in a responsible, consenting relationship.

The few criminals who are truly bisexual have found it necessary to make a choice that we do not dictate. To be married and have a secret homosexual liaison violates the open channel and the trustworthiness that they know are essential to all their relationships. Their past homosexual episodes have all been exploitative and not reflective of their true sexual preference. In marriage, they have deterred homosexual thinking and action and have committed themselves to their wives. The one criminal in the program who is single and bisexual has chosen an exclusively heterosexual adjustment.

We now present a case that illustrates problems that arise with *all* criminals as they learn to relate responsibly to women.

Before he was in our program, C had known R for several years. Now, out of prison and participating in our program, C learned that he was not ready for romantic involvement. He wanted female companionship, however, so he contacted R. R had little romantic interest in C, but had enjoyed his company. The two resumed their friendship, with C being totally candid about his criminal background and his participation in the program. C and R met once a week, went to a concert or museum, had a meal together, or just spent time talking. This worked out to their mutual satisfaction. However, as they grew closer, C realized that sexual involvement might become a primary factor for both of them. He decided that he would not be the one to push the issue, but would face it if it arose. After several months of seeing each other, C and R discussed the possibility of a consenting sexual relationship. They had been spending increasing amounts of time with each other and had developed great closeness. R was afraid that she could not satisfy C, who had the reputation of being sexually very active. Finally, with apprehension on the part of both, sex occurred. For C, this was the first time that he had had sex with a woman whom he had begun genuinely to care for. There was tenderness and consideration, rather than exploitation; at the same time, there was disciplined deterrence in his thinking about other women.

As C and R spent more time together and sex became more frequent, C began to become disenchanted with R, because she appeared to live in a fantasy world with respect to her own importance. She also clung to him for advice in even the smallest decision. She began to expect him to spend all his spare time with her and often phoned him at work. In his customary manner of thinking in extremes, C went back and forth between viewing R as the most wonderful woman in the world and as the most unsuitable neurotic. Sometimes, he wanted to see her every day; at other times, he wanted to terminate the relationship completely. With his usual secrecy, there was not a forthright discussion of problems. R was increasingly insecure as she picked up C's reservations about the relationship, although she did not know what they were.

We knew that C's cooling off about R had to do with more than R's neuroticism. C had conquered R sexually. Now that she was his, he wanted greater excitement. In the past, C had maintained contacts with several women at a time. Despite being responsible, attractive, and intelligent, R did not have all the physical features that he sought in the harem that he had always kept.

C continually found fault with R in his thinking. He did not always express what he thought, but R picked up the fact that not all was well. C was actually seeking things to pick on. When he tried to phone her and the line was busy for an hour, he took this as evidence that he did not count for much in her life; otherwise, she would leave the line free. He objected to the triviality of some of her conversation. He was critical of numerous other features. Again, the issue of continuing the relationship came to a head. R said that she valued C very much. If C left, she would be miserable, but she would be even more miserable if he stayed and continued to find fault with her. After talking, they decided to continue their relationship.

From the beginning of their relationship, and even before C had gone to prison, C has misrepresented himself to R as a man of wealth. He had promoted himself as a person who could offer her anything she wanted in life. As R now became short of funds, C indicated that he could easily afford to help her out and gave her several hundred dollars. This depleted his savings, but R did not know that. By giving her this money, C built up his opinion of himself and strengthened his control over R.

By this point, every criminal feature had asserted itself in C's relationship with R. Because of R's particular personality, she permitted this.

As C eliminated criminal thinking and action patterns and the relationship became more stable, C began to evaluate its pros and cons. He valued R as a person—she was attractive, affectionate, intelligent, and vivacious and shared many of his interests—but her indecision, unrealistic expectations of him, and clinging to him bothered C. He knew that she could resolve these problems with some outside help. In the past, he would have tried to act as her therapist. Now he refrained from advice-giving and left her to work out her own problems. For himself, C had to resolve whether he wanted to adapt to her idiosyncrasies in the interest of a long-term relationship. In the past, C had adapted to no one and did not tolerate others' foibles. In this situation, C had immeasurably complicated the difficulties by his irresponsibility and criminal patterns. What was most important here was that C was beginning to value another person, to see things from that person's point of view, and to develop an interdependent relationship.

At the time of this writing, the two are still spending time with each other and are good friends. Not only have they ruled out sex with each other, but sex plays a minimal role in C's *thinking*. C has become less controlling of R, less critical of her, and more critical of his own functioning. Our experience has been that the criminal who is progressing in change blames himself for anything that goes awry in a relationship, because he knows that he is the one who needs most to change. This account illustrates what occurs in an important arena for change, as the criminal learns for the first time what a human relationship requires of him.

OUR CONTACTS WITH OUTSIDE SOURCES

The more we can learn from people close to the criminal, the more effective we can be in helping him to achieve change. We require access to outside sources both to check on the criminal's progress and to be of assistance in working out problems. A condition of his participation in this program is that the criminal must agree in advance to our making regular checks on him with someone responsible—usually his wife, a relative, or a steady girlfriend. We require that these meetings with others be conducted in the criminal's presence whenever possible, so that possibilities for misinterpretation are minimized.

It is often difficult to obtain the cooperation of outside informants. Irresponsible relatives do not want to meet with us at all, mainly because they think that their own behavior will be scrutinized. Responsible relatives are sometimes afraid to tell the truth, because they have long been intimidated by the criminal. Many a criminal has untruthfully complained that outside informants refused to meet with us, when the fact was that he had forbidden them to do so.

However, once contact is made and we have had an initial meeting, responsible relatives cooperate with us eagerly and sometimes call us spontaneously, seeking counsel in handling particular situations. Often, the contact is continued for a long time, less for purposes of factual checking than for reconciling differences and pointing out problems that require attention.* In fact, even after their husbands have completed the intensive part of the program, some wives phone us for guidance, especially if the couple has had an argument.

We sometimes help a criminal's wife to make changes in her own attitudes or ways of doing things. Usually, her undesirable patterns of behavior do not emerge until the criminal has progressed in change. In two cases, when a wife and a girlfriend had neurotic problems, we advised them to seek help and referred them to psychotherapists. In most cases, however, these women do not need a course of therapy, but only informed instruction.

Initially, some wives are skeptical of our approach, because they think that we are advocates for the criminal, or because, being inexperienced in examining their own patterns of functioning, they find exposure to our methods disagreeable. The test of our effectiveness is not whether there is instant agreement in our office, but whether our approach makes an impact afterward. In every instance, when our informant has been responsible, he or she has been responsive to our suggestions and welcomed our perspective, whatever the initial reservations.

---

*When the criminal closes the channel of communication, a meeting with an outside informant is helpful to us.

The wives with whom we have dealt have shown an amazing tolerance of their husbands. Most have endured the stresses imposed upon them because of their dread of loneliness, others (usually those who are irresponsible) because of a fascination with their husbands' criminality. Most wives have had to assume their husbands' duties and obligations. After doing this for a long time, they have developed set ways of doing things. As their husbands begin to show evidence of change, their methods are challenged. They believe that they have been right, if for no other reason than that their husbands have contributed so little. After exposure to our program, the two parties learn to share in responsible decision-making. Some old solutions can be reconsidered, and problems can be approached more responsibly than before. In most cases, the wives function much more stably and with greater confidence and flexibility, because, for the first time, they can count on their husbands' cooperation.

When husband and wife are both amenable, we meet with them together to discuss actual and potential difficulties in their relationship. We do this only when we are reasonably certain that the criminal is functioning responsibly. Otherwise, all we are likely to hear are his wife's justifiable complaints and accusations. The following is an example of issues that arise in our meetings with couples.

> C's wife, P, pointed out that C was up tight about many things that seemed relatively trivial to her—the choice of a route to work, how to mow the lawn, when to do the shopping, and so on. She said that it was difficult to tolerate C's continually making mountains out of molehills. We pointed out that, when a person like C decides at the age of thirty to make a total change in his thinking and action patterns, there is a tremendous amount to learn. We assured P that C's tension would subside as he gained greater experience in functioning responsibly. In fact, from our point of view, such tension was an indicator that change was occurring.

> C stated that his wife was simplistic, dogmatic, and closed-minded on many issues. P, willing to listen and to be self-critical, stated that she had not realized how her abruptness could impede communication. She pointed out that C was often silent and that this made her more irritable. C said that he thought he had improved, in that, in the past, he had become angry and had intimidated her. Now, he was silent, because he really had nothing to say and did not want to stir up an argument. The upshot of the discussion was that P said that she would try to watch herself and react less dogmatically. She realized that it had become so habitual for her to speak this way that sometimes she sounded closed-minded, when in reality it was a manifestation of her own uncertainty.

The emphasis was on clarifying issues for C's wife. However, attention is never restricted to one person. Later in that meeting, some of C's mistakes were identified, and correctives were suggested.

A more basic problem is that many wives, girlfriends, and relatives expect too much from the criminal too soon. If the criminal has reduced his anger reactions by eighty percent, his wife thinks only about the unpleasantness of the other twenty percent, which she regards as evidence of a failure to change. Our function is to establish a sounder perspective and to counsel patience. Some criminals complain that their wives remain skeptical about the genuiness of change, even after substantial change has occurred. The wives have been disappointed so often that they do not place much hope in any enterprise, for fear of being disappointed again. It is reasonable, then, to require the criminal to be patient and put himself in his wife's place, recognizing that her skepticism is warranted. If his wife's doubts are part of an underlying neuroticism and do not become less intense with the criminal's evident change, we explain to her how her attitude retards the constructive building of the relationship. We have found that she responds constructively to our suggestions.

Wives who are highly irresponsible or criminal resent us and our approach. After meeting with us once or twice, these women perceive us as intrusive and reject invitations for further meetings. They inform us of their husbands' activities only when they are trying to use us as instruments to control their husbands. Once the criminal eschews irresponsibility, his irresponsible wife or girlfriend rejects him, because he is no longer the same exciting man. Marriages to irresponsible women often break up, despite efforts by the changing criminal to hold them together and effect change.

We meet with outside sources both for verification purposes and to help counsel the criminal. These sources include parents, siblings, employers, and others who have frequent contact with the criminal, such as counselors and therapists. Privileged communication is always maintained, and the criminal is usually present.

EMERGING SELF-RESPECT

Ours is not a program for raising the self-esteem of criminals. In fact, we stress the opposite—eliminating their criminal pride and sense of uniqueness by making them realistically face what they are. The criminal's self-esteem is based on a misconception of his power and status in the world. He thinks well of himself when responsible people who know him do not. The term *self-respect* is applied to a changing criminal who realistically appraises himself as functioning responsibly. This self-assessment may not be corroborated immediately by others; but, when it finally is, the criminal's self-respect is reinforced.

The criminal slowly builds a new life as a result of his own initiative, endurance, and persistence. Having corrected old patterns, he is afraid of losing what he has achieved. A sense of self-respect emerges that at first is based on honest acquisition of things that did not come easily and are therefore valued. First of all, the criminal values his freedom from confinement and does not want to jeopardize that.

> As C expressed it, while he was a criminal he lived in the tiny corner of the world of the criminal element. It was a world in which he was forever creating problems for himself, having to look over his shoulder for fear of detection. Now, as a responsible person, C lives in a bigger and better world that has a multitude of opportunities and possibilities. This he would not give up for anything.

The criminal well along in change experiences another kind of freedom—the inner freedom of not having to deter criminal ideas endlessly. He is so programmed with new tasks that criminal thinking is progressively less frequent: "I don't have time for criminal thinking." It has been replaced by a new outlook on life, and his mind is occupied with the many tasks required to achieve his new objectives.

The criminal begins to acquire material possessions. He is afraid of losing what he has earned. He has banked some money, rents an apartment that is within his means, owns furnishings and other possessions paid for with honestly earned wages, and, despite our disapproval, has established a good credit rating that is valuable to him.

> C was laid off from his job. Although this was a setback, he was determined not to give up. He said he would wash dishes if he had to, because "I don't want to lose my apartment." He was proud of the apartment; he was paying for it with money honestly earned. He saw it as both a symbolic and a tangible reward of responsible conduct. As it turned out, C did wash dishes until he found another job.

The changing criminal also perceives the developing good will of others. Those who know his history are generous in their approval. In addition, new friendships grow, and strangers respond favorably to his courtesy and trustworthiness.

> C had explored the possibility of working at a store. Having discovered a more promising opportunity elsewhere, he called the store's manager to tell him that he had taken another position. His call was received courteously, and the manager thanked him for calling and said that he

would be interested in hiring C if he were available in the future. C was very gratified by this reception and saw it as a reward for responsible behavior.

Too frequently, the unchanged criminal has conned his way into the good graces of others. However, when they discover that their trust in him has not been justified and that they have been betrayed, they turn against him.

The changing criminal does not want to jeopardize himself. He no longer imperils blossoming relationships with his family, neighbors, co-workers, and people with whom he does business. In addition, he values the respect of the A.C. and of other group members.

Self-respect honestly earned is indicative of an emerging concern about morality. True, the criminal values the freedom that comes with not being tripped up by lies, crimes, or other irresponsible conduct. But most important is the inner freedom that derives from the effective, sustained operation of conscience. Previously, crime has been the criminal's oxygen; now, he regards crime as a form of pollution. He has an inner sense of cleanliness.

Six years before, C illegally obtained and irresponsibly disposed of thousands of dollars. A substantial amount of the money was spent at the very restaurant where he was working as a busboy. There he had wined and dined women whom he later exploited. Now he had two dollars in spending money in his pocket. Six years before, he did not have even two dollars that had been earned honestly. Although C was in financial poverty now, there was no poverty of morality.

*   *   *

Four chairs were delivered to C's home by mistake. He thought about the value of the chairs and had the fleeting idea of selling them, rather than returning them to the rightful owner. Then C thought, "It's what those chairs are worth compared to what I'm worth." He said to us in his report, "I guess you have to weigh these. It's a matter of values."

The criminal knows that, if he is responsible, he can experience a freedom from personal jeopardy that he never knew before. One criminal called this new state simply "freedom," because he was free from arrest and free to avail himself of many new opportunities. Another called it a state of being "clear," because he experienced a mental clarity about life that was new to him. Some have used the word "clean," and others refer to "inner peace." All are describing the same phenomenon—the consequence of thinking in terms of what is moral, although they do not use the word *morality*.

A different perspective on success and failure emerges with self-respect.

> C said that, with a criminal gang, "you try to prove to others that you're somebody." Now he was trying to prove to himself that he was responsible. In his view, he could fail financially, fail to achieve a promotion, or fail in some other way, but "I'm still a winner as long as I keep my nose clean."

There is a growing sense of conviction about the way the criminal lives. His experiencing the rewards of responsibility reinforces the idea that "there is only one way to live." He fears doing anything to imperil the gains that he is making.

> "When you are concerned about yourself making progress in the world, you get very stingy, not only with money, but with the gains made. You don't want to lose anything you worked hard for. You gain another set of values that you don't want to lose. You gain self-respect, which you don't want to lose. A person gets stingy with the things that he values."

No criminal uncritically adopts the Protestant ethic or becomes a pawn of responsible people. Indeed, many are interested in current affairs and develop firm beliefs about the need for social change. But they realize that, as one put it, "to be effective in changing the system, you have to be clean yourself. Otherwise, people won't listen." To date, our people have not been politically active, mainly because they are wary of the criminal equivalents (power thrusts) that could be involved. They think independently and have their own views, but they do not try to teach others or propagandize for causes. This program *never* tries to influence their opinions. We are interested only in the process by which the criminal arrives at his opinions, not in the substance of the opinions themselves.

When the criminal starts in this program, he thinks that responsibility is easily achieved and that it offers the path to happiness. But happiness, as he conceives it, is a state of problemlessness and euphoria, like a criminal high or power state. These expectations are radically altered in the course of change.

> C's co-workers remarked that C seemed so happy as he performed the routine duties of busboy. C thought about how in the past he had put on a facade of being happy to impress others. Now, however, he was genuinely happy as he experienced not the euphoria he had expected but an inner cleanliness that was altogether new.

One criminal observed of his life, "Things are really changing." He had achieved a harmonious relationship with his wife, he had received a promotion at work, he had cleared his debts, and he had become the owner of a home. He had a general sense of well-being and believed that life was worth while. However, his observation that "things are changing" was in error. Little had changed around him; it was *he* who was changing, and this was evoking a change in others' responses to him. He had respect for himself, and others had respect for him that was based on his functioning responsibly.

MAJOR INDICATORS OF ADVANCE IN CHANGE

Most workers in programs designed to rehabilitate criminals have a concept of change that is limited to the criminal's holding a job and not being arrested. Many criminals fulfill these criteria, but remain active in crime. We know of dozens of situations in which criminals whom others considered changed were committing felonies.

Our criteria of change go far beyond crimelessness and holding a job. Often a criminal in our program has received praise from others, but severe criticism from us.

C went to meet with his probation officer. The latter was not there, so C met with the supervisor. This man asked C whether he was working and whether he was saving money. C replied that he was working ten hours a day and had banked one thousand dollars after spending a substantial sum on clothes that he said he needed for the job. The officer praised him for his appearance, his work, and his savings. However, we knew that C was being massively irresponsible. That very morning in the group, C had been criticized for extravagant spending and for using money as an instrument for controlling women.

The key indicator that change is taking place is implementation of new patterns of thought and action both in our office and outside, the latter being verified by outside sources. Fear accompanying that implementation is evidence of effort—fear of not doing well enough and fear of slipping into old patterns.

Our criteria of change do not call for subjective appraisal, but are based on what can be readily observed. The *extent* of participation in the group is one such assessment. Does the criminal attend regularly? Is he prompt? Is he willing to meet sometimes on weekends or, if necessary, on a holiday? Does he contact us between meetings when critical situations arise?

The criminal's *attitude* as he participates in group discussion is another clue in assessing change. The changing criminal's reports are well-organized and contain the details of the thinking and action of the preceding period. The reports are conceptual, showing scope in thinking, rather than preoccupation with concrete events. The channel is wide open as a criminal progresses. Despite fear of looking foolish or of being attacked in the group, he discloses totally and includes reports of his inner debates as to whether to reveal something. The criminal pays close attention to others' reports to learn from them, rather than simply to criticize. He is responsive to our question, "What did you learn?" He concentrates on our summary dictations at the conclusion of each meeting. The changing criminal reflects on themes developed in the previous meeting and elaborates on them in successive sessions.

The criminal's attitude is self-critical, both in the meeting and outside it. When adversities arise, the changing criminal does not blame others and no longer presents himself as a victim. He does not complain about the strains of daily living, but endures them and patiently looks for ways to overcome them constructively. In change, the criminal blames only himself if he fails to do something well and falls short of excellence.

An early sign of change is the disappearance of tactics that have blocked his effective transactions with responsible people. Instead of vagueness, there is clarity. Instead of silence, there is participation. Instead of assent, there is thoughtful consideration and discussion. Instead of feeding us what he thinks we want to hear, the criminal expresses his opinion forthrightly, whether he agrees with us or not, and states his differences calmly. Instead of minimizing his faults, he magnifies them and tries to correct them.

Major indicators of change are the elimination of anger reactions, the abdication of control, and the elimination of power thrusts. Power words are eliminated, including profanity, and there is less hyperbole in speech. There is rational dialogue, not a power contest. There are disagreements, but not angry tirades.

The criminal in change applies deterrents (D1 through D5) as necessary, but with decreasing reliance on D1 and D2. Instead, moral inventories that prompt self-disgust become prevalent and are a central focus of meetings. These moral inventories are instrumental in creating and sustaining a mental set against crime. The criminal is so programmed with the many tasks and problems of responsible living that there is little occasion for criminal thinking, but what little there is gets quickly deterred. Even when the criminal reads accounts of crime and sees television programs or movies that portray crime, he does not savor the criminal excitement, but instead puts himself in the place of the victim.

If the criminal is continuing for many weeks or months to use D1 and D2, it indicates that his choice to change is not firm. If, during such an interval, he deters the same kind and amount of criminal thinking again and again, this demonstrates that he has not shut the door on crime and has failed to commit himself to the program. Criminal thinking is eliminated only when the criminal broadly reshapes his view of himself and the outside world. As this occurs, progressively less recourse to the more elementary deterrents is required.

The criminal's dreaming patterns reflect the extent of change. In three overlapping stages, dreams parallel the change process. First, there are full-scale criminal dreams in which the criminality is exciting. Of course, if the criminal is not disclosing criminal thinking, then he is not likely to report a crime dream. These dreams are enjoyed and savored after awakening. In the second stage, the criminality is just as intense, but there is deterrence in the dream itself. The dream becomes a nightmare in which the criminal is arrested or becomes the victim of a crime himself. From these, the criminal often awakens in shock and terror. In the third stage, with greater change, such dreams occur less frequently. Increasingly, dreams contain elements of daily concerns about family, job, and social situations, and criminal themes are seldom present. If a dream with crime in it occurs, the criminal worries a great deal about having had the dream at all, even if it is the first such dream in weeks. We do not give special attention to dreams. Rather we regard a dream as an indicator of a criminal's progress in change, especially with respect to the effectiveness of deterrence.* To interpret dreams and concern ourselves with the dynamics of the unconscious would only take us far afield from our approach.

> C dreamed of being with a friend who had an ounce of marijuana. Both smoked it and then went to a dance. C was awakened by his alarm and reported that he awoke relieved that the event was only a dream. In his report to the group, C revealed that he had been thinking that he might smoke marijuana again sometime.

Here a dream made a statement about a criminal's current attitude toward change. Instead of interpreting the dream, we utilized it as a signal that C had failed to foreclose criminal activity as a possibility. Indeed, several weeks later, C did smoke marijuana. A dream often reveals something more than what a criminal has previously reported to us, thereby reflecting some additional information about the progress of change.

The criminal goes from one extreme to another as he changes. From total lack of concern about obligations, he becomes overconcerned and perfectionistic about them. The criminal worries greatly over anything he does that he thinks could in any way be interpreted as a sign of irresponsibility. The result of all this may be a neurotic reaction with inordinate self-doubt, insomnia, and psychosomatic symptoms. We have described these phenomena in chapters 7 and 8. There are extreme shifts in attitudes toward many things. The criminal is now thoroughly disgusted with his criminal past and with others who are criminal. His moral inventories heighten his disgust. He wants nothing to do with criminals. He shows

*This is hardly surprising. As Hall and Lindzey (1970, p. 575) observed: "In fact, a person's mode of existence as portrayed in his dreams often duplicates his mode of existence in waking life."

intolerance to minor irresponsibility on the part of otherwise responsible people.

The changing criminal becomes financially prudent. He permits his funds to be controlled by a responsible person. As he becomes more responsible, he controls his own money and manages it very carefully. Not only does he live within his means, but he puts himself on an austerity program. Some take sandwiches to work, instead of buying lunch. Most do not make a major purchase unless it is on sale. Although they may obtain credit ratings, most of our people buy very little on credit. Criminals are totally open with us about financial transactions. They bring checkbooks and bankbooks for review and advice, and they learn to keep accurate financial records.

Generally, the criminal lives an austere life, certainly so in comparison with his past. He does not go out on the town, and he socializes very little. Instead, he prefers to stay home with his wife and children, read, watch television, and do household chores. Most changing criminals have little recreation and seek little variation in their daily routine. In fact, if a criminal does very much socializing, it indicates that he is neglecting other necessary things. With a full-time job, with a commitment to spend at least fifteen hours a week with us, and with a family at home (which most have), the criminal has no time for extensive socializing.

With so much to occupy his time and energy, and with conquest and triumph elements no longer present, the criminal's desire for sex drops off markedly. He has an entirely new perspective on the place of sex in life: A woman is a person, not just breasts, buttocks, or vagina. Sex is a relatively minor part of a responsible relationship that has many other dimensions. Sexual activity occurs once or twice a week, with greater competence and pleasure than ever before. The married criminal limits himself to one woman and effectively deters desires for other women.

When a criminal presses to be released from the court's control, this indicates a lack of change. His willingness to remain on probation and his valuing of it as a safeguard are solid signs of change. This is not to suggest that the criminal wants to remain under the control of the court. Rather, he accepts the idea that court control works for him rather than against him; a few years of probation may help to ensure decades of freedom from confinement in the future.

Finally, the changing criminal, no matter how great his progress, still regards himself as a criminal much in the manner that a chronic alcoholic who has abstained for ten years still regards himself as an alcoholic. Evidence of smugness or complacency in his own assessment of his progress is a sufficient indicator that change is not occurring at a suitable rate. The criminal knows that the work of change is never finished. He applies "once a criminal, always a criminal" to himself, because he is well aware that if he fails to be watchful of himself and fails to continue his efforts to change, a return to old patterns is inevitable.

By way of summation, we list thirty-seven indicators of change.

A Checklist for Gauging Change

1. Opening the channel wide
   a. Full disclosure through phenomenologic reporting and truthfulness outside the office
   b. Receptivity
   c. Self-criticism
2. Elimination of the victim stance
   a. No sociologic or psychologic excuses
   b. No blame of others
3. Elimination of the "I can't" attitude
4. Achieving a time perspective
   a. Applying the past to the future
   b. Elimination of "instancy"
   c. Responsible long-range planning
5. Effort (doing what one does not want to do and not doing what one wants to do in responsible pursuits)
6. Putting oneself in another's position
7. Not injuring others
8. Fulfilling obligations
9. Elimination of the ownership attitude
10. Self-generation of responsible initiatives
11. Fear guiding action in responsible living
12. Basing interest on experience
13. Interdependence
14. Trust
    a. Trusting others discriminately
    b. Being trustworthy
15. Replacing pretensions with reasonable expectations
16. Sound decision-making
17. Redistributing energy
18. Elimination of anger
19. Replacing criminal pride with self-respect
20. Elimination of zero-state thinking
21. Elimination of criminal power and control
22. Elimination of the "unique number one" attitude
23. Excellence, but not criminal perfectionism
24. Sustained sentimentality expressed responsibly

25. Sustained cognitive self-disgust
26. Conceptual, rather than only concrete, thinking
27. Elimination of fragmentation
28. Elimination of criminal suggestibility (severance of ties to criminals)
29. Changing sexual patterns
    a. Sexual activity an integrated part of a consenting relationship
    b. Tenderness
30. Elimination of superoptimism
31. Elimination of complacency
32. Elimination of criminal tactics
33. Implementation of deterrents (especially D-4, the moral inventory)
34. Elimination of criminal thinking
35. Thrift and responsible money management
36. Efficient, effective performance at work
37. No deferment of responsible initiatives and obligations

FOLLOW-UP OF CHANGING CRIMINALS

We have been critical of programs that claim to rehabilitate criminals, but that fail to include a follow-up of their functioning over a significant period. We have taken extraordinary measures to conduct thorough follow-ups, because we know that periodic monitoring of the criminal is necessary, no matter how far change has progressed. It is similar to a routine medical examination which is desirable even if there is no evident physical problem. We have followed some of our people for as long as twelve years after they had participated intensively in the program. Although they may be working and are not arrestable, some criminals have been asked to attend an intensive series of weekly meetings, usually in the company of other criminals in earlier phases of change. In such groups, new material is presented to assist them substantially in decision-making.

If all is going well after a year of intensive daily participation, the criminal enters a phase of the program in which he meets with us in prolonged sessions once a week minimally for a full year. These meetings occur on an evening, on a day off, or on a weekend at a time compatible with the criminal's work schedule. The reporting requires notes for the week organized thematically: family, work, sex, and money. Increasingly, the emphasis is placed on the criminal's moral inventories (D-4) as he continues to reevaluate himself. Irresponsible thinking is always discussed, with emphasis on the incipient. We are most concerned with the process of making decisions, both important and trivial. It is the mental discipline and the process by which decisions are made, rather than the substance of the decisions themselves, that are critical. We know that prejudgment, failure to find facts, or lack of consideration of alternatives can open the gates of criminal thinking. The changing criminal not only is thorough and comprehensive in his reporting, but has thought about issues that require decisions, much as noncriminals do who seek counseling for their problems.

C went into elaborate detail in his reporting from the copious notes that he had assembled during the week. In fact, we thought that a great deal of the material did not require our attention. However, we did nothing to discourage C's attempt to cover all aspects of his life thoroughly. C said that, unless he met with us weekly and presented complete reports, his thinking would grow fuzzy. He was in his third year of voluntary attendance at the weekly sessions.

After the second year of the program, some criminals request less frequent contact with us. We agree to this, but suggest that they call us for assistance whenever they have difficulty in making major decisions. This attitude can be compared with that of the golf champion who, in a slump, periodically returns to his instructor for correction. The professional athlete who never wanes in his pursuit of excellence continues to be self-critical and show concern for the quality of his performance. We have succeeded in establishing this attitude in most, but not all, of our changed people. In a few cases, criminals have phoned us to set up appointments to discuss developing problems before they become serious. If a criminal has not been in touch with us for a year or two, we take the initiative and schedule a meeting.

Not having talked to C in several months, we phoned him and asked him to come in. C reported no criminal thinking and extremely few instances of anger. Although he was not even remotely arrestable, he admitted that he was not functioning as effectively as he might. He had been careless with expenditures of money and was not programming his time. When he could have been working to pay off debts incurred earlier, he was lying around his apartment, somewhat bored, listening to music, and indulging in sexual fantasy. C readily acknowledged that he was not being as constructive as he should. He then met with us in a weekly evening group to correct some of his continuing errors of thinking.

In these meetings, decision-making processes are reviewed, and usually further opinions are offered. The latter is often our most important contribution.

During our regular meetings over a two-year period and in sporadic meetings thereafter, we not only review the criminal's written notes, but also cover our checklist of indicators of change. The following are illustrations of our assessments.

Work and Money

C had been excessively and unrealistically fearful of assuming increased responsibility at work, because he did not think that he could do an adequate job. Having worked for two years on a construction crew, he had earned several promotions and was the number two man among thirty and the fifth in seniority. His interpersonal relations at work were excellent, and he took problems in stride. C reported a total absence of anger reactions at work. For example, every so often he got a lemon in the form of an instrument that did not make proper calibrations for laying out the work. He found himself reacting to this as a challenge, not as a cause for anger. He tried to do his best, despite the defective equipment. Saving money from his paycheck was extremely important. Earning one hundred fifty dollars per week plus overtime, he had saved close to four thousand dollars. Whenever overtime work was available, C grabbed it. C said that, if only he had the work, he would work seven days a week, especially because he would earn double time for the seventh day. Over the two years, C had achieved job stability, advancement, and, most important, a sense of self-respect and pride in his work. C said that his prospects for the future were good. It was strictly up to him to see opportunities and to make the most of them. There was nothing that he could see that would block him from further promotions.

This was the functioning of a criminal who had never held a steady job and who had committed thousands of crimes, mainly thefts and arson.

Marital

C said that he had stayed away from us for several months because he believed that he should develop some independence. He had been having problems in his marriage, but believed that he could handle them on his own. We had spoken with C by phone several times and suggested that he come for a follow-up interview. C's wife had talked about returning to her native country to visit her family. This she did, with C contributing four hundred dollars of his earnings toward the trip. He bought presents for her parents, her sisters, and even the child of a sister. In addition to his wife's own earnings and the four hundred dollars, she had pocket money that C had given her. She was away for a month and, during that time, C wrote her a half-dozen long letters. In return, all that he received from her was one letter addressed to her stepchildren. She failed to return from her trip on the date specified. C waited ten days past that date, figuring that she may have been delayed by illness in her family. Having heard nothing, he contacted her place of employment and learned that she had been back for a week. Clearly, she had decided to return to the United States, but not to rejoin him. Remaining calm, C called her and asked her to come over to talk, which she did. C wanted to resume their former relationship, but did not want to exert pressure. He had several times requested that they both come to see us and have a talk, but she had refused. C reported that he was functioning responsibly and without anger through all this. He had been tense but had placed his obligations ahead of his feelings. There had been no drinking, other women, or criminal thinking. C said that one of the most important things that he had learned was that, if things go wrong, he has to assume one hundred percent of the responsibility and take steps to improve them.

This criminal did not want to jeopardize all that he had worked for. This was the same man who had committed a homicide in reaction to a putdown by a woman. Now, he did not regard himself as put down and was working conscientiously to solve problems in the relationship with his wife.

Criminal Thinking

Despite enormous pressure from work and having many chores to do at home, C set for himself the task of carefully observing any criminal thought, even if it lasted only five seconds. One week, he retrieved eight brief flashes, and the next week five. The purpose of trying to remember these was to determine their content, so that he could conduct a moral inventory and preempt their recurrence. C was resolute about eliminating all vestiges of criminal thinking.

Social-Sexual

C had made an exclusively homosexual adjustment. He had two or three responsible companions with whom he socialized and occasionally had sex. There was no soliciting or cruising for pickups. C decided to spend weekends with one of his friends, who was the affluent manager of a company. After three weeks of this, a problem arose. This manager enjoyed elegant living, and there had been expensive dining out and nightclubbing. C had tried to be thrifty and found to his alarm that he was not at all staying within his budget. Consequently, he decided to terminate this arrangement. After doing so, he concluded that his sexual life was over and became very depressed. He developed a psychosomatic ailment in the form of stomach trouble and took several antispasmodic pills. He then called us. We advised him to go to the nearest hospital emergency room. C was hospitalized overnight and then released to go to work the next day.

This criminal had lost perspective. C was genuinely depressed and used poor judgment. However, there was no incipient thinking that would lead to an arrestable act. If C had contacted us earlier, we could have anticipated the difficulties inherent in the proposed weekend living arrangement, the least of which were financial. After the pill episode, C met with us for a year on a triweekly basis.

There is no particular point at which one can say that a criminal has become a changed man. The criminal is constantly in the process of changing. We seek verification of change from others, usually family members. We have found that all our changed people are accountable to and considerate of others. Most importantly, they still consider themselves criminals. There is no smugness about having changed. They all despise what they were and fear the possibility that if they are not watchful of themselves, they will revert to former patterns.

As of May 1976, thirteen men who were hard-core criminals are now living in the community and fulfill our strict criteria of responsible functioning. To be sure, given the number of years that we have been working, this is not a large number. However, as we explained in chapter 1 of volume 1, our effectiveness has increased notably over the last several years. Many formative years were spent pioneering new techniques and acquiring the knowledge that led to the present format.* Consequently, we are now able to achieve positive results much faster than we could earlier. We are more effective in our initial contact, as well as in implementing our program for achieving basic change.

An interesting phenomenon that we have observed is that, if we ask the criminal to name the correctives for thinking errors that he learned while in the program, he cannot name them, even though he is implementing them. One man explained this when he said, "After you have lived for ten years in a house that you have built, you don't remember every board of lumber or every nail."

We have been extreme in our insistence on *total* elimination of criminal thinking and action. That is, we have warned that the least irresponsibility is the crack in the door that will eventually result in the criminal's being confined. Our follow-up has continued for years. Some of our changing criminals maintain total and meticulous adherence to the program even years after they leave the intensive group sessions. In some, we find instances of what we regard as substantial irresponsibility. Occasionally, there have been anger reactions, careless financial expenditures, unjustified job mobility, an occasional drink, a failure to plan for the long haul sufficiently, and

---

*Well over two-thirds of the criminals with whom we have had extended contact have not participated in our program for change. They agreed to be interviewed at length as part of our factfinding.

imprudent decision-making. We have found that these *have not resulted in arrestability*, despite our earlier warning that this would surely occur. Although these changing criminals are not as efficient and productive as they might otherwise be, there has been no compromise in basic integrity. After long, careful follow-up, we conclude that these criminals have deviated from the program, to a degree, but no further, *because we had required "saintliness" during the intensive part of the program*. Earlier, when our requirements were less strict, we found that they did indeed return to criminal patterns; we became stricter because of this. Now we find some backsliding in total responsibility, but never to the point of arrestability.

When we assess these criminals years after they have left the intensive program, they do not attempt to justify any deviation from the program's standards. They are still self-critical, and they are receptive to our views. They become frightened as the possible ramifications of their irresponsibility are discussed.

> C reported that he had been having an "occasional beer." A few times, he admitted, he got "bombed." One such time was at a family celebration, where C said that he had a "happy drunk." This may have seemed innocuous enough, except that C also reported that he had been driving when intoxicated. One time, he had an accident in which he damaged no other vehicle, but did extensive damage to his own. The seriousness of this incident spoke for itself. Reflecting on his drinking, C saw that there was in fact a *pattern* of drinking, not just an occasional beer. He stated, "From now on, it's water."

As we reviewed other aspects of C's current living, he realized that he had let down in his adherence to program standards in other ways. In pledging not to drink, C had no points to score with us; he was meeting with us voluntarily. But he was frightened about possible consequences of not following the program, and he therefore arranged to be in touch with us on a regular, although infrequent, basis.

The criminals who follow this program the most strictly are the most recent participants. They have had the benefit of a more comprehensive program with its refined techniques. Some criminals, like C in the example above, were in this program years ago, before the evolution of such concepts as the system of deterrence (chapter 9), with its emphasis on the moral inventory. We have found that, largely because we are more knowledgeable and efficient, criminals now in the program are more effective in deterring irresponsibility and push themselves harder to implement new patterns of thought and action. There is a momentum and a zest for change that persists long after they have finished with the intensive part of the program and its daily monitoring.

THE DESTINATION OF UNCHANGED CRIMINALS

We will describe here a follow-up of unchanged criminals with whom we have had extensive interviews. These are both dropouts from our program and criminals who were included in our studies but have never been in the program. One source of the follow-up information is changed criminals who have demonstrated their reliability. Although they no longer have personal contact with other criminals, they occasionally receive information that we have found to be reliable about the fate of someone whom they once knew well. Our major source of information has been unchanged criminals themselves who have sought us. In doing so, they state that they are appreciative and trusting of us, because they respect out knowledge, commitment, and integrity. Some participated in our studies over a period of many months. Others had only brief contact wtih us, but, because the interviews were extensive, they made an impact. In either case, the intense relationship that developed has facilitated effective follow-up. We receive their Christmas cards, their occasional letters from all parts of the country, and phone calls.* Some write to us from confinement (both in the Washington area and outside it), because they want something from us—perhaps a listening ear, but usually our intervention to offer them admission to our program, which they expect will expedite their release from prison. There is yet another factor in the unchanged criminal's maintaining contact. Some criminals drop by, because they want to boast to us about how, contrary to our predictions, they are actually doing well. They claim that they have changed, but in saying this they adopt the current conventional definition of change—that is, they are holding a job and have not been arrested. Without fail, we have found on interviewing them that they are substantially arrestable. This has been true both of program dropouts and of those whom we have interviewed intensively but who never entered the program.

There are other means of follow-up. Being based at Saint Elizabeths Hospital, we keep abreast of returns to the forensic division. Many times, we have interviewed criminals who are back at the hospital after being released, arrested for another crime, and then returned for evaluation or treatment. There are several indirect (and sometimes less reliable) sources of information: unchanged criminals who tell us about others, hospital staff, and, occasionally, newspaper accounts of the arrests, convictions, and deaths of criminals whom we have known.

We have diligently sought to discover whether any criminal who has not completed our program and who has been judged rehabilitated by others has remained nonarrestable. Of the criminals whom we have interviewed

---

* In a few cases, we have received calls from parents worried about their criminal offspring. This has helped us to update our information.

(program dropouts and criminals never in the program), every one has been arrestable many times for a variety of offenses.

What do those who dropped out of our program say about it? They do not dispute our understanding of the criminal personality, nor do they fault the philosophy or specific requirements of our program. However, unless they are currently seeking help from us, they assert that, although the program is good for others, it is not necessary for them. For some, a temporary deterrent effect results from prolonged contact with us. One criminal said, "You ruin us," meaning that he derived enough from the program so that conscience factors sometimes intruded as he was contemplating a crime. Another criminal reported the following experience:

> He had purchased a gun and was thinking about several possibilities for holdups. Having been in this program for several months before dropping out, he reported that he became so worried and frightened that "I was unable to shoot a gun." He said that he was so angry that he cursed his ever having met us. Then he decided to get stoned on amphetamines. Even the drugs did not eradicate his fears. The deterrent was much less the thought of injury to others than fear for his own life—he might be injured or killed in the course of the dangerous crimes that he was contemplating. The external deterrent held, at least for a while. Within a few weeks, it, too, was cut off, and he committed an armed robbery.

This criminal reported that, for a time, he was using our program in a way that made him a more effective criminal. Being keenly aware of the dangers of superoptimism, C reported that he had resolved to be more cautious in committing crimes. However, this caution was short-lived, and C went the full route in crime and was finally convicted of a major felony.

To provide the flavor of the interviews and the communication that we have received over the years, we include sample material both from program dropouts and from criminals who participated in our studies without ever being in the program.

Program Dropout: A Letter from Prison

He describes his legal entanglements and then says: "I only wish all this baloney would have been avoided—why didn't you kick me in the seat of the pants a few times? That's where my brains are! How could I have been so *stupid* to leave the program? I have the highest S.Q. [stupidity quotient] vs. I.Q. in existence. Well enough crying over spilt milk. If God gives me the grace to return to your program I *will* bind myself to it— legally and morally and totally! My only problem is a moral one and if I can reach inside and conquer my own deficiencies and inadequacies and lack of intestinal fortitude, I shall be truly reborn, a man for the first time. ... God bless you for the effort and unceasing work you are doing—it offers hope for a truly new kind of mankind.

Your errant son,"

This exceedingly intelligent criminal had been in our program for many months before deciding that he preferred his criminal way of life. Confined and faced with the prospect of serving a long sentence, C was hoping to find a way to be released to our custody, so that he could once again be in our program and leave the penitentiary. This has not happened, nor are we promoting it. We shall accept C only if he is on a strict and long probationary sentence.

Program Dropout: A Series of Phone Calls

Six years from the time we had last heard from C, he phoned us long distance, asking whether we would help him locate a good clinic for some elective surgery. He agreed to come to see us and talk the matter over, as well as discuss his life since he had left the program. Several weeks later, there was another phone call. C requested that we speak with a friend of his and answer that person's questions about the type of person C was. A third call came early in the morning several days later. C said that he had to see us immediately, maintaining that "the Feds are after me." C asked whether we could help him get admitted to Saint Elizabeths. Clearly, he wanted to use the hospital to escape prosecution on criminal charges. C arranged an appointment to meet with us. On the appointed day, C called us from an airport and said that he had missed his plane. During the course of the discussion, C said that he was living on a Veterans' Administration pension of one hundred thirty dollars a month. He had had many jobs and lost them and had rarely remained in the same part of the country for long. C made another appointment to meet with us. Again, he called long distance and cancelled it, leaving word with the secretary that he was going to the West Coast.

We expect that we shall hear from C again. It appears that he wanted to use us to escape legal difficulties, but then changed his mind.

Program Dropout: A Letter from an Indirect Source

"I had misplaced that letter you had sent to [C and his wife]. However they have had it long enough now that they should have answered it. Why they haven't, I don't know. For one thing, I know things are rough for them. [C] hasn't had but a few days work this past month and not much before that. So now with the new baby coming, both are very upset."

In this letter from C's mother, not much specific information was provided. However, we could safely conclude that the antiwork pattern of this intelligent and skilled criminal was continuing and that he still had not settled down.

Not in the Program for Change, but Included in Our Studies: A Letter from Prison

"For some reason, I seem to get something out of your letters. A sentence will be food for thought. . . . I got the impression you felt that the kind of life we live, we are programmed to end up in a place like this. I hate to think that everything about my life was a waste, as you once said. . . . Not any of the people you inquired about are here. . . . This I'm sure will surprise you. I have been talking to a fellow here. I guess you would say somewhat in a counselor sense. He knows about you and I was telling him how long it was before you made me realize I was a criminal. His reply was that he did not consider himself one and I could not convince him he was. He is nice to children and little old ladies, so I guess he considers himself a nice guy. I thought about myself when I was seeing you. One day when I'm up to it, I'll do him like you did me and go back to his childhood."

This criminal, eager for contact with us, requested that we visit him in prison. Using his inadequate and outdated understanding of this program (he was in the early history-taking phase), he was trying to counsel others. This was a power thrust (a criminal equivalent), in that he put himself above the other prisoners by functioning as their teacher and regarding himself as having something of an inside track on "truth."

Not in the Program for Change, but Included in Our Studies: An Interview with a Criminal Returned to the Hospital

C, a criminal whom we had interviewed several times previously, had been returned to the hospital for determination of mental competence to stand trial. C maintained that he had reformed for a while. He had stopped using heroin and was restricting himself to marijuana. Then came a period in which he was very religious. His religiosity did not preclude crime, and he was arrested for two robberies. However, he was acquitted for lack of sufficient evidence. C was also gambling, was receiving stolen goods, and was in a liquor sales racket. Finally, he was arrested, this time for a third robbery, in which he and a partner commandeered a passing car and kidnapped the driver. C's lawyer suggested that he use the insanity defense, owing to his having a history as a mental patient.

This is the kind of case in which others may well have thought that the criminal was doing well, because he had ceased hard-drug use, was employed, and, before his third robbery, had not been convicted of a crime. To the community, he appeared to be a changed man, when actually he was an unchanged criminal still active in crime.

Not in the Program for Change, but Included in Our Studies: An Interview with a Criminal Not in Confinement

One of our current group members was contacted by his friend, C, a man whom we had interviewed some years before. C agreed to meet with us several times. However, he spent most of the sessions defending his criminality on the basis of what society had done to him as a member of an oppressed minority. C was more interested in defending his position and debating social issues than in revealing thinking and action patterns. We did learn that C had been married five times and had lived with numerous women. He had stopped using heroin within the preceding five months and was not smoking marijuana and drinking large amounts of liquor. He admitted to being a chronic liar, but justified his lying as necessary. C said that he did some stealing, but less than before. He defended stealing from stores, on the basis of their large profits. Constantly, we had to penetrate a thicket of excuses and pervasive criminal pride and self-righteousness. In the course of these meetings, we learned enough to confirm that C was an unchanged criminal.

This criminal had his freedom. He came to see us out of curiosity. Finding our probing disagreeable and his attempts to convince us of his point of view unsuccessful, C elected not to attend any more meetings.

Not in the Program for Change, but Included in Our Studies: A Letter (Written out of Sentiment on a Holiday)

"I'll bet I can tell you what you are thinking; 'How the hell did he do it?' or 'It's got to be phony; he can't really be the Executive Director of the biggest wire service in the world.' No, you want to bet I can't. If you need verification of the validity of this letter, call———.... O.K. now you've verified my I.D., you are saying to yourself, 'Well, he's conned his way to the top this time!!' You know something? You are so right! This time I'm sitting on top of the heap smelling like a rose. . . . Check your schedule and figure out when you can spare some time and I'll arrange to meet you if I can. I am not always able to get away when I'd like, but most of the time I can. I sincerely hope and pray you are well and enjoying life and are having a great deal of success in your work."

Actually, C had not conned his way to the top. He had set up another in a series of obscure companies with false fronts. Within a few years, C's criminality had expanded to the point where he was arrested, convicted, and sentenced to a long term in prison for crimes other than setting up companies.

All the criminals whom we have followed and who did not complete our program remained unchanged and were still in crime. After almost fifteen years of our studying the criminal, this is no longer surprising to us. The only change that endures is that which involves change of the inner man. The unchanged criminal lacks the thinking processes to function responsibly. He can choose to acquire these; he is not a victim of the processes that he does have. However, he requires a program like ours to train him in the new thinking patterns set forth in this volume.

BIBLIOGRAPHY

Aristotle (1952). *Nicomachean Ethics. Great Books of the Western World*, vol. 9. Chicago: Britannica.

Hall, C. S., and Lindzey, G. (1970). *Theories of Personality*, 2nd ed. New York: Wiley.

Shakow, D. (1975). What *is* clinical psychology? Invited address delivered at the 83rd annual convention of the American Psychological Association, Chicago, August.

Chapter 11

Criminal Patterns
in Confinement

THIS CHAPTER DEMONSTRATES how criminals have responded to rehabilitation measures implemented at Saint Elizabeths Hospital. This material has been drawn from many sources, but we have relied mainly on our own observations. We have spent much time with criminals who have been confined in federal, state, and municipal prisons. In no instance do we report what a criminal says about his experience before our study of him. Rather we have weighted more heavily the reports of criminals whom we have seen in our own daily sessions for years. Our most significant material is derived from the disclosures of criminals who, under close scrutiny, have shown substantial change as verified by others' observations of their functioning on the outside. After they have left Saint Elizabeths Hospital, some criminals have written extensive reports on their experiences at the hospital. Much important information has also been contributed by responsible nursing assistants.

Confinement, whether in a prison, a halfway house, or a hospital, provides still another arena for criminal thought and action. The criminal is what he is, whether on the street or confined. His alteration of behavior in confinement is part of his adaptation to achieve his objectives. The patterns of thinking and action described in chapters 4 through 8 of volume 1 are operative wherever the criminal lives. In this chapter, we discuss the impact of the institution on the criminal and the criminal's impact on the institution. It is not our intention to focus on Saint Elizabeths Hospital in particular. This chapter has relevance to almost any institution in which criminals are confined or treated. We are, however, fortunate in working at Saint Elizabeths Hospital because the facilities here are better than in most penal institutions.

The physical plant in which the forensic division is now located is relatively new, and the personnel per forensic patient are more abundant than in any prison or hospital within our knowledge. A sizable professional staff administers and conducts a wide spectrum of activities designed to achieve rehabilitation and to make life more pleasant for the residents. The hospital environment is attractive and livable. Most forensic wards house no more than thirty patients, and each ward is well covered by personnel. With such resources, by no stretch of the imagination could Saint Elizabeths Hospital be called a warehouse for forensic patients. This chapter provides background to chapters 12 and 13, which present suggestions for improved selection and training of change agents and a proposal for establishing more effective outpatient and inpatient services.

Saint Elizabeths Hospital, in Washington, D.C., was established in 1855 by an act of Congress to provide "the most humane and enlightened curative treatment" for the mentally ill. In 1967, Saint Elizabeths was placed under the jurisdiction of the National Institute of Mental Health (NIMH), a division of the National Institutes of Health.

Most of the hospital's patients are residents of the District of Columbia who voluntarily seek treatment for mental illness or are committed through the courts, but not in connection with a crime. However, it is the patients sent to Saint Elizabeths as a result of criminal offenses with whom we are concerned. They are sent for determination of competence to stand trial and for determination of their mental responsibility at the time of the crime. Because it is a federal institution, some of the patients reside in other states and are sent here either because they committed crimes in Washington, D.C., or federal offenses outside Washington. If criminals are adjudged by the court as "not guilty by reason of insanity" (NGBRI), they may then be sent to Saint Elizabeths for treatment.* Saint Elizabeths Hospital is the only facility in the United States for the mental examination of women who have committed federal offenses. Also admitted to the hospital are prisoners considered to have become psychotic while serving sentences, most of them at the District of Columbia Correctional Facility at Lorton, Virginia. These prisoners are sent to Saint Elizabeths for confirmation of psychosis; those considered mentally ill are retained for treatment until they have recovered.

At the time we began our work in 1961, the courts were operating under the Durham rule. In 1972, the U.S. District Court adopted the ruling of the American Law Institute,** but the District of Columbia Superior Court still

---

*Previously, patients on forensic wards were referred to as "prisoner-patients." The *prisoner* designation was dropped and *patient* alone used because these people had been adjudicated "not guilty by reason of insanity." In line with preceding chapters, we refer to them as criminals. *Patient* is used only to describe a situation from the hospital's viewpoint.

**According to the American Law Institute, "a person is not responsible for criminal conduct if at the time of such conduct as a result of mental disease or defect, he lacked substantial capacity either to appreciate the wrongfulness of his conduct or to conform his conduct to the requirements of the law" (American Law Institute Model Penal Code, Sec. 4.01 [1] Official Draft, 1962).

applied the Durham rule. Under the 1954 Durham rule (Durham v. United States, 214 F. 2d 862), three questions were asked of the hospital. The first was whether the person was competent to stand trial; this entailed his having a factual and rational understanding of the charge, so that he could assist in his own defense. The second question was whether the person had been suffering from a mental disease or defect at the time of the crime. The third, and key, question was whether the crime had been the product of such mental disease or defect.

In the early 1960s, criminals were admitted to the hospital for a ninety-day observation period. Today, the evaluation may be limited to two weeks. While here for pretrial observation, all criminals are housed in maximum security at the John Howard Pavilion (JHP), opened in 1959 and presently capable of housing 284 patients.* In 1969 the hospital's Facilities Work Group, composed of representatives of hospital departments, surveyed the utilization of various facilities. John Howard was termed "the most modern and most ideally equipped for residential treatment" (p. 12). This building has tiled walls and floors, a modern dietetic kitchen, a gymnasium and outdoor recreational facilities (walled for security reasons), and complete occupational therapy facilities. Security is tight, with television monitoring, electric doors at the entrance, and locked doors, elevators, and windows.

In the 1960s, if a criminal were adjudged NGBRI, he would be placed in maximum security. When judged safe for lesser security, he was transferred to minimum security, where more privileges were granted. The other buildings were not as modern as JHP, but criminals housed in them had access to additional facilities on the grounds. At the time, the hospital's administration believed that patients of one diagnostic type should not be separated from all the others. For example, it was regarded as a poor practice to have an entire ward of deteriorated hebephrenic patients and a separate ward for forensic patients. The administration thought it more beneficial to mix patients at various levels of alertness and functioning. With the passage of time and the accumulation of experience, that attitude changed. In their 1969 report, the hospital's Program Development Work Group on Forensic Services suggested that the objective of continuity of treatment could be met better by having each security division retain its own patients from admission through conditional release (p. 30). Many hospital personnel already believed that patients were shifted around too often, experiencing too many changes of doctors. Thus, in the summer of 1970, unitization of service became hospital policy, and all forensic patients were moved to JHP. This consolidation necessitated having maximum and minimum security in the same building.

*John Howard has held as many as 400 residents, but this crowding now has been eliminated by reducing the actual number of beds to 284.

Elevators were adjusted to stop at some floors but not at others to help accomplish this, and patients leaving the facility to go onto the grounds or into town had to show identification cards before being permitted to leave.

The administrative methods for assigning patients to wards have also changed. With unitization, assignment of a forensic patient to a specific ward at John Howard has been based solely on legal status. As of August 1975, the ward organization was as follows:

Before Trial

Wards 7, 8, and 9 (Male)

Felony and misdemeanor criminals are combined on these wards, but just prior to 1975, the men charged with major felonies were housed separately on Ward 8. Patients declared incompetent to stand trial were housed on pretrial wards until recently. In 1976, such patients were placed in a separate treatment unit for the mentally incompetent.

Ward 2 (Female)

The only female ward, houses pretrial and post-trial patients

Admitted While Serving a Sentence Elsewhere

Ward 10 (Male)

After Trial

Wards 3, 11, and 12 (Male)	*Wards 4, 5, and 6 (Male)*
Maximum Security	Minimum Security

It is commonly acknowledged that the seriousness of a charge is correlated with the length of stay in the hospital. If a man were found NGBRI for murder in 1961, he was likely to stay at least ten years. In the 1970s, forensic patients of all types tend to stay in the hospital for shorter periods than in the early 1960s. This, in part, is because of a shift in the type of patients sent to the forensic division. As the result of a court reorganization, there have been far fewer criminals admitted for severe felonies and many more for minor felonies and misdemeanors.

ADMISSION TO THE HOSPITAL

We described in chapters 3 and 6 of volume 1 how a criminal often tries to get into the hospital in order to beat a charge. If the evidence against him appears almost incontrovertible and the crime is serious, the criminal is especially disposed to seek admission. Jail is virtually a classroom where the criminal learns how to make himself a candidate for an insanity hearing. Criminals whom we have studied report that much lore about Saint Elizabeths floats around the District of Columbia Jail. We have confirmed this repeatedly in that they have told us what they have learned. Although criminals know that they will be committed to the hospital for an indeterminate period, they believe that, at least for a major felony, confinement in the hospital will be far shorter than confinement in a prison. Furthermore, the criminal hears that the hospital offers better conditions and more freedom than prison. He may also learn that, once he works his way into minimum security, Saint Elizabeths is a relatively easy place from which to elope. But some criminals resist the idea of pleading insanity, because they do not want to be considered crazy. A few prefer a long jail sentence to any period in the "nut house." Nevertheless, to most criminals who face serious charges, admission to a mental hospital is a desirable way out. Once a criminal decides this, he begins scheming and anticipates eventual triumph in getting admitted. First, he must convince personnel at the jail that something is mentally wrong with him. Some criminals resort to elaborate measures.

C had done considerable reading about epilepsy. He learned about both the physical and mental aspects of the disorder—the size of the pupils, defecation, urination, and so forth. He even practiced simulating an epileptic seizure. He became so proficient at this that he convinced twelve doctors that he had epilepsy and was subject at times to violent behavior that he could not control and was not responsible for.

*   *   *

C assumed that a suicidal gesture would have the effect he wanted. He told someone that he was going to hang himself, so that the person would know when to alert the authorities and have him cut down. This succeeded; the staff viewed him as a suicidal risk who belonged in a hospital rather than a jail.

The criminal may be advised by other criminals to take less extreme measures.

C was told by other prisoners to be a loner: he should say nothing to others and avoid watching television, playing cards, or doing anything else that involved relating to people.

C was instructed that getting into fights would be helpful in proving his lack of control and demonstrating general instability. However, he chose the device of lying about not remembering what he had done, so that he would appear to be suffering from amnesia.

In chapters 3 and 6 of volume 1, we described other ploys used to gain admission to the hospital. Innumerable forms of malingering are recommended by many other prisoners or arise out of the criminal's own resourcefulness.

Even if a criminal is not facing a particularly serious charge, his life situation may be so distressing that he chooses hospitalization, not for the purpose of change, but to get others off his back. His weary and desperate family may believe that he really is sick because of his actions and may pressure him to get help. Even if he resists his family's entreaties, a wife (for example) collaborating with a lawyer may be persuasive.

C's wife turned him in to the police. She and the family lawyer wanted him hospitalized. C objected to this plan, because he knew that Saint Elizabeths was for crazy people, and he did not regard himself as crazy. He wanted to serve his one to three years and get it over with. However, C knew that he was faced with losing his wife if he did not get treatment. His wife had called him "sick" for quite a while, but to him this meant having something wrong with him that the doctor would cure. He was not thinking about mental sickness; this was anathema. Finding himself forced into a corner by his wife and lawyer, C consented to being admitted to the hospital.

If the criminal has anything sounding even remotely like a psychiatric history, he and his lawyer capitalize on it. It may be previous psychiatric consultation, treatment, or confinement. Also helpful is a physician's view that a physical condition was of psychiatric origin or that psychiatric factors played a role in it. The criminal and his lawyer may go far back and cite something from his childhood, such as bed-wetting until the age of nine, to demonstrate that he had a long-standing psychiatric problem. Any of this helps to establish the presence of mental disease or defect.

C had a long history, going back to the age of fourteen, of crimes that were regarded as symptomatic of mental illness. He had been seen at mental clinics even earlier. He had spent most of his life either in jail or in mental institutions. While in jail, he had often convinced others that he was crazy and was moved to a section for the mentally ill and sometimes from there to a state hospital. Had he not been counting on his well-documented history of mental illness, C said he might not have chanced committing some of his more serious offenses. He had been arrested for almost fifty felonies and had beaten every charge but one. All his actions were seen as manifestations of mental illness, including his calculated publicity-seeking efforts. Even before he committed a crime, he knew that mental illness would be a way out.

It could accurately be said that a history of mental illness is a license for crime. C was one of a triumvirate who in a systematic, coordinated way managed to beat charges for serious crimes for years. Another member of the threesome, who had avoided prison terms for fifteen years by feigning insanity, finally was recognized as a malingerer and sentenced to life imprisonment for hijacking *(New York Times 7/28/73)*.

Criminals scheme and malinger with various degrees of sophistication and success. Convincing the authorities that they belong in a hospital and not a prison is the first victory. Then, during an observation period of two weeks to ninety days, they must convince the hospital authorities that they are mentally ill and require treatment.

PRETRIAL EVALUATION

The process that began in jail continues in the hospital. When the criminal arrives, he is counseled by other criminals as to how to put on a convincing demonstration of mental illness. He may be referred by other inmates to one of their number considered especially sophisticated and enlightened about this; he is told, "See ———." The ward often includes people placed there for re-evaluation of competency. Nearly everyone is ready to give advice, so the listener has to choose among conflicting options. He may be advised to ingratiate himself with the staff, on the grounds that, if he is too troublesome, the staff may find him without mental illness in order to get rid of him, which means that he will wind up in jail. He may be told to be contentious, if not openly hostile, to convince others of his abnormal mental condition. Each bit of advice reflects the experience of the man giving it. As he does with any crime, the criminal analyzes the situation to determine how he will operate. Significantly, what is considered criminal on the outside may well be considered insane when it occurs on the ward. In other words, if the criminal simply continues a pattern of violation but makes an open show of it, he may aid his cause.

When C came to the hospital to beat a murder charge, one of his tactics was to engage in homosexual acts so openly that it was assumed that he would have to be insane to do it. His purpose was to avoid a trial where most probably he would be convicted of homicide. His activity was calculated to make him appear mentally ill, and it worked.

Throughout life, when held accountable, the criminal tells others what he thinks they want to hear. He does the same thing on the pretrial ward. The specific form of malingering and the tactics depend on what the criminal discerns about the orientation of whoever has decision-making power—resident, chief of service, clinical director. By talking with others, he attempts to learn in advance what questions will be asked and what biases the doctor has.

During the pretrial period, the criminal resides in maximum security. No treatment is offered, because the hospital's function at this point is only to observe and evaluate. In the few cases in which a criminal is in a genuine psychotic phase and thus incompetent to stand trial, the hospital provides treatment to restore competence, but it does not provide a long-term program of rehabilitation. During the pretrial period, there are few organized patient activities. Ward meetings are held to discuss administrative matters and problems of patient management. Patients may be taken to the recreation area and, upon request, arts and crafts or other projects are offered on the ward. Otherwise, the pastimes are reading, playing pool, listening to records, playing cards, watching television, and talking with one another.

Until recently, the pretrial wards were administered by psychiatric residents or U.S. Public Health Service officers. A team headed by a physician had the responsibility for conducting a thorough evaluation, including a mental examination, psychosocial study, psychologic testing, and a physical examination. Also included were the observations of nursing assistants who were asked to make regular entries on patients' charts.

In the 1960s, criminals usually remained the ninety days allowed by court order for observation. During our several years' tenure at John Howard, the residents were often instructed by a hospital administrator not to interview criminals until the last month of their stay. Now, dispositions are often made within three weeks, because the caseload is heavy and there is pressure to process patients rapidly.

Until 1969, it was mandatory that conferences be held for every pretrial patient. All staff members involved in the case and the clinical director usually attended. These conferences were to serve the purpose of compiling, discussing, and evaluating all information obtained during the observation period. In 1969, the requirement of a conference for *every* patient was discontinued, owing to a huge backlog of some one hundred eighty patients. However, conferences were not totally abolished. In that year, David L. Chambers, assistant professor of law at the University of Michigan, was hired as a consultant at John Howard Pavilion. As an outside observer, he cited problems touching what we had known was only the tip of a very large iceberg. His report of situations and events (1969) confirmed what we had been seeing right along.* With respect to the conferences, he stated:

> For most patients, opinions were ultimately sent to the courts without formal staff conferences. Indeed, because of the loss of one of the doctors, almost no staff conferences were being held at the time I left. When conferences were held, only a few people attended (usually two doctors and perhaps a psychologist or social worker). (p. 7)

[A footnote on the conference issue] The problem for John Howard is that the conferences are not even attended by all those with important information about the particular patient. Most notably absent are nursing staff who are the only personnel who observe the patient closely during his stay.

The dozen staff conferences that I attended were, however, often quite lengthy, running two or three hours. Despite this, dissatisfaction was expressed with the conference process.

The conference was reinstituted in 1970 for two reasons: the courts asked that a sizable amount of information be collected for presentation, and it was thought by the hospital to be a poor policy to have the fate of a patient decided by one person.

At these conferences, residents often rendered opinions based on a single interview of fifteen minutes or a half-hour with a patient.** Doctors at the conference were sometimes unfamiliar with whatever background material was available on a patient. The nursing assistants' reports were heavily relied on, but they were often sketchy and biased. Psychologic testing, when done, was at times an exercise in futility, in that the psychologists were under pressure to back up the doctor's diagnostic findings; otherwise, their report would be passed over and rarely filed. In talking with staff members, we often picked up an attitude of discouragement, if not demoralization. A social worker said of her report "They won't read it anyway." Some social workers

*In this chapter, we shall make occasional reference to Chambers' report, which was not easily available. Even the hospital library did not contain a copy, but we were able to obtain one through the hospital Superintendent. Our continuing attempts to inform the administration of the types of things that Chambers observed were ignored.

**We were on the wards of John Howard every working day for a year. Thus, we know that these very brief interviews took place; we also were told about them by staff and patients.

and psychologists thought that they were going through the motions, because the doctors seemed to have already made up their minds before the conferences were held. Many of the personnel reported to us that they were errand boys and nothing more. Chambers (1969) stated:

> The psychologists felt that they were hardly ever listened to and thus rarely bothered to attend. Even some doctors expressed dissatisfaction. They complained of the questions that were asked or not asked at the conference and of the questionable soundness of the judgments rendered by doctors who had never seen the patient except at the conference. One in John Howard referred to the conferences there as "farces." A former staff physician referred to them as "bad jokes." (pp. 7, 8)

Chambers suggested that "greater candor" be the practice in setting forth findings to the court.

> Generally, only a single opinion is provided and conflicting opinions of psychologists and junior physicians are omitted. They should be included in the letter. (p. 25)

During these conferences, the criminal was asked questions, usually perfunctory. These dealt with the circumstances of the crime for which he was charged, his background, and his plans for the future. Each staff department having information to contribute gave its report. Opinions were rendered as to the disposition favored. However, those opinions were not binding on the clinical director, who often arrived at an opposite decision. In the 1970s, the staff psychiatrist took care to interview each criminal or delegated the task to an outside consultant brought in by the hospital. The consultant saw a criminal one or two times and made a recommendation. The staff doctor interviewed the criminal at most three times—before the conference, during the conference, and sometimes after the conference. At conferences held now, a psychologic report, a psychosocial history, an admission note, and a physical examination report are supposed to be included for every evaluation. It is acknowledged that the psychology department does not have time to test every pretrial patient, but a psychologist who has neither tested nor examined the patient is asked to vote, anyway, because he is legally permitted to testify on matters of competence and mental illness.

Our source of information about these conference proceedings are interviews with staff personnel and criminals with whom we spent thirty to seventy hours while they were in JHP for observation. Before they were seen by staff doctors, and thus before their conference, they told us how they planned to operate with the doctor and the rest of the staff. In every case, the criminal was armed with self-serving stories calculated to achieve his objective—usually to be adjudged NGBRI. Thus the doctor's write-up was based largely on inaccurate, distorted data provided by the criminal himself. Some criminals did not plan lies in advance, because they believed that they would lie better spontaneously during the interview. They thought it best to see what the doctor wanted and then give it to him. At the conference itself, most offered self-serving stories. As we described in chapter 3 of volume 1, a few malingered on psychologic tests. Information from psychosocial histories was meager (noted by Chambers 1969, p. 9), and much of what was offered was unreliable, having been tailored by families eager to protect their kin.

The nursing assistants' observations potentially carry considerable weight with the doctor, because they spend eight hours a day with the criminal and thus have more contact with him than do other staff members. By deciding what to report and what not to report, they can greatly affect the decisions to be made. Therefore, competent nursing assistants who can give objective and accurate evaluations to the doctor are of great importance.

In short, very important decisions are often made on the basis of unreliable data, self-serving stories, and outright lies. Close to half of the criminals with whom we have worked and who were tested, have attempted to fake responses to psychologic tests. Social work reports are based on information given by family and friends who sometimes shade the truth to protect the criminal; in many cases, reports of past hospitalizations are not obtained; the criminal's own testimony is fraudulent from beginning to end; some nursing reports lack objectivity and are sketchy; and the doctor's evaluation is based on one or two interviews, and sometimes not even that. Despite the many ploys that criminals use to convince others that they are mentally ill, in the majority of cases, they are not successful. Currently, only twenty percent are found "not guilty by reason of insanity."

After their interviews or conferences, the criminals whom we talked to usually remembered almost none of the specific events that had taken place in them, so little impact did the proceedings have on them. All they cared about was the outcome. When we asked these men what questions they had been asked, we got vague, disinterested replies—"Oh, the doctor asked me about my childhood." In the interviews or conferences, only that which related to their immediate objectives was important.

Perhaps most interesting of all, however, is how practices change with respect to the proportion of criminals found NGBRI. Diagnosis, some administrators have admitted, varies with the environment in the hospital and the environment in the community, as well as with the assessment of the individual. This has been observed over a period of time. For example, in a law-and-order atmosphere, fewer criminals are likely to be found mentally ill. Weihofen (1960, p. 5) pointed out that "the existence or non-existence of mental illness is not solely a factual question to be determined by objective observation or examination." A study by Steinberg (1964) illustrates this. From 1954 to 1964, the percentage of patients committed to Saint Elizabeths by the District Court and found to be *without* mental disorder increased.

> We are left finally with the most likely explanation of the data being that patients are now being diagnosed as without mental illness who would previously have been diagnosed as character disorder.

Steinberg went on to say that this reflected the impact of the Leach decision of 1957* that made sociopathic personality a form of mental disorder, a diagnosis that psychiatrists were reluctant to make:

> If a character disorder was a mental disease then most criminals in the District would have to be considered mentally ill and acquitted not guilty by reason of insanity. (p. 11)

This diagnosis was then made less and less frequently. Certainly the nature of man has not changed; and there is little to suggest that the prevalence of mental illness has been decreasing. Thus, one has to conclude that it is more a matter of the hospital's eagerness to avoid admitting sociopathic patients.

Chambers pointed out that even within the hospital's forensic services, there seemed to be a marked disparity in diagnostic findings that was difficult to account for.** Although he knew that he was out of his field when it came to diagnosis, Chambers (1969, p. 23) did raise a question about the diagnostic process:

> My complaints regarding candor are most specifically directed towards a few kinds of testimony. . . . [One is] the meaningfulness of the diagnostic labels. (That John Howard consistently finds twenty to twenty-five percent of those it examines mentally ill, while West Side finds over ninety percent, can hardly be explained in terms of the differences in their clientele. Rather, it illustrates either the differing political contexts in which the two services operate or the uncertain content of the diagnostic labels.)

Overholser v. Leach, 103 U.S. App. D.C. 289, 257 F. 2d. 667 (1957); cert. denied 359 U.S. 1013.

**Numerous articles have appeared on the lack of validity and reliability of psychiatric diagnoses, for example, Rossi (1974) and Stoller (1974). A further comment on this issue is a highly publicized study by Rosenhan (1973) in which sane pseudopatients who gained admission to mental hospitals were found by hospital staffs to be insane. Rosenhan stated that "psychiatric diagnosis betrays little about the patient but much about the environment in which an observer finds him" (p. 251).

David Bazelon, Chief Judge of the U.S. Court of Appeals for the District of Columbia Circuit, questioned the manner in which diagnostic labels were being used.

> Psychiatrists argued about whether a defendant had a "personality defect," a "personality disorder," a "disease," an "illness," or simply a "type of personality." How could a jury or any one else really make any sense out of this when the psychiatrists couldn't agree on the definitions? It was as if to maintain an illusory elitism psychiatrists resorted to deliberate obscurantism.

> What the psychiatrist has apparently never been able to understand is that conclusory labels and opinions are no substitute for facts derived from disciplined investigation. Labelling a person "schizophrenic" does not make him so. (Oct. 12, 1973)

> Do the various diagnostic labels—explaining everything yet understanding nothing—reflect an attempt to cover up the crucial conflicts of interest between patient and institution? Why is it that in the hospital's written official report to the court of diagnostic conclusions, differing viewpoints within the hospital's staff are not included? Attempts to obtain records or tapes of clinical conferences have consistently been opposed and thwarted by the psychiatric staff at St. Elizabeths. (Jan. 19, 1974)

The pretrial period is supposed to be one in which observation and evaluation take place. In our years of being on JHP wards, we have regarded this as a period of sitting around for the criminal. Chambers shared this view. He pointed out that, after the patient is seen in conference, it is "unlikely that [he] will see any professional staff member for diagnostic purposes" for the following several weeks.

> The only function that will arguably be served by the weeks and weeks that he will sit around is "observation." It is highly questionable whether any real observation takes place in John Howard, for whatever nursing staff observations are made, or even recorded, were rarely mentioned in staff conferences. (1969, p. 6)

LIFE IN MAXIMUM SECURITY

In nearly all felony cases and in some misdemeanor cases, the criminal declared NGBRI begins his stay on a posttrial ward in maximum security. In the early days of our study, a few patients of special interest were used as training cases for psychiatric residents who wanted to conduct individual psychotherapy. Some patients were also treated individually by psychologists and social workers. More recently, trainees in various disciplines worked with individual patients. Almost all the forensic patients have received no individual attention. Owing to their maximum security status, they are excluded from programs in areas away from their wards or on the hospital grounds

WARD MEETINGS

Once or twice a week for about an hour, all the patients on a ward meet as a group with the ward administrator (a medical doctor, psychologist, or social worker). The rest of the staff may sit in and offer comments. (Ward meetings sometimes are convened in the absence of the ward administrator, with a staff member in charge.) There is at least a rudimentary attempt to follow parliamentary procedure. The format varies from ward to ward, as does the comprehensiveness of the matters dealt with. Some ward administrators run very businesslike sessions; others attempt to promote a therapeutic-community atmosphere. The purpose of the ward meetings is to establish something approaching a participatory democracy, in which patients can have a say in the matters that affect their lives. Authority-patient contact is a primary objective; if it were not for these meetings, many patients might go for weeks or months at a time without being seen by the ward administrator. A second objective is to handle administrative matters and patient requests—phone privileges, plans for a ward party, and so forth. A third objective is to help patients express their feelings about ward life and to give an airing to problems between patients and staff. One physician described the ward meeting as an opportunity to "give the patients a push to help themselves get what they want."

In practice, the criminal does not have to be helped to get what he wants. Most of his time in ward meetings is spent in his using whatever tactics he thinks necessary to push for what he wants. A newly admitted patient discusses his case—usually the charge for which he was admitted—and then submits to questions. Later, he asks for privileges. The criminal is untruthful in the history that he gives and is deceptive in making a case for privileges. Men have cried at these meetings about wanting to go to funerals of people whom they hardly knew or about desiring to visit nonexistent offspring. In at least one instance, a criminal was permitted to attend his mother's funeral, but instead went drinking with the nursing assistant who accompanied him, continuing a pattern begun when he had left the hospital to see his mother when she was ill.

The staff is constantly being put on the defensive. Complaints, requests, and more complaints are the order of the day. The ward administrator is berated if he delays in signing a form or in endorsing a privilege. Although some ward administrators maintain a hard line in the face of the numerous pressures of a criminal group, most want things to run smoothly. We observed a meeting in which a doctor was asking for understanding and almost pleading for the patients to realize that he was doing what he could to expedite their requests for privileges and changes in status. The doctor read aloud the names of all those who had asked for various changes in status and was apologetic because he could not get things done as quickly as he wanted. In fact, he said that there was competition among doctors to advance patients from maximum to minimum security; he assured his own patients that he would do his very best to assist them. On another ward, patients complained about the closed staff meetings that followed the open ward meetings. The doctor then initiated staff meetings open to the patients. Few patients attended the open staff meetings. In fact, even patients whose cases were being discussed sometimes chose not to attend. The patients' objective clearly is to keep the staff on the defensive, no matter what the issue.

These meetings rarely feature a calm, truthful discussion of a substantive issue. Except when it is expedient, there is little honest disclosure, minimal receptivity, and virtually no self-criticism. The meetings are forums for exercises in control; their form depends on the personalities of the staff members, especially the ward administrator. There might be a crude shouting match or a smooth-running meeting of cooperation and ingratiation to score points.

One doctor who conducted ward meetings admitted his skepticism about their effect. He thought that it might not matter whether he came to the ward at all. But, he mused, perhaps he was not doing enough; perhaps the meetings should be held three times a week, rather than once. He said that he did not know of anything that a psychiatrist could offer to make a difference. He thought that perhaps the forensic division should be one big experiment, with no doctors on some wards, social workers running others, and nursing assistants in charge of others. He was thoroughly discouraged with what he was doing in these meetings, but believed that he had to continue to do something rather than nothing.

MILIEU THERAPY

Criminals in maximum security are not allowed on the grounds; thus, the milieu of the ward must be the arena in which change takes place, if it is to take place at all. In milieu therapy, the criminal is to learn interpersonal and other skills in a controlled environment. The totality of the program and services available in maximum security is brought to bear in an integrated effort at change. The various activities are the vehicles for the new learning that is to occur. In all aspects of milieu therapy, the staff assumes that the criminal has a mental illness from which he needs and wants to recover. Assignment to particular programs is part of the prescription for change. Each ward administrator is supposed to know each of his patients well enough to make referrals to the appropriate adjunctive services. Within the limits of the setting, it is possible to have informal recreation, recreational therapy, and occupational therapy, which, for a while, included the publication of a journal. Volunteers organize various projects, parties, and educational programs. The activity programs are fully described later in this chapter.

The discrepancy between the ideal and the actual in milieu therapy is great. No sooner has the criminal deceptively gained admission to the hospital than he is eager to leave. He realizes that he must take a series of steps before he is released. An occasional criminal scoffs at this gradual process and demands release immediately, on the grounds that he is not mentally ill.

> Although C had convinced the staff in the pretrial evaluation that he was ill, he did a complete turnabout after he was adjudged NGBRI. He stated that he did indeed "beat the rap" and contended that, because he never really was mentally ill, he should be unconditionally released immediately. C was regarded as dangerous, but it was clear that he had malingered before and was without mental disorder. Thus, the hospital, having no alternative, presented him to the court for release.

C had been in the hospital several times before. He figured that these tactics would succeed, because the hospital was eager to discharge him. Most criminals, however, play the game. The first step after being found NGBRI is to convince others that one is ready for minimum security. To do this, the criminal attends activities. That is a relatively pleasant way to spend time, but what is more important is that each criminal knows that his improvement is evaluated partly by his participation. Most seek to satisfy others without making too many compromises. Thus, they cooperate and do what is expected. Having played by the system's rules, they believe that they merit release. One criminal said:

> "The idea seemed to be that if you pursued all of these things (art, education, etc.) faithfully and behaved yourself on the ward, you somehow gained 'insight' into what was wrong with you and became better. A chronic complaint among many patients was that they had done everything expected from them, and still had not been released. It was as

if they were being denied that which was owed them for playing the game well."

Some criminals consider it a putdown to do as the establishment expects. They contest authority and are considered troublemakers. They hope that the hospital will discharge them, and sometimes it does.

Most criminals, however, follow an intermediate course. They appear cooperative, but they violate secretly. The guiding rule is to be discrete. As the criminal's mind works, getting caught is wrong, not violating. Getting caught is not that great a threat. Some staff members overlook violations and do not report them. They do not want to bother with having to do a writeup, provide supporting evidence, and answer questions, thus, as a consequence, antagonizing the patient. Some nursing assistants do not see anything objectionable in some of the infractions. If a criminal believes that a staff member is conscientious about reporting or that someone has it in for him, he is much more cautious.

Although there is a charge in point-scoring, most criminals desire greater excitement. The patterns are similar to those used on the street. Because the criminal is under surveillance, the risks are greater. For some, surveillance adds to the challenge. Criminals steal from each other, from the staff, and from the hospital. Fights occasionally break out among patients and between patient and staff member. Gambling is a part of ward life. Patients may indulge in heterosexual activities with nonpatients and exploitative homosexual acts with each other. In short, the whole gamut of violation is present, although on a reduced scale which depends on how the criminal group sizes up the staff on the ward.

If the staff responds to a violation, the practice is to view the offender as responsible, even though he is hospitalized because he has been adjudged insane and therefore not responsible. Restriction is applied in the name of treatment. At one point, a buddy system was introduced in which one man was paired with another; if one violated, both were punished. Whenever restriction is applied, endless power contests and legalistic maneuvers occur, as the criminal tries to beat the rap.

What is done when a man is caught violating is basically up to the nursing assistants and depends on current hospital policy, the doctor's policies and personality, and the attitude of the particular nursing assistant. We have observed that most of the criminal's violations have been either undetected or ignored. When a criminal is written up, it is often because what he did was so brazen that it captured everyone's attention or because a nursing assistant had a personal vendetta. In the early 1960s, nonreporting was due to the punitive policy of the hospital administration. If a person were reported for even a relatively minor violation, he could be retained in maximum security for a long time. At that time, the forensic ward personnel punished frequently and severely. In the 1970s, there is a much stronger tendency to ignore violations unless they are major or someone is hurt.

THE NURSING ASSISTANTS*

We have had numerous reports of criminality occurring in training schools, prisons, and hospitals among criminals, among staff, and among criminals and staff. This situation has been serious enough to warrant notices in the news media.** The sources of our information about nursing assistants (N.A.'s) in the forensic division of Saint Elizabeths are nursing assistants, physicians, other staff personnel, criminals (unchanged and changed, in the hospital and after unconditional release), and our own observations on the wards. For this section, most of our material came from nursing assistants who are dedicated to their jobs and of proven responsibility over the years. Under conditions of confidentiality, they gave us their views of people and programs in the forensic division. Their accounts confirmed reports of criminals whom we interviewed and worked with over a fifteen-year period. We have pointed out that the criminal is a liar and says anything that he thinks suits his purposes, but the reader will recall that we were seeing these men daily in a privileged communication arrangement. We were carefully probing the events of their lives and details of their thinking. Unchanged criminals whom we interviewed at different times reported the same behavior on the part of the same personnel. Their version of events was confirmed over the same period by criminals who showed substantial change. This material applies both to maximum and minimum security. We have omitted unusual situations and reference to particular individuals or groups. Instead, our emphasis is on *patterns* of behavior.

The majority of nursing assistants are responsible and conscientious about their jobs. However, an irresponsible *minority* (estimated by our sources as being from 25 to 40 percent) have been able to hamper and corrode the morale of many who are trying to do their best under difficult circumstances.

Right on the ward, those nursing assistants who are irresponsible aid and abet the criminal enterprises of forensic patients. However, most N.A.'s who

*We have in the forgoing writings in this study used the term *Nursing Assistant* in referring to the ward attendant, and we shall continue to do so. However, as of July 1973, in the Forensic Services Division (John Howard Pavilion) the designated term used has been changed to *Forensic Psychiatric Technician* (F.P.T.), and continues to be so as of February 1977.

**News reports of brutal guards, drug-using counselors, and personnel who violate in collusion with inmates are not uncommon (*Washington Post* 6/14/71; *Evening Star and News* 7/13/72).

are irresponsible do not collaborate in violation on the wards. There are in this work innumerable opportunities for the exercise of control and power in a nonarrestable form. Some N.A.'s enjoy the roles of detective, judge, and jailer. There is excitement in outwitting the criminal, catching him in a lie or violation, and then determining his fate. The criminal has relatively little contact with the doctor, which means that it is the N.A. who makes the countless daily decisions, such as when a man can make phone calls, get his medicine, see a doctor, or go to an activity. Most importantly, the data from nursing assistants influence the doctors' decisions. Most doctors are assigned to a ward for a limited period before being rotated to another service or moving on to a new position. Swamped with paperwork and administrative duties, they must rely on those who seem to know the criminal best. Many N.A.'s are around long before the doctor arrives on the scene and will be there long after he departs. They are the ones who interpret policies and decide whether to enforce the rules. In the days when doctors rarely visited some of the wards, a patient had to go through an N.A. to be transferred to minimum security. A request to see a doctor had to be routed through an N.A. and then through a nonmedical administrator. If the N.A. did not like a particular criminal, the request reached a dead end. If the N.A. did not trust a particular doctor, he might not convey information. The N.A. could also decide not to supply information because of a belief that the doctor would mete out too severe a penalty without giving the patient a chance to tell his side of the story. When a doctor came onto some of the wards, some nursing assistants resented it, perceiving an immediate threat to their power. Even now, much power is delegated to nursing assistants. They are asked to function as advisers and counselors, in addition to their regular duties. Power and control are built into the job and are often exercised. Thus, there are invariably power contests, not only among the staff members, but also between staff members and criminals.

There have been property violations of many types by N.A.'s, including the theft of clothing and money entrusted to them by patients. The fencing of stolen items sometimes occurs between N.A.'s and criminals and on the grounds between N.A.'s and other hospital personnel and patients. Sexual repartee occurs between criminals and some of the N.A.'s; and sexuality has gone beyond talk. After sexual activity or collaboration between N.A. and criminal in any crime, each party has something on the other. The criminal can always threaten to report the N.A. and thus, in a form of blackmail, receive favors. The N.A., because of his position, has power over the criminal and can make life relatively pleasant or difficult for him. Inequities in treatment of patients become obvious to all and then constitute the subject of grievances on the ward.

Another kind of violation by N.A.'s is assault or misuse of force. Assaults are difficult to conceal, however, and as the deterrents are so great, they occur less frequently than other types of violations.

The importation of contraband items has been accomplished with the help of N.A.'s. This is especially common with respect to drugs. Needles are available from ward supplies, and a few N.A.'s bring drugs to work. At one time, it was generally known that a dozen nursing assistants were using drugs. It was suggested that perhaps a treatment program should be offered to these N.A.'s, but difficulties in approaching them prevented its establishment. Those who have brought in drugs have been very resourceful. For example, heroin has come in in the center of cored apples and as powder on candy. Shooting galleries (places for the injection of drugs) were known by ward personnel to exist on some wards but were disregarded until they became too blatant.*

Similarly there has been use of liquor in maximum security. We have observed this firsthand. Other contraband items brought in through collusion with N.A.'s included hacksaws. At one time, duplicate keys to ward doors were available for purchase.

Other types of violations are gambling and usury. It was only rarely reported when patients had large sums of money on the ward, and then the money was not locked up for safe keeping. It was to the criminal's benefit to make a loan to an N.A., not only because of the interest he could charge, but also because of the privileged status he would enjoy. Criminals have loaned money at such usurious rates as 125 percent per week.

> "If the attendant N.A. has your money, you are the number one boy. You can stay in bed when you're not supposed to, have booze in your room during a shakedown, and so forth."

In addition to these violations by nursing assistants, there have been numerous incidents of neglect of duty. One N.A. expressed an all-too-often encountered attitude: "This is an easy job, the easiest and best I can get. I can eat, sleep, and get paid." Although these N.A.'s constitute a *minority*, the more responsible personnel have a hard time trying to provide the level of patient care they think is desirable. Of course, there have been occasions when N.A.'s wanted to act responsibly but were thwarted not by other N.A.'s, but by administrative indifference.

> An N.A. related that, while he was transferring a patient with another N.A., the criminal pulled a gun and escaped. As a result, the nursing assistants asked for a shakedown. It did not take place for a full week.

*Chambers (1969, p. 30) noted the use of heroin by criminals in ward bathrooms.

In another incident, a criminal pulled a knife on an N.A. at the medical and surgery service. The N.A.'s on that patient's ward in the forensic division asked for a shakedown, and nothing was done.

Nursing assistants can violate with little fear of disciplinary action, because hard proof is required for administrative action. One N.A. covers for another, and those who are opposed to this activity are not likely to inform and risk retaliation by their irresponsible coworkers. In practice, disciplinary action is taken only when an N.A. is caught *in the act* of violating. Supervisors are reluctant to enforce rules and regulations, largely because of the fear of retaliation. Efforts to reduce active violation and the neglect of duty have often resulted in driving the behavior further underground.

Before leaving the topic of how nursing assistants conduct themselves, we want to emphasize the double game some play. On the one hand, most N.A.'s try not to alienate the criminals; on the contrary, they court their favor. On the other hand, N.A.'s must stay on good terms with their superiors if they want promotions. Consequently, a criminal thinks that his interests will be served by the N.A., but the N.A. may act in his own behalf when he deals with the administration. For example, an N.A. may indicate to a criminal that he will press for the criminal's transfer to minimum security. However, if he knows that the attitude of the administration is unfavorable to such an action, he may not even present the request. Nevertheless, he will let the criminal think that he is working in the criminal's interest, making others on the staff the bad guys while keeping his own standing with the criminal untarnished.

In all fairness, it must be emphasized that some nursing assistants are afraid of their patients. Many of the N.A.'s come from the very neighborhoods in which their patients reside. They fear retaliation by the criminal when he is released. Sometimes the N.A. is overtly threatened, although at other times, the threat is not explicit. In any event, the security of the N.A. and that of his family is a consideration in his not wanting to antagonize the criminal.

In such a milieu, it is difficult for the responsible N.A. to do his job. Several very conscientious N.A.'s talked with us. We learned that the N.A. who complains to his superior about a fellow N.A. may be on trial himself. Unless he has in hand evidence of wrongdoing, his complaint backfires and he becomes unpopular. The greatest dilemma is the problem of carving out a useful role for oneself in such an environment. It is a problem of morale. The nursing assistants who take their work seriously (a majority) know that they have a difficult patient group to deal with. When their efforts are hampered by irresponsible coworkers (a minority), they become disillusioned, dispirited, and defensive. The responsible employee has the challenge of trying to contribute something under adverse conditions. When he tries to help someone, he may be accused of having a pet or be ridiculed for trying to do too much for the person. An honest N.A. has to be blind to much that goes on around him, not just to maintain morale, but to survive.

We have two purposes in describing these patterns by the minority of irresponsible N.A.'s. One is to emphasize the importance of selection and training procedures. More will be said about this in the following chapter. The other purpose is to point out the effect of irresponsible N.A.'s on the criminal.

For the criminal, life in confinement reflects life on the street, in that he avoids responsibility and consorts with those who are irresponsible. His reaction to the institution is based on that irresponsible minority, not the responsible majority. The criminal is not corrupted by the institutional environment. It does not make him any worse. However, he takes advantage of whatever opportunities there are to continue his way of life.

The criminal views the N.A. (and the rest of the staff) as he does the policeman. A good N.A. allows him to do largely what he wants to do, does not enforce the rules, and may even collaborate with him. A "bad" N.A. interferes by enforcing the rules and trying to change him against his will to be responsible. Violations are planned according to who is on duty, the criminal being temporarily deterred when the bad N.A. is on.

Of course, in accountability reasoning, the criminal justifies his own criminality by pointing to the irresponsibility of staff members who consort with him, are irresponsible in their own right, or do not take measures to stop him. A criminal is difficult to change to begin with. However, even in an institution that has the excellent resources that Saint Elizabeths has, the best conceived therapeutic and corrective programs are largely subverted, and thus it is difficult to establish change in the criminal.

CRIMINAL EQUIVALENTS

We have described the types of infractions and violations that occur in maximum security. In confinement, due to the limitations imposed on him, most of the criminal's thrusting for power occurs via criminal equivalents. Conceiving and executing strategies for getting into and out of the hospital have many criminal equivalents. This series of maneuvers contains all the thinking processes operative in a crime. These nonarrestable thrusts for power provide the same impact as do arrestable crimes. There is great excitement in the nearly constant talk about sex, crime, and getting out.* Getting out is such an important part of a man's thinking that talk about it goes on day and night.

---

*Letkemann (1973) put in perspective the notion that confinement is a school of crime. What he observed of prisons, we have found to hold true wherever the criminal lives with others like himself: "Inmates think of such learning primarily in terms of 'contacts' or associations that facilitate crime upon release. They agree that the techniques of crime are not ordinarily systematically taught in prison, but rather communicated informally (p. 122).

On one ward, meetings were held by criminals without staff members present. The topic was how to advance from maximum security. The criminals called these sessions "seminars." These were the ward meetings that mattered to them. They began at night and often continued into the morning.

"There were four of us who assembled most evenings. We would have coffee and tea and what food might be available from the kitchen or sent in by friends. and we would talk. The talk would go from sex to personal history and ambitions to how to get out. Of this latter topic we made a real study. We analyzed the case of every one of the patients on the ward— about twenty-five in number—and discussed how long each patient had been on the ward, the crime for which he had been committed, how he conducted himself and when he thought he would be slated to leave or what was holding him back. We reviewed the cases of past patients as far back as our collective memories could recall. Our senior member developed what he called his 'two year rule.' On the basis of all the data he could collect about other patients, past and present, on both maximum security wards, he decided that no matter how heinous the offense for which you had been committed, so long as you conducted yourself properly, your maximum stay was about two years on maximum security and another year to a year and a half on minimum.

"During these sessions we tested each others' defenses against the day when they might have to be presented to a doctor or to a group of physicians at a conference.

"I realize that it sounds as if these 'seminars' were formalized meetings deliberately organized and structured to enable us to con our way out. But this was not so. What the get togethers were, they were basically coffee clatches of people who liked each other and had a use for each other."

Most hospital programs are used by the criminal to his own advantage. There are criminal equivalents in point-scoring, in directing an activity, and in heading a committee (showing what others regard as leadership). During confinement, most of the criminal's interpersonal transactions are characterized by building himself up at the expense of other people.

The criminal is fragmented, so his stance toward the hospital sometimes changes. He has periods of vulnerability and phases in which he is serious about reforming. Thus, there are times when he enters programs with some enthusiasm, cooperates with the staff, and lives harmoniously within the patient community. As we have pointed out, such periods of sincerity are without conviction. They do not last. Many criminals maintain an exploitative stance throughout and have no intention of changing. They remain single-minded in their objectives—to get in to beat the charge, and then to get out. Many of these criminals, while telling the hospital staff that they intend to be crimefree, have concurrently told us that they plan to resume their old style of life when they leave the hospital, except that they will be more careful so as not to get caught.

THE DOCTORS

Most of the doctors who come to the forensic division begin in good faith. They try to do the best possible job with what they already know. We have indicated above that until recently the brunt of responsibility for criminals on most forensic wards has rested on the shoulders of young, relatively inexperienced psychiatric residents or Public Health Service officers.* This corps of youthful talent has been essential; as Chambers pointed out, without it treatment standards would have been unattainable because of the small number of other doctors available. In speaking of doctors here, we include Ph.D. psychologists who have had both therapeutic and administrative experience.

Most of the young doctors are enthusiastic, responsible, and dedicated, but they have been trained to treat noncriminals, and they are inexperienced with criminals. Their ideas as to what techniques are effective are derived from their earlier work. They approach the criminal not only with concepts useful for another psychiatric population, but with a frame of reference based on current sociologic and psychiatric views as to who the criminal is, as we did when we began. Thus, the doctors believe that they are dealing with mentally ill people who are victims of both inner and outer forces. These doctors use analytic interpretations or rational, behavioral, or pharmacologic procedures. Some use group therapy to treat volume; others believe that group therapy is truly the method of choice. When one approach does not work, the more flexible among them shift to another. As time passes, their work with criminals elicits from doctors responses that are not elicited by work with other patient groups. Enthusiasm wanes and is replaced by a sense of futility; eventually, interest diminishes. Many reduce their contact with criminals to an absolute minimum and limit themselves to administrative duties, of which there are plenty to keep them busy. Finally, most leave. The observations in this section apply to doctors in both maximum and minimum security forensic wards.

---

*The forensic division currently has neither residents nor Public Health Service officers. The division maintains that our description of its doctors does not apply to the current (1976) staff.

As he would with a noncriminal, the doctor depends on the criminal to raise important issues. His questions and responses are guided by his theoretical framework. This makes him vulnerable to the criminal's leading him by the nose, once the latter figures out the doctor's orientation. As a result, the doctor may obtain information that confirms what he believes but is not valid. That is followed by the demoralizing experience of being surprised to learn that things are not what they seem to be. The doctor then questions the original sincerity of the criminal and eventually, as this recurs, comes to doubt the effectiveness of his procedure. The young doctor quickly finds himself pressured and buffeted about as he deals with criminals individually and, particularly, in groups. Once criminals pick up a doctor's unsureness and inexperience, they view him as a mark, someone easy to influence. They then apply pressure in various forms. If a doctor candidly acknowledges his unsureness, he is not respected for his openness, but scorned and exploited. Any doctor who takes a sincere interest and is compassionate is taken advantage of. The criminal regards kindness as weakness.

"The consensus on the ward was that Dr.———was a kind man, sincerely devoted to helping his patients and working as hard as he could toward that end within the limitations imposed on him by the system. Of course, as ward doctor, he was also in charge of the movement of his patients off the ward toward eventual freedom and that stood in the way of any possible therapeutic relationship because we were all too busy trying to con him into releasing us."

Some doctors respond to criminals by becoming hard-liners. They do not start out this way, but it happens with time. The criminal thinks of these doctors who act like prosecuting attorneys as policemen. Hard-liners may elicit more information than other examiners, but they are no more effective in dealing with it.

"He was nasty, bitingly sarcastic and so deliberately rude that I decided he must be trying to provoke an angry reaction from me. I played it cool and listened to him carefully. . . . There was a mixture of truth, taunts and barbs. I left that meeting as I was to leave the next, aware that I had failed to recruit Dr. ———, the one person I had to recruit, . . . and feeling blazingly angry, frustrated and humiliated."

The criminal who has not previously dealt with a psychiatrist arrives at the hospital with no set image. In his experience, a doctor helps and is kind, understanding, and sympathetic. In relatively short order, the criminal's attitude shifts to fit the circumstances of his situation. Like a prison, the hospital confines him; thus, it is viewed as prison. The added factor is that in the hospital he is considered sick, and by playing the psychiatric game, he can get out more rapidly than from prison. The criminal sees the doctor as his keeper, warden, or jailer. A doctor can be a helper in only one way, to help him get out of the hospital.

The inexperienced doctor is fearful as he works with this group; even doctors who are not afraid are perceived that way by the criminal. The doctor is uncertain how to manage a ward filled with criminal patients. He is afraid of what these criminally insane men might do to disrupt the ward and inflict injury, perhaps even on him. He is afraid that he will not gain the respect of the criminals and that his authority will be undermined. He is apprehensive about making important decisions of legal and social consequence. Most of all, the doctor feels vulnerable to being made a fool of by men who con, lie, and exploit others as a way of life. A cycle of fear and suspicion may mount, with the doctor becoming increasingly skeptical about anything the criminal says or does. Even the doctor who is initially compassionate eventually develops a somewhat hard-bitten attitude. Skepticism is expressed openly or transmitted by the doctor's tone and actions. The criminal, of course, picks this up and capitalizes on it. Giving the doctor tidbits of information, which are in fact revealing (truthful), can be very effective in relieving the doctor's fears and scoring points.

In addition to fearing the criminals, many ward doctors fear antagonizing nursing assistants. A doctor is on a service for a short time and encounters established ways of operating and hardened attitudes in people who may have been at the hospital for decades. Many of them do not want to change their ways. Power issues sometimes are expressed in racial terms. The real issue, however, is status—often, professional staff against ward staff. The new doctor certainly does not want to be viewed as a racist. If he recognizes that this can be used against him, he may tread lightly in exercising his authority. Psychiatrists new to a ward are usually anxious more about whether they can relate effectively to their ward staffs than about whether they can treat criminals effectively. That is not surprising; without the cooperation of the nursing assistants, doctors have been sabotaged continually.

The doctor's superiors are basically on the sidelines. It has been the administration's position that it should not interfere with or stifle the work of the young doctor. Actually, there is a fear of upsetting the applecart above and below. The administration does not want to tell the doctor what to do and get embroiled in a contest. The doctor in most cases wants to go his own way and does not request help from above; at the same time, he does not want to get embroiled with those below, the nursing assistants. No one wants to tread on anyone else's toes. This results in poor supervision by those who are experienced, and, as a consequence, the criminal has greater leeway.

We emphasize that most of the doctors are responsible, although many are inexperienced and not knowledgeable about the criminal. However, just as some nursing assistants are attracted to work with the criminal for the excitement, so are a few doctors. They may not have chosen this patient group to work with, but, once assigned, they find gratifications that they might not have anticipated. Some doctors working with criminals have said that they themselves are sociopaths and therefore enjoy work with this group. Several doctors have approached criminals whom they found fascinating, volunteered to help them out, and continued to associate with them after release.

Those who work with the criminal for the excitement have little genuine concern for the patient. A few doctors have openly adopted the position that the criminal should learn to be content with himself as a person. Getting caught is seen as the problem more than criminality itself. In more than one instance, the doctor has faulted a criminal, not for violating, but for being stupid enough to get caught. He is urged to be more careful. Such an attitude is compatible with the criminal's objectives.

Generally, the longer the doctor is around, the more perfunctory his evaluations become. He may not know vital things about a patient, because he has neglected to talk to his staff or read the record. Instead, he emphasizes the details of the crime for which the patient was arrested and goes into other violations. The irresponsibility of these doctors shows itself in their defaulting on particular obligations of their job. Recommendations for privileges and the writing of specific orders are promised, but not acted on. There have been some gross examples of physical neglect of patients. In some cases, criminals have gone three to five years without physical examinations. Sometimes, a patient's physical distress is assumed to be a manifestation of his mental illness. One criminal, for example, complained of itching in his groin. This was ignored, so he eloped and went to a local hospital, where he was found to be infested with crab lice and was given a prescription. He then returned to his ward. Incidents such as this only add to the criminal's antagonism toward the institution.

A much more basic problem than the quality of medical care is the accessibility of the doctor. It is difficult to get an opportunity even to speak with a doctor for a few minutes. Chambers found what we had been seeing for years.

On most wards the patients rarely saw their doctor, except for a passing "How do you feel?" or an occasional sick call. The doctor, nevertheless, had sole control over the patient's progress through and out of the hospital. He was expected to make decisions regarding the patient's recovery and an individualized conclusion regarding his likely dangerousness. (1969, p. 27)

The doctor is often not on the ward, being tied up in meetings, at court, and in the writing of reports, summaries, and referrals. He is simply too busy. Some are reluctant to visit the ward, because they know that they will be hounded with a siege of requests, demands, and complaints. Usually, it takes a major violation or an impending court proceeding for a doctor to see a patient individually. Occasionally, even criminals who have committed crimes on the ward are not seen by a doctor. On some wards, when a criminal is asked to see a doctor at the doctor's request, he is certain that it is because a reprimand is forthcoming. In the 1960s especially, there were few instances of doctors seeing patients to find out how they were getting along. One reason for the current popularity of the therapeutic community among some doctors is that the doctor sees patients once a day in a group, rather than having to deal with them individually. Before the therapeutic community, it was a common experience to have criminals surround us when we came to the ward. On one occasion, Dr. Yochelson was told, "Watch out, doctor, we have a trap set for a doctor if he happens to come on the ward." No doctor had interviewed anyone on that ward for eleven weeks. Some criminals filed writs solely to get to see a doctor. In the 1960s, some criminals went years without a note in their records by a doctor. In some cases, it is the criminal who is hesitant to approach the doctor, because of biases that the doctor is reputed to have. With the absence of the doctor from the ward, more decision-making power is entrusted to or appropriated by the nursing assistants. One ward doctor signed a pad of seclusion slips and left it with the N.A.'s, telling them to fill in the rest of the information. Thus, without the doctor's supervision, the N.A.'s had complete freedom to put a person in seclusion.

Actual violations involving a doctor and a criminal are uncommon, or at any rate rarely known about. However, they do occur. There have been some cases of collaboration in crime. When this occurs, the relationship is mutually exploitative. A criminal has greater leverage to get what he wants and takes advantage of it. In short, each has something that he can threaten the other with. A few doctors have offered to help criminals in ways that are ethically compromising or frankly illegal. The details of these situations are not as important as how criminals react to a few corrupt people who are in positions of power over them. Criminals in such situations gain more room to maneuver. If a staff member finds them fascinating or wants something from them, the power relationship is radically altered to the criminal's advantage.

Criminals are nearly always submitting requests, appealing decisions, and doing whatever else is necessary to seek privileges leading to their discharge from the institution. As a consequence, the administrative paper work is heavy. Criminals have had great difficulty in finding out about the status of a request. Some of this has to do not with the workload of the administrators but rather with interpersonal politics. Some decisions are deferred indefinitely, as the buck is passed up through the hierarchy. Criminals are told only that they must wait. Prejudices against individual criminals may also be operative. When a criminal is a source of controversy and has had publicity in the community, he is likely to be treated differently than others. We pick a case in which we were involved as an example. The issues are less what the staff did than its impact on the criminal.

Dr. Yochelson had spent approximately thirty hours within one month with a man accurately regarded as dangerous, more time than all the doctors combined had spent with him over a period of years. During our contact and during all the turmoil that followed, this man showed us that he wanted to be in our program. We thought his desire sincere enough to warrant accepting him. Arrangements had to be made so that he could come to our office, on another part of the grounds. By precedent, a security risk patient could participate in a program elsewhere in the hospital if it were deemed important to his rehabilitation. He would then be escorted by guards to the building. The following is the sequence of events.

Discussion began in May about permitting C's transfer to minimum security so he could attend our program. By September, no decision had been made, and the Public Defender Service threatened to intervene with legal action if there were further delay. The public defender cited the Covington decision, which interprets the right to treatment and freedom from undue restriction. The matter was referred to the Superintendent, who delayed taking action. Meanwhile, an administrative doctor of the forensic division declared that he was against C's participation and would present his objection in court. C then alleged that his ward doctor had tried to discourage him from pressing any further.

"Dear Dr. Yochelson:

"I know that I might see you Friday but I just have to get this off my chest. I saw Dr. ——— today and he gave me what he called friendly advice; he said that if I knew what was good for me I should stop messing around with [the administrative doctor] and you because I was going to get hurt as there was no love lost between you and [him], and in effect he was telling me that [the administrative doctor] would get to me somehow. Well let me say that I got quite up tight about [Dr. ———'s] statement. I asked him if he would repeat it under oath in court; he said, "There you go again, starting something." I told him straight up that sure [the administrative doctor] hurt me and I knew that; but what was better—to be hurt by [him] for trying to get help for myself even if it was with you or to go on the way I had already in my life and set up here and keep my mouth shut and not fight for what was right. I can't do it for Christ sake here once I want to really change and see a way of doing it; and all I get is bullshit from the authority; but like we have talked about, do I really have any right to complain because I am really a lot worse than they could ever be a million times over."

By November, when still no decisive action had been taken, C changed his mind and decided to press no longer. He feared that even if he won in court, certain staff members would make things unpleasant for him. In November, he eloped from the hospital, taking three very dangerous men with him.

For six months, this forensic patient had been serious about wanting to avail himself of a program for change. He had conducted himself on the ward with propriety and without violating, so eager was he to enter our program. Many times, when things looked bleak during that half-year, C devised numerous escape plans. These schemes were not implemented, because he still had hope that he could soon embark on an effort to change his life. The public defender was disappointed, not only because the criminal had become so discouraged that he eloped, but also because he believed that he (the public defender) had a cogent case to present in court.

C stayed out of the hospital for quite some time, but he kept in touch with us by phone. In the following calendar year, tired of the life he was leading and with an accidentally self-inflicted wound, C returned to the hospital. Finally, in July, with a new director of the forensic division in command, C was permitted to enter our program. C was still an unchanged criminal and clearly a great elopement risk, especially in the light of his latest successful escape. The new director recognized the risks, as did we, but he operated according to what he believed was best for the criminal. C never eloped again. In fact, he obtained a conditional release, got a job, and developed a sound relationship with a responsible girl. What is most important, more than three years after this story began, C was participating conscientiously in our program and satisfying its severe requirements satisfactorily.

LIFE IN MINIMUM SECURITY

In minimum security, the criminal is less restricted. Freedom of movement is commensurate with privilege status. The criminal may attend activities off the ward or out of the building. He may be permitted to go into the city for designated purposes, such as work, school, or visiting his family. Privileges are granted in stages:

A status—no privileges

B status—criminal may go to activities off the ward accompanied by a staff member

C status—different degrees or limits of unaccompanied ground privileges

D status—unaccompanied ground privileges from 9 a.m. to 5 p.m., and then 9 a.m. to 9 p.m.

A criminal is permitted off the grounds on a regular basis when he is granted a conditional release.

There is no uniform procedure for assignment to minimum security. Sometimes, a full staff conference is convened, with the administrative doctor from the criminal's prospective new ward attending. This may resemble the pretrial conference in format. Although there cannot be absolute certainty as to whether a criminal is ready for the new step, the staff has, as one psychologist put it, "a feel for the patient"; the staff members pool their ideas, with particular emphasis on the criminal's history of dangerousness and his present deportment. Psychologic tests may be administered, in the hope that they will shed some light on the criminal's readiness. Often, the process is much more informal: a ward doctor chats with staff members, reaches a decision, and then clears the transfer with the appropriate people on the ward that will receive the criminal. On maximum security wards that have a therapeutic community or something similar, a criminal's name is brought up for discussion. The other criminals then have a chance to express their opinions about his prospective transfer.

We have already described the types of violations in maximum security by criminals and some staff members. Violations occur in minimum security, too, but to an even greater degree. Minimum security is a step toward getting out. The hospital offers more treatment and places greater confidence in the criminal than earlier; he is being prepared for reentry into society. With greater freedom, there are more opportunities to violate; violations actually increase in number and extent.

Many take advantage of the new freedom once they are permitted outside the building where they have been confined. They leave the grounds without authorization and violate. Some criminals alter privilege cards by forging the doctor's name. Others have been known to obtain passes already bearing the doctor's signature and sell them. At one time, criminals were going through the hospital gates with forged passes sold at two dollars apiece. In some cases, hospital employees have driven criminals into the city without authorization. But usually criminals leave simply by walking through the gates unnoticed or unimpeded by guards.

Thefts occur at almost any site on the grounds, and stolen articles are fenced on the grounds. In addition, there is stealing off the grounds. Some criminals leave the grounds on Monday and steal so that they will have items to sell on Tuesday, the employees' payday. The criminality has been so brazen that crimes have been planned openly.

One criminal was shouting from a ward window to another man standing outside. They were planning a bank robbery in pig Latin. When the inmate had his time out on the grounds, he eloped, held up a bank, and then returned to the hospital without being apprehended, flashing the proceeds.

The criminal finds sex easily available. He locates patients wandering the grounds who are willing to cooperate for token payment, such as cigarettes or some change. There have also been instances of criminals having sex with employees both on and off the grounds.

Some criminals have misrepresented themselves to establish sexual liaison with other patients.

C posed as a caseworker and gained access to another ward in the hospital under the guise of providing social work services for a female patient. He arrived on the ward dressed conservatively in tie and jacket and with briefcase in hand. The appearance of a stranger raised questions in the minds of staff members, who made inquiry and asked him to leave the premises. However, no further attempt was made to determine who he was or what he was doing there.

This criminal did not have to go to such lengths for sex, it being readily obtainable on the grounds. But he derived excitement from being admitted to the ward while representing himself as a staff person.

A confirmed episode occurred in which a criminal kept a girl in his room for four days and three nights.

C's girlfriend came to see him on Saturday. In order to look as though she were leaving at the end of visiting hours, she took her pocketbook with her when she left C's room, but went into the bathroom nearby. When she came out, a nursing assistant, who was about to go off duty, allowed her back on the ward. She stayed in C's room the entire holiday weekend, during which on-duty staff members were fairly few and supervision lax. On Tuesday, she left with the visitors who had come that day during visiting hours.

Particular activities have been known to afford especially good opportunities to violate. One is the weekly movie. Some criminals simply walk out during the film to transact business, whether it be having sex, procuring drugs and liquor, or anything else. Some depart for action outside the hospital gates and return before the lights go on at the end of the film. Violations may occur just outside the room where the film is being shown. A criminal may find a woman who is partially out of contact with reality and either bribe or coerce her to come into a bathroom to have sex. Sometimes this is arranged in advance, so that someone meets him for sex. Some criminals have chosen the darkness of the movie as the occasion to elope from the hospital.

Once he is in minimum security, the criminal finds it much easier to procure drugs, liquor, and other contraband. He does not have to depend on others to bring them in, but can do it himself. The result is private parties at which these substances are used. Some N.A.'s ignore this. Drugs have long been sold in maximum security and on the hospital grounds, with sellers in competition with each other. A numbers game used to be run daily in front of one of the canteens. At one point in the 1960s, there was so much liquor and drugs around that some of the doctors were saying that they did not care so much about the drinking, that it was more important for drugs at least to be kept off the wards. Meanwhile, in some cases, their own nursing assistants were peddling drugs from the ward medical supply, as well as from outside sources. Prescriptions for amphetamines forged by criminals were filled by unknowing hospital pharmacists. The pills were sold on the grounds and on the street. A wide variety of contraband items found their way on to the wards, including weapons.

In short, the violations that occurred in maximum security continued and increased in minimum security. Our sources of information are criminals who have changed, criminals in the process of change, and staff with whom we have repeatedly checked, as well as our own personal observations. It is not hard, once one knows who the forensic patients are, to observe them leaving the grounds when they are not supposed to. We have seen some returning from the streets carrying bags of stolen items.

When the eloping criminal returns to the ward, it may not even have been observed that he was gone. In more than one instance, the only comment by nursing assistants has been to ask whether he had a good time. Of course, if the patient is in disfavor or if there is a current policy of cracking down, the man may be punished by being restricted. As in maximum security, violations are planned according to whether a good or bad N.A. (from the criminal's point of view) is on a particular shift. The criminal decides on the basis of who is on duty whether he can afford to come in late, or perhaps arrive drunk.

Violations of hospital rules and regulations occur with great frequency. Overstaying a curfew, for example, is a frequent event. Misrepresenting one's privileges to unknowing family members and friends is also common.

> C visited his girlfriend at her house often. The woman was horrified and embarrassed to learn that she had been unwittingly assisting C in almost daily violation. C had told her that he had permission to go off the grounds when in fact he did not.

In the early 1960s, the hospital administration reacted punitively to violations, which sometimes resulted in a man's being returned to maximum security and confined for a long period. A criminal could be placed in maximum security on the basis of little more than a second-hand report that he had been seen off the grounds. In part, it was this attitude that led even some of the very responsible nursing assistants to ignore violations, because a writeup based on a rumor could result in a severe penalty.

That period was followed by one of greater laxity in policies about penalty and privilege. A criminal was likely to be shifted back to maximum security only if he were involved in an episode of violence, and even then concrete evidence was required. The following event is indicative of how attitudes have changed.

> C had sex with a patient in the basement of another building at the hospital. He enjoyed himself more than he had anticipated; when he looked at his watch, C realized that he was thirty-five minutes late. He rushed back to the ward. His defense was that it is better to have sex on the grounds than to go off and violate. Emphasis was on the lateness, and not the sex on the grounds, which some years before would have resulted in confinement in maximum security.

A doctor distinguished between little sins and major offenses. A little sin was a violation that did not harm anyone physically or pose a threat to the ward, such as a theft, getting drunk, or having sex on the grounds. A little sin tended to be ignored unless the criminal was so brazen about what he did that the staff would obviously be negligent not to respond. With less deterrence, violations have become more frequent. Minimum security patients, in some cases, leave the grounds almost any time they want to.

> C described a continuing pattern of violation. Sometimes, he was driven off the grounds by a housekeeper at the hospital. At other times, he left by a hole in the fence or simply walked out the gate. He had been to his brother's house several times. When he got hungry, he went to the grocery store across from the hospital. Once, he met some strangers on the street, and they invited him to a crap game. C reported that he was not particularly fearful of getting in trouble, because the general attitude of the staff was that a little drinking, gambling, and sex made little difference. C knew that this would not retard his progress in getting out of the institution.

The practice of leaving the grounds to cross the street for food or drink was so common that the stores became *de facto* an extension of the grounds of Saint Elizabeths. Then criminals pressed for it to be *de jure* an extension.

Some nursing assistants have shown carelessness or indifference toward the elopement of criminals. A man might be missing for hours before anyone was even aware of it, and still longer before it would be reported. In several situations, N.A.'s have seen criminals who have eloped but refused to turn them in, in one case because, as the N.A. put it, she saw him "after working hours." Perhaps the most surprising aspect of the indifference toward elopement is that repeatedly criminals return to the hospital grounds for short visits while on unauthorized leave, converse with fellow criminals under the very noses of the authorities, and suffer no consequences.

Some members of the security force have shown attitudes similar to those of the nursing assistants. There is a continuum of dedication and responsibility on the part of the security force. Most guards are conscientious and do the best they can, but are demoralized by what goes on around them. Others are irresponsible in their work habits and do not interfere with much of the violating that they witness. And a few themselves have violated in a variety of ways, sometimes collaborating with patients.*

Guards have told us that some members of their force simply did not think it worthwhile to enforce rules and regulations. Some compromise, such as the guard who tells the criminal that he may consume liquor outside the gate, but does not want to see it brought on to the grounds. A few guards believe that there is no point turning the criminal in, because he would soon be freed and would repeat the offense.

From time to time, this general attitude of indifference and carelessness has worried the courts and the community at large. Starting in 1971 and for several years thereafter, the community went through a period of awareness and alarm at the high incidence of elopements.** News of elopements and crimes committed by patients on elopement periodically appears in the press (*Washington Post* 5/11/71, 11/28/71, 4/25/72, 6/23/73.) Indeed, the problem had become critical with the general loosening of deterrence in the management of the forensic division. During July, August, and September 1972, the hospital's Biometrics Branch reported thirty criminals on unauthorized leave from the minimum security wards, which hold about ninety patients. (The number thirty reflects criminals on unauthorized leave for even the briefest period at any time during that quarter of the year.) During fiscal 1972, Biometrics reported 4,416 patient-days of elopement from *one* minimum security ward.

Police officials have complained that the hospital administration often fails

---

*In the last several years, changes have been made in the security force so that, compared to the past, there is relatively little irresponsibility.

**An article in *Evening Star* (11/12/71) noted that "the record of escapes is one of the worst in the nation." The article reported that the hospital's security staff charged hospital administrators with indifference in the matter.

to notify them immediately, if at all, when a person elopes. Sometimes, the hospital's own security force is totally in the dark.

> In checking the security force notifications to see whether three dangerous elopees were listed, we found that they were not. Looking through the elopement records for three months, we saw only three or four sheets of paper, with the names of far fewer patients than even we knew had left. The guards were not to be faulted for this; they reported that frequently they are not told of elopements. They cannot be alerted or alert others to pick up these criminals if they believe that these criminals are still residing in the hospital.

In the last few years, notification has improved.

The hospital has several ways of dealing with criminals on elopement without involving legal authorities. If a so-called sexual psychopath is released on convalescent status (living in the community while still on the hospital rolls) and is apprehended for a crime other than one of a sexual nature, he may still be unconditionally released from hospital rolls as having recovered from sexual psychopathy.

> C, designated as a sexual psychopath, was placed on convalescent status, even though he was known to be using drugs at the time. He was eventually discharged as recovered from his sexual psychopathy. Unknown to the authorities, he was continuing his sexual practices.

If C had been caught for another sex crime, he would have been returned to the hospital. When a patient on conditional release (still residing in the hospital) elopes, he may also be placed on convalescent status without being returned to the court. Thus, in addition to whatever elopees are on official records, the criminals from these two groups must also be counted. If the hospital is embarrassed by an incident and fears adverse publicity, it may take sterner measures. When two men got away from a marshal, fired a shot, and fled to New York, they were picked up in New York quickly. They were not even caught in a crime. One was sent to serve a pre-existing sentence, and the other was returned to the hospital and placed in seclusion.

When a criminal on conditional release elopes, it may be relatively easy for him to avoid trouble. If he returns to the hospital, and if he promises to report periodically, he may well be assured of being kept on convalescent status. That is one reason that the convalescent status roll is so large. Those who elope stay on the hospital census, even though some administrators have little interest in tracking them down and exercising jurisdictional authority over them. Thus, frequently no bench warrants are issued. Metropolitan police have told us that the police are reluctant to pick up known elopees; doing so takes much time and entails red tape that officers think is not worth going through, inasmuch as they realize that the same criminals may be back on the streets again within a short time.

Some hospital officials have done little to retrieve criminals, even when they have information as to their whereabouts. It may take a crime to initiate action to pick up an elopee.

C, who was on elopement, occasionally hung around the hospital grounds. No one paid any attention to him. When C killed a man in a neighboring state, the hospital and police made extensive efforts to locate him. By contacting a former patient associate of his, the police were able to track him down and make the arrest.

In short, deterrence of elopement is weak. In a recent court decision, a man deemed legally insane cannot be subjected to criminal prosecution (that is, held responsible) for leaving the institution in which he has been confined.* While this helps protect the rights of the individual, another deterrent is eliminated.

THERAPY DESIGNED TO BE PROBATIVE

Most of the treatment in the forensic division is milieu therapy. There have also been limited offerings of individual, group, and psychodrama therapy that purported to probe more deeply into the personality of the criminal than do other activities.

INDIVIDUAL THERAPY

Two or possibly three of the 271 committed patients receive individual psychiatric therapy. Staff psychologists treat another half dozen patients individually and thirty to thirty-five more in groups. Around 200 patients do not receive individual or group therapy, but several John Howard doctors thought such therapy had limited value anyway for most of these patients. (Chambers 1969, p. 27)

What Chambers observed in 1969 has been true right along, with even less individual therapy being offered in the years since. If a doctor finds a criminal

*United States v. Powell 503 F. 2 195 (1974).

particularly interesting, he may offer him individual sessions. It is usually the trainees in psychology and social work who select individuals for psychotherapy. A few staff members in other disciplines also conduct therapy with individual criminals. In the late 1960s, nursing assistants started functioning as counselors.

Criminals play both sides of the issue with respect to the availability of individual therapy. They protest if it is not available, claiming that the institution offers no treatment. There are criminals who are in a transient phase of self-disgust. They are genuinely tired of the criminal life that has landed them in confinement and they sincerely want treatment, but this phase does not last. If treatment is not offered to them when they are receptive, they reject it when it is offered and blame the institution for offering help too late. They then negate any form of help offered them. The few who are offered individual therapy eventually view it as interfering with their getting out. They believe that the more they reveal of themselves, the longer they will remain confined. They reason that, once the staff regards them as patients who will profit by therapy, they may be kept in the hospital to work on their problems. Here is a typical statement by a criminal who has grown restless, is no longer interested in therapy, and wants only to be released:

"Doctor, I am well now. I don't need to be in Saint Elizabeths anymore. I may try to go to court now and see if I can seek an early release. . . . The time is ripe I feel for my release now. And I want to go out and do good. I am not afraid of the street anymore. I know that I can make a go of it. I dig myself."

The fragmented criminal changes his mind as to what he wants. The following notes by a psychiatric resident illustrate what even a dedicated, intelligent therapist has to face.

From the notes of Dr. ———
[Sessions began early in August]

8/14   He intimated that if released in October that our sessions would no longer be necessary since he had become wise enough to seek psychiatric aid on the outside, and this of course would prevent him from committing any further criminal acts.

9/4   He threatened me into understanding that he was being backed into a position where he would not be responsible shortly for his actions [because he had not received privileges].

9/10 [When told he had to go through a stepwise procedure for privileges] he could not see the sense of continuing our therapy if we couldn't "put our lessons to good use."

9/11 I have no doubt that in his way of thinking he would provide narrative in exchange for my intercession with Dr. ——— for his privileges. Bit by bit he is coming to understand that I cannot be bought or manipulated to his advantage.

10/15 [The patient] seemed genuinely thankful that "unlike the 99% of fellows here with my problems, at least I can get more of what I consider treatment."

11/30 We sat out in the warm sun. . . . There was much more nonverbal communication and mutual reassurance that a new phase of understanding and rapport had been reached.

12/18 He moved into the area of wanting to get me a Christmas gift.

1/15 [Last session before elopement]

6/30 [In a call to the doctor, the patient] said he had eloped because his city privileges and conditional release had been denied.

We ourselves spent many hours with this criminal after he was readmitted to the hospital several years later and again was declared NGBRI. Speaking of his earlier individual therapy, the criminal said that he had truly liked Dr.———. He also made the following observations:

"I had good bull sessions with him but that would be all you could call them."

"I just played him by ear and gave him what he wanted, but we only played 'ring around the roses.'"

"I didn't intentionally lie to him [but] I played it up real big."

"I just seemed to lead him where he wanted to go."

C had seventy-four therapy sessions with Dr. ——— in five-and-a-half months—far more intensive work than forensic patients are usually offered.

As it turned out, what Dr. ——— considered therapy, C often perceived as a con operation. Finally, he eloped from the hospital and continued to be heavily in crime. Another criminal reflected on the individual therapy that he had had with another conscientious and perceptive resident:

> "I am sure that most of the information I fed Dr. ——— was fed to him with the sole purpose of impressing him, getting on his good side . . . [as long as it] wouldn't be harmful to me insofar as my release from the hospital [went]. . . . In other words, if I was sitting in the doctor's chair and I could help, what would I want to hear?"

In their 1969 report, the Program Development Work Group on Forensic Services recommended that, to adjust to staff shortages, greater reliance be placed on "subprofessionals" to provide "treatment under supervision." The report pointed out that programs at other institutions had depended "almost exclusively" on nursing assistants as "primary or sole behavior change agents" (p. 31). The implementation of this recommendation has resulted in some compromising situations. Nursing assistants do not receive extensive training to counsel criminals (although the forensic division is currently offering more training than it did formerly). Also, as we have pointed out, some of these counselors are themselves highly irresponsible. Incidents like the following have occurred.

> C's counselor urged him to come into a room away from the mainstream of ward activity. She had been drinking and offered him some scotch. Along with it she issued an invitation to him to go to the races, first mentioning a boyfriend and then changing it to include him and a party of others. She also advised him to be a companion to a female criminal patient. When he was on conditional release, the counselor expressed annoyance with him for failing to attend a party to which she had invited him. The way in which she conducted herself around him was just shy of explicit sexual solicitation.

Setting up this counseling system makes it appear that more services are being offered and relieves the doctors of having to deal with some questions or requests that they do not have time for anyway.

GROUP THERAPY

From time to time, various therapeutic groups have been organized on the forensic wards. They have seldom been extensive enough to involve more than a small number of patients at a time. Occasionally, a staff psychiatrist runs a group. For example, one therapist met with some sex offenders and focused on the nature of the offense, with an attempt to get to the causative factors. Resolution of questions of sexual identity was considered to be at the heart of the change process. Criminals who join such therapy groups usually do so to indicate to others that they are motivated to work on their problem. Groups have become increasingly popular, for three reasons: (1) they are a way to treat large numbers of people (if a man is not seen in a group, he may receive no individual attention at all); (2) they offer training opportunities for students (trainees in psychology, social work, and nursing); and (3) they permit a doctor to say that he observed and treated a particular man, which is important when the doctor has to go to court to testify about him.

Instead of a learning experience, group therapy for criminals becomes an operation controlled by criminals. Group meetings become gripe sessions and forums for venting perceived injustices. Criminals attending these sessions often try to run them, pushing the therapist aside. When the therapist directs the discussion, he elicits in response self-serving stories, power plays, lies, and silence. The tone of the group meeting varies with the personality and style of the therapist. It should be noted that in some of these groups, control by the criminals is compatible with the doctor's philosophy of letting the patient decide what he wants to discuss. The gripe sessions too may be by design.

We present accounts of two meetings of therapeutic groups that we observed. In the first, the leader was earnestly trying to be empathic. In the second, the leader was himself a power-thruster who was challenging and provocative.

Meeting 1

Dr. ———— decided that, rather than try to cope with thirty men at a weekly ward meeting, it would be preferable to have three groups meeting once a week. In that way, there would be more individual attention and thus a greater therapeutic advantage.

The meeting began with an opening attack on the doctor's inefficiency in following up particular requests for conditional release. Dr. ———— then saw that Doug (a criminal) was sitting in the corner, apparently sleeping. He asked Doug what was going on, to which Doug responded that he had nothing to say. Dr. ———— then asked the group whether it thought that Doug should talk or not. He got responses to the effect that it was up to Doug. Furthermore the criminals pretty much concurred that talking is not likely to do one much good. One criminal claimed that a man could not win—that if he did not talk, it could be used against him, but if he did talk, he would be seen as "bugging the doctor," and that this also could be used against him. Dr. ——— tried to make it a group problem as to what they thought about Doug and why he was acting the way he was. In particular, the doctor asked what the group thought of the fact that Doug seemed to "mess up" just before he was to get out.

What ensued was a discussion of patients staying too long and becoming institutionalized, with one of the criminals applying this to Doug. The N.A. who was sitting next to Dr. ——— nodded in vigorous agreement. Doug remained silent. When pressed by Dr. ———, he declared that he was content, had a place to stay, had his meals, and was sleeping well. The discussion of institutionalization wore on, with Tom, also a criminal, quoting Menninger. Several other criminals complained that they too were becoming institutionalized. One criminal said about Doug, "My ass he is institutionalized. He would walk out of here any time he could. He is a good jailhouse lawyer. He is doing all kinds of writing here. He writes and writes, but he can't write worth a damn, and he misspells what he does write, but he is trying anyway." Tom said that Doug had a criminal mind. This brought an outburst from Doug, who insisted that everybody is a criminal and asked, who is more criminal, the person who shoots dope in the city or the people on Wall Street? Tom replied that this was not what he had in mind and said that he and Doug both had criminal minds.

The discussion was punctuated by various interruptions. The men were yelling, outshouting one another, cutting one another off, but then perfunctorily saying, "I don't mean to cut him off, but———." At one point during all the yelling, Dr. ———, knowing that he could not be heard above the group, tried to talk under the din. Dr. ——— asked an older, white man, who had been quiet, what he had to say about institutionalization. The man said that he had nothing to say about it, other than that he figured that he was here for punishment. At this point, the doctor incredulously asked him whether he really thought that this was the case. Dr. ——— pointed out that he had never been found guilty of the crime, but had been declared incompetent to stand trial. Thus, he could not be at Saint Elizabeths for punishment. A young black criminal said that he hoped that the man got twenty years. He claimed that black patients were never judged incompetent. Dr. ——— asked this man why he hated the older man so much—was it because of his robbing the bank or because he was stupid enough to get caught? The man replied that he hated someone who was so stupid as to be caught. The group then proceeded to discuss why these people do some of the things they do. Three reasons were listed: curiosity, the influence of others, and a desire to impress older criminals. Tom had a lot to say about this. The others scornfully referred to him as "doctor," and one yelled that he seemed to be a doctor, philosopher, and everything else.

During this exchange, one criminal walked out. There was then a discussion about him and how his problem was homosexuality. This brought an outburst from a criminal who proclaimed that he himself was a homosexual and would suck off anyone on the ward. He stated that he liked homosexual women and would "flop one over on a church floor." He went on a tirade, in which he referred to Tom as a "no-good nigger" and went on and on, while the doctor sat helplessly by. Dr. ——— did ask the nursing assistant to bring back the man who had left.

When the criminal returned, the question of snitching, or informing, arose. He was clearly annoyed that the others had talked about him in his absence. One criminal stated that, even in therapy, one man should not snitch on another. The doctor asked, if it were a matter of a man's losing an eye or somebody snitching to prevent this, which was preferable. The criminal who had just returned stated that the loss of the eye was preferable. Dr. ——— then said that each man should be concerned about the other and not view giving information as snitching. He said that people must get along together and interact. He said that he thought that Tom perhaps was truly concerned about someone other than himself.

Occasionally, the discussion returned to Doug. This was usually prompted by Doug's making some rather dramatic statement. One criminal said that he loved and hated Doug and did not know what to do, because Doug was so pigheaded. Doug admitted that he was stubborn, but said he had learned his lesson about the evils of pride in an earlier incident, which had resulted in his being set back in his privileges.

The doctor tried hard to salvage something useful out of chaos, but to no avail. With the best intentions and using the techniques he knew, he was trampled by the group. They were shouting and profane with each other, although rarely directly abusive of the doctor. Obviously uncomfortable throughout, Dr. ——— took off his coat, raised his voice, and twice resorted to profanity himself, which was out of character. A nursing assistant and a nurse attending the meeting contributed little. Dr. ——— told us that these groups were intended to help the criminal to get in touch with his feelings and express them, so that he does not need to act them out. Dr. ———'s view of the criminal is that he has low self-esteem, which he tries to compensate for by turning to crime. He recalled a moving event when one criminal turned to another and said, "I dig you." Dr. ——— said that he tends to become maudlin in such situations, primarily because he is so dedicated to fostering brotherhood. He said that the criminal has to learn how to deal with other people. He pointed out that the criminal has some of the same gripes about society as everyone else, but in addition has the problem of his own feelings of inferiority. This therapist was not experienced in treating the criminal. Like many others among the professional staff (especially younger staff), he was sincere and dedicated but lacked the knowledge and techniques to be effective. Not many months after we saw him struggling so hard, he left the forensic division.

Meeting 2

Dr. ——— was meeting for an hour and a half once a week, conducting group therapy with four criminals, at the time we observed. Dr. ———'s style was flamboyant, dramatic, profane, and loud. In response, the group members were equally flamboyant, profane, loud, and belligerent. Dr. ——— called what he was doing confrontation. He perspired throughout and tugged at his beard. When he shouted at someone, which was frequent, he did not look at the person, but only cast a fleeting glance his way when that individual appeared to be not looking.

Matt, a criminal, began talking about his brother's near brush with death. Dr. ——— told him that he was not going to listen to him "go around Robin Hood's barn." Matt asked him whether mental illness was hereditary. Dr. ——— was silent and then said loudly, "You want that as an excuse?" His irritation rising, Matt eventually walked out of the group, with Dr. ——— storming down the hall after him yelling, "Walking out of this like you walked out on your wife twelve fucking times."

Dr. ——— seemed pleased with the way in which he dealt with Warren, another criminal, whom he nailed down whenever he could. He told Warren that he could not speak the English language, that he had no insight, that his thinking was sick, and that, if he were making the decision, he would never let Warren out of the hospital. Warren had been involved in armed robbery, rape, arson, and theft. This criminal rose to the challenge by staying calm during Dr. ———'s tirades.

During the meeting, several criminals made comments about the therapist. One surmised that Dr. ——— "smoked pot and sucked pussy," but then acknowledged that "that is up to him. It's what he does in here that counts." Another commented to the doctor that he should get a haircut and a shave. One of the criminals called the doctor "rude." Dr. —

——'s response to all this was a silence followed by, "We are not here to analyze the therapist."

Later, when we asked Dr. —— about his techniques, he stated that he was trying to make Warren "face his inferiority." With great relish, he described how he had made Warren "eat shit in front of authority" when he caught him stealing. Just after the session we observed Dr. —— saw Warren in the hall and tried to provoke him again. He asked Warren why he did not steal some medicine that had been carelessly left lying around in a hallway. Warren replied that he would be justified in doing so, because it had been left out and there was none on the ward. Dr. —— responded, "Why don't you go ahead and steal it, and then I will make you apologize before authority." Dr. —— had used a similar technique of provocation with an alcoholic in the group. He told the man that he really wanted a drink, "Wouldn't a drink be nice?" In the past he had taunted the same person by saying, "Wouldn't it be nice if we both had a great big bottle of delicious Jack Daniels Scotch?"

These two examples confirm what criminals have reported to us for years. The criminal modifies his tactics to fit the personality of the staff member. In groups like these, talk is valued for itself. Often, there is greater emphasis on volume of talk than on substance. This offers the criminal an opportunity to score points. The group leaders rebuke the more silent members for not talking enough. Both sessions reported here accomplished little of value. The fact that they were held enabled the hospital to say that it was offering therapy.

Social workers have run groups on wards variously designated as insight, reentry, or remotivation groups. Nursing assistants have also led small groups that were to serve a discussion-counseling function. In some instances, N.A.'s have been skeptical, even cynical, about the professional staff's emphasis on insight. The criminal is supposed to recognize that he is ill and then gain insight into his problems. Many N.A.'s either do not understand or do not share this perspective, although some pay lip service to it by adopting the jargon. One exasperated Menninger-trained social worker left the forensic division because she thought that the N.A.'s were basically jailers and that the environment was not therapeutic. She declared that none of the nursing assistants had any concept of mental illness and that they offered more impediments to the recovery of the patients than the patients themselves did. She believed that if she and her colleagues could proceed with their group work unhampered by the punitive attitude of the N.A.'s, the patients would achieve insight and recover from their illnesses.

From our standpoint, it is absurd to talk about reentry of people who have never entered society in the first place or remotivation of people who are strongly motivated for their kind of life, but not for a responsible life. Insight in traditional therapy amounts to "incite"—giving criminals an opportunity to vent anger at others. However, the therapists are gratified when a criminal admits that he has problems, does a lot of talking about them, and indicates that he understands why he does what he does. The therapist explains any setback as a regression. Actually, the life of most therapy groups has been brief. The perception of accomplishment is often short-lived, as criminals continue old patterns. Criminals are likely to drop out of group therapy after a few meetings, except for those who are convinced that remaining would score points. In some cases, disillusioned therapists abandon what they are doing and try something else. Some do what the Menninger-trained social worker did, quit.

In general, there is little coordination of points of view, treatment strategy, or substantive themes. Thus, what a criminal learns in group therapy may be contradicted in conflicting advice given by personnel at various levels. This is because, within one ward, there are different approaches among the staff members, sometimes in direct opposition to one another. Competing factions of personnel often differ strongly in their views of the criminal and how to deal with him.

PSYCHODRAMA

Saint Elizabeths was one of the first public hospitals to offer psychodrama as a therapeutic tool. This therapeutic intervention has been used in the forensic division, as well as in other parts of the hospital. One objective, as the program was described to us, is to examine patient role relationships, past and present. One psychodramatist stated that health involves assuming the appropriate role at the appropriate time; a person is sick when he is unable to take the appropriate role. At psychodrama sessions, the criminal is asked to examine both the role relationships that he fantasies and those that he actually has. Then, he is urged to consider how he can alter his relationships to make them more like what he wants. Psychodrama sessions are also seen as having cathartic value, in that patients are encouraged not only to express, but also to act out, feelings.

Some of these sessions function as therapy groups meeting regularly once or twice a week. The focus is on helping the criminal to learn to respond to the demands of living. Emotional education is central: the criminal is to become aware of his needs and learn how to fulfill them in a socially acceptable manner.

The format of the groups varies. One psychoanalyst decided that it would be best to have a group meet off the ward, making participation voluntary. He wanted to de-emphasize the discussion of getting out and the attitude of "keep your nose clean and your mouth shut and don't let others know what you're thinking." He believed that if psychodrama were held on the ward, criminals would be too guarded in expression and that little of value would occur. Both men and women were included, so that they could work on their sexual hangups. Initially, this was unsuccessful, because there was a lot of unproductive banter, and some patients were reported to be scared of the opposite sex. So the men and women met separately for one session and together for the other. In August 1972, a full-time psychodramatist was assigned to the forensic division. He decided to have all his groups meet right in the ward dayrooms. This was a low-key program, with patients being invited to drop in if they felt like it. This therapist also wanted to eliminate the "no snitching" attitude and secretiveness. However, he thought that the way to accomplish this was to have everything in the open, to show patients that the ward could be a place to share intimate things. Once there, there was little pressure to attend or to talk. If no one showed up, the session was canceled. If a person came and wanted to leave, he was allowed to do so. The therapist attempted to gear the intensity of the meeting to what he called the ward's level of emotional comfort. That is, he wanted the patients to be able to live together after a session if emotionally laden material were stirred up.

We observed psychodrama in action on one ward with a very dedicated therapist who was just beginning to apply this form of treatment to the criminal.

"Psychodrama time" was announced on the ward. Over a period of forty minutes, only a few criminals wandered in. Realizing that there was a dearth of interest, the therapist canceled the session. A discussion followed in the nursing office as to why people were not attending. The therapist (T) thought that too much "threatening material" had been stirred up at the previous meeting. A nursing assistant dismissed this and said that the patients were simply retaliating for not being allowed to go to recreation on the preceding night. Cigarette butts were on the floor, water was spilled and not cleaned up, and the patients were taking an attitude of "To hell with everything," including psychodrama. T then changed his mind and agreed that this was a more plausible explanation.

The next day, three or four criminals showed up, and the session was held. Two of these were in a psychotic phase, one criminal talking about his having seen God. T decided that this criminal, who had never known his father, was in need of fathering that he had never received and therefore was turning to the "Holy Father." the group then engaged in role-playing, going back to the criminal's youth. In C's view, his next-door neighbor had a good relationship with his father. What made him a good father was that he gave his son everything that the son wanted, such as money or clothing. The father-son relationship was re-enacted, with an N.A. articulating what must have been going on in C's head as he watched his buddy next door: "Gee, I wish I had a father like that," and so forth.

T stated afterwards to the staff that C needed fathering from the nursing assistants. The idea was to have the criminal understand what his needs were and then to have him learn how to fulfill these needs now.

In this psychodrama, two problems were evident. One was the notion of what a father is; the definition was concrete and typical of the criminal: a good father is one who gives his son whatever he wants. C was seen as deprived because he lacked this. The second was that the whole issue had no bearing on the patient's criminality. The therapist believed that change would be promoted if the criminal were aware of unmet needs that were still striving to be fulfilled. In this meeting, at least, there was an attempt, no matter how contrived, to focus on the individual. Many psychodrama sessions amount to a playing out of grievances against the system. This may be a reflection more of the criminal's operations than of the therapist's competence. For example, one criminal complained, "This hospital does not deal with anyone's problems. It is interested only in its system." Actually, it was the criminals who continued to bring up the system, not the therapist. ·

Some criminals have been genuinely involved during a session, but their enthusiasm beyond a particular episode is short-lived. In addition, what they have gained does not make a lasting difference in their thinking and action, for two reasons: the issues addressed are usually irrelevant, and the reenactment of life situations is concrete. The criminal may be asked to put himself in another's place literally by standing so as to assume a different position physically. The criminal who is watching is supposed to identify with what is being acted out and apply it to his own life. The problem is that the criminal does not conceptualize and remains focused on a specific situation. Furthermore, each man thinks that what applies to someone else does not apply to him. Thus, the identification with the other person does not occur. The most formidable obstacle is the closed channel. The material is tailored to suit the criminal's purpose.

Psychodrama provides an arena for criminal equivalents. There is opportunity for a criminal to attack whomever he wishes and then to be commended for honesty and for expression of feelings.

In a psychodrama meeting, C grew increasingly abusive and virtually took over the session. When the distraught therapist asked the group how to return the session to the issues of the psychodrama, C retorted, "This *is* psychodrama. I was acting out. I was telling you what I thought."

C expected to be lauded for his tirade, with its accompanying racial invective. In such situations, emotional expression is valued. In theory, ventilation of feelings is regarded as cathartic; in practice, it results in an increase, not a diminution, in anger. Anger expressed by one criminal elicits anger from others. Anger feeds anger, rather than draining it.

Usually nothing new is dealt with in psychodrama sessions. Cognitive processes are overlooked in favor of feelings, and an issue gets lost in the criminal's diversions and other tactical maneuvers. Generally, the quantity of adrenalin generated is considered more important than the content of what is said. Something trite is often endowed with significance, simply because it is said with feeling. A psychodramatist not experienced in working with criminals may think that something important is being revealed. However, what is new to him is laughed at by the criminal. The following incident illustrates attempts to analyze an event.

> The issue was that C had defecated on the shower-room floor. The chairman of the patient group brought this up as a serious issue. C was to be questioned about it. However, because C rarely said much, at least in a group, the discussion was turned into a psychodrama with criminals cast in different roles and the doctor acting as an alternate for C. It turned out that the act had followed a homosexual incident with M, another criminal. Thus, there were two issues: why C had defecated on the floor and why he had gone along with M to have a sexual act. The question was raised as to whether he had done this voluntarily. This raised a further question about other acts of coercion on the ward.

> Criminals then played M and C. However, because M was off the ward, his position was pure conjecture. C was reluctant to speak. The other criminals tended to mock him, one asking him how short he wore his skirts. The past ward chairman bragged about how tough he was and how he would never be in the position C was in. Many criminals were quite willing to dispose of the whole matter by having C transferred to another ward, so that there would not be any further trouble. The role-playing was of the approach that M made to C. It was stated that C had acted out in his defecating on the floor, because he was so angry and felt so worthless after the episode with M that he decided to shit (literally) on everyone.

> It was considered something of a success merely to get C to talk, because he was viewed as being passive. The session ended with C saying that he wanted help with his problem, which he had had since he was ten years old. He could not say no when offered money, a drink, or other favors to engage in homosexual relations.

In the staff meeting afterward, a nursing assistant stated that the group never brings out anything that is very important, even when it is clear that a lot is going on with the patients on the ward. He said that it took someone to defecate on the floor to mobilize the group. This N.A. had continually maintained that the patient community was not working as it should and that very little responsibility was assumed, except when someone was inconvenienced and outraged. Then the patients would be willing to talk about someone else's behavior. They would censure him or vote to restrict or get rid of him. The doctor pointed out that perhaps the important outcome of the psychodrama was that an entree now existed to other things occurring on the ward that the staff did not know about. It was noted, however, that C had told the staff about many incidents that the staff had ignored. This was not explored by the doctor, either with the staff or at the patient meeting.

A shortcoming of the psychodrama as staged was that one of the three participants involved in the original incident was not present, and much was left to speculation as to what was going on in the mind of the absentee. This session was ostensibly intended to be helpful to C, but there was little in the way of an attitude of helpfulness on the part of the other criminals and the staff. It was more of an interrogation that put the criminal on display. What psychodrama offers is an open arena for the criminal to tailor a situation to his advantage and then to dramatize it. He makes himself look good, puts others down, and scores some points for his participation.

One rule of procedure is that anyone attending psychodrama may be asked to participate, including the doctor. There have been instances in which the psychodramatist has encouraged the doctor or a nursing assistant to express his feelings and then commended him for it. In such meetings, the subject of discussion is the doctor or N.A., not the criminals.

Psychodrama has potential value. Instead of providing an arena for point-scoring, power-thrusting, searching for excuses, and bringing out what is obvious or irrelevant, psychodrama could be used as a format for the dissection of thinking processes and the teaching of concepts. As it is now used, even its sponsors acknowledge that they do not know whether there is carryover beyond the sessions to life itself. Indeed, one psychodramatist stated that he does not believe that cognitive change occurs, but rather experiential change. In other words, there is an expression of feeling, a catharsis, and that is about the extent of it.

Two criminals whom we worked with had Industrial Therapy assignments at the psychodrama theater for several hours a day. They had successfully participated in psychodrama as patients. At Industrial Therapy they were asked to function as patient-aides to explain some of the psychodrama procedures to other patients. These two criminals reported to us that their psychodrama participation was solely to score points. Concurrently, they had been violating on the side. In no way had psychodrama had an impact on them, despite their exposure to it over many months.

Psychodrama participation will not result in the criminal's achieving responsibility, but it may be useful after responsibility is firmly established.

THE THERAPEUTIC COMMUNITY

Maxwell Jones (1953) pioneered a concept in group treatment in which patients were to serve as resources to one another, supplanting the more traditional authority relationships in institutions. From the moment the patient entered an institution, he was to participate in an entire subculture designed to change attitudes. Jones' idea was to convert all human interactions into learning situations. The therapeutic community (T.C.) was to be a participatory democracy in human relations whose important principles were bilateral communication, confrontation, decision-making by consensus, and multiple leadership. The T.C. was to accomplish the opposite of warehousing patients; it was to recognize them as individuals with rights.*

At Saint Elizabeths Hospital, the therapeutic community was organized originally with these ideas in mind. The entire ward, criminals, doctor, nursing assistants, and other staff members, constituted the T.C. As explained by doctors in charge of forensic wards, the prevailing concept was that patients would become increasingly responsible by participating in the making of decisions that affected their lives. The T.C. was designed to create stress and thereby prepare patients to cope more effectively with stresses outside the institution. With peer pressure operating, the criminal was required to take stock of himself, become more sensitive to others, and develop the habit of listening to other people and considering their viewpoints seriously. Another objective was to break what was regarded as an unhealthy dependence on the doctor and the institution.

The therapeutic community as implemented on the forensic wards offers benefits to the doctor, the ward staff, and the hospital administration. On wards that have this extension of milieu therapy, the T.C. offers the only direct contact between the doctor and most of his patients. We have already described the inaccessibility of most doctors. The Rouse decision** maintains

---

*As Kiger (1967, p. 192) pointed out, the "heart" of all therapeutic community programs is the daily community meeting. We shall be describing mainly what occurs at these meetings (as well as the staff's view of the entire process). Chapter 2 contained a review of literature on the therapeutic community as applied to criminals at other institutions.

**Rouse v. Cameron, 125 U.S. App. D.C. 366, 373, F. 2d. 451 (1966).

that patients under mandatory commitment have the right to be treated. Thus, the hospital is accountable to the courts in this respect. The therapeutic community protects the doctor and the hospital, inasmuch as it can be said that each criminal is seen every day at the T.C. meeting. Although a doctor may spend only fifteen or twenty minutes with a criminal before he goes to court, he can nonetheless say that the criminal has had many hours of treatment in the T.C. In practice, many criminals in these groups choose to remain silent, and the doctor learns little about them. Even those who do participate remain unknown, because their contributions are usually superficial or self-serving. Yet, for legal purposes, the doctor can maintain that he sees patients regularly and is in touch with what is going on. The psychiatrist who is skeptical about treating the criminal may convince himself that something of value is being done toward rehabilitation. The term *therapeutic* in therapeutic community implies some kind of "therapy."

The T.C. helps to preserve staff sanity, as one doctor put it. Dealing with the requests of each of thirty criminals consumes considerable time. Furthermore, criminals divide staff members by playing the advice of one off against that of another. Hours of wasted energy, discussion, and dissension are saved by requiring the criminal to bring all requests and complaints to the community meeting. With the group as the decision-making body, a heavy burden is lifted from the shoulders of the staff. One doctor pointed out that a long-range and very practical advantage for the criminal is that the T.C. format allows a man to get out faster, because he no longer has to wait to see the doctor for every decision.

The criminal is given an option as to whether he will join the community. However, because he knows that he may never get out of the hospital unless he is a member, he really has little choice. Once a criminal is on the roster of names that come up for discussion, his fate depends largely on what happens in the T.C. meetings. From the criminal's point of view, the T.C. formalizes the method of exodus from the institution. The rules are spelled out. Usually, he is asked to discuss his charge. Then, whenever he wants to make a request or seek a change in status, he has to appear before the group to state his case. If he is caught violating, he is accountable to the T.C.

The staff continually urges criminals to work on their problems. However, the criminal has only one problem—that he is confined. The forcefulness and candor with which criminals voice this vary. On one ward, a criminal accepted the post of T.C. secretary with the candid statement that he wanted to get out and that the meetings offered the only way to accomplish this. Although all criminals have this view, most do not proclaim it openly. The following is an excerpt from a meeting in which it became clear to the doctor that his patients attached importance only to getting out.

C had eloped eight times during his stay in minimum security. The result each time he did so was that all the criminals were restricted to the ward, because the community was deemed responsible. Various proposals were made at the T.C. meeting to deal with C, including returning him to maximum security. The criminals said that this should be the decision of the staff. The doctor saw this as a copout and urged the criminals to assume responsibility. C presented a bunch of feeble excuses for his conduct, and was questioned very little by his fellow criminals. When it appeared that the tide could turn in favor of his going back to maximum security, C stated that what he really needed was individual help from a staff member who was sympathetic to him. The criminals then declared that they refused to play a part in sending a man back to maximum security. The doctor questioned them as to how they could be so self-defeating as to vote this man privileges time and again, when it worked to their own detriment—restriction. The doctor tried to convince the men that it would be therapeutic for C to take a step backward in order to go forward. One man angrily retorted that the doctor was trying to shove his opinion down the throats of the group. Another criminal declared that the group was no darn good and kept insisting that it was up to the doctor. A vote was finally taken; only five of the twenty-five criminals voted to send C to maximum security. The doctor stated then that he did not know whether he would use his veto power, which he retained on all decisions.

In a postgroup meeting with the staff, the doctor expressed discouragement, saying that things seemed to be working out poorly. He wanted to help the criminals to exercise good judgment and be responsible. However, he was finding that the overriding orientation of both criminals and staff was how to get out, with little regard for other issues that the doctor deemed important. He stated that perhaps he was wrong in imposing his view, because it flies in the face of patient democracy.

The doctor did not know how to prevent the therapeutic community from being used merely as a forum for getting out.

In this participatory democracy, the criminals and staff members are equal, in that each person has one vote. What happens to an individual is determined by majority vote. Because criminals outnumber staff personnel, they can be sure of prevailing, unless the doctor exercises a veto, which he occasionally does. This varies with each T.C. The objective is to give the criminal power in the decision-making process. Every time he makes a decision about someone else, he bears in mind what he will be asking for later: "You scratch my back, and I'll scratch yours." However, a man may tear down another community member (a patient) and thereby score points with the staff. Criminals support the staff, even against a fellow criminal, if it appears to be in their best interest.

The T.C. provides another outlet for criminality. As in crime, M.O.'s vary. Some con their way along, appearing cooperative and compliant. If they violate, they are discrete and do not run big risks. Another common pattern is to try to get out by causing as much trouble in the community as possible. The criminal who does this shows his refusal to bow to the establishment. He scorns the criminal who cooperates, seeing him as gutless. A criminal who operates in this manner is likely to be voted down by the community in his requests for privileges. Fellow criminals may rebuff him for making life more difficult and because they are supposed to show that they recognize and disapprove of irresponsible behavior. Staff members are obliged to oppose such criminals' requests, even though they are eager to have them leave.

The T.C. provides a daily opportunity for point-scoring. Here is where one criminal outdoes another in feeding the doctor and the rest of the staff what they want to hear. The following episode indicates how swiftly the criminal alters his position, so as to be compatible with what he thinks satisfies those in authority:

> C was presenting himself as being virtually a helpless victim of the "disease" of alcoholism. For about twenty minutes, the group challenged him on this. Then C did an about-face and stated flatly, "I want to drink. That's why I drink."

When enough pressure is put on a criminal and he wants to show that he has acquired insight, he agrees with whatever position he thinks he is supposed to take. Here, the victim stance was not accepted by the others, so C changed from a victim of a disease to a person who was responsible for his own drinking. This stopped the badgering, and the discussion took another tack. Antagonism decreased, and the group turned to how it could help C.

The currency for transactions in most of these groups is feelings. A criminal is considered to be improving when he expresses his feelings.

> At one meeting, a man refused to talk. He was criticized because he did not express feelings. Later, when he grew very angry and threatened to smash chairs and windows, this was considered healthy, and he was credited with improvement.

Confrontation is valued by many mental health practitioners. A direct expression of thoughts and feelings is considered therapeutic. Usually, anger increases, the thinking becomes more illogical, but this is viewed as valuable.

In the T.C. (as elsewhere), self-criticism is minimal.

Dr. ——— was dissatisfied because every criminal was presenting himself as a model patient at the T.C. meetings, although it was known many were violating. Dr. ——— exhorted the fellows to talk about their bad features and not to limit themselves to their good points, which they constantly emphasized to promote their getting privileges. He tried to compel a more self-critical attitude by saying that no more matters could be voted on until such a stance was forthcoming.

This doctor tried to mandate a practice that is totally alien to the criminal. He was trying to foster self-examination in a group of men who viewed self-criticism as self-incrimination. However, these criminals took the cue. When a criminal knows that confession and self-incrimination are valued as evidence of insight, and thus of improvement, he cooperates. When the doctor puts a premium on honesty, then this is the best policy for the criminal.

C stated that he wanted privileges to be on the grounds from 9 a.m. to 5 p.m. in order to get off the ward. Dr. ——— was quite impressed with his having put it this way, because he believed that many people wanted privileges for just this reason. C was telling the truth. C went on to say that a lot of the talk that went on in the community was nonsense. Dr. ——— again was impressed with his candor.

Selected portions of the truth can be the best con. Even when a criminal gets abusive in these meetings, he may be lauded by staff members for expressing himself.

C prided himself on "telling it like it is." He would mention others by name and even incriminate himself as he described the activities in which they were collaborating. If another criminal challenged him, C exposed the things that he had engaged in with the questioner—liquor, drugs, homosexuality, and so on. Then he pointed to others with whom he had been violating. As these people were shot down by him, questions addressed to him ground to a halt. As he did all this, C derived great excitement. He would tell others to sit down, to be quiet, and to come back if they started to walk out.

No one criticized C for acting like a prosecutor or for putting others down. Exposure of himself and others cost him little, because he was regarded as "honest." C eventually eloped from the hospital and returned to crime.

When honesty entails incriminating someone else, the criminal usually has some initial reluctance. This is snitching, which the criminal wants to avoid, because he has to count on the support of others. Besides, snitching provokes retaliatory snitching. However, when a man can advance himself by informing, he does so. Informing is valued by the doctor, because it is a source of information which is otherwise hard to acquire. A criminal may appear inconsistent in the T.C. when it comes to informing.

> At a meeting, C said that he was a constructive member of the T.C., in that, if he knew of a violation, he would turn the violator in. A few days later, he objected to the questioning of a criminal on the grounds that the purpose was to get that criminal into trouble, and this was not constructive.

On the surface, this appears to be a 180-degree reversal. First, the criminal would inform without reservation; later, he would protect a man and refuse to talk. Looked at from the criminal's frame of reference, both positions are compatible with a larger objective, scoring points and exercising power. In the first instance, he is going to put the other down and, while doing so, show that he is an upholder of the law. In the second, he can self-righteously maintain that each man must be responsible for himself and that it is irresponsible for one person to start tearing into another when his own house is not in order. The second position is shakier, but in some T.C.'s, either one wins approval.

Generally, the best defense is a good offense. When the criminal puts others on the grid, he diverts the discussion from himself. In doing so, he may be credited for being an astute observer. The harshest interrogators are likely to be the most severe offenders, and it is significant that chairmen of therapeutic communities are often the most serious violators. On one ward, for example, one chairman had eloped and committed a rape, another had eloped and participated in an armed robbery, and the new secretary was on restriction at the time of the election.

Interest in becoming a ward chairman is often very low, because the criminal is either totally uninterested or does not wish to reveal that he desires the position. A criminal who wants to hold office rarely pursues it, but waits for others to come to him. The doctor or other staff members then nominate criminals in an effort to increase participation. The men nominated decline, unless they believe that it is to their advantage to serve. If more than one person wants the position, he and his rivals arrange for one to succeed the other. Sometimes, a group of criminals try to elect a chairman without staff participation.

> A gang of criminals on the ward wanted the nomination and election of the ward chairman to occur without being subjected to the critical eye of the day staff, which was the most enlightened of the three nursing shifts. They arranged to have the voting at a late afternoon meeting attended by

the evening shift, rather than hold it during the regular morning meeting, as scheduled.

Basically, the criminal in the T.C. wants to have his cake and eat it. He violates and requests privileges at the same time. It usually takes a brazen offense for an incident to arouse action by the T.C. Most violations are never detected or are overlooked. When an infraction is considered serious, patients who are diagnosed mentally ill are held responsible for their actions. To make the members of the group responsible to each other, it is the policy of some T.C.'s to punish all for the violation of one. On one ward, criminals were given a chance to vote on whether they wanted a T.C. They voted it down, because they did not want the entire group to be held accountable for what an individual member did. On wards where only the violator is restricted, the community often votes to mete out a lighter penalty than might normally be called for.

C, a regular violator, was finally caught and restricted. Mr. A, another criminal, observed at a T.C. meeting that restriction was not helping C. He proposed that C be given back his privileges, which would permit him to be on the grounds. Such a status would permit him to go to an Industrial Therapy assignment with the grounds crew, so that he could establish a work pattern. The criminals voted in favor of this. The doctor did not veto the decision, even though he knew that it would establish a precedent that would cause difficulties later.

Generally speaking, policies for determining the length and degree of restriction are not uniform from ward to ward; they are not consistently adhered to even within a single ward.

In the T.C., the criminals function as judge, jury, and witness, as well as plaintiff. The T.C. as jury hears both sides and supplies the evidence. The doctor abides by the verdict of the jury, rarely exercising his veto power, because he believes that it would undermine the patient democracy or cause other problems. When a defendant is in a tight spot, he becomes legalistic, demanding hard evidence. Although he has trampled on the rights of others, he protests that his rights are being violated. The need for proof is brought up frequently. On one ward where criminals were permitted to determine penalties, the staff grew so dissatisfied that it withdrew this prerogative.

Frequently, a criminal is so scornful of the entire setup that he refuses to participate.

C stated that he did not care whether he ever joined the T.C. He called it bullshit and maintained that the doctors had no idea what they were doing. He declared openly that he would elope at the first opportunity and that no one would do anything about it.

The contempt is often expressed in the way the criminal responds to the doctor.

> A doctor from another ward was attending a T.C. meeting. C addressed this new doctor, not his own. When urged to speak to his own doctor, C replied that his doctor was one of the patients himself, pointing scornfully to the doctor's mustache, long hair, and unkempt appearance. C declared that, if the doctor removed his mustache, it would be hard to tell if he were male or female. His doctor's response was to question what C was getting out of the program. C said that it was "doing something for somebody, mainly helping him to get out." By this he meant that participating in the T.C. meetings would create a favorable impression and therefore be beneficial to getting discharged from the hospital.

In the T.C., as in many therapy groups, insight is valued, particularly with respect to the criminal's alleged mental illness. If a criminal admits that he has been mentally ill, even though he is not now, he is considered to be showing at least some rudimentary insight.

> In a dialogue between Dr. ——— and C, the crucial question was whether C realized that he was sick. The criminal said that he was not sick. The doctor replied that, if C wanted to get out, he had to show progress. Of course, he could not do this if he were not sick. Then C was asked to explain why he had said that he was sick when he was first admitted. C was frank, stating that he never was sick, but why put in thirty years to life if he could get out faster by saying that he was sick and going to a hospital?

C was open in his statement of why he had sought admission to the hospital. Usually, the criminal is more discreet:

> "Dr.——— posed 'The Patient's Dilemma'. As he puts it, 'Having convinced the doctors you're insane so that you can get into the hospital (i.e., beat your criminal charge) how do you then convince them you're sane so you can get out?' He remarked that some patients tackled the problem by insisting that they pled insanity only on advice of counsel but were really sane all along. Others said they were sick but had become well. [One patient], quite involved in ward activities, combined these approaches. He said he'd faked insanity to get in, but once in, he found he

really had some problems which he thought he now had pretty well resolved. I handled the quandary by saying that I was sick when I came and was still sick, but that I could receive better treatment on the outside. Eventually, the staff agreed with this."

If the criminal uses the proper terminology and formulations and can demonstrate an understanding of his illness, he is viewed as improving. The staff believes that a man is doing well when he accepts the fact that he is ill and when he goes along with the therapeutic programs without causing trouble. The criminal knows this and bears testimony that the therapeutic community has had a role in curing him. This is an intrinsic part of the strategy of going along with the program.

Much time is taken up with parliamentary maneuvers—contesting procedures, making points of order, rewriting the constitution, drawing up new formats. All this does not grow out of a genuine concern for order and efficiency. Rather, parliamentary contests are further devices to obtain more privileges, modify rules, and minimize punishment. Such maneuvers (objectives that fit well with society's thinking) preclude getting to matters of substance. In these meetings, thinking processes are not altered. The entire approach is concrete. Problem-solving consists of the criminal's bailing himself out of trouble. The word responsibility is bandied about, but it has little operational significance. Responsibility is evaluated by the degree to which a man does what he is supposed to. He is responsible if he completes his work detail, if he cleans his room, if he is on time for meetings, and if he returns from the grounds on time.

Some doctors are very conscientious about trying to individualize their handling of criminals. That is hard to do, because they do not have much individual contact with T.C. members. They usually meet with problems, in that a concession or exception granted to one criminal becomes the prerogative of all. If one man desires a holiday pass, all claim that they are entitled to it. Of course, nearly all requests are supported by unreliable information. The doctor is faced with having to make most decisions without sufficient facts. Most of all, the doctor wants to avoid protracted struggles with man after man. Consequently, he may get beaten down to the point where he gives blanket permissions, rather than reject requests and have to defend himself.

In chapter 1 of volume 1, we described our early experiences with criminals in which they functioned far more like gangs than therapeutic groups. That is exactly what happens in the therapeutic community. Because of either misguided idealism or expediency in dealing with volume, a format that has been used with some success with the noncriminal has been selected as the program of choice for the criminal. The staff has been spared some inconvenience, and the hospital (honestly) can say that it offers treatment. But, in practice, the therapeutic community has turned out to be a battleground. It has become a series of encounters or confrontations with confined criminals maneuvering against the staff to fight their way out. Criminals vote each other privileges, and the staff rarely intervenes. Instead of a true meeting of minds with genuine disclosure, it is a ritualistic gathering of people who exploit each other for their own gain.

The T.C. is often an exercise in scapegoating. It is not only a case of criminals versus staff, but also of criminals exploiting differences among individual staff members. The criminal is adept at spotting rivalries and jealousies between people in different disciplines and within a single discipline. So it is doctor versus criminal, criminal versus nursing staff, nursing staff versus doctor, and even N.A. versus N.A. A community meeting may be the occasion for an airing of staff problems. The focus sometimes shifts from criminals to staff, depending on the particular doctor and the state of staff interpersonal relations at the time.

> The community had not finished its discussion of C. In the meantime, C had asked an N.A. whether he could go to a dance; the N.A. said no, because the discussion on C's status had not been completed. C then pointed out that the doctor had taken him off restriction and recorded this in the orders. This being true, C attended the dance.

> Mrs. ———, a black N.A., on hearing this, stated that again a white man was getting a break from the doctor, who was also white. She pointed out that standard procedure was for the doctor to write the order lifting the restriction only after the community had completed its discussion. She decided to bring this out at the next meeting, making the case that whites and blacks should be treated equally. The ward chairman and other criminals knew that she was going to do this. Some of these criminals, who had no racial ax to grind, decided that this would be a good opportunity to take some verbal swings at the doctor.

Here, a few of the nursing personnel were planning to use the group to attack a doctor on a problem that was not a general ward issue. It is not unusual for members of the staff, either spontaneously or calculatingly, to use the group to subvert, attack, or circumvent a doctor. What is significant about this episode is that it was planned in advance.

Clearly, not everyone is enthusiastic about or supportive of the therapeutic community. Some nursing assistants oppose it, because they believe that their authority is undermined by the criminals and also by the doctor. The N.A.'s are often in accord with the criminals and may openly vote with them against the doctor, knowing that he is unlikely to veto the decision or to reprimand them later. Staff members who are so inclined use the T.C. for their own power-thrusting. This can include challenging the doctor, putting down a criminal, and giving advice. Most N.A.'s and some doctors recognize the limitations of the community and know that it is not accomplishing what it purports to. The N.A.'s may show their attitudes in a not so subtle manner by the things they say and do. For example, an N.A. may excuse a criminal from attending a meeting to do something that the N.A. wants him to do. Or an N.A. may be slow to assemble the criminals when the community is about to convene.

Most doctors, whatever their reservations, plug away as well as they can with this, their major and perhaps only treatment program. Doctors hope that the T.C. format will help the criminal to face up to things that he might not otherwise. However, some doctors admit that they are uncertain as to whether any significant learning is occurring. There is considerable skepticism about whether any enduring change occurs, or whether only lip service is being paid to a few concrete ideas.

> Dr. ———, a Public Health Service officer, stated that the therapeutic community had been operating on his ward for five years before he had come on the scene. He believed that, with his own personality and ideas, he would have some impact in making changes for the better. He said that he had no illusions about the criminal's changing his basic personality. This would be the province of the other therapies. However, he did hope that these patients would get a clue that perhaps "something in their head makes them do the things they do." Dr. ——— observed that every doctor is faced with the dilemma of running a ward and treating the impulse-ridden sociopath. He stated that he did not even know where to read something that was helpful about this. As he saw the situation, there were two choices: a more traditional format, in which he would have to deal with the constant conning and scapegoating of the staff by the patients, and the T.C. which offered hope of a constructive way of working things out. Because he was assigned to a ward where there was a T.C., he continued with it.

The critical statement here is that the doctor did not expect the therapeutic community to contribute significantly to personality change. In one case, a doctor became so fed up with the whole operation that he suspended the T.C. for a week. However, he stated that, without it, the criminal has to "get all the privileges from Papa"; they were going to him with every little request. He found this even less tolerable, so he reinstated the T.C. One psychiatrist issued a memorandum to all criminals, presenting his evaluation of the T.C. as it was operating at the time.

> "The present T.C. is based on a rationale that patients are responsible enough to decide whether one of their number is ready to move further through the steps, and have a special insight to offer on the matter. . . . Let's face it, it isn't working. The basic conditions here lead instead to the patients using this structure to avoid responsibility and to hold their insights in check for less mature purposes. Some patients tell me that this is a natural expression of the 'oppressed" within an 'oppressive structure.' The result is that case discussions are perceived as mock court hearings, and the person under discussion as being 'on the spot.'

> "Dealing with the underlying realities and resultant feelings that prevent more therapeutic behavior is prevented by a system that allows only for emergencies and roster business. Almost anything constructive is 'out of order.' The therapeutic energy of the group is locked."

He then proposed that meetings be structured as a forum for a discussion of problems, leaving privileges to be taken care of elsewhere. He urged members of the T.C. to "therapeutically confront themselves." On his list of remaining problems, he had at the top, "Where does this leave the issue of patient responsibility?"

On the basis of our knowledge of the criminal, we have concluded that the therapeutic community format is guaranteed to fail, no matter how dedicated the staff. Until criminal thinking patterns are replaced by responsible ones, a T.C. can be only one more arena for criminality. There is no substitute for the arduous work of dissecting existent thinking patterns and teaching new ones. We have not seen this done in the T.C.; it is not a means to basic change. In some settings, one has to contend with a group of criminals and an untrained, partially irresponsible staff. Irresponsible patients and irresponsible staff cannot deal responsibly with issues of responsibility.

In 1975, the therapeutic community was still in existence at the forensic division. However, a doctor intimately acquainted with it said that it existed in name only. With the introduction and widespread use of the T.C. with criminals, there has been a rise in the rate of elopement from Saint Elizabeths. Unchanged criminals are more readily gaining privileges, which they vote each other. And there is less and less deterrence of violations, which frequently are not taken very seriously, unless they occur so often and are so obvious that they cannot be ignored.

OTHER THERAPEUTIC PROGRAMS OFFERED TO FORENSIC PATIENTS AT SAINT ELIZABETHS HOSPITAL: DESCRIPTION AND CRITIQUE

There are two critical issues in our evaluation of how the unchanged criminals in our study have utilized forensic programs at Saint Elizabeths Hospital. One is how each program is run: Does the way in which it is operated offer still another outlet for criminal activity? The second issue is whether the desired objectives are achievable with a criminal group and, if they are, whether they promote enduring changes in the criminal. We are describing here programs in both maximum and minimum security.

EDUCATIONAL THERAPY

The purpose of educational rehabilitation is twofold in that the school activity provides an adjunct to the patients' therapy program by raising his self-esteem, building his self-confidence, etc. and/or gives him an opportunity to rehabilitate himself by obtaining skills which will enable him to more easily qualify for employment or function better in the community. (From a statement by the Educational Rehabilitation Unit, Occupational Therapy Section)

The education department offers three types of instruction: basic academic, business and commercial, and tutoring. On referral by his ward doctor, a criminal is enrolled and evaluated for placement at the proper academic level. The process of referral is actually governed by the pressure principle. That is, the criminals who request educational programs are the ones who are referred, not necessarily those who would profit most from it.

The chief obstacle presented by forensic patients was summed up in two words by a staff member: "no motivation." Most criminals do not believe that educational programs are inherently valuable for them. Some ask to attend classes only to get off the ward. It is also a good way to score points. The few who seem to want to learn usually lose interest quickly, but continue to attend for a while to impress others. When we talked to a chief educational therapist, only two of ninety eligible forensic patients were going to the educational center for classes. Educational services within the forensic division itself were perfunctory. The lack of participation in educational therapy was noted in Chambers' report:

There is a full-time educational therapist on the service, but no educational therapy. An outside teacher did give classes last year, but the therapist has apparently been unable to conduct classes this year himself, unable to find teachers to give them, and during the three months I was there, no educational courses of any kind were given. None were projected for the immediate future. (1969, p. 29)

That was written in 1969; the situation persisted for some time afterward.

One therapist stated that an advantage in working with forensic patients (when they show up), is that, in contrast with other patients, they are in contact with reality and can function well. With respect to the verbal facility of forensic patients, he observed enough of their conning to realize one can be taken in. They talk a lot, he said, but their talk often has little substance. The educator rarely finds out how well his students do in the future. There is little or no followup. Faced with unmotivated criminals whose interest is short-lived, a very dedicated therapist searched for reasons why. He wanted to understand criminals better, so that he could achieve better results. He attributed their poor performance to deficiencies in the schools that they attended as children, to impaired auditory discrimination for some, and to poor object relations. Of this last, the therapist commented, "Sometimes I wonder if these people remember they are here from one day to the next." This could well be a commentary on what we term the criminal's concreteness and fragmentation. The therapist stated that, despite the acumen of many forensic patients, he found psychotics to be more rewarding to work with, because they at least develop a strong attachment to a place or person, even if they are not in contact with reality. Discouraged by the forensic situation, this educator was directing his efforts more toward the adolescent patients at Saint Elizabeths, whom he called "the real dropouts" and the future inmates of John Howard.

Our experience has been that most criminals consider participation in educational programs a blow to their self-esteem, rather than a boost. The criminal believes that he already knows it all and has no need for academic routine. Thus, only a relatively small number of criminals consider enrolling in educational activities in confinement. Those who do participate need education only to the extent that it furthers their grand plans—the immediate purpose of release from confinement or gaining credentials for a future criminal objective. In fourteen years, not one of the criminals whom we have followed (other than those in our program) has used his newly acquired knowledge and skills responsibly. To be sure, criminals in confinement have earned highschool equivalency diplomas and prepared themselves in particular subjects in which they were deficient; but rarely have they used this education for any substantial period. Most begin classes, but become bored and drop out. Those who stay in, do so to score points; others think well of them if they show eagerness for self-improvement via education. In some instances, a criminal has attended one or two class meetings and dropped out. Weeks have elapsed until teacher and ward communicated about this. The teacher assumed the criminal was on the ward; the ward staff assumed that he was in class. Actually, he had been in neither place, but off the grounds during classtime. Some of the criminals who attended classes in hospital facilities outside maximum security used the occasion to get out of the ward and pick up girls.

The reader familiar with the material preceding this chapter recognizes that it is inconceivable for the criminal to utilize the educational program in a responsible way. As we pointed out in chapter 3 of volume 1, most criminals have the intelligence for scholastic achievement. However, a criminal with an education is as much a criminal as one without an education.* The primary change must be in the thinking processes and the resultant global change in living. From our point of view, the program of the education department would be a valuable adjunct to a program that had achieving a baseline of responsibility as its primary objective.

OCCUPATIONAL THERAPY

A printed statement outlines the scope, objectives, and method of operation of the Occupational Therapy Unit (Saint Elizabeths 1971). The ward doctor refers the criminal, indicating his "present condition and treatment goals." The criminal is then assigned to one of five areas where he is to be "guided into therapeutically purposeful activities." Those areas are:

1. Clinical sessions (treatment and evaluation) utilizing the media of arts and crafts
2. Observation and evaluation
3. Workshops in woodworking and carpentry, in steno pool and in sewing
4. Activity program for female patients
5. Consultation service to nursing personnel

The occupational therapist is to note the criminal's attendance and behavior and submit evaluative reports to the ward administrator. In the clinical sessions, the staff member is supposed to be a therapeutic agent:

---

*The fact that good grades have no bearing on basic change is reflected in our followup of certain criminals who have performed well academically but continued in crime. In one case that we know of, a criminal was attending school off the grounds. He was doing well and considered by hospital staff to be most promising in terms of rehabilitation and change. His educational career ended abruptly when he was arrested for bank robbery. This is typical of what has happened.

a. To provide an opportunity to establish a better or more constructive relationship
b. To provide an opportunity through structured media and environment to learn how to handle limits in exercising their behavior
c. To provide an opportunity for reality-testing and orientation
d. To provide an opportunity for increasing self-esteem

In some activities, the emphasis is on learning and improving skills, broadening vocational opportunities, improving "work tolerance," learning interpersonal skills, and reinforcing "gender identity." With respect to the last objective, it is thought that men should be comfortable at masculine activities, such as woodworking, and women should be comfortable in such activities as sewing.

The occupational therapy (O.T.) facilities at John Howard Pavilion are extensive. A criminal has his choice of a variety of media to work with, including ceramics, metal, leather, plastic, tile, and cloth. There is a classroom with typewriters and a sewing room with machines. The woodworking shop is large and well equipped with power tools. Unfortunately, there is a considerable gap between the objectives and the achievements of the program. The staff indicates that it has so many tasks to accomplish that not enough time is available for working directly with patients. The training of university students, interminable paperwork (including the ordering of equipment), housekeeping chores (janitorial service is sparse), and various meetings all consume valuable time. Only maximum security patients participate in O.T. Minimum security patients are not involved, because they are seen as being ready for more complex tasks, which industrial therapy is supposed to offer; furthermore, minimum security criminals could bring contraband into maximum security areas.

In the fall of 1972, only 26 of nearly 180 eligible patients were participating in O.T. A few O.T. projects were underway on the wards, but there was little enthusiasm on thê part of the N.A.'s who were asked to supervise the work. There was no place to store equipment on the wards, and there was fear of the consequences of allowing some tools to be in the hands of maximum security criminals. When we asked an occupational therapist what his caseload was, he replied that he had one group for two hours twice a week and that, when others came, he was available in his office to talk to them, but it was up to his assistant to carry on. In April 1974, steno pool training and training in tailoring were no longer in existence. The death of these programs was reportedly due to a lack of patient interest and to a lack of anyone at that level of functioning. Under the sponsorship of O.T., *The John Howard Journal* was published for a while. It contained stories, features, poems, and other writing by forensic patients. Among patient publications of mental hospitals and prisons, the *Journal* was a prizewinner. It flourished because two industrious, capable, articulate criminals in succession assumed responsibility for the entire project while in maximum security. They solicited stories, edited, and prepared the material for printing. When we asked about the demise of the publication, the answer was short and simple—"[C] moved to minimum security." When we studied the two criminals who headed the paper, it became clear that they were interested in the newspaper as a vehicle for scoring points with the staff and for pushing others around to do their bidding.

It is hard to see how O.T. fulfills a stated goal of broadening vocational opportunities. Few criminals will earn livelihoods in ceramics, leatherwork, and woodwork. The typewriters and sewing machines usually go unused day after day. It is occupational therapy, in the sense that it occupies the time of some criminals who might otherwise be idle on the wards and makes their stay more pleasant. It also affords criminals with artistic talent a chance to do something they like. As for fulfilling some of the other goals, O.T. falls short of the mark, as Chambers indicated:

> Some of the goals of O.T., such as increasing self-esteem and providing outlets for hostility, were unassailable, but even the staff occupational therapist had doubts about the effectiveness of his own program. Doctors, he complained, seemed to assign patients more because they asked to come than because the doctor had found they needed it. Moreover, the doctors apparently made little effort to check up on the patient's progress. The current therapist had been on the service for about two months when I met with him, and only once or twice had an administrative doctor consulted with him about the progress of a patient or sat down with him to review his program. No doctor had come to watch the program operate on site. Evaluation sheets on each participating patient were written every month, but remained in the O.T. office files. (1969, p. 28)

Criminals subverted O.T. objectives and pursued their own. They scored points with the staff and met their fellow patients from other wards, who were also assigned to O.T. and with whom they engaged in exciting talk and collusive action.

INDUSTRIAL THERAPY

> In the field of job training anything would be an improvement. (Chambers 1969, p. 36)

In most rehabilitation programs for criminals, job training is central. Criminals are in contact with reality, so they are expected to assume responsibility in work. Once criminals are in minimum security, they are eligible for industrial therapy (I.T.), which is actually a work assignment. I.T. is considered a bridge between the hospital and the outside world. The program's objectives are to teach skills, increase "work tolerance," and "restore work habits." At first, there was no pay. Criminals complained about working without compensation. In the later 1960s, a cash-incentive therapy program was offered for some kinds of work, paying $2.50 per week if a criminal worked a minimum of fifteen hours.* By 1975, this arrangement had been changed. A patient had the opportunity after one month of evaluation (earning 35¢ an hour) to earn as much as the hospital employee with whom he was working. Thus, if a grounds crew employee earned $3.50 per hour, the patient who worked on the grounds with him could receive the identical salary if he received a "one-hundred percent" evaluation. Otherwise, his earnings were prorated according to how good his evaluation was. Even when there was a monetary incentive, the criminals' attitudes did not change. In fact, their performance remained poor. Ideally, the job is to be suited to the criminal. The referral form lists therapeutic objectives that the doctor can check off as appropriate: increase self-esteem, increase sense of responsibility, encourage socialization, relieve anxiety, and promote useful adjustment to prolonged hospitalization. The referring doctor can also indicate in general terms whether the staff should take a permissive or firm attitude or something in between.

At Saint Elizabeths, forensic patients are barred from some kinds of work as security risks, especially from work in areas in which women are employed. Thus, the locations for I.T. assignments have been mainly trucks, the grounds, the barber shop, the bakery, and occasionally clinics. The supervisor of the unit spoke heatedly of his fights to get acceptance and proper supervision of forensic patients in other areas of the hospital. He said that after some unfavorable publicity about the hospital appeared in a local newspaper, the administration finally appeared more responsive to the idea of beefing up the program.

In October 1972, only thirty minimum security criminals were listed as having been assigned to I.T. Some criminals wanted to work, simply to have time away from their wards. It is not unusual for a criminal to protest when assigned to a job with close supervision, such as in an office, rather than to an

---

*There is a "transitional workshop" where, at an hourly wage of $0.31–2.00 per hour, patients work on projects contracted out by government offices. We do not have first-hand information about this program, because our criminals have not participated. As of January 2, 1975, about a half dozen forensic patients were working in this thirteen-week work adjustment and evaluation program.

area where he can do as he pleases. As far as the wards are concerned, what matters is that a man leaves for work on time and returns on time. Supervision on many assignments is almost nonexistent. Criminals check in at their assignments, are recorded as present, and leave as soon as the supervisor is out of sight. Criminals assigned to ground crews are picked up by trucks in the morning and deposited at sites to work. Others walk to their assignments. Some disappear for hours at a time and then return to meet the trucks to go back to the wards. The supervisor might ask if they have completed their assignments, but no one has actually observed them. At one I.T. location, a supervisor reported a man to be working two weeks after he had been dismissed from that very job. Another supervisor pointed out that it is difficult to know where the men are, because of the constantly changing schedule of ward meetings and other activities. We know of a number of instances in which a supervisor had no idea of when a particular criminal was scheduled to be on the job. Thus, a criminal could claim that he was leaving the ward for I.T. and immediately leave the grounds, with no checking at either end by the ward or the I.T. supervisor. There have been cases in which a criminal *by arrangement* with his supervisor has reported to work and left for the day. One supervisor asked a criminal to give him some figure for the number of hours that he was supposed to have worked, so that it could be turned in for administrative and payroll purposes.

For some criminals, an assignment to I.T. provides the perfect opportunity to leave the hospital for good. One criminal eloped during the first fifteen minutes of work on the first day of his I.T. assignment. He simply jumped off one of the trucks and disappeared, leaving the grounds. Often the doctor who is responsible for recommending privileges does not know the criminal well enough to evaluate whether he is trustworthy. Furthermore, there is no strictly enforced system of controls. Even when there is a phone check, the criminal is resourceful enough to get around it.

> C told the ward staff that he was leaving for his I.T assignment. Enroute, he called his I.T. supervisor informing him that he was ill and would remain on the ward. C then called back to the ward and, disguising his voice, misrepresented himself as the I.T. supervisor. He stated to the N.A. responsible for the phone check: "Mr. —— has arrived." . . . He then left the grounds.

Some criminals who are either brought back or return on their own after elopement are put right back on I.T. assignments.*

*The *Evening Star* (11/12/71), in an article about escapes from the hospital, noted that elopement often occurs from industrial therapy assignments.

Every month, the criminal's I.T. supervisor is supposed to send an evaluation sheet to the ward physician. The criminal is to be rated on seventeen items, including promptness, productivity, socialization, and appearance. Whereas industrial therapy helps out-of-contact patients to function better, it is doubtful that it offers a criminal anything other than time away from the ward and a larger arena in which to violate. Having a job does not make a criminal responsible.* Criminals have abused the relative freedom of I.T. by seeking out sexual contacts, stealing, and engaging in other criminal acts, both on and off the grounds. The laxness in the program has made it easier for criminals to participate in numbers and gambling, make drug connections, buy liquor, and commit other violations while going to and from work assignments, while on the job itself, and while taking breaks. We have seen criminals leaving the grounds via gates or holes in the fence when they were supposed to be at I.T. We have watched them get into cars and later return carrying stolen items. Recently, one criminal walked off his job and, with another man wanted by the police for a homicide, committed an armed robbery. In short, just as the criminal has subverted other programs, so he subverts this one, but it is easier, because he is outside the immediate view of the forensic division staff.**

A chief I.T. supervisor stated that he himself is not a "liberal, permissive person." Rather, he believes that the hospital is obliged to offer opportunities to men who want to work. He knows that some violate at the first chance they have. That is why he has urged tighter supervision and security at job assignments.

Some criminals do fulfill I.T. assignments conscientiously because they know that a good evaluation will help to show the staff that they are ready to take a productive place in society. The criminal who puts in his time at I.T. regards himself as having earned his release. In his opinion, he has worked long enough and for absurdly low wages. The state of mind is not that of a person to be evaluated, but that of a person whose rights are being violated if he is not regarded as ready for release. All other behavior is to be ignored; he deserves payment for his labor, and that payment is discharge.

---

* In chapter 2, we reviewed work-release and vocational rehabilitation as these efforts have been applied to the criminal.

**Letkemann (1973) observed that what criminals learn in vocational training may be "deliberately exploited for illegitimate purposes." That is, some of what the criminal learns "directly help [s] . . . improve his criminal activity. . . . Prison opens up new work possibilities, both legitimate and illegitimate. Recidivism rates suggest that the illegitimate alternatives are the more probable" (p. 128). Our point is that even the best programs offered at a prison or hospitals are likely to be exploited to serve the criminal's own illegitimate ends (which seem legitimate to him).

RECREATIONAL THERAPY

A recreational therapist with whom we spoke detailed several objectives of his program. The first he described as diversionary, with such activities included as playing cards, watching movies, and attending performances by outside theater groups. The therapist warned that the practice of offering diversion, if extended, could serve a repressive function, in that it is sometimes translated into an attitude of "keep the patients busy and tired out." He emphasized instead the "sociotherapeutic positive force" that recreational therapy offers. Patients may experience the "pleasures and outlets of normal circumstances which they are deprived of due to confinement." More important is that the program can offer a person alternatives that were lacking before, because of "social, cultural, or psychopathological limitations." In other words, if a man sings in a hospital choir, this activity may be carried over to the outside. Another category was described as a "new frontier" involving personal expression in movement, poetry, and creative writing.

The therapist who outlined these possibilities was newly in charge of the program of recreational therapy (R.T.). He commented that he was getting quite an education; he had to learn a new language even to establish basic communication. He indicated that he was ever sensitive to "relaxing too much," because he could be conned by these patients, who had been "super street-wise since age six." For about twenty-five hours per week, six volunteers came to the wards for art, writing, and table games. But the therapist had to spend considerable time supervising the volunteers, because "of the kind of people that come to do this kind of thing." He had to help these people to avoid "getting taken in and getting involved in a variety of situations which would be anything but therapeutic."

For the pretrial criminal in maximum security, there is no R.T., because he is there for evaluation and not treatment. Such a criminal is offered recreational opportunities in the yard and gymnasium. In working with criminals from posttrial wards, one recreational therapist convened a recreational council of criminals, which he considered to be something of a therapeutic work group. He hoped that this would be a task-oriented group in which men would establish common interests and recommend the kinds of programs that they wanted. In no time, the criminals were calling the shots on the basis of what fit their idea of R.T. Thus, R.T. at times consisted of listening to records or devising ways to win cigarettes from one another.

A miniscule number of criminals were participating in R.T. At one time in the early 1970s, of seventy criminals on three posttrial wards that the recreational therapist was working with, he described twelve as actively involved. Another dozen or so he called passively involved, which meant that as spectators they attended such events as basketball games. Minimum security posttrial criminals had no R.T. One reason was the possibility of bringing contraband to maximum security patients. Another was that it was thought that these criminals should not be offered too much at the hospital, because they needed to be weaned from the institution. The upshot is that, of about three-hundred criminals then on various forensic wards, only a dozen were actively involved in R.T.

Chambers referred to the quantity of service being offered during the three months that he observed at the hospital. We are in a position to speak of the quality of what has happened over fifteen years. In one of our early groups, twelve unchanged criminals were discussing hospital programs. They criticized all but R.T., for which they had praise. R.T. was popular because it was indeed recreation of a kind that the criminal liked: loosely structured activity in which he could do as he wished. Patient activity here was broadly labeled as "socializing," to make it respectably therapeutic. Often, it was nothing more than sitting around and talking, sometimes with sexual repartee. During recreation, criminals have had the opportunity to associate with their friends from other maximum security wards. R.T., then, is an arena in which to expand criminal talk, to scheme, and to deliver various items to one another. When criminals were housed on parts of the grounds other than at John Howard, R.T. was conducted in places that they could easily leave. The staff had a generally permissive attitude. Consequently, violations were numerous, and substantial amounts of R.T. equipment were stolen.

R.T. has continued to be popular. Exercise and the special activities that it sponsors make life more pleasant. The weekly movie shown on the grounds outside the forensic division has afforded an opportunity for a few criminals to walk out and do other things, once the lights go off. Some have sex with female patients from other parts of the hospital. Others leave the grounds for various purposes—getting food, liquor, and drugs. So many have used this as an opportunity to elope that such added security measures as increasing the guard force were taken. Dances provide another opportunity for violation. Responsible nursing assistants are reluctant to attend, but irresponsible N.A.'s let the criminals do much as they please.

R.T. objectives are laudable, and some staff members are very much in earnest about seeing those objectives accomplished. But the discrepancy between what has been proposed and what is being practiced is wide. The facilities that have been utilized most are the gym and the baseball diamond. These have offered fine opportunities for exercise and diversion for the criminal. However, there is little concept of a change process for him. No significant change takes place in this permissive, sometimes collusive environment. This is quite unlike the success that R.T. enjoys with the other groups of patients in the hospital, who have mental disorders, but are without criminal patterns.

THE ROLE OF THE CLERGY

The forensic division has had available a full-time Protestant chaplain, a full-time Catholic chaplain, and a part-time Jewish chaplain. Because Saint Elizabeths has one of the oldest and largest mental hospital training programs for clergy in the nation, trainees often have been assigned, in addition to regular staff. Hence, coverage is adequate.

The chaplain is supposed to make contact with each criminal early in his stay, to determine the patient's religious and spiritual needs. Pressure is rarely exerted. A clergyman may drop in and chat with any criminal, regardless of that person's professed faith. Usually, however, each clergyman concentrates on his own potential flock. The number of hours of contact per criminal is very small. The clergymen may have duties elsewhere in the hospital. Even if assigned to the forensic division, they spend hours in meetings and staff conferences. Seminars, meetings, writing reports, and supervisory hours consume a large share of the trainees' time. Aside from this, patient turnover is so high that it is hard even to make initial contact with all the patients, much less develop a relationship. Some clergymen are discouraged by a lack of interest and consequently visit the forensic wards only infrequently. But there have been a few clergymen with unflagging energy who made themselves available whenever possible. As we shall explain, the main reason for lack of contact is that very few criminals are interested.

The priest, minister, or rabbi who works with forensic patients believes that the criminal, like other people, is a child of God and that the resources of religious faith should be offered to him. That the criminal shows token religious interest gives the chaplain sufficient entree. Most criminals have been exposed to religion earlier in life, and some clergymen think that they can reactivate religious beliefs and thus have a salutary effect on the criminal's immoral behavior.

Some of the clergy have limited themselves to supplying the material and ritualistic aspects of religion. They approach the criminal mainly in terms of asking him what he needs, a prayerbook, a Bible, and so on. They reason that if the criminal makes contact with God and grows in favor with God, he will mend his ways. Some clergymen give personal counseling to the criminal that extends well beyond religious issues. In taking a psychologic approach, many excuse the criminal for what he has done and highlight his good points. Some approach the criminal by trying to court his favor. They do this by playing cards, having bull sessions, or running errands. A small number of clergymen who are fascinated by the criminal and by crime dwell on the details of the crimes that the criminal has committed.

Most clergymen believe that they should show an understanding and compassionate attitude. A few are hard-nosed and subscribe less to the criminal's self-serving accounts of how forces beyond his control made him what he is. The chaplain's approach is often low-key and indirect. He tries to establish rapport, perhaps without even mentioning religion. One chaplain, for example, reported that he began playing chess with a female patient who was opposed to any church. As the game went on, she became less antagonistic, and the minister gently exhorted her to make some changes in her way of life.

Chaplains work on other than an individual basis. They hold after-church discussions and in a few instances have held seminars. From time to time, there has been a choir composed of patients. One chaplain gave criminals the opportunity to discuss the Scripture reading and sermon immediately after each Sunday service. He also ran a group once a week that discussed the relevance of parts of the Bible to daily living. He commented that he was surprised to find at one meeting that several criminals were familiar with the Book of Ruth. However, he quickly pointed out that these criminals did not apply its wisdom to their own lives, especially as it touched on family solidarity.

Most important is the individual counseling, which varies in format and objective. Some clergymen look for good points in the criminal and try to build his self-esteem. There is counseling in which the criminal is told, "Be yourself," or, in street language, "Dig yourself." Its focus is on self-acceptance. Others try to offer deeper therapy. One clergyman spoke of his serving as a father figure to gain the criminal's acceptance and trust. He believed that he could proceed from there to deal with more personal themes.

Generally, the criminal does not want to have anything to do with a clergyman who opposes his way of life. He is not interested in organized religion and is quick to find fault with the clergyman and dismiss him as a hypocrite. The criminal who has fragments of religious sentiment but no strong religious beliefs also has no need of a clergyman; he usually keeps his sentiment to himself and does not want it exposed to others.

Even those who scorn the clergyman do not want to lose a potential ally.

> "I attended weekly Mass. I was registered as a Catholic and decided it was expected of me. Also, it gave me a chance to get off the ward. Besides, who knew when the chaplain might come in handy?"

Some exploit the clergy as they do everyone else. If a minister appears to be interested in helping him, the criminal does not turn his back. In fact, some criminals have misstated their religion, in order to avail themselves of contact with a particular clergyman; one never knows when the clergyman will be useful.

In the hospital's forensic services, there has been less point-scoring with the clergy than there is in prison. (Criminals have reported that, in some institutions in which they have served sentences, the clergy has a strong voice in decision-making.) Nevertheless, in the hospital if the criminal makes a good impression, he is in a better position to ask the clergyman for favors. The less experienced and more idealistic minister who acts in good faith is vulnerable to being made into an errand boy. Although the criminal has no interest in religious services, he may play along and feign some interest with the idea of exploiting the clergyman. In time, he is asking him to make calls, buy cigarettes, arrange social services, and put in a good word with the doctor.

> "When I saw the chaplain, he said, 'I see by the record that you have put yourself down as a Catholic.' I said, 'Yes, I was brought up as a Catholic but I haven't been to church regularly for twenty years.' . . . I felt that I didn't want to be back in the fold—certainly not under these circumstances. At the end of the conversation on that subject, he said, 'Is there anything that I can do for you?' So I told him that I hadn't had any contact with my family and that I had a brother here and I gave him all the particulars. I told him what church he attended and he said he would do what he could to get in touch with him. Then he said, 'You realize that I am not supposed to do this. I have agreed with the hospital that I won't interfere with any of their social work . . . but I know the pastor of the church you mentioned and I will get in touch with him.' Well, this was the first of a series of contacts that I had with chaplains."

There have been rare instances in which the clergyman who elects to minister to the criminal has been in collusion with him. The criminal features of such a person come to the fore in working with this patient population. Chaplains have taken criminals off the grounds without authorization. Some clergymen have aligned themselves with criminals and used whatever influences they could to help the criminals to get out of confinement. The clergyman who is a violator is gravitated to and admired.

In fifteen years, we have dealt with only four criminals who we thought valued religion. The staff members on their wards also regarded them as genuinely religious people. We and the staff were both wrong. One man was in a true monastic phase (at the time we had not conceptualized it this way). He attended confession and daily Mass. He was very dogmatic in his beliefs about sin, punishment, and redemption. He impressed a priest with the intensity of his self-condemnation, to the extent that the priest told him not to be so hard on himself. This criminal wanted to enter a monastery and wrote some letters to inquire about the possibility. The monasticism did not last and eventually, he was again in massive crime, and the fervent dedication to self-purification came to an end. Another criminal was thought to be monastic. He was a prison-wise criminal who gave a convincing display of religiosity while active in crime. Two other criminals totally compartmentalized religion. One railed against the permissiveness of the church and its hypocrisy. Although he attended church regularly, he was active in crime. The other held on to his desire to become a minister, but was a constant violator. Thus, of the only four men who we thought were religious, the religiosity was insignificant when set against their criminal way of life.

Even the most well-intentioned clergyman can do little to change criminals.* A person must be responsible first if he is to be truly religious. Those among the clergy who accentuate the positive features of the criminal only reinforce the criminal's notion that he is a good person. In the long run, this misguided effort can only facilitate crime. The services of the clergy would indeed be useful in conjunction with a comprehensive program that dissects religious instruction could add a new and enriching dimension to life, but only after there were a responsible base on which to build.

OVERVIEW OF THE "THERAPEUTIC" PROGRAMS

Saint Elizabeths Hospital has a good physical plant, many resources, and conscientious, dedicated people in the forensic division. Most certainly, it does not warehouse criminals, but instead has genuinely attempted to offer opportunities to the criminal to rehabilitate himself. The primary failure has resulted from a lack of knowledge of the criminal and his patterns of thinking and action and from a tendency to excuse him because of sociologic and psychologic considerations, most notably mental illness.

Many criminals have no organized programs. According to some activity heads, staff shortage and scheduling problems account in great part for the paucity of participation by criminals in the activities offered. For those who do participate, the various activities make life less onerous. However, excellent facilities go unused for considerable periods. Referrals work largely by the pressure principle. Doctors who do not know most of the criminals refer those who make the most noise about wanting to do something. Chambers (1969) indicated the scope of the staff's failure to provide substantive activities for over half the patients.

> The principal activities of vast numbers of patients are walking the halls and watching television. Morale is at its nadir among both patients and staff. (p. iii)

> In sum, well over half of the patients are involved in practically nothing in the hospital. Some have participated in the past, become tired and bored,

---

*In chapter 2, there is a discussion of religious rehabilitative approaches tried elsewhere with the criminal.

and dropped out. Others have drifted into the woodwork, are rarely seen and even more rarely urged to participate. (p. 29)

Attached to the 1969 Covington decision was an appendix in which an ad hoc committee (1968) reported its evaluation of security programs and facilities at Saint Elizabeths. The following excerpt from that group's report concurs with Chambers's findings:

There is too much "sitting around" on the wards at the present time. Adjunctive therapy should be greatly expanded.... All adjunctive treatment must be related to therapeutic goals and not be merely time fillers. . . . Merely supplying [patients] with socializing experience is no substitute for interpreted experience which will modify personality operations. (p. 52)

We concur with the committee and Chambers. However, even with "interpreted experience" designed to "modify personality operations" implemented to the hilt, we contend that, with the present state of knowledge of the criminal, this would not achieve basic change. The programs are intended to help the criminal acquire various skills, including the interpersonal, to build self-esteem, and to increase self-confidence. O.T., R.T., I.T., and other programs discussed here are of proven value in approaching such goals with mentally ill, noncriminal patients. By themselves, they do not achieve significant change in the criminal. A man may be a skilled craftsman and cooperate with others, but remain a criminal. Some therapists and other agents of change believe that if a man has success experiences and receives recognition and if the good in him is brought out, this will contribute significantly to change. Bringing out the good in a criminal ultimately only gives him greater license for crime. It bolsters his view of his own decency. For him to be a criminal and do as he does, he must have this reservoir of good in him, as he views himself. He has plenty of self-esteem and confidence when it comes to doing the criminal things that he wants to do. What he lacks is the self-respect that can come only through the hard work and accomplishment that responsible living can bring. No painting, music, or poetry can provide this. An entire view of life must change, along with all the thinking patterns. Therapeutic programs like those just described may be useful adjuncts to a program that calls for a total change to a new way of life and instructs the criminal in how to make that change. As things stand at the forensic division, there are uncoordinated, underutilized programs that many staff members have little faith in when it comes to significantly changing the criminal.

The activities made available to criminals are pleasant diversions from being cooped up on the ward. Criminals enjoy the recreation or projects that they work on, but that does not mean that they even attend them regularly, because they might be enjoying something else more. Essentially, they approach the programs as they would any criminal enterprise. They are aware that looking good at an activity results in a favorable evaluation being sent to the doctor. A criminal knows what is needed to convince the staff that he is recovering from a mental illness. Good conduct and good performance are the important avenues to the way out. The motivation that appears to be lacking in the criminal suddenly emerges, when it becomes clear to him that release depends on participation in some activities. In addition, when staff members hold a favorable attitude toward the criminal, it is easier for him to get away with violations on the side. Violations occur at the site of some of the activities, but usually go undetected or unreported. The criminal also seeks personal gains from criminal equivalents. His personal triumphs are often seen by others as manifestations of leadership.

From the point of view of the staff, many hopes are raised and then shattered. Most activity heads and their assistants care; they want to be effective. They do not know what happens later in the lives of their patients, so they rarely know whether they have accomplished anything lasting. Some are content with their subjective evaluations of the gains that they perceive. If they value self-expression and see a criminal, when he has previously appeared withdrawn, expressing hostility, they believe that he is opening up and that something good is happening. However, some voice serious doubts as to whether their efforts are having a constructive, lasting impact on the criminal. The basic questions that emanate from such doubts not only go unanswered, but, in time, stop being asked.

We have had entensive contact with about 220 criminals from Saint Elizabeths. From the criminal's perspective, these programs offered by the forensic division at best were time-consumers and provided opportunity for scoring points. Once he spent time in I.T., O.T., R.T., or any other program, the criminal believed that he was entitled to his release—a *quid pro quo* exchange: he had served his time, made his contributions, done what the hospital wanted, and thus he had earned his discharge.

We have said repeatedly that the milieu and the programs in confinement do not make a criminal worse: they only offer him an institution-accepted arena for criminal expression, whether arrestable or a criminal equivalent. However, his recognition that the hospital has not achieved its objectives with him gives him further fortification for his argument that he might as well be released. He does not view himself as mentally ill to begin with. If he is mentally ill, little is occurring to contribute to his recovery. The hospital's failure is known to him, and he exploits it in pressing for release.

RELEASE

There are three stages in getting out of the hospital: conditional release (C.R.), convalescent status (C.S.), and unconditional release (U.C.R.). Every criminal used to have to go through all stages with the court's approval of each step. The court's involvement was mandatory in the early 1960s, to the extent that a criminal out of the hospital on C.S. would have to return to the hospital and be taken to court handcuffed.* C.S. is now left to the discretion of the hospital. The court still sets the terms for conditional release.

To gain approval for C.R., some criminals have filed with the court writs of habeas corpus. These are usually of little merit, being crudely written and containing little favorable evidence that would stand up in court. Criminals know that they have little chance of succeeding with such writs, but writing them is a way of pressuring the hospital. From their point of view, it is better to submit a writ and lose than to remain inactive. Although they know that a favorable outcome is unlikely, their thinking while waiting for the hearing is, "I'm going to get out." It is known that the hospital prefers not to appear in court on such matters. Consequently, there have been instances in which someone in the administration has tried to work out an arrangement mutually satisfactory to the hospital and the criminal. Compromises have been offered, such as giving a criminal ground privileges in return for his tearing up a writ.

The criminal on conditional release continues to reside in the minimum security part of the forensic division. He is then allowed to go into the city for designated purposes—school, work, family visits. A curfew is imposed for returning to the hospital. The court expects the hospital to keep track of patients and to see that court-imposed conditions are adhered to.

In practice, the C.R. arrangement works poorly, because the criminal is unchanged. With greater freedom, infractions and violations usually become more numerous. Some men are on the streets with the pretense of holding a job, but are actually working only part-time or, in some cases, not at all. Supervision is such that criminals have successfully signed out for school when school was not even in session. Curfew violation is common; the criminal always has an excuse ready, such as working overtime, missing a bus, or having car trouble. Sometimes a criminal returns to the ward drunk. This may be ignored, unless he creates a commotion and his condition is obvious to everyone. Criminals bring drugs and liquor into the hospital, as well as stolen goods. When it comes to enforcement, there is little consistency; some men seem to get away with numerous violations, whereas others are watched carefully by those who are waiting for them to make a mistake.

---

*This was because the prisoner-patient was regarded more as a prisoner at that time.

On convalescent status, the criminal is no longer residing at the hospital, but is required to report to the outpatient department at designated times. Supervision is limited. At one point, in an attempt to remedy this, the hospital scheduled meetings on Sunday mornings that C.S. patients were required to attend. Few appeared. Drug use and drinking occurred on the premises. Some criminals came to the meetings already intoxicated or on drugs. The sessions were held by a rotating series of doctors, most of whom knew very few of the patients. The format was, Anyone got a problem? These men had only one problem: how to satisfy the doctor that they were keeping their noses clean. There was no discussion of functioning at work and home. The Sunday morning meetings were discontinued when it became clear that they were failing to achieve their purpose of follow-up. Other attempts at systematic outpatient follow-up have been instituted. When the social service department played a role in administering the outpatient clinic, a spokesman admitted that the clinic was poorly attended and understaffed. Now the outpatient clinic is staffed by a psychologist administrator and several counselors.

Criminals in our program have reported to us that outpatient sessions that they have attended mostly have been brief, with a few perfunctory questions being asked as to whether they are employed and whether they are using drugs. No inquiry is made into patterns of thought and action. The criminals simply go through the motions.

> When he attended the outpatient clinic, C was not asked what he was doing. Instead, the staff member asked what needed to be done *for* him. C asked about getting permission to go out of town to visit relatives and a girlfriend. The answer was that, although permission could not be given officially, if he were careful he could go, and no one would know the difference. C (in our program at the time) then said that he wanted to do this responsibly and asked that the clinic help him obtain permission from the court.

Many criminals during these interviews appear able to keep the hospital off their backs. The information gathered then is a major source of data for the hospital to use as a basis for recommending unconditional release. Some criminals who have not been seen for months can, nevertheless, have the benefit of a doctor's testifying for them for U.C.R. In such cases, the criminal is called and told to come for an interview just before a court hearing.

The hospital does not keep criminals on the active rolls any longer than necessary. In fact, the success of this hospital, and many other mental institutions, is often judged by the number of patients who get out. Sometimes, a criminal is released unconditionally when he has another charge pending and there is assurance that he will go to jail, rather than being on the street, where he can embarrass the hospital if he gets into trouble. Release sometimes seems to be a function of staff fatigue.

C, a long-time drug user, was in poor physical condition. Even so, he was still involved in drug sales and continued to use drugs. This man who was unable to get out of bed at times, groaning and walking with a cane, was taken to court and granted a U.C.R. On the basis of our detailed knowledge of C, we advised one of the doctors that C was a danger to himself and society. The doctor simply shrugged, and the hospital rid itself of a man whom it did not want. C had been a patient for more than a decade and was in worse physical and mental condition than ever. His personality was the same, but his activity in crime was reduced because of his physical disabilities. Out of the hospital, he stayed on drugs and was in crime. He quickly spent over $1,000 inherited from his mother. He wrecked his car and was admitted to a medical facility, from which he was discharged. He returned to Saint Elizabeths in deteriorated physical condition and was placed on a service other than a forensic ward, because the forensic division wanted no part of him. Shortly after readmission, C died of a condition related to years of drug use.

At many points in his later years, the staff had tried to push C out—totally unchanged and in poor physical condition.

There have been instances in which staff members have desired to get rid of criminals who are hard to manage, especially criminals representing a physical danger to other patients and staff. Some unorthodox practices have helped to accomplish this.

C was a troublemaker on the ward. Of greatest concern to the staff was his assault pattern. C was advised by staff members that, if he did not get into trouble for thirty days, he would be released. C messed up this arrangement twice. Finally, thirty days passed without a major incident, and he was discharged.

We know of several occasions when staff members have offered NGBRI criminals a *choice* of whether to continue in that status. These were criminals whom the staff wanted to discharge. In each case, the criminal was told that, if he chose to remain NGBRI, he would be buried and never gain his freedom; otherwise, he would be released directly from maximum security. Most criminals, of course, would choose outright release—being found without mental disorder, but not those who had charges to face elsewhere or backup time to serve in prison on other charges.

A very dangerous man was given the choice of getting out immediately or staying in the hospital. The latter choice might have been tempting, because he had charges to face immediately on discharge from the institution. However, he chose to be released, for several reasons. He disliked the idea of an indeterminate sentence. As he put it, he would have to "kiss everybody's ass for everything" to work his way out. Furthermore, he considered the work at the hospital "slave labor." Instead, he prefered to take his chances in court, about which he was superoptimistic. His status would be to be out on bond until he went to trial for attempted robbery and assault with a deadly weapon. The patient wanted to have his lawyer delay the trial, so that he would have time to establish a work record. Then, he thought, he could convince the judge to place him on probation for 5 years.

This criminal served a six month sentence and then went on probation. He killed someone not long after.

The staff may delay U.C.R. if it thinks that the release of a criminal may cause future embarrassment to it in the community. But there have been exceptions to this, as in the following situation when the institution recommended a U.C.R., even though evidence was available that a criminal was still dangerous.

C's doctor was asked by the court whether he considered the patient still dangerous. The doctor replied that he was not sure. The court's response was that C should remain at the hospital a couple of months more, so that a more thorough evaluation could be made. The doctor went on vacation, during which time C attacked a woman on the grounds of the hospital. Saint Elizabeths decided to go ahead with the U.C.R. The doctor returned and, not knowing of the hospital's decision, stated that C was dangerous.*

Some criminals do not want unconditional release. Remaining on the hospital rolls gives them some protection against going to prison. One man had detainers issued for him in four states. Were he to be discharged from Saint Elizabeths, he might receive penalties elsewhere totaling fifteen years in

---

*This situation was reported in the press (*Evening Star and . . . News* 7/13/72). The judge in one case talked about hospital politics playing a role in the evaluation of the criminal. He called the hospital staff's change of opinion in this situation "highly irregular" and noted that "people have a tendency to rid themselves of whatever bothers them." The judge stated that, for over a year, the hospital had given "an unbroken line of testimony," saying that the criminal was sick, and had then issued "a dramatic reversal" in which the criminal was not mentally ill.

prison. If a criminal is apprehended for a crime while he still has the status of a mental patient, he may be returned to the hospital, rather than put in jail. This is especially likely if he has committed a crime similar to the offense that led to his admission to the hospital in the first place. Other advantages of a mental illness diagnosis may accrue. A diagnosis may serve as a convenient excuse for not doing what is expected, such as working, or for doing what is not supposed to be done, such as making irresponsible expenditures. Furthermore, with a psychiatric diagnosis, he remains eligible for pensions, if he has been receiving any in connection with mental disability. He is also eligible to continue to receive hospital medical services without charge. We have repeatedly witnessed thousands of dollars being given to the criminal through federal, state, and local subsidy (service-connected disability, social security, etc.). We have yet to see a case in which an unchanged criminal uses this money for his rehabilitation. Instead, it goes mainly to further his criminal pursuits.

Since the late 1960s, the hospital has reduced its patient census. This is in line with the practice of mental hospitals nationwide; it is considered desirable by mental health personnel to keep patients in the community, if at all possible. As we pointed out, in the early 1960s and before, the hospital was much more careful about whom it released. Now it is far less so. Every criminal *not* in our program who has left this hospital and whom we have retained contact with has committed more crimes. We know of homicides, child molestations, rapes, drug sales, numerous thefts, and other crimes for which these criminals have not been apprehended. The cost to society of the discharge of unchanged criminals is high. Criminals repeatedly say that, if the staff had total knowledge of what happened during every twenty-four-hour period for every forensic patient, no patient would be clean enough to be presented for conditional release.

SUMMARY

We have pointed out here (as well as in volume 1) that the criminal enters the hospital to escape longer confinement elsewhere. Once he is admitted, he seeks to get out. He is not interested in change, but only in convincing the authorities that he is no longer mentally ill and that he should therefore be discharged. The hospital's forensic division has a mammoth job, to produce change in criminals who want only to continue their criminal life style. Even the excellent resources that the hospital has are of minimal assistance in having an impact on the criminal, who wants only to get out of the institution.

The hospital provides another arena for criminals to continue their patterns of thought and action. Using the thinking patterns of a lifetime, the criminal exploits what is a permissive and inconsistent milieu. Participation in programs offered is mainly for point-scoring purposes. Those programs, however conceived and implemented, do not change criminal thinking patterns. The criminal continues to violate, although with more caution, and does so in part by collaborating with the minority of staff members who are themselves irresponsible. Under these conditions, the institution does not worsen existing criminal patterns, but it does nothing to change them.

In the next two chapters, we shall discuss prerequisites for being an effective change agent with criminals, and we shall present a proposal for a new kind of institution.

BIBLIOGRAPHY

Ad Hoc Committee for the Evaluation of Security Programs and Facilities at Saint Elizabeths Hospital. (1968). Report. Appendix to Covington v. Harris, 136 U.S. App. D.C. 35, 419 F 2d 617 (1969).

Bazelon, D. L. (1973). Is the adversary process essential to due process in psychiatry? Joint meeting of the Cleveland Bar Association and the Cleveland Psychiatric Society, Cleveland, Ohio, October 12.

―――― (1974). Institutional psychiatry—'the self inflicted wound'? Conference on Mental Health and the Law at Catholic University, Washington, D.C., January 19.

Chambers, D. L. (1969). A report on John Howard Pavilion at Saint Elizabeths Hospital. Submitted to Saint Elizabeths Hospital and the National Institute of Mental Health, June 4.

Evening Star 11/12/71. Escape rate at St. Elizabeths is growing concern to police.

Evening Star and The Washington Daily News. 7/13/72. Sanity ruling disputed.

―――― 7/13/72. Inmates, 5 guards at Lorton indicted.

Facilities Work Group (1969). Report. Washington, D.C.: Saint Elizabeths Hospital.

Jones, M. (1953). *The Therapeutic Community.* New York: Basic Books.

Kiger, R. S. (1967). Treating the psychopathic patient in a therapeutic community. *Hospital & Community Psychiatry*: 191-196.

Letkemann, P. (1973). *Crime as Work.* Englewood Cliffs, N.J.: Prentice-Hall.

New York Times 7/28/73. ――――sentenced to life for hijacking of airliner.

Program Development Work Group on Forensic Services (1969). Report. Washington, D.C.: Saint Elizabeths Hospital, October 1.

Rosenhan, D. L. (1973). On being sane in insane places, *Science* 179 (January): 250-258.

Rossi, J. J. (1974). Challenges and issues in private practice in working with addicted people. Paper presented at the 82nd annual convention of the American Psychological Association, New Orleans, August.

Saint Elizabeths Hospital (1971). Program plan for John Howard Occupational Therapy Unit, rev. ed. Washington, D.C.

Steinberg, G. G. (1964). Change in psychiatric diagnosis of male patients sent for evaluation by the District Court of D.C. since the Leach decision. Washington, D.C.: n.p.

Stoller, R. J. (1974). "Psychiatric diagnoses do not work." Paper presented at the 127th annual convention of the American Psychiatric Association, Detroit, May.

Washington Post. (5/11/71). 2 escape deputy marshals.

——— (6/14/71). Moundsville Prison: cruel and unusual.

——— (11/28/71). 2 Saint Elizabeths patients arrested.

——— (4/25/72). Rapist walks out, returns to hospital.

——— (6/23/73). Man fleeing robbery fatally shot by guard.

Weihofen, H. (1960). The definition of mental illness. *Ohio State Law Journal* 21: 1-16.

Chapter 12

The Personality of
the Agent of Change

THE CHANGING PATTERN WITH respect to utilization of staff at Saint Elizabeths that we described (chapter 11) obtains in other institutions, especially in mental hospitals housing forensic patients. At Saint Elizabeths, intensive individual treatment was offered to some patients by staff and residents ten years ago. These careful and often prolonged efforts to achieve change were discontinued as a new orientation was deemed more practical. Increasingly, the group treatment format was used in which large numbers of criminals could be seen frequently. With an emphasis on milieu therapy, activity therapies, and the therapeutic community, the doctors' time became taken up more and more with administrative matters. Doctors who were supposed to function as therapists were increasingly occupied with ward policy, deportment problems, emergencies, and paperwork. They became remote from the criminal, often having little or no individual contact with him. Counseling was relegated to untrained nursing assistants. This has been a trend in other situations where treatment has become more group-oriented, and paraprofessionals have come to play a major role.

The 1960s saw the emergence of a social movement dedicated to improving the lot of the offender. People became sensitive to the fact, as White (1971, p. 14) put it, that "the basic handling of the convicted offender is little different than it was more than 100 years ago." The National Advisory Commission on Criminal Justice Standards and Goals (1973, p. 466) stated that corrections had previously been a very unappealing field. The Commission noted that the field had failed especially to retain "many of its highly trained, young, and creative staff members, particularly those who come from minority groups." The wave of social consciousness in the 1960s created pressure to reform the correctional system. People with interest, but no formal training, began to work in the field. The Task Force on Corrections (1967, p. 100) pointed out that over half the agencies responding to its questionnaire reported that they had no organized training programs. Another finding was that

> only 96 (16 percent) of a sample of 602 colleges and universities offered courses in corrections or correctional administration. . . . More than three-quarters of [the 96] required no practical field work with the course. (p. 99)

People began to look to the universities to play a greater role "in meeting the research and training needs of corrections" (Waldo 1971, p. 62). Beto and Marsh (1974, p. 35) stated that in the 1960s criminal-justice education programs had proliferated. In late 1974, more than 1,000 institutions of higher learning were offering some kind of degree in criminal justice. Beto and Marsh observed, however, that many academic institutions "developed programs with little guidance or forethought."

The new wave of people entering the corrections field had little specific training and showed little evidence of being selected on the basis of personal characteristics. A show of interest has been sufficient to qualify one for a job. Faust (1965) said that it was because of demands on the system that untrained people were shouldering responsibility for offenders. Faust used the following analogy in speaking of this trend:

> When a person is seriously injured and a physician is not available, the proper application of first-aid will certainly make the injured party more comfortable and may even save his life, despite the fact that the practitioner's technical knowledge of medicine is limited. (p. 350)

Faust used untrained staff members for group counseling. He said that this allows "you to do a better job with what you have." The National Advisory Commission urged that paraprofessionals be hired, to reduce case loads and "spread scarce professional services." A part of this trend was to seek workers among people with the same backgrounds as many of the offenders.

> Many persons with less than a college education can be of special use in corrections, since they understand the problems of offenders who are likewise without higher education. (National Advisory Commission 1973, p. 472)

Not only did programs seek workers who had similar backgrounds, but they began to hire offenders after they were released and clear of the legal process. The Task Force stated unequivocally that "ex-offenders are a promising source of manpower for corrections" (p. 103). Claiborne (1971) observed that many ex-convicts were being attracted to careers in social work and were functioning as counselors and supervisors in community clinics, halfway houses, and other facilities. Ex-convicts have even been successful in obtaining grants to run rehabilitation projects for youth *(Washington Post 6/6/71)*.

Many who enter corrections, or a related discipline, do so with enthusiasm. However, they grow disenchanted and experience a sense of futility, because their programs do not achieve constructive results. Many decide that they want no part of working with criminals. In private psychiatry, there has been a progressive decline in interest in this group, and no form of therapy has been effective with it. Competent private psychiatrists who want to help those who genuinely seek help rarely choose to treat criminals. Institutions have developed no programs that have produced lasting change. At a time when society is asking for more personnel and better programs, the sense of futility is very high in institutions that are asked to provide them. The situation is not much better in community health centers and outpatient clinics. Very few criminals seek treatment voluntarily. Those who are followed by clinics, outpatient departments, or probation services receive little treatment. Followup is perfunctory, because there is little interest in doing the extensive checking and cross-checking that are necessary with criminals.

Thus, the field has largely been left to those who simply show some eagerness and willingness to work in it. The increase in interested people, however, has not been accompanied by an increase in qualifications required. There is little, if any, specific training for working with the criminal. A corrections worker simply applies whatever approach is compatible with his knowledge and interest provided it is within the constraints of his organization. In many cases, a person takes what he has used with noncriminals (if he has had any training) and applies it to criminals. Some workers enter the field solely out of interest, with no training whatsoever. Some of these are seeking excitement and prefer to work with criminals rather than any other group. Those who have criminal components in their own personalities often function in collusion with their criminal charges (as described in the preceding chapter).

We have presented a specific program that works—it has achieved change in hard-core criminals. To implement this change process, there must be personnel qualified to function as agents of change. Clearly, not everyone who has a graduate degree is suited, by virtue of that degree alone, to work with the criminal, just as not everyone who wants to be a physician necessarily has the aptitude and personality to do so. Even if one has the aptitude and other personal characteristics for a profession, he must receive proper training. Just as one should not expect a patient to be operated on successfully unless his surgeon is well-trained, so criminals should not be expected to change if assisted by those who are not qualified with respect to temperament and training.

In this chapter, we shall focus on what we have concluded are the personal characteristics most conducive to success in working with the criminal. We have arrived at the conclusions expressed here through four routes: (1) We have observed how criminals have functioned with other change agents. (2) We have interviewed professionals who work with criminals in a variety of settings (prisons, hospitals, and clinics); these professionals have been candid in assessing their own discouragement and lack of impact, and they have revealed a great deal about their own personalities—from the dedicated and responsible to the frankly criminal. (3) Criminals, changed and unchanged, have told us how they have dealt with other change agents. (4) Finally, during our fifteen years of working with criminals, we have sought out and recorded criminals' observations about the effectiveness of our approach. Whenever we modified our procedures, we received significant feedback. More than a decade's experience has been indispensable in formulating the personal and professional qualities necessary to deal effectively with the criminal population.

THE AGENT OF CHANGE AS A MODEL

An important aspect of human development is the process of identification: "The act or process of becoming like something or someone in one or several aspects of thought or behavior" (Brenner 1957, p. 44). In literature on the criminal, delinquent, or psychopath, the failure to make positive identifications with responsible, stable people is viewed as a significant contributing factor to antisocial behavior. Aichhorn (1965, p. 225) maintained that there are some "dissocial types" who "lack the inherited capacity for object cathexis and identification" owing to some "inborn defects." The most frequently encountered formulation is that the criminal lacks stable, responsible models at home, therefore considers himself betrayed, and with hostility turns to socially unacceptable members of his peer group, with whom he identifies.

> There is no doubt that a warm tie between father and son is of great significance in helping a boy to develop a wholesome set of ideals through the process of emotional "identification" with his father. Should this bond not be close, the growing child may seek a substitute in companionship with delinquent children. (Glueck and Glueck 1952, p. 62)

The defects of the "typical antisocial reaction" are marks left by the betrayals suffered in childhood within the family, by the lack of stable, dependable, protecting identification models in the parents. (Cameron 1963, p. 658)

In the absence of other models in the home or school whose emulation or influence could be constructive in their lives, your boys did the natural thing. They took what was available, which was to adopt the code for behavior as laid down by their ghetto peers and the wolves of their neighborhood. (Henry 1972, p. 80)

Although lack of a stable model may be conducive to a child's identifying with people outside the family, some think that a child identifies with the negative, often aggressive, qualities of his parents. Shields (1962, p. 160) spoke of "projective identification with the aggressor," which "intensifies the antisocial behavioural traits in these children." Erikson (1968, p. 88) has described the choice of a "negative identity," a condition that "prevails in the delinquent."

Most therapists, no matter what their theoretical persuasion, appear to believe that identification with a stable, responsible role model is an integral part of the therapeutic process. Aichhorn, writing about the role of the teacher in a residential, analytically oriented program, maintained that

the teacher, as a libidinally charged object for the pupil, offers traits for identification that bring about a lasting change in the structure of the ego-ideal. This in turn effects a change in the behaviour of the formerly dissocial child. (p. 235)

Slavson (1965, p. 609), who has done extensive residential and group psychoanalytic work with delinquents, has also described the process of "identification with the therapist as an ideal." The caseworker who undertakes field work with delinquents also expects to serve as a model for identification (New York City Youth Board 1960, pp. 53–54). The behavior therapy literature contains many statements on learning from social models. In discussing behavior therapy with delinquents, Bishop (1973, p. 64) has recommended providing "models to the young offender, and models who behave and are successful in our society."

Fifteen years of working with the criminal has taught us that neither the unchanged nor the changed criminal identifies with other people. In growing up, the criminal has regarded responsible people as people to be used. He has not wanted to be like them. Furthermore, he has opposed them because they have been antagonistic to his way of life. The stability of his home did not determine identification. If one is wedded to the identification theory one can find features in any home that may be viewed as deleterious to the process of identification. However, most of our criminals came from homes where the parents were responsible and emotionally stable; in the homes that were broken, there was usually a stabilizing force in the form of the remaining parent or a relative (see chapter 3 of volume 1). The criminal did not function according to parental expectations and chose a different way of life. Yet his own siblings identified with the very parents that he departed from. The same is true with relatives, teachers, employers, and other responsible people in his life; the criminal has chosen not to pattern himself after the models whom others have found worthy of imitation. This does not mean that the criminal rejected those people. In fact, many criminals were very fond of their parents and respected and sometimes envied responsible people whom they knew. But they simply had no use for the responsible way of life.

One could postulate that the criminal made an identification with deviant and delinquent people in his environment instead. But this is not the case either. The criminal has always considered himself unique, even vis-a-vis other criminals, and does not identify with other criminals. He collaborates with them, shares interests with them, and uses them, but there is nothing like a process of identification. The criminal has always considered himself apart from and superior to others. It is a putdown for him to copy others. He may ask another criminal for his thinking or for information and use it to his own advantage. But this is not identification. In fact, he may well regard the other criminal as foolish for talking.

During the fifteen years of our work with criminals, we have examined many aspects of our relationship with them. In doing so, we have inquired into the matter of identification. We have spent hundreds and in some cases thousands of hours with particular criminals. In that time, they have learned what we have taught, but they have not become like us. Criminals give us gifts at Christmas, compliment us, speak favorably about us to others, show concern about our health, and learn what we have to teach, but insist on remaining individuals. They do not dress or speak like us, nor do they adopt our hobbies or political and social views. In fact, changed criminals are hypersensitive to any suggestion that they are becoming like us. They take nothing from us except the substance of the program, which they choose to implement.

We have had an impact as effective teachers, not as models. It is as though one were learning mathematics from a gifted teacher. The teacher might not be the kind of person one is particularly fond of or chooses to be like. However, this would not preclude learning the subject matter from him. The criminal is favorably disposed toward us, but in no way regards us as models.

Even a criminal who said, "You're more of a father to me than any father I ever had," was not identifying with us. We were functioning as teachers and consultants to him; he did not want to be like us. The critical element in change is the merit of the material that we present, and not the interpersonal relationship.

If a criminal thinks that the agent of change expects him to serve as a model, he may appear to be identifying with an A.C. by taking on one or more aspects of his behavior. This is not an authentic identification. He is merely feeding the A.C. what he thinks the A.C. wants to hear.*

Total responsibility on the part of the A.C. is necessary, *independent* of whether he serves as a model. The A.C. cannot allow himself to be vulnerable to a valid charge of irresponsibility, because it would destroy his credibility.

The role of the A.C. as a deterring force should not be confused with any identification with him as a model of thinking and conduct. In a very concrete manner, the criminal may invoke the A.C. as a deterrent. A specific conversation, a visual image, or the thought of the agent's name may deter him from some violation. The criminal always wants to avoid an accountability situation, and the very thought that he will have to face the A.C. and the group and report irresponsible thinking or action may deter him. The A.C. is then an inhibitor, not a model for identification. Like all the other deterrents, the A.C.'s deterring force can be cut off.

When the criminal admires us for operating in a particular manner, he emulates us only if he thinks it will work for him, not because of an identification. For example, one man who had been implementing the program for some time admired the A.C.'s endurance of an allergic reaction to penicillin. It was a lesson for him, and he valued the teaching. He increased his tolerance to physical distress, because he saw the pragmatic value of the endurance. But admiration and identification are not the same.

The criminal has always done things his own way. He continues to operate in this manner when he has become responsible. When the criminal is faced with two options that are equally responsible, he is as likely as not to choose differently from the way we would. Those change agents who require a process of modeling and identification as a basic component of the change process will not be successful. A program based on reason does not require identification, whereas a program not so based may well use it. The criminal does not go through a process of identification, either before or after change. As operative as the concept of identification is with the noncriminal, it is inoperative with the criminal.

---

*Sometimes there are cases in which the imitation is genuine and not for point scoring purposes. For example, the criminal may use some of the same phrases as the A.C. Such isolated imitative acts do not contribute to basic change.

INTEGRITY

It is essential that the A.C. be a person of total integrity, not because he is providing a model for the criminal, but for reasons essential to leading a program which is firmly grounded in moral values. We have described at length in volume 1 the criminal's total lack of integrity. Lying is a way of life. It is essential for survival. When used to deceive someone, it is a source of power. The criminal frankly admits that he will lie whenever it is necessary. In fact, he asserts that everyone lies, and regards lying as the great common denominator between himself and responsible people. He sees his massive lying and the occasional small lie told by the noncriminal as the same. In fortifying his position that everyone lies, he points to the dishonesty in the corporate structure and in the political arena. If a person denies lying, the criminal says that such a denial itself constitutes a lie.

The criminal is all too ready to criticize a change agent in any matter— dress, manners, choice of words, and so forth. If he spots any behavior of the A.C. that appears irresponsible, he dwells on it and tries to put the A.C. on the defensive. He is always alert to anything that indicates insincerity or deception on the part of an adversary who is in a position of authority. If an A.C. gives even the slightest indication that he does not live by the integrity that he espouses, the criminal concludes that he is "one of us"—a criminal.

In the hands of an irresponsible person, the most profound knowledge and the soundest techniques cannot succeed in effecting lasting change in the criminal. New information and techniques can be readily acquired, but sound, responsible functioning must be there to begin with. Personal integrity in his own life is mandatory if an A.C. is to help a criminal arrive at the firm, moral position on which this program is based. Although most traditional forms of psychiatry eschew moralizing by the change agent, moral issues are at the heart of our work (although these issues are discussed only after substantial change has occurred). An A.C. who is not totally responsible cannot convincingly convey the concepts of responsible thinking and action to the criminal.

When we say that the agent of change must live responsibly, it does not mean that he accepts the world the way it is. If he condoned the imperfections, inequalities, and injustices that occur daily, the criminal would regard him as a bigot, hypocrite, or simple conformist. The A.C. would in effect be condoning in society some of the very same behavior that he condemns and tries to change in the criminal. The particular views of the A.C. on current issues do not matter, so long as his thinking and action are responsible and constructive. He must be forthright in expressing his views, being critical of irresponsibility not only in the criminal, but in all others. The test of responsibility applies to all.

Candor and directness are called for from the very first contact with the criminal. As we pointed out in chapter 3, we inform the criminal of our view of him immediately. This entire program calls for total honesty and open expression of a point of view on both sides. Our view is anything but complimentary to the criminal. This type of candor is unusual in the criminal's experience with change agents and with others who have had some authority over him. It is necessary to open the channel.

> "Since you're brutally frank, you encourage frank expression. . . . In other words, your frankness encourages frankness in return."

The integrity of the A.C. is often challenged with respect to the highly charged issue of confidentiality. Whatever stance the A.C. adopts, he must stick by what he says. The A.C. must anticipate that others will come to him seeking information, but he must make it clear to the criminal that nothing will be revealed—except that the A.C. will intercede when there is an impending homicide. Difficult situations occur with legal authorities in search of information.

> When a representative from the Secret Service came to ascertain the status of C, we had C present information on himself at the meeting. The A.C. made a general statement about the program and C's cooperation with it at that time. The Secret Service agent was then free to question C. Everything was in the open, and it was up to C how much he wanted to talk about his life before and during the program.

We do not encourage the criminal to be an informer. If he desires to inform in the interest of what he considers to be the social good, we do not play an active role, but we have arranged meetings and sat in while information was passed.

In fifteen years, we have testified in court seven times. Each time, we insisted on being subpoenaed. In three cases, the only issue was whether a criminal had exhibited sufficient change to warrant being released to the community. One case involved our testifying on behalf of a changed criminal's application to have a professional license reinstated. In another instance, we testified on behalf of a criminal who was requesting transfer from maximum to minimum security so that he could participate daily in our program. Of course, we were aware of the risk in this. The man had been receiving little in the way of treatment in maximum security and had expressed interest over many months in entering our program. On one occasion, we were asked to testify concerning the mental state of a man at the time of an assault, the testimony being limited solely to this issue. Finally, there was a trial in which we were requested to testify with respect to a criminal's legal sanity, after he had been apprehended for an armed robbery. We claimed privileged communication, but the judge determined that it did not hold in cases in which the defendant uses the insanity defense. Our testimony was limited to the sanity issue; we held that the criminal was sane, and revealed no other information. The criminal realized that we had been required by law to testify. After receiving a substantial sentence, he wrote to us that he respected us for our candor. He pleaded that we again accept him in our program whenever he received parole.

The A.C. must be discriminating when it comes to evaluating adverse outside information or grapevine reports about the criminal. He must have the knowledge, so that he can gauge whether the criminal is in such a state of mind that the reports can be discussed directly with him. Some of the reports are mere gossip and not worth pursuing. If a criminal on the outside is clear in his thinking, we inform him of the grapevine and discuss it. We have found that the criminal has respected us all the more for our forthrightness in presenting him with the outside information, rather than concealing it and convicting him on the basis of it before we confronted him with it or otherwise ascertained the facts. When the A.C. is forthright, the criminal sees that nothing is being withheld, and this may well encourage him to report more fully.

The term *integrity* embraces a wide range of personal attributes and behavior beyond those mentioned. To work with the criminal, an A.C. must respond to questions forthrightly without ambiguity. When he does not know, he must say so. There is to be no hiding behind psychiatric language or passing the buck to others (including administrators). When asked a yes-or-no question, if the A.C. wants time to think the answer over, he should always respond within an agreed-on time. Otherwise, the delay is likely to be interpreted by the criminal as duplicity. An A.C. with integrity makes no promises that cannot be promptly fulfilled. If he makes an error and realizes it, he volunteers that fact; if the error is called to his attention by the criminal, he acknowledges it. Throughout this discussion, we have stressed the openness of the A.C. in dealing with the criminal. This is in total contrast with the secrecy with which the criminal has chosen to envelop himself. When the A.C. disagrees, he states his disagreement explicitly. He does not disguise his opinion of the criminal. In fact, he makes his written records available to the criminal. At no time does the A.C. contrive questions or responses to test a criminal. Testing is a devious process that has no place in a program that requires a wide-open channel. If a criminal takes a particular stance and fails and terms it testing, this tactic is exposed for correction. Such a forthright exposure is an exercise in integrity by the A.C.

Our position here is in marked opposition to those who maintain that the agent of change who is like the criminal has an advantage in trying to change him. For example, Kiger (1966), who runs a therapeutic community for "psychopaths," has said that "being imbued with just the right touch of the psychopath's characteristics is a definite asset." To judge by our observations of staff members at Saint Elizabeths Hospital and by reports from a wide variety of sources, this is not true. The criminal is quick to view such an A.C. as a criminal himself. If a criminal perceives a psychopathic attitude, he readies his con operation, knowing that an irresponsible person is more vulnerable to it. What is most important is that once a criminal believes that an A.C. is like him, it destroys the A.C.'s credibility, because it creates the patently absurd situation of an irresponsible person's using the criminal's tactics while urging the criminal to be responsible.

STRENGTH AND FIRMNESS

In chapter 8 of volume 1, we described in detail nineteen tactical maneuvers used by the criminal to control an examiner, interviewer, or agent of change. Some tactics are subtle, others blatant. In any adversary proceeding, a criminal examines others more than he himself is being examined. He tries to determine what others want to hear and feeds it to them. He finds and uses opportunities for digression and diversion. He discloses as it suits his purposes. He slants his version of events to make himself a victim and blames others for his plight in life. He tries whatever he thinks will impress the examiner or A.C., enlist his sympathy and compassion, or convince him of a particular point of view. Failing this, he uses a variety of tactics to put an A.C. on the defensive. These may be couched in highly intellectual terms as the criminal argues the meaning of a word, disputes a philosophic issue, and generalizes a point to absurdity. However, there are also open power plays as he intimidates, threatens, ridicules, and erupts with angry reactions.

The agent of change has no hope of being successful if he allows a criminal to set the conditions of a meeting. The criminal tries to manage others, whether in individual or in group sessions, and makes efforts to revise the format to suit himself. The A.C. must stand firm and not allow the criminal to do this. An A.C. who is indecisive or lacks confidence does not instill confidence or respect in a criminal. Nor can an A.C. who is permissive later establish himself as a firm authority. Many criminals have had experience with permissive change agents and have exploited them. A person who is shy, timid, or reserved may do well in many endeavors, but he will fail to effect change in criminals.

Firmness, as we are describing it, means that the A.C. does not shift his position to mollify a criminal. Whereas a compromise might be expedient for the short run to retain a criminal in the program, that criminal will eventually be lost. Once the criminal finds that the A.C. is willing to shift his position to accommodate him, he will attempt to erode the A.C.'s position on other points. When the A.C. decides to yield no further, the criminal will respond by quitting. Shifting one's position to avoid disagreement with the criminal is a precedent that cannot be overcome later. It is preferable that the criminal drop out sooner than later and that the integrity of the program's principles and requirements remain intact.

The A.C. must show firmness by stating unequivocally his attitude toward the criminal's life style. This firmness is necessary from the outset, to inform the criminal of where he stands. The A.C. must have the confidence and strength to assume control of the interview right away. Allowing the criminal to state his case opens the door to hours of victor-victim discussion, to be followed later by periods of silence when these are not subscribed to. The early transactions are not dialogues; the criminal is not interested in discussion. As opposed to the noncriminal, who comes in distressed and asking for help, all the criminal wants to do is dominate. The A.C. must be able to establish his dominance immediately and inform the criminal that he is so doing. This helps to establish that he is not one of the ordinary agents of change whom the criminal can use.

Firmness and strength should not be confused with harshness. An A.C. who is belligerent or antagonistic will certainly fail, because his very manner will invite counterproductive power conflicts. If the A.C. is a power-wielder, the criminal will be quick to perceive this. Cornering a criminal and interrogating him to get him to talk, breeds either silence or contests. So, too, does undue skepticism. In dealing with this population, one is naturally skeptical if for no other reason than to avoid being gullible. But when skepticism reaches the point of deprecating whatever the criminal does, it cannot contribute to progress in change.

The A.C. must be able to create a sober, "let's get down to business" atmosphere, which the criminal will eventually respect. The objectives are to make the best use of time and to keep the criminal focused on the issue; as one criminal said, "If you are not rugged, I will get away," meaning that he would quickly divert the discussion if given a chance. Relevance can be maintained only if the A.C. has the knowledge of how the criminal mind works and if he adheres to a well-thought-out format, covering material that he deems important while making it pertinent to the criminal's life experiences.

> "Your method allows you to maintain control and cuts down needless time-wasting dialogue, and I'm just going to have to learn to get used to it."

The A.C. must have the tenacity to stick to his convictions and format without exception. He must be neither swayed by tears and complaints nor intimidated by anger. If the A.C. can be budged from his position by the criminal's point scoring, persuasion, or sad stories, he is at a disadvantage, because the criminal interprets kindness as weakness, and understanding or sympathy as agreement.

A show of firmness is necessary, because the criminal is without convictions as we define them. From meeting to meeting, his state of mind varies. Our job is to help him to function responsibly in a consistent manner. The criminal is fragmented, so the A.C. must be firm and consistent. The criminals with whom we have worked maintain that we drive a hard bargain. This has been said in tribute to our firm, uncompromising attitude toward what is required to become responsible.

In more than one instance, the criminal has brought to us a relative or prospective spouse who has insisted on finding out what the criminal's situation really is. In such a meeting, with the criminal present, we have laid out in a straightforward manner the criminal patterns of his entire life, without breaching confidentiality.

> C brought his girlfriend to see Dr. Yochelson. He had never before in the program, but over the years had developed a great deal of respect for the doctor when they had some conversations. He knew that the doctor would tell his prospective wife what kind of person he had beeen, namely a very criminal one. But an essential reason for his coming was that he thought that Dr. Yochelson would hold out some hope for change if he married a decent, honest woman.
>
> As the three of them chatted, Dr. Yochelson stated that C had been a thoroughbred criminal, participating in almost every conceivable kind of crime. The doctor did this without violating any details of privileged communication. He pointed out that C did not have an honest bone in his body and that this relationship could not be considered "love," because the criminal does not know the meaning of the word.
>
> C said that the fact that his wife-to-be knew the truth was proof that he had only the best of intentions and was not conning her. The doctor responded that one of the best cons was to tell the truth. From here on, he pointed out that C's criminal thinking processes would prevent him from becoming a responsible husband and citizen. Obviously, a marriage to a responsible woman would not produce change in him.

The A.C. was firm without being strident or carping. He was uncompromising, yet cordial, as he had been over the years when he had dealt with C on an occasional basis. However, he provided something beyond an indictment of a man's character by offering to meet with C frequently if C was sincere about change. It was a show of firmness, but tempered by compassion, in the sense of wanting to help C undertake something constructive. The criminal received all this calmly, without rancor and objection.

The A.C. must recognize that, although he can and must control the interviews in the beginning and intermediate stages, he cannot push the buttons to control the criminal's life. Firmness excludes making decisions for a man, persuading, exhorting, or acting as a missionary. As we have indicated, our firmness entails being direct in format, in procedures, and in setting up the ground rules. It is a matter of unflagging adherence to a basic position and setting forth the requirements that the criminal must follow if he is to succeed.

Firmness is also essential any time the criminal attempts to justify not doing what he is supposed to do. We do not accept his excuses for tardiness, unwise expenditures of money, failure to make an examination of conscience, or anything else that is required.

> C made an appointment with a doctor at the neighborhood clinic for 9 a.m. This was a perfectly legitimate appointment in the light of an injury to C's arm for which a cast had to be checked. We had no objection to his making the appointment, but required that he change the appointment to the afternoon in order not to miss the group meeting.
>
> *   *   *
>
> C stated that he had no time to conduct a "moral inventory" because he had been working such long hours and had a great deal to do at home. We informed him that there was no point to his continuing in this program unless he made the time for the examination of conscience.

Firmness comes into focus most clearly when, after several months, we find that either the criminal is arrestable or that he is not cooperating with us. After months of our knowing the most intimate aspects of his life, it calls for unequivocal firmness to turn him in to the authorities. This is the most extreme instance of firmness.

ENDURANCE AND PATIENCE

Tremendous endurance and patience are required in work with the criminal. The criminal mind is so fragmented that the A.C. has to anticipate and remain calm in the face of numerous shifts in the former's commitment and implementation. The criminal may comprehend a major principle one day but seem to have obliterated it from memory the next day, as he persists in his habitual errors of thinking. The A.C. must remain calm and assured in the face of whatever happens. He must not draw conclusions prematurely about the success or failure of the enterprise. He must expect to discover violation and with it evidence that the channel has been closed for some time. Instead of abandoning the task, he must take this in stride, viewing it simply as indicative of insufficient change. If one becomes exasperated by incessant repetition (which is required), he would do better working with another group. The repetition is necessary, not only because of the criminal's fragmentation but also because of the concreteness of his thinking. Teaching a man to think conceptually about even the most elementary things is a trying task and requires a great deal of patience.

Rather than trying to read the barometer of change after every session or every few weeks, the A.C. must be able to view the whole process of change in a long-range perspective. Knowing how fragmented the criminal mind is, he must adopt a "time will tell" approach with respect to the criminal's progress. Along the way, he must be fully prepared for a surprising turn of events. If it finally becomes evident that the enterprise has not been successful, the A.C. must recognize that the failure of a criminal to choose a different life is not necessarily a reflection on his own competence. If a patient is given a prescription and refuses to take the medicine, the doctor cannot be faulted.

Patience and endurance are also required in facing the criminal's trying barrage of tactics. The A.C. must endure lying, point scoring, expressions of undiluted scorn, and everything else that we have described. Indeed, the A.C. may be witness to outbursts of violence in which the criminal smashes property. On a few occasions, criminals have broken ash trays or other handy objects, but never with physical injury to any person. Criminals have misquoted us to others and, although praising our efforts in our presence, have condemned us in quarters where they thought that they could gain something by so doing. The A.C. must also endure the criminal's continual probing in which the criminal appears to be testing the A.C.'s reactions and the limits of acceptable conduct in the program.

Knowing the criminal, an A.C. will not be surprised by these tactics and will be prepared to meet them. As we have pointed out, silence as a response only leads the criminal to believe that the agent agrees with him. The A.C. who uses the same tactics as the criminal puts himself on the same level of operation as the criminal. The agent has to let the criminal know that the war being waged is one-sided. The criminal may be out for a victory, but the A.C. wants to enlighten and to produce change. Abuse, irrationality, and power-thrusting must be met by composure, rationality, and quiet but firm adherence to a position of absolute responsibility. If the A.C. does not join battle, but effectively maintains his position, a criminal who is at all interested in change will react in the following manner, at least inwardly:

"I engage in a manipulative struggle with all around me. It's a continuous exercise within my own mind. However, so far with you, it's like throwing a punch at a guy who isn't there."

He will in time recognize that there is no adversary. This—coupled with the A.C.'s "it's your life" position—may help to put the discussion on a more rational basis. The A.C. must recognize that some criminals will drop out and do so angrily. After all, the program opposes their entire way of life. Some criminals have left cursing us. Some have called later, asking to return. Such exits and reentries must be handled patiently and calmly, regardless of what the criminal said or did. There is no room for vituperation.

Knowing in advance what to expect contributes to one's mental stamina in dealing with the criminal's fluctuating state of mind. Knowledge helps one to endure, and endurance leads to acquiring more knowledge.

"It is a pretty grim day; Arthur crying, Matt exploding in crime, and Charlie groggy with drugs. If one isn't willing to live through these storms, he shouldn't have anything to do with this kind of patient." (Our note from a session)

The A.C. must react to such situations by working harder, rather than by becoming discouraged and giving up. Instead of growing cynical or in any way retaliating, the A.C. should view all difficulties as stimuli to self-questioning about his procedures. What we used to take personally as disappointments, we have learned to use as opportunities. With such a perspective, we are more dispassionate in our demeanor, conduct, and inner state of mind. One criminal, who posed a great danger to society, decided to leave the program after we had expended tremendous time and energy attempting to help him. When he decided to quit, Dr. Yochelson dictated the following:

"This is where a man tends to call names. I don't think we should cheapen our position by calling him an animal in the jungle or wild or immature or anything of the sort. You look a man right in his eye; you say to him, 'You are evil, cruel, you voluntarily hurt people. Your contribution to society is worthless.' What I have is a privilege to dictate these statements very calmly, sadly, and to tell a man he has chosen the devil rather than God, only because he is more congenial with the devil. It is a sad state."

Patience and endurance pay off, regardless of whether the A.C. succeeds with any given criminal. Any person is gratified when he achieves positive results. But we have found that it is essential not to view this work in terms of success and failure. By having the patience and interest to continue to learn from men who choose not to live responsibly, we have gained new knowledge that we can use in helping those who do choose to live responsibly. In this, as in any investigation, patience is rewarded by knowledge, and any knowledge gained is all to the good. Perhaps the most important thing to keep in mind is that it is the criminal's life that is at stake, and that the A.C. puts responsibility for that life directly in the criminal's hands. Thus, if the criminal tries to score points, the A.C. can endure this, but it will eventually be the criminal's road to ruin. If we think in terms of a batting average, our involvement and concern become liabilities, rather than assets, because they afford the criminal a chance to control us. We need to remember whose life is at stake.

Another way of putting this is to say that stubbornness is a virtue in a change agent working with the criminal. Obstacles, insults, and ordeals are all in a day's work. An unyielding tenacity is a virtue, if one is tenacious about the right things. Anyone who is not dispassionate enough to endure the many ups and downs in working with these fragmented people will find serving as an agent of change very demoralizing, because he is unlikely to achieve the ratio of success to failure that he would like.

How the A.C. reacts to the criminal's obstacles obviously conveys a great deal about the kind of person he is. In chapter 11, we referred to personnel who met the criminal's anger with anger, his deceptions with deceptions of their own, and so forth. Instead of enduring and persisting in a prolonged relationship for the purpose of change, these people participated in power contests and got nowhere.

The A.C. must show that he endures adversities and setbacks in the conduct of his program and in his own life. For example, when the A.C. encounters administrative obstacles in a bureaucracy, he must show the same patience that he expects the criminal to learn to display. In fact, the criminal perceives any show of impatience by the A.C. as anger, He then perceives the A.C. as being no different from him.

PERSISTENCE IN PROBING

In earlier chapters, we presented conceptually and with examples the need for careful probing of thinking processes in the correcting of thinking errors. In the beginning and intermediate stages of change, these errors stand out; they are not hard to identify and correct. On some days, however, the criminal presents reports in which he appears to be functioning responsibly. Particularly as he accomplishes more toward eliminating old patterns and implementing new ones, there may be little that is obvious to criticize. The A.C. must probe thinking processes tenaciously, even when this happens. Compliments only encourage complacency. As we pointed out earlier, complacency in the criminal is the prelude to erosion of progress. When a criminal thinks that he has it made, he monitors himself less and does not attack life's problems as efficiently and responsibly as he should. He is not as quick to catch and deter old thinking patterns.

The A.C. must never take the "let well enough alone" attitude. The more he probes and the more actively he searches for errors in thinking, the more he discovers. This is essential in fighting complacency and promoting further change. For example, a criminal may be describing transactions with his wife over a twenty-four-hour period. This may be against a backdrop of several weeks or even months in which he has drastically altered former patterns of thinking and action. He no longer controls her, ignores her wishes, or criticizes her every flaw. He has indicated that things have, therefore, gone much more smoothly. The A.C. must then scrutinize the relationship closely and start raising questions about what the criminal has done *for* his wife. True, he is not abusive and domineering; but what has he done on the positive side?

The A.C. can be even more microscopic than this. From small incidents that seem to offer nothing obvious to comment on, he can draw out something that reflects important considerations for total change.

> C recommended a particular concert to a woman that he worked with. She took his recommendation and attended. She was enthusiastic and told C that she had looked for him at the concert, but had not seen him. C replied, "I was too busy to go." Actually, he was not busy, but did not want to promote a relationship between himself and the co-worker.

C had done what many responsible people might do and think no further about. However, we brought out another way in which he could have handled the situation. His reasoning about not promoting himself with the woman was sound, given C's past patterns. But he could have told her, "I decided not to go." This would have been a more truthful response. The emphasis is on the elimination of even a petty lie of the type that he told here. Another example of the same type is the following:

> C planned to inform his girlfriend that he had arrived in his home town safely. He was going to call her, let the phone ring three times, and hang up, thus saving the cost of a long-distance call.

We took the position that this was cheating the phone company, a practice that the criminal must not allow himself, even though it is common among people not considered criminals. We could well have let the deceptions in each example pass inasmuch as there was no obvious injury to another person and each of these criminals had almost entirely eliminated lying. However, we know that a small deception opens the door to larger deceptions. This necessary microscopic probing requires intense, prolonged concentration.

A failure to persist in probing for details will leave major issues for change buried.

> We had discussed C's sexual relationship with his wife in some detail. Because of the way C had treated her, she had become disinterested in sex. C made considerable progress in changing his attitudes and behavior through participation in our program. However, his wife's attitude about sex remained unchanged, despite her being treated in a most thoughtful and considerate manner by C. It sounded to us both from what C said and from our interviews with his wife, that she was frigid, and we counseled C to be patient and to endure her lack of interest. This was our basic position for some time. Over a period of weeks, this issue came up repeatedly as C reported his thinking about their dormant sexual life. We decided that perhaps we had not explored the details of their sexuality sufficiently and that more needed to be understood.

> It turned out that C's wife had learned nearly all she knew about sex from C. What she had learned was that sex involved biting, roughness, and little tenderness. She had rejected sex because nothing in it met her needs. Her lack of response to C was not comprehensible to us until we inquired into the details of C's approach.

We had spent many months dissecting C's patterns of thinking and action. Because C was no longer committing sex crimes or going to adult book stores and had very few if any rape-homicide fantasies (which he had had repeatedly each day), and because he was functioning responsibly toward his wife (to her satisfaction) in almost all ways, we had attributed the sexual problem to her. Once we found out C's patterns and talked with him and his wife about them, it did not take long for change to occur, and her interest in sex grew with more frequent, satisfying experiences.

If the A.C. listens to a criminal's report and raises no substantive issues, his failure to comment is interpreted as blanket endorsement. Even if he cannot ferret out an error, the A.C. can raise broader issues that relate to future conduct. That is, if a criminal demonstrates that he is putting new concepts to work, the A.C. can discuss with him how these changes came about and anticipate situations in which the new patterns of thought and behavior can be implemented in the future.

A basic error on the part of an A.C. in working with a criminal is silence; it is not golden. The criminal's point of view is that the A.C. has an opinion. If it is not expressed, the criminal assumes, at least in the early stages of the program, that the A.C. is double-dealing—thinking one thing, but expressing another or hiding his opinion entirely. Sometimes, silence is viewed as timidity or ignorance, in which case the criminal responds with contempt for the A.C. At all stages of the change program, the A.C. must be outspoken. He must constantly persist in raising new issues, probe further, and never permit himself or the criminal to be satisfied with the current state of change, no matter how far advanced it seems.

FLEXIBILITY

The criminal is quick to criticize a change agent for being rigid. If the A.C. operates from a moral base, as we do, he is criticized for being moralistic. However, if he departs from this position, he may be criticized for not standing by what he says. The criminal criticizes him for being flexible or inflexible, depending on the particular objectives of the criminal at the time. If an A.C. yields to a criminal's point of view, attacks, or criticisms, he is in danger of surrendering control to the criminal. However, if he does not alter his approach to suit the criminal's objectives, the criminal derides his rigidity. The criminal scorns an A.C. as weak when he does not assume control. When the A.C. does take charge, the criminal faults him for using criminal tactics and thus for being a criminal himself. The A.C. obviously cannot please the criminal. As we have maintained all along, he should not try.

A rigid, unwavering stance is mandatory with respect to the program's requirement of total responsibility everywhere. Here, there is no room for flexibility. However, the A.C. should not be rigid on procedural matters in his day-to-day dealings with the criminal. On the basis of his knowledge of how the criminal mind works, the A.C. should be prepared for each day's session, but some danger exists in this. He can be so intent on one line of inquiry that he inadvertently overlooks significant aspects of life experiences. The A.C. must be flexible in evaluating each day's report and in choosing topics for discussion.

> Dr. Samenow was working with a group of three 14-year-old delinquent boys at an outpatient clinic. Having been trained by Dr. Yochelson, he knew that he would have to take a strong, controlling position from the beginning and know what he was going to do at each session. He had a particular topic in mind for discussion, because one of the youngsters had just been arrested. As he started to discuss the superoptimism before the crime, the group members began laughing, joking, and otherwise diverting the discussion. The A.C. persisted with the topic, but never got very far. He was so focused on what he wanted to probe that the tactics

preventing a meaningful discussion were not handled. Time was wasted because of the failure to shift focus and deal with the tactics directly.

The A.C. was too bound by what he thought was the most important issue. Having failed to deal directly with the interpersonal obstacles, he nearly lost control of the session. The failure was twofold: there was no productive discussion, and the delinquents were not confronted directly with the A.C.'s knowledge of why they were using such tactics. We have pointed out the disastrous consequences of tubular vision in the criminal; the same is true as it applies to the A.C.

The A.C. must be flexible in being able to shift from one level of discourse to another. That is, he may be emphasizing a glaring, obvious error, but it might be more effective to shift to a broader perspective than to remain fixed on the one concrete issue. Being alert enough to shift from a tree to the forest or from the forest to a tree as appropriate is an important aspect of flexibility. The A.C. must also be willing to defer issues that are less important, rather than persevere with them at the expense of other, more significant issues.

Flexibility is not shown by going along with the criminal's diversionary tactics. For example, an A.C. may believe that he is being flexible if he discusses Buddhist philosophy, when in fact this is not flexibility, but rather being duped by the criminal.

Flexibility is necessary in determining how much control of the session the A.C. needs to maintain. Strong, unwavering domination of a session is not always called for. When the criminal is in a cooperative frame of mind, the A.C. may unnecessarily stir up a contest if he appears more domineering than the occasion warrants. The A.C. must gauge the degree of control necessary and yield accordingly, allowing greater independence as the criminal shows that he is ready for it.

When we call for flexibility on the part of the A.C., we are not referring to an alteration of basic values or attitudes toward irresponsibility and violating patterns. We remain steadfast in our condemnation of criminal thinking and action. Flexibility is necessary in assessing the changing nature of the A.C.'s relationship with very fragmented people. We are speaking, then, of flexibility with respect to procedure, but not with respect to basic premises and substantive content.

OPEN-MINDEDNESS

Our present program is the outcome of a long search, rather than research, into existing concepts and procedures. We described the fifteen-year evolution of our program in chapter 1 of volume 1. Adherence to an established school of thought was not likely to yield something new. We have continued to be open-minded, especially about deficiencies within our own system. We know full well that we could become so absorbed by our own concepts and procedures as to develop a cult of our own. However, we still continue the process of changing, refining, and adding to our fund of information and thereby to our procedures.

The A.C. who approaches work with the criminal with an unbending allegiance to a particular theory or school of thought is at a tremendous disadvantage. In chapter 8 of volume 1, we pointed out how readily the criminal evaluates the A.C.'s orientation and feeds him what he thinks the A.C. wants to hear. In effect, the criminal masters the system. Of course, noncriminals also do this, but they do not pervert a system the way the criminal does. The criminal intends to use the system, not for change, but for preventing confinement or seeking release from confinement or mitigating some other restriction. An A.C. who is wedded to one viewpoint and is not open to new points of view may be satisfied easily if the expectations of his orientation are met. As one criminal said of his therapist, "When I satisfied the doctor's theory, I was considered cured."* We have reported the experiences of change agents at Saint Elizabeths and elsewhere. Some of these have invested years of their lives in using specific procedures based on their training. Some regard themselves as effective change agents, because their criteria for change are met: The criminal achieves insight, maintains good work performance, and is not arrested. From our studies, we have found that even with these criteria being met, criminals still engage in criminal thinking and action. Other A.C.'s know that they have failed, but they persist with the same approaches, not knowing what else to do.

Another problem arising from an A.C.'s being wedded to a particular interpretive approach is that the criminal is likely to resent it and stir up a contest. The criminal is quick to know if he is being "boxed and packaged," as one man put it. He regards himself as a totally unique individual and fights being categorized. He even fights our identifying him as a criminal and objects to our presentation of facts about his life. The problems for an A.C. are still greater when a criminal is trying to dismantle an entire theoretical system, idea by idea, because he is rejecting being boxed and packaged.

The criminal hears, but does not listen. The A.C. must both hear and listen. An open mind is necessary, if the A.C. is truly to receive what the criminal is saying. The A.C. is likely to view most situations differently from the criminal. However, he must listen with an open mind, so that he can find out what the criminal's position is, without prejudging it. The A.C. should always be alert

*As we indicated earlier, the criminal can also, and sometimes does, feed us what he thinks we want to hear. However, with our "de-lying" techniques and our "time will tell" approach, which indicates that we are not necessarily being taken in, the feeding is not as effective.

to the possibility of learning something new from the criminal—not with respect to an M.O. but with regard to a pattern of thought. Several years from now, we shall probably provide more information on criminal thinking, because we not only are open to new information but are actively seeking it.

A practitioner sometimes needs to listen closely in order to discover thinking errors; some are obvious, but others have to be ferreted out. It is counterproductive for the A.C. to curtail a criminal's report on the basis of a prejudgment of what will be important. A report may have to be abbreviated if it is repetitive or clearly diversionary or when time is limited. But dismissing something that a criminal reports without carefully examining its ramifications can result only in a loss of effectiveness. An A.C. who is truly open-minded does not reject even material that appears unrelated to criminal thinking. Instead, he explores it by probing more deeply to determine whether it contains anything substantive.

The A.C. must remain open-minded in the sense of not prejudging a criminal's progress or his own effect on the criminal. Moreover, this open-mindedness should be expressed to the criminal. Neither excessive pessimism nor excessive optimism about change is warranted. The A.C. must not be too quick to evaluate the impact of a meeting or a series of meetings on a criminal. Emerging from a session, he may despair that he has been engaged in a futile enterprise, that he has not put his point across. But the seeds planted bear fruit only later. There is also the danger of being overly pleased about a good session. The A.C. must be open-minded enough to suspend judgment and wait for time to tell the story. An A.C. seeking quick answers and immediate success would be well-advised not to work with criminals.

SELF-CRITICISM

Self-criticism is the basic component of the wide-open channel, a *sine qua non* in dealing with a criminal. The criminal is taught to question his established thinking patterns so as to focus on his own shortcomings. Similarly, the A.C. must be critical of his own thinking and action patterns, especially as they affect his procedures in the change process. Consequently, he constantly takes stock of his personal and professional life, striving for personal growth, as well as improving the quality of his professional work. Chapter 1 of volume 1 narrates a story of a fourteen-year enterprise that could not have developed without persistent self-criticism that resulted in alteration after alteration of concepts of the criminal mind and of procedures designed to change it. Only experience and the recognition of errors permitted many revisions and refinements to occur. Had we been intent on proving that our procedures were sound and had we failed to criticize ourselves, we would not have improved. The choice is between proving and improving; what is crucial in the attempt to improve is active self-criticism.

In our procedures, we sometimes openly question and criticize what we are doing. Often, this self-criticism is not expressed, but it is later incorporated in a revision of a concept or a new procedure; then the criminal learns of it. What he sees us doing is what we insist that he do. This self-criticism, however, is *not* designed to serve as a model. Rather, it is to improve our own performance.

When the criminal is confronted with an A.C. who rigidly persists in an approach that is clearly failing, he either becomes contemptuous (sometimes openly) or finds an opportunity for a power struggle. In contrast our process of self-criticism does have an impact on him, although we must emphasize that it is not calculated to have an impact. When the "know it all" criminal deals with a trained A.C. who is self-critical and eager to improve, one who not only tolerates reasonable criticism but even invites it, a power struggle may well be preempted.

The A.C. who is not self-critical ceases to learn and then ceases to improve his services. Indeed, we have often commented to our groups, "This year we are doing better than last year, and next year we shall do even better than this year." This is not a contrived statement to impress the criminal. It is a statement of fact, and we find that such statements by a firm A.C. result in fewer power contests, more valid reporting, and greater commitment to change.

COMPASSION

Compassion is expressed in two ways in our program, neither of them immediately obvious. A visitor to our program would not be able to observe compassion in our attitude or procedures. Compassion is not visible, but it can easily be inferred if one grasps the overall thrust of our work. What is absent is the kind of compassion often expressed in maudlin sympathy and in attempts to help the criminal feel better about himself and about life in general. However, compassion is built into this hard-line program. The toughness of the program is designed to change criminals, so that they will live responsible lives and no longer injure others. We actively show concern for the criminal's wife, children, and parents and for society at large. The toughness of the program is intended to make the criminal consider other people and his own future. We are concerned about potential victims as well as about the suffering of those who already have become victims. We want to do our part to make the streets safe for citizens to go about their business unintimidated by the threat of theft, vandalism, assault, and other crimes. This is one element of compassion, with the least compassion being shown toward the plight of the criminal himself.

The criminal initially does not comprehend the broad social dimensions of the problem being attacked, but he does perceive that vast amounts of time and energy are being expended in behalf of his changing. The A.C. shows his compassion by what he is willing to do and endure. This is communicated by the A.C.'s failure to be discouraged or personally affronted by the criminal's abuse, violations, and mistakes. We are describing a person with an intense, unflagging commitment, one willing to take the consequences of this approach.

Compassion and respect for the individual are shown by treating all criminals equally. Some A.C.'s find a specific person or type of crime so offensive that it precludes their dealing with the criminal effectively. This kind of bias is as detrimental to the change process as would be the inability of a surgeon to stand the sight of blood during an operation. Fascination for a particular crime is equally disadvantageous, for reasons pointed out earlier.

Lack of ethnic, racial, or religious prejudice is mandatory. The A.C. must be convinced that crime is within the man and is not a matter of race, religion, or social station. Biased attitudes must be overcome *before* beginning the work. Whatever the background of the criminal, the A.C. must work with unequivocal dedication.

The A.C. is at a disadvantage if he believes that compassion should be demonstrated by special efforts to establish rapport. If the A.C. is the kind of professional worker who expresses himself by being helpful and doing things for others, the criminal is an unsuitable client. The A.C. who functions in this manner will end up as an errand boy, exploited by the criminal, and not as a change agent. Being excessively compassionate is as disqualifying as being overtly antagonistic. Compassion toward the criminal is unrelated to liking or acceptance; we neither like nor accept the criminal as he is. Acceptance of the criminal constitutes approval in his eyes—the opposite of what must be communicated. If the A.C. is oriented toward building the criminal's self-esteem, he should not work with criminals. Even when the criminal is in a zero state, the role of the A.C. is not to do things for him or to help him to feel better. The best way to show compassion is to help the criminal to change his thinking patterns. There will then be fewer zero states.

Compassion is shown through the A.C.'s hard work. He devotes himself to criminals who are serious about change and gives abundantly of his time and energy to promote this change. In our experience, it has involved making time available outside regular working hours to meet with criminals who have jobs. It has also entailed working with criminals long after they have left the institution. The ingredients of the A.C.'s commitment, and therefore his compassion, are seriousness of purpose, availability, persistence, and, perhaps most important, such a thorough knowledge of the criminal mind that the criminal knows that he has at last found someone who understands how he thinks (even though the A.C. does not agree with his thought) and can help the criminal help himself to change.

SUMMARY

Except for personal integrity, the personality characteristics described in this chapter can be developed or learned through experience. In fact, we have had to develop some of them, as we realized what was required for effective work with the criminal. Agents of change will be variously practiced in firmness, endurance, persistence in probing, flexibility, openmindedness, self-criticism, and compassion. Deficiency in some of these would not disqualify a person from functioning as an A.C. As he gains experience, if he so desires, he will be increasingly effective with respect to all the characteristics described. We must underline that experience is vital; none of the attributes described here can be learned didactically. They must be learned in the field.

Objection in principle to any of the requirements described does disqualify a person from this job. If he refuses to be firm, insists on setting the criminal at ease, and wants to do things for him, he will fail.

If a person has all the attributes described and is well-trained, his achievement will, nevertheless, be seriously hampered if he is working in a facility that is not administratively compatible with the objectives and methods of our program. We turn now to recommendations for an institution where our program could be implemented.

BIBLIOGRAPHY

Aichhorn, A. (1965). *Wayward Youth.* New York: Viking.

Beto, G. J. and Marsh, R. (1974). Problems in development of an undergraduate criminal justice curriculum. *Federal Probation,* 38 (December): 34-40.

Bishop, B. (1973). Self control is learned: external control precedes internal control. In *Behavior Therapy with Delinquents,* ed. Stumphauzer, J. S., Springfield, Illinois: Charles C Thomas. pp. 54-65.

Brenner, C. (1957). *An Elementary Textbook of Psychoanalysis:* New York: Anchor.

Bromberg, W. (1948). *Crime and the Mind.* Philadelphia: Lippincott.

Cameron, N. (1963). *Personality Development and Psychopathology.* Boston: Houghton Mifflin.

Claiborne, W. L. (1971). Careers as social workers attract many ex-convicts. *Washington Post,* December 26.

Erikson, E. H. (1968). *Identity: Youth and Crisis.* New York: Norton.

Faust, F. L. (1965). Group counseling with juveniles by staff without professional training in casework. *Crime and Delinquency,* 11: 349-354.

Glueck, S., and Glueck, E. (1952). *Delinquents In The Making.* New York: Harper.

Henry, N. (1972). *When Mother Is A Prefix: New Directions in Youth Correction.* New York: Behavioral Publications.

Kiger, R. S. (1966). Myth of the psychopath. n.p.

National Advisory Commission on Criminal Justice Standards and Goals. (1973). *Corrections.* Washington, D.C.: U.S. Government Printing Office.

New York City Youth Board. (1960). *Reaching the Fighting Gang.* New York: New York City Youth Board.

Shields, R. W. (1962). *A Cure of Delinquents.* New York: International Universities Press.

Slavson, S. R. (1965). *Reclaiming the Delinquent.* New York: The Free Press.

Task Force on Corrections (1967). *Task Force Report: Corrections.* Washington, D.C.: U.S. Government Printing Office.

Waldo, G. P. (1971). Research and training in corrections? The role of the university. *Federal Probation,* 35 (June): 57-62.

Washington Post (6/6/71). Ex-convict gets U.S. grant to run youth project.

White, E. (1971). Penology—the new science. *Corrective Psychiatry and Journal of Social Therapy* 17: 14-17.

Chapter 13

A Recommendation for
a Rehabilitation Program

HOW CAN TOTAL AND LASTING change be produced in hard-core criminals with a minimum of confinement and at minimal cost? In this volume, we have described a program that has achieved total and basic change in some criminals. This program can be applied on a wide scale without requiring vast sums of money for buildings and personnel. We present here a proposal for such an application of our program. This is not a blueprint, but rather a recommendation conceptually framed, with many details to be worked out before implementation.

We advocate that our proposal be implemented on a trial basis in the form of pilot programs. In the past, too many programs have been enthusiastically endorsed, generously funded, and implemented on a large scale, only to fail. They result in disillusionment and cynicism in those responsible for such programs, the presumed beneficiaries, and the public at large. Our program, applied in institutions or in the community, should be accompanied by two or three years of further research, development, and evaluation. On the basis of fifteen years of experience, we believe that our proposal is practical, economical, and promising.

The emphasis in corrections has changed from confining criminals for the protection of the community to offering criminals opportunities for rehabilitation in the community with little or no confinement beforehand. Whereas large penal facilities have been built over the years to house criminals, the recent trend is to halt construction and reduce utilization of these facilities and to fund instead community corrections programs. In fact, there has been such a proclivity for placing criminals in the community that protests have been raised that the community's safety is being jeopardized. Our proposal does not call for the criminal's sacrifice of his opportunity for change or for the community's sacrifice of its safety. It is designed to change the criminal in the community (which we have already accomplished) and to avoid injury to society. We protest warehousing criminals, which often occurs either by determinate or indeterminate confinement in institutions. Our program does not serve retributive purposes, nor is it designed with the specific intention of deterring others.

Although we are in line with the current trend toward working with criminals in the community, we advocate reasons for doing so that are different from the current rationale for community corrections. Community-based corrections has had wide advocacy for two basic reasons. One is that society has become largely convinced that prisons only warehouse inmates, but do not produce change. In fact, some contend that prisons make the criminal worse.

> To subject anyone to custodial coercion is to place him in physical jeopardy, to narrow drastically his access to sources of personal satisfaction, and to reduce his self-esteem. That all these unfavorable consequences are the outcome of his own criminal actions does not change their reality. (National Advisory Commission 1973, p. 222)

The second reason is economic. It has been estimated that constructing an institution to house criminals costs approximately twenty-two-thousand dollars per bed (NIMH 1971, p. 34). Community corrections programs, costing much less, have taken many forms—probation, parole, residence in halfway houses and noninstitutional boarding facilities, and treatment in clinics and day-care centers. Rehabilitation in the community has been thought to offer the criminal opportunities to learn job skills, improve his education, and in other ways integrate himself into the community (see chapter 2). However, as we have pointed out throughout this volume, such measures do not make substantial contributions to change and never produce lasting change. Rather, a change in thinking processes is necessary for a criminal to utilize job skills or an education responsibly. Furthermore, the community programs have lacked the necessary intensive supervision and followup.

In our program, we have found definite drawbacks to working with criminals while they are confined. Their milieu and routine are constricted. Therefore, day after day, there is a sameness to the phenomenologic report. A criminal who is changing refrains from interaction with other criminals not in our program. He fills his time with whatever legitimate activities are available. We then obtain his thinking about the other criminals with whom he is confined, the staff (some of whom may also be irresponsible or frankly criminal), books he is reading, television programs he is watching, visitors who come to see him, and any other topic that he happens to think about. The material for change provided us is extremely meager because of the restricted criminal world in which the criminal lives. A further obstacle is that the orientation of most confined criminals, even those sincere about change, is toward getting out. The tremendous amount of thinking directed toward that objective also limits the scope of their reports. We have found that once these criminals are in the community, there is a much wider arena for implementing the program and we thus have more data to work with, as the criminal interacts with his family, employer, fellow employees, friends, and so on. We advocate working with the criminal in the community, not because he needs to learn particular skills while there, but because he benefits most from having a wider arena in which to implement new patterns of thinking and acting thereby enriching the scope of phenomenologic reports, which provide the meat of the change process.

To operate the program in the community, a clinic would have to earn the confidence of the court. It is anticipated that the court would play an active role in the program from the outset and throughout a criminal's participation. Some of the participants would be convicted criminals to whom the court would offer the alternatives of coming to the program or serving a prison sentence. Others would be criminals whom the court had no intention of sending to jail, but who, in a probationary arrangement, would be assigned instead to an intensive program like ours. A minority would come as voluntary participants, seeking us out because they were experiencing self-disgust, wanted to change some particular aspect of their behavior, or were being subjected to other outside pressures than those stemming from an arrest.

For those choosing our program as an alternative to jail, a strong external deterrent would be operative immediately: under such an arrangement, the criminal would enter the program with the understanding that if he did not fulfill the requirements, he would be returned to court and would probably have to serve his sentence. The criminal could be dismissed from it in either of two ways: by selecting himself out (as described in chapter 3) or by failing to change, as evidenced by patterns of point scoring, violation, or general lack of implementation of the program. Obviously, the tendency to enter the program and score points by specious cooperation would be great, at least initially. But this program places responsibility for one's life totally on the criminal. It also includes patient assessment to determine whether intentions are transformed into convictions. If the criminal is interested only in scoring points, this becomes evident in time, because the channel is closed and violations eventually occur. The A.C. decides what constitutes sufficient reason for dismissal. At no time in the program does an agent of change bail a criminal out of difficulty.

In volume 1, we described the criminal's feigning a mental illness to earn a diagnosis satisfying the legal definition of insanity and thereby avoiding a prison term. Chapters 6 and 7 of volume 1 demonstrated that the diagnosis of mental illness should be limited to those who are clearly out of contact with reality. This seldom occurs except in occasional cases of toxic psychosis or psychosis developing between arrest and trial. As we have pointed out, we have not found any criminal to be psychotic at the time of the crime. From our point of view, a criminal should be hospitalized only if he fulfills the criteria for psychosis at the time of sentencing. The fact that he committed a crime would be irrelevant to the diagnosis. That is, the psychiatric evaluation would not be different from that of a noncriminal. Thus, if a criminal were disoriented or conceivably dangerous to himself, he would not be eligible, at that time, for our program. Again, we stress that very few criminals would be eliminated from eligibility for our program on the basis of mental illness.

As he entered the program, the criminal would know that he had to remain in it for four years, with a mandatory minimum of a year of attendance at daily meetings. Thereafter, a regular follow-up would take place on a schedule arranged with the change agent. The change agent, or perhaps a different person from the clinic, might handle the follow-up depending on scheduling. The criminal might report to an individual, or he might be assigned to a special follow-up group. However, the format of each meeting would remain as it had always been, with the criminal's presenting detailed phenomenologic reports and subjecting his thinking to criticism and correction. Assessments of change would not be in terms of arrest, money saved, holding a job, and so forth. The criterion of total change is impeccability in thought and action—total responsibility everywhere. The specific indices are described in chapter 10. Our program is working most efficiently with criminals who have spent little or no time in confinement, but who have maintained themselves in the community and attended our program as a requirement of probation. If they do not implement the program, they are subject to having their probation or parole revoked and then being reconfined.

The basic unit of a community clinic would consist of two people—a change agent and an assistant. The A.C. would be responsible for operating the program for approximately a dozen criminals at a time. His assistant would make family contacts, maintain liaison with probation officers, and relieve the A.C. of whatever teaching chores he could—instruction about money management, for example. The assistant could be a paraprofessional. A group of such units would constitute a clinic, which would require an administrator.

Each criminal would participate three hours a day, five days a week, in a continuing group. These groups would be open; when one member left, another would join immediately. Thus, in any given group, criminals would be at different stages in the change process, a practice that, as we have explained in chapter 6, has considerable advantage. Obviously, close supervision is built into this program. Although close ties would need to be maintained with the probation department, the supervisory function of its personnel would be reduced.

In this program, the criminal would obtain a full-time job compatible with the scheduling of the daily sessions. We have had no difficulties with this over the years, in that employment on an evening or night shift has been available. The criminal would obtain the job, no matter how demeaning, on his own; no help from the clinic staff would even be offered. Furthermore, the understanding would be that he would be totally honest about himself in talking with prospective employers. The criminal would be required to find a job with little opportunity for power thrusting, in a setting where there would be little free time, and with an organization in which advancement were possible.

Changing the individual criminal and protecting the community are responsibilities of which we are equally cognizant. Our clinic program differs from most others in scope and intensity. If a criminal is meeting with an A.C. daily for three hours, his thinking and action are being monitored very closely. A criminal is accountable for all his time—eight hours at work, three hours in the program meetings, eight hours of sleep, and five remaining hours, which are to be programmed. In addition, the criminal is required to program his time in advance on weekends. The A.C. would check with outside sources to confirm the veracity of the criminal's reports of how he spends his time. In this work, one has to be ever mindful of his obligation to society, in terms both of protecting society and of changing the individual criminal, which, in the end, is the greatest protection to society of all.

Some criminals will be considered by the courts or clinic to be too dangerous to live in the community. Protection of the community will demand confinement, but only in a minority of cases, if the current trend prevails. Thus, there is a need for a maximum security facility from which the criminal can begin participation in the program. We make no pretense that confinement it elf is a habilitative measure. However, it is a place where the criminal can begin to participate in the program. The court, advised by the change agent, would decide when the criminal could be released to continue in the program through the community clinic. The maximum security facility would be staffed by change agents, a few administrators, and a larger adjunctive staff than that required by the clinic. That is, there would be need for attendants and some personnel to staff activity programs. Coordination between maximum security and the community clinic would be essential to ensure continuity and follow-through as the criminal is released by one to the other. Optimally, the two facilities would be in geographic proximity. All units would be coordinated with the courts and the probation department.

Maximum security status would not be synonymous with isolation and inactivity, as it is in some institutions. Our maximum security program would differ from others, in that the criminal would immediately begin to spend fifteen hours a week in a process designed to change his thinking and action patterns by rational methods. All other activities would be subordinate and complementary to that objective. Adjunctive personnel in the institution would staff such elective activities as education, vocational training, and recreation to occupy the criminal's time constructively. Again, there would be no pretense that these activities change thinking processes. They would simply be arenas in which the criminal could be observed, implement what he was learning in the group, and at the same time acquire a skill that might be useful later. When transferred to the community clinic, the criminal would switch to a different group and A.C. We estimate that criminals who are evaluated as implementing the program would remain in maximum security no longer than six months.

In both the community clinic and the maximum security facility, it is essential that the staff be carefully selected and thoroughly trained, so that there is a consistent, uniform implementation of the program. We described in chapter 11 the serious problems that occur when there is no common approach, set of procedures, or objectives. In working with criminals, each staff member must be personally qualified, meeting the standards described in the preceding chapter. Once selected, he must have a well-defined sphere of influence and authority within the clinic or institution compatible with the program's overall objectives.

Work as a change agent is not the exclusive province of the psychiatrist, psychologist, or social worker. In fact, a person from any one of these professions who is wedded to a particular approach and is not open to being trained in a new program is unsuitable. Professionals hired from these disciplines would not function in traditional roles in our program. Therefore, in the hiring process, they would have no advantage over clergymen, educators, or applicants from other fields seeking to be trained. It is not one's interest, zeal, or education and previous training that are of primary importance. Rather, it is having the personality and the willingness to apply oneself to learning our approach that counts. Every staff member would have to participate in training sessions offering a rigorous, intensive indoctrination in our approach. Of course, not everyone would be expected to have the same depth of knowledge. That is, the housekeepers in the maximum security facility would not have to know as much about details of criminal thinking patterns or change procedures as would assistants to the change agent. But everyone would have to be schooled in the overall philosophy and the specifics of the program, be in agreement with its moral tenets, and implement them in daily living.

The criminal has led other change agents astray. To a great extent, this has happened because there has been no specific program for correcting his thinking patterns in a rational manner and requiring discipline in implementation. The criminal, encountering the psychiatric fisherman who casts about aimlessly, has tried to mold the change agent's thinking along his own lines. Our program offers a cohesive approach and empirical procedures based on it. The value of this is observable in the results that have been produced.

In our program, sessions are not up for grabs. The A.C. is thoroughly equipped with information and procedures that are specific, pragmatic, and relevant. The material is specific, in that, instead of knowing things *about* the criminal, the A.C. knows *what* he is and how his mind operates. It is pragmatic, in that the concepts are usable and not obscure; the A.C. deals with the criminal's daily thoughts and actions. The material is relevant, in that it has succeeded in bringing about change. There is a great impact on the criminal when he encounters *all* the personnel applying this body of information in a total institutional (clinic) program.

Training of a change agent requires the candidate's being totally familiar with the concepts of volumes 1 and 2, having the information in mind, and being ready to apply it to situations as they arise. The candidate should also be familiar with the techniques of change agents schooled in other approaches. This is helpful background when he begins to work with a criminal who has encountered other approaches previously.

The outcome of our proposed selection and training is that all A.C.'s will function essentially alike. That is, they will base what they do on the same information and be well-versed in a common set of procedures. They will differ in style of presentation and in some personality features, but they will all have what is necessary to do the job. When new knowledge comes to light and becomes an accepted part of the fund of information and procedures, it will be incorporated into everyone's approach. We emphasize that the program requires a disciplined consistency and uniformity. Continuing evaluation of the staff is mandatory to achieve this. Admittedly, this uniformity is easier to talk about than to accomplish—not so much in the community center, where the criminal is in contact with one, or at most two, staff people, but in the maximum security facility. However, of the need for uniformity there can be no doubt. It has been achieved in other programs that are devoted to noncriminals*, and it can be achieved here.

---

*A notable example of this is the adolescent service at the Neuropsychiatric Institute of the University of Michigan Medical Center, where, under Dr. Willard Hendrickson, a thoroughly coordinated, consistent, effective approach was used with noncriminals.

It might appear that it would be difficult to attract and train enough people to meet the demand for trained personnel in the program that we propose. One change agent and one assistant will be responsible for only twelve criminals. At present, there is an urgent sense of need for effective programs but a sense of disenchantment and futility with observed results. Consequently, work with the criminal is unattractive, although it has become apparent during the last few years that there is a reservoir of suitable and interested people. Many have abandoned such efforts and instead entered fields in which they can help human beings who want help. We anticipate that once it is seen that there is a clearly defined and effective program for changing criminals, many people will become involved. This is even more likely in view of the present extent of social consciousness about crime and the offender. It might be argued that two trained workers for only a dozen criminals is too costly, but it is less expensive than building institutions and staffing them. We remind the reader, as we pointed out in volume 1, that the criminal inflicts injuries far beyond the crimes for which he is arrested. For example, we mentioned a young man who did millions of dollars worth of damage in thefts, fires, and vandalism by the time he was eighteen. The injury to people who were affected by this is incalculable in monetary terms. With every changing of a hard-core criminal, society saves hundreds of thousands of dollars (as well as saving in ways not measurable monetarily). The cost of unchanged criminals is incomparably higher than the cost of this program.

BIBLIOGRAPHY

National Advisory Commission on Criminal Justice Standards and Goals (1973). *Corrections.* Washington, D.C.: U. S. Government Printing Office.
National Institute of Mental Health (1971). *Community Based Correctional Programs.* Washington, D.C.: U. S. Government Printing Office.

Index

Abrahams, D. Y., 52, 57
Adelson, J., 248
admission, hospital, criminal patterns in confinement and, 449-451
agents of change (A.C.)
  criminal group therapy and, 179-186
  firmness in, importance of, 390-393
  as model, 534-538
  personality of, 531-556
    compassion in, 554-556
    endurance and patience in, 544-547
    flexibility in, 550-551
    integrity in, 538-541
    open-mindedness in, 551-553
    persistence in probing in, 547-550
    self-criticism in, 553-554
    strength and firmness in, 541-544
Aichorn, A., 47-48, 534, 535
alcohol, in maximum security, 477
Alexander, F. 46, 74, 215
Allport, G. W., 146
American Bar Association, 32
American Correctional Association, 38, 39
American Law Institute, 446
  Model Penal Code, 19n, 446

American Psychiatric Association, 46-47
Amos, W. E., 85
Andy, O., 23
anger, elimination of, in correction of thinking errors, 270-276
Arieti, S., 149
Aristotle, 189, 239, 366
Assagioli, R., 69n, 149, 340n
assistants, nursing, See nursing assistants
Averill, S., 52, 53
Ayllon, T., 80
Azrin, N., 80

Barnes, H. E., 25, 31
Barr, N. I., 35, 91n
Bazelon, Judge D., 74, 88, 457
Bedau, H. A., 78
Bennett, I., 51
Bentham, J., 73
Berne, E., 40, 66
Beto, G. J., 532
Binstock, J., 241
Binswanger, L., 70
Bishop, B., 535
Borriello, J. F., 54-55
Boslow, H. M., 33, 34, 56, 57, 85
Boss, M., 70n, 164, 164n
Bradley, C., 22
Brandes, N. S., 55